DEAR STUDENTS:

Most or you will start your careers as functional specialists—as account[...] sales people, finance specialists, and so on. If you are successful in [...] job, you will be promoted, and more than likely, before long you will [...] of other people. At this point, you will have become a manager. As a manager, further advancement will depend upon your ability to get things done through others—to motivate, persuade, encourage, and coach others so that they perform better. This book is about what it takes to become an effective manager. It is about how to make good decisions, how to exert influence on the strategies and policies of your employer (even when you are an entry-level employee), how to motivate and lead others, how to communicate effectively, how to manage change, and much more. Becoming a *good* manager is not easy, but it is a way to have a successful career and have an impact on the organizations in which you work. Becoming a *great* manager is more than that—great managers build organizations that change the world. Great managers of the last quarter century include Sam Walton, who built Wal-Mart from nothing into the world's largest retailer; Jack Welch, who transformed General Electric from a lumbering conglomerate into a dynamic and productive enterprise; Howard Schultz, who was the inspiration behind the growth of Starbucks; and Michael Dell, who starting from his dorm room created the world's largest manufacturer of personal computers.

We have written this book to help you get started on the road to becoming a good—or even a great—manager. We have tried to put together a book that is written in a lively and accessible style, crammed full of interesting and relevant examples, and that introduces you to the most useful concepts and theories for managers, yet presents these concepts and theories in a way that is easy to understand.

We hope you enjoy the book, but more than that, we hope that the ideas contained herein stay with you for the rest of your careers and help you to advance in the world of work.

Charles W.L. Hill

Steven L. McShane

Charles W.L. Hill   **Steven L. McShane**

PRINCIPLES OF **MANAGEMENT**

Charles W.L. Hill
UNIVERSITY OF WASHINGTON

Steven L. McShane
UNIVERSITY OF WESTERN AUSTRALIA

McGraw-Hill Irwin

Boston   Burr Ridge, IL   Dubuque, IA   Madison, WI   New York   San Francisco   St. Louis
Bangkok   Bogotá   Caracas   Kuala Lumpur   Lisbon   London   Madrid   Mexico City
Milan   Montreal   New Delhi   Santiago   Seoul   Singapore   Sydney   Taipei   Toronto

McGraw-Hill
Irwin

PRINCIPLES OF MANAGEMENT

Published by McGraw-Hill/Irwin, a business unit of The McGraw-Hill Companies, Inc., 1221 Avenue of the Americas, New York, NY, 10020. Copyright © 2008 by The McGraw-Hill Companies, Inc. All rights reserved. No part of this publication may be reproduced or distributed in any form or by any means, or stored in a database or retrieval system, without the prior written consent of The McGraw-Hill Companies, Inc., including, but not limited to, in any network or other electronic storage or transmission, or broadcast for distance learning.

Some ancillaries, including electronic and print components, may not be available to customers outside the United States.

This book is printed on acid-free paper.

1 2 3 4 5 6 7 8 9 0 DOW/DOW 0 9 8 7 6

ISBN   978-0-07-353012-3 (student edition)
MHID 0-07-353012-3 (student edition)
ISBN   978-0-07-331626-0 (instructor's edition)
MHID 0-07-331626-1 (instructor's edition)

Editorial director: *John E. Biernat*
Senior sponsoring editor: *Ryan Blankenship*
Developmental editors: *Natalie Ruffatto and Laura Griffin*
Senior marketing manager: *Anke Braun*
Media producer: *Greg Bates*
Lead project manager: *Mary Conzachi*
Lead production supervisor: *Michael R. McCormick*
Senior designer: *Kami Carter*
Senior photo research coordinator: *Jeremy Cheshareck*
Photo researcher: *Keri Johnson*
Supplement producer: *Ira C. Roberts*
Senior media project manager : *Susan Lombardi*
Cover and interior design: *Kami Carter*
Cover image: © *Corbis Images*
Typeface: *10/12 Times New Roman*
Compositor: *Techbooks*
Printer: *R. R. Donnelley*

Library of Congress Cataloging-in-Publication Data

Hill, Charles W. L.

    Principles of management / Charles W.L. Hill, Steven L. McShane.
      p. cm.
    Includes index.
    ISBN-13: 978-0-07-353012-3 (student edition : alk. paper)
    ISBN-10: 0-07-353012-3 (student edition : alk. paper)
    ISBN-13: 978-0-07-331626-0 (instructor's edition : alk. paper)
    ISBN-10: 0-07-331626-1 (instructor's edition : alk. paper)
    1. Management. I. McShane, Steven Lattimore. II. Title.
HD31.H4885 2008
658--dc22

                                     2006033368

www.mhhe.com

For Lane

—C.W.L.H.

Dedicated with Love
and devotion to Donna,
and to our wonderful
daughters, Bryton and
Madison

—S.L.M.

about the // AUTHORS

Charles W. L. Hill

Charles W. L. Hill is the Hughes M. Blake Professor of International Business at the School of Business, University of Washington. Professor Hill received his PhD from the University of Manchester's Institute of Science and Technology (UMIST) in Britain. In addition to the University of Washington, he has served on the faculties of UMIST, Texas A&M University, and Michigan State University.

Professor Hill has published over 40 articles in peer-reviewed academic journals, including the *Academy of Management Journal, Academy of Management Review, Strategic Management Journal,* and *Organization Science.* He has also published two college texts: one on strategic management and the other on international business. Professor Hill has served on the editorial boards of several academic journals, including the *Strategic Management Journal* and *Organization Science.* Between 1993 and 1996 he was consulting editor at the *Academy of Management Review.*

Professor Hill teaches in the MBA, Executive MBA, Management, and PhD programs at the University of Washington. He has received awards for teaching excellence in the MBA, Executive MBA, and Management programs. He has also taught customized executive programs.

Professor Hill works on a consulting basis with a number of organizations. His clients have included ATL, Boeing, BF Goodrich, Hexcel, House of Fraser, Microsoft, Seattle City Light, Tacoma City Light, Thompson Financial Services, and Wizards of the Coast.

Steven L. McShane

Steven L. McShane is Professor of Management in the Graduate School of Management at the University of Western Australia, where he receives high teaching ratings from students in Perth, Singapore, and other cities in Asia where UWA offers its programs. He is also an Honorary Professor at Universiti Tunku Abdul Rahman (UTAR) in Malaysia and previously taught in the business faculties at Simon Fraser University and Queen's University in Canada. Steve has conducted executive seminars with Nokia, Wesfarmers Group, ALCOA World Alumia Australia, and many other organizations. He is also a popular visiting speaker, having given four dozen talks to faculty and students in almost a dozen countries over the past three years.

Steve earned his PhD from Michigan State University in organizational behavior, human resource management, and labor relations. He also holds a Master of Industrial Relations from the University of Toronto, and an undergraduate degree from Queen's University in Canada. Steve has served as President of the Administrative Sciences Association of Canada (the Canadian equivalent of the Academy of Management) and Director of Graduate Programs in the business faculty at Simon Fraser University.

Along with co-authoring *Organizational Behavior,* 4e, Steve is the author of *Canadian Organizational Behaviour,* 6th ed. (2006), co-author (with Tony Travaglione) of *Organisational Behaviour on the Pacific Rim,* 2e (2007), and co-author (with Mary Ann von Glinow) of *Organizational Behaviour: Essentials* (2007). He has also published several dozen articles, book chapters, and conference papers on diverse topics, including managerial decision making, organizational learning, socialization of new employees, gender bias in job evaluation, wrongful dismissal, media bias in business magazines, and labor union participation.

Steve enjoys spending his leisure time swimming, body board surfing, canoeing, skiing, and traveling with his wife and two daughters.

/// BRIEF **CONTENTS**

// TABLE OF CONTENTS

PART 4
Leading

\\ PREFACE \\\

The management textbook market is crowded, so why did we write another one? The answer, quite frankly, is that a huge gap exists between what managers actually do or think about and what the existing gaggle of management books say are contemporary practices. Some topics that managers say are important (such as strategizing and shaping corporate culture) need much more attention in management courses; other concepts and practices long forgotten by most managers shouldn't be required reading in a college management course. Management theory has also moved forward, and in some cases has become well-established practice in the corporate world. Again, we were surprised by the gap in what students have been reading. So, this book was crafted to close that gap, to help students have a more realistic understanding about what managers actually do and what management theory actually recommends. We offer this relevant view of management in a way that has a logical flow of content, is succinct and clear in its writing style, rich in real-world examples, and remains focused on the role of managers.

// RELEVANCE: A BOOK FOR THE TWENTY-FIRST CENTURY

Almost 100 years ago, French industrialist Henri Fayol proposed five functions of management, four of which (planning, organizing, leading, and controlling) have become the foundation of management books over the past 40 years. While some management functions are timeless, we firmly believe that the late-1800s managers who inspired Fayol to describe these functions are markedly different from effective managers today. In other words, it is time for a 21st-century management book written for 21st-century managers. At the same time, we recognize that Fayol's management functions have become deeply entrenched in management courses, so this book proposes an evolutionary rather than revolutionary approach to change. We retain four management functions, and with similar names to the past, but these subtle differences are more pronounced in the chapters and emphasis throughout this book. Let's look at a few of these emerging perspectives.

Planning and Strategizing

Most management books focus on planning, whereas we write about planning and strategizing. A trivial difference? Hardly! While planning is a formal process for periodically (e.g., once a year) generating organizational strategies, strategizing is a *continual* process for thinking through what a firm should pursue to attain its goals. In other words, successful managers are continually strategizing, sometimes in the absence of planning. Thus, we repeatedly emphasize how managers strategize. And to avoid perpetuating the error that planning and strategizing are interchangeable terms, this book has the distinction of presenting separate chapters for both practices.

Organizing and Controlling—Organization Architecture

Most management textbooks treat *organizing* and *controlling* as completely separate functions. Yet managers will tell you that organizing people into departments and teams is an important form of control. They also point out that various control systems—such as incentive systems and budgets—are closely connected to the organization's structure. Furthermore, managers emphasize that organizational culture is an important control system, no matter how difficult it is to shape; it should never be viewed as an untouchable fixture of the internal environment (as other books assume). Thus, we apply the contemporary management view that organizing and controlling belong together as two parts of the underlying management process, called *organizational architecture*.

Leading and Developing Employees

Leadership is important; in fact, it is vital for guiding the organization toward its objectives and for applying the other management functions. But managers today do more than motivate, influence, and direct others. Although missing from Fayol's original functions, this book highlights the fact that managers also devote much of their time to developing staff. In fact, General Electric and other top-performing companies insist that managers give the highest priority to hiring, training, mentoring, and rewarding employees. In contemporary management parlance, these companies consider human capital as their competitive advantage, and managers play a vital role in enhancing the value of that resource.

// ORGANIZATION: A LOGICAL INTEGRATED FLOW OF TOPICS

We held several meetings, transmitted numerous e-mail messages, and consulted with dozens of instructors to hammer out the right organization of chapters and topics for this book. The fact is, by finding the right sequence of chapters and topics, we can more successfully help students to understand management roles and their interconnections. The chapter sequence also reflects how managers actually think and act, which explains why this book is organized somewhat differently from management textbooks that rely on past models. For example, the chapters on organizational structure and controls are side-by-side for the reasons noted earlier. We also organize staffing, motivating, and maintaining the well-being of employees in a sequence, because this is how managers actually view the process of building human capital. More generally, this book moves from macro, through midlevel issues, to micro issues, and closes by switching back to a macro perspective (managing innovation and change).

This book also takes an integrated rather than piecemeal approach to management topics. This means that later chapters build upon concepts introduced in earlier chapters. Students can't make sense of planning and strategizing, for example, unless they have learned about the external environment. The goal is to get students to see the big picture, and to understand the important linkages between different aspects of management. To drive this home, we frequently refer to concepts introduced in prior chapters, and show how they related to the material being discussed in the current chapter. At the same time, we are sensitive to the desire of some instructors to skip certain chapters. We have not pushed the level of integration so far that this cannot be done.

// SUCCINCT: FOCUSING ON WHAT IS IMPORTANT

The field of management covers a large territory, but we were amazed at how many pages the leading management textbooks required to cover this territory. Most management courses are one semester, which makes it very difficult for students to read through their textbook. Even in a two-semester course, the reading requirements could potentially undermine rather than improve the learning process. Although deciding what to include and exclude from a textbook is never easy, we were determined to keep this book to a more reasonable length. This book has no chapter on management history, choosing instead to discuss historical developments where appropriate throughout the book. We also avoided special chapters found in other books (entrepreneurship, information systems, and so on). These topics are peripheral to the management discipline and, indeed, are usually the focus of other courses. Through these and other adjustments, we have crafted a management book with a manageable 18 chapters and a more reasonable number of pages of reading.

// CONTENT: UP-TO-DATE

Along with its contemporary management structure, this book offers students up-to-date management concepts and examples. Current management thinking is apparent throughout, such as recognizing social concerns with globalization (Chapter 3), practicing backchannel control methods (Chapter 9), building an employer brand (Chapter 12), improving customer satisfaction through better job satisfaction (Chapter 14), and recognizing the effects of disruptive technologies (Chapter 18).

Students want real-world examples that are fresh, not ancient history (like the 1980s or even the 1990s), so we scanned the latest sources to link management concepts to recent events. For instance, we describe how Chick-Fil-A CEO Dan Cathy serves as a figurehead by camping out with customers (Chapter 1), how Intel CEO Paul Otellini is steering the microchip makers toward a new strategic plan (Chapter 5), how Unilever has reconfigured its organizational structure in recent years to find the right balance among competing demands in the marketplace (Chapter 8), how Dell executives have attempted to shift the computermaker's corporate culture (Chapter 10), how Google attracts top talent by engaging in guerrilla recruitment practices (Chapter 12), and how Xerox CEO Anne Mulcahy led the company's dramatic turnaround despite her status as an "outside-insider."

// READABILITY: INTERESTING AND ACCESSIBLE

Management textbooks don't have to be dense, boring, and dull. Our tactic for engaging students has been to illustrate concepts through stories, using examples that are current, interesting, and, when appropriate, provocative. We are story tellers, and we believe that the evocative stories throughout this book will help students to understand the content and motivate them to read through the assigned pages. At the end of the day, we have written this book for students; we want to reach them through lively and accessible communication.

To improve readability, we have also cleared out the clutter found in most management books. Gone is the weighty boxed material because instructors and students alike told us that content or anecdotes placed in boxes are not read. Instead, these examples are embedded in the text so they are more clearly interwoven with the discussion of key concepts. Each chapter also opens not with the traditional boxed case, but with a brief story that is used to illustrate the concepts covered in the chapter. The goal, again, is to capture the attention of students and draw them in.

// MANAGEMENT CENTRIC

A management textbook should write about what managers do and how they can perform their jobs more effectively. This principle seems obvious, but it is often lost in practice as management textbooks become steeped in theory without connecting back to management practice. Aware of this tendency, we have tried to make managers the centerpiece of this book. Essentially, we adopt an action-oriented approach by focusing on what successful managers do and why those actions work well (and under what conditions they work well). We repeatedly emphasize why the concepts discussed in a chapter matter for managers. We also drive these points home at the end of every chapter with a closing section appropriately entitled "Why does it matter?"

// HIGH-QUALITY SUPPORT MATERIALS

Unlike revised texts/resource packages, where materials are refitted, resized, and repurposed, the resources supporting this text have been freshly created in close conjunction with the text and each other to provide you with a truly integrated support package organized by chapter learning objectives, measures learning outcomes, and incorporating AACSB standards.

The Instructor's Manual (authored by Barbara Carlin, University of Houston, and Chris Quinn-Trank, Texas Tech University) closely follows the textbook's learning objectives and includes extra war stories and teaching tips. The Instructor's Manual also incorporates ideas and guidelines for implementing the Management Portfolio Project into your management course.

The Test Bank (authored by Carol Johnson, University of Denver) includes over 150 questions per chapter, including multiple-choice, true/false, and short answer questions at various levels of Bloom's Taxonomy. Every test bank question is tagged to the corresponding textbook page, learning objective, Bloom's Taxonomy, and the AACSB requirement it assesses. A test table is also provided to help you easily choose questions to fit your needs. An additional set of practice quizzes, also written by the test bank author, is available on the text's Online Learning Center.

PowerPoint Package (authored by Amit Shah, Frostburg State University) includes over 350 slides, each tied to the textbook page and learning objective. Slides include teaching notes to help reduce your prep time. A set of student slides is available on the text's Online Learning Center.

Instructor's Resource CD. All of our instructor supplements are available in this one-stop, multimedia resource, which includes the PowerPoint Package, Test Bank, and Instructor's Manual.

Videos. A set of new videos on management issues accompanying this text is suitable to support your classroom or student lab, or for home viewing. These thought-provoking video clips are available upon adoption of this text.

PrepCenter. Let McGraw-Hill/Irwin save you time preparing for class with PrepCenter! On one easy screen you can access the entire library of resources available with *Principles of Management* by Hill/McShane. Browse for available assets by chapter, concept, or media type, and then preview and organize them for your course.

Online Learning Center (OLC). Our Web site mirrors the text chapter-by-chapter. OLCs can be delivered in multiple ways—professors and students can access them directly through the textbook Web site, through PageOut, or within a course management system such as WebCT, Blackboard, TopClass, or eCollege.

Enhanced Cartridge. McGraw-Hill/Irwin is pleased to offer an enhanced cartridge to help you organize your course. Not only do you receive the instructor's material, but we also provide you with additional student exercises such as threaded discussion questions, quizzes, and more!

// ADDITIONAL RESOURCES FOR YOUR PRINCIPLES OF MANAGEMENT COURSE

Group and Video Resource Manual: An Instructor's Guide to an Active Classroom. This electronic manual for instructors includes a menu of items they can use as teaching tools in class. Included are detailed teaching notes and PowerPoints for self-assessments, test your knowledge exercises, the Manager's Hot Seat DVD, as well as new group exercises, complete with any handouts or worksheets you'll need to accompany them.

Manager's Hot Seat. This interactive, video-based software puts students in the manager's hot seat where they have to apply their knowledge to make decisions on the spot on hot issues such as ethics, diversity, working in teams, and the virtual workplace. This resource is available for student purchase with the Hill/McShane text. Resources to support these videos are located in the Group and Video Resource Manual.

Team Learning Assistant (TLA). This online tool makes it easy for you to implement team learning in your class. Monitor the team process, facilitate peer feedback and evaluation, teach the value of team contracts and conflict resolution, and grade individual performance quickly and easily by using TLA.

Hill/McShane in eBook format. Real Texts—Real Savings! Are you interested in giving your students the option to access the textbook contents digitally, with interactive, dynamic features and save your students some money? If so, our eBooks are for you. They are identical to our printed textbooks but cost about half as much. Your students will be able to search, highlight, bookmark, annotate, and print the eBook! McGraw-Hill Higher Education's eBooks can be viewed online on any computer with an Internet connection or downloaded to an individual's computer. For more information, please visit http://ebooks.primisonline.com/or contact your McGraw-Hill rep.

You can customize this text. **McGraw-Hill/Primis Online's** digital database offers you the flexibility to customize your course including material from the largest online collection of textbooks, readings, and cases. Primis leads the way in customized eBooks with hundreds of titles available at prices that save your students over 20 percent off bookstore prices. Additional information is available at 800-228-0634.

***BusinessWeek* Edition.** Your students can subscribe to *BusinessWeek* for a specially priced rate of $8.25 in addition to the price of the text. Students will receive a pass code card shrink-wrapped with their new text. The card directs students to a Web site where they enter the code and then gain access to *BusinessWeek*'s registration page to enter address info and set up their print and online subscription as well. Passcode ISBN 007-251530-9.

***The Wall Street Journal* Edition.** Your students can subscribe to the *The Wall Street Journal* for a specially priced rate of $20.00 in addition to the price of the text. Students will receive a "How To Use the *WSJ*" handbook plus a pass code card shrink-wrapped with the text. The card directs students to a Web site where they enter the code and then gain access to the *WSJ* registration page to enter address info and set up their print and online subscription, and also set up their subscription to Dow Jones Interactive online for the span of the 10-week period. Passcode ISBN 007-251950-9.

// FOR STUDENTS

Most or you will start your careers as functional specialists—as accountants, engineers, salespeople, finance specialists, and so on. If you are successful in your entry-level job, you will be promoted, and more than likely, before long you will be put in charge of other people. At this point, you will have become a manager. As a manager, further advancement will be dependent upon your ability to get things done though others—to motivate, persuade, encourage, and coach others so that they perform better. This book is about what it takes to become an effective manager. It is about how to make good decisions, how to exert influence on the strategies and policies of your employer (even when you are an entry-level employee), how to motive and lead others, how to communicate effectively, how to manage change, and much more. Becoming a *good* manager is not easy, but it is a way to have a successful career and have an impact upon the organizations in which you work. Becoming a *great* manager is more than that—great managers build organizations that change the world. Great managers of the last quarter-century include Sam Walton, who built Wal-Mart from nothing into the world's largest retailer, Jack Welch, who transformed General Electric from a lumbering conglomerate into a dynamic and productive enterprise, Howard Schultz, who was the inspiration behind the growth of Starbucks, and Michael Dell, who starting from his dorm room created the world's largest manufacturer of personal computers.

We have written this book to help you get started on the road to becoming a good—or even a great—manager. We have tried to put together a book that is written in a lively and accessible style, that is crammed full of interesting and relevant examples, and that introduces you to the most useful concepts and theories for managers, yet presents these concepts and theories in a way that is easy to understand.

We hope you enjoy the book, but more than that, we hope that the ideas contained herein stay with you for the rest of your careers, and help you to advance in the world of work.

PRINCIPLES OF **MANAGEMENT**

1

MANAGEMENT

LEARNING OBJECTIVES

After Reading This Chapter You Should Be Able to:

1 Describe the basic functions of management.

2 Identify where in an organization managers are located.

3 Discuss the challenges people encounter as they become first-time managers.

4 Describe the roles managers adopt to perform the basic functions of management.

5 Outline the competencies managers must have to be effective.

The Essence of Hip—
The Burberry Trench
Coat
Under the leadership
of Rose Marie Bravo,
London fashion house
Burberry underwent a
renaissance. Between
1997 and 2003 profits
increased almost
fivefold as Burberry
was repositioned as a
hip, high-end global
brand.

© McGraw-Hill Companies/
Lars A. Niki Photographer.

When Rose Marie Bravo, the highly regarded president of Saks Fifth Avenue, announced in 1997 that she was leaving to become CEO of ailing British fashion house Burberry, people thought she was crazy. Burberry, best known as a designer of raincoats with trademark tartan linings, had been described as "an outdated business with a fashion cachet of almost zero." Seven years later Bravo was being heralded in Britain and the United States as one of the world's best managers. In her tenure at Burberry she engineered a remarkable turnaround, leading a transformation of Burberry into what one commentator called an "achingly hip" high-end fashion brand whose raincoats, clothes, handbags, and other accessories were must-have items for well-heeled, fashion-conscious consumers. When asked how she achieved the transformation, Bravo explained that hidden value in the brand was unleashed by constant creativity and innovation. Although she hired good designers to re-energize the brand, she also noted that "creativity doesn't just come from designers…ideas can come from the sales floor, the marketing department, even from accountants, believe it or not. People at whatever level they are working have a point of view and have something to say that is worth listening to." Bravo also emphasized the importance of teamwork. "One of the things I think people

overlook is the quality of the team. It isn't one person, and it isn't two people. It is a whole group of people—a team that works cohesively toward a goal—that makes something happen or not." She notes that her job is to build the team and then motivate them, "keeping them on track, making sure that they are following the vision."[1]

By all accounts Rose Marie Bravo is a remarkable manager. Her story illustrates the important and powerful role that managers can play in an organization. Bravo didn't redesign Burberry's tired fashion line; she didn't personally create the ads featuring supermodel Kate Moss that helped reposition the brand; it wasn't her job to coordinate Burberry's global manufacturing system to make sure suppliers adhered to Burberry's exacting quality standards; nor did she directly participate in the redesign of Burberry's retail stores. But she did help to hire, motivate, lead, and reward the people who did these things. Bravo saw the hidden value in the Burberry brand, pushed for a new hip vision, asked people at all levels in the organization for ideas, and built and managed the teams that transformed Burberry. Rose Marie Bravo embodies what great managers do: They make things happen; they develop strategy; they organize people, projects, and processes; they energize others in the organization; and they lead.

management
The art of getting things done through people.

This book is about **management**, which can be defined as the art of getting things done through people in organizations.[2] As we will see, management can be an enormously creative endeavor. Managers are not bureaucrats. They do more than just keep the trains running on time. Managers can also give organizations a sense of purpose and direction. As Wal-Mart's founder Sam Walton was fond of saying, they can motivate "ordinary people to do extraordinary things."[3] They can transform organizations; they can create new ways of producing and distributing goods and services; and they can change how the world works through their actions. Think about what some of the greatest managers of this era have done. Sam Walton built Wal-Mart from scratch into the largest retailer in the world. Lou Gerstner repositioned IBM from a troubled manufacturer of mainframe computers into the dominant provider of computer software services in the world. Jack Welch reenergized General Electric, transforming a tired engineering conglomerate into an efficient, vibrant, entrepreneurial enterprise that set the standard for excellence in many industries in which it competed. In the late 1970s Steve Jobs of Apple Computer gave the world the first mass-marketed, easy-to-use personal computers; today Apple under Jobs's management is still driving innovation with its iPod music player. Meg Whitman provided the leadership that helped eBay become the world's first and most successful online auction house, revolutionizing the auction industry.

Throughout this book we will discuss how great managers like these work through people to do remarkable things. First, however, we must better understand the basic functions of management, where you can find managers in an organization, how one becomes a manager, the nature of managerial work, the roles managers adopt to get things done through people, and the different competencies that are required to become a good manager.

■ // The Functions of Management

In the early 20th century a French industrialist named Henri Fayol stated that management had five main functions: planning, organizing, commanding (that is, leading), coordinating, and controlling.[4] A lot of water has passed under the bridge since Fayol wrote about management, and we have learned much about the theory and practice of management; but in a testament to the robustness of Fayol's original formulation, a modified version of Fayol's list is still widely used. This list identifies four management functions: planning, organizing, controlling, and leading (Fayol's fifth function, coordinating, is now treated as an aspect of organizing). In this book we focus on these four main functions of management, but we have broadened the definition of those functions somewhat to better represent the realities of management practice in the 21st century. The four functions that we discuss are (1) planning and strategizing, (2) organizing, (3) controlling, and (4) leading and developing employees.

planning
A formal process whereby managers choose goals, identify actions to attain those goals, allocate responsibility for implementing actions to specific individuals or units, measure the success of actions by comparing actual results against the goals, and revise plans accordingly.

// PLANNING AND STRATEGIZING

Planning is a formal process whereby managers choose goals, identify actions to attain those goals, allocate responsibility for implementing actions to specific individuals or units, measure the success of actions by comparing actual results against the goals, and revise plans accordingly. Planning takes place at multiple levels in an organization and is an ingrained part of a manager's job. Planning is used by senior managers to develop overall strategies for an organization (a **strategy** is an action that managers take to attain the goals of an organization). Planning, however, goes beyond strategy development to include the regulation of a wide variety of organizational activities. Managers plan expenditures every year in a budgeting process. Managers draw up plans for building new factories, opening new offices, implementing new information systems, improving inventory control systems, introducing new products, launching new marketing campaigns, rolling out employee benefits programs, dealing with

strategy
An action that managers take to attain the goals of an organization.

crises, and so on. To be sure, many of these plans are linked to the strategy of the enterprise. The allocation of financial resources specified in an organization's budget for the coming year, for example, should be driven by the strategy of the organization. However, planning is often about formalizing a strategy that has already been selected and documenting the steps that managers must follow within the organization to put that strategy into effect.

Although planning is a useful process for generating strategies, strategizing involves more than planning. **Strategizing** is the process of thinking through on a continual basis what strategies an organization should pursue to attain its goals. Strategizing involves being aware of and analyzing what competitors are doing; thinking about how changes in the external environment, such as changes in technology or government regulations, impact the organization; weighing the pros and cons of alternative strategies; anticipating how competitors might respond to these strategies; and choosing a course of action. When Rose Marie Bravo decided to reposition Burberry as a hip, high-end fashion brand, she was strategizing.

Whereas planning is a formal process for generating the strategies of an organization, strategies can also arise in the absence of planning.[5] For example, anyone who has walked into a Starbucks store may have noticed that in addition to various coffee beverages and food, the company also sells music CDs. Most Starbucks stores now have racks displaying about 20 CDs. Reports suggest that when Starbucks decides to carry a CD, it typically ranks among the top four retailers selling it. The interesting thing about Starbucks' entry into music retailing is that it was not the result of a formal planning process. The company's journey into music retailing started in the late 1980s when Tim Jones, then the manager of Starbucks' store in Seattle's University Village, started to bring his own tapes of music compilations into the store to play. Soon Jones was getting requests for copies from customers. Jones told this to Starbucks' CEO Howard Schultz and suggested that Starbucks start to sell its own music. In other words, *Jones was strategizing*. At first Schultz was skeptical, but after repeated lobbying by Jones he eventually took up the suggestion. Today Starbucks not only sells CDs; it is also moving into music downloading with its Hear Music Starbucks stores, where customers can listen to music from Starbucks' 200,000-song online music library while sipping their coffee and burning their own CDs.[6]

Starbucks' strategy to enter the music retailing business emerged from the grass roots of the organization in the absence of planning. It was the result of strategizing by an individual store manager, and only after some time was the strategy adopted by senior managers. As we will see later in this book, strategy often develops in this way. Managers at all levels in an organization spend a lot of time strategizing. It is an important aspect of their jobs. Sometimes they do this as part of a formal planning process, but strategic thinking also goes on without planning. This is not to belittle the importance of planning, which has an important role in organizations. However, strategizing is more than just planning—it involves constantly thinking through strategic alternatives.

// ORGANIZING

Organizing refers to the process of deciding who within an organization will perform what tasks, where decisions will be made, who reports to whom, and how different parts of the organization will coordinate their activities to pursue a common goal. In a business, organizing typically involves dividing the enterprise into subunits based on functional tasks—such as procurement, R&D, production, marketing, sales, customer service, human resources, accounting, and finance—and deciding how much decision-making authority to give each subunit. Organizing is part of planning and strategizing: As we discuss later in this book, strategy is implemented through organization. For example, to implement the decision to expand Starbucks' operations into online music, Howard Schultz set up a separate unit within Starbucks called Hear Music; placed an executive, Don MacKinnon, in charge of that unit; and gave him the task of rolling out Hear Music in Starbucks' stores across the country. MacKinnon, together with his unit, is thus responsible for implementing the strategy of growing Starbucks' music business.

strategizing
The process of thinking through on a continual basis what strategies an organization should pursue to attain its goals.

■ Strategy development at Starbucks.

■ Organizing at Starbucks.

organizing
The process of deciding who within an organization will perform what tasks, where decisions will be made, who reports to whom, and how different parts of the organization will coordinate their activities to pursue a common goal.

// CONTROLLING

Controlling is the process of monitoring performance against goals, intervening when goals are not met, and taking corrective action. Controlling is just as important as planning, strategizing, and organizing. Without control systems to verify that performance is hitting goals, an organization can veer off course. Controlling is also linked to planning and strategizing and to organizing. Drafting plans is the first step in controlling an organization. Controlling requires managers to compare performance against the plans to monitor how successful an organization is at implementing a strategy. Thus at Starbucks, Don MacKinnon has been given goals related to the rollout and sales of Hear Music, and his success at implementing the strategy will be assessed by comparing actual performance against the goals.

An important aspect of controlling is creating incentives that align the interests of individual employees with those of the organization, helping to ensure that everyone is pulling in the same direction. An **incentive** is a factor, monetary or nonmonetary, that motivates individuals to pursue a particular course of action. Starbucks, for example, has a long history of giving stock-based compensation to employees. The thinking here is that stock-based incentive pay will induce employees to look for ways to improve the performance of the organization, thus increasing the company's stock price and their own wealth. So perhaps it is no surprise that Tim Jones, who was not only a store manager but also a stockholder, actively lobbied senior management to persuade them to sell music in the stores. With the right incentives in place, employees will work productively and control their own behavior, which reduces the need for close personal supervision and other intrusive control methods.

Caffeine Music   Starbucks has a profitable sideline selling select music CDs. Since 2004 customers have been able to download music and burn their own CDs at its Hear Music stores. The strategy to enter the music retailing business was not planned—it was adopted after lobbying by an individual store manager.

© Axel Koester, Axel Koester Photography.

// LEADING AND DEVELOPING EMPLOYEES

Leading is the process of motivating, influencing, and directing others in the organization to work productively in pursuit of organization goals.[7] Leading also entails articulating a grand strategic vision for an organization and becoming a tireless advocate for that vision. Rose Marie Bravo was thought of as a great manager in part because she was good at persuading other employees to accept her transformational strategic vision for Burberry, and she excelled at motivating, influencing, and directing people. As in the case of Rose Marie Bravo, leading also involves listening to others, learning from them, and empowering them to pursue actions that benefit the organization.

An important aspect of leading is developing employees. **Developing employees** refers to the task of hiring, training, mentoring, and rewarding employees in an organization, including other managers. It is often said that people are the most important asset of an organization.

Academics talk about the value of the **human capital** of an enterprise, by which they mean the skills and motivations of its employees; they assert that human capital can be a source of competitive advantage.[8] Rose Marie Bravo recognized the importance of human capital when she took on the top management position at Burberry. One of her first actions was to recruit a top-notch team of managers and creative designers through which she could get things done. Management expert Peter Drucker has emphasized that hiring and promoting the right people are among the most important management tasks because they have lasting consequences for the organization and are difficult to reverse. Unfortunately Drucker also estimates that many managers are not good at this function. According to Drucker, about one in three selection and promotion decisions is only minimally effective.[9] The legendary former CEO of General Electric, Jack Welch, seen by many as one of the best managers of the 20th century, estimated that he spent 70 percent of his time as CEO developing and selecting other managers, mentoring them, and evaluating their performance.[10]

Leading and developing employees are in many ways the core connection among planning and strategizing, organizing, controlling, and creating incentives. Skilled leaders

- Drive strategic thinking (strategizing) deep within the organization while articulating their own vision for the organization.
- Have a plan for their organization and push others to develop plans.
- Proactively structure the organization to implement their chosen strategy.
- Exercise control with a deft hand, never seeming too overbearing or demanding, while at the same time never taking their eyes off the ball.
- Put the right kinds of incentives in place.
- Get the best out of people by persuading them that a task is worthy of their effort.
- Build a high-quality team of other managers and employees through which they can work to get things done.

Without skilled leaders strategy may fail. The organization may become bureaucratic; control may be lost; employees will lack incentives and motivation; and the organization may suffer insufficient human capital.

■ // Types of Managers

Managers are found at multiple levels in an organization. They may lead an entire organization as Rose Marie Bravo did at Burberry; or they may head functions, departments, or units. There are three main types of managers: general managers, functional managers, and frontline managers. **General managers** are responsible for the overall performance of an organization or one of its major self-contained subunits or divisions. **Functional managers** lead a particular function or a subunit within a function. They are responsible for a task, activity, or operation such as accounting, marketing, sales, R&D, production, information technology, or logistics. **Frontline managers** manage employees who are themselves not managers. They are found at the lowest level of the management hierarchy.

For illustration, consider a large diversified enterprise like General Electric. General Electric is active in many different businesses: Among other things, it makes jet engines, power plants, medical equipment, railway locomotives, and lighting products. GE also sells insurance, owns NBC, and offers a wide range of financial services, particularly to industrial customers. GE is organized into different business divisions, and each division has its own functions, such as R&D, production, marketing, sales, and customer services. GE is thus known as a *multidivisional* enterprise (see Figure 1.1). Multidivisional enterprises like GE have four main levels of management: the corporate level, the business level, the functional level, and frontline managers. General managers are found at the corporate and business levels. Functional managers are found within the divisions where they manage functions or subunits within those functions. Frontline managers are found deep within functions managing teams of nonmanagement employees.

---

human capital
The knowledge, skills, and capabilities embedded in individuals.

■ Leadership at Burberry.

general managers
Managers responsible for the overall performance of an organization or one of its major self-contained subunits or divisions.

functional managers
Managers responsible for leading a particular function or a subunit within a function.

frontline managers
Managers who manage employees who are themselves not managers.

FIGURE 1.1

A Multidivisional
Management Hierarchy

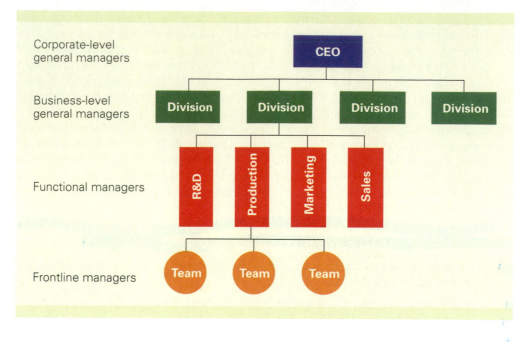

■ Corporate management
at GE.

// CORPORATE-LEVEL GENERAL MANAGERS

The principal general manager at the corporate level is the chief executive officer (CEO), who leads the entire enterprise. In a multidivisional enterprise the CEO formulates strategies that span businesses—deciding, for example, whether to enter new businesses through acquisitions or whether to exit a business area. The CEO decides how the enterprise should be organized into different divisions and signs off on major strategic initiatives proposed by the heads of divisions. The CEO exercises control over divisions, monitoring their performance and deciding what incentives to give divisional heads. Finally, the CEO helps develop the human capital of the enterprise.

At General Electric Jeffery Immelt has been the CEO since 2001. Immelt has articulated a grand vision that includes pushing GE into environmentally friendly technologies.[11] Immelt is doing this because he thinks it makes good business sense. He believes that tighter environmental standards are inevitable, that environmentally friendly technologies are also cost-efficient, and that customers will increasingly demand them. Thus GE is investing in more fuel-efficient locomotives and jet engines; coal-based power plants that use technologies to strip almost all pollutants out; technologies for sequestering carbon dioxide emissions; water purification systems; and power-generating windmills. Under Immelt GE is also exiting some businesses that do not fit his strategic vision, including GE's insurance business, which he sold to Swiss Reinsurance Co. in 2006 for $6.8 billion.[12]

The CEO of a corporation also manages relationships with the people who own the company—its shareholders. The CEO reports to the board of

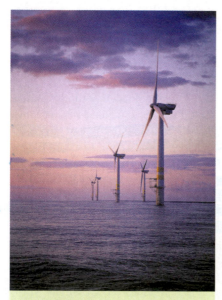

Green in Green   The vision of CEO Jeffery Immelt for General Electric calls for the company to invest in green technologies. GE now sells over $2 billion worth of power-generating windmills annually.

Courtesy of GE Energy

directors, whose primary function is to make sure the strategy of the company is consistent with the best interests of shareholders. The CEO also normally sits on the board and spends considerable time describing company strategy to shareholders.

Members of the top management team help the CEO in all of this. The team normally includes a chief financial officer (CFO), who is responsible for the overall financing of the corporation. It may also include a chief operating officer (COO), who makes sure operations are run efficiently within the company; and in some high-technology enterprises a chief technology officer (CTO) is responsible for developing new technologies and products within the corporation.

// BUSINESS-LEVEL GENERAL MANAGERS

With a multidivisional enterprise such as General Electric, business-level general managers head the different divisions. GE has general managers running its power generation business, medical equipment business, lighting business, and so on. These general managers report directly to Jeffery Immelt. Within an organization that is active in just one line of business, such as Burberry or Starbucks, the business and corporate levels are the same.

Business-level general managers lead their divisions—motivating, influencing, and directing their subordinates—and are responsible for divisional performance. Business-level general managers translate the overall strategic vision for the corporation into concrete strategies and plans for their units. Thus the head of GE's locomotive business, together with that team, has formulated strategies for making locomotives more environmentally friendly. These include the development of diesel locomotives with lower emissions and hybrid diesel–electric engines. Business-level managers often have considerable latitude to develop and implement strategies that they believe will improve the performance of their divisions, so long as those strategies are consistent with the overall goals and vision for the entire corporation. Business-level general managers organize operations within their division, deciding how best to divide tasks into functions and departments and how to coordinate those subunits so that strategy can be successfully implemented. Business-level general managers also control activities within their divisions, monitoring performance against goals, intervening to take corrective action when necessary, and developing human capital.

■ Business-level managers at GE.

// FUNCTIONAL MANAGERS

Below general managers we find functional managers, who are responsible for specific business functions that constitute a company or one of its divisions. Thus a functional manager's sphere of responsibility is generally confined to *one* organizational activity (purchasing, marketing, production, or the like), whereas general managers oversee the operation of the entire company or a self-contained division.

The head of each function leads that function. Functional managers motivate, influence, and direct others within their areas. Although they are not responsible for the overall performance of the organization, functional managers nevertheless have a major strategic role: to develop functional strategies and draft plans in their areas that help fulfill the strategic objectives set by business- and corporate-level general managers. In GE's aerospace business, for instance, manufacturing managers develop manufacturing strategies consistent with the corporate objective of producing environmentally friendly products and generating high performance. They might, for example, decide to implement process improvement programs to improve quality and boost employee productivity. Moreover, functional managers provide most of the information that makes it possible for business- and corporate-level general managers to formulate realistic and attainable strategies. Indeed, because they are closer to customers than are typical general managers, functional managers themselves may generate important ideas that subsequently may become major strategies for the company. Thus it is important for general managers to listen closely to the ideas of their functional managers. An equally great responsibility for managers at the functional level is strategy implementation: the execution of corporate- and business-level strategies.

■ Functional managers at GE.

The heads of functions are responsible for developing human capital within their organizations. They also organize their functions into subunits such as departments or teams; exercise control over those subunits; set goals; monitor performance; provide feedback; and make adjustments if necessary. Thus the manufacturing function might be further subdivided into departments responsible for specific aspects of the manufacturing process. There might be a procurement department, a production planning department, an inventory management department, and a quality assurance department. Each department will have its own managers, who report to their superiors, the functional heads; those managers will be responsible for leading their units, organizing and controlling them as necessary, strategizing for the tasks under their control, and developing employees within their units.

// FRONTLINE MANAGERS

Furthest down the management hierarchy are frontline managers, who manage employees who are themselves not managers. A frontline sales manager might manage 10 salespeople; a frontline manager in manufacturing might manage a work group of employees who physically assemble a product; and a frontline engineering manager in a software company might manage a group of developers writing computer code. Most complex organizations have many frontline managers. For example, the oil and energy company BP has some 10,000 frontline managers who oversee 80 percent of the organization's 100,000 employees. They work in every part of the company—from solar plants in Spain to drilling rigs in the North Sea and marketing teams in Chicago. Their decisions, in aggregate, have an enormous impact on BP's performance.[13] Most successful managers begin their managerial careers as frontline managers. In this job they encounter the realities of management, which as we will see in the next section often differ from their expectations.

■ Frontline managers at BP.

Frontline managers are critical to maintaining the performance of an organization. They lead their teams and units. They strategize about the best way to do things in their units and about the best strategies for their functions and the company. They plan how best to perform the tasks of their units. They organize tasks within their teams, monitor the performance of their subordinates, and try to develop the skills of their subordinates. As we saw in the case of Tim Jones at Starbucks, who was a frontline manager responsible for the performance of an individual store, frontline managers can have an impact significantly beyond their jobs. In some cases they can influence the destiny of an entire organization.

■ // Becoming a Manager

As we have just seen, managers are found at multiple levels within an organization. Although their precise roles and responsibilities vary depending on their levels in the organization, all managers have to lead and develop other employees, plan and strategize for their units, organize their units, and apply controls and incentives. How do people become managers, and what is the job like?

// FROM SPECIALIST TO MANAGER

■ Becoming a manager at Microsoft.

The journey into management typically begins when people are successful at a specialist task for which they were initially hired. For example, Microsoft hires many software engineers. Initially these people are recruited for their ability to write computer code; but if they succeed at this job, they may find themselves in charge of other software engineers, becoming development leads (a frontline position at Microsoft). At this point their management skills are just as important as their technical skills in fulfilling their responsibilities. People who cannot get things done through other people will not advance further. If they are successful, they may be promoted again and one day become general managers. A relevant case is John DeVaan, who was hired to write computer code after finishing an undergraduate computer science program at Oregon State University in 1985. Initially he worked on Excel. DeVaan's technical success soon brought him to the attention of his superiors, and he was promoted, becoming a development lead. He managed this successfully too, and further promotions followed. He directed software development for Office 95 and Office 97 and was ultimately promoted to lead Microsoft's Desktop Applications Business (the unit responsible for Office), growing that to a $7 billion business. DeVaan then became the general manager of Microsoft's TV division. Today he is senior vice president of engineering excellence at Microsoft and part of the business leadership team. To be sure, DeVaan was valued and promoted for his technical skills; but he would not have advanced had he not also been a great manager who excelled at leading and developing employees, planning and strategizing, organizing, and controlling.

More generally, whatever people's disciplinary backgrounds and initial functional assignments, if they are successful they may find themselves promoted into managerial roles. Accountants and finance professionals may manage other accounts and finance professionals; engineers working in production may manage other engineers; scientists in R&D may manage other scientists; and salespeople might find themselves managing part of the sales force. In these new roles technical skills remain important, but now people also have to manage. If they succeed, like John DeVaan they may find themselves promoted to general management positions, running entire divisions of an organization where their ability to lead, plan, develop strategy, organize, control, and motivate through incentives becomes of paramount importance. So the art of management is relevant to almost anyone who joins an organization with ambition and the ability to succeed, whatever his or her disciplinary background.

// MASTERING THE JOB

Harvard Business School Professor Linda Hill wanted to discover what work life was like for functional specialists who had been newly appointed to management positions, so she followed 19 newly appointed frontline managers through their first year as managers.[14] These managers had all been star performers as functional specialists, and their promotions to management positions were seen as rewards and an opportunity for career advancement. Hill documented the enormous difference between their expectations as they entered the job and the reality they soon encountered. Initially the new managers believed that their job was to exercise formal authority, making decisions and telling others what to do—in effect, to be the "boss." They also thought they would be able to continue doing the technical work they had been doing, "only with more power and control."[15] These expectations were shattered by reality.

After six months the new managers found themselves struggling with the fast-paced nature of the job. The managers found that they were in constant demand from subordinates, peers, and their own bosses. There was little time for quiet reflection. The workload was heavier than they had anticipated, and the job was more fragmented with many issues requiring attention during a typical day. Some yearned for the "simple days" when all they had to do was focus on their functional tasks. Now they had to process a significant amount of mail, deal with personal issues, and meet with peers and their own bosses, customers, suppliers, and so on. These observations echoed work by Henry Mintzberg, who followed managers around and found that on average they processed 36 pieces of mail each day, attended eight meetings, and took a tour through the building or plant.[16] Recent work by Mintzberg confirms the impression that a day in the life of an average manager is fragmented, full of different tasks, and characterized by constant interruptions and involves significant interpersonal networking.[17]

Before long most of the new managers in Linda Hill's study discovered that formal authority was a limited source of power: Their subordinates didn't necessarily listen to them! Moreover, they found out that to get things done, they had to work closely with peers and their bosses—people over whom the new managers had no formal authority. Hill noted that the most demanding issues managers encountered in their first year on the job all had to do with

Software Man The career of John DeVaan at Microsoft exemplifies how many people become managers. DeVaan started out as a software engineer writing code, but he was promoted to become a software development lead and then a general manager. DeVaan, a 20-year Microsoft veteran, is now a member of the business leadership team at Microsoft and senior vice president for engineering excellence.

© Microsoft Corporation.

"people challenges." They had to learn how to influence subordinates, peers, and their own bosses to get things done, and they had to establish trust and credibility with their subordinates, peers, and bosses before they could influence them. Being known as a star individual contributor is rarely enough; managers earn trust and credibility largely through interpersonal interactions on the job.

Over time the managers in Hill's study discovered that they had two sets of responsibilities: agenda setting for their teams and network building within the organization. Most new managers grasped the importance of agenda setting quickly, but the importance of building networks took longer to sink in. Managers must realize that to get things done and to help their own team succeed, they must work closely with a network of peers and superiors, persuading them to buy into the agenda of the manager's team. They have to be network builders, good at managing relationships. Hill concluded that new managers go through a psychological change during their first year on the job. They learn through experience to see themselves not as technical experts or functional specialists, but as leaders and network builders—not as bosses who get things done through command and control, but as people who get things done through their ability to influence and persuade others.

■ // Managerial Roles

managerial roles
Specific behaviors associated with the task of management.

Managerial roles are specific behaviors associated with the task of management. Managers adopt these roles to accomplish the basic functions of management just discussed—planning and strategizing, organizing, controlling, and leading and developing employees. One of the earliest and most enduring descriptions of managerial roles comes from Henry Mintzberg, who (as we have already noted) shadowed managers observing what they did during the day.[18] Mintzberg developed a list of roles that he grouped into three categories: interpersonal roles, informational roles, and decisional roles (see Figure 1.2). Mintzberg emphasized that managing is an integrated activity, so these roles are rarely distinct. Visiting clients, for instance, usually relates to two or more roles simultaneously.

FIGURE 1.2

Management Roles

Source: Based on H. Mintzberg, *The Nature of Managerial Work* (New York: Harper & Row, 1973).

Mintzberg's work has been replicated many times. Most researchers have found similar sets of roles (although there are some variations in labels and categories).[19] The roles that Mintzberg identified flesh out the richness of managerial work and tell us how managers behave and what they do when trying to perform the main functions of management.

// INTERPERSONAL ROLES

Interpersonal roles are roles that involve interacting with other people inside and outside the organization. Management jobs are people-intensive: Research suggests that managers spend somewhere between 66 and 80 percent of their time in the company of others.[20] Seldom do managers work alone for long periods without outside communication. As Linda Hill noted, managers get things done through their network of interpersonal relationships. Mintzberg identified three types of interpersonal roles: a figurehead role, a leader role, and a liaison role.

Managers at all levels are *figureheads*. They greet visitors, represent the company at community events, serve as spokespeople, and function as emissaries for the organization. For example, when Atlanta-based Chick-fil-A opens a new restaurant, it gives a year's worth of free meal coupons to the first 100 customers. This incentive draws big crowds, who camp outside the restaurant before opening day in the hope of being among the first 100 customers. The chain's president, Dan Cathy, joins them, camping outside the night before the opening, chatting with them, and then signaling the grand opening by playing his trumpet. By doing this, Cathy is acting as a figurehead for Chick-fil-A. At lower levels in a company, functional and frontline managers perform a variety of figurehead roles. They welcome new staff, help their teams celebrate performance milestones, give performance awards to employees, accompany senior executives or outside visitors on tours through the work area, and so on.

Earlier we noted that leadership is one function of management, and it is perhaps the most pivotal. However, leadership is more than a function that managers must fulfill. Managers also take on a *leadership* role to get things done within organizations. Managers behave as leaders to influence, motivate, and direct others within organizations and to strategize, plan, organize, control, and develop. A central task of leaders is to give their organizations a sense of direction and purpose. They do this by identify and articulating strategic visions for the organizations (by strategizing) and then by motivating others to work toward this vision. This is exactly what Rose Marie Bravo did at Burberry: She gave the organization a strategic vision, repositioning it as a hip, high-end brand, and she engaged Burberry's employees in that vision.

In their *liaison* role managers connect with people outside their immediate units.

The CEO as a Figurehead Dan Cathy, the president and COO of Atlanta-based Chick-fil-A restaurants, blows his trumpet to signal a new store opening. Cathy takes his figurehead role seriously. He particularly enjoys participating in the grand opening of a new store.[21]

Photo courtesy of Chick-fil-A, Inc. Photograph by Joe Siebold.

These may be the managers of other units within the organization or people outside the organization, such as suppliers, buyers, and strategic partners. An important purpose of such liaisons is to build a network of relationships. Managers can use their networks to help coordinate the work of their units with others, to gain access to valuable information, and more generally to get things done and further their own agendas within the organization. As Linda Hill observed in her research, building a network is one of the most important tasks that new managers face.

// INFORMATIONAL ROLES

Informational roles are concerned with collecting, processing, and disseminating information. Managers collect information from various sources both inside and outside the organization, process that information, and distribute it to others who need it. Mintzberg found that managers spend 40 percent of their time in these tasks. Mintzberg divided the information roles of management into three types: monitor, disseminator, and spokesperson.

As *monitors* managers scan the environment both inside and outside the organization. At Microsoft, for example, CEO Steve Ballmer is constantly reviewing competitive, technological, and regulatory trends in the markets in which Microsoft competes. He also monitors the performance of the different units within Microsoft, assessing, for example, how well the Windows, Office, and Xbox businesses are performing against targets.

Managers rely on both formal and informal channels to collect the information required for effective monitoring. Formal channels include the organization's own internal accounting information systems and data provided by important external agencies. Managers at Microsoft, for example, can access through the company's intranet a vast electronic library of research reports produced by external consulting companies and stock analysts that profile competitive trends and competitors in all the relevant markets. Informal channels include the manager's own personal network, which can be a great source of qualitative information and useful gossip. By monitoring the external competitive and internal organizational environment for information, managers try to gain knowledge about how well the organization is performing and whether any changes in strategy or operational processes are required. At Seattle-based retailer Nordstrom, for example, the first thing President Blake Nordstrom does when he gets to his desk every day is review sales figures from all company stores for the previous day. He compares these figures against targets; looks for trends; and if there is variance considers whether the company should take corrective action. In this respect the monitoring role of management is part of the controlling function. In addition, the information collected from monitoring can help managers think more clearly about the company's strategy.

One thing managers do with this information is disseminate it to direct reports and others inside the organization. In their *dissemination* role managers regularly inform staff about the company's direction and sometimes about specific technical issues. At the supervisory level, the disseminator role often takes the form of one-to-one informal conversations with specific employees about particular matters.

In their *spokesperson* role, managers deliver specific information to individuals and groups located outside their department or organization. Sales managers communicate with business partners regarding new sales strategies. Division heads give presentations to their colleagues in other divisions about strategies and resource requirements. CEOs meet with investors, government officials, community leaders, and others to convey information about company developments of interest to those stakeholders. These are more than figurehead activities: They communicate valuable information to important constituencies, and in doing so they can help to shape their perception of the organization and the way they interact with it. For example, if by sharing information the CEO of a company can successfully persuade investment analysts that his company is pursuing a good strategy, they may write a favorable investment report. In turn, this might lead to an increase in the company's stock price, making it easier for the company to raise additional capital from investors in the future by issuing new stock.

■ Information roles at Nordstrom.

// DECISIONAL ROLES

Management guru Peter Drucker once wrote that whatever managers do, they do through making decisions.[22] The information collected through monitoring is directed toward discovering problems or opportunities, weighing options, making decisions, and ensuring that those decisions are put into action. Whereas interpersonal roles deal with people and informational roles deal with knowledge, decisional roles deal with action. They translate the people and information into processes with the purpose of moving the organization toward its strategic goals. Mintzberg identified four decision roles: entrepreneur, disturbance handler, resource allocator, and negotiator.

To survive in competitive markets, firms must be entrepreneurial. They must pioneer new products and processes and quickly adopt those pioneered by others. In their role as *entrepreneurs*, managers must make sure that their organizations innovate and change when necessary, developing or adopting new ideas and technologies and improving their own products and processes. They must make decisions that are consistent with such entrepreneurial behavior. If they do not, their organizations will be quickly outflanked by more nimble competitors. Rose Marie Bravo is a good example of what happens when a manager successfully adopts the entrepreneur role. She made decisions that encouraged creativity within Burberry, leading directly to the development of new product offerings that appealed to a wider customer base.

■ Decision roles at Burberry.

Managing is full of paradoxes, and this is partly apparent when we contrast the proactive entrepreneurial role with the reactive *disturbance handler* role. Disturbance handling includes addressing unanticipated problems as they arise and resolving them expeditiously. In managerial work unanticipated problems arise often. Sales may grow more slowly than anticipated; excess inventory may accumulate; production processes may break down; valuable employees might leave for jobs elsewhere; and so on. Managers must decide what to do about these unanticipated problems—often quickly.

An important class of management decisions involves *resource allocation*. Organizations never have enough money, time, facilities, or people to satisfy all their needs. Resources are scarce and can be used in many different ways. A crucial decision responsibility of managers is to decide how best to allocate the scarce resources under their control between competing claims in order to meet the organization's goals. As a resource allocator, a manager in charge of product development, for example, may have to assign people, money, and equipment to three different product development teams. A marketing manager may apportion money between media advertising and point-of-sale promotions. A production manager may have limited funds for new equipment. In general, resource allocation decisions should be guided by the strategy of the organization.

Negotiating is continual for managers.[23] They negotiate with suppliers for better delivery, lower prices, and higher-quality inputs. They negotiate with customers over the pricing, delivery, and design of products and services. They negotiate with peers in their own organization over shared resources and cooperative efforts. They negotiate with their superiors for access to scarce resources, including capital, personnel, and facilities. They even negotiate with subordinates in their own work unit, trying to allocate employees between tasks to meet the goals of both the organization and individual employees. Managers who are successful when making negotiation decisions can lower input costs, strike better deals with customers, gain access to more high-quality resources within the organization, and better organize their own subordinates. Skilled negotiators are more likely to successfully implement strategy and raise the performance of their organizations.

// SOME QUALIFICATIONS

Mintzberg's work is useful for what it tells us about the nature of managerial work and the behaviors managers must adopt to execute successfully the functions of management. Nevertheless, his model of managerial roles has limitations. First, the model tells us what managers do, but it does not tell us what they *should* do. Remember, the model was derived by watching managers at work. Simply because managers routinely engage in an activity does not mean that they should pursue that activity. As a practical matter, all of the roles described in Mintzberg's model seem important, and most successful practicing managers probably engage in all of them at least occasionally. However, some roles may be more important than others and more deserving of management time and effort. The leader role, for example, is probably far more important than the figurehead role for managerial success.

Second, Mintzberg does not mention some important roles of managers. For example, evidence shows that managers can improve strategic thinking and decisions within their organization by taking on the role of *devil's advocate*, questioning the logic underlying proposed decisions to expose flawed thinking.[24] Similarly, many successful managers adopt a *mentoring* role with their subordinates. As mentors, managers draw on their own experiences to offer important insights to their subordinates, coaching them on how to become better managers.

A further limitation of Mintzberg's managerial roles model is that it is context dependent. The managerial roles model tries to describe what all managers do in all situations. The reality, of course, is that what managers do depends partly on the situation. For instance, one study noted that chief executives in local government agencies do not perform the public figurehead role because it is assigned to politicians. Similarly, some decision-making roles are limited for managers in government agencies because key decisions are made by politicians. Other studies have reported that the size of an organization has an impact on management roles. One study reported that managers of small growth-oriented businesses experience more brevity and fragmentation in their work than do managers in large companies. The absence of formal structure in these companies also changes the amount of time spent on some roles versus others. Studies also report that the importance of specific managerial roles varies across cultures.[25]

A final limitation of the model is that it does not reveal much about *how* to perform these different roles. To be sure, it is interesting to know that managers engage in negotiations all the time, that they have an important monitoring role, and that they allocate resources between competing claims. But what a practicing manager really wants to know is how to improve the performance of these tasks. This is precisely the focus of this book.

■ // Management Competencies: Do You Have What It Takes?

competencies
A manager's skills, values, and motivational preferences.

To fulfill the roles that were just described, managers need to have the "right stuff." They must possess several **competencies**—skills, values, and motivational preferences—that allow them to perform their jobs effectively and become proficient at planning and strategizing, organizing, controlling, developing, and leading.[26] We might be gifted with some competencies at birth, but most are developed through upbringing, education, and experience. No single set of competencies represents the perfect combination for successful management. Instead managers can be equally effective with different combinations of these personal characteristics.

// MANAGERIAL SKILLS

Management is a challenging and complex task, and performing it effectively requires a variety of skills. These skills are organized into three categories: conceptual, technical, and human. They apply in varying degrees of importance to managers at all levels in an organization.[27]

conceptual skills
The ability to see the big picture.

Conceptual Skills When 3,600 managers at 250 companies in several regions of the world ranked the importance of 24 competencies for midlevel managers, two of the top five categories in every culture studied were "analyze issues" and "sound judgment."[28] These categories fall under the domain of **conceptual skills**—the ability to see the "big picture," understand how the various parts of the organization affect each other, and conceptualize how those parts can be organized to improve the performance of the overall organization. In other words, conceptual skills are the foundation for strategizing and organizing.

A common misunderstanding is that conceptual skills for managers are all about the capacity for structured analysis. Rational, logical thinking is certainly important; but managers also require conceptual skills to think outside the box.[29] Many issues on managers' desk are exceptions with no existing solutions. Thus managers must be able to creatively figure out the real problem (or opportunity), the variety of options available to solve that problem, and the best choice in the context of that novel situation.

Managers at all levels require conceptual skills, but they are paramount in top management positions. This makes sense because CEOs and vice presidents have more scope to understand. They also face more novelty and uncertainty, which require plenty of creative thinking. In general, managers further down in an organization, such as frontline managers, face narrowly focused tactical issues as opposed to bigger strategic issues, and the problems they confront tend to be routine rather than exceptional.

Technical Skills **Technical skills** enable managers to perform specific activities involving methods, processes, or techniques. These skills include mastery of specific equipment (such as configuring intranet servers) or correctly following procedures (such as conducting an accounting audit). Frontline managers work directly with employees with technical expertise, so they typically require some of this expertise themselves to monitor employee performance, provide meaningful feedback, and help employees solve unusual problems. As an example, call center managers spend up to half of their time monitoring customer calls and giving employees feedback about how to improve their dialogue in the future. These managers would be ineffective in this mentoring role if they lacked sufficient knowledge about the product and the correct procedures for handling customer calls.

> **technical skills**
> Skills that include mastery of specific equipment or following technical procedures.

The general rule is that technical knowledge and skills are more important for frontline managers than for more senior management positions. The reasoning is that managers in the lower part of the hierarchy work directly with technical staff, whereas managers further up the hierarchy work more with other managers. Studies of management careers report that managers need to shift away from reliance on technical skills to more reliance on conceptual skills as they advance within an organization. The breakpoint occurs when a manager is responsible for people across functional units, such as managing a plant where employees have various forms of expertise.[30]

Although the demand for technical skills diminishes as a manager is promoted up the hierarchy, they remain important for managers at all levels. In fact, higher-level managers usually require technical knowledge and skills across a broader spectrum of functional areas (marketing, production, accounting, and so on) than is necessary for lower-level managers operating within one functional area. For instance, consider Ed Dunlap, the chief financial officer of Wild Oats Markets, a health food supermarket chain based in Boulder, Colorado. Dunlap had acquired considerable financial expertise throughout his career and retained many of those technical skills as chief financial officer. However, Dunlap's promotion to chief operating officer required him to learn technical skills beyond finance and accounting, such as in-store operations. "One thing I still need experience in is merchandising, so I'm working very closely with our merchandising staff to develop an eye for that side of the business," says Dunlap. "That starts to give me all the pieces to take on even greater responsibility if it's presented to me."[31]

■ Technical skills: at Wild Oats Markets.

Human Skills Star employees are often promoted into management jobs due to their technical prowess, but many soon get into trouble because they lack the requisite human skills. Several years ago this began to emerge as an endemic problem at Microsoft, where great software programmers, once promoted into management positions, often exhibited poor human skills. Many subordinates complained that their managers had poor communication skills and organization capabilities, that they engaged in micromanagement, that they could be abrasive and arrogant, and that they demoralized rather than motivated team members. To fix this problem, for more than a decade Microsoft has devoted a great deal of attention to training its new managers, teaching them how to be more effective in their new role.[32]

The Technical CEO   People in top management positions generally use their conceptual and human skills more than technical skills. However, the latter remain important; some experts even suggest that CEOs need enough technical bench strength to effectively execute strategies developed with their conceptual skills. Apple CEO Steve Jobs is a case in point. Jobs closely inspects many of Apple's products, even suggesting initial designs and features. "The interesting thing about the iPod is that since it started, it had 100 percent of Steve Jobs's time," says Ben Knauss, who worked on Apple's digital music player while a senior manager at Portal Player. "Every day there were comments from Steve saying where it needed to be." Knauss claims the iPod is even a little louder than other players because Steve Jobs has less than ideal hearing.[33]

© AP Photo/Marcio Jose Sanchez.

human skills

Skills that managers need, including the abilities to communicate, persuade, manage conflict, motivate, coach, negotiate, and lead.

The **human skills** that managers need include the abilities to communicate, persuade, manage conflict, motivate, coach, negotiate, and lead. Effective managers understand the needs of their subordinates and act on this knowledge to improve employee well-being while also achieving organizational objectives. Human skills include working with other units, not just with employees within the manager's own unit. In other words, successful managers use their human skills to reconcile the needs and goals of their own team members with people in other work units, as well as with the needs of customers, suppliers, and others outside the organization.

Human skills go beyond interacting effectively with others. They include the manager's self-awareness and self-management.[34] Good managers know how to manage themselves, which lets them manage others more effectively. They are mindful of their own needs, emotions, and impulses and can control or apply them at appropriate times and places. After all, managers are role models, so they must manage their emotions, words, and deeds accordingly. They must be able to lead by example.

Human skills are important whether you are a night manager at a 7-Eleven store, a development manager at Microsoft, or the chief executive officer at Bank of America. This makes sense when we recall that, by definition, managers accomplish organizational goals through others. You cannot get employees to work together toward common goals if you lack the ability to manage yourself and others. A recent study of thousands of managers at IBM, Lucent, PepsiCo, British Airways, and hundreds of other diverse organizations revealed that human skills are more important than technical and conceptual skills for managers across a wide range of levels.[35] The analysis showed that people get promoted into management, and promoted from lower to higher levels of management, by demonstrating acceptable levels of technical and cognitive skills. However, these skills are secondary to human skills when it comes to distinguishing between successful and mediocre managers

// MANAGERIAL VALUES

Another important characteristic of successful managers is the values they hold and the strength of those values.[36] **Values** are stable, evaluative beliefs that guide our preferences for outcomes or courses of action in a variety of situations.[37] They are perceptions about what is good or bad, right or wrong. Values tell us what we "ought" to do. They serve as a moral compass that directs our decisions and actions. People organize the dozens of values that exist into a hierarchy of importance. Values at the top take priority over values further down the hierarchy. Some individuals value new challenges more than they value conformity. Others value generosity more than frugality. We are referring here to the values that actually guide behavior (**enacted values**), not what people say is important to them (**espoused values**).

Values have gained a lot of respect in business circles over the past decade.[38] Top executives in most *Fortune* 500 companies have carefully identified the core values that they believe employees should embrace in the workplace. These **shared values**—values held by several people—are important because they create a sense of collective purpose, which increases loyalty and satisfaction within the team and organization. Equally important, when employees embrace and follow shared values, their actions are more consistent with team or organizational objectives.

This point brings us to the two reasons why values represent an important characteristic of successful managers. Across all levels of the organization, managers are ultimately responsible for forming, strengthening, and, where necessary, reprioritizing the shared values of their staff. To accomplish this, they must personally hold the values that steer the team and organization in the right direction. "You can't lead other people unless you have a strong set of beliefs," advises former New York mayor Rudy Giuliani.[39] Managers who act by their values are more likely to instill those values in others. Thus the personal values of middle and frontline managers need to echo and amplify the values that top management wants to spread throughout the organization.

The other reason why values represent an important characteristic of successful managers is that they stabilize and guide managers through ambiguous circumstances.[40] Managers are constantly buffeted by many forces, some of which are strong enough to steer them toward ineffective or unethical results. Values serve as beacons that keep managers steadfastly on course under these conditions. "I've always thought that values are a core part of leadership," says Richard Brajer, CEO of LipoScience, a diagnostic testing and analytical company headquartered in Raleigh, North Carolina. "Why? … Because, quite frankly, the stresses of a leadership role are very strong. You need to have a solid foundation."[41] The stabilizing effects of values not only steer managers clear of bad decisions; they also improve the consistency of their decisions and actions. Through this consistency, employees learn that managers have integrity and can be trusted.[42]

Managing with the Right Values   Managers don't just require strong values; they require the *right* values. What are these? The answer to this question has two parts. First, managers need to embrace values that are consistent with the situation in which they work. If precision and accuracy are critical, then managerial values should emphasize conformity and tradition more than stimulation and change. If the company's success is threatened by a shortage of talent, then managers need values that place employee well-being near the top of the priority list.

The second part of the answer is that all managers in all situations must always engage in ethical behavior, so they must embrace ethical values. **Ethical values** are values that society expects people to follow because they distinguish right from wrong in that society. These values are unwavering across time and, according to various studies, are similar across most cultures. For example, when 70,000 respondents located on six continents were asked what values they

values
Stable, evaluative beliefs that guide our preferences for outcomes or courses of action in a variety of situations.

enacted values
Values that actually guide behavior.

espoused values
What people say is important to them.

shared values
Values held in common by several people.

ethical values
Values that society expects people to follow because they distinguish right from wrong in that society.

look for and admire in a leader, well over 80 percent included honesty in their lists. Honesty remained the most often identified value in three sets of surveys over 15 years. It was also at the top of the list in most cultures and was in the top four traits (out of 225 traits) in others.[43]

// MANAGERIAL MOTIVATION

Along with the right combination of managerial skills and values, truly great managers also possess needs that motivate them to manage others effectively. Several specific managerial motivations have been discussed over the years, but the four discussed here stand out.[44]

Desire to Compete for Management Jobs Managers are more successful when they are motivated to compete for their jobs. Even in collegial firms, managers vie for promotion to positions further up the hierarchy. These tournaments are so pronounced for top-level jobs that we often read about executives leaving the company because they lost the fight. For example, Jeffery Immelt, the current CEO of General Electric, was one of three managers groomed by Jack Welch to succeed him as CEO. When Immelt won the competition to become CEO, the other two managers left GE. Effective managers thrive rather than wither in the face of this competition. The desire to compete for managerial jobs is so important that one expert warns that if this motivation declines, the United State could face a shortage of high-performance leaders in the future.[45]

personalized power orientation

Seeking power for personal gain.

Desire to Exercise Power Successful managers are motivated to seek power. However, they don't want this power for personal gain or for the thrill they might experience from wielding power over others (called **personalized power orientation**). Instead good managers have a **socialized power orientation**. They do not seek power for its own sake; rather they accumulate power to accomplish organizational objectives. Management theorist Jeffery Pfeffer has argued that organizations are political entities characterized by different centers of power and influence. To get things done in such a setting, Pfeffer argues that managers need to accumulate power and use that power in a constructive way.[46] Power comes not just from formal authority: It also comes from personal traits, such as ability to influence others through communication; from a network of allies; and from control over crucial information or resources. According to Pfeffer, the wise and constructive use of power is an important characteristic of successful managers.

socialized power orientation

Accumulating power to achieve social or organizational objectives.

Desire to Be Distinct or Different Successful managers need to be—or at least feel comfortable being—different from the people they lead. Why? One reason is that managers need to broker the interests of many stakeholders, so the need to be distinct or different from others allows them to act neutrally. This is consistent with studies reporting that effective managers have a moderately low *need for affiliation*—they have less concern about being liked and are less sensitive to the pressure others impose to conform to their wishes.[47] The other reason for the need to be different is that managers need to take center stage to communicate and symbolize the organization's or work unit's future direction. Employees look to managers as guides and role models of future behavior. Managers who feel uncomfortable with standing out from the group have difficulty leading people in new directions.

■ Allied Signal looks for action oriented managers.

Desire to Take Action One of the most important challenges for managers is to create momentum—motivating employees (as well as suppliers and other stakeholders) to achieve the organization's ambitions for the future. A recent survey of 3,600 bosses identified the "drive for results" as one of the five most important competencies of effective managers. This evidence is backed up by Larry Bossidy's experience leading thousands of managers. "When assessing candidates, the first thing I looked for was energy and enthusiasm for execution," says the former CEO of Honeywell and Allied Signal. Bossidy says that this bias for action is so important that "if you have to choose between someone with a staggering IQ…and someone with a lower IQ who is absolutely determined to succeed, you'll always do better with the second person."[48]

IN CONCLUSION WHY DOES IT MATTER?

If you are on track to become an accountant, a finance professional, an engineer, a salesperson, a creative marketer, you may wonder, "Why am I studying management"? The answer is straightforward: If you are successful as a functional specialist within an organization, it is almost inevitable that you will be offered a management position. If you have ambition, you will see that offer as a route to career advancement. As you transition into the job of management, however, you will discover what many others before you have realized—management is a very different and challenging job. Being a good manager requires more than technical skills. It requires an ability to get work done through others; planning and strategizing; organizing; controlling; and developing and leading a team, unit, function, or entire organization. It requires you to perform multiple roles effectively. You must be a good leader, figurehead, and liaison; be able to collect, analyze, and disseminate information; and function effectively as a negotiator, resource allocator, disturbance handler, and entrepreneur. It requires that you have the right human and conceptual skills, the right values, and the right motivations. It requires that you know how to craft a strategic vision, energize others through communication, build networks, accumulate power, and use that power wisely and constructively. Some people may be born with these skills, but many of us have to learn them. This book is designed to help you do that. It represents the first step on the road toward becoming a successful manager.

MANAGEMENT CHALLENGES

1. Every January *BusinessWeek* produces a list of "The Best and Worst Managers of the Year." Take a look at the most recent list and pick one of the best managers and one of the worst managers:
   a. What makes them good or bad?
   b. Can you find an example of a management function they performed well or poorly?
   c. Can you find examples of management roles they performed well or poorly?
   d. What are the strongest and weakest skills of these managers?

2. Jack Welch, the CEO of General Electric from 1981 to 2001, was regarded by many as one of the best managers in recent business history. Do some research to identify the characteristics and behaviors that made Welch so admired. Can you see drawbacks to his management style?

3. What skills and competencies must a newly appointed frontline manager develop to perform his or her job effectively? How do these skills and competencies differ from those required to perform a technical specialist job effectively?

4. Why might strategizing be an important part of the job of a frontline manager? Can you find examples of frontline managers who have influenced the strategies of their organizations?

MANAGEMENT PORTFOLIO

There is a management portfolio exercise at the end of every chapter in this book. To complete this exercise, you are asked to pick an organization that you can track as you work through the chapters in this book. At the end of each chapter you will be asked to look into an aspect of the organization that matches the content of the chapter. It is probably best if you pick a large business organization that is well known and has publicly traded stock. For such an organization you can typically find lots of information in news reports and magazine articles. Students at most universities can now access much of this material online through their libraries. In addition, a wealth of information can often be extracted from company Web sites, including Securities and Exchange Commission (SEC) documents and annual financial reports. It can also help if you know someone who works at the organization (a family member perhaps) who can be a source of information.

FOR THE ORGANIZATION YOU HAVE CHOSEN TO FOLLOW:

1. Describe the firm. How old is it? What industry (or industries) is the firm active in? What products or services does it sell? Who are its principal competitors? Is it active internationally? How many employees does it have? What are its sales and profits?

2. How well has the firm performed recently compared to rivals? Has it outperformed rivals or underperformed them? Why?

3. Who is the CEO? How long has she or he been in this position? What has been the career track of the CEO?

4. Can you find examples of how the CEO has performed the basic tasks of management—strategizing, planning, organizing, controlling, developing, and leading his or her organization?

CLOSING CASE   GEORGE DAVID

George David has been CEO of United Technologies Corporation (UTC) for more than a decade. During that time he has received numerous accolades and awards for his performance as a CEO. Under his leadership UTC, a $343 billion conglomerate whose operating units include manufacturers of elevators (Otis Elevator), aerospace products (including Pratt & Whitney jet engines and Sikorsky helicopters), air conditioning systems, and fire and security systems, has seen earnings grow at 10–14 percent annually—impressive numbers for any company but particularly for a manufacturing enterprise.

According to David, a key to United Technologies' success has been sustained improvements in productivity and product quality. The story goes back to the 1980s when David was running the international operations of Otis Elevator. There he encountered a Japanese engineer, Yuzuru Ito, who had been brought in to determine why a new elevator product was performing poorly. David was impressed with Ito's methods for identifying quality problems and improving performance. When he was promoted to CEO, David realized that he had to lower the costs and improve the quality of UTC's products. One of the first things he did was persuade Ito to work for him at UTC. Under David, Ito developed a program for improving product quality and productivity, known as Achieving Competitive Excellence (ACE), which was subsequently rolled out across UTC. The ACE program has been one of the drivers of productivity improvements at UTC ever since.

Early in his tenure as CEO, David also radically reorganized UTC. He dramatically cut the size of the head office and decentralized decision making to business divisions. He also directed his accounting staff to develop a new financial reporting system that would give him good information about how well each division was doing and make it easier to hold divisional general managers accountable for the performance of the units under them. He then gave them demanding goals for earnings and sales growth and pushed them to improve processes within their units by implementing the ACE program.

At the same time David has always stressed that management is about more than goal setting and holding people accountable. Values are also important. David has insisted that UTC employees adhere to the highest ethical standards, that the company produce goods that have minimal environmental impact, and that employee safety remain the top consideration in the workplace.

When asked what his greatest achievement as a manager has been, David refers to UTC's worldwide employee scholarship program. Implemented in 1996 and considered the hallmark of UTC's commitment to employee development, the program pays the entire cost of an employee's college or graduate school education, allows employees to pursue any subject at an accredited school, provides paid study time, and awards UTC stock (up to $10,000 worth in the United States) for completing degrees. Explaining the program, David states, "One of the obligations that an employer has is to give employees opportunities to better themselves. And we feel it's also very good business for us because it generates a better workforce that stays longer."

David states that one of his central tasks has been to build a management team that functions smoothly over the long term. "People come to rely upon each other," he says.

Values Manager! George David, the CEO of United Technologies, is seen as something of a paradox. A tough no-nonsense manager who holds people accountable for measurable performance, he also stresses the importance of helping employees improve themselves and maintaining the highest ethical, environmental, and safety standards.
Courtesy of United Technologies Corporation.

"You have to have the same trusting relationships. You know people; they know you. You can predict them; they can predict you. All of that kind of begins to work, and it accelerates over the tenure of a CEO. If you have people bouncing in and out every two to three years, that's not good."

According to Sandy Weill, former chairman of Citicorp and a UTC board member, David has the right mix of toughness and sensitivity. "When somebody can't do the job he'll try to help; but if that person is not going to make it work, that person won't be on the job forever." At the same time Weill says, "He does a lot of things that employees respect him for. I think he is a very good manager. Even though David is demanding, he can also listen—he has a receive mode as well as a send mode."[49]

CASE DISCUSSION QUESTIONS

1. What makes George David such a highly regarded manager?

2. How does David get things done through people?

3. What evidence can you see of David's planning and strategizing, organizing, controlling, leading, and developing?

4. Which managerial competencies does David seem to possess? Does he seem to lack any?

ENDNOTES

1. Quotes from S. Beatty, "Bass Talk: Plotting Plaid's Future," *The Wall Street Journal*, September 9, 2004, p. B1. Also see C.M. Moore and G. Birtwistle, "The Burberry Business Model," *International Journal of Retail and Distribution Management* 32 (2004), pp. 412–22.

2. The definition was first offered by Mary Parker Follett in the 1920s. See P. Graham (ed.), *Mary Parker Follett: Prophet of Management* (Boston: Harvard Business School Press, 1995).

3. S. Walton, *Made in America* (New York: Doubleday, 1992).

4. This view dates back to the French industrialist Henri Fayol, although Fayol talked about "planning" rather than "strategizing." See H. Fayol, *General and Industrial Management* (London: Pitman, 1986). Original edition published in 1916.

5. H. Mintzberg, "Patterns in Strategy Formulation," *Management Science* 24 (1978), pp. 934–48.

6. S. Gray and E. Smith, "Coffee and Music Create a Potent Mix at Starbucks," *The Wall Street Journal*, July 19, 2005, p. A1.

7. G. Yukl and R. Lepsinger, "Why Integrating the Leading and Managing Roles Is Essential for Organizational Effectiveness," *Organizational Dynamics* 34, no. 4 (2005), pp. 361–75.

8. N.W. Hatch and J.H. Dyer, "Human Capital and Learning as a Source of Sustainable Competitive Advantage," *Strategic Management Journal* 25 (2004), pp. 1155–79; J. Pfeffer, *Competitive Advantage through People* (Boston: Harvard Business School Press, 1996).

9. P. Drucker, *Peter Drucker on the Profession of Management* (Boston: Harvard Business School Press, 1998), pp. 33–34.

10. *GE's Two Decade Transformation,* Harvard Business School Case #9-399-150.

11. D. Fisher, "GE Turns Green," *Forbes*, August 15, 2005, pp. 3–5.

12. K. Kranhold, "GE Takes Big Steps in Its Strategy to Exit Insurance," *The Wall Street Journal*, November 21, 2005, p. C7.

13. A. Priestland and R. Hanig, "Developing First Level Leaders," *Harvard Business Review*, June 2005.

14. L.A. Hill, *Becoming a Manager* (Boston: Harvard Business School Press, 1992).

15. L.A. Hill, "What It Really Means to Manage," *Harvard Business School Teaching Note* #9-400-041 (February 2000).

16. H. Mintzberg, "Managerial Work: Analysis from Observation," *Management Science* 18 (1971), pp. B97–B110.

17. H. Mintzberg, "The Yin and the Yang of Managing," *Organizational Dynamics* 29 (2001), pp. 306–12; H. Mintzberg, "Managing Exceptionally," *Organization Science* 12 (2001), pp. 759–71.

18. H. Mintzberg, *The Nature of Managerial Work* (New York: Harper & Row, 1973).

19. Mintzberg, *The Nature of Managerial Work;* H. Mintzberg, "The Manager's Job: Folklore and Fact," *Harvard Business Review,* July–August 1975, pp. 49–61; L.B. Kurke and H. Aldrich, "Mintzberg Was Right! A Replication and Extension of *The Nature of Managerial Work*," *Management Science* 29, no. 8 (August 1983), pp. 975–84; C.P. Hales, "What Do Managers Do? A Critical Review of the Evidence," *Journal of Management Studies* 23, no. 1 (January 1986), pp. 88–115; S. Chareanpunsirikul and R.C. Wood, "Mintzberg, Managers, and Methodology: Some Observations from a Study of Hotel General Managers," *Tourism Management* 23 (2002); pp. 551–56. Mintzberg recently proposed a revised model of managerial work, but few writers have taken up this model, possibly due to its messiness and gaps. See Mintzberg, "Managing Exceptionally."

20. Hales, "What Do Managers Do? A Critical Review of the Evidence."

21. C. Salter, "Customer-Centered Leader Chick-fil-A," *Fast Company*, October 2004, pp. 83–84; L. Cannon, "2005 Golden Chain: Dan T. Cathy," *Nation's Restaurant News*, September 19, 2005; H. Jett, "Businesses Use Grand Openings to Attract Audience, Establish Roots," *Free Lance-Star* (Fredericksburg, VA), March 24, 2005.

22. P. Drucker, *The Practice of Management* (New York: Harper & Row, 1954), Chapter 28.

23. L. Hill, *Becoming a Manager: How New Managers Master the Challenges of Leadership* (Boston: Harvard Business School Press, 2003), pp. 41–42.

24. J.S. Valacich and C. Schwenk, "Structuring Conflict in Individual, Face-to-Face, and Computer-Mediated Group Decision Making," *Decision Sciences* 26 (1995), pp. 369–94; D.N. Stoe, M.P. Sivitanides, and A.P. Magro, "Formalized Dissent and Cognitive Complexity in Group Processes and Performance," *Decision Science* 25 (1994), pp. 243–62.

25. C. Dargie, "The Role of Public Sector Chief Executives," *Public Administration* 776 (Spring 1998), pp. 161–77; M. Noordegraaf and R. Stewart, "Managerial Behavior Research in Private and Public Sectors: Distinctiveness, Disputes, and Directions," *Journal of Management Studies* 37, no. 3 (May 2000), pp. 427–43; C. O'Gorman, S. Bourke, and J.A. Murray, "The Nature of Managerial Work in Small Growth-Oriented Businesses," *Small Business Economics* 25 (2005), pp. 1–16.

26. R. Boyatzis, *The Competent Manager: A Model for Effective Performance* (New York: John Wiley & Sons, 1982), p. 21; R. Jacobs, "Using Human Resource Functions to Enhance Emotional Intelligence," in *The Emotionally Intelligent Workplace*, ed. C. Cherniss and D. Goleman (San Francisco: Jossey-Bass, 2001), pp. 159–81; S.L. Tubbs and E. Schulz, "Exploring a Taxonomy of Global Leadership Competencies and Meta-Competencies," *Journal of American Academy of Business* 8, no. 2 (2006), pp. 29–34.

27. R.L. Katz, "Skills of an Effective Administrator," *Harvard Business Review* 52, no. 5 (September–October 1974), pp. 90–102.

28. D. Nilsen, B. Kowske, and A. Kshanika, "Managing Globally," *HRMagazine*, August 2005, pp. 111–15.

29. M.D. Mumford et al., "Leadership Skills for a Changing World: Solving Complex Social Problems," *Leadership Quarterly* 11, no. 1 (2000), pp. 11–35.

30. R.E. Hill and J. Collins-Eaglin, "Technical Professionals, Technical Managers, and the Integration of Vocational Consciousness," *Human Resource Management* 24, no. 2 (Summer 1985), pp. 177–89; H.G. Enns, S.L. Huff, and B.R. Golden, "CIO Influence Behaviors: The Impact of Technical Background," *Information & Management* 40, no. 5 (2003), p. 467.

31. D. Buss, "How to Pick Your Number 2," *Financial Times* (London), December 16, 2004, p. 16.

32. The author consults with Microsoft on these issues and teaches several in-house management development programs.

33. L. Kahney, "Inside Look at Birth of the iPod," *Wired News*, July 21, 2004.

34. D. Goleman, R. Boyatzis, and A. McKee, *Primal Leaders* (Boston: Harvard Business School Press, 2002).

35. L.M. Spencer and S.M. Spencer, *Competence at Work: Models for Superior Performance* (New York: John Wiley & Sons, 1993), Chapter 16; D. Goleman, "Emotional Intelligence: Issues in Paradigm Building," in *The Emotionally Intelligent Workplace*, ed. C. Cherniss and D. Goleman (San Francisco: Jossey-Bass, 2001), pp. 13–26.

36. E.E. Ghiselli, "Interaction of Traits and Motivational Factors in the Determination of the Success of Managers," *Journal of Applied Psychology* 52, no. 6 (1968), pp. 480–83.

37. B.M. Meglino and E.C. Ravlin, "Individual Values in Organizations: Concepts, Controversies, and Research," *Journal of Management* 24, no. 3 (1998), pp. 351–89; B.R. Agle and C.B. Caldwell, "Understanding Research on Values in Business," *Business and Society* 38, no. 3 (September 1999), pp. 326–387; S. Hitlin and J.A. Pilavin, "Values: Reviving a Dormant Concept," *Annual Review of Sociology* 30 (2004), pp. 359–93.

38. J.C. Collins and J.I. Porras, *Built to Last: Successful Habits of Visionary Companies* (London: Century, 1995); C.A. O'Reilly III and J. Pfeffer, *Hidden Value* (Cambridge, MA: Harvard Business School Press, 2000).

39. R. Giuliani, "Rudy Giuliani on Leadership," *Leadership Excellence*, June 2005, pp. 17–18.

40. J.L. Badaracco Jr., "The Discipline of Building Character," *Harvard Business Review* 76, no. 2 (March–April 1998), pp. 114–24; J.M. Kouzes and B.Z. Posner, *The Leadership Challenge*, 3rd ed. (San Francisco: Jossey-Bass, 2002), Chapter 3.

41. "Building a Solid Foundation on Value-Driven Principles," *Business Leader* 14 (June 2003), p. 6.

42. T. Simons, "Behavioral Integrity: The Perceived Alignment between Managers' Words and Deeds as a Research Focus," *Organization Science* 13, no. 1 (January–February 2002), pp. 18–35.

43. Kouzes and Posner, *The Leadership Challenge*, Chapter 2.

44. J.B. Miner, *Studies in Management Education* (Atlanta: Organizational Measurement Systems Press, 1965); J.B. Miner, "Twenty Years of Research on Role Motivation Theory of Managerial Effectiveness," *Personnel Psychology* 31 (1978), pp. 739–60; B.P. Ebrahimi, S.A. Young, and V.W.M. Luk, "Motivation to Manage in China and Hong Kong: A Gender Comparison of Managers," *Sex Roles* 45, no. 5–6 (2001), pp. 433–53.

45. J.B. Miner, B.P. Ebrahimi, and J.M. Wachtel, "How Deficiencies in Motivation to Manage Contribute to the United States' Competitiveness Problem (and What Can Be Done about It)," *Human Resource Management* 34, no. 3 (1995), pp. 363–86.

46. J. Pfeffer, *Managing with Power* (Boston: Harvard Business School Press, 1992).

47. D.C. McClelland and D.H. Burnham, "Power Is the Great Motivator," *Harvard Business Review* 73 (January–February 1995), pp. 126–39 (reprint; original article published in 1976).

48. R. Charan, C. Burke, and L. Bossidy, *Execution: The Discipline of Getting Things Done* (New York: Crown Business, 2002). The survey of managerial competencies is reported in Nilsen, Kowske, and Kshanika, "Managing Globally."

49. Sources: J.S. McClenahen, "UTC's Master of Principle," *Industry Week*, January 2003, pp. 30–34; D. Brady, "The Unsung CEO," *BusinessWeek*, October 25, 2005, pp. 74–75; W.J. Holstein, "George David Steps Out," *Chief Executive*, May 2005, pp. 3–35.

2

THE EXTERNAL AND INTERNAL ENVIRONMENTS

Managers in the airline industry have their work cut out for them; they face one of the most challenging environments in business. Since 2001 this industry has been characterized by volatile demand conditions and intense competition from low-cost carriers such as Jet Blue, Air Tran, and Southwest Airlines. Consumers have plenty of options to choose from, and they tend to select carriers with the lowest prices, putting downward pressure on pricing. When adjusted for inflation, the price consumers paid to fly one mile in the United States fell from $0.091 in 1980 to $0.042 in 2004. Moreover, the cost structure of airlines is closely linked to volatile fuel prices. Every 5 percent increase in fuel costs reduces airline profitability by 1 percent, and the price of jet fuel increased from $0.71 a gallon on average in 2002 to $1.80 a gallon in late 2005. To complicate matters, many long-established airlines also have to work with powerful labor unions that historically have resisted attempts to reduce employee pay and introduce flexible work processes. This has kept labor costs high. Due to these conditions, between 2001 and 2004 the industry lost a staggering $32.3 billion.[1]

external environment

Everything outside a firm that might affect the ability of the enterprise to attain its goals.

task environment

Actual and potential competitors, suppliers, and buyers (customers or distributors); firms that provide substitute products to those sold in the industry; and firms that provide complements.

general environment

Political and legal forces, macroeconomic forces, demographic forces, sociocultural forces, technological forces, and international forces.

If managers in the airline industry are going to run their organizations efficiently, they have to understand the *external* environment confronting them, anticipate how changes in the environment might affect the profitability of their airlines, and take appropriate actions. These actions might include reducing capacity as demand declines, purchasing more fuel-efficient jets, avoiding price wars with low-cost airlines if possible, and reducing labor costs. At the same time the ability of managers to take such actions is shaped by the airlines' *internal* environment. For example, some long-established airlines, such as United, have powerful labor unions that have resisted attempts by managers to cut pay for pilots, flight attendants, and ground staff, or to introduce flexible work practices that boost labor productivity. This constraint has kept costs high and made it more difficult for managers to do what is required to make the airline profitable.

The situation confronting managers in the airline industry, while dramatic, is not unique. The work of all managers is affected by two main environments: the external environment and the internal environment. The **external environment** constitutes everything outside a firm that might affect the ability of the enterprise to attain its goals. The external environment itself can be subdivided into two main components (see Figure 2.1). There is the industry or **task environment** confronting the organization, which typically includes actual and potential competitors, suppliers, and buyers (customers or distributors); firms that provide substitute products to those sold in the industry; and firms that provide complements. Then there is the more encompassing **general environment** within which the task environment is embedded. The general environment includes political and legal forces, macroeconomic forces, demographic forces, sociocultural forces, technological forces, and international forces. The general environment impacts the firm through its influence on the task environment.

When managers analyze the external environment they typically look for opportunities and threats. *Opportunities* arise from circumstances or developments in the external environment that, if exploited through strategies, enable managers to better attain the goals of their enterprise. For example, according to the most recent forecast from Boeing, airline travel is predicted to grow at 4.8 percent per year compounded over the next 20 years, which is considerably faster than the growth rate over the last 20 years.[2] Rising demand for airline travel can be seen

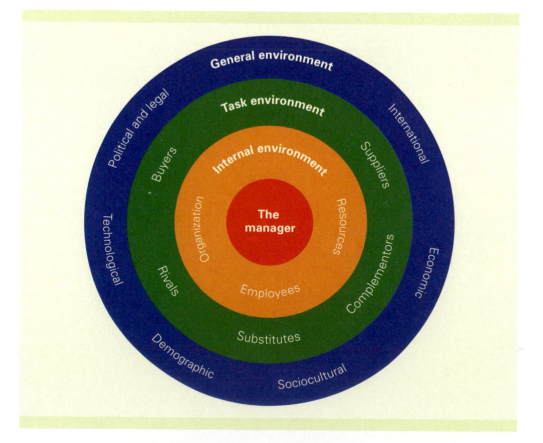

FIGURE 2.1

The Environment of Managers

as an opportunity, the exploitation of which might better enable airlines to increase revenues and profits. *Threats* arise from circumstances or developments in the external environment that may adversely affect the ability of managers to attain the goals of their enterprise. Thus the entry of budget carriers into the airline industry is a threat to the position of established carriers such as United and American Airlines, which have a higher cost structure than firms like South West Airlines and Jet Blue. Rising fuel costs are another significant threat.

The **internal environment** constitutes everything inside the firm that might affect the ability of managers to pursue certain actions or strategies. The internal environment includes the *organization* of the firm (its structure, culture, controls, and incentives), the *employees* of the firm (its human capital), and the *resources* of the firm (its tangible and intangible assets). As we will see, each of these elements can be a strength or a weakness. A *strength* is an activity the organization is good at; it is a potential source of competitive advantage. A *weakness* is an activity that the organization does not excel at; it may be a source of competitive disadvantage.

When managers analyze the internal environment of their own firm, they often do so by identifying its strengths and weaknesses. This inward focus complements the identification of opportunities and threats in the external environment. Taken together, an inventory of internal strengths and weaknesses and external opportunities and threats can help managers develop strategy. This methodology, which is often referred to by the acronym of **SWOT** analysis (**s**trengths, **w**eaknesses, **o**pportunities, and **t**hreats), is a standard part of strategic planning and decision making; we will discuss it in more detail in Chapter 5.

In this chapter we take a close look at the components of the external and internal environments and discuss how they shape managerial actions and give rise to opportunities, threats, strengths, and weaknesses. We start with the external environment, looking first at the task environment and then at the general environment. We discuss the task environment first because it is closest to the firm and thus of most immediate concern for managers. Moreover, because the general environment affects the firm through its impact on the task environment, we cannot discuss the importance of the general environment until we understand the task environment. We close the chapter with a discussion of the internal environment.

■ // The Task Environment

One of the most popular frameworks for analyzing the task or industry environment is a model developed by Michael Porter known as the **five forces model** (see Figure 2.2).[3] According to Porter, the ability of a firm to make a profit is influenced by five competitive forces: the

internal environment
Everything inside a firm that affects managers' ability to pursue actions or strategies.

SWOT
Strengths, weaknesses, opportunities, and threats.

Five forces model:
Model of competitive forces that determine the intensity of competition in an industry.

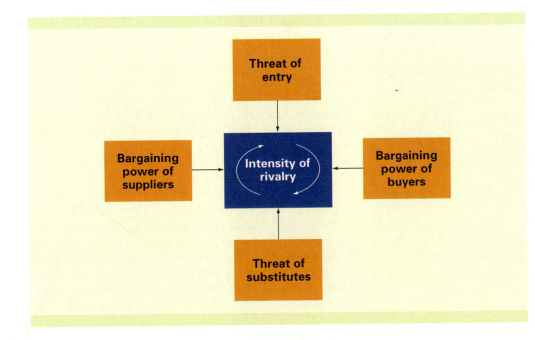

FIGURE 2.2

Porter's Competitive Forces Model

threat of entry by potential competitors, the power of buyers, the power of suppliers, the threat of substitute products, and the intensity of rivalry between firms already in the industry. In Porter's framework, the stronger each of these forces, the more difficult it will be for incumbent firms in an industry to make profits. A strong force thus constitutes a threat, whereas a weak force often gives managers the opportunity to increase sales, raise prices, and make higher profits. Porter also notes that by getting their firm to pursue the right strategies, managers can alter the strength of the various forces. Thus managers might pursue strategies that reduce the bargaining power of buyers, thereby decreasing the threat posed by this force. In this section we look at each force in turn.

// THE THREAT OF ENTRY

In general, if an industry is profitable new enterprises will enter, output will expand, prices will fall, and industry profits will decline. Managers often strive to reduce the threat of entry by pursuing strategies that raise barriers to entry.[4] **Barriers to entry** are factors that make it costly for potential competitors to enter an industry and compete with firms already in the industry. High entry barriers protect incumbent firms from new competition even when they are making good profits; they reduce the threat associated with a potential increase in the number of competitors in a market.

Economies of scale, which are the cost reductions associated with a large output, represent an important barrier to entry. When incumbent firms enjoy significant economies of scale, they may have a cost advantage over new entrants that lack sales volume. Another important barrier to entry is the brand loyalty enjoyed by incumbents. **Brand loyalty** is the preference of consumers for the products of established companies. Other things being equal, the higher the brand loyalty enjoyed by incumbents, the harder it is to enter an industry and the fewer competitors there will be. In the market for cola, for example, Pepsi and Coke enjoy substantial brand loyalty. It would be expensive for another company to enter the cola market and try to break down the brand loyalty enjoyed by these enterprises. By pursuing strategies that enable their firms to reap economies of scale and brand loyalty, managers in incumbent enterprises can limit new entry.

For an example of an industry where incumbents are protected from competition by scale and brand-based entry barriers, consider the small package express delivery market in the United States. Since the late 1980s this market has been dominated by two firms, FedEx and UPS, which together accounted for over 80 percent of the market in the early 2000s. Both FedEx and UPS have spent heavily on advertising to build their brands, which has deterred entry. Furthermore, success in this market requires substantial capital expenditures amounting to billions of dollars to purchase a nationwide network of aircraft, delivery trucks, tracking systems, sorting facilities, and drop-off locations. FedEx and UPS have achieved the shipment volumes required to cover the fixed costs associated with such a network and enjoy substantial economies of scale. As a result, from the early 1980s until 2003 there was no new entry into this market: entry barriers kept competitors locked out.

In 2003 this changed when German-owned DHL entered the industry by purchasing Airborne Express, a struggling enterprise in the market with a share of less than 7 percent. DHL's entry, however, illustrates how hard it is to gain share in this industry. The company spent $1.02 billion to acquire the assets of Airborne Express; committed itself to spending another $1.2 billion to expand Airborne's capacity; and launched a nationwide advertising campaign, which cost another $150 million, in an attempt to erode the brand loyalty enjoyed by FedEx and UPS. Due to heavy spending DHL lost

barriers to entry
Factors that make it costly for potential competitors to enter an industry and compete with firms already in the industry.

economies of scale
Cost reductions associated with large output.

brand loyalty
The preference of consumers for the products of established companies.

■ Entry barriers in the express delivery market.

Not Much Bang for the Buck DHL has spent over $2 billion trying to gain share from FedEx and UPS in the U.S. market for small package delivery, but it has little to show for it. The entry barriers into the U.S. market are very high.

© AP Photo/Roberto Pfeil.

$638 million in the United States in 2004 and another $380 million in 2005. What did DHL get for its money? Not much. In 2005 DHL's share of the U.S. market stood at 7 percent, barely more than the share enjoyed by Airborne Express before DHL acquired the outfit. It would seem that the costs of entering the market are indeed high. DHL is finding it difficult and expensive to overcome the brand loyalty enjoyed by UPS and FedEx and to achieve the volumes necessary for economies of scale.[5]

// BARGAINING POWER OF BUYERS

The next competitive force is the bargaining power of buyers. An industry's buyers may be the individual customers who ultimately consume its products (its end users) or the intermediaries that distribute the industry's products to end users, such as retailers and wholesalers. For example, although detergents made by Procter & Gamble and Unilever are ultimately purchased by individual consumers, the principal buyers of detergents from P&G and Unilever are supermarket chains and discount stores, which then resell the products to consumers. The **bargaining power of buyers** is the ability of buyers to bargain down prices charged by firms in the industry or to raise the firms' costs by demanding better product quality and service. By lowering prices and demanding better service, powerful buyers can squeeze profits out of an industry. Thus powerful buyers should be viewed as a threat. Alternatively, when buyers are in a weak bargaining position, firms in an industry may have the opportunity to raise prices and increase the level of industry profits.

Buyers are most powerful when one or more of the following conditions holds: (1) they are few in number and purchase large quantities, (2) they can choose between equivalent products from many different firms, and (3) they can switch easily between the offerings of different firms (their switching costs are low). Consider the power that Wal-Mart has over manufacturers of detergents. Wal-Mart is the largest retailer in the world, accounting for some 8 percent of U.S. retail sales, so it buys in huge quantities. Its volume purchases give it considerable leverage over producers like Procter & Gamble and Unilever: Wal-Mart can demand that they lower prices in return for access to shelf space. Moreover, Wal-Mart can easily adjust the amount of shelf space it devotes to detergents from P&G and Unilever, and it uses this fact, along with the threat of devoting more shelf space to its own brands, as a bargaining tactic to get firms like P&G and Unilever to lower their prices. Thus Wal-Mart has considerable bargaining power over firms in the detergent industry. It purchases in great quantities, it can choose between many products, and it can switch easily between different offerings.

Buyers are in a weak position when (1) they are plentiful and purchase in small quantities, (2) they have little choice, and (3) they cannot switch easily between the offerings of different firms. For an example of buyers who are in a weak position, consider the buyers of operating systems for personal computers. Most such buyers purchase in small amounts relative to the size of the market, so they lack the leverage that comes from volume. More than 90 percent of the world's personal computers use Microsoft's Windows operating system; the only other viable choice is Apple's operating system. Thus buyers have little choice. Moreover, if people use Microsoft's Windows operating system and have libraries of related software applications, it is expensive to switch to another computer operating system because in addition to purchasing the operating system itself, they would have to purchase new software applications.[6] In other words, the switching costs facing buyers are high and their bargaining power is low.

As the Microsoft example illustrates, high switching costs can significantly reduce the bargaining power of buyers. **Switching costs** arise when it costs a buyer time, energy, and money to switch from a product offered by one enterprise to that offered by another. When switching costs are high, buyers can be *locked in* to the product offerings of a firm, even if other enterprises offer better products.[7] Managers often try to gain bargaining power over buyers by trying to increase the switching costs they must bear to adopt a rival product. To the extent that they are successful, this enhances the ability of the firm to raise prices. For example, wireless telephone providers try to induce customers to sign multiyear contracts in return for new telephones—a strategy that increases switching costs. As a result, wireless

---

bargaining power of buyers
Ability of buyers to bargain down prices charged by firms in the industry or to raise the costs of firms in the industry by demanding better product quality and service.

■ Buying power at Wal-Mart.

■ Switching costs and Microsoft.

switching costs
The time, energy, and money required to switch from the products offered by one enterprise to those offered by another.

firms have been able to charge higher prices than would otherwise have been the case. On the other hand, anything that lowers switching costs should be viewed as a threat. In 2003 just such a threat emerged in the wireless telephone industry when the government allowed customers to take their phone numbers with them when they switched from one carrier to another. Prior to this legislation, the inconvenience associated with changing telephone numbers when customers changed carriers constituted a powerful switching cost.

// BARGAINING POWER OF SUPPLIERS

bargaining power of suppliers

Ability of suppliers to bargain up prices charged by firms in the industry or to raise the costs of firms in the industry by supplying lower-quality products and service.

Suppliers provide inputs to the firm. These inputs may be raw materials, partly finished products, or services. Suppliers include the employees of a firm, who supply their skills and time in return for pay. Whether suppliers represent an opportunity or threat to a firm depends on the extent of their control over inputs the firm needs to function.[8] In the extreme case, where there is only a single supplier of an important input, that supplier has substantial bargaining power over the firm and can use this power to raise input prices and increase costs. Such a situation constitutes a threat. Managers try to reduce this threat by finding alternative suppliers. A good example of this situation has occurred in the personal computer industry, where chip maker Intel has long been the dominant supplier of microprocessors to personal computer makers. This has given Intel substantial bargaining power over PC manufacturers and enabled Intel to charge higher prices. Managers at PC firms have responded by encouraging Intel's sole competitor, AMD, to increase its supply of microprocessors. This effort has met with limited success. Intel's brand loyalty among consumers is high, and their preference for computers with Intel microprocessors has limited the ability of PC firms to develop this alternative supply source.

■ Intel's bargaining power.

Suppliers represent an opportunity when incumbent firms have bargaining power over them and can reduce the prices they pay for inputs. As noted earlier, Wal-Mart has such enormous bargaining power that it has been able to drive down the prices it pays suppliers for goods and service, which increases the profitability of Wal-Mart. The bargaining power of an enterprise over its suppliers is greater if one or more of the following conditions holds: (1) the firm purchases in large quantities, (2) it can choose between multiple suppliers, (3) the costs of switching between suppliers is low, and (4) the firm is not dependent on any single supplier for important inputs.

// THE THREAT OF SUBSTITUTES

substitute products

The goods or services of different businesses or industries that can satisfy similar customer needs.

Another competitive force in Porter's model is the threat of **substitute products**: the goods or services of different businesses or industries that can satisfy similar customer needs. For example, firms in the coffee industry compete indirectly with those in the tea and cola drink industries because all three serve customer needs for nonalcoholic caffeinated drinks. The existence of close substitutes is a strong competitive threat because this limits the prices that companies in one industry can charge for their products, and thus industry profitability. If the price of coffee rises too much relative to that of tea or cola, coffee drinkers may switch to those substitutes.

If an industry's products have few close substitutes, so that substitutes are a weak competitive force, then other things being equal, firms in the industry have the opportunity to raise prices and earn additional profits. For example, there is no close substitute for microprocessors, which lets companies like Intel and AMD charge higher prices.

Substitutes based on new technologies can be a particularly potent threat. Consider what happened to the typewriter industry after the spread of personal computers and word processing software during the 1980s. From the 1870s through the 1980s the typewriter industry enjoyed significant growth with firms like Smith Corona, IBM, and Olivetti deriving substantial revenues from this market. By 1996 the industry was dead. The last great typewriter manufacturer, Smith Corona, went bankrupt that year and closed its doors for good. It was killed by the rise of the substitute: personal computers with word processing software.

// THE INTENSITY OF RIVALRY

Last in Porter's model, but by no means least, is the intensity of rivalry between firms in an industry. Intense rivalry between incumbents, such as we currently see in the airline industry, is a threat that reduces the profits of established enterprises. Conversely, anything that reduces the intensity of rivalry between incumbent firms, allowing them to raise prices and make greater profits, can be seen as an opportunity. A number of different factors determine the intensity of rivalry in an industry: the nature of the product, demand and supply conditions, the cost structure of firms, and the competitive structure of the industry.

The Nature of the Product Some products can be thought of as commodities or as being commoditylike. A **commodity product** is one that is difficult to differentiate from those produced by rivals. Pure commodities include raw materials, such as oil, natural gas, and coal, along with many agricultural products—like wheat, corn, beef, and pork. In such cases rival firms' products are close substitutes for each other, if not exactly the same thing. Thus it might be difficult for a consumer to distinguish between the gasoline sold by different service stations, the wheat produced by different farmers, and the gold from different mines. An inability to differentiate a product from those produced by competitors can result in competition defaulting to the lowest common denominator: price! An inability to compete on attributes other than price tends to be a threat, because this can lead to a downward price spiral and lower profits, particularly if demand conditions are weak.

> **commodity product**
> A product that is difficult to differentiate from those produced by rivals.

Managers try to deal with this threat by finding ways to differentiate their products. This has been a surprisingly successful strategy in some industries where the products might seem difficult to differentiate. Take the water industry: In many ways water is the ultimate commodity, yet clever marketing coupled with a little bit of natural carbonation and a slice of French cunning has enabled Perrier to successfully differentiate its carbonated bottled water from that produced by other enterprises.

Some products that are not pure commodities, such as airline travel, are commoditylike because many firms provide products that are almost identical and thus are close substitutes for each other. Most airline passengers view the service of competing airlines as similar and thus choose between them on the basis of price. Managers in the airline industry have pursued all sorts of tactics to try to differentiate their product offerings—from frequent flyer programs to in-flight entertainment systems—but with only limited success. Those offerings are often quickly imitated by competitors, in which case competition again defaults to price.

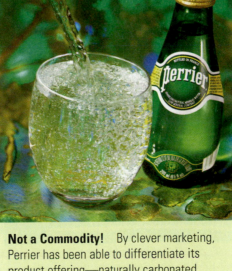

Not a Commodity! By clever marketing, Perrier has been able to differentiate its product offering—naturally carbonated sparkling water—to create a powerful brand for which it can charge a premium price.

Courtesy of Nestlé Waters North America, Inc.

Demand and Supply Conditions If overall customer demand for a product or service is growing, the task environment can be viewed as more favorable. Firms will have the opportunity to expand sales and raise prices, both of which may lead to higher profits. Of course the converse also holds: Stagnant or falling demand is a threat that leads to lower profits. Thus falling demand for airline travel due to an economic slowdown and the terrorist attacks of September 11th, 2001, resulted in net profits in the U.S. airline industry of $2.49 billion in 2000 turning into a net loss of $11.3 billion in 2002.

■ Demand for Boeing planes.

Demand trends in an industry are determined by several factors. Among the more important are economic growth and rising income levels. For example, as noted earlier, Boeing predicts that demand for air travel will grow by 4.8 percent yearly between 2005 and 2025. This is primarily because Boeing believes that the world economy will grow at 2.9 percent per year over this period; income levels will rise accordingly, and as people get richer they tend to fly more. This is good news for Boeing, which expects robust demand for commercial aircraft over the next 20 years, with nearly 26,000 jets valued at over $2 trillion being sold.[9] It could also be good news for the beleaguered airline industry if growing demand translates into higher prices and greater profits.

In addition to demand, supply conditions are also important to consider. Specifically, a major determinant of the intensity of rivalry in an industry is the amount of productive capacity (supply) relative to demand. If demand for the goods or services produced by firms in an industry exceeds capacity (supply) in the industry—if a situation of *excess demand* exists—prices will be bid up by consumers and rivalry will be reduced. Conversely, if supply exceeds demand—if a situation of *excess capacity* exists—firms will compete vigorously for enough sales volume to efficiently utilize their capacity, rivalry will be intense, and prices and profits will trend lower. Excess demand thus represents an opportunity and excess capacity a threat.

Between 2004 and 2006 the world oil market was experiencing excess demand. Demand had expanded faster than predicted, driven partly by surging demand from the rapidly industrializing nation of China. There was insufficient readily available supply in the world to meet this demand. So oil prices increased from around $20 a barrel in 2003 to over $70 a barrel in April 2006. This was a great environment for oil producers, who saw their profits surge.

■ Excess capacity in the market for bandwidth.

The market for high-speed Internet bandwidth is a good example of what can occur when capacity exceeds demand (when there is a situation of excess capacity). Between 1996 and 2001 a number of enterprises, including WorldCom, Global Crossing, XO Communications, and 360 Networks, made multi-billion-dollar investments in fiber optic cable to carry Internet data. These investments were made in the belief that demand for Internet bandwidth was growing by 1,000 percent a year. This turned out not to be the case (it was actually growing by 100 percent per year), and by 2002 it was apparent that there was far too much fiber optic cable in the ground given demand conditions (supply exceeded demand). Indeed, more than 90 percent of all fiber optic cables were "dark"—they were transmitting no data. This excess capacity resulted in plunging prices and triggered a wave of corporate bankruptcies. All of the companies just mentioned went bankrupt because they could not generate sufficient revenues to service the debt they had taken on to build their fiber optic networks.

Most industries go through periods of both excess demand and excess capacity. A critical thing for managers to understand is how long the excess is likely to persist because that helps define the scale and longevity of the associated opportunity or threat. In other words, managers need to understand how fast the market in which their organization competes adjusts and how quickly demand and supply will be brought back into balance.

The speed of the adjustment process is partly determined by barriers to entry and barriers to exit. We have already discussed barriers to entry. **Barriers to exit**, the opposite of barriers to entry, are factors that stop firms from reducing capacity even when demand is weak and excess capacity exists.[10] Barriers to exit include (1) the fixed costs of closing down capacity, such as the financial charges that must be taken to shut down a plant and lay off employees; (2) an unwillingness to reduce capacity due to a belief, which may be misplaced, that demand will soon rebound; and (3) government regulations, such as Chapter 11 bankruptcy rules in the United States, that allow insolvent enterprises to reorganize their debt and keep operating under the protection of a bankruptcy court.

barriers to exit

Factors that stop firms from reducing capacity even when demand is weak and excess capacity exists.

Figure 2.3 summarizes the possibilities here. If excess demand exists and barriers to entry are high, the entry barriers will lock potential rivals out of the market, the intensity of rivalry within the industry will remain low, and the period of plenty will persist for some time. Such a situation represents a significant opportunity for the firm. Conversely, if excess demand exists but entry barriers are low, new enterprises are likely to enter the industry, attracted by the high prices and profits of incumbents; supply will expand and prices fall until supply and

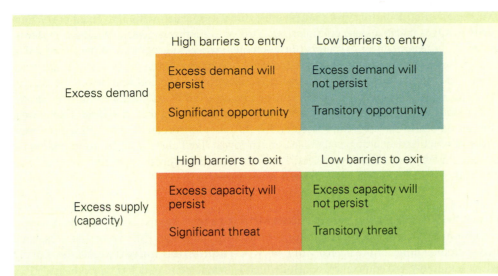

FIGURE 2.3
Adjustment Processes

demand are brought into balance. Thus the opportunity associated with excess demand in such a situation is transitory.

If excess supply (capacity) exists but barriers to exit are low, it is likely that supply will be quickly reduced until it is in line with demand, and the intense rivalry will be relatively short-lived. However, if excess capacity exists and barriers to exit are high, this represents a significant threat that may persist for some time, with unfortunate consequences for enterprises in the industry. This has long been the case in the steel industry. Demand for steel in the United States has been declining since the 1960s as other materials, including composites, plastics, and aluminum, have replaced steel in many product applications. Excess capacity began to emerge in the 1970s and has been a persistent feature of the industry ever since, with as much as 40 percent of U.S. steel capacity standing idle at any time. Although many steel enterprises went bankrupt, Chapter 11 regulations allowed these companies to keep operating until they emerged from bankruptcy protection. As a result, the excess capacity did not go away fast. Not until the late 1990s and early 2000s did many of the old steel companies finally shut down. Because of these factors, the steel industry has been characterized by intense rivalry, low prices, and low or negative profits for years. Thus the combination of excess capacity and high exit barriers constituted a significant and persistent threat.

The Cost Structure of Firms Fixed costs are those that must be borne before a firm makes a single sale. For illustration, before they can offer service, cable TV companies have to lay cable in the ground; this is a fixed cost. Similarly, to offer air express service a company like FedEx has to invest in planes, package sorting facilities, and delivery trucks. These are fixed costs that require significant capital investments. In industries where the fixed costs of production are high, if sales volume is low, firms cannot cover their fixed costs and will not be profitable. This creates an incentive for firms to cut their prices and increase promotion spending to raise sales volume, thereby covering fixed costs. In situations where demand is not growing fast enough and too many companies are cutting prices and raising promotion spending, the result can be intense competition and lower profits.[11] Thus high fixed costs should be viewed as a threat, particularly when combined with weak demand conditions or excess capacity.

■ Exit barriers in the steel industry.

fixed costs
The costs that must be borne before the firm makes a single sale.

Fixed Costs! These workers are laying fiber optic cables in the ground. A communication company has to lay tens of thousands of miles of such cable before it can offer high-speed Internet service—a process that can cost hundreds of millions if not billions of dollars.

© Getty Images.

■ Reducing fixed costs at Cisco.

Managers often look for ways to reduce the threat associated with high fixed costs. One strategy involves trying to push off high fixed costs onto another organization. Cisco Systems, the world's largest producer of routers (the computer switches at the heart of the Internet that direct traffic), has significantly reduced its fixed costs by outsourcing much of the manufacturing of its routers to independent contract manufacturers. Cisco concentrates on the design, marketing, sales, and support functions of the business, all of which have low fixed costs. Another strategy involves developing new methods of production that have lower fixed costs. In the automobile industry, for example, Toyota has pioneered the development of new flexible production technologies that have much lower fixed costs than the traditional mass production methods used in the industry. This has reduced the threat associated with having a high fixed cost structure and weak demand conditions.[12]

competitive structure

The number and size distribution of incumbent firms in an industry.

fragmented industry

An industry with many small or medium-sized companies.

consolidated industry

An industry dominated by a few large companies.

Competitive Structure The **competitive structure** of an industry is the number and size distribution of incumbent firms. Industry structures vary, and different structures have different implications for the intensity of rivalry. A **fragmented industry** consists of many small or medium-sized companies, none of which is in a position to determine industry price. A **consolidated industry** is dominated by a few large companies (an oligopoly) or in extreme cases by just one company (a monopoly); here companies often are in a position to determine industry prices. Examples of fragmented industries include agriculture, dry cleaning, and radio broadcasting. Consolidated industries include the aerospace, soft drink, and the small package express industries.

Fragmented industries are characterized by low entry barriers and commodity products that are hard to differentiate. The combination of these traits tends to result in boom and bust cycles as industry profits rise and fall. Low entry barriers imply that whenever demand is strong and profits are high, new entrants will flood the market, hoping to profit from the boom. The explosion in the number of video stores, health clubs, and sun tanning parlors during the 1980s and 1990s exemplifies this situation. Often the flood of new entrants into a booming fragmented industry creates excess capacity, so firms cut prices to use their spare capacity. The difficulty firms face when trying to differentiate their products from those of competitors can exacerbate this tendency. The result is a price war, which depresses industry profits, forces some companies out of business, and deters potential new entrants. For example, after a decade of expansion and booming profits, many health clubs are now finding that they have to offer large discounts to hold their members. In general, the more commoditylike an industry's product is, the more vicious will be the price war. This bust part of the cycle continues until overall industry capacity is brought into line with demand, at which point prices may stabilize again.

In general, a fragmented industry structure constitutes a threat rather than an opportunity. Most booms are relatively short-lived because of the ease of new entry; they will be followed by intense price competition and bankruptcies. Because it is often difficult to differentiate products in these industries, the best strategy for managers is to try to minimize costs so their enterprises will be profitable in a boom and survive any subsequent bust. Alternatively, managers might try to adopt strategies that change the underlying structure of fragmented industries and lead to a consolidated industry structure in which the level of industry profitability is increased. For example, at one time the video rental industry was very fragmented and characterized by many small independent video rental stores. In the 1990s, however, managers at two firms, Blockbuster and Hollywood Video, pursued strategies that consolidated the industry. They built national brands though aggressive marketing, gained a differential advantage over their competitors by offering a wide availability of popular videos in large stores, and as they grew were able to use their bargaining power to drive down the costs they paid film studios for videos. In other words, by their choice of strategies, managers at Blockbuster and Hollywood Video transformed the industry structure, making it more favorable.

■ Blockbuster Video: Consolidating a fragmentary industry.

In consolidated industries firms are *interdependent* because one firm's competitive actions or moves (with regard to price, quality, and so on) directly affect the market share of its rivals and thus their profitability. When one firm makes a move, this generally forces a response from its rivals. The consequence of such interdependence can be a dangerous competitive spiral. Rivalry increases as firms attempt to undercut each other's prices or offer customers more value in their products, pushing industry profits down in the process. The fare wars that have periodically created havoc in the airline industry provide a good illustration of this process. Similarly, in the automobile industry if General Motors offers discounts to try to sell more cars (zero rate financing and cash-back rebates, for example), this will hurt the sales of Ford, which then has to respond in kind or lose market share.

Competitive interdependence in consolidated industries is thus a threat. Managers often seek to reduce this threat by pursuing strategies to differentiate their products from those offered by rivals, thereby making demand less vulnerable to price cuts by rivals. In the automobile industry firms try to differentiate their offerings by styling and quality. This has worked for Toyota, whose reputation for superior quality has insulated the firm from price competition; but it has not worked for Ford and GM, whose products are seen by consumers as roughly equivalent to each other.

// A SIXTH FORCE: COMPLEMENTORS

Although Porter's model is based on five forces, many observers believe that a six force is also important: complementors.[13] **Complementors** are firms that provide goods or services that are *complementary* to the product produced by enterprises in the industry. For example, a complementary product for video game consoles such as the Sony PS2 and Microsoft Xbox are the games themselves. Complementors to Sony and Microsoft include independent firms that produce video games such as Electronic Arts and Activision. Complementors can be important drivers of demand conditions in some industries.[14] Demand for video game consoles depends on a good supply of games from independent firms. Similarly, demand for the SoundDock speaker system produced by Bose (a set of powerful high-quality speakers that can play music from an Apple iPod) depends on the installed base of iPods. As more iPods are sold, demand increases for the speaker system produced by Bose.

As suggested by these examples, in industries where complements are important, strong complementors that make products consumers demand represent a substantial opportunity for a firm to increase its own revenues. Conversely, weak complementor product offerings can constitute a significant threat to a firm. In the early 2000s, for example, Sega introduced a powerful video game console, the Dreamcast, ahead of both Sony's PS2 system and Microsoft's Xbox. But demand for the Dreamcast was weak because there were few compelling games to play on the machine, and in the end Sega was forced to withdraw its console from the market.

complementors
Firms providing goods or services that are complementary to the product produced by enterprises in the industry.

■ Complementors for Microsoft and Sony.

// SYNTHESIS

Figure 2.4 summarizes the various elements we have discussed so far. When analyzing the task environment using Porter's five forces model (or six forces if complementors are included), remember that the forces interact with each other, and some forces may be more important than others depending on the industry setting. Managers need to look at the big picture when trying to understand the competitive forces that determine the nature of rivalry in their industry.

For example, the task environment confronting a firm may be particularly challenging if its industry is characterized by commoditylike products, powerful buyers with low switching costs who can bargain down prices, powerful suppliers who can raise input costs (or stop them from being reduced), high fixed costs, weak demand conditions, excess capacity, and easy new entry. These were the conditions prevailing in the airline industry between 2001 and 2005, and the results were awful for many firms in this industry. Conversely, if an industry is characterized by differentiated product offerings, relatively weak buyers who face high switching costs, an absence of powerful suppliers and substitutes, low fixed costs, high entry barriers, few rivals, and steady demand growth, it will be favorable for incumbent enterprises. Microsoft, of course, faces just such an environment in the market for computer operating

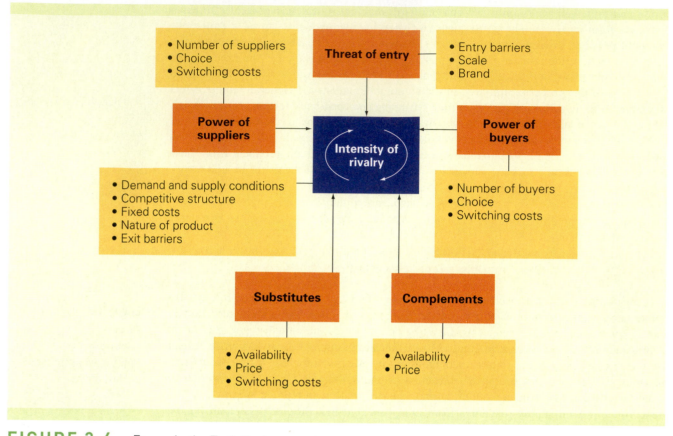

FIGURE 2.4   Forces in the Task Environment

systems and office productivity software (such as Microsoft Office). Not surprisingly, the firm's performance has been very strong.

The power of this approach lies not only in the identification of opportunities and threats in the task environment, but also in the help it gives managers when thinking through the various strategies they might pursue to take advantage of opportunities, and to counter threats, to better attain the goals of their enterprise. For example, an industry analysis by managers at FedEx during the early 1990s concluded that buyers were powerful due to low switching costs and their perception that the offerings of FedEx and UPS were similar. The same analysis revealed growing demand from corporate customers who wanted FedEx to take over their logistics operations, shipping components between different manufacturing locations and finished goods to retailers. The managers at FedEx saw this as an opportunity to pursue a different strategy that would add value to their product offering and increase switching costs. Specifically, FedEx managers realized that they could use their network to offer logistics services to customers, and that once customers had integrated their own operations with those of FedEx, it would be more difficult for them to switch—thereby reducing their tendency to periodically use the threat of switching as a device for getting volume discounts. This strategy has been successful for both FedEx and for UPS allowing both firms to increase revenues and profits.

■ FedEx reduces buyer power.

■ // The General Environment

The general environment is the larger environment within which the task environment is embedded. It includes political and legal forces, macroeconomic forces, demographic forces, sociocultural forces, technological forces, and international forces. Elements in the general environment impact the organization through the medium of the task environment. That is, the general environment helps shape the task environment, thus determining the magnitude of the opportunities and threats confronting the organization. The general environment is remote and less easy to shape than the task environment, but it is no less important.

// POLITICAL AND LEGAL FORCES

Political and legal forces are the result of changes in laws and regulations. Political processes shape a society's laws, which constrain the activities of organizations and thus create both opportunities and threats.[15] For example, throughout much of the industrialized world during the last 20 years there has been a strong trend toward deregulation of industries and the privatization of organizations once owned by the state. In the United States deregulation of the airline industry in 1979 allowed 29 new airlines to enter the industry between 1979 and 1993. The increase in passenger carrying capacity after deregulation led to excess capacity on many routes, intense competition, and fare wars.

The interplay between political and legal forces and industry competitive forces is a two-way process in which the government sets regulations that influence competitive structure, and firms in an industry often seek to influence the regulations that governments enact. For example, in 2002 the United States Steel Industry Association was a prime mover in persuading President Bush to impose a 30 percent tariff on imports of foreign steel into the United States. The purpose of the tariff was to protect American steelmakers from foreign competitors, thereby reducing the intensity of rivalry in the U.S. steel market.

Industry-specific regulators are an important and often overlooked aspect of the general environment of many firms. **Industry-specific regulators** are government agencies with responsibility for formulating, interpreting, and implementing rules specific to a particular industry. These rules shape competition in an industry; thus government regulators can have a profound impact on the intensity of competition in a firm's task environment and on the opportunities and threats confronting its managers. Some important industry-specific regulators include the Federal Drug Administration (which has to approve all new drugs for marketing), the Federal Communications Commission (which licenses firms to offer communication services), and the Federal Aviation Authority (which regulates the airline industry).

For an example of the influence exerted by industry regulators, consider the Federal Communications Commission (FCC), which licenses companies to deliver communication services. In 1997 the FCC created a huge opportunity when it agreed to allow firms to offer satellite radio service. The FCC set up an auction, and the two highest bidders in the auction, Sirius and XM Radio, were granted exclusive licenses to offer satellite radio in the United States until 2012. By 2005 over 5 million people were subscribing to satellite radio services, and demand was growing rapidly. Although those licenses will probably be renewed, the FCC could transform this opportunity into a threat for XM Radio and Sirius if it decides to offer additional licenses in the future, thereby increasing the number of satellite radio providers and competitive intensity in the market. Note that this decision to license two satellite radio operators has been a threat to established terrestrial radio stations, which face new competition from satellite radio firms.

Managers try to influence industry-specific regulators, lobbying both them and the politicians who oversee the regulators to get them to introduce legislation that is in the interests of the firm. When the FCC was considering whether to license spectrum to satellite radio providers, for example, established radio companies, who correctly saw satellite radio as a threat to their business, lobbied the FCC, arguing that it would be a mistake to allow satellite radio because that would lead to the demise of socially valuable local radio services.[16] Fortunately for satellite radio firms, these efforts were not successful.

// MACROECONOMIC FORCES

Macroeconomic forces affect the general health and well-being of a national or the regional economy, which in turn affect the profitability of firms within that economy. Four important factors in the macroeconomic environment are the growth rate of the economy, interest rates, currency exchange rates, and inflation (or deflation) rates. *Economic growth,* because it leads

political and legal forces
Industry changes resulting from changes in laws and regulations.

industry-specific regulators
Government agencies with responsibility for formulating, interpreting, and implementing rules specific to a particular industry.

■ Government regulator, Sirius, and XM Radio.

macroeconomic forces
Forces that affect the general health and well-being of a national or the regional economy, which in turn affect the profitability of firms within that economy.

Interest-Sensitive Product Demand for housing is influenced by the level of interest rates of mortgage loans. Interest rates are influenced by the policy of the Federal Reserve, which adjusts interest rates on government debt in response to economic conditions. When the economy is weak, the Federal Reserve lowers interest rates to stimulate demand, and vice versa.

© The McGraw-Hill Companies, Inc./John Flournoy, photographer

demographic forces

Outcomes of changes in the characteristics of a population, such as age, gender, ethnic origin, race, sexual orientation, and social class.

to an expansion in customer expenditures, tends to produce a general easing of competitive pressures within an industry. This lets firms expand their operations and earn higher profits. Because economic decline (a recession) leads to a reduction in customer expenditures, it increases competitive pressures. Economic decline frequently causes price wars in mature industries whose products are commoditylike and where buyers are powerful.

The level of *interest rates* can determine demand for a firm's products. Interest rates are important whenever customers routinely borrow money to finance their purchase of products. The most obvious example is the housing market, where mortgage rates directly affect demand. Interest rates also affect the sale of autos, appliances, and capital equipment, to give just a few examples. For firms in such industries, rising interest rates are a threat and falling rates an opportunity.

Currency exchange rates define the value of different national currencies against each other. Movement in currency exchange rates has a direct impact on the demand for a firm's products in the global marketplace. Between 2002 and 2004 the dollar fell in value against the euro, the currency used by many members of the European Union. The result was to make U.S. products cheaper in Europe. In general, a low or declining dollar reduces the threat from foreign competitors while creating opportunities for increased foreign sales. Conversely, a rising dollar can be a threat because it makes U.S. products more expensive, which can hurt sales.

Price inflation can destabilize the economy, producing slower economic growth, higher interest rates, and volatile currency movements. If inflation keeps increasing, investment planning becomes hazardous. The key characteristic of inflation is that it makes the future less predictable. In an inflationary environment it may be impossible to predict with any accuracy the real value of returns that can be earned from a project five years hence. Such uncertainty makes firms less willing to invest. In turn, low investment depresses economic activity and ultimately pushes the economy into a slump. Thus high inflation is a threat to organizations.

// DEMOGRAPHIC FORCES

Demographic forces are outcomes of changes in the characteristics of a population, such as age, gender, ethnic origin, race, sexual orientation, and social class. Like the other forces in the general environment, demographic forces present managers with opportunities and threats and can have major implications for an organization. Changes in the age distribution of a population represent an example of an important demographic force. Currently most industrialized nations are experiencing the aging of their populations as a consequence of falling birth and death rates and the aging of the baby boom generation. In Germany the percentage of the population over age 65 is expected to rise from 15.4 percent in 1990 to 20.7 percent in 2010. Comparable figures for Canada are 11.4 and 14.4 percent; for Japan, 11.7 and 19.5 percent; and for the United States, 12.6 and 13.5 percent.[17]

The Shape of Things to Come Demographic trends strongly suggest that the population of the United States will get older over the next few decades, driving demand for goods and services that cater to older people.

© Keith Brofsky/Getty Images.

The aging of the population is increasing opportunities for firms that cater to older people; the home health care and recreation industries are seeing an upswing in demand for their services. As the baby boom generation from the late 1940s to the early 1960s has aged, it has created a host of opportunities and threats. During the 1980s many baby boomers were getting married and creating a surge in demand for the appliances normally bought for first households. Companies such as Whirlpool Corporation and General Electric capitalized on the resulting demand for washing machines, dishwashers, dryers, and the like. In the 1990s many of these same baby boomers were starting to save for retirement, creating an inflow of money into mutual funds and a boom in the mutual fund industry. In the next 20 years many of these same baby boomers will retire, increasing demand for retirement communities.

> **sociocultural forces**
> The way in which changing social mores and values affect an industry.

// SOCIOCULTURAL FORCES

Sociocultural forces refer to the way in which changing social mores and values affect an industry. Like the other forces discussed here, social change creates opportunities and threats. One major social movement of recent decades has been a trend toward greater health consciousness. Its impact has been immense. Firms that recognized the opportunities early have often reaped significant gains. PepsiCo was able to gain market share from its rival Coca-Cola by being the first to introduce diet cola and fruit-based soft drinks. At the same time the health trend has created a threat for many industries. The tobacco industry, for example, is in decline as a direct result of greater customer awareness of the health implications of smoking.

■ TheStreet.com: Beneficiary of technological change.

// TECHNOLOGICAL FORCES

Over the last century the pace of technological change has accelerated.[18] This has unleashed a process that has been called a "perennial gale of creative destruction."[19] Technological change can make established products obsolete overnight and simultaneously create a host of new product possibilities. Thus technological change is both creative and destructive—both an opportunity and a threat.

One of the most important impacts of technological change is that it can affect the height of barriers to entry and therefore radically reshape industry structure. The pervasive Internet has changed the competitive structure of many industries. It has lowered entry barriers and reduced customer switching costs, increasing the intensity of rivalry in many industries and lowering both prices and profits.[20] For example, the Internet has lowered barriers to entry into the news industry. Providers of financial news now have to compete for advertising dollars and customer attention with new Internet-based media organizations that sprang up during the 1990s such as TheStreet.com, the Motley Fool, and Yahoo's financial section. The increase in rivalry has given advertisers more choices, enabling them to bargain down the prices they pay to media companies. Similarly, in the automobile industry, the ability of customers to comparison-shop for cars online and purchase cars online from a number of distributors such as Auto Nation has increased customers' ability to find the best values. Customers' increased bargaining power enables them to put downward pressure on car prices and squeeze profits out of the automobile industry.

> **The Mad Man of Wall Street** In 1997 the iconoclastic Jim Cramer founded TheStreet.com, an online financial news site to compete with established print media such as *The Wall Street Journal* and *Investors Business Daily*. Online sites like TheStreet.com have increased rivalry in the market for financial information and commentary, making it harder for established news organizations to capture advertising dollars.
>
> Courtesy of TheStreet.com, Inc.

// INTERNATIONAL FORCES

The last half century has witnessed enormous changes in the world economic system. We review these changes in detail in the next chapter when we discuss the global environment. For now the important points to note are that barriers to international trade and investment have tumbled, and an increasing number of countries are enjoying sustained economic growth. Economic growth in places like Brazil, China, and India is creating large new markets for goods and services, giving enterprises an opportunity to profit by entering these nations. Falling barriers to international trade and investment have also made it much easier to enter foreign nations. For example, 20 years ago it was almost impossible for a Western company to set up operations in China. Today Western and Japanese companies are investing over $50 billion a year in China. By the same token, however, falling barriers to international trade and investment have made it easier for foreign enterprises to enter the domestic markets of many firms (by lowering barriers to entry), thereby increasing the intensity of competition and lowering profitability. Because of these changes, many formerly isolated domestic markets have now become part of a much larger, more competitive global marketplace, creating myriad threats and opportunities for firms. We will return to this topic in detail in the next chapter.

// Dynamic Changes in the External Environment

It should be clear from the discussion so far that the external environment confronting managers is not stable. Indeed, the opposite is the norm. Elements of the general and task environments are always changing. Changes in the general environment, such as those in regulations, macroeconomic trends, demographics, social mores, or technology, impact the nature of competition in a firm's task environment. For example, new technology and deregulation can lower barriers to entry into an industry and increase the intensity of competition. Similarly, strong economic growth and falling interest rates can lead to greater customer demand in the task environment, whereas an economic recession and climbing interest rates may result in a contraction in demand.

Even when the general environment is relatively stable, changes in the task environment can still occur. By their own actions firms can change the nature of competition in their industries. Price cutting by one firm can spark a price war; introduction of a new product might spur greater demand growth; bankruptcy of marginal players in the industry can reduce capacity and create a more favorable competitive environment; and so on.

// INCREMENTAL VERSUS DISCONTINUOUS CHANGE

incremental change

Changes that do not alter the basic nature of competition in the task environment.

Managers must address two types of external environmental change: incremental change and discontinuous change. **Incremental change** refers to changes that do not alter the basic nature of competition in the task environment. Most task environments are characterized by ongoing incremental change. Demand might accelerate or decelerate in response to changes in the macroeconomy; competition may be more or less intense depending on the balance between demand and capacity; the entry of a new competitor might increase competition; and the bankruptcy of a competitor might reduce competitive pressures. Such changes, although not trivial, do not fundamentally alter the nature of competition.

discontinuous change

Change that fundamentally transforms the nature of competition in the task environment.

A **discontinuous change** is one that fundamentally transforms the nature of competition in the task environment. Discontinuous changes are normally triggered by discrete events, such as the emergence of a powerful new technology that changes the basis of competition, or substantial changes in the regulations governing an industry. Discontinuous changes are often characterized by the emergence of new competitors and, in many cases, by the decline of long-established enterprises that cannot adapt to the new environment (a primary reason for such failure to adapt is organization inertia, which we consider in Chapter 18).

■ Discontinuous change in the music industry.

The growth of the Internet, for example, when coupled with the development of small portable music players such as Apple's iPod, may now be ushering in a period of discontinuous change in the music industry. Increasingly music is being downloaded over the Internet, as opposed to being purchased at retail stores. This is hurting music retailers. Illegal downloading over the Internet has depressed the sales of music labels. The rise of legal sales through services such as Apple's iTunes may also be a mixed blessing for music companies: Customers can purchase individual songs and no longer have to purchase the dud "filler tracks" that are included on many CDs. In the long run these developments may lead to a lower sales base for music publishing companies and a decline in the number of music retailers with physical stores. This is definitely not business as usual for music companies! And that is the essence of discontinuous change—it represents a sharp break from business as usual.

Most task environments seem to go through long periods of relative stability, when changes are incremental in nature, punctuated by short periods of discontinuous change when the nature of competition is revolutionized, often by the arrival of new technology or a significant change in government regulations. This process is referred to as **punctuated equilibrium**.[21] The computer industry provides a classic example. During the 1960s and 1970s the industry was dominated by manufacturers of large computers such as IBM. In the mid-1980s personal computer technology revolutionized the industry. IBM lost its market dominance, and several new competitors, most notably Microsoft and Intel, grew with the new technology and seized industry leadership. For a period during the late 1980s and early 1990s the industry once again became stable. Then in the mid-1990s the Internet ushered in another period of revolutionary change. Although Microsoft and Intel survived with their dominance intact, several enterprises took advantage of this period to substantially grow their businesses. Most notably, Dell harnessed the power of the Internet to manage both its customer interface and its supply chain, driving down its costs in the process and gaining significant revenues at the expense of other computer manufacturers. The industry has been relatively stable since 2000, and change is once more incremental.

Incremental change is something that managers must learn to handle because all industries are characterized by this. Coping with discontinuous change is far more problematic and requires actions of an entirely different order. We discuss managing change and innovation in detail in Chapter 18.

// ENVIRONMENTAL UNCERTAINTY

To complicate the manager's life, not only is the external environment constantly changing, but the nature of change is frequently difficult to predict. The world is characterized by significant **uncertainty**, which in this context means an inability to predict with accuracy the nature, magnitude, timing, and direction of change in the environment. Managers typically seek to reduce the amount of environmental uncertainty they face by collecting more information and by trying to exert some control over the environment.[22]

Collecting Information By collecting information about different aspects of the environment they face, managers hope to reduce uncertainty, increase their knowledge, and thus make better decisions. However, although uncertainty can be reduced by collecting more information, it can never be eliminated altogether. The world is an inherently uncertain and unpredictable place. The best that can be hoped for is to reduce the uncertainty to some manageable level.

Collecting information can involve a number of tactics. *Market research* can improve managers' knowledge about customer needs and preferences, enabling them to better predict future demand trends. Boeing's market research group, for example, routinely talks to customers about their own plans as a way of trying to gauge future customer demand for commercial aircraft, thereby reducing the uncertainty associated with demand projections. *Competitive intelligence* can be gathered to better understand what competitors are doing. Thus Boeing carefully tracks the financial performance, investments, and strategic decisions of its global rival Airbus to better understand what Airbus is planning and to predict how Airbus will react to Boeing strategic initiatives, thereby reducing the uncertainty associated with such initiatives. Managers might also meet with industry-specific regulators to better anticipate what they might do in the future. Again consider Boeing: Managers at the company may talk with the Federal Aviation Authority (FAA) to predict how FAA regulations might affect aircraft design. In a famous example, when the company was building the Boeing 777 (the first wide-bodied long-haul jet to have only two engines), Boeing's managers consulted regularly with the FAA to make sure the agency would certify the aircraft for long-distance flights over the world's oceans (until the 777, only aircraft with four engines had been thus

punctuated equilibrium:
A view of industry evolution asserting that long periods of equilibrium are punctuated by periods of rapid change when industry structure is revolutionized by innovation.

■ Punctuated equilibrium in the computer industry.

uncertainty
An inability to predict with accuracy the nature, magnitude, timing, and direction of change in the environment.

■ Boeing: Collecting infromation to reduce uncertainty.

Multiple Acquirer   Cisco Systems, the maker of Internet routers, has reduced the technological uncertainty it faces in its environment by acquiring smaller enterprises that are developing new router technology.

© Getty Images.

■ Cisco Systems: Making acquisitions to control technology.

certified). In other words, by consulting with the FAA, Boeing's managers reduced the uncertainty associated with this aspect of the task environment.

Exerting Control   In addition to collecting information, managers try to reduce the environmental uncertainty they face by increasing their ability to exert control over it.[23] Various strategies can be used to do this. For example, facing uncertainty about the future trajectory of technology in an industry, incumbent enterprises often acquire or partner with smaller enterprises that are developing new technology, thereby trying to exercise some control over the development of that technology. Cisco Systems, the world's largest manufacturer of Internet routers, is famous for doing this. Cisco has a long history of acquiring smaller enterprises that are developing technology that might possibly supersede Cisco's own technology. If that technology subsequently turns out to be an improvement, Cisco is often the first to incorporate it. By making such acquisitions Cisco reduces the uncertainty associated with technological change.

More generally, firms use a variety of means to control their environments. They may acquire, merge with, or collaborate with competitors, thereby reducing the uncertainty associated with competitive rivalry. For example, the early 1990s saw considerable uncertainty over which technology would be used in DVDs. Rather than compete with each other by developing different and incompatible variations of DVD technology, leading consumer electronics firms formed an industry association known as the DVD Forum. Through the DVD Forum they established a common standard.

Similarly, to reduce uncertainty firms may acquire distributors, key suppliers, or important complementors to increase their control over them. To make sure there would be sufficient compelling games to accompany its Xbox video game console (that is, to reduce the uncertainty associated with the supply of games) in 2000 Microsoft acquired an important complementor, Bungie Studios. At the time Bungie was working on a science fiction game, *Halo*. After the acquisition *Halo* was developed exclusively for the Xbox, and the popularity of this game (and its successor, *Halo 2*) helped drive demand for the Xbox against its rival, the Sony PS2. Firms also enter cooperative ventures with distributors, suppliers, or complementors to exert similar control over the environment.

■ // The Internal Environment

In addition to the external environment, managers also face the internal environments of their own organizations. As noted in the chapter introduction, the internal environment includes the organization of the firm (its structure, culture, controls, and incentives), its employees (human capital), and its resources (tangible and intangible assets). Each of these elements can be a strength, enabling managers to attain the goals of the enterprise, or a weakness that makes it more difficult for managers to work productively toward attaining enterprise goals. When managers analyze the internal environment of their firm, they often do so by identifying its strengths and weaknesses. This inward focus complements the identification of opportunities and threats in the external environment. Taking such an inventory (a *SWOT* analysis) can help managers develop strategy.

// INTERNAL ORGANIZATION

The internal organization of a firm can create an environment that is easy or difficult to work in. It might be an enlightened meritocracy that offers a host of opportunities for advancement, rewards skilled and creative managers, and fosters high productivity; or it might be an inert bureaucracy that punishes those who advocate change, rewards only those who promote the status quo, and inhibits the attainment of productivity. The internal environment can be a liberating place that lets a manager reach his or her full potential, or it can be stifling. It can be a place where it is easy to do good things or where it is hard to do anything. It can also be changed by the actions of managers. Managers can transform their firms from dull bureaucracies into progressive meritocracies. Unfortunately the opposite can happen too: Bad managers have taken over good organizations and left them in worse shape than they found them in![24]

It is common to think of the internal organization of a firm in terms of its **organizational culture**—the basic pattern of values and assumptions shared by employees within an organization.[25] As important as organizational culture is, the organization comprises far more than culture. It is also determined by the structure of the organization, its control systems, its incentives, and the kind of people who work there. Collectively we refer to structure, controls, incentives, and culture as aspects of the *organization architecture* of a firm. We discuss the basic elements of organization architecture in detail in Chapters 8 through 11. For now, however, remember that each of these elements is critical in determining the kind of place in which a manager works.

Culture is important because the shared values and assumptions of an organization influence what a manager can and cannot do, as well as what is encouraged or discouraged by the organization. Structure defines who has responsibility for what in an organization, where power and influence are concentrated in an organization, and thus whose support is critical for getting things done. Controls and incentives tell the manager what kind of behavior the organization expects, what is being tracked, and what will be rewarded. If a manager is going to get things done in an organization, he or she must figure out how the organization works, how decisions get made, and what to do to exert influence. To be successful, and to handle external environmental challenges, the manager must understand the internal organization in which he or she is based.

Although we discuss internal organization in more detail later in the book, two points are of note now. First, the internal organization of an enterprise can be a strength or a weakness. An internal organization that encourages and rewards high productivity and enables managers to respond rapidly to external opportunities and threats can be considered a strength. Conversely, an internal organization that inhibits productivity and is characterized by political infighting and inertia forces can be considered a weakness.

Second, just as managers can pursue strategies to take advantage of opportunities and counter threats in the external environment, they can also pursue strategies to build on organizational strengths and counter weaknesses. For example, when Jack Welch became CEO of General Electric in 1981, a position he held until 2001, he quickly realized that the internal organization of GE was a weakness. Among other things, he thought it was too centralized, bureaucratic, and hierarchical, with far too many layers of management (on average there were 11). His strategy for the organization was to delayer (reducing the number of management layers to as few as four), decentralize responsibility for operating and strategic decisions to self-contained business divisions, and create positive incentives for managers to pursue strategies that boosted productivity and profit growth. Over time this change in internal organization had the desired effect, and what had been a weakness became a strength.

// EMPLOYEES (HUMAN CAPITAL)

The employees of an enterprise can be a source of sustained competitive advantage, or they can represent a weakness. Employees constitute what economists call the **human capital** of an organization, by which they mean the knowledge, skills, and capabilities embedded in individuals. Human capital is a crucial source of productivity gains and economic growth.[26] Stanford Business School Professor Jeffery Pfeffer has argued that people are the most important source of sustainable competitive advantage.[27] Hire the right people, train them well, create an internal organization that allows them to fully express their potential, and reward them appropriately by putting the right incentives in place, and the firm will be rewarded by superior performance. By the same token, if employees lack the knowledge,

organizational culture
The basic pattern of values and assumptions shared by employees within an organization.

■ Organizational weaknesses at GE.

human capital
The knowledge, skills, and capabilities embedded in individuals.

■ Building human capital at Microsoft.

skills, capabilities, and motivation to work productively and pursue opportunities for improving performance, Pfeffer's arguments suggest that this can constitute a source of competitive disadvantage.

The strategy of Microsoft illustrates the role of people in building a successful enterprise. Microsoft has always tried to hire the best and the brightest, to reward them for high performance through incentive-based pay (stock options and grants), and to give them plenty of opportunities for expressing their potential. Over the years this strategy made people a unique *strength* for Microsoft. This produced significant gains, enabling the company to make and effectively market a range of software products that became industry standards (specifically Windows and Office). In recent years, however, it has become more difficult for Microsoft to execute this strategy. Today many of the best and brightest are going to work for competitors such as Google, which they perceive as a more vibrant enterprise. Moreover, many of Microsoft's original employees became very wealthy during the 1990s and retired early. This drained some of the firm's human capital. As a result, it is no longer clear that people represent a unique strength for the company. In fact, relative to competitors, Microsoft's employees could become a weakness if the company does not take steps to correct the gradual erosion of its human capital.

In some cases the employees of an organization can indeed be a source of weakness. For example, as we saw in the introduction to the chapter, the ability of managers at some U.S. airlines, such as United, to implement strategies addressing tough competitive conditions in the task environment has been hampered by the fact that many of the people within the organization belong to unions that have resisted the proposed changes. It has been easier for managers at other airlines, such as SW Airlines and Jet Blue, to introduce flexible work practices that boost productivity and reduce costs, partly because their workforces are not unionized.

We further discuss strategies for managing people and upgrading human capital later in this book. For now remember that people can be a distinctive strength or a weakness relative to competitors; managers can exert influence over the human capital of the organization through human resource practices and by putting the right internal organization architecture in place.

// RESOURCES

resource-based view
A view that resources of an enterprise can be a source of sustainable competitive advantage.

resources
Assets that managers have to work with in their quest to improve the performance of an enterprise.

tangible resources
Physical assets, such as land, buildings, equipment, inventory, and money.

intangible resources
Nonphysical assets that are the creation of managers and other employees, such as brand names, the reputation of the company, processes within the firm for performing work and making decisions, and the intellectual property of the company, including that protected through patents, copyrights, and trademarks.

An important line of work in academic literature known as the **resource-based view** of the firm argues that the resources of an enterprise can be a source of sustainable competitive advantage.[28] The **resources** of a firm are the assets that managers have to work with in their quest to improve the performance of the enterprise. **Tangible resources** are physical assets, such as land, buildings, equipment, inventory, and money. **Intangible resources** are nonphysical assets that are the creation of managers and other employees, such as brand names, the reputation of the company, processes within the firm for performing work and making decisions, and the intellectual property of the company, including that protected through patents, copyrights, and trademarks.

The resource-based view argues that a resource can constitute a unique strength if it meets the following conditions (see Figure 2.5). First, the firm must *own* the resource in question; if it does not, the resource owner will capture the benefits. Second, the resource must be *valuable*, increasing the performance of the firm relative to that attained by competitors either by lowering costs or by differentiating the product offering and helping the firm to raise prices and sell more. Third, the resource must be *rare*: Competing enterprises lack similar quality resources. Fourth, the resource must be *inimitable*: It is difficult for competitors to imitate or replicate it. Fifth, the resource must be *nonsubstitutable*: Competitors cannot use a different resource that is easy to acquire to achieve the same effect.

■ Aramco's valuable resources.

For a simple example, consider Aramco, the state-owned Saudi oil company. Aramco owns a valuable resource: the sole right to pump oil out of the giant Saudi Ghawar field, the largest ever discovered. The resource is valuable because the cost of extracting oil from

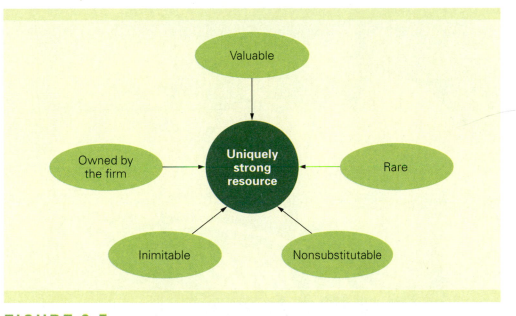

FIGURE 2.5   Uniquely Strong Resources

Ghawar, at around $10 a barrel, is far below the price of oil (which in early 2006 stood at $70 a barrel). The resource is rare because very few oil fields are as big as Ghawar, and the cost of oil extraction at Ghawar has long been among the lowest in the world. The resource is inimitable because other oil companies cannot simply copy the Ghawar—there is only one Ghawar. The resource is nonsubstitutable because there is no other way of producing oil that is substitutable for production at Ghawar. Thus ownership of the right to pump oil out of Ghawar represents a unique strength of Aramco.[29]

As another example, consider the Coca-Cola trademark. An intangible asset, the trademark is the exclusive property of the Coca-Cola Company, its owner. It is a valuable resource because it signifies the Coca-Cola brand and all that implies in the minds of consumers. Most notably, the trademark allows Coca-Cola to differentiate its cola from that of other companies. The trademark is a rare resource because it is intellectual property that is exclusively owned by Coca-Cola; it is inimitable because trademark law prohibits other enterprises from using a lookalike trademark. One can also argue that the trademark is nonsubstitutable because there is no commonly available substitute for the Coca-Cola trademark—except perhaps the Pepsi-Cola trademark, which was built at great expense by PepsiCo. In sum, the Coca-Cola trademark seems to constitute a unique strength of Coca-Cola. It is a resource that managers can work with to improve the firm's performance. Indeed, when managers noticed that growth in demand for cola in the United States was starting to mature, they decided to use the Coca-Cola trademark to help sell other beverages such as bottled water, which is sold under the Dasani brand name but also sports the Coca-Cola trademark on every bottle.

More generally, resources that are unique strengths for a firm—*uniquely strong resources*—can take on all sorts of forms. The process that 3M uses to generate new products may be a uniquely strong resource, given the history and success of that company in doing just that. Similarly, the production systems of leading manufacturing companies such as Toyota and Dell Computer may be based on uniquely strong resources. Some would also say that internal organization and human capital, two aspects of the internal environment we have already considered, may in the right conditions be considered uniquely strong resources.[30]

■ Coca-Cola's valuable resource.

A Unique Strength   The Coca-Cola trademark is a valuable resource, owned by the firm, that is rare, inimitable, and nonsubstitutable. Coca-Cola has invested heavily in promoting and protecting this trademark.

© Getty Images.

The resource-based view of the firm suggests three things. First, when reviewing a firm's assets for strengths and weaknesses, managers should evaluate the firm's tangible and intangible resources with respect to the five characteristics discussed here: ownership, value, rareness, inimitability, and nonsubstitutability. Such resources can be a source of unique strength. Second, managers should be aware that they need to protect such resources and make sure they continue to be a source of strength in the future. For example, to protect the value of the Coca-Cola trademark, Coca-Cola invests in brand promotions, makes sure that its product quality is good (ultimately the trademark is a symbol of product quality), and uses its legal staff to sue enterprises that make unauthorized use of the trademark. Third, managers can create resources that constitute unique strengths if they make the right kinds of investments over time. The Coca-Cola trademark, for example, was initially not that valuable. It became so over time only as managers at Coca-Cola built the brand through marketing, promotions, and product extensions and used the legal system to stop others from copying the trademark.

IN CONCLUSION   WHY DOES IT MATTER?

An organization does not exist in a vacuum; as we have seen, it is embedded in a task (industry) environment, and that environment is embedded in a wider general environment. Developments in the general environment can shape the task environment, and the task environment determines the ability of an organization to attain its goals. The task environment can present opportunities that if exploited make it easier for the organization to attain its goals; it can also give rise to threats that make attaining goals more problematic. Managers need an intimate understanding of the environment that confronts their firm. They need this to craft actions and strategies to take advantage of opportunities and counter threats. Without a detailed understanding of the environment confronting their organization and how that environment might change over time, managers are unlikely to be effective.

Managers also need to understand that the external environment is not just something they passively respond to; it is something they can influence and shape through their actions. In a dramatic example, David Margolese, the former CEO of Sirius Radio, lobbied the Federal Communications Commission for several years, finally persuading the FCC to grant licenses allowing companies to offer satellite radio service in the United States. Today two satellite radio providers, XM Radio and Sirius, are growing rapidly and presenting traditional radio broadcasters with a significant competitive challenge. Through his actions Margolese significantly altered the task environment confronting radio broadcasters. This is what the best managers do: They see the external environment not as it is, but as it might be, and they push their firms to take actions that dramatically change that environment.

To manage effectively, to address emerging opportunities and threats, and to proactively shape the external environment in ways that benefit their firm, managers must be able to get things done within their enterprise. To do this they must understand the internal environment confronting them, particularly its strengths and weaknesses. They need to review the internal organization of their enterprise, as well as its human capital and resources, and ask themselves what can be done to improve these factors, eradicating weaknesses and building on strengths, so they have better assets to work with as they attempt to exploit external environmental opportunities.

MANAGEMENT CHALLENGES

1. Identify an industry in which the task environment facing firms is hostile and makes it difficult for firms to make good profits. Explain how the task environment is hostile.

2. Identify an industry in which the task environment facing firms is favorable and makes it relatively easy for firms to make good profits. Explain how this task environment is favorable.

3. Over the last 20 years the telecommunications industry in the United States has been radically transformed.
   a. What has driven these changes?
   b. How has the nature of competition in the industry changed?
   c. What are the implications of these changes for firms in the industry?
   d. How have managers at these firms tried to deal with the changing industry?

4. How will the aging of the baby boom generation change the task environment in the health services industry? Who will benefit from these changes? Why?

5. What are the barriers to entry into the soft drink industry in the United States? What are the implications of these entry barriers for incumbent companies such as Coca-Cola and PepsiCo?

6. What are the strengths and weaknesses of Microsoft? What are its strengths based on? What can the company do to upgrade its resources so that more are sources of strength?

MANAGEMENT PORTFOLIO

FOR THE ORGANIZATION YOU HAVE CHOSEN TO FOLLOW:

1. Describe the nature of the task environment the firm is facing. What are the opportunities here, and what are the threats?

2. Has the task environment been influenced by trends in the general environment over the last decade? If so, what are these trends and how have they changed things?

3. What are the sources of uncertainty in the task environment confronting the firm? What strategies have managers at the firm adopted to try and cope with this uncertainty?

4. What are the strengths of the organization? What are the weaknesses?

CLOSING CASE   THE PHARMACEUTICAL INDUSTRY

Managers in pharmaceutical firms face a dynamic and challenging task environment that creates both opportunities and threats. Demand for pharmaceuticals is strong and has been growing steadily for decades. Between 1990 and 2005 there was a 12.5 percent annual increase in spending on prescription drugs in the United States. This strong growth was driven by favorable demographics. As people grow older they tend to consume more prescription medicines, and the population in most advanced nations has been growing older as the post–World War II baby boom generation ages.

Moreover, successful new prescription drugs can be extraordinarily profitable. Consider Lipitor, the cholesterol-lowering drug sold by Pfizer. Introduced in 1997, by 2005 this drug generated a staggering $12 billion in annual sales for Pfizer. The costs of manufacturing, packaging, and distributing Lipitor amounted to only about 10 percent of revenues, or around $1.2 billion. Pfizer spent close to $400 million on advertising and promoting Lipitor and perhaps as much again on maintaining a sales force to sell the product. That still leaves Pfizer with a gross profit from Lipitor of perhaps $10 billion.

Lipitor is highly profitable because the drug is protected from direct competition by a 20-year patent. This temporary monopoly allows Pfizer to charge a high price. Once the patent expires, other firms will be able to produce generic versions of Lipitor, and the price will fall—typically by 80 percent within a year—but that is some time away.

Competing firms can produce drugs that are similar (but not identical) to a patent-protected drug. Drug firms patent a specific molecule, and competing firms can patent similar, but not identical, molecules that have a similar pharmacological effect. Thus Lipitor does have competitors in the market for cholesterol-lowering drugs—such as Zocor, sold by Merck, and Crestor, sold by AstraZeneca. But these competing drugs are also patent protected. Moreover, due to Federal Drug Administration regulations and requirements for demonstrating that a drug is safe and effective, the costs and risks associated with developing a new drug and bringing it to market are very high. Out of every 5,000 compounds tested in the laboratory by a drug company, only five enter clinical trials, and only one of these will ultimately make it to the market. On average, estimates suggest that it costs some $800 million and takes anywhere from 10 to 15 years to bring a new drug to market. Once on the market, only 3 out of 10 drugs ever recoup their R&D and marketing costs and turn a profit. Thus the high profitability of the pharmaceutical industry rests on a handful of blockbuster drugs. To produce a blockbuster, a drug company must spend great amounts of money on research, most of which fails to produce a product. Pfizer, for example, spent over $7.4 billion on R&D in 2005 alone, equivalent to 14.6 percent of its total revenues.

In addition to R&D spending, the incumbent firms in the pharmaceutical industry spend much money on advertising and sales promotion. Although the $400 million a year that Pfizer spends promoting Lipitor is small relative to the drug's revenues, it is a large amount for a new competitor to match, making market entry difficult unless the competitor has a significantly better product.

There are also some big opportunities on the horizon for firms in the industry. New scientific breakthroughs in genomics portend that within the next decade pharmaceutical firms might be able to bring new drugs to market that treat some of the most intractable medical conditions, including Alzheimer's, Parkinson's disease, cancer, heart disease, stroke, and HIV.

On the other hand, managers in the industry face serious challenges. Many patent-protected medicines are scheduled to come off patent in the next decade, and to maintain profitability, pharmaceutical firms must find new drugs to replace them. In addition, as spending on health care rises, seniors are complaining about the high costs of prescription medicines, and politicians are looking for ways to limit this. One possibility is some form of price controls on prescription drugs. Pharmaceutical price controls are already in effect in most developed nations, and although they have not yet been introduced in the United States, that could happen. Another possibility is to make it easy for U.S. residents to purchase pharmaceuticals from foreign nations where prices are lower.

A further challenge is associated with the growth of large health care providers, who have millions of subscribers and are starting to use their power to reduce the drug prices their subscribers pay. In some cases they are refusing to provide insurance coverage for high-priced pharmaceuticals when lower-priced generic alternatives are available.[31]

CASE DISCUSSION QUESTIONS

1. What are the barriers to entry into the pharmaceutical industry? To what extent do you think these entry barriers protect established pharmaceutical companies from new competitors?

2. The pharmaceutical industry has long been one of the most profitable in the United States. Why do you think this is the case?

3. What forces in the general environment influence the nature of competition in the task environment facing pharmaceutical firms?

4. Are there reasons for believing that the profitability of the industry might come under threat over the next decade? What do you think managers in the industry should do to counter this threat?

ENDNOTES

1. Sources: "Flying on Empty," *The Economist,* May 22, 2005, p. 73; "Turbulent Skies: Low-Cost Airlines," *The Economist,* July 10, 2004, pp. 68–72; *"Silver Linings, Darkening Clouds," The Economist,* March 27, 2004, pp. 90–92; W. Zellner and M. Arndt, "Big Airlines: Not Much Runway Left," *BusinessWeek,* July 5, 2004, p. 50; Economic data from the Air Transport Association at www.airtransport.org.

2. Boeing Commercial Airplane Group, Current Market Forecast, 2005. Available at www.boeing.com/commercial/cmo/pdf.

3. M.E. Porter, *Competitive Strategy* (New York: Free Press, 1980). Also see J. Pfeffer and G.R. Salancik, *The External Control of Organizations* (New York: Harper & Row, 1978).

4. J.E. Bain, *Barriers to New Competition* (Cambridge, MA: Harvard University Press, 1956). For a review of the modern literature about barriers to entry, see R.J. Gilbert, "Mobility Barriers and the Value of Incumbency," in *Handbook of Industrial Organization,* vol. 1, ed. R. Schmalensee and R.D. Willig (Amsterdam: North-Holland, 1989). Also see R.P. McAfee, H.M. Mialon, and M.A.Williams, "What Is a Barrier to Entry?" *American Economic Review* 94 (May 2004), pp. 461–68.

5. Sources: J. Ewing and D. Foust, "DHL's American Adventure," *BusinessWeek,* November 29, 2004, pp. 126–67; "Shares at a Cost," *Traffic World,* April 11, 2005, pp. 1–2; R. Brooks, "DHL Plans to Spend $1.2 Billion in Challenge of FedEx and UPS," *The Wall Street Journal,* June 25, 2004, p. B2.

6. For details see C. Shapiro and H.R. Varian, *Information Rules: A Strategic Guide to the Network Economy* (Boston: Harvard Business School Press, 1999).

7. A detailed discussion of switching costs and being locked in can be found in C. Shapiro and H.R. Varian, *Information Rules: A Strategic Guide to the Network Economy.*

8. Pfeffer and Salancik, *The External Control of Organizations.*

9. Boeing Commercial Airplane Group, Current Market Forecast, 2005.

10. For a review, see F. Karakaya, "Market Exit and Barriers to Exit: Theory and Practice," *Psychology and Marketing* 17 (2000), pp. 651–68.

11. M. Busse, "Firm Financial Condition and Airline Price Wars," *Rand Journal of Economics* 33 (2002), pp. 298–318.

12. J.P. Womack, D.T. Jones, and D. Roos, *The Machine That Changed the World*; J. Palmer, "Can Anyone Stop Toyota?" *Barron's,* September 13, 2004, pp. 25–29.

13. A.S. Grove, *Only the Paranoid Survive* (New York: Doubleday, 1996).

14. For details and further references, see C.W.L. Hill, "Establishing a Standard: Competitive Strategy and Technology Standards in Winner Take All Industries," *Academy of Management Executive* 11 (1997), pp. 7–25; and Shapiro and Varian, *Information Rules.*

15. For a detailed discussion of the importance of the structure of law as a factor explaining economic change and growth, see D.C. North, *Institutions, Institutional Change, and Economic Performance* (Cambridge: Cambridge University Press, 1990).

16. B. McLean, "Satellite Killed the Radio Star," *Fortune,* January 22, 2001, pp. 94–99.

17. *Economist, The Economist Book of Vital World Statistics* (New York: Random House, 2000).

18. See M. Gort and J. Klepper, "Time Paths in the Diffusion of Product Innovations," *Economic Journal,* September 1982, pp. 630–53. Looking at the history of 46 products, Gort and Klepper found that the length of time before other companies entered the markets created by a few inventive companies declined from an average of 14.4 years for products introduced before 1930 to 4.9 years for those introduced after 1949.

19. The phrase was originally coined by J. Schumpeter in *Capitalism, Socialism, and Democracy* (London: Macmillan, 1950), p. 68.

20. M.E. Porter, "Strategy and the Internet," *Harvard Business Review,* March 2001, pp. 62–79.

21. The term *punctuated equilibrium* is borrowed from evolutionary biology. For a detailed explanation of the concept, see M.L. Tushman, W.H. Newman, and E. Romanelli, "Convergence and Upheaval: Managing the Unsteady Pace of Organizational Evolution," *California Management Review* 29, no. 11 (1985), pp. 29–44; C.J.G. Gersick, "Revolutionary Change Theories: A Multilevel Exploration of the Punctuated Equilibrium Paradigm," *Academy of Management Review* 16 (1991), pp. 10–36; R. Adner and D.A. Levinthal, "The Emergence of Emerging Technologies," *California Management Review* 45 (Fall 2002), pp. 50–65; F.T. Rothaermel and C.W.L. Hill, "Technological Discontinuities and Complementary Assets: A Longitudinal Study of Industry and Firm Performance," *Organization Science* 16 (2005), pp. 52–70.

22. J.D. Thompson, *Organizations in Action* (New York: McGraw-Hill, 1967).

23. The classic summary of such strategies is given in Pfeffer and Salancik, *The External Control of Organizations*.

24. J.P. Kotter and J.L. Heskett, *Corporate Culture and Performance* (New York: Free Press, 1992).

25. A. Williams, P. Dobson, and M. Walters, *Changing Culture: New Organizational Approaches* (London: Institute of Personnel Management, 1989); E.H. Schein, "What Is Culture?" in *Reframing Organizational Culture*, ed. P.J. Frost et al. (Newbury Park, CA: Sage, 1991), pp. 243–53.

26. G.S. Becker, *Human Capital*, 2nd ed. (Chicago: University of Chicago Press, 1993).

27. J. Pfeffer, *Competitive Advantage through People* (Cambridge, MA: Harvard Business School Press, 1994).

28. The material in this section relies on the resource-based view of the company. For summaries of this perspective, see J.B. Barney, "Company Resources and Sustained Competitive Advantage," *Journal of Management* 17 (1991), pp. 99–120; J.T. Mahoney and J.R. Pandian, "The Resource-Based View within the Conversation of Strategic Management," *Strategic Management Journal* 13 (1992), pp. 363–380; R. Amit and P.J.H. Schoemaker, "Strategic Assets and Organizational Rent," *Strategic Management Journal* 14 (1993), pp. 33–46; M.A. Peteraf, "The Cornerstones of Competitive Advantage: A Resource-Based View," *Strategic Management Journal* 14 (1993), pp. 179–91; B. Wernerfelt, "A Resource-Based View of the Company," *Strategic Management Journal* 15 (1994), pp. 171–80; and K.M. Eisenhardt and J.A. Martin, "Dynamic Capabilities: What Are They?" *Strategic Management Journal* 21 (2000), pp. 1105–21.

29. Paul Roberts, *The End of Oil* (Boston: Houghton Mifflin, 2004).

30. This seems to be the position advocated by Jay Barney, one of the founders of this approach. See J.B. Barney, "Company Resources and Sustained Competitive Advantage," *Journal of Management* 17 (1991), pp. 99–120.

31. Source: Staff reporter, "Pharm Exec 50," *Pharmaceutical Executive*, May 2004, pp. 61–68; J.A. DiMasi, R.W. Hansen, and H.G. Grabowski, "The Price of Innovation: New Estimates of Drug Development Costs," *Journal of Health Economics* 22 (March 2003), pp. 151–70; Staff reporter, "Where the Money Is: The Drug Industry," *The Economist*, April 26, 2003, pp. 64–65; Value Line Investment Survey, *The Drug Industry*, April 22, 2005.

3

GLOBALIZATION AND THE MANAGER

LEARNING OBJECTIVES

After Reading This Chapter You Should Be Able to:

1 Explain what globalization is.

2 Describe the processes driving globalization.

3 Identify the implications of globalization for business enterprises.

4 Discuss different constraints limiting the pace of globalization.

5 Outline the benefits of going global for a business firm.

6 Discuss some of the challenges of managing in a global enterprise.

India Calling!—This call center in India deals with customer service inquiries for American companies. Until the advent of global communications networks, it was impossible to outsource such service activities.

© Sherwin/Crasto/ Reuters/Corbis

Outsourcing manufacturing activities to foreign producers is nothing new. American companies have been doing this for decades. But until recently few service firms outsourced work to third parties overseas. Thanks to modern communications technologies, that is now changing. Consider individual tax returns in the United States. Until the beginning of this decade, all individual U.S. tax returns were compiled in the United States by U.S.–trained accountants. Then some small accounting firms started to experiment with outsourcing to India the "grunt work" involved in preparing tax returns. In 2003 some 25,000 tax returns were compiled in India; in 2004 the figure was 100,000; and in 2005 the number exceeded 250,000. Although still just a tiny fraction of the 130 million individual U.S. tax returns compiled each year, industry experts expect the numbers to grow rapidly. The reasons are simple: (1) There are not enough trained accountants in the United States to handle the flood of work that occurs every tax season; (2) foreign accountants are cheaper—the average accountant in India earns just a fraction of a U.S. counterpart's salary; and (3) because India is on the other side of the world from the United States, Indian accountants can compile returns while their American partners are asleep, cutting preparation time in half, which translates into better customer service.[1]

Outsourcing tax return preparation to foreign producers is one example of a fundamental transformation occurring in the world economy. We have been moving rapidly away from a world in which national economies were relatively self-contained entities, isolated from each other by barriers to cross-border trade and investment; by distance, time zones, and language; and by national differences in government regulation, culture, and business systems. And we have been moving toward a world in which barriers to trade and investment are tumbling; perceived distance is shrinking due to advances in transportation and telecommunications technology; material culture is starting to look similar the world over; and national economies are merging into an integrated and interdependent global economic system—a process commonly referred to as *globalization*.

Globalization is pushing deeper into national economies. For example, service activities used to be performed when the service was delivered. However, modern communications technologies such as the Internet have allowed firms to outsource to foreign producers many service activities that don't require face-to-face contact. Not only are tax returns being outsourced; so are credit card applications, mortgage loan processing, software debugging, and the diagnosis of MRI scans. Like manufacturing firms before them, service firms are now shifting productive activities to different locations around the globe where they can be performed most efficiently, creating a globally dispersed production system.

This new world is challenging and exciting for managers. Globalization is radically altering the environment confronting managers, giving rise to opportunities and threats that did not exist two decades ago and creating new uncertainties that are much harder to reduce or control. In this chapter we look first at the process of globalization. Then we discuss what globalization means for managers.

■ // The Process of Globalization

globalization
The process whereby national economies and business systems are becoming deeply interlinked with each other.

Globalization is the process whereby national economies and business systems are becoming deeply interlinked with each other. The world is moving away from relatively independent national economies toward a single global system. The process of globalization, however, has markedly accelerated since the 1980s. There are three main reasons for this: the spread of market-based economic systems, the decline of barriers to international trade and foreign direct investment, and falling costs of communication and transportation.[2]

// THE SPREAD OF MARKET-BASED SYSTEMS

market economy
An economy in which businesses are privately owned and prices are set by the interaction of supply and demand.

In a **market economy**, such as that of the United States, most businesses are privately owned (as opposed to being owned by the state); prices are set by the interaction of supply and demand; and government regulation is limited to ensuring that competition between individual enterprises is free and fair and that the system does not produce outcomes judged to be unacceptable by society (poor working conditions, false advertising, harmful industrial pollution).[3]

socialist economy
An economy in which businesses are owned by the state and prices are set by state planners.

Until recently only a minority of countries operated with market-based systems. As little as 25 years ago much of the world's population lived in **socialist economies.** There most businesses were owned by the state; private producers were excluded from certain industrial and commercial activities; prices were set by the state; and state planners decided what was produced where, in what quantity, and by whom. China, Russia, and most of Eastern Europe operated with tightly controlled socialist economies. In addition, the economies of many other nations, from India and Brazil to Britain and Sweden, had significant socialist elements in some sectors. In Britain, for example, 30 years ago state-owned enterprises dominated many sectors of the economy, including steelmaking, shipbuilding, coal mining, transportation, and telecommunications services.

By their nature, socialist economies are antithetical to globalization. They inhibit rather than encourage cross-border trade and investment. Foreign businesses are excluded from many sectors of the economy, if not the entire economy, and state-owned enterprises often focus inward on their own economy. In the 1970s, for example, Britain's telecommunications industry was monopolized by British Telecom, which focused exclusively on providing telecommunications services to the British economy. No other telecommunications companies were allowed to compete in Britain, and British Telecom had no overseas ventures.

Socialist economies trace their roots to Marxist-inspired political movements, which advocate that the "commanding heights" of an economy should be controlled by the state and managed in the public interest.[4] By the 1970s it was apparent that this ideology had failed to deliver on its promise to improve the lot of working people. Indeed, the opposite seemed to be the case, with socialist economies lagging market economies in economic growth rates and living standards. Consequently, by the early 1980s a pronounced move was under way in many nations from socialism toward market-based economics. The movement started in Britain, spread throughout the social democratic states of Western Europe, and following the collapse of Communism in Eastern Europe and the former Soviet Union, spread into Eastern Europe and Russia by the early 1990s. By the mid-1990s market-based systems were spreading worldwide. Large countries such as India and Brazil had embraced market-

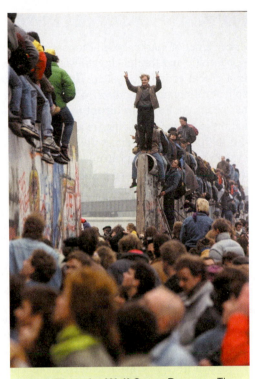

More Than the Wall Came Down.   The demolition of the Berlin Wall, a powerful symbol of Soviet domination in Eastern Europe, signaled the end of Communism there. The collapse of Communism was quickly followed by the introduction of market-based economic systems in many formerly Communist and socialist nations.

© AP Photo/Lionel Cironneau

based economic reforms, and even several nominally Communist nations, including most notably China, moved rapidly toward market based systems.[5] By 2005, according to an annual survey conducted by the Heritage Foundation, market-based economic systems were more widespread than at any time in modern history.[6]

The shift toward market-based systems has four main elements: privatization of state-owned enterprises, dismemberment of former state-owned monopolies, deregulation of markets (including abandonment of price controls and laws restricting investment by foreign enterprises), and establishment of a legal system that supports private enterprise and protects property rights. For example, in Brazil the state-owned telecommunications monopoly was privatized and split into 12 separate companies that could compete with each other; the government also allowed foreign telecommunications companies to enter the Brazilian market.

In sum, the worldwide shift toward market-based economic systems has supported globalization. Market economies are more open to foreign investment and international trade than the socialist alternative. Moreover, the transformation of economies such as China's and India's to more open systems has created a plethora of opportunities and threats for Western businesses. Outsourcing of manufacturing and service activities to these nations has accelerated, as have investments in these nations. China in particular has become an engine of *global* economic growth, a major market for many imports (particularly commodities such as oil), and a source of substantial exports.

// FALLING BARRIERS TO TRADE AND INVESTMENT

international trade
The sale of a good or service across borders.

A key tenet of market-based economic systems is the belief that removing barriers to international trade and foreign direct investment is in the best interests of all nations that participate in a global economic system.[7] **International trade** occurs whenever a good or service is sold across national borders. When Boeing sells planes to Japan Airlines, international trade has occurred. **Foreign direct investment** refers to investments by a company based in one nation in business activities in another nation. When Ford builds a car factory in Russia, as it did in 2003, foreign direct investment has occurred. The global shift toward market-based systems has been accompanied by a decline in barriers to international trade and foreign direct investment, a surge in such trade and investment, and an increase in the economic interdependence between nations.

foreign direct investment
Investments by a company based in one nation in business activities in another nation.

Trade barriers take two main forms: the application of tariffs to imports from a foreign country and quotas. **Tariffs** are taxes on imports, which raise their prices and make them less attractive. **Quotas** are limits on the number of items of a good that can be imported from a foreign nation. In 1947 nineteen developed nations signed a treaty known as the General Agreement on Tariffs and Trade (or GATT), which committed the signatories to a progressive reduction in trade barriers on manufactured goods. In 1995 the GATT was superseded by the World Trade Organization (WTO).

tariffs
A tax on imports.

Over 120 nations are now members of the WTO, including all significant trading nations. As a result of efforts by the GATT and WTO, tariff rates have tumbled and most quotas on imports of manufactured goods into developed nations have been abolished. Between 1950 and 2002 the average tariff rate on manufactured goods imported into the United States fell from 14 percent to 4 percent; in Germany tariffs fell from 26 percent to 4 percent; and in Britain they dropped from 24 percent to 4 percent.[8] The WTO is now pushing forward with negotiations to reduce or remove tariffs on trade in agricultural products and a wide range of services. Although progress has been slow, agreement may be reached by the end of this decade.

quotas
A limit on the number of items of a good that can be imported from a foreign nation.

In addition to global agreements brokered by the WTO, there has been a sharp increase in **regional trade agreements** to remove barriers to trade and foreign direct investment between adjacent nations. The most notable of these has been the European Union (EU), which now has 25 member nations. The EU has progressively removed barriers to trade, investment, and labor flows between member nations, creating a continental economy similar in scale and scope to that of the United States. The North American Free Trade Agreement (NAFTA) between the United States, Canada, and Mexico is another significant regional trade agreement. Established in 1994, by 2004 NAFTA had removed tariffs on 99 percent of the goods traded between the three countries.

regional trade agreements
Agreements to remove barriers to trade between nations within a geographic region.

Although both the WTO and various regional groupings have made progress in removing barriers to foreign direct investment (FDI), so far much of the reduction in barriers to FDI has come from bilateral agreements. As of 2004 there were 2,392 such treaties in the world involving more than 160 countries—a 12-fold increase from the 181 treaties that existed in 1980.[9] According to the United Nations, some 93 percent of the 2,156 changes made worldwide between 1991 and 2004 in the laws governing foreign direct investment created a more favorable environment for FDI.[10]

// TUMBLING COMMUNICATION AND TRANSPORTATION COSTS

The lowering of barriers to international trade and FDI made globalization a theoretical possibility; technological change has made it a tangible reality. Over the past 30 years, global communications have been revolutionized by developments in satellite, optical fiber, and wireless technologies, as well as the Internet. The costs of global communications are plummeting, which lowers the costs of coordinating and controlling a global organization. Between 1930 and 1990 the cost of a three-minute phone call between New York and London fell from $244.65 to $3.32.[11] By 1998 it had plunged to just 36 cents for consumers, and much lower rates were available for businesses.[12] Indeed, over the Internet the cost of an international phone call is rapidly plummeting toward just a few cents per minute.

The rapid growth of the World Wide Web is the latest expression of this development. In 1990 fewer than 1 million users were connected to the Internet. By 1995 the figure had risen to 50 million. By 2007 the Internet may have more than 1.47 billion users, or about 25 percent of the world's population.[13] The World Wide Web has developed into the information backbone of the global economy. Web-based transactions hit $657 billion in 2000 (up from nothing in 1994) and reached some $6.8 trillion in 2004.[14]

Included in the expanding volume of Web-based traffic is a growing percentage of cross-border trade. Viewed globally, the Web is emerging as an equalizer. It rolls back some constraints of location, scale, and time zones.[15] The Web makes it much easier for buyers and sellers to find each other, wherever they may be located and whatever their size. The Web allows both small and large businesses to expand their global presence at a lower cost than ever before.

In addition to developments in communication technology, several major innovations in transportation technology have occurred since the 1950s. The most important are probably the development of commercial jet aircraft and superfreighters and the introduction of containerization, which simplifies transshipment from one mode of transport to another. The advent of commercial jet travel, by reducing the time needed to get from one location to another, has effectively shrunk the globe. In terms of travel time, New York is now closer to Tokyo than it was to Philadelphia in the colonial days.

Containerization has revolutionized the transportation business, significantly lowering the costs of shipping goods over long distances. Before the advent of containerization in the 1970s and 1980s, moving goods from one mode of transport to another was labor-intensive, lengthy, and costly. It could take days and several hundred workers to unload a ship and reload its goods onto trucks and trains. With containerization the whole process can be executed by a handful of workers in a couple of days. Since 1980 the world's containership fleet has more than quadrupled, reflecting in part the growing volume of international trade and in part the switch to this mode of transportation. As a result of the efficiency gains associated with containerization, transportation costs have plummeted, making it much more economical to ship goods around the globe and thereby helping to drive globalization. Between 1920 and 1990 the average ocean freight and port charges per ton of U.S. export and import cargo fell from $95 to $29 (in 1990 dollars).[16] The cost of shipping freight per ton–mile on railroads in the United States fell from 3.04 cents in 1985 to 2.3 cents in 2000, largely as a result of efficiency gains from the widespread use of containers.[17] An increased share of cargo now travels by air. Between 1955 and 1999 average air transportation revenue per ton–kilometer fell by more than 80 percent.[18] Reflecting the falling cost of airfreight, by the early 2000s air shipments accounted for 28 percent of the value of U.S. trade, up from 7 percent in 1965.[19]

Twenty-First Century Camel The development of containerships has reduced the costs of shipping goods across oceans by two-thirds, helping to drive the globalization of production.
© Getty Images/Steve Allen

■ // Implications of Globalization

The implications of the trends we have just discussed are profound. First, these trends have resulted in a massive surge in the volume of international trade and foreign direct investment. According to data from the World Trade Organization, from 1970 to 2004 the volume of world merchandise trade expanded almost 26-fold, outstripping world production, which grew about 7.5 times in real terms. (World merchandise trade includes trade in manufactured goods, agricultural goods, and mining products, but *not* services. World production and trade are measured in real, or inflation-adjusted, dollars.) As suggested by Figure 3.1, due to falling barriers to international trade, the growth in world trade seems to have accelerated since the early 1980s.

FIGURE 3.1

Volume of World Trade and World Production, 1950–2004

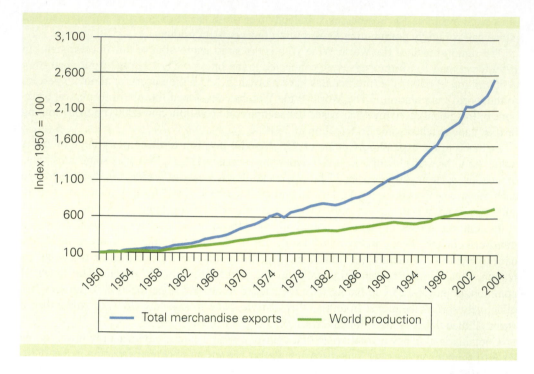

Foreign direct investment (FDI) has increased even more dramatically. The average yearly outflow of FDI increased from $25 billion in 1975 to a record $1.3 trillion in 2000 before falling back to around $900 billion in 2005.[20] Despite the slowdown in 2001–2005, the flow of FDI not only accelerated over the past quarter century, but also accelerated faster than the growth in world trade. Between 1992 and 2005 the total flow of FDI from all countries increased by about 420 percent, while world trade doubled and world output grew by 35 percent.[21] Because of the strong FDI flow, by 2004 companies had some $9 trillion in foreign assets. In total, at least 70,000 parent companies had 690,000 subsidiaries in foreign markets that collectively employed some 54 million people abroad and generated value accounting for about one-tenth of global GDP. The foreign affiliates of multinationals had an estimated $19 trillion in global sales—nearly twice as high as the value of global exports of goods and service combined, which stood at $11 trillion.[22]

These are dramatic figures, but what do they mean for individual enterprises and their managers? They suggest first that the globalization of production is well under way; second, that the globalization of markets is also starting to occur; and third, that advances in technology are facilitating these trends. The result is an environment facing today's managers that is dramatically different from the one their predecessors faced a generation ago.

// THE GLOBALIZATION OF PRODUCTION

globalization of production

Sourcing goods and services from locations around the globe to take advantage of national differences in the cost and quality of factors of production.

■ Boeing: Outsourcing production to foreign producers.

The **globalization of production** refers to the sourcing of goods and services from locations around the globe to take advantage of national differences in the cost and quality of factors of production (such as labor, energy, land, and capital). By doing this, firms hope to lower their overall cost structure and improve the quality or functionality of their products, allowing them to compete more effectively. We have already considered one example of this trend: the outsourcing of U.S. tax return preparation to India. Consider also the Boeing Company's 777 jet airliner. Eight Japanese suppliers make parts for the fuselage, doors, and wings; a supplier in Singapore makes the doors for the nose landing gear; three suppliers in Italy manufacture wing flaps; and so on.[23] In total, some 30 percent of the 777, by value, is built by foreign companies. For its next jet airliner, the 787, Boeing is pushing this trend even further, with some 65 percent of the total value of the aircraft scheduled to be outsourced to foreign companies, 35 percent of which will go to three major Japanese companies.[24]

Part of Boeing's rationale for outsourcing so much production to foreign suppliers is that these suppliers are the best in the world at their particular activities. A global web of suppliers yields a better final product, which enhances Boeing's chances of winning a greater share of total orders for aircraft than its global rival, Airbus Industrie. Boeing also outsources some production to foreign countries to increase the chance that it will win significant orders from airlines based in that country.

Although historically significant outsourcing has been primarily confined to manufacturing enterprises such as Boeing, increasingly companies are taking advantage of modern communications technology, and particularly the Internet, to outsource service activities to low-cost producers in other nations. For example, the Internet has allowed hospitals to outsource some radiology work to India, where images from MRI scans and the like are read at night while U.S. physicians sleep; the results are ready for them in the morning. Similarly, in December 2003 IBM announced that it would move the work of some 4,300 software engineers from the United States to India and China (software production is counted as a service activity).[25] Many software companies now use Indian engineers to maintain software designed in the United States. Due to the time difference, Indian engineers can run debugging tests on software written in the United States when U.S. engineers sleep, transmitting the corrected code back to the United States over secure Internet connections so it is ready for U.S. engineers to work on the following day. Dispersing business activities in this way can compress the time and lower the costs required to develop new software programs. Other companies from computer makers to banks are outsourcing customer service functions, such as customer call centers, to developing nations where labor is cheaper.

Built by Boeing—in Japan, Singapore, Italy, Britain... Some 65 percent of Boeing's new jet, the 787, will be built by foreign suppliers. Japanese suppliers will build 35 percent of the 787. Final assembly will take place in the United States. The 787 is an example of a truly global product.

■ Reading MRI scans in India.

■ Outsourcing by IBM.

// THE GLOBALIZATION OF MARKETS

The **globalization of markets** refers to the merging of historically distinct and separate national markets into one huge global marketplace. Falling barriers to international trade have made it easier to sell internationally. It has been argued for some time that the tastes and preferences of consumers in different nations are beginning to converge, thereby helping to create a global market.[26] Consumer products such as Citigroup credit cards, Coca-Cola soft drinks, Sony PlayStation video games, McDonald's hamburgers, and Starbucks coffee are frequently cited as examples of this trend. Firms such as Citigroup, Coca-Cola, McDonald's, Starbucks, and Sony are more than just beneficiaries of this trend; they have also facilitated it. By offering the same basic products worldwide, they help create a global market.

In many global markets the same firms frequently confront each other as competitors in nation after nation. Coca-Cola's rivalry with PepsiCo is a global one, as are the rivalries between Ford and Toyota; Boeing and Airbus; Caterpillar and Komatsu in earthmoving equipment; and Sony, Nintendo, and Microsoft in video games. If one firm moves into a nation that is not currently served by its rivals, those rivals are sure to follow to prevent their competitor from gaining an advantage.[27] As firms follow each other around the world, they bring with them many of the assets that served them well in other national markets—including their products, operating strategies, marketing strategies, and brand names—creating some homogeneity across markets. Thus greater uniformity replaces diversity.

globalization of markets

The merging of historically distinct and separate national markets into one huge global marketplace.

// TECHNOLOGY: THE GREAT FACILITATOR

As we have seen, due to technological innovations the real costs of information processing and communication have fallen dramatically. These developments allow managers to create and then manage a globally dispersed production system, further facilitating the globalization of

■ Dell Computer: Using the Internet to control global production.

production. A worldwide communication network has become essential for many international businesses. For example, Dell uses the Internet to coordinate and control its globally dispersed production system to such an extent that it holds only two days' worth of inventory at its assembly locations. Dell's Internet-based system records orders for computer equipment as they are submitted by customers via the company's Web site, and then immediately transmits the resulting orders for components to various suppliers around the world, which have a real-time view of Dell's order flow and can adjust their production schedules accordingly. Given the low cost of airfreight, Dell can use air transportation to speed up the delivery of critical components to meet unanticipated demand shifts without delaying the shipment of final products to consumers. Dell also has used modern communication technology to outsource its customer service operations to India. When U.S. customers call Dell with a service inquiry, they are routed to Bangalore in India, where English-speaking service personnel handle the call.

The Internet has been a major force facilitating international trade in services. The Web allows hospitals in Chicago to send MRI scans to India for analysis, tax accountants in San Francisco to outsource routine tax preparation work to the Philippines, and software testers in India to debug code written by developers in Redmond, Washington, the headquarters of Microsoft. We are probably still in the early stages of this development. Before long almost any work processes that can be digitized will be, and in theory this will allow that work to be performed wherever in the world it is most efficient and effective to do so.

In addition to the globalization of production, technological innovations have also facilitated the globalization of markets. Low-cost global communication networks such as the World Wide Web are helping to create electronic global marketplaces. Inexpensive transportation has made it more economical to ship products around the world, thereby helping to create global markets. For example, due to the tumbling costs of shipping goods by air, roses grown in Ecuador can be cut and sold in New York 24 hours later while they are still fresh. This has created an industry in Ecuador that did not exist 20 years ago and that now supplies a global market for roses. Global communication networks and global media are creating a worldwide culture. U.S. television networks such as CNN, MTV, and HBO are now received in many countries, and Hollywood films are shown the world over. In any society the media are primary conveyors of culture; as global media develop, we can expect the evolution of something akin to a global culture. A logical result of this evolution is the emergence of global markets for consumer products. The first signs of this are already apparent. It is now as easy to find a McDonald's restaurant in Tokyo as it is in New York, to buy an iPod in either Rio or Berlin, and to buy Gap jeans in both Paris and San Francisco.

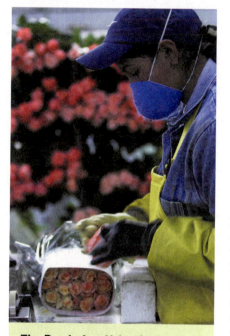

The Day before Valentine's An Ecuadoran worker packs roses prior to shipping them to the United States. Within 24 hours these flowers, grown in ideal conditions in the highlands of Ecuador, will be sold in U.S. stores. On Febuary 13 Ecuador ships twice its normal volume of roses, some 30,000 boxes, to international buyers.

© AP Photo/Dolores Ochoa

■ // Constraints on Globalization

Despite the historic nature of the trends we have just reviewed, we must be careful not to overemphasize their importance. Globalization is not inevitable. Powerful countervailing forces are constraining the pace at which production and markets are becoming global. These constraints limit the ability of managers to disperse production activities to locations in the world where they can be performed at the lowest cost, as well as managers' ability to treat the entire world as a single homogeneous marketplace.

// PROTECTIONIST COUNTERTRENDS

The worldwide march toward market-based economic systems with few or no barriers to cross-border trade and investment is not guaranteed to continue. History is full of reversals away from progressive trends. The first bloom of modern global trade in the late 1800s and early 1900s was brought to an end by protectionist policies in major trading nations during the 1920s and 1930s, which led to a slump in international trade and helped usher in the Great Depression.

This could happen again. Many politicians and media commentators have argued that international trade destroys jobs and that outsourcing production to foreign nations is akin to exporting jobs and hollowing out the American economy (the CNN commentator Lou Dobbs frequently voices such concerns). They also suggest that globalization is promoting a "race to the bottom," with wage rates being driven down in developed nations.

Supporters of free trade reject these arguments. They point out that the gains from international trade far exceed its costs and that international trade promotes economic growth and raises living standards.[28] For example, although free trade in textiles means that American textile workers in South Carolina might lose their jobs as production moves to other nations where production costs are lower, the result will be lower prices for clothes, increasing the disposable income of American consumers. Thus as a result of free trade in textiles Americans can purchase more clothes and purchase more of other goods and services. The consequence is greater economic growth in America, which helps to create additional jobs that offset those lost as a result of free trade in textiles. Moreover, free trade opens foreign markets, allowing American businesses to sell more overseas, which further stimulates economic growth. Thus even though jobs are lost in low-technology, labor-intensive industries such as textiles, the American economy as a whole can reap substantial benefits if free trade allows U.S. firms to sell more commercial jet aircraft, software, pharmaceuticals, computers, and the like in other nations. This is not just a theoretical argument; economic evidence suggests that international trade promotes economic growth for *all* nations that participate in a free trade system.[29] The problem, as economists often point out, is one of public relations: The gains from international trade are widely distributed, but the pain is concentrated in a few sectors where people lose their jobs, and focusing on the pain makes for better news copy.

Despite the substantial theory and evidence in support of free trade, some politicians would like to engineer a return to the days of high barriers to cross-border trade and investment, which would inhibit the process of globalization. Indeed, there is still substantial protectionism in the world economy. Recent WTO talks to lower barriers to cross-border trade in agriculture, for example, have been stalled by the unwillingness of several developed nations, including the United States, Japan,

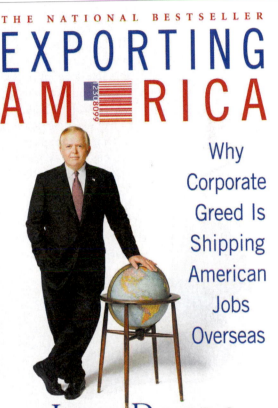

The Modern Mercantilist Lou Dobbs has used his position as a CNN host to promote his views of international trade. Dobbs has no objection to American businesses profiting from selling overseas, but he doesn't like the idea that foreigners can profit from selling to Americans. This viewpoint harks back to a discredited 19th-century economic philosophy known as mercantilism, which saw international trade as a zero-sum game in which the goal was to accumulate as much wealth from foreigners as possible while not letting those same foreigners compete in your markets.

© Courtesy of Warner Books. Used with permission.

and particularly the European Union, to remove tariffs and quotas that currently protect their agricultural sectors from foreign competition. The rise of China as a major export power is also straining the world trading system, much as the rise of Japan did in the 1980s, and is leading to renewed calls for protectionism against "unfair" competition. If some of the advances of the last 50 years are turned back and barriers to cross-border trade and investment are raised, national markets will once more be segmented from each other, and the globalization of production and markets will stall. Such a scenario seems unlikely at present but is not impossible.

// NATIONAL DIFFERENCES IN CONSUMER BEHAVIOR

It is important not to overstate the globalization of markets. Although many goods and services are sold globally—from Boeing jets and Nokia cell phones to Starbucks coffee and McDonald's hamburgers—there are still often substantial differences between the tastes and preferences of consumers in different nations. Many enterprises have discovered (at their cost) that foreign consumers differ from domestic consumers, and that accounting for these differences requires them to customize goods and services to better match local demand. In other words, truly global markets may be some way off.

For example, the American automobile market is very different from the European market. Driving in Europe you see few of the large SUVs so beloved by Americans. There are two good reasons for this: Gas prices are much higher in Europe, so fuel economy is valued over vehicle size and power, and smaller roads and parking spots in Europe's historic cities and towns makes a smaller car more practical. Thus even though automobile firms such as Toyota and Ford might like to design cars they can sell the same way worldwide to realize substantial scale economies, reality requires that cars and their marketing be tailored to different regions.

Even in a young industry such as the cell phone business, important national differences in consumer usage patterns can be observed. Americans, for example, tend to think of cell phones primarily as devices for talking, not as devices that can also send e-mail and browse the Web. Consequently, when selling to U.S. consumers, cell phone manufacturers focus more on slim good looks and less on advanced functions and features. This contrasts with Asia and Europe, where text messaging and Web browsing functions have been much more widely embraced. A cultural issue seems to be at work here. People in Europe and Asia often have more time to browse the Web on their phones because they spend more time commuting on trains, whereas Americans tend to spend more time in cars, where their hands are occupied.[30]

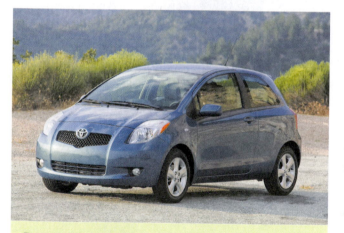

European Drivers Only   The Toyota Yaris was designed specifically for the European market. This small, fuel-efficient car is perfect for Europe's high fuel costs and crowded cities.

© Courtesy of Toyota Motor Sales, USA, Inc.

// NATIONAL DIFFERENCES IN BUSINESS SYSTEMS

There are still major differences between nations in business systems, legal systems, infrastructure, and overall level of economic development, and this works against treating the world as a single global marketplace. In the pharmaceutical industry, for example, Americans are used to seeing advertisements for drugs on television; but in many nations direct advertising of drugs to consumers is prohibited by law (the belief being that such advertising interferes with the doctor–patient relationship). Thus pharmaceutical companies have to use different marketing strategies in different countries. Moreover, in many nations pharmaceuticals are still subject to government price controls, so firms charge different prices in different nations (prices tend to be higher if they are not controlled by the government). Competition can also vary from nation to nation. Due to differences in patent law, for example,

Amgen's best-selling drug Epogen will be subject to competition in Europe much sooner than in the United States.

Distribution channels may vary significantly from nation to nation, and this can require different approaches. Whereas Coca-Cola cans are distributed by trucks in much of the world, in parts of rural China they are distributed on the backs of motorcycles, and in Nepal on the backs of yaks or human porters.

Differences in income levels also have a major impact. In the West Unilever sells shampoo and soap in the larger bottles we are used to seeing in our supermarkets; but in poor nations such as India and much of Africa, it sells the same products in much smaller containers because local consumers cannot afford to purchase the larger ones.

Many similar examples can illustrate the same basic point: Business systems, legal systems, infrastructure, and income levels differ from nation to nation. Handling these differences requires adaptation, and the process of adaptation (customizing the product offering, marketing message, sales strategy, pricing, and distribution system) runs counter to viewing the world as a single homogeneous global marketplace.

// DIFFERENCES IN SOCIAL CULTURE

Finally, it is important to realize that differences in social culture across nations are often profound. As such, they make it harder for firms to view the world market as homogeneous and more difficult to manage operations in different countries. By **social culture** we mean the system of values and norms that are held in common by people living in a society.[31] Values (discussed in Chapter 1) are abstract ideas about what a group believes to be good, right, and desirable; they are shared assumptions about how things ought to be.[32] **Norms** are the social rules and guidelines that prescribe appropriate behavior in particular situations.

To pick a vivid example of cultural differences and why they matter, consider the differences between the cultures of Saudi Arabia and the United States. Saudi views diverge from those of many Americans about the role of women in society, the consumption of alcohol (which is illegal in Saudi Arabia), the nature of time, and the connection between religion and the state. Saudi culture is strongly influenced by a strict interpretation of Islam and by the traditions of the nomadic Bedouin society that gave birth to modern Saudi Arabia. These antecedents of Saudi culture support restrictions on the role of women in society and the prohibition against alcohol. It would represent a lack of cultural sensitivity, therefore, for an American firm to send a woman to run its subsidiary in Saudi Arabia, particularly if that subsidiary were staffed by local Saudi employees. Similarly, offering alcohol might offend a visiting Saudi businessman.

Moreover, Americans need to understand how cultural values influence the way a Saudi does business. Reflecting the traditions of Bedouin society, Saudis will often conduct business only after trust has been established—a process that might require many face-to-face meetings. Saudis may resent being rushed into a business decision, preferring to let discussions proceed in a more relaxed fashion—something that Westerners with their attachment to precise rather than approximate time might find taxing. Business meetings may be long because many Saudis maintain an "open office" and will interrupt a meeting to conduct other business. This can be traced back to the Bedouin tradition in which all tribal members have a right to visit and petition their leaders without a prior appointment. In addition, given the cultural importance attached to status, Saudi executives will not react well if a foreign company sends a junior executive to transact business.[33]

More generally, managers need to be sensitive to cultural differences across nations, and they need to understand how cultural differences can require adaptation not only of marketing and sales strategy, but also of basic management practices. Not everybody thinks and acts like Americans, and the American way of conducting business does not always succeed in a foreign land. Even in countries that seem much more similar to the United States than Saudi Arabia, deep-seated cultural differences affect how business is conducted. For example, anthropologist Edward T. Hall has described how Americans, who tend to be informal, react strongly to being corrected or reprimanded in public.[34] This can

social culture
The system of values and norms that are held in common by people living in a society.

norms
Social rules and guidelines that prescribe appropriate behavior in particular situations.

■ Saudi Arabia and the United States: Cultural differences.

Cruising the Mall in Riyadh   Saudi women have access to the physical trappings of the modern world—fast food, shopping malls, cell phones—but have to wear traditional dress when outside the home, which covers them from head to foot.

© AFP/Getty Images

cause problems in Germany, where a cultural tendency toward correcting strangers can shock and offend most Americans. For their part, Germans can be surprised by the tendency of Americans to call everyone by first name. This is uncomfortable enough among executives of the same rank; but it can be seen as insulting when a young, junior American executive addresses an older, more senior German manager by first name without having been invited to do so. Hall concludes that it can take a long time to get on a first-name basis with a German; if you rush the process you will be perceived as overly friendly and rude, and that may not be good for business.

Another common cultural difference concerns attitudes about personal space, which is the comfortable amount of distance between you and someone you are talking with. In the United States the customary distance apart adopted by parties in a business discussion is five to eight feet. In Latin America it is three to five feet. Consequently many North Americans unconsciously feel that Latin Americans are invading their personal space and can be seen backing away from them during a conversation. Indeed, the American may feel that the Latin American is being aggressive and pushy. In turn, the Latin American may interpret such backing away as aloofness. The result can be a regrettable lack of rapport between two businesspeople from different cultures.

■ // The Benefits of Going Global

multinational enterprise (MNE)

A business that has productive activities in two or more countries.

As globalization progresses, an increasing number of businesses are expanding across national borders, becoming multinational enterprises in the process. A **multinational enterprise (MNE)** is any business that has productive activities in two or more countries. There are four main reasons why the managers of many enterprises, both large and small, seek to expand their operations across national borders: Doing so lets a firm expand the market for its products, realize scale and location economies, and benefit from global learning.

// EXPANDING THE MARKET

International expansion enlarges the market a firm can address, enabling it to increase its sales and profits faster. The growth of Starbucks, for example, owes much to the rapid international expansion of the company. Starbucks opened its first international store in 1996, when it was operating some 700 stores in the United States. By 2005 the company had over 3,200 locations in 34 countries outside the United States (plus 7,000 more in the United States). In just a decade Starbucks grew from a midsized national company to a world entity with a powerful world brand. Going forward, Starbucks sees continued international expansion as a major engine of growth. The company's aim is to make Starbucks as ubiquitous internationally as other great American consumer brands, such as McDonald's and Coca-Cola.

■ Starbucks: Global expansion.

More generally, many enterprises develop a core skill at home and then try to earn greater returns from that competency by applying it to foreign markets where indigenous competitors lack the same skills. Thus McDonald's developed a core competency in managing fast-food franchise operations in the United States, and then earned greater returns from that competency by entering foreign markets that lacked American-style fast-food restaurants. Similarly, Procter & Gamble established core competencies in the development and mass marketing of household consumer products, including shampoos, detergents, and diapers, and it has earned greater returns from those competencies by applying them to foreign markets that lacked enterprises with the same skill set. In short, when the managers at a firm have built a valuable competency or skill, going global is often the best way to maximize the return on their investment in that skill.

// REALIZING SCALE ECONOMIES

The larger sales base associated with serving a global market can allow enterprises to attain economies of scale, lower their costs, and boost their profits. In the automobile industry, for example, an efficiently scaled factory is one designed to produce about 200,000 units a year. Automobile firms would prefer to produce a single model from each factory because this eliminates the costs associated with switching production from one model to another. If domestic demand for a particular model is only 100,000 units a year, the inability to attain a 200,000-unit output will drive up average unit costs. However, by serving international markets and exporting some production, the firm may be able to push production volume up to 200,000 units a year, thereby reaping greater scale economies.

More generally, by serving domestic and international markets a firm may be able to utilize its production facilities more intensively. For example, if Intel sold microprocessors only in the United States, it might be able to keep its factories open for only one shift, five days a week. By serving international markets from the same factories, Intel can run three shifts seven days a week for lower costs and greater profitability.

// REALIZING LOCATION ECONOMIES

Different locations around the world are more or less suitable for performing different business activities. For example, China is a good location for making textiles due to the combination of low labor costs (textile manufacturing is labor-intensive) and good infrastructure. The United States is not as good for making textiles due to relative high labor costs; so textile manufacturing has been migrating out of the United States for the last 20 years. On the other hand, New York, Paris, and Rome are all good locations for fashion design due to the high concentration of successful design firms and design schools and the abundant supply of skilled designers. Similarly, the United States is a good place for developing new software products because of its many skilled software programmers and the high rate of innovation in the U.S. computer industry. By the same token, Bangalore is a great location for performing software testing and debugging due to a high supply of software engineers, relatively low wage rates, the widespread use of English, and the fact that Bangalore is 12 time zones away from the American West Coast, where many software firms are concentrated. Thus software code written during the day on the West Coast can be tested and debugged by engineers at night in Bangalore and sent back to programmers in America in the morning. As a result of these factors, Bangalore is home to India's rapidly developing software industry and its two largest high-technology firms: Wipro and Infosys.

Location economies arise from exploiting such differences; they are the economies that arise from performing a business activity in the optimal location for that activity, wherever in the world that might be (transportation costs and trade barriers permitting). Locating a business activity in the optimal location can have one of two effects. It can lower the costs of performing that activity, and it can enable the firm to add value to its final product offering and thus better differentiate its offering from that of competitors. The task facing managers in a global economy is to look at the various activities of a firm and decide where in the world they should be located to realize location economies.

■ IBM and location economies.

For illustration, consider IBM's ThinkPad X31 laptop computer (this business was acquired by China's Lenovo in 2005).[35] The ThinkPad was designed in the United States by IBM engineers because IBM believed that the United States was the best location in the world to do the basic design work. The case, keyboard, and hard drive were made in Thailand; the display screen and memory were made in South Korea; the built-in wireless card was made in Malaysia; and the microprocessor was manufactured in the United States. These components were manufactured in the optimal locations given managers' assessment of the relative costs of performing each activity at different locations. These components were shipped to an IBM operation in Mexico, where the product was assembled before being shipped to the United States for final sale. IBM assembled the ThinkPad in Mexico because IBM's managers calculated that due to low labor costs, the costs of assembly could be minimized there. The marketing and sales strategy for North America was developed by IBM personnel in the United States, primarily because IBM believed that due to their knowledge of the local market, U.S. personnel would add more value to the product through their marketing efforts than personnel based elsewhere.

In theory, a firm that realizes location economies by dispersing each of its different activities to the optimal location should have a competitive advantage over a firm that bases all of its value creation activities at a single location. It should be able to better differentiate its products and keep its cost structure lower than its single-location competitor. In a world where competitive pressures are increasing, such a strategy may become imperative for survival.

// GLOBAL LEARNING

Implicit in our discussion so far is the idea that valuable skills are developed first at home and then transferred to foreign operations. Thus Wal-Mart developed its retailing skills in the United States before transferring them to foreign locations. However, for more mature multinationals that have already established a network of subsidiary operations in foreign markets, the development of valuable skills can just as well occur in foreign subsidiaries.[36] Skills can be created anywhere within a multinational's global network of operations, wherever people have the opportunity and incentive to try new ways of doing things. The creation of skills that help lower the costs of production, enhance perceived value, and support higher product pricing is not the monopoly of the corporate center.

■ Global learning at McDonald's.

Leveraging the skills created within subsidiaries and applying them to other operations within a firm's global network may create value. For example, McDonald's increasingly is finding that its foreign franchisees are a source of valuable new ideas. Facing slow growth in France, its local franchisees have begun to experiment not only with the menu but also with the layout and theme of restaurants. Gone are the ubiquitous golden arches, as well as many of the utilitarian chairs and tables and other plastic features of the fast-food giant. Many McDonald's restaurants in France now have hardwood floors, exposed brick walls, and even armchairs. Half of the 930 or so outlets in France have been upgraded to a level that would make them unrecognizable to an American. The menu, too, has been changed to include premier sandwiches, such as a chicken on focaccia bread, priced some 30 percent higher than the average hamburger. In France the strategy seems to be working. Following the changes, increases in same-store sales rose from 1 percent annually to 3.4 percent. Impressed with the impact, McDonald's executives are now considering adopting similar changes at other McDonald's restaurants in markets where same-store sales growth is sluggish, including the United States.[37]

For the managers of a multinational enterprise, this phenomenon creates important new challenges. First, they must have enough humility to recognize that valuable skills and competencies can arise anywhere within the firm's global network—not just at the corporate center. Second, they must establish an incentive system that encourages local employees to acquire new skills, which is not as easy as it sounds. Creating new skills involves a degree of risk: Not all new skills add value. For every valuable idea created by a McDonald's subsidiary in a foreign country, there may be several failures. The management of the multinational firm must install incentives that encourage employees to take the necessary risks. The company must reward people for successes and not sanction them unnecessarily for taking risks that did not pan out. Third, managers must have a process for identifying when valuable new skills have been created in a subsidiary. Finally, they need to act as facilitators, helping to transfer valuable skills within the firm.

You're Not in Kansas Anymore   The interior of this McDonald's restaurant in France is different from many of those found in the United States. The French operation changed the layout of its restaurants and the menu to better meet the needs of its consumers and to evolve with the changing times. The effects have been dramatic. The French operation is now one of the best performing of all McDonald's subsidiaries.

© Used with permission from McDonald's Corporation

■ // Management Challenges in the Global Enterprise

We have just seen that there are clear advantages to going global, and an increasing number of firms are doing just that. However, managing a global enterprise represents a significant challenge. When a firm goes global, it encounters a whole set of decisions that managers in purely domestic enterprises do not face. These decision include (1) whether to treat the world as a single market or customize the firm's products to reflect differences across nations; (2) the best mode for entering a foreign market; (3) where to locate different business activities; and (4) how best to manage subsidiaries. Here we look at each issue in turn.

// GLOBAL STANDARDIZATION OR LOCAL CUSTOMIZATION

One of the most important decisions managers face is whether to treat the world as a single market or customize products for different nations. When a firm treats the world market as a single entity, selling the same basic product around the globe, we say that it is pursuing a **global standardization strategy**.[38] Alternatively, when an enterprise varies some aspect of its products or marketing messages to take country or regional differences into account, we say that it is pursuing a **local customization strategy**. The global standardization strategy enables a firm to realize substantial scale economies by mass-producing a standardized output and using the same marketing strategy worldwide. However, such a strategy ignores local differences in consumer tastes and preferences, local business systems and culture, and so on. If such differences are profound, the firm may do better with a local customization strategy, even though that may mean fewer scale economies and higher costs. Choosing between these strategic postures is not easy, and firms often seek a balance between standardization and customization.

For an example of balance between global standardization and local customization, consider MTV Networks. MTV has been expanding outside its North American base since 1987 when it opened MTV Europe. Despite its domestic success, MTV's global expansion got off to a weak start. In 1987 it piped a single feed across Europe composed almost entirely of

global standardization strategy

Treating the world market as a single entity, selling the same basic product around the globe.

local customization strategy

Varying some aspect of product offerings or marketing messages to take country or regional differences into account.

■ MTV: Responding to local demands.

American programming with English-speaking veejays. Naively, the network's U.S. managers thought Europeans would flock to the American programming. But although viewers in Europe shared a common interest in a handful of global superstars, their tastes turned out to be surprisingly local. What was popular in Germany might not be popular in Great Britain. Many staples of the American music scene left Europeans cold. MTV suffered as a result. Soon local copycat stations were springing up in Europe to focus on the music scene in individual countries. They took viewers and advertisers away from MTV. As explained by Tom Freston, chairman of MTV Networks, "We were going for the most shallow layer of what united viewers and brought them together. It didn't go over too well."

In 1995 MTV changed its strategy and offered regional feeds in Europe (there are now eight). The network adopted the same localization strategy elsewhere in the world. For example, in Asia it has an English–Hindi channel for India, separate feeds for China and Taiwan, a Japanese feed for Japan, and so on. All the feeds have the same familiar frenetic look and feel of MTV in the United States, but much of the programming is now local. In Italy *MTV Kitchen* combines cooking with a music countdown. *Erotica* airs in Brazil and features a panel of youngsters discussing sex. The Indian channel produces 21 homegrown shows hosted by local veejays who speak "Hinglish," a city-bred breed of Hindi and English. Hit shows include *MTV Cricket in Control,* appropriate for a land where cricket is a national obsession; *MTV House-full,* which hones in on Hindi film stars (India has the biggest film industry outside Hollywood); and *MTV Bakra,* modeled after *Candid Camera.* The localization push has reaped big benefits for MTV, capturing viewers back from local imitators[39]

// ENTRY MODE

There are five main modes for entering a foreign market: exporting, licensing, franchising, entering a joint venture with a local enterprise, and setting up a wholly owned subsidiary.[40] **Exporting** involves producing a good at home and then shipping it to another country. **Licensing** involves an enterprise licensing a foreign firm to produce its product in a country or region in return for royalty fees on any sales that the licensee makes. **Franchising** is

exporting
Producing a good at home, and then shipping it to another country.

licensing
Licensing a foreign firm to produce its product in a country or region in return for royalty fees on any sales that the licensee makes.

franchising
Licensing the right to offer a service in a particular format.

Indian Rap   Sukhbir and Josh perform live in Mumbai at the MTV India "Immies" awards. The Immies are MTV India's annual music awards, analogous to the Grammies in the United States.

similar to licensing, but here what is licensed to the foreign enterprise is not the right to produce a physical good, but the right to offer a service in a particular format. Franchising is popular among fast-food enterprises (like McDonald's and KFC) as well as international hotel chains. **Joint ventures** are agreements between a firm and its foreign partner to establish a new enterprise, the joint venture, in which they each take an equity stake. **Wholly owned subsidiaries** are foreign subsidiaries that are 100 percent owned by the firm.

The choice between these different entry modes is complex, and a full discussion is beyond the scope of this book. A few brief points can be made, however. First, exporting is a good strategy when the firm can mass-produce at a single location, thereby realizing economies of scale and lowering its costs. In this regard, exporting is consistent with a global standardization strategy. But many firms have found advantages to producing in local markets. Basing production in a country or region can facilitate local customization (because products are designed and built closer to where customers are), and it may be more politically acceptable to produce locally. For example, Toyota has set up production facilities in all its major markets—Japan, North America, and Europe. These facilities produce products that are customized to local requirements. Thus Toyota's European operation makes small cars designed for European customers and not sold in the United States. Similarly, Toyota products sold in America, such as the Toyota Tundra truck, are not made or sold in Europe. Toyota also established production facilities in America and Europe to reduce the threat that high levels of exports from Japan might result in the imposition of trade barriers.

Second, licensing is not often used, primarily because it gives the firm little ongoing involvement in a foreign market beyond the current licensing contract. In addition, many firms are reluctant to license products that incorporate valuable technology because they fear that ultimately the licensee might develop its own version of the technology and no longer need to license from the firm. To forestall this possibility, many firms enter using other modes.

Third, joint ventures are favored when a local partner can bring valuable expertise to the partnership, such as local market knowledge. In addition, in some countries a joint venture may be more acceptable to the government than a wholly owned subsidiary. This was certainly the case in China for a while, and many early Western entrants into the Chinese market began with joint ventures. The problem with joint ventures, however, is that disputes between partners over strategy and investments can lead to their failure.

Fourth, although wholly owned subsidiaries involve the highest up-front cost (the firm must bear all costs of opening a foreign market), this entry mode gives the firm maximum control over the future direction of the subsidiary. Moreover, the firm captures all profits from the venture, as opposed to having to share them with a joint venture partner or taking only a share of them in the form of royalty payments from a licensee. Thus many managers prefer to enter foreign markets through a wholly owned joint venture. Even when a product is manufactured elsewhere and exported to a country, they might still establish a wholly owned subsidiary to market, sell, and distribute the product in that country.

// LOCATING ACTIVITIES

Another key decision is where to locate the various activities of the enterprise. As we have seen, there are advantages to dispersing the activities of an enterprise to locations around the globe where they can be performed most efficiently. Making the right choice involves two steps. First, managers have to break the operations of the firm into discrete steps or activities—such as product design, purchasing, production, marketing, sales, service and customer care, and so on. Second, each activity has to be located in the best place given a consideration of factors such as country differences in labor costs and infrastructure, transportation costs, tariff barriers, likely currency exchange rates, and strategic orientation. Managers need to evaluate the cost of performing an activity at a given location and how much value can be added to a product at a certain location—which is not easy.

Moreover, the attractiveness of key locations changes over time. Ten years ago, for example, few American software firms outsourced software testing and debugging activities to

joint venture
An agreement between a firm and a partner to establish a new enterprise in which they each take an equity stake.

wholly owned subsidiary
A foreign subsidiary that is fully owned by a firm.

■ Toyota's entering strategy.

Indian companies. Now such a move is commonplace. Similarly, as discussed in the introduction, only in the last few years have American accounting firms started to outsource the work associated with compiling individual tax returns to accountants located in India. The attractiveness of locations varies over time as local economies advance (or decline), labor costs change, infrastructure is added, and exchange rates shift. For example, if the value of the Chinese currency rises against the U.S. dollar, over time China will become less attractive as a location for performing labor-intensive activities (such as textile manufacturing), and manufacturing will migrate to other parts of the globe.

// MANAGING PEOPLE IN THE MULTINATIONAL FIRM

Managing people in a multinational firm represents one of the most difficult tasks facing managers. Consider the mature multinational enterprise with activities in several different nations. Managers have to decide how best to staff foreign operations—and specifically whether senior managers should be nationals of the foreign (or host) country where operations are based or come from the home country of the enterprise. If a firm uses home country personnel or **expatriates** as they are commonly known, it must prepare them for the foreign posts and make sure that their eventual return to the home country is well managed. Research evidence suggests that this is not easy. Between 16 and 40 percent of all American employees sent abroad to developed nations return from their assignments early, and almost 70 percent of employees sent to developing nations return home early.[41] The inability of a spouse to adjust, the inability of the manager to adjust, or other family problems are major reasons for the failure of expatriates to succeed in foreign posts. One study found that 60 percent of expatriate failures occur due to these three reasons.[42] Another study found that the most common reason for assignment failure is lack of partner (spouse) satisfaction, which was listed by 27 percent of respondents.[43]

The inability of expatriate managers to adjust to foreign posts seems to be caused by a lack of cultural skills on the part of the managers being transferred. According to one human resources management consulting firm, this is because the expatriate selection process at many firms is fundamentally flawed. "Expatriate assignments rarely fail because the person cannot accommodate to the technical demands of the job. Typically, the expatriate selections are made by line managers based on technical competence. They fail because of family and personal issues and lack of cultural skills that haven't been part of the selection process."[44] Expatriate failure such as this is expensive for the firm, but it can be reduced through the implementation of proper policies for selecting, training, managing, and repatriating expatriates.[45]

In addition, managers have to decide how to vary the compensation structure from nation to nation to reflect different local norms. They also have to think hard about how cultural differences will impact management practices in a nation. What works in a firm's home country may not in a foreign nation. For illustration, one researcher reported the case of a U.S. manager who introduced participative decision making while working in an Indian subsidiary.[46] The manager subsequently received a negative evaluation from host country managers because in India strong social stratification means managers are seen as experts who should not have to ask subordinates for help. The local employees apparently viewed the U.S. manager's attempt at participatory management as an indication that he was incompetent and did not know his job.

Managers also have to decide what staffing and management development programs to put in place to make the best use of their human capital. Nowadays many multinational firms are gravitating toward a **geocentric staffing** policy, that seeks the best people for key jobs throughout the organization, regardless of nationality.[47] This can be compared to an **ethnocentric staffing** policy, in which all key management positions are staffed by home country nationals, and a **polycentric staffing** policy, where key management positions in a subsidiary are staffed by host country nationals.

---

expatriates

Home country executives sent to a foreign post.

geocentric staffing

A staffing policy that seeks the best people for key jobs throughout the organization, regardless of nationality.

ethnocentric staffing

A staffing policy in which all key management positions are staffed by home country nationals.

polycentric staffing

A staffing policy in which key management positions in a subsidiary are staffed by host country nationals.

An *ethnocentric approach* relies on expatriate managers to run foreign operations. This may ensure a common organization culture, but an ethnocentric approach limits advancement opportunities for host country nationals. This can lead to resentment, lower productivity, and increased turnover among that group. Resentment can be greater still if, as often occurs, expatriate managers are paid significantly more than home country nationals. An ethnocentric policy can also lead to cultural myopia—a failure to understand that host country cultural differences require different approaches to marketing and management. Moreover, the adaptation of expatriate managers can take a long time, during which they may make major mistakes. For example, expatriate managers may fail to appreciate how product attributes, distribution strategy, communication strategy, and pricing strategy should be adapted to host country conditions. The result may be costly blunders. They may also make decisions that are unethical because they do not understand the culture in which they are managing.[48] In one highly publicized case in the United States, Mitsubishi Motors was sued by the federal Equal Employment Opportunity Commission for tolerating extensive and systematic sexual harassment in a plant in Illinois. The plant's top managers, all Japanese expatriates, denied the charges. The Japanese managers may have failed to realize that behavior that would be viewed as acceptable in Japan was not acceptable in the United States.[49] Finally, as we have seen, many expatriate managers return home early, which is expensive for the firm.

■ Mitsubishi Motors: The costs of ethnocentric staffing.

In many respects a *polycentric approach* is a response to the shortcomings of an ethnocentric approach. One advantage of adopting a polycentric approach is that the firm is less likely to suffer from cultural myopia. Host country managers are unlikely to make the mistakes arising from cultural misunderstandings to which expatriate managers are vulnerable. A second advantage is that a polycentric approach may be less expensive to implement, reducing the costs of value creation, given how costly expatriate managers can be to maintain.

However, a polycentric approach also has its drawbacks. Host country nationals have limited opportunities to gain experience outside their own countries and thus cannot progress beyond senior positions in their own subsidiaries. As in the case of an ethnocentric policy, this may cause resentment. Perhaps the major drawback with a polycentric approach, however, is the gap that can form between host country and parent country managers. Language barriers, national loyalties, and a range of cultural differences may isolate the corporate headquarters staff from the various foreign subsidiaries. The lack of management transfers from home to host countries, and vice versa, can exacerbate this isolation and lead to a lack of integration between corporate headquarters and foreign subsidiaries.

A *geocentric staffing* policy is thought to overcome the limitations of both ethnocentric and polycentric approaches. Under a geocentric policy, not only do managers move from home country to host nation; they also move between host nations and from host nation to the home nation, where they may ultimately take on senior management positions. Managers have to decide how best to select, train, develop, and compensate a cohort of qualified managers, irrespective of their national origin. Such a policy lets a firm make the best use of its human resources, promoting the best people to key jobs throughout the organization, regardless of nationality. In addition, the multinational composition of the management team that results from geocentric staffing tends to reduce cultural myopia and to enhance adaptation to local conditions. For all of these reasons, many of the leading multinationals in America have adopted a geocentric approach.

The Geocentric CEO Born and raised in India, Indra Nooyi (left) became president and chief financial officer of PepsiCo in 2001 at the age of 45 and CEO in 2006. Prior to joining Pepsi, Nooyi held senior management positions at Asea Brown Boveri, a European engineering company, and Motorola. Her rise to the top rank of management at a major U.S. corporation was made possible by the geocentric staffing policies of all these companies.

© AP Photo/John Keating

IN CONCLUSION   WHY DOES IT MATTER?

Managers must understand the nature of the global environment because ongoing changes in that environment are creating a plethora of opportunities, threats, and challenges. As we have seen, the world is moving rapidly toward a global integrated economic system characterized by the emergence of global markets and the development of global production systems. Although countervailing forces are putting a brake on the pace of globalization, and a reemergence of protectionism certainly could halt the march toward globalization, for now at least the trajectory is well established. If present trends continue, 25 years from now far more countries will have joined the ranks of developed nations. Brazil, China, and India will have established themselves as economic superpowers on a par with the United States, Japan, and the European Union. Barriers to cross-border trade and investment will be lower than they are today. Material culture will be increasingly homogeneous across developed nations, and markets will be more global.

In this global world managers will increasingly take advantage of opportunities to expand the business of their enterprise into foreign nations, to lower costs by realizing economies of scale from global volume and locating different business activities where they can be performed most efficiently, and to enhance competitiveness by transferring valuable skills within the globally dispersed network of the firm's operations. At the same time they will face threats from new foreign competitors. In the 1970s and 1980s, Western businesses faced competitive threats from emerging Japanese enterprises. In the next 20 years Chinese, Indian, and Russian enterprises may well emerge as major players in the global economy, entering the markets of Western businesses and presenting Western firms with new competitive challenges. Indeed, this is already starting to occur. In 2005 China's Lenova acquires IBM's PC operations, signaling the company's intention to become a major player in the global computer industry. Similarly, Infosys and Wipro of India have become key competitors in the global market for information technology service, and Lukoil of Russia now operates 1,200 gas stations in the United States. The message in these developments is clear: The world is changing! Even if an enterprise does not do business across national borders, it may still be affected by the entry of new foreign competitors into its domestic marketplace.

Finally, globalization matters because in a global enterprise (and in the future far more firms will be global enterprises) managers have to grapple with a host of issues that do not occur in purely domestic enterprises, only a few of which we have discussed here. As we have seen, managers in a global enterprise have to decide on entry mode; strategic posture; where to locate different business activities; what to outsource to foreign producers; and how best to staff, compensate, motivate, train, develop, and manage the human capital of their organization. There are also substantive issues associated with deciding the timing of entry into different markets, managing currency exchange rates, adjusting marketing and sales strategy to accommodate country differences, managing globally dispersed supply chains, dealing with different accounting and tax rules, and so on. Taken together, these factors make managing the global enterprise a complex and challenging task, but one that is also exciting for the skilled manager.

MANAGEMENT CHALLENGES

1. How are the processes of globalization affecting the nature of competition in the textile industry? Who are the winners in this process? Who are the losers in this process?

2. How might the process of globalization ultimately affect the nature of competition in the health services industry? Who will be the winners in this process? Who will be the losers in this process?

3. If the world pulls back from lowering barriers to cross-border trade and investment, and instead raises them, what do you think will happen to the American economy?

4. What are the implications of continuing globalization for a computer manufacturer based in a developed nation? What are the opportunities and challenges associated with globalization?

5. What are the implications of globalization for the hiring and promotion strategy of a firm headquartered in a major developed nation that has significant international operations?

6. How do you think the rise of anti-Americanism might affect the international prospects of a firm like Microsoft? What, if anything, can Microsoft do to counter the adverse affects of anti-Americanism?

MANAGEMENT PORTFOLIO

FOR THE ORGANIZATION YOU HAVE CHOSEN TO FOLLOW:

1. Outline how the processes of globalization have impacted your firm and might affect it in the future. What challenges is globalization creating? What opportunities are emerging as a result of globalization?

2. Is your firm active outside its home market? How much of its business comes from foreign sales?

3. What is the largest foreign market of your firm? How does it do business in that market (through wholly owned subsidiaries, joint ventures, exporting)? Why do you think managers at the firm chose that entry mode?

4. In what ways has your firm benefited from going global?

CLOSING CASE   PLANET STARBUCKS

Thirty years ago Starbucks was a single store in Seattle's Pike Place Market selling premium roasted coffee. Today it is a global roaster and retailer of coffee with over 8,400 stores, more than 2,000 of which are found in 31 countries outside the United States. Starbucks Corporation embarked on its current course in the 1980s when the company's director of marketing, Howard Schultz, came back from a trip to Italy enchanted with the Italian coffeehouse experience. Schultz, who later became CEO, persuaded the company's owners to experiment with the coffeehouse format—and the Starbucks experience was born. The basic strategy was to sell the company's own premium roasted coffee, along with freshly brewed espresso-style coffee beverages, a variety of pastries, coffee accessories, teas, and other products, in a tastefully designed coffeehouse setting. The company also stressed providing superior customer service. Reasoning that motivated employees provide the best customer service, Starbucks' executives devoted a lot of attention to employee hiring and training programs and progressive compensation policies that gave even part-time employees stock option grants and medical benefits. The formula met with spectacular success in the United States, where Starbucks went from obscurity to one of the best-known brands in the country in a decade.

In 1995, with almost 700 stores across the United States, Starbucks began exploring foreign opportunities. Its first target market was Japan. Although Starbucks had resisted a franchising strategy in North America, where its stores are company owned, Starbucks initially decided to license its format in Japan. However, the company also realized that a pure licensing agreement would not give Starbucks the control needed to ensure that the Japanese licensees closely followed Starbucks' successful formula. So the company established a joint venture with a local retailer, Sazaby Inc. Each company held a 50 percent stake in the venture, Starbucks Coffee of Japan. Starbucks initially invested $10 million in this venture, its first foreign direct investment. The Starbucks format was then licensed to the venture, which was assigned responsibility for growing Starbucks' presence in Japan.

To make sure the Japanese operations replicated the Starbucks experience in North America, Starbucks transferred some employees to the Japanese operation. The licensing agreement required all Japanese store managers and employees to attend training classes similar to those given to U.S. employees. The agreement also required that stores adhere to the design parameters established in the United States. In 2001 the company introduced a stock option plan for all Japanese employees, making it the first company in Japan to do so. Skeptics doubted that Starbucks would be able to replicate its North American success overseas; but by 2005 Starbucks had almost 550 stores in Japan, and it plans to continue opening them at a brisk pace.

After getting its feet wet in Japan, the company began an aggressive foreign investment program. In 1998 it purchased Seattle Coffee, a British coffee chain with 60 retail stores, for $84 million. An American couple, originally from Seattle, had started Seattle Coffee with the intention of establishing a Starbucks-like chain in Britain. In the late 1990s Starbucks opened stores in Taiwan, China, Singapore, Thailand, New Zealand, South Korea, and Malaysia.

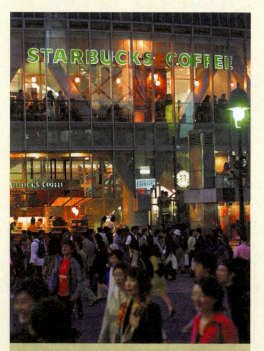

Konnichiwa Japan was the first foreign market for Starbucks, and it remains one of the largest. Starbucks now has around 550 stores in the country, where it has become part of the local scene.

© AP Photo/Shizuo Kambayashi

In Asia Starbucks' most common strategy was to license its format to a local operator in return for initial licensing fees and royalties on store revenues. Starbucks also sold coffee and related products to the local licensees, who then resold them to customers. As in Japan, Starbucks insisted on an intensive employee training program and strict specifications regarding the format and layout of the store. However, Starbucks became disenchanted with some of the straight licensing arrangements and converted several into joint venture arrangements or wholly owned subsidiaries. In Thailand, for example, Starbucks initially entered a licensing agreement with Coffee Partners, a local Thai company. Under the terms of the licensing agreement, Coffee Partners was required to open at least 20 Starbucks coffee stores in Thailand within five years. However, Coffee Partners found it difficult to raise funds from Thai banks to finance this expansion. In July 2000 Starbucks acquired Coffee Partners for about $12 million. Its goal was to gain tighter control over the expansion strategy in Thailand. A similar development occurred in South Korea, where Starbucks initially licensed its format to ESCO Korea Ltd. in 1999. Although ESCO soon had 10 successful stores open, Starbucks felt that ESCO would not be able to achieve the company's aggressive growth targets, so in December 2000 it converted the licensing arrangement into a joint venture with Shinsegae, the parent company of ESCO. The joint venture enabled Starbucks to exercise greater control over the growth strategy in South Korea and to help fund that operation while gaining the benefits of a local operating partner. By October 2000 Starbucks had invested some $52 million in foreign joint ventures.

By the end of 2002, with more than 1,200 stores in 27 countries outside North America, Starbucks was initiating aggressive expansion plans into mainland Europe. The company's plans called for opening stores in six European countries, including the coffee cultures of France and Italy. As its first entry point on the European mainland (Starbucks had 150 stores in Great Britain), Starbucks chose Switzerland. Drawing on its experience in Asia, the company entered a joint venture with a Swiss company, Bon Appetit Group, Switzerland's largest food service company. Bon Appetit was to hold a majority stake in the venture, and Starbucks would license its format to the Swiss company using an agreement similar to those it had used successfully in Asia. This was followed by a joint venture in Germany with KarstadtQuelle, one of the country's largest retailers. Under that agreement Starbucks held 18 percent of the equity in the venture, and Karstadt held the remainder. In early 2005, with more than 2,000 international stores, Starbucks announced that it believed there was the potential for up to 15,000 stores outside the United States.[50]

CASE DISCUSSION QUESTIONS

1. What are the benefits to Starbucks from expanding internationally?

2. Why do you think Starbucks has been so successful internationally?

3. Initially Starbucks expanded internationally by licensing its format to foreign operators. It soon became disenchanted with this strategy. Why?

4. Why do you think Starbucks has now elected to expand internationally primarily through local joint ventures to which it licenses its format, as opposed to a pure licensing strategy?

5. What are the advantages of a joint venture entry mode for Starbucks over entering through wholly owned subsidiaries? On occasion, though, Starbucks has chosen a wholly owned subsidiary to control its foreign expansion (such as in Britain and Thailand). Why?

ENDNOTES

1. E.D. Cook et al., "Outsourcing Tax Returns Raises Legal and Ethical Concerns," *Practical Tax Strategies*, vol. 75 (August 2005), pp. 68–74; J.F. Reeves, "CPAs and Foreign Outsourcing," *The Practical Accountant*, June 2004, p. 23; R.A. Davis, "Outsourcing Sparks Returns," *Accounting Technology*, vol. 21 (January 2005), pp. 37–43.

2. For details, see T.L. Friedman, *The World Is Flat* (New York: Farra, Straus and Giroux, 2005); R.B. Reich, *The Work of Nations* (New York: A.A. Knopf, 1991); and J.A. Frankel, *Globalization of the Economy* (National Bureau of Economic Research: Working Paper no. 7858, 2000).

3. For a detailed but accessible description, see M. Friedman and R. Friedman, *Free to Choose* (London: Penguin Books, 1980).

4. For a classic summary of the tenets of Marxism details, see A. Giddens, *Capitalism and Modern Social Theory* (Cambridge: Cambridge University Press, 1971).

5. S. Fisher, R. Sahay, and C.A. Vegh, "Stabilization and the Growth in Transition Economies: The Early Experience," *Journal of Economic Perspectives* 10 (Spring 1996), pp. 45–66.

6. Heritage Foundation, *2005 Index of Economic Freedom,* www.heritage.org.

7. For details, see Chapters 5 and 7 in C.W.L. Hill, *International Business*, 6th ed. (New York: McGraw-Hill, 2007).

8. World Trade Organization, *2004 Annual Report* (Geneva: WTO, 2005).

9. United Nations, *World Investment Report 2005* (New York & Geneva: United Nations, 2005).

10. United Nations, *World Investment Report 2005.*

11. Frankel, *Globalization of the Economy.*

12. J.G. Fernald and V. Greenfield, "The Fall and Rise of the Global Economy," *Chicago Fed Letters,* April 2001, pp. 1–4.

13. Data compiled from various sources and listed by CyberAtlas at http://cyberatlas.internet.com/big_picture/.

14. www.forrester.com/ER/Press/ForrFind/0,1768,0,00.html.

15. For a counterargument, see "Geography and the Net: Putting It in Its Place," *The Economist,* August 11, 2001, pp. 18–20.

16. Frankel, *Globalization of the Economy.*

17. Data from Bureau of Transportation Statistics, 2001.

18. Fernald and Greenfield, "The Fall and Rise of the Global Economy."

19. Data located at http://www.bts.gov/publications/us_international_trade_and_freight_transportation_trends/2003/index.html.

20. United Nations, *World Investment Report 2005;* United Nations Conference on Trade and Development, "Data Show That Foreign Direct Investment Climbed Sharply in 2005," UNCTAD press release, January 23, 2006.

21. World Trade Organization, *International Trade Statistics 2005* (Geneva: WTO, 2005); United Nations, *World Investment Report 2005;* United Nations Conference on Trade and Development, "Data Show That Foreign Direct Investment Climbed Sharply in 2005."

22. United Nations, *World Investment Report 2005.*

23. I. Metthee, "Playing a Large Part," *Seattle Post-Intelligencer,* April 9, 1994, p. 13.

24. D. Pritchard, "Are Federal Tax Laws and State Subsidies for Boeing 7E7 Selling America Short?" *Aviation Week,* April 12, 2004, pp. 74–75.

25. W.M. Bulkeley, "IBM to Export Highly Paid Jobs to India," *The Wall Street Journal,* December 15, 2003, pp. B1, B3.

26. T. Levitt, "The Globalization of Markets," *Harvard Business Review,* May–June 1983, pp. 92–102.

27. See F.T. Knickerbocker, *Oligopolistic Reaction and Multinational Enterprise* (Boston: Harvard Business School Press, 1973); and R.E. Caves, "Japanese Investment in the U.S.: Lessons for the Economic Analysis of Foreign Investment," *The World Economy* 16 (1993), pp. 279–300.

28. See J. Bhagwati, *In Defense of Globalization* (New York: Oxford University Press, 2004).

29. A large body of evidence supports the proposition that free trade stimulates economic growth. See J.D. Sachs and A. Warner, "Economic Reform and the Process of Global Integration," *Brookings Papers on Economic Activity,* 1995, pp. 1–96; J.A. Frankel and D. Romer, "Does Trade Cause Growth?" *American Economic Review* 89, no. 3 (June 1999), pp. 379–99; and D. Dollar and A. Kraay, "Trade, Growth, and Poverty," Working Paper, Development Research Group, World Bank, June 2001. Also, for an accessible discussion of the relationship between free trade and economic growth, see T. Taylor, "The Truth about Globalization," *Public Interest,* Spring 2002, pp. 24–44.

30. K. Belson, "In U.S., Cell Phone Users Are Often All Talk," *The New York Times,* December 13, 2004, pp. C1, C4.

31. J.Z. Namenwirth and R.B. Weber, *Dynamics of Culture* (Boston: Allen & Unwin, 1987), p. 8.

32. R. Mead, *International Management: Cross Cultural Dimensions* (Oxford: Blackwell Business, 1994), p. 7.

33. G. Rice, "Doing Business in Saudi Arabia," *Thunderbird International Business Review*, January–February 2004, pp. 59–84.

34. E.T. Hall and M.R. Hall, *Understanding Cultural Differences* (Yarmouth, ME: Intercultural Press, 1990).

35. D. Barboza, "An Unknown Giant Flexes Its Muscles," *The New York Times,* December 4, 2004, pp. B1, B3.

36. See J. Birkinshaw and N. Hood, "Multinational Subsidiary Evolution: Capability and Charter Change in Foreign Owned Subsidiary Companies;" *Academy of Management Review* 23 (October 1998), pp. 773–95; A.K. Gupta and V.J. Govindarajan, "Knowledge Flows within Multinational Corporations," *Strategic Management Journal* 21 (2000), pp. 473–96; V.J. Govindarajan and A.K. Gupta, *The Quest for Global Dominance* (San Francisco: Jossey-Bass, 2001); T.S. Frost, J.M. Birkinshaw, and P.C. Ensign, "Centers of Excellence in Multinational Corporations," *Strategic Management Journal* 23 (2002), pp. 997–1018; and U. Andersson, M. Forsgren, and U. Holm, "The Strategic Impact of External Networks," *Strategic Management Journal* 23 (2002), pp. 979–96.

37. S. Leung, "Armchairs, TVs, and Espresso: Is It McDonald's?" *The Wall Street Journal,* August 30, 2002, pp. A1, A6.

38. C.K. Prahalad and Y.L. Doz, *The Multinational Mission: Balancing Local Demands and Global Vision* (New York: Free Press, 1987). Also see J. Birkinshaw, A. Morrison, and J. Hulland, "Structural and Competitive Determinants of a Global Integration Strategy," *Strategic Management Journal* 16 (1995), pp. 637–55.

39. Sources: M. Gunther, "MTV's Passage to India," *Fortune,* August 9, 2004, pp. 117–22; B. Pulley and A. Tanzer, "Sumner's Gemstone," *Forbes,* February 21, 2000, pp. 107–11; K. Hoffman, "Youth TV's Old Hand Prepares for the Digital Challenge," *Financial Times,* February 18, 2000, p. 8; presentation by Sumner M. Redstone, chairman and CEO, Viacom Inc., delivered to Salomon Smith Barney 11th Annual Global Entertainment Media, Telecommunications Conference, Scottsdale, AZ, January 8, 2001. Archived at www.viacom.com.Viacom 10K Statement, 2003.

40. C.W.L. Hill, P. Hwang, and W.C. Kim, "An Eclectic Theory of the Choice of International Entry Mode," *Strategic Management Journal* 11 (1990), pp. 117–28; C.W.L. Hill and W.C. Kim, "Searching for a Dynamic Theory of the Multinational Enterprise: A Transaction Cost Model," *Strategic Management Journal* 9 (Special Issue on Strategy Content, 1988), pp. 93–104.

41. Shay and Bruce, "Expatriate Managers." Also see J.S. Black and H. Gregersen, "The Right Way to Manage Expatriates," *Harvard Business Review,* March–April 1999, pp. 52–63; Y. Baruch and Y. Altman, "Expatriation and Repatriation in MNCs—A Taxonomy," *Human Resource Management* 41 (2002), pp. 239–59; *Cornell Hotel and Restaurant Administration Quarterly,* 38 (1997) pp. 30–35.

42. C.M. Solomon, "Success Abroad Depends upon More Than Job Skills," *Personnel Journal,* April 1994, pp. 51–58.

43. C.M. Solomon, "Unhappy Trails," *Workforce,* August 2000, pp. 36–41.

44. Solomon, "Success Abroad Depends upon More Than Job Skills."

45. For details, see Chapter 18 in Hill, *International Business.*

46. G. Oddou and M. Mendenhall, "Expatriate Performance Appraisal: Problems and Solutions," in *International Human Resource Management,* ed. G. Mendenhall and M. Oddou (Boston: PWS-Kent, 1991).

47. S.J. Kobrin, "Geocentric Mindset and Multinational Strategy," *Journal of International Business Studies* 25 (1994), pp. 493–511.

48. M. Banai and L.M. Sama, "Ethical Dilemma in MNCs' International Staffing Policies," *Journal of Business Ethics,* June 2000, pp. 221–35.

49. Reitman and Schuman, "Men's Club: Japanese and Korean Companies Rarely Look Outside for People to Run Their Overseas Operations;" *Wall Street Journal,* September 26, 1996, p. R17.

50. Sources: Starbucks 10K, various years; C. McLean, "Starbucks Set to Invade Coffee-Loving Continent," *The Seattle Times*, October 4, 2000, p. E1; J. Ordonez, "Starbucks to Start Major Expansion in Overseas Market," *The Wall Street Journal*, October 27, 2000, p. B10; S. Homes and D. Bennett, "Planet Starbucks," *BusinessWeek*, September 9, 2002, pp. 99–110; "Starbucks Outlines International Growth Strategy," *Business Wire*, October 14, 2004.

4

STAKEHOLDERS, ETHICS, AND
CORPORATE SOCIAL RESPONSIBILITY

In their quest to boost profitability, during the 1990s managers at Nike contracted out the production of sports shoes to producers in the developing world. Unfortunately for Nike, the working conditions at several of these producers were very poor, and the company was subsequently attacked for using "sweatshop labor." Typical of the allegations were those detailed in the CBS news program *48 Hours*. The report told of young women at a Vietnamese subcontractor who worked six days a week, in poor working conditions with toxic materials, for only 20 cents an hour. The report also stated that a living wage in Vietnam was at least $3 a day, an income that could not be achieved without working substantial overtime. Nike was not breaking any laws, nor were its subcontractors; but this report and others like it raised questions about the ethics of using "sweatshop labor." It may have been legal, helping the company increase its profitability. But was it ethical to use subcontractors who by Western standards exploited their workforce? Nike's critics thought not, and the company found itself the focus of a wave of demonstrations and consumer boycotts.[1]

The Nike story illustrates what should be a cardinal principle of business: The quest to maximize profitability should be constrained not just by the law but also by ethical obligations. It is often argued that the goal of managers in business enterprises should be to take actions that maximize long-term shareholder value and that the best way to do this is to maximize the long-term profitability of the enterprise. However, in this chapter we argue that managers must also behave in an ethical and socially responsible manner when pursuing this goal. They must do so because it is the right thing to do—and also because doing so can help an organization maintain and enhance its reputation with key constituencies or stakeholders, whose support is necessary for the survival of the enterprise. By using "sweatshop labor" Nike damaged its reputation and alienated some members of a key stakeholder group—its customers, who chose to purchase sneakers from other suppliers. To repair the company's reputation and rebuild support among customers, managers at Nike formulated a code of conduct that requires suppliers to adhere to certain labor standards. The company has also hired independent auditors to regularly monitor suppliers to make sure they comply with the code. From being the target of vociferous criticism, Nike has become a case study in how to incorporate ethical issues into management decisions.

We open this chapter with a discussion of stakeholders and stakeholder management. Next we turn our attention to a discussion of business ethics, and we assert that behaving ethically can help an organization maintain the support of key stakeholders. The chapter closes with a discussion of corporate social responsibility, which is the notion that managers should take the social consequences of economic actions into account when making decisions.

■ // Stakeholders and Stakeholder Management

stakeholder

An individual, institution, or community that has a stake in the operations of an organization and in how it does business.

A **stakeholder** is an individual, institution, or community that has a stake in the operations of an organization and in how it does business.[2] Stakeholders include those who regularly transact directly with the organization, most notably employees, customers, suppliers, distributors, shareholders, and creditors. Stakeholders also include institutions that are more remote but still have a stake in how the organization operates and does business, including government, local communities, and the general public (see Figure 4.1).

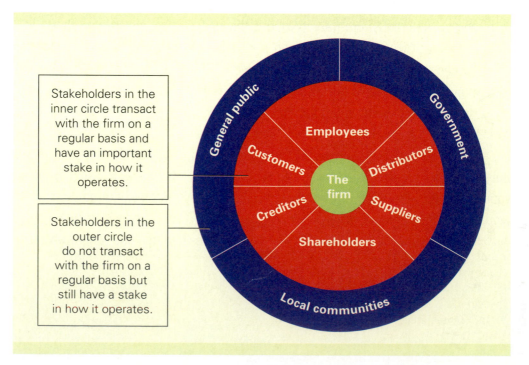

Stakeholders in the inner circle transact with the firm on a regular basis and have an important stake in how it operates.

Stakeholders in the outer circle do not transact with the firm on a regular basis but still have a stake in how it operates.

FIGURE 4.1

Stakeholders

// STAKEHOLDERS AND THE ORGANIZATION

All stakeholders are in an exchange relationship with an organization. Each stakeholder group supplies the organization with important resources (or contributions), and in exchange each expects its interests to be satisfied (by inducements).[3] Employees provide labor and skills and expect commensurate income, job satisfaction, job security, and good working conditions. Customers provide revenues and want reliable products that represent value for money. Suppliers provide inputs to the organization and seek prompt payment and dependable buyers. Distributors help sell an organization's output, and in return they seek favorable payment terms and products that will sell well. Shareholders provide a corporation with risk capital. They are also its legal owners. In exchange they expect management to maximize the return on their investment in the corporation. Creditors such as bondholders provide the organization with capital in the form of debt, and they expect to be repaid on time with interest.

Governments provide an organization with rules and regulations that govern business practice and maintain fair competition. In exchange they want businesses to adhere to rules and regulations and pay their taxes on time. Local communities provide organizations with local infrastructure and want businesses that are responsible citizens. The general public provides organizations with national infrastructure and seeks some assurance that the quality of life will be improved as a result of the organization's existence.

// TAKING STAKEHOLDERS INTO ACCOUNT

Managers need to take the various claims of stakeholders into account when making decisions. If they do not, stakeholders may withdraw their support. Shareholders may sell their shares, bondholders demand higher interest payments on new bonds, employees leave their jobs, and customers buy elsewhere. Suppliers may seek more dependable buyers, and distributors may favor the products of other enterprises. Unions, as the representatives of employees, may engage in disruptive labor disputes. Government may take civil or criminal action against a firm and its top officers, imposing fines and in some cases jail terms. Communities may oppose a firm's attempts to locate its facilities in their area, and the general public may form pressure groups, demanding action against businesses that impair the quality of life. Any of these reactions can have a damaging impact on an enterprise. In other words, catering to the claims of different stakeholder groups is good business strategy and will help the organization to survive and prosper in the long run.[4]

Unfortunately managers cannot always satisfy the claims of all stakeholders. The goals of different groups may conflict. In practice few organizations have the resources to simultaneously satisfy all stakeholder claims.[5] For example, employee claims for higher wages can conflict with consumer demands for reasonable prices and shareholder demands for higher returns. Often managers must choose between the competing claims of different stakeholders. To do so, they must identify the most important stakeholders and give highest priority to pursuing actions that satisfy their needs. Stakeholder impact analysis can provide such identification. Typically stakeholder impact analysis follows the steps illustrated in Figure 4.2.[6]

Such an analysis enables managers to identify the stakeholders most critical to the survival of their organization, making sure that the satisfaction of their needs is paramount. Most businesses that have gone through this process quickly come to the conclusion that three stakeholder groups must be satisfied above all others if a firm is to survive and prosper: customers, employees, and shareholders.[7] If customers defect, financial performance will decline. If skilled employees leave the organization for work elsewhere, the human capital that the firm can draw upon will decline, productivity will fall, costs will increase, and financial performance will again fall. And if shareholders sell their shares, the stock price of the firm will decline, its cost of capital will rise, and the firm will find it difficult to raise fresh capital from investors.

In general, if managers can satisfy the claims of the customers and employees of the firm, financial performance will be strong, the share price will rise, and this will satisfy the claims of shareholders.[8] In other words, in the long run satisfying the claims of shareholders

FIGURE 4.2

Evaluating Stakeholder Claims

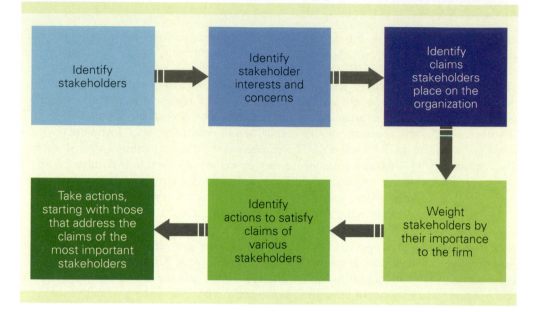

requires managers to *first* pay close attention to their customers and employees. If customers are satisfied, they will continue to purchase from the firm and sales will be strong. If employees are satisfied, they will work hard, productivity will increase, costs will fall, and financial performance will improve. Enterprises like Southwest Airlines and Starbucks have made a virtue out of satisfying the demands of their customers and creating a good environment for their employees. It is not surprising that both enterprises have been rewarded with robust financial performance and a strong stock price, thereby satisfying the claims of shareholders.

■ Monsanto: The cost of ignoring stakeholders.

Although it is important to focus on the claims of customers, employees, and shareholders, managers must be careful not to ignore the claims of other stakeholder groups. Monsanto, for example, spent billions of dollars to develop genetically modified crops that were resistant to common pests. Monsanto's belief was that these products would benefit farmers, Monsanto's customers, who could spend less money on chemical insecticides. The company also thought that the resulting profits would benefit shareholders through appreciation in the company's stock price, as well as employees, who would have more secure employment. However, Monsanto failed to anticipate the adverse reaction from another important stakeholder group: the general public. Monsanto's introduction of genetically modified crops has met stiff resistance from the general public in both Europe and Latin America. The public has several concerns. One is that genetically modified food might constitute a health risk and cause cancer. A second is that in the long run, Monsanto's insect-resistant crops might make matters worse because over time insects will evolve resistance to the "natural pesticides" engineered into Monsanto's plants, rendering the plants vulnerable to a new generation of "superbugs." A third concern, termed "genetic pollution," is the possibility that the DNA inserted into Monsanto's plants might jump across species into plants it was never intended for, there producing a pesticide harmful to insects that do not damage crops. Public concern led to action by pressure groups such as Friends of the Earth and Greenpeace. These pressure groups successfully lobbied governments in Europe and Latin America to prohibit the sale of certain genetically modified foods, which hurt Monsanto's shareholders and employees.

Critics argue that Monsanto hurt itself by initially dismissing public concerns. Managers, claiming that protestors ignored scientific evidence, stated that genetically modified seeds had beneficial effects on agricultural productivity and would lead to lower food prices. The general public in Europe and parts of Latin America perceived Monsanto's approach, which seemed reasonable to the firm's managers, as arrogant and insensitive. Monsanto may have helped its case if it had first invested in a carefully crafted public education campaign designed to inform both the public and government officials that genetically modified food poses no health risks, and that concerns regarding superbugs and genetic pollution are vastly exaggerated. The reality is that the scientific evidence is on Monsanto's side; but by ignoring public perceptions and failing to anticipate the hostile reaction from an important stakeholder group, Monsanto hurt rather than helped its case.[9]

Another problem arises when managers make the mistake of putting the claims of shareholders in front of all other claims. It is true that a business corporation should try to maximize the return associated with holding its stock; but it is also true that if managers focus obsessively on that goal, they may take actions that not only run counter to the interests of other important stakeholder groups, but also are not in the best long-term interests of shareholders themselves. Most notably, in an attempt to boost the stock price, managers may cut investments in employees, productive assets, and technology that are essential for the health of the corporation. The increased cash flow may boost the short-term performance of the firm; however, in the long run the lack of investment in employees, production facilities, and new technology can lead to a decline in performance that leaves all worse off.

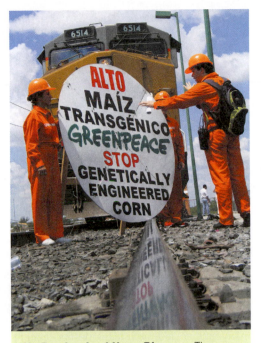

No Frankenfood Here, Please   These Greenpeace activists in Sweden were part of a wide European movement to stop Monsanto from selling genetically modified seeds in Europe. Because it initially dismissed protests from powerful interest groups that opposed the introduction of genetically modified food, Monsanto found it harder to introduce its seeds in Europe.

© Greenpeace

For example, when Al Dunlap joined the troubled small appliance maker Sunbeam, shareholders expected great things. In his previous job as CEO of Scott Paper, Dunlap had engineered a tough turnaround. Within three months of joining Sunbeam, Dunlap had fired many senior managers and announced plans to cut the workforce in half and close 18 of the company's 26 factories. At the same time he claimed that his cost-cutting strategy would soon boost profits and revenues, richly rewarding stockholders. The stock price did surge from $18 when Dunlap was first hired to $53 a share over the next 18 months as the cost-cutting strategy initially boosted the bottom line. Then Sunbeam's performance began to falter. It soon became clear that Dunlap had so gutted Sunbeam's workforce, facilities, and product development pipeline that the company lacked the capability to meet his ambitious growth goals. Worse still, Dunlap had apparently been urging his managers to engage in ethically dubious practices to hit financial performance goals and keep the stock price up. One of these practices, known as "bill and hold," involved Sunbeam selling its products to retailers at a large discount to normal prices, and then holding them in warehouses for delivery later. In effect the company had been inflating its financial performance by shifting sales from the future to the current period. When this practice was discovered, the board of directors fired Dunlap. It was too late for Sunbeam, however, which never did recover from Dunlap's tenure and ultimately went bankrupt.[10]

In sum, by trying to boost the short-term share price, Dunlap damaged Sunbeam and did considerable harm to all stakeholder groups, including shareholders. The lesson in the Monsanto and Sunbeam examples is that managers must pay attention to all stakeholder groups, balancing their claims and taking actions that are in the best long-term interests of key stakeholders—employees, customers, and shareholders—while being careful not to alienate

■ Al Dunlap: The king of destructive downsizing at Sunbeam.

other key stakeholders, such as the general public. As we will see in the next section, if managers have a strong ethical foundation, they are far less likely to take actions that damage stakeholder interests.

// Business Ethics

business ethics
Accepted principles of right or wrong governing the conduct of businesspeople.

ethical dilemmas
Situations in which there is no agreement over exact accepted principles of right and wrong.

The term *ethics* refers to accepted principles of right or wrong that govern the conduct of a person, the members of a profession, or the actions of an organization. **Business ethics** are the accepted principles of right or wrong governing the conduct of businesspeople. Ethical decisions are those that are in accordance with those accepted principles of right and wrong, whereas an unethical decision is one that violates accepted principles. This is not as straightforward as it sounds. Managers may face **ethical dilemmas**, which are situations where there is no agreement over exactly what the accepted principles of right and wrong are, or where none of the available alternatives seems ethically acceptable.

In our society many accepted principles of right and wrong are not only universally recognized but also codified into law. In the business arena there are laws governing product liability (tort laws), contracts and breaches of contract (contract law), the protection of intellectual property (intellectual property law), competitive behavior (antitrust law), and the selling of securities (securities law). Not only is it unethical to break these laws—but it is illegal. However, many actions, although legal, do not seem to be ethical. As we saw in the introduction, Nike's use of "sweatshop labor" in developing nations was not illegal, but many considered it unethical. Behaving ethically, in other words, goes beyond staying within the bounds of the law.

// ETHICAL ISSUES IN MANAGEMENT

The ethical issues managers confront cover a wide range of topics; but most arise due to a potential conflict between the goals of the organization, or those of individual managers, and the fundamental rights of important stakeholders. Stakeholders have basic rights that should be respected, and it is unethical to violate those rights. Shareholders have the right to timely and accurate information about their investments (in accounting statements). Customers have the right to be fully informed about the products and services they purchase, including how those products might harm them or others, and it is unethical to restrict their access to such information. Employees have the right to safe working conditions, to fair compensation for the work they perform, and to be treated in a just manner by managers. Suppliers and distributors have the right to expect contracts to be respected, and a firm should not take advantage of a power disparity to opportunistically rewrite contracts. Competitors have the right to expect that a firm will abide by the rules of competition and not violate the basic principles of antitrust laws. Communities and the general public, including their political representatives in government, have the right to expect that a firm will not violate the basic expectations society places on enterprises—for example, by dumping toxic pollutants into the environment or overcharging for work performed on government contracts.

Those who take the stakeholder view of business ethics often assert that it is in the enlightened self-interest of managers to behave in an ethical manner that recognizes and respects the fundamental rights of stakeholders, because doing so will ensure the support of stakeholders, which ultimately benefits the firm and its managers.[11] Others go beyond this instrumental approach to ethics to argue that in many cases acting ethically is simply the right thing to do. They argue that businesses need to recognize their moral responsibility to give something back to the society that made their success possible.

Unethical behavior tends to arise when managers decide to put the attainment of their own personal goals, or the goals of the organization, above the fundamental rights of one or more stakeholder groups. The most common examples of such behavior involve self-dealing, information manipulation, anticompetitive behavior, opportunistic exploitation of suppliers and distributors, the maintenance of substandard working conditions, environmental degradation, and corruption.

Self-Dealing Self-dealing occurs when managers find a way to feather their own nests with corporate funds. Classic examples of this behavior include (1) senior managers who treat corporate funds as their own personal treasury, raiding them to support a lavish lifestyle; (2) senior managers who use their control over the compensation committee of the board of directors to award themselves multi-million-dollar pay increases or stock option grants that are out of proportion with their contribution to the corporation; and (3) instances where individual managers award business contracts not to the most efficient supplier but to the one that provides the largest kickback. In these cases managers are not acting in the best interests of their shareholders and are instead consuming funds that should legitimately go to shareholders. Some of this behavior is illegal; some is technically legal but unethical because it violates the basic right of shareholders to a fair return on their investment.

For an example of self-dealing, consider the former CEO of Tyco International, Dennis Kozlowski. Kozlowski treated Tyco as his personal treasury, drawing on company funds to purchase a $30 million Manhattan apartment and a world-class art collection. Kozlowski even used company funds to help pay for a lavish $2.2 million birthday party for his wife in Italy! Kozlowski ultimately was charged with securities fraud, found guilty of looting Tyco of $97 million, and was sentenced to jail term of $8\frac{1}{3}$ to 25 years.[12]

The Fall of the Self-Dealing CEO   Dennis Kozlowski, the former CEO of Tyco International, was sentenced to a minimum of $8\frac{1}{3}$ years in jail after being convicted of looting Tyco of nearly $100 million.

© AP Photo, Ed Bailey.

Information Manipulation Information manipulation occurs when managers use their control over corporate data to distort or hide information to enhance their own financial situations or the competitive position of the firm. Many of the accounting scandals that swept through American companies in the early 2000s involved cases of information manipulation. For example, the now-bankrupt energy trading firm Enron hid significant debt from shareholders in off–balance sheet partnerships. This practice misled investors about the level of risk Enron had assumed and supported a much higher stock price than was justified. Not surprisingly, this higher stock price enabled managers to exercise stock option grants for considerable personal gain (a case of information manipulation to support self-dealing). When the scale of hidden debts was finally revealed, Enron quickly collapsed into bankruptcy, resulting in losses of over $100 billion for shareholders. Information manipulation is unethical because it violates the right of investors to accurate and timely information.

Information manipulation can also take place with nonfinancial data. This occurred when managers at tobacco companies suppressed internal research that linked smoking to health problems, violating the right of consumers to accurate information about the dangers of smoking. When evidence of this came to light, lawyers brought class action suits against the tobacco companies, claiming they had intentionally caused harm to smokers. In 1999 the tobacco companies settled a lawsuit brought by several states, which sought to recover health care costs associated with tobacco-related illnesses; the total payout to the states was $260 billion!

Anticompetitive Behavior Anticompetitive behavior includes a range of actions aimed at harming actual or potential competitors, most often by using monopoly power to enhance the prospects of the firm. For example, in the 1990s the Justice Department claimed that Microsoft used its monopoly in operating systems to force PC makers to bundle Microsoft's Web browser, Internet Explorer, with Windows and to display Internet Explorer prominently on the computer desktop. Microsoft reportedly told PC makers that it would not supply them with Windows unless they did this. Because the PC makers had to have Windows to sell their machines, this was a powerful threat. The alleged aim of the action, which is an example of *tie-in sales* (illegal under antitrust laws), was to drive a competing browser maker, Netscape, out of business. The courts

■ Self-dealing at Tyco.

■ Information manipulation at Tyco.

self-dealing
Situations in which managers find a way to feather their own nests with corporate funds.

information manipulation
Situations in which managers use their control over corporate data to distort or hide information to enhance their own financial situations or the competitive position of the firm.

anticompetitive behavior
Behavior aimed at harming actual or potential competitors, most often by using monopoly power.

■ Microsoft: Anticompetitive behavior.

ruled that Microsoft was indeed abusing its monopoly power in this case, and in a 2001 consent decree the company agreed to stop the practice.

Putting the legal issues aside, action such as that allegedly undertaken by managers at Microsoft is unethical in at least three ways. First, it violates the rights of end consumers by unfairly limiting their choice; second, it violates the rights of downstream participants in the industry value chain, in this case PC makers, by forcing them to incorporate a particular product in their design; and third, it violates the rights of competitors to free and fair competition.

opportunistic exploitation

Unilaterally rewriting the terms of a contract with suppliers, distributors, or complement providers in a way that is more favorable to a firm, often using its power to force the revision through.

Opportunistic Exploitation Opportunistic exploitation of other players in the value chain in which the firm is embedded is another example of unethical behavior. **Opportunistic exploitation** of this kind typically occurs when the managers of a firm seek to unilaterally rewrite the terms of a contract with suppliers, distributors, or complement providers in a way that is more favorable to the firm, often using the firm's power to force the revision through. For example, in the late 1990s Boeing entered a $2 billion contract with Titanium Metals Corp. to buy certain amounts of titanium annually for 10 years. In 2000, after Titanium Metals Corp. had already spent $100 million to expand its production capacity to fulfill the contract, Boeing demanded that the contract be renegotiated, asking for lower prices and an end to minimum purchase agreements. As a major purchaser of titanium, managers at Boeing probably thought they had the power to push this contract revision through, and the investment by Titanium Metals meant that firm would be unlikely to walk away from the deal. Titanium Metals Corp. promptly sued Boeing for breach of contract. The dispute was settled out of court, and under a revised agreement Boeing agreed to pay monetary damages to Titanium Metals (reported to be in the $60 million range) and entered an amended contract to purchase titanium.[13] Irrespective of the legality of this action, it seems unethical because it violated the rights of a supplier to be dealt with in a fair and open way.

■ Boeing opportunism.

substandard working conditions

Tolerating unsafe working conditions or paying employees below-market rates to reduce costs of production.

Substandard Working Conditions **Substandard working conditions** arise when managers tolerate unsafe working conditions or pay employees below-market rates to reduce costs of production. The most extreme examples of such behavior occur when a firm establishes operations in countries that lack the workplace regulations found in developed nations such as the United States. The example of Nike, given earlier, falls into this category. In another recent example, the Ohio Art company ran into an ethical storm when newspaper reports alleged that it had moved production of its popular Etch a Sketch toy from Ohio to a supplier in Shenzhen province, where employees, mostly teenagers, worked long hours for 24 cents per hour, below the legal minimum wage of 33 cents an hour there. Moreover, production reportedly started at 7:30 a.m. and continued until 10 p.m., with breaks only for lunch and dinner. Saturdays and Sundays were treated as normal workdays. This translated into a workweek of seven 12-hour days, or 84 hours a week, well above the standard 40-hour week set by authorities in Shenzhen. Such working conditions clearly violated the rights of employees in China as specified by local regulations (which were poorly enforced). Is it ethical for the Ohio Art company to use such a supplier? Many would say not.[14]

■ Ohio Art company: Using sweatshops.

environmental degradation

Taking actions that directly or indirectly result in pollution or other forms of environmental harm.

Environmental Degradation **Environmental degradation** occurs when managers take actions that directly or indirectly result in pollution or other forms of environmental harm. Environmental degradation can violate the rights of local communities and the general public to clean air and water; land that is free from pollution by toxic chemicals or excessive deforestation that causes land erosion and floods; and so on.

The issue of pollution takes on added importance because some parts of the environment are a public good that no one owns but anyone can despoil. No one owns the atmosphere or the oceans, but polluting them, no matter where the pollution originates, harms all.[15] The atmosphere and oceans can be viewed as a global commons from which everyone benefits but for which no one is specifically responsible. In such cases a phenomenon known as the *tragedy of the commons* becomes applicable. The tragedy of the commons occurs when a resource held in common by all, but owned by no one, is overused by individuals, resulting in its degradation. The phenomenon was first named by Garrett Hardin in describing a particular problem in 16th-century England. Large open areas called commons were free for all to use as pasture. The poor put out livestock on these commons to supplement their meager incomes. It was advantageous for each family to put out more and more livestock, but the consequence was far more livestock than the commons could handle. The result was overgrazing and degradation of the commons to the point where they could no longer support livestock.[16]

In the modern world corporations contribute to the global tragedy of the commons by moving production to locations in developing nations where environmental regulations are lacking or less strict than they are at home. There the firms are freer to pump pollutants into the atmosphere or dump them in oceans or rivers, thereby harming these valuable global commons. Although such action may be legal, is it ethical? Again, if seems to violate basic societal notions of ethics and clearly harms important stakeholder groups, including the general public and local communities.

Corruption Corruption can arise in a business context when managers pay bribes to gain access to lucrative business contracts. A recent example of corruption concerns the allegation that the Texas-based energy company Halliburton participated in a consortium that made $180 million in illegal payments to government officials (that is, bribes) to secure a $4.9 billion contract to build a liquefied natural gas plant in Nigeria.[17] Corruption is clearly unethical: It violates several rights, including the right of competitors to a level playing field when bidding for contracts and, when government officials are involved, the right of citizens to expect that government officials will act in the best interest of the local community or nation, and not in response to corrupt payments that feather their own nests.

Corruption is widespread in much of the world. According to Transparency International, an independent nonprofit organization dedicated to exposing and fighting corruption, businesses and individuals worldwide spend some $400 billion a year on bribes related to government procurement contracts alone![18] Transparency International has also measured the level of corruption among public officials in different countries.[19] As can be seen in Figure 4.3, the

There Goes the Global Commons   It may be legal to shift production to countries where environmental controls are much laxer than in the United States, but is it ethical to do so? Most think not.

© Digital Vision/PunchStock

■ Halliburton: Allegations of corruption.

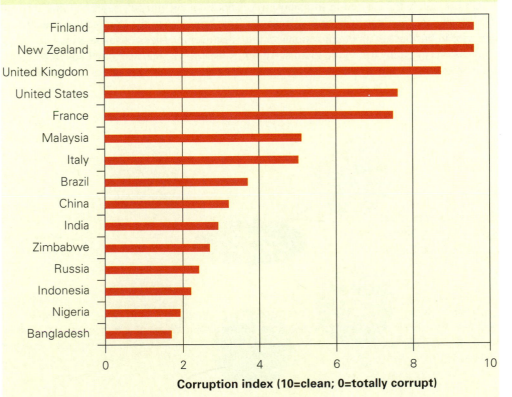

Corruption index (10=clean; 0=totally corrupt)

FIGURE 4.3

Rankings of Corruption by Country: 2005

Source: Based on source data from Transparency International's Corruption Preceptions Index (2005), www. transparency.org.

organization rated countries such as Finland and New Zealand as very clean, whereas countries such as Russia, India, Indonesia, and Zimbabwe were seen as corrupt. Bangladesh ranked last out of all 146 countries in the survey; Finland ranked first.

// THE ROOTS OF UNETHICAL BEHAVIOR

Why do some managers behave unethically? What motivates them to engage in actions that violate accepted principles of right and wrong, trample on the rights of stakeholder groups, or simply break the law? There is no simple answer to this question, but a few generalizations can be made (see Figure 4.4).[20] First, business ethics are not divorced from personal ethics. As individuals we are taught that it is wrong and unethical to lie and cheat and that it is right to behave with integrity and honor and to stand up for what we believe to be right and true. The personal ethical code that guides our behavior comes from a number of sources, including our parents, schools, religion, and the media. Our personal ethical code exerts a profound influence on how we behave as businesspeople. An individual with a strong sense of personal ethics is less likely to behave in an unethical manner in a business setting—and in particular is less likely to engage in self-dealing and more likely to behave with integrity.

Second, many studies of unethical business behavior have concluded that businesspeople sometimes do not realize they are behaving unethically, primarily because they simply fail to ask the relevant question: Is this decision or action ethical?[21] Instead they apply a straightforward business calculus to what they perceive as a business decision, forgetting that the decision may also have an important ethical dimension. The fault here lies in processes that do not incorporate ethical considerations into business decision making. This may have been the case at Nike when managers originally decided to subcontract work to businesses in developing nations that had poor working conditions. Those decisions were probably made on the basis of good economic logic. Subcontractors may have been chosen on the basis of business variables such as cost, delivery, and product quality, and the key managers simply failed to ask how the subcontractors treated their workers. If they thought about the question at all, they probably reasoned that it was the subcontractors' concern, not theirs.

Unfortunately the climate in some businesses does not encourage people to think through the ethical consequences of business decisions. This brings us to the third cause of unethical behavior in businesses: an organizational culture that deemphasizes business ethics, reducing all decisions to purely economic factors. Author Robert Bryce has explained how the organizational culture at now-bankrupt energy company Enron was built on values that emphasized

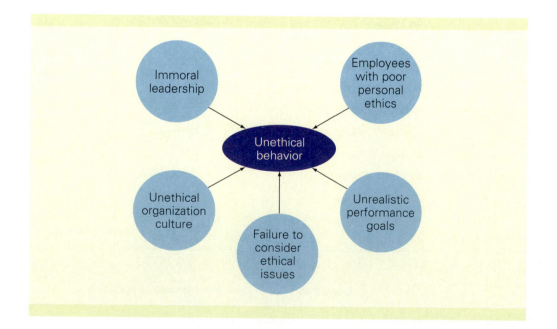

FIGURE 4.4

Roots of Unethical Behavior

greed and deception.[22] According to Bryce, the tone was set by top managers who engaged in self-dealing to enrich themselves and their own families. Bryce tells how former Enron CEO Kenneth Lay made sure his own family benefited handsomely from Enron (which is an example of self-dealing). Much of Enron's corporate travel business was handled by a travel agency partly owned by Lay's sister. When an internal auditor recommended that the company could do better by using another travel agency, he was fired. In 1997 Enron acquired a company owned by Kenneth Lay's son, Mark Lay, which was trying to establish a business trading paper and pulp products. At the time Mark Lay and another company he controlled were targets of a federal criminal investigation of bankruptcy fraud and embezzlement. As part of the deal, Enron hired Mark Lay as an executive with a three-year contract that guaranteed him at least $1 million in pay over that period, plus options to purchase about 20,000 shares of Enron. Bryce also details how Lay's grown daughter used an Enron jet to transport her king-sized bed to France. With Kenneth Lay as an example, it is perhaps not surprising that self-dealing soon became endemic at Enron. Another notable example was CFO Andrew Fastow, who set up the off–balance sheet partnerships that not only hid Enron's true financial condition from investors, but also paid tens of millions of dollars directly to Fastow (Fastow was subsequently indicted by the government for criminal fraud and went to jail).

■ Enron: Culture and ethics.

We're the Smartest Guys in the Room   Kenneth Lay and Jeff Skilling (pictured here) used to think of themselves as the smartest guys in the room. The company they built, Enron, was one of the most admired enterprises of the late 1990s—until it was revealed that the company's success was built upon systematic and massive accounting fraud.

© AFP/Getty Images.

A fourth cause of unethical behavior has already been hinted at. This is pressure from top management to meet performance goals that are unrealistic and can be attained only by cutting corners or acting in an unethical manner. Again, Bryce discusses how this may have occurred at Enron. Lay's successor as CEO, Jeff Skilling, put a performance evaluation system in place that weeded out 15 percent of "underperformers" every six months. This created a pressure-cooker culture with a myopic focus on short-term performance. Some executives and energy traders responded to that pressure by falsifying their performance (such as by inflating the value of trades) to make it look as if they were performing better than was actually the case.

The lesson from the Enron debacle is that an organizational culture can appear to legitimize behavior that society would judge as unethical, particularly when this culture is mixed with a focus on unrealistic performance goals, such as maximizing short-term economic performance no matter what the costs. In such circumstances there is a high probability that managers may violate their own personal ethics and engage in behavior that is unethical. By the same token, an organizational culture can do just the opposite and reinforce the need for ethical behavior. At Hewlett-Packard, for example, Bill Hewlett and David Packard, the company's founders, propagated a set of values known as the HP Way. These values, which shape the way business is conducted both within and by the corporation, have an important ethical component. Among other things, they stress the need for confidence in and respect for people, open communication, and concern for the individual employee.

■ Hewlett-Packard and ethics.

The Enron and Hewlett-Packard examples suggest a fifth root cause of unethical behavior: leadership. Leaders help to establish the culture of an organization, and they set an example that others follow. Other employees in a business often take their cue from business leaders; and if those leaders do not behave in an ethical manner, other employees may see this as justification for their own unethical behavior. It is not what leaders say that matters, but what they do. Enron, for example, had a code of ethics that Kenneth Lay himself often referred to; but Lay's own actions to enrich family members spoke louder than any words.

// PHILOSOPHICAL APPROACHES TO ETHICS

Soon we will discuss what steps managers can take to make sure that they and their coworkers act in an ethical manner. Before doing this, however, let's take a closer look at the philosophical underpinnings of business ethics. These theories have a practical purpose: They provide guidance that can help managers navigate their way through difficult ethical issues and make better decisions.

Utilitarian The utilitarian approach to business ethics was developed in the 18th and 19th centuries. Although it has been superseded by more modern approaches, it is also part of the tradition upon which newer approaches have been constructed. Thus it is important to review this approach.

> **utilitarian approach**
> The view that the moral worth of actions or practices is determined by their consequences.

The **utilitarian approach** to ethics holds that the moral worth of actions or practices is determined by their consequences.[23] An action is judged to be desirable if it leads to the best possible balance of good over bad consequences. Utilitarianism is committed to the maximization of good and the minimization of harm. Utilitarianism recognizes that actions have multiple consequences, some of which are good in a social sense, and some of which are harmful. As a philosophy for business ethics, it focuses attention on the need to carefully weigh all social benefits and costs of a business action and to pursue only actions that have more benefits than costs. The best decisions, from a utilitarian perspective, are those that produce the greatest good for the greatest number of people.

Many businesses have adopted specific tools, such as cost–benefit analysis and risk assessment, that are rooted in utilitarian philosophy. Managers often weigh the benefits and costs of a course of action before deciding whether to pursue it. An oil company considering drilling in Alaska must weigh the economic benefits of increased oil production and the creation of jobs against the costs of environmental degradation in a fragile ecosystem.

Utilitarian philosophy has some serious drawbacks. One problem is measuring the benefits, costs, and risks of a course of action. In the case of an oil company considering drilling in Alaska, how does one measure the potential harm to the fragile ecosystem of the region?

The second problem with utilitarianism is that the philosophy does not consider justice. The action that produces the greatest good for the greatest number of people may result in the unjust treatment of a minority. Such action cannot be ethical because it is unjust. For example, suppose that in the interests of keeping down health insurance costs, the government decides to screen people for the HIV virus and deny insurance coverage to those who are HIV positive. By reducing health costs, such action might produce significant benefits for many people; but the action is unjust because it discriminates unfairly against a minority.

> **rights theories**
> The view that human beings have fundamental rights and privileges.

Rights Theories Developed in the 20th century, **rights theories** recognize that human beings have fundamental rights and privileges. Rights establish a minimum level of morally acceptable behavior. One well-known definition of a fundamental right construes it as something that takes precedence over or "trumps" a collective good. Thus we might say that the right to free speech is a fundamental right that takes precedence over all but the most compelling collective goals; it overrides, for example, the interest of the state in civil harmony or moral consensus.[24] Moral theorists argue that fundamental human rights form the basis for the *moral compass* managers should navigate by when making decisions that have an ethical component. In a business setting, stakeholder theory provides a useful way for managers to frame any discussion of rights. As noted earlier, stakeholders have basic rights that should be respected, and it is unethical to violate those rights.

Along with rights come obligations. Because we have the right to free speech, we are also obligated to make sure we respect the free speech of others. Within the framework of a theory of rights, certain people or institutions are obligated to provide benefits or services that secure the rights of others. Such obligations also fall upon more than one class of moral agent (a moral agent is any person or institution that is capable of moral action, such as a government or corporation).

For example, in the late 1980s, to escape the high costs of toxic waste disposal in the West, several firms shipped their waste in bulk to African nations, where it was disposed of at a much lower cost. In 1987 five European ships unloaded toxic waste containing dangerous poisons in Nigeria. Workers wearing thongs and shorts unloaded the barrels for $2.50 a day and placed them in a dirt lot in a residential area. They were not told about the contents of the barrels.[25] Who bears the obligation for protecting the rights of workers and residents to safety in a case like this? According to right theorists, the obligation rests not on the shoulders of one moral agent, but on the shoulders of all moral agents whose actions might harm or contribute to the harm of the workers and residents. Thus it was the obligation not just of the Nigerian government, but also of the multinational firms that shipped the toxic waste, to make sure that it did no harm to residents and workers. In this case both the government and the multinationals apparently failed to recognize their basic obligation to protect the fundamental human rights of others.

Justice Theories **Justice theories** focus on attaining a just distribution of economic goods and services. A just distribution is one that is considered fair and equitable. One of the most influential justice theories was developed by the philosopher John Rawls.[26] Rawls asserts that all economic goods and services should be distributed equally except when an unequal distribution would work to everyone's advantage. According to Rawls, valid principles of justice are those to which all people would agree if they could freely and impartially consider the situation. Impartiality is guaranteed by a conceptual device that Rawls calls the *veil of ignorance.* Under the veil of ignorance, everyone is imagined to be ignorant of all his or her particular characteristics (such as race, sex, intelligence, nationality, family background, and special talents). Rawls then asks what system people would design under such a veil of ignorance. Rawls's answer is that under these conditions, people would unanimously agree on two fundamental principles of justice.

The first principle is that each person should be permitted the maximum amount of basic liberty compatible with similar liberty for others. Roughly speaking, Rawls takes these to be political liberty (such as the right to vote), freedom of speech and assembly, liberty of conscience and freedom of thought, the freedom and right to hold personal property, and freedom from arbitrary arrest and seizure. The second principle is that once equal basic liberty is ensured, inequality in basic social goods—such as income and wealth distribution and opportunities—is to be allowed only if it benefits everyone. Rawls accepts that inequalities can be just so long as the system that produces inequalities is to the advantage of everyone. More precisely, he formulates what he calls the *difference principle,* which says that inequalities are justified if they benefit the position of the least advantaged person. So the wide variations in income and wealth that we see in the United States can be considered just if the market-based system that produces this unequal distribution also benefits the least advantaged members of society. One can argue that a well-regulated market-based economy, by promoting economic growth, benefits the least advantaged members of society. In principle, at least, the inequalities inherent in such systems are therefore just.

In the context of business ethics, Rawls's theory creates an interesting perspective. Managers could ask themselves whether the policies they adopt would be considered just under Rawls's veil of ignorance. Is it just, for example, to pay foreign workers less than workers in the firm's home country? Rawls's theory might suggest that it is, so long as the inequality benefits the least advantaged members of the global society. Alternatively, it is difficult to imagine that managers operating under a veil of ignorance would design a system in which employees are paid subsistence wages to work long hours in sweatshop conditions and are exposed to toxic materials. Such working conditions are clearly unjust in Rawls's framework, and therefore it is unethical to adopt them. Similarly, operating under a veil of ignorance, most people would probably design a system that imparts protection from environmental

■ Violating rights: Dumping toxic waste in Nigeria.

justice theories
Theories that focus on attaining a just distribution of economic goods and services.

degradation, preserves a free and fair playing field for competition, and prohibits self-dealing. Thus in a real sense Rawls's veil of ignorance is a conceptual tool that contributes toward a moral compass that managers can use to navigate through difficult ethical dilemmas and make decisions that are ethically robust.

// BEHAVING ETHICALLY

What is the best way for managers to make sure ethical considerations are taken into account when decisions are made? In many cases there is no easy answer to this question: Many of the most vexing ethical problems arise because they contain real dilemmas and no obvious right course of action. Nevertheless, managers can and should do many things to ensure that basic ethical principles are adhered to and that ethical issues are routinely inserted into business decisions.

Here we focus on seven things that a business and its managers can do to make sure that ethical issues are considered in business decisions (see Figure 4.5):

1. Favor hiring and promoting people with a well-grounded sense of personal ethics.
2. Build an organizational culture that places a high value on ethical behavior.
3. Make sure that leaders within the business not only articulate the rhetoric of ethical behavior, but also act in a manner that is consistent with that rhetoric.
4. Put decision-making processes in place that require people to consider the ethical dimensions of business decisions.
5. Develop strong governance processes.
6. Appoint ethics officers.
7. Act with moral courage.

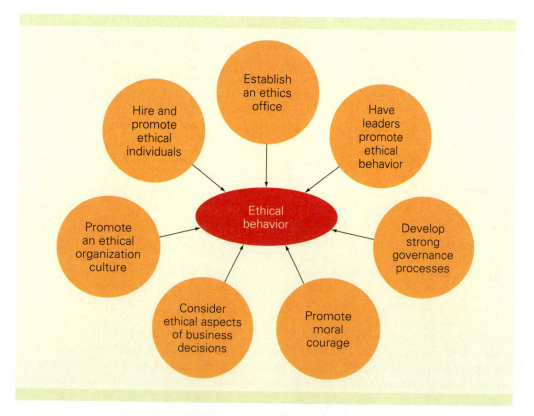

FIGURE 4.5

Building a Positive Ethical Climate

Hiring and Promotion It seems obvious that businesses should strive to hire people who have a strong sense of personal ethics and would not engage in unethical or illegal behavior. Similarly, you would rightly expect a business to not promote people, and perhaps fire people, whose behavior does not match generally accepted ethical standards. But when you think about it, doing so is difficult. How do you know that someone has a poor sense of personal ethics? In our society we have an incentive to hide a lack of personal ethics from public view. Once people realize that you are unethical, they will no longer trust you.

Is there anything businesses can do to make sure they do not hire people who subsequently turn out to have poor personal ethics? Businesses can give potential employees psychological tests to try to discern their ethical predisposition, and they can check potential employees' references. And people who have displayed poor ethics should not be promoted in a company where the organization culture places a high value on the need for ethical behavior, and where leaders act accordingly.

Not only should businesses strive to identify and hire people with a strong sense of personal ethics, but it is also in the interests of prospective employees to find out as much as they can about the ethical climate in an organization. After all, nobody should want to work at a firm like Enron.

Organizational Culture and Leadership To foster ethical behavior, businesses need to build an organizational culture that places a high value on ethical behavior. Three things are particularly important in building an organizational culture that emphasizes ethical behavior. First, businesses must explicitly articulate values that place a strong emphasis on ethical behavior. Many companies now do this by drafting a code of ethics, which is a formal statement of the ethical priorities a business adheres to. Others have incorporated ethical statements into documents that articulate the values or mission of the business. For example, the food and consumer products giant Unilever has a code of ethics that includes the following points: "We will not use any form of forced, compulsory, or child labor" and "No employee may offer, give, or receive any gift or payment that is, or may be construed as being, a bribe. Any demand for, or offer of, a bribe must be rejected immediately and reported to management."[27] Unilever's principles send a clear message about appropriate ethics to managers and employees within the organization.

■ Unilever's code of ethics.

Having articulated values in a code of ethics or some other document, it is important that business leaders give life and meaning to those words by repeatedly emphasizing their importance *and then acting on them*. This means using every relevant opportunity to stress the importance of business ethics and making sure that key business decisions not only make good economic sense but also are ethical. Many companies have gone a step further, hiring independent firms to audit the company and make sure employees are behaving in a manner consistent with their ethical code. After its experience in the 1990s, for example, Nike hired independent auditors to make sure subcontractors used by the company live up to Nike's code of conduct.

Finally, building an organizational culture that places a high value on ethical behavior requires incentive and reward systems, including promotion systems, that reward people who engage in ethical behavior and sanction those who do not. At General Electric, for example, former CEO Jack Welch has described how he reviewed the performance of managers, dividing them into several different groups. These included overperformers who displayed the right values, who were singled out for advancement and bonuses, and overperformers who displayed the wrong values, who were let go. Welch's point was that he was not willing to tolerate leaders within the company who did not act in accordance with the central values of the company, even if they were in all other respects skilled managers.[28]

Decision-Making Processes In addition to establishing the right kind of ethical culture in an organization, businesspeople must be able to think through the ethical implications of decisions in a systematic way. To do this they need a moral compass, which both rights theories and Rawls's theory of justice help to provide. Beyond these theories, some ethics experts have proposed a straightforward practical guide—an ethical algorithm—to determine whether a decision is ethical.[29] A decision is acceptable on ethical grounds if a businessperson can answer yes to each of these questions:

1. Does my decision fall within the accepted values or standards that typically apply in the organizational environment (as articulated in a code of ethics or some other corporate statement)?
2. Am I willing to see the decision communicated to all stakeholders affected by it—for example, by having it reported in newspapers or on television?
3. Would the people with whom I have a significant personal relationship, such as family members, friends, or even managers in other businesses, approve of the decision?

Ethics Officers To ensure that a business behaves in an ethical manner, a number of firms now have ethics officers. These are individuals who make sure that all employees are trained to be ethically aware, that ethical considerations enter the business decision-making process, and that the company's code of ethics is adhered to. Ethics officers may also be responsible for auditing decisions to make sure they are consistent with this code. In many businesses an ethics officer acts as an internal ombudsperson—handling confidential inquiries from employees, investigating complaints from employees or others, reporting findings, and making recommendations for change.

■ Ethics officers at United Technologies.

United Technologies, a large aerospace company with worldwide revenues of over $28 billion, has had a formal code of ethics since 1990.[30] There are now some 160 ethics officers within United Technologies who are responsible for making sure the code is adhered to. United Technologies also established an ombudsperson program in 1986 that lets employees inquire anonymously about ethics issues. The program has received some 56,000 inquiries since 1986, and 8,000 cases have been handled by an ombudsperson.

Strong Corporate Governance Strong corporate governance procedures are needed to ensure that managers adhere to ethical norms, and in particular to make sure senior managers do not engage in self-dealing or information manipulation. The key to strong corporate governance procedures is an independent board of directors that is willing to hold top managers into account for self-dealing and is able to question information provided by managers. If companies like Tyco, WorldCom, and Enron had strong boards of directors, is it unlikely that they would have been subsequently racked by accounting scandals, and top managers would not have been able to view the funds of these corporations as their own personal treasuries.

There are five foundations of strong governance. The first is a board of directors that is composed of a majority of outside directors who have no management responsibilities in the firm, who are willing and able to hold top managers accountable, and who do not have business ties with important insiders. The outside directors should be individuals of high integrity whose reputation is based on their ability to act independently. The second foundation element is a board of directors in which the positions of CEO and chairperson are held by separate individuals, and the chairperson is an outside director. When the CEO also chairs the board of directors, he or she can control the agenda, thereby furthering a personal agenda (which may include self-dealing) or limiting criticism of current corporate policies. The third foundation element is a compensation

Enforcing Ethics: Sarbanes–Oxley President Bush signs into law the Sarbanes–Oxley Act. By tightening corporate governance, the Sarbanes–Oxley law is designed to make it more difficult for managers to engage in self-dealing and information manipulation.

© AP Photo/Doug Mills.

committee of the board of directors that is composed entirely of outside directors. The compensation committee sets the level of pay for top managers, including stock option grants and the like. If the compensation committee is independent of managers, the scope for self-dealing is reduced. Fourth, the audit committee of the board, which reviews the financial statements of the firm, should also be composed of outsiders, thereby encouraging vigorous independent questioning of the firm's financial statements. Finally, the board should use outside auditors who are truly independent and do not have a conflict of interest. This was not the case in many recent accounting scandals, where the outside auditors were also consultants to the corporation and therefore were less likely to ask hard questions of management for fear that doing so would jeopardize lucrative consulting contracts. In the United States the 2002 Sarbanes–Oxley Act significantly strengthened corporate governance by legally requiring that accounting firms that audit a corporation do not also provide consulting services to the enterprise, and by requiring that CEOs affirm that a firm's financial accounts represent a true and accurate picture of a corporation.

Moral Courage It is important to recognize that on occasion managers may need significant moral courage. This enables managers to walk away from a decision that is profitable but unethical. Moral courage gives an employee the strength to say no to a superior that tells her or him to pursue actions that are unethical. And moral courage gives employees the integrity to blow the whistle on persistent unethical behavior in a company. Moral courage does not come easily—there are well-known cases in which individuals have lost their jobs because they blew the whistle on corporate behaviors they thought unethical, telling the media about what was occurring.[31]

Companies can strengthen employees' moral courage by committing themselves to not take retribution against employees who exercise moral courage, say no to superiors, or otherwise complain about unethical actions. For example, consider the following extract from Unilever's code of ethics:

■ Unilever: Giving permission to exercise moral courage.

> Any breaches of the Code must be reported in accordance with the procedures specified by the Joint Secretaries. The Board of Unilever will not criticize management for any loss of business resulting from adherence to these principles and other mandatory policies and instructions. The Board of Unilever expects employees to bring to their attention, or to that of senior management, any breach or suspected breach of these principles. Provision has been made for employees to be able to report in confidence, and no employee will suffer as a consequence, of doing so.[32]

This statement gives "permission" to employees to exercise moral courage. Companies can also set up ethics hotlines, which allow employees to anonymously register complaints with a corporate ethics officer.

Summary All of the steps discussed here can help ensure that when managers make business decisions, they are fully cognizant of the ethical implications and do not violate basic ethical precepts. But we must remember that not all ethical dilemmas have a clean and obvious solution; that is why they are dilemmas. At the end of the day, there are clearly things that managers should not do and things they should do; but there are also actions that present true dilemmas. In these cases a premium is placed on the ability of managers to make sense out of complex messy situations and make balanced decisions that are as just as possible.

■ // Social Responsibility

In addition to recognizing stakeholders and their claims, acting legally, and behaving ethically, many believe that businesses should also act in a socially responsible manner. For a business firm, **social responsibility** is a sense of obligation on the part of managers to build certain social criteria into their decision making. The concept implies that when managers within a business evaluate decisions, there should be a presumption in favor of adopting courses of

social responsibility
A sense of obligation on the part of managers to build certain social criteria into their decision making.

action that enhance the welfare of society at large. The goals selected are often quite specific: to enhance the welfare of communities in which a business is based, improve the environment, or raise the education level of employees.

// ARGUMENTS FOR SOCIAL RESPONSIBILITY

In its purest form, social responsibility can be supported for its own sake simply because it is the right way for a business to behave. Advocates of this approach assert that businesses, and particularly large successful businesses, need to give something back to the society that has made their success possible. More pragmatic are arguments that socially responsible behavior is in a firm's self-interest and can lead to better financial performance.[33] Economic actions have social consequences affecting a company's outside stakeholders. Therefore, to retain the support of these stakeholders, the company must take those social consequences into account when formulating strategies. Otherwise it may generate ill will and opposition. For example, if a community perceives a company as having an adverse impact on the local environment, it may block the company's attempts to build new facilities in the area.

The pragmatic approach, you might realize, is an extension of the stakeholder management approach that we discussed earlier in the chapter. In contrast, the purer approach emphasizing the social responsibility of successful businesses goes beyond a pragmatic stakeholder management approach to advocate that businesses should take actions to enhance the welfare of society that exceed what is necessary to maintain the support of key external stakeholders. For example, a business with a strong sense of social responsibility may invest in the community where it is located beyond the level necessary to maintain community support.

BP, one of the world's largest oil companies, is a good example of a business that has taken the notion of social responsibility to heart in recent years.[34] BP was the first oil company to

Tastes Better without the Salt   In communities near the Algerian operations of BP, the company has built four desalination plants to bring pure drinking water to local inhabitants. This is just one of the social investments undertaken by BP, one of the world's largest oil companies.

Courtesy of BP photographer Barry Halton.

accept that greenhouse gas emissions may be changing the world's climate in unpredictable and potentially harmful ways. BP embraced a goal of doing no harm to the environment—a difficult goal for an oil company because its products are a primary source of greenhouse gas emissions. Since the late 1990s BP has invested in the development of technologies designed to reduce emissions of greenhouse gases from oil-burning electric plants and from automobiles. In 1998 BP set a target of reducing the greenhouse gas emissions from its own operations by 10 percent from a 1990 baseline level by 2010. The company actually met this target in 2001, nine years ahead of schedule. Moreover, savings associated with greater fuel efficiency and reductions in the amount of gas flared or vented from its facilities achieved this reduction without raising costs.

■ BP: Social responsibility.

BP has also embraced its responsibility to the communities in which it does business and has invested in trying to improve the quality of life in those communities. In Algeria, for example, where BP is the largest foreign oil enterprise, the company has a social investment program that, among other things, has invested in facilities to improve the quality of the local water supply. In the desert community of In Salah, where groundwater supplies of drinking water were contaminated with salt, BP has built four desalination plants so that all of the town's 27,000 inhabitants can have access to 20 liters of pure water a day for drinking and cooking. Nor is this an isolated case; wherever BP does business, the company has established social investment programs both because the company believes that this is the right thing to do and because it is in BP's long-term interests to take actions that enhance its reputation. If BP is seen as a good corporate citizen in the communities where it does business, this will probably make it easier for BP to expand its operations in those communities in the future or to enter other communities.

// THE FRIEDMAN DOCTRINE

Some people argue that a business firm has no obligation to pursue social goals. Nobel laureate Milton Friedman, for one, insists that social responsibility considerations should not enter the business decision process:[35]

> There is one and only one social responsibility of business—to use its resources and engage in activities designed to increase its profits so long as it stays within the rules of the game, which is to say that it engages in open and free competition without deception or fraud.[36]

Friedman explicitly rejects the idea that businesses should undertake social expenditures beyond those mandated by law and required for the efficient running of a business. For example, he suggests that improving working conditions beyond the level required by the law *and* necessary to maximize employee productivity will reduce profits and is therefore not appropriate. His belief is that a firm should maximize its profits because that is how to maximize the returns that accrue to the owners of the firm, its shareholders. If shareholders wish to use the proceeds to make social investments, that is their right according to Friedman; but managers of the firm should not make that decision for them.

Although Friedman's position is well stated, he would probably not object to social expenditures by businesses that have positive spillover effects for the firm. For example, BP clearly derives economic benefits from the positive publicity and goodwill that result from its social investments. Beyond this, it can be argued that socially responsible behavior by businesses can change society for the better, and that all benefit from such action. For example, in the 1980s many large, successful American businesses withdrew their investments in South Africa to protest the white apartheid regime that denied political representation to people of African and Asian descent, who happened to be the vast majority of people living in South Africa. This action precipitated an economic crisis in South Africa, which was a contributing factor in the ultimate collapse of apartheid and its replacement by a democratic government. What this example illustrates is that corporations can be an instrument for social change and progress—and given this, many people believe that businesses should take social considerations into account when choosing their actions.

IN CONCLUSION WHY DOES IT MATTER?

Why should managers care about stakeholders, ethics, and social responsibility? If managers ignore the claims that stakeholders place on an organization, those stakeholders will withdraw their support, and the performance of the organization will falter. In other words, it is in managers' self-interest to take stakeholder claims into account.

There are several reasons why managers should adhere to high ethical standards. First, by doing so they can enhance their own personal reputations, which will be valuable for them in the long run. Second, considering the ethical aspects of business decisions is a good way of making sure that the rights of different stakeholder groups are respected. And third, behaving ethically is simply the right and moral thing to do. Ethical behavior should be valued for its own sake. People who behave in an ethical manner have greater self-respect, and that goes a long way toward ensuring psychological security.

Finally, managers should consider issues of social responsibility when they make business decisions because all economic decisions also have social consequences that impact stakeholders. Making socially responsible investments is thus another way of recognizing stakeholder claims and improving stakeholder relations, which benefit the firm. Moreover, as with ethical behavior, managers should take social factors into account when making business decisions because this is the right thing to do. Large corporations in particular have gained a great deal from the societies in which they do business, and it is incumbent upon them to repay those societies with social investments that improve human well-being.

MANAGEMENT CHALLENGES

1. What makes someone a stakeholder?

2. Should managers address stakeholder concerns by going beyond the steps required by the law?

3. You are the manager of a firm that outsources work to a subcontractor in India. On a site visit you discover that the subcontractor employs children between 12 and 16 years old to work long hours for low pay.

   a. Are you morally responsible for this situation?

   b. What action should you take?

   c. What if you are told that those children are breadwinners for their families, and without the work they might be forced to resort to begging, theft, or prostitution? Would that change your position? Would you do anything different to resolve the situation?

4. In 2003 it was revealed that Frank Quattrone, once a star investment banker at Credit Suisse First Boston, had been allocating shares in upcoming initial public offerings (IPOs) of technology companies to "movers and shakers" in Silicon Valley, known as the "friends of Frank," in return for the understanding that they would push future IPOs to his unit at Credit Suisse (Quattrone and Credit Suisse earned huge fees from IPO deals).[37] The shares were difficult to obtain and typically appreciated significantly immediately following the IPO. Is this behavior ethical?

5. In 2004 Boeing's CFO, Mike Sears, offered a government official, Darleen Druyun, a lucrative job at Boeing while Druyun was still involved in evaluating whether Boeing

should be awarded a $17 billion contract to build tankers for the Air Force. Boeing won the contract against strong competition from Airbus, and Druyun was subsequently hired by Boeing. Do you think the job offer may have had an impact on the Air Force decision? If you were a member of Boeing's board, would you approve of Sears's action? If you disapproved, what action would you take?

MANAGEMENT PORTFOLIO

FOR THE ORGANIZATION YOU HAVE CHOSEN TO FOLLOW:

1. Is it satisfying the claims of key stakeholders, including employees, customers, shareholders, and the general public? If so, how? If not, why not?

2. How would you characterize the ethical climate of the organization you have chosen to follow? What evidence is there to support your conclusion?

3. Find out if the organization has been the focus of any adverse ethical issues in recent years (look at historic news reports). If it has, try to determine whether this was due to the isolated actions of rogue managers or to more systemic, organizationwide problems.

4. Does the organization undertake social investments that go beyond its narrow economic self-interest? If so, what kind of investments has it made? Whom do these investments benefit? Do you approve of these investments?

CLOSING CASE WORKING CONDITIONS AT WAL-MART

When Sam Walton founded Wal-Mart, one of his core values was that if you treated employees with respect, tied their compensation to the performance of the enterprise, trusted them with important information and decisions, and provided ample opportunities for advancement, they would repay the company with dedication and hard work. For years the formula seemed to work. Employees were called "associates" to reflect their status within the company; even the lowest-paid hourly employee was eligible to participate in profit-sharing schemes and could use profit-sharing bonuses to purchase company stock at a discount from its market value; and the company made a virtue of promoting from within (two-thirds of managers at Wal-Mart started as hourly employees). At the same time Walton and his successors always demanded loyalty and hard work from employees—managers, for example, were expected to move to a new store on very short notice—and base pay for hourly workers was low. Still, as long as the upside was there, little grumbling was heard from employees.

In the last 10 years, however, the relationship between the company and its employees has been strained by a succession of lawsuits claiming that Wal-Mart pressures hourly employees to work overtime without compensating them, systematically discriminates against women, and knowingly uses contractors who hire undocumented immigrant workers to clean its stores, paying them less than minimum wage.

For example, a class action lawsuit in Washington State claims that Wal-Mart routinely (1) pressured hourly employees not to report all their time worked, (2) failed to keep true time records, sometimes shaving hours from employee logs, (3) failed to give employees full rest or meal breaks, (4) threatened to fire or demote employees who would not work off the clock, and (5) required workers to attend unpaid meetings and computer training. Moreover, the suit claims that Wal-Mart has a strict "no overtime" policy, punishing employees who work more than 40 hours a week, but that the company also gives employees more work than can be completed in a 40-hour week. The Washington suit is one of more than 30 actions that have been filed around the nation in recent years.

With regard to discrimination against women, complaints date back to 1996 when an assistant manager in a California store, Stephanie Odle, came across the W2 of a male assistant manager who worked in the same store. The W2 showed that he was paid $10,000 more than Odle. When she asked her boss to explain the disparity, she was told that her coworker had "a wife and kids to support."

When Odle, who is a single mother, protested, she was asked to submit a personal household budget. She was then granted a $2,080 raise. Subsequently Odle was fired; she claims this action was taken in retribution for her complaint. In 1998 she filed a discrimination suit against the company. Others began to file suits around the same time, and by 2004 the cases had evolved into a class action suit that covered 1.6 million current and former female employees at Wal-Mart. The suit claims that Wal-Mart did not pay female employees the same wages as their male counterparts and did not provide them with equal opportunities for promotion.

In the case of both undocumented overtime and discrimination, Wal-Mart admits to no wrongdoing. The company says that with 1.4 million employees, some problems are bound to arise; but it claims that there is no systematic, companywide effort to get hourly employees to work without pay or to discriminate against women. Indeed, the company claims that this could not be the case because hiring and promotion decisions are made at the store level.

Critics charge that although the company may have no policies that promote undocumented overtime or discrimination, the hard-driving cost containment culture of the company has created an environment where abuses can thrive. Store managers are expected to meet challenging performance goals, and in an effort to do so they may be tempted to pressure subordinates to work additional hours without pay. Similarly, company policy requiring managers to move between stores at short notice unfairly discriminates against women, who often lack the flexibility to uproot their families and move them to another state at short notice.[38]

CASE DISCUSSION QUESTIONS

1. Do you think that the values and practices that Wal-Mart founder Sam Walton articulated recognized the claims that employees, as stakeholders, have on the firm?

2. What might have changed in the ethical climate of Wal-Mart in recent years to contribute to the lawsuits by disgruntled employees?

3. Do you think Wal-Mart has an ethical problem? Is the company right to claim that with 1.4 million employees, some problems are bound to arise?

4. If you were running Wal-Mart, what steps would you take to address any potential ethical issues, particularly with regard to employees?

ENDNOTES

1. "Boycott Nike," *CBS News 48 Hours,* October 17, 1996; D. Jones, "Critics Tie Sweatshop Sneakers to 'Air Jordan,'" *USA Today,* June 6, 1996, p. 1B; S. Greenhouse, "Nike Shoe Plant in Vietnam Is Called Unsafe for Workers," *New York Times,* November 8, 1997.

2. E. Freeman, *Strategic Management: A Stakeholder Approach* (Boston: Pitman Press, 1984).

3. C.W.L. Hill and T.M. Jones, "Stakeholder–Agency Theory," *Journal of Management Studies* 29 (1992), pp. 131–54; J.G. March and H.A. Simon, *Organizations* (New York: Wiley, 1958).

4. S.L. Berman, A.C. Wicks, S. Kotha, and T.M. Jones, "Does Stakeholder Orientation Matter?" *Academy of Management Journal* 42 (1999), pp. 488–506; J. Post and L. Preston, *Redefining the Corporation: Stakeholder Management and Organization Wealth* (Palo Alto, CA: Stanford University Press, 2002).

5. Hill and Jones, "Stakeholder–Agency Theory."

6. I.C. Macmillan and P.E. Jones, *Strategy Formulation: Power and Politics* (St. Paul, MN: West, 1986).

7. J.P. Kotter and J.L. Heskett, *Corporate Culture and Performance* (New York: Free Press, 1992).

8. Freeman, *Strategic Management: A Stakeholder Approach;* E. Freeman, "The Stakeholder Approach Revisited," *Zeitschrift fur Wirtschafts* 5 (2004), pp. 228–42; Hill and Jones, "Stakeholder–Agency Theory"; Post and Preston, *Redefining the Corporation: Stakeholder Management and Organization Wealth.*

9. Sources: C.W.L. Hill, "Monsanto: Building a Life Sciences Company," in C.W.L. Hill and G.R. Jones, *Strategic Management: An Integrated Approach* (Boston: Houghton Mifflin, 2001); A. Barrett, "Rocky Ground for Monsanto?" *Business-Week,* June 12, 2000, pp. 72–76; J. Rifkin, "Perils of Unnatural Science," *Financial Times,* June 20, 1998, p. 9; J. Forster and G. Smith, "A Genetically Modified Comeback," *BusinessWeek,* December 24, 2001, pp. 60–61.

10. Sources: J. Byrne, "How Al Dunlap Self-Destructed," *BusinessWeek,* July 6, 1998, p. 58; G. DeGeorge, "Al Dunlap Revs Up His Chainsaw," *BusinessWeek,* November 25, 1996, p. 37; Staff reporter, "Exit Bad Guy," *The Economist,* June 20, 1998, p. 70; E. Pollock and M. Brannigan, "Mixed Grill: The Sunbeam Shuffle," *The Wall Street Journal,* August 19, 1998, p. A1.

11. Freeman, *Strategic Management: A Stakeholder Approach;* Freeman, "The Stakeholder Approach Revisited."

12. "Money Well Spent: Corporate Parties," *The Economist,* November 1, 2003, p. 79; M. Maremont, "Tyco Figures Will Be Jailed for at Least 7 Years," *The Wall Street Journal,* September 20, 2005, p. C1.

13. Anonymous, "Timet, Boeing Settle Lawsuit," *Metal Center News* 41 (June 2001), pp. 38–39.

14. J. Kahn, "Ruse in Toyland: Chinese Workers' Hidden Woe," *The New York Times,* December 7, 2003, pp. A1, A8.

15. P. Singer, *One World: The Ethics of Globalization* (New Haven, CT: Yale University Press, 2002).

16. G. Hardin, "The Tragedy of the Commons," *Science* 162, no. 1, pp. 243–48.

17. See N. King, "Halliburton Tells the Pentagon Workers Took Iraq Deal Kickbacks," *The Wall Street Journal,* January 23, 2004, p. A1; Anonymous, "Whistleblowers Say Company Routinely Overcharged," Reuters, February 12, 2004; and R. Gold and J.R. Wilke, "Data Sought in Halliburton Inquiry," *The Wall Street Journal,* February 5, 2004, p. A6.

18. Transparency International, *Global Corruption Report 2005,* www.transparency.org, 2005.

19. www.transparency.org.

20. S.W. Gellerman, "Why Good Managers Make Bad Ethical Choices," in *Ethics in Practice: Managing the Moral Corporation,* ed. K.R. Andrews (Harvard Business School Press, 1989).

21. D. Messick and M.H. Bazerman, "Ethical Leadership and the Psychology of Decision Making," *Sloan Management Review* 37 (Winter 1996), pp. 9–20.

22. R. Bryce, *Pipe Dreams: Greed, Ego, and the Death of Enron* (New York: Public Affairs, 2002).

23. See T.L. Beauchamp and N.E. Bowie, *Ethical Theory and Business,* 7th ed. (Upper Saddle River, NJ: Pearson Prentice-Hall, 2001), pp. 17–23.

24. T. Donaldson. *The Ethics of International Business* (Oxford: Oxford University Press, 1989).

25. Donaldson, *The Ethics of International Business.*

26. J. Rawls, *A Theory of Justice,* rev. ed. (Boston: Belknap Press, 1999; original edition 1971).

27. Unilever Web site: http://www.unilever.com/company/ourprinciples/.

28. J. Bower and J. Dial, *Jack Welch: General Electrics Revolutionary* (Harvard Business School Case # 9-394-065, April 1994).

29. For example, see R.E. Freeman and D. Gilbert, *Corporate Strategy and the Search for Ethics* (Englewood Cliffs, NJ: Prentice-Hall, 1988); T. Jones, "Ethical Decision Making by Individuals in Organizations," *Academy of Management Review* 16 (1991), pp. 366–95; and J.R. Rest, *Moral Development: Advances in Research and Theory* (New York: Praeger, 1986).

30. United Technologies Web site: http://www.utc.com/profile/ethics/index.htm.

31. C. Grant, "Whistle Blowers: Saints of Secular Culture," *Journal of Business Ethics,* September 2002, pp. 391–400.

32. Unilever Web site: http://www.unilever.com/company/ourprinciples/.

33. S.A. Waddock and S.B. Graves, "The Corporate Social Performance–Financial Performance Link," *Strategic Management Journal* 8 (1997), pp. 303–19.

34. Details can be found on BP's Web site at www.BP.com.

35. M. Friedman, "The Social Responsibility of Business Is to Increase Profits," *New York Times Magazine,* September 13, 1970. Reprinted in Beauchamp and Bowie, *Ethical Theory and Business.*

36. Friedman, "The Social Responsibility of Business Is to Increase Profits."

37. L. Himelstein, S. Hamm, and P. Burrows, "Inside Frank Quattrone's Money Machine," *BusinessWeek,* October 13, 2003, pp. 104—9.

38. Sources: S. Holt, "Wal-Mart Workers' Suit Wins Class Action Status," *The Seattle Times,* October 9, 2004, pp. E1, E4; C. Daniels, "Women v. Wal-Mart," *Fortune,* July 21, 2003, pp. 79–82; C.R. Gentry, "Off the Clock," *Chain Store Age,* February 2003, pp. 33–36; M. Grimm, "Wa-Mart Uber Alles," *American Demographic,* October 2003, pp. 38–42.

5

PLANNING AND
DECISION MAKING

LEARNING OBJECTIVES

After Reading This Chapter You Should Be Able to:

1 Describe the different levels of planning in an organization.

2 Explain the difference between strategic, tactical, operating, and unit plans.

3 Outline the value of single-use plans, standing plans, and contingency plans.

4 Describe the main components of a typical strategic planning system.

5 Identify the main pitfalls that managers encounter when engaged in formal planning processes, and describe what can be done to limit those pitfalls.

6 Discuss the major reasons for poor decisions, and describe what managers can do to make better decisions.

GROWTH is back

For 20 years Intel grew by making microprocessors, the chips that are the brains of personal computers. By the early 2000s this strategy was no longer delivering the growth Intel wanted. There were two reasons for this: The growth rate in the personal computer industry had slowed down, and Intel's main rival, AMD, was matching Intel's microprocessors on features and taking a larger market share. So the company's CEO, Paul Otellini, drafted a new strategic plan. This plan called for the company to build "platforms" of multiple chips that will work together to perform specific functions for computer users. There will be a platform for corporate computers, for home computers, for laptop computers, and for computers designed for use in the health services industry. Each platform will focus on providing utility to a specific customer set. Thus the platform for home computers will combine a microprocessor with chips and software for a wireless base station (for home networking), chips for showing digital movies, and chips for three-dimensional graphics processing (for computer games). The hope is that these platforms will allow Intel to capture more of the value going into every computer sold—and that should increase the company's growth rate.[1]

FIGURE 5.1

Main Steps of Planning

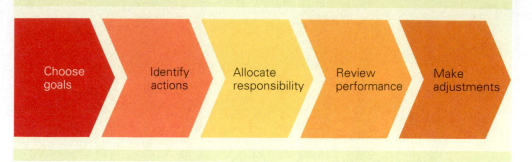

| Choose goals | Identify actions | Allocate responsibility | Review performance | Make adjustments |

planning

A process whereby managers select goals, choose actions (strategies) to attain those goals, allocate responsibility for implementing actions to specific individuals or units, measure the success of actions by comparing actual results against the goals, and revise plans accordingly.

■ Planning at Intel.

As the Intel story illustrates, planning is a primary function of management. **Planning** is a process whereby managers select goals, choose actions (strategies) to attain those goals, allocate responsibility for implementing actions to specific individuals or units, measure the success of actions by comparing actual results against the goals, and revise plans accordingly (see Figure 5.1). In other words, it is a structured process for making important decisions. A plan can provide direction for an organization. It tells everybody what the organization is trying to do, what its priorities are, where it is going, and how it is going to get there. It is a process for marshalling resources and deciding who should do what—for allocating roles, responsibilities, and money. It is also a control mechanism: By comparing actual results against the plan, managers can determine whether the organization is attaining its goals and make adjustments if required.

For example, as part of his plan, Otellini decided to reorganize Intel into four market-focused divisions, allocating specific roles, responsibilities, and resources to each division. One division will develop a platform for corporate computers, another for home computers, another for laptop computers, and a fourth for computers targeted at health services. Going forward, Otellini can compare the performance of each division against its specific goals and make necessary adjustments. If the top manager of the laptop computer division brilliantly executes the plan, he or she may receive a big performance bonus and become a leading candidate to replace Otellini when he retires. If the home computer division stumbles in its efforts to develop a platform, Otellini may allocate more engineering resources to the unit while simultaneously altering the senior management of the unit. In this way the plan becomes a control mechanism for managing the business.

In this chapter we look closely at the nature of planning and its benefits as a process for making strategic decisions and controlling the organization. We will discover that planning has limitations. Not everything can be planned for. The world has a way of rendering even the best plans obsolete. Things happen that cannot be easily predicted, and good ideas about strategy can emerge without planning. Moreover, planning processes are far from perfect. Many spectacular strategic failures have been based on supposedly comprehensive planning. Often these mistakes are due to a failure by managers to effectively use the information at their disposal. In other words, poor decision making is a major reason for planning blunders. Thus in this chapter we also look at the nature of managerial decision making. We identify common errors in decision making, and we discuss how managers can avoid these. We begin by looking more closely at the nature of planning within organizations and at the components of a typical plan.

■ // Planning within Organizations

The plans managers formulate within an organization can be differentiated by the levels in the organization to which the plans apply (strategic or operational plans), the time horizon of the plans (short-term or long-term), the number of times the plans are used (standing plans versus single-use plans), and the contingent nature of the plans. We consider each of these dimensions in turn.

// LEVELS OF PLANNING

Planning is performed at multiple levels within an organization. Planning starts at the top of an organization with a **strategic plan**, which outlines the major goals of the organization and the organizationwide strategies for attaining those goals. In complex organizations, such as a large diversified corporation with multiple business units, there may be three layers of strategic planning. Planning at the corporate level focuses on corporate-level strategy; plans made at the business level focus on business-level strategy; and planning done at the operating level focuses on operational strategy. **Corporate-level strategy** is concerned with deciding which industries a firm should compete in and how the firm should enter or exit industries. **Business-level strategy** is concerned with deciding how the firm should compete in the industries in which it has elected to participate. **Operating strategy** is concerned with the actions that should be taken at the level of individual functions, such as production, logistic, R&D, and sales, to support business-level strategy. (We look in detail at corporate, business, and operating strategies in subsequent chapters.) Normally an operating plan is embedded within a business-level strategic plan, and in turn that is embedded within the corporate-level strategic plan.

For illustration consider 3M, which is a large diversified company with over 5,000 different products, ranging from Post-it notes and Scotch tape to LCD display screens and surgical dressings. It is organized into more than 40 different business units that collectively generate over $20 billion in sales. Within a firm of this scale and scope, strategic planning takes place at multiple levels. At the corporate level, the CEO and his or her direct reports set overall goals for the organization, choose corporate-level strategies that span the entire organization, and allocate responsibility for implementing those strategies. Recently 3M has operated with a goal of increasing profits by 12–14 percent per year. The plan for attaining that goal includes a number of strategies, such as requiring all business units to implement programs to improve their productivity, making strategic acquisitions to strengthen the competitive position of 3M, and focusing R&D dollars on product development projects that are likely to produce big breakthroughs and result in substantial sales revenues and profits.[2]

At the business level, such as 3M's office supplies division, which makes Post-it notes and Scotch tape among other products, the business-level strategic plan details the specific actions that will be taken by this unit to attain the goals of the business and establish a competitive advantage. These might include, for example, developing new products, exiting product lines that are not performing well, and taking actions to rationalize its supply chain.

Embedded within business-level strategic plans are **operating plans**, which specify the goals for individual functions, the actions they will take to attain these goals, and who is responsible for those actions. Within 3M's medical division there may be an operating plan to develop a new product—let's say sterile surgical drapes coated with a substance that acts as an antibiotic. The plan may contain goals relating to development time and costs and assign responsibility to a team drawn from research and development, marketing, and manufacturing to develop the drapes and launch the product. In the same division, manufacturing personnel might develop an operating plan for reducing inventory costs. The plan will have a goal—perhaps to reduce inventory costs by 20 percent—and assign responsibility to specific individuals to attain that goal. Similarly, human resource personnel might develop an operating plan for hiring a sales force to sell a new product the division has developed; information systems personnel might develop an operating plan for using the Internet and e-business software to coordinate the supply chain of the division; marketing personnel might develop an operating plan for promoting the products of the division to consumers to enhance the 3M brand and grow revenues and profits.

Planning might not stop here; embedded within operating plans might be **unit plans**, which are plans for departments within functions, work teams, or even individuals. Within the manufacturing function in 3M's office supplies division, for example, a quality assurance department could draw up its own unit plan for improving quality in the division's manufacturing process. Similarly, within the R&D function of the same division several teams of researchers may be focusing on the development of different technologies; each team will draw up its own unit plan that specifies goals, actions, responsibilities, and resource requirements.

strategic plan
A plan that outlines the major goals of an organization and the organizationwide strategies for attaining those goals.

corporate-level strategy
Strategy concerned with deciding which industries a firm should compete in and how the firm should enter or exit industries.

business-level strategy
Strategy concerned with deciding how a firm should compete in the industries in which it has elected to participate.

operating strategy
Strategy concerned with the actions that should be taken at the level of individual functions, such as production, logistic, R&D, and sales, to support business-level strategy.

operating plans
Plans that specify goals, actions, and responsibility for individual functions.

■ Planning at 3M.

unit plans
Plans for departments within functions, work teams, or individuals.

FIGURE 5.2

Levels of Planning

In sum, unit plans are embedded within operating plans, operating plans are embedded within business-level strategic plans, and business-level strategic plans are embedded within corporate-level strategic plans (see Figure 5.2). Embedded means that higher-level plans set the context for lower-level plans. Thus at 3M the corporate-level plan calls for productivity improvement programs to be rolled out across 3M; the plan of a business division outlines how that is being done within that division; the plan of a function describes how productivity is being improved within the function; and the plan of a department says how that is being done within the department. At the same time, higher-level plans are not formulated in a vacuum; they are formulated after consultation with lower-level managers. When the CEO at 3M decides how to allocate development funds to projects within 3M, he or she does so only after consulting extensively with the managers responsible for those projects and the business and functional levels. Similarly, business-level managers decide which productivity improvement projects to pursue within their divisions only after consultation with functional and department managers.

// PLANNING HORIZONS

planning horizon

How far out a plan is meant to apply.

The **planning horizon** refers to how far out a plan is meant to apply. Most strategic plans, whether at the business or corporate level, are multiyear plans. They are meant to stay in place for several years (a three- to five-year horizon is typical). If successful, Paul Otellini's plan for Intel, which we discussed earlier, will drive strategy at the company for years to come. Indeed, it would be dangerous to change strategic plans frequently: This would confuse important stakeholders such as employees, suppliers, customers, and investors about the direction of the organization, and they might lose confidence in top management.

There is an exception to the generalization that strategic plans are long-term plans. Organizations sometimes adopt short-term plans to address specific and transitory opportunities or threats. Such short-term plans are known as *tactical plans,* which are plans for pursuing transitory competitive tactics. **Tactical plans** outline the actions managers must adopt over the short to medium term to cope with a specific opportunity or threat that has emerged. For example, when Lilly-ICOS, a pharmaceutical company, launched its new drug Cialis for erectile dysfunction in 2004, the firm found it difficult to gain share against the market leader, Viagra, even though Cialis worked for up to 36 hours, compared to just 4 hours for Viagra. So in mid-2004 managers at Lilly-ICOS came up with a tactical plan to get men to try Cialis. The plan was to roll out a program known as the Cialis Promise. Under this program, men with erectile dysfunction could receive a voucher for a free trial. If they liked Cialis, they could get

tactical plans

The actions managers adopt over the short to medium term to deal with a specific opportunity or threat that has emerged.

■ ICOS: Tactical planning.

a second trial for no charge. If they were not satisfied with Cialis, ICOS committed itself to pay for a competing erectile dysfunction drug (such as Viagra). The idea behind this tactic was to get men to switch from Viagra to Cialis. It seems to have worked—the market share of Cialis doubled to 25 percent in a year.

Operating and unit plans tend to have shorter time horizons than strategic plans. Whereas an organization might function with the same basic strategic plan for years, operating and unit plans might change regularly as the tasks outlined in them are completed and managers turn their attention to the next task. For example, it may take only six months to implement and complete a productivity improvement program identified in an operating or unit plan at 3M, so next year that program will not be in the plan, although it may be replaced by another one. Moreover, operating and unit plans often drive the annual budgeting process at organizations, so they have to be revisited annually.

In sum, strategic plans normally have a three- to five-year time horizon, although an organization could in theory pursue the same strategy for much longer. Tactical plans typically have a short-term horizon (often less than a year) and are adopted to deal with emerging and transitory opportunities and threats. Operating and unit plans tend to have short to medium time horizons (one to three years) because they address specific tasks that have a well-defined beginning and end. But there are exceptions to these generalizations. An organization might be forced to change its strategic plan after a year if it clearly is not working, and an operating plan may be in place for more than five years if its specific tasks take that long.

Beating Viagra—The Cialis Promise   To take market share from Viagra, ICOS adopted the Cialis Promise program. This tactical plan seems to have worked—Cialis doubled its market share to 25 percent in a year, largely at the expense of Viagra.

© Sonda Dawes/The Image Works.

// SINGLE-USE PLANS AND STANDING PLANS

In addition to level and time horizon, plans can be differentiated by their frequency of use. Some plans are **single-use plans**: They address unique events that do not reoccur—they are plans for attaining a one-time goal. For example, in 2002 the Boeing Corporation decided to move its corporate headquarters from Seattle, where they had been since the company was founded, to Chicago. The decision involved the relocation of 330 employees, primarily senior managers and their support staff, and Boeing had to create a single-use plan to execute this move as quickly and seamlessly as possible. Once the move was completed, however, the plan was obviously no longer needed. Other cases of single-use plans include plans for converting office files from paper to digital format, plans for establishing an organizationwide intranet, or plans for rebranding an organization and rolling out a new corporate name and logo.

In contrast, **standing plans** are used to handle events that reoccur frequently. The idea behind standing plans is to save managers time by giving them a playbook to which they can refer when a certain type of event occurs. Standing plans relieve

Yet Another Starbucks Store
Starbucks has been able to open stores at a rapid rate because it has a standing plan that outlines the steps required to identify a suitable location and open a store.

© The McGraw-Hill Companies, Inc. /Jill Braaten, photographer.

single-use plans
Plans that address unique events that do not reoccur.

■ Boeing: Single-use plans.

standing plans
Plans used to handle events that reoccur frequently.

managers from having to reinvent wheels. One reason why Starbucks has been able to grow from just 17 stores in 1987 to almost 9,000 stores by 2005 is that managers developed a standing plan that outlines the steps required to find the best store locations, ensure that the stores have the same look and feel as other Starbucks stores, and open stores quickly. But standing plans like these are not rigid. Intelligent managers recognize that no plan is perfect, and they use their cumulative experience to fine-tune standing plans, improving them over time.

// CONTINGENCY PLANNING

Many organizations are based in environments characterized by considerable uncertainty and the possibility that certain events might require a rapid response or an overall change of strategy. To anticipate such events, managers might formulate contingency plans. **Contingency plans** are plans formulated to address specific possible future events that might have a significant impact on the organization. There are two types of contingency plans: crisis management plans and scenario plans.

contingency plans
Plans formulated to address specific possible future events that might have a significant impact on the organization.

crisis management plan
Plan formulated specifically to deal with possible future crises.

Crisis Management Planning A *crisis* is a discrete event that can have a severe negative impact on an organization or its stakeholders. A **crisis management plan** is a plan formulated specifically to deal with possible future crises.[3] In the wake of the September 11, 2001, terrorist attacks on the United States—an obvious crisis if ever there was one—a number of government organizations drew up crisis management plans that detailed how they would respond to specific terrorist incidents, including the deliberate release of biological pathogens (such as smallpox or anthrax) or chemicals (such as sarin gas). One of the companies experiencing the largest loss of life on September 11 was the bond trading company Cantor Fitzgerald, which occupied the top floors of one of the destroyed twin towers. Nearly 700 of its 1,000 U.S. employees died that day. Yet the company was able to resume business almost immediately because after the 1993 bombing of the World Trade Center, the company had formulated a crisis management plan that included backup computer systems in New Jersey.[4]

Crises take many different forms—from terrorist attacks and industrial disasters, such as the gas leak from a Union Carbide plant in Bhopal, India, that killed almost 4,000 people to natural disasters like the December 26, 2004, tsunami that devastated parts of Southeast Asia and left 180,000 people dead. Drafting a plan to effectively manage a crisis involves three main steps: prevention, preparation, and containment.[5]

The best way of dealing with a crisis is to *prevent* it from happening in the first place if possible. In the wake of the September 11, 2001, attacks the U.S. government took a number of steps to prevent future terrorist attacks, including creating the Department of Homeland Security and implementing new regulations for screening passengers and baggage at airports. Another prevention tactic is to build positive relationships with key stakeholders, such as customers, suppliers, investors, and communities. These relationships can act as an early warning system, providing managers with information about an impending crisis. In some cases quick action can avert an impending crisis or limit its impact.

Not all crises can be prevented. Nobody could have predicted or stopped the December 26, 2004, tsunami. So managers need to plan for such events. This is the *preparation* stage of a crisis management plan. Preparation requires an organization to designate a crisis management team and a spokesperson that will cope with crises that arise. Preparation also requires a detailed plan of the steps that will be taken to deal with the crisis, to coordinate crisis management efforts, to manage its aftermath, and to communicate important information to affected people and organizations.

Mt. Rainier, the heavily glaciated volcano in Washington State, is a place of staggering beauty; but it is also one of the most dangerous volcanoes in the world. An eruption, an earthquake, or simple weakening of rock caused by erosion could trigger a massive mudslide known as a *lahar* that could sweep a wave of debris 100 feet high at 50 miles an hour down valleys where 100,000 people live. To limit the effects of such a crisis, managers at the U.S. Geological Survey and Washington State government agencies have prepared a

Beautiful—and Very Dangerous Mt. Rainer looms over surrounding communities. To deal with the impact of a potential lahar, Washington State has a crisis management plan in place.
© Ken Straiton/Corbis.

detailed plan that includes a crisis management team, a permanent lahar detection system and emergency communication systems, plans for rapid evacuation of towns in the path of a lahar, regular evacuation training for schools, establishment of shelters for the displaced, and procedures for search and rescue. Although a lahar cannot be prevented, these preparations are designed to limit the loss of human life associated with such a cataclysmic event.

Finally, there is the *containment* stage of crisis management. Containment is concerned with the steps that need to be taken after a crisis has occurred to limit its effects; these actions need to be part of the overall crisis management plan. Containment involves (1) rapid response to limit the immediate effects of the crisis; (2) communication because the truth will emerge anyway, and plenty of evidence suggests it is better to face reality immediately rather than try to deny that a crisis is occurring; (3) meeting the needs of those affected by the crisis; and (4) returning to business as rapidly as possible. The classic example of successful containment of a crisis is the response of Tylenol maker Johnson & Johnson to a crisis that arose when four people died after taking cyanide-laced Tylenol capsules. Even though the capsules were tampered with after the Tylenol had left the factory, the company immediately recalled all Tylenol and stopped making the product until it had redesigned the product packaging to minimize the risk of future tampering. This quick action cost Johnson & Johnson some sales, but it enhanced the company's reputation and quickly rebuilt consumer confidence in the safety of the product.

Scenario Planning Scenario planning is based on the realization that the future is inherently unpredictable and that an organization should plan for a range of possible futures. **Scenario planning** involves formulating plans that are based on "what if" scenarios. In the typical scenario planning exercise, some scenarios are optimistic and some pessimistic. Teams of managers are asked to develop specific strategies to cope with each scenario. A set of indicators is chosen as "signposts" to track trends and identify the probability that any particular scenario is coming to pass. The idea is to get managers to understand the dynamic and complex nature of their environment, to think through problems in a strategic fashion, and to generate a range of strategic options that might be pursued under different circumstances.[6]

scenario planning
Plans that are based on "what if" scenarios about the future.

FIGURE 5.3

Scenario Planning

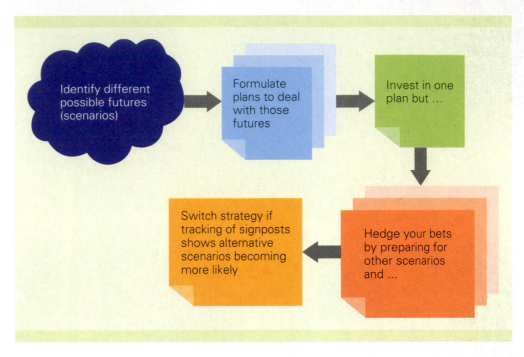

■ Royal Dutch Shell: Crisis planning.

The scenario approach to planning has spread rapidly among large companies. One survey found that over 50 percent of *Fortune* 500 companies use some form of scenario planning methods.[7]

The oil company Royal Dutch Shell has perhaps done more than most to pioneer the concept of scenario planning, and its experience demonstrates the power of the approach.[8] Shell has been using scenario planning since the 1980s. Today the firm uses two main scenarios to refine its strategic planning. The scenarios relate to future demand for oil. One ("Dynamics as Usual") sees a gradual shift from carbon fuels such as oil and natural gas to renewable energy. The second scenario ("The Spirit of the Coming Age") looks at the possibility that a technological revolution will lead to a rapid shift to new energy sources.[9] Shell is making investments that will ensure the profitability of the company in either scenario, and it is carefully tracking technological and market trends.

The great virtue of the scenario approach to planning is that it can push managers to think creatively, to anticipate what they might have to do in different situations, and to learn that the world is a complex and unpredictable place that places a premium on flexibility. As a result of scenario planning, organizations might pursue one dominant strategy related to the scenario that is judged to be most likely while making some investments that will pay off if other scenarios occur (see Figure 5.3). Thus the current strategy of Shell is based on the assumption that the world will only gradually shift away from carbon-based fuels; but the company is also hedging its bets by investing in new energy technologies and mapping out a strategy to pursue should its second scenario come to pass.

■ // Strategic Planning: A Closer Look

As noted earlier, most plans within an organization are embedded within the overall strategic plan of the enterprise. Strategic plans form the context within which operating and unit plans are formulated. Because strategic planning is such an important activity, here we examine the steps involved in formulating and implementing a strategic plan and how that plan drives operating and unit plans. Figure 5.4 charts what can be viewed as an archetypal strategic planning process.[10]

The process starts with a statement of the mission, vision, values, and goals of an organization. Then it moves on to an analysis of the external operating environment and the internal environment of the organization. As noted in Chapter 2, the aim here is to identify

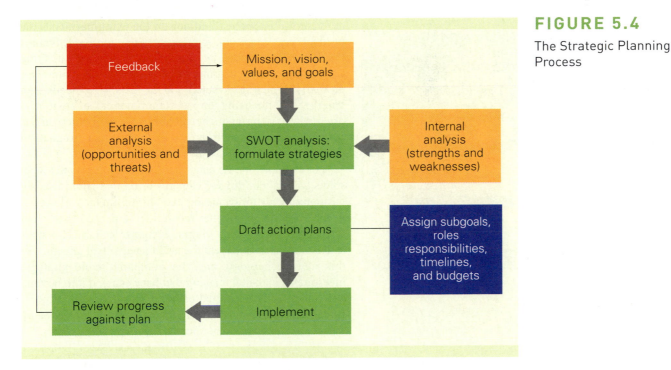

FIGURE 5.4
The Strategic Planning
Process

the strengths and weaknesses of the organization and the opportunities and threats in the external environment. Next, in a process known as *SWOT analysis,* managers choose strategies. The aim is to select strategies that are consistent with the vision, values, and goals of the organization and that exploit environmental opportunities, counter threats, build on organizational strengths, and correct weaknesses. Then managers draft action plans. **Action plans** specify with precision how strategies will be put into effect; they include subgoals, responsibilities, timelines, and budgets. Action plans are drafted at the business level, operating level, and unit level within functions. In other words, *each strategic, operating, and unit plan should have a component that is an action plan.* Once action plans have been drafted and agreed on, they are implemented. The process does not stop here, however; planning is also a control mechanism. Thus managers compare actual performance against the plan, and through a feedback process make necessary adjustments to goals and strategies. Planning, in other words, is an iterative process in which plans are adjusted over time in response to new information. Next we take a closer look at each of these elements.

action plans
Plans that specify with precision how strategies will be put into effect.

// SETTING THE CONTEXT: MISSION, VISION, VALUES, AND GOALS

The mission, vision, values, and goals of an organization are the starting points of strategic planning. They set the context for the rest of the process and for the operating and unit plans that are embedded within a strategic plan.

Mission The **mission** of an organization describes its purpose. For example, the mission of Kodak is to provide "customers with the solutions they need to capture, store, process, output, and communicate images—anywhere, anytime."[11] This mission focuses on the customer needs that Kodak is trying to satisfy (the need for imaging) as opposed to the products the company currently produces (film and cameras). Kodak's mission statement is a *customer-oriented* mission statement, not a *product-oriented* one.

There is general agreement that a good mission statement focuses on the *customer needs* an organization is satisfying rather than the goods or services it is producing.[12] A product-oriented mission statement, which focuses on the attributes of the products

mission
The purpose of an organization.

■ Kodak: Mission statement.

Mission Fulfilled Kodak's mission helped to take the company into digitized imaging.

© Used with permission of Eastman Kodak Company.

delivered to customers and not on the customer needs the products are satisfying, is inherently dangerous. It ignores the fact that there may be more than one way of satisfying a particular set of customer needs, and that over time new products, which do a better job of satisfying needs, can emerge. By focusing on customer needs, a customer-oriented mission statement can help an organization anticipate changes in its environment and adopt new products to satisfy those needs.

For example, for the better part of a hundred years Kodak sold silver halide film and cameras using that film to satisfy customer needs for capturing and storing images. However, in the early 1990s another technology emerged that could satisfy those same needs—digital imaging. Kodak's customer-oriented mission statement focused management attention on this new technology, and the company made strategic investments in digital imaging that have enabled it to become a major provider of digital cameras and imaging software. Kodak's mission helped it to adopt a new product technology that better served customer needs.

vision

A desired future state.

Vision The **vision** of an organization articulates a desired future state; it describes, often in bold, evocative, and succinct terms, what the management of an organization would like to achieve. The vision of Ford is "to become the world's leading consumer company for automotive products and services." This vision is challenging: Judged by size Ford is currently the world's number three company behind General Motors and Toyota. Attaining this vision will be a stretch for Ford—but that is the point. Good vision statements are meant to stretch a company by articulating some ambitious but attainable future state that will help to energize and motivate employees at all levels in the organization and unite them in a common purpose.[13] A good vision can help employees make sense out of the organization's strategy. The vision tells them what the strategy is meant to achieve.

A good vision can also generate strategies by communicating to employees what the ultimate goal of a strategy should be and motivating them to search for and formulate strategies that help to attain that goal. For example, at General Electric under the leadership of its legendary former CEO, Jack Welch, the vision was simple yet clear: GE was to be number one or number two in every major business in which it competed. Welch did not tell the managers heading GE's various divisions what strategies they should pursue—that was left up to them; rather, by articulating a clear and compelling vision Welch helped set the context for strategy formulation at the business level. He in effect told his managers, "Whatever strategies you pursue, they should enable your business unit to become number one or two in your market."

values

The philosophical priorities to which managers are committed.

Values The **values** of an organization state the philosophical priorities to which managers are committed. Values outline how managers and employees should conduct themselves, how they should do business, and what kind of enterprise they should build to help the organization attain its mission and vision. Given that they help shape behavior within an organization, values can help to determine an organization's culture, which as you might recall from Chapter 2 refers to the basic pattern of shared values and assumptions adopted by employees within an organization. The culture of a business organization can be an important source of competitive advantage, and because values shape this, they are extremely important.[14] (We discuss the issue of organizational culture in depth in Chapter 10.) For

■ Nucor Steel: Values.

example, Nucor Steel is one of the most profitable steel firms in the world. Its competitive advantage is based in part on the extremely high productivity of its workforce, which, the company maintains, is a direct result of its cultural values that influence how employees are treated at Nucor:

- "Management is obligated to manage Nucor in such a way that employees will have the opportunity to earn according to their productivity."
- "Employees should be able to feel confident that if they do their jobs properly, they will have a job tomorrow."
- "Employees have the right to be treated fairly and must believe that they will be."
- "Employees must have an avenue of appeal when they believe they are being treated unfairly."[15]

Nucor's values emphasizing pay for performance, job security, and fair treatment for employees help create an egalitarian culture within the company that leads to high employee productivity. In turn this has given Nucor one of the lowest cost structures in the steel industry, which helps explain the company's profitability in a very price-competitive business.

Goals After the mission, vision, and key values of the organization have been stated, the final step in setting the context for strategic planning is to establish organizationwide goals. A **goal** is a desired future state that an organization attempts to realize. In this context the purpose of goals is to specify exactly what must be done so the company can attain its mission and vision. Well-constructed goals have four main characteristics:[16]

1. They are *precise* and *measurable.* Measurable goals give managers a yardstick or standard against which they can judge their performance.

2. They *address important issues.* To maintain focus, managers should select a few major goals to assess the performance of the company. The selected goals should address crucial issues.

3. They are *challenging but realistic.* They give all employees an incentive to look for ways to improve the performance of the organization. If a goal is unrealistic, employees may give up; but a goal that is too easy may fail to motivate managers and other employees.[17]

4. They *specify a time period* in which they should be achieved. Time constraints tell employees that success requires a goal to be attained by a given date. Deadlines can inject a sense of urgency into goal attainment and act as a motivator. However, not all goals require time constraints.

> **goal**
>
> A desired future state that an organization attempts to realize.

Well-constructed goals also provide a means by which to assess strategy effectiveness and evaluate the performance of managers.

Most business organizations establish goals for profitability and profit growth. Thus a company might aim for attaining at least a 10 percent return on invested capital (a key measure of profitability) and growing profits at 15 percent per year. However, managers must not make the mistake of overemphasizing current profitability to the detriment of long-term profitability and profit growth.[18] The overzealous pursuit of current profitability to maximize short-term performance can encourage such misguided managerial actions as cutting expenditures judged as nonessential in the short run—for instance, expenditures for research and development, marketing, and new capital investments. Although cutting current spending increases current profitability, the resulting underinvestment, lack of innovation, and diminished marketing can jeopardize long-term profitability and growth. These expenditures are vital if a company is to pursue its long-term mission and sustain its competitive advantage and profitability. But managers may make such decisions because the adverse effects of a short-term orientation may not materialize and become apparent to shareholders for several years or because they are under extreme pressure to hit short-term profitability goals.[19]

To guard against such behavior, managers need to adopt goals whose attainment will increase the long-term performance and competitiveness of their enterprise. Long-term goals emphasize specific targets concerning such things as productivity, product quality, customer satisfaction, employee satisfaction, and innovation. The idea here is that if managers take actions that, for example, boost productivity, in the long run that will lead to \\ lower costs and higher profitability, even if it requires sacrificing some profits today to support higher investments in productivity-enhancing technologies. To do this, it is often recommended that managers adopt a *balanced scorecard* of goals that couple traditional financial measures (such as profitability) with goals linked to customer satisfaction, the efficiency of internal processes, and innovation. (We discuss the balanced scorecard approach in more detail in Chapter 9.)[20]

// EXTERNAL AND INTERNAL ANALYSIS

Having set the context for strategic planning by defining the mission, vision, values, and major goals of the organization, the next step in the strategic planning process is to analyze the environment of the organization. Two distinct environments are looked at: the external environment within which the organization operates and the organization's own internal environment. Managers must analyze the organization's external environment—including the task (or industry) environment in which it competes and the general environment—for opportunities and threats. (We reviewed the external and internal environments in Chapter 2.) Opportunities arise when competitive or general environmental trends create enhanced potential for the organization to attain its vision and associated goals. For example, deregulation of the U.S. telecommunications industry in 1996 created an opportunity for phone companies to merge with each other and offer an expanded range of services (for example, before 1996 local phone companies could not offer long-distance service). In addition, around the same time two new technologies entered the mainstream: wireless telephony and high-bandwidth Internet access via digital subscriber line (DSL) technology. These two changes created enormous opportunities for phone companies to expand their services. Thus by 2005 Verizon, which was formed by the merger of two local telephone companies in 2000, was also offering Internet access via DSL service, long-distance telephone service, and wireless service.

Threats arise when competitive or general environmental trends make it more difficult for an organization to attain its vision and associated goals. This can also be illustrated by considering the telecommunications industry in the United States. Despite all the opportunities created by deregulation and technological change, these trends also created distinct threats. The entry of new enterprises into the wireless market depressed prices and made it difficult to make a profit. Moreover, new technologies have made it possible for cable companies (not traditionally a competitor) to offer phone service and Internet access over TV cables, enabling companies such as Comcast and Time Warner to emerge as potent competitors to established telephone companies such as Verizon. The resulting increase in competition has put pressure on prices and profits.

■ Verizon: Environmental analysis and strategy.

Having analyzed the external environment for opportunities and threats, managers should look inside the organization and identify its strengths and weaknesses. A strength is an activity the organization is good at and is a potential source of competitive advantage. A weakness is an activity the organization does not excel at; it may be a source of competitive disadvantage. At Verizon's wireless business, for example, the quality of its telephone service and the excellence of its customer service are seen as strengths that have helped the company outperform rivals.[21]

// SWOT ANALYSIS: FORMULATING STRATEGIES

Once managers have identified the strengths, weakness, opportunities, and threats that confront their organization, they use a SWOT analysis to list these and then start the process of choosing strategies. The goal at this stage is to formulate strategies at the corporate, business, and operating levels that build on organization strengths, correct weaknesses, use strengths to exploit opportunities in the environment, and block threats so the organization can execute its mission, realize its vision, meet or beat its major goals, and do so in a manner that is consistent with its values.

The strategies identified through a SWOT analysis should be congruent with each other. Operating strategies should be consistent with the business-level strategy of the company. Moreover, as we will see in the next chapter, corporate-level strategies should support business-level strategies. Thus as a result of a SWOT analysis, managers should have identified a set of corporate, business, and operating strategies that support each other and enable the organization to attain its goals. The trick now is to put those strategies into action!

// ACTION PLANS

As noted earlier, action plans specify precisely how corporate-level, business-level, and operating strategies will be put into effect. Action plans should include subgoals, responsibilities, time lines, and financial budgets. Consider again the case of Verizon Wireless. A key Verizon strategy has been to differentiate its service by superior geographical coverage. To put this strategy into action, Verizon had to build more cell towers than its competitors (so its wireless signal would cover a larger geographical area, resulting in fewer dropped calls). An action item of this strategic plan might therefore have given operations managers in Illinois, for example, a subgoal of adding 100 cell towers in the state within a year. Responsibility for hitting this goal might have been assigned to a particular individual; let's call her Allison Jones, vice president for operations in Illinois. Jones would have been given a budget containing sufficient funds to achieve this objective. In practice, Verizon would have had similar action plans for every state where it offered service. Action plans thus turn broad statements of strategic intent into concrete actions that have to be undertaken within a given period. Action plans are where strategic planning gets practical.

■ Verizon Wireless: Action plans.

// IMPLEMENTATION

Once action plans have been drawn up and all members of the organization know what they are supposed to do to execute the strategy, it is on to implementation. At the most basic level, **strategy implementation** consists of putting action plans into effect. At a higher level of abstraction, however, strategy implementation also requires that the enterprise have the right kind of organization structure, incentives, control systems, and culture, as well as the right mix of people. Put differently, strategy is implemented by people, but the way that people work is influenced by the internal organization of the enterprise. (We discuss internal organization architecture in depth in Chapter 8.)

Again consider Verizon Wireless; making sure that Allison Jones, the VP for operations in Illinois, performs up to her potential might require Verizon to create positive incentives for Jones. Thus her annual bonus might be determined in part by how well her unit executes its action plan. Moreover, to let Jones work quickly and make decisions that are appropriate for her unit, Verizon might decentralize all relevant operating decisions concerning the building out of cell towers in Illinois to Jones. Jones's boss, in other words, would leave it up to her to determine a precise schedule for building cell towers and let her decide where the towers should be placed. The design of incentive systems and decisions concerning the decentralization of operating responsibilities are both aspects of the organization architecture of Verizon. In this example higher-level managers at Verizon are adjusting the company's internal organization architecture to create an internal environment in which Jones is most likely to meet the goals outlined in her unit's action plan. More generally, this is what higher-level managers do: They make decisions about the structure, incentives, controls, culture, and people of the organization in an attempt to create an internal environment that best supports lower-level managers and employees in their quest to implement action plans.

strategy implementation
Putting action plans into effect.

// REVIEW AND ADJUSTMENTS

The final step in the strategic planning process is to periodically review actual performance against the plan and make any needed adjustments. A plan can be viewed as a control mechanism. If parts of an organization (or the entire organization) do not reach the goals outlined in the plan, senior managers will start to ask questions and seek an explanation for the variance between the plan and actual results. Once they understand why the variance is occurring, they may take corrective action to reach the plan; they may decide the plan itself needs tuning; or in extreme situations, they may decide that the plan needs to be scrapped and a new plan formulated. Thus if the unit headed by Allison Jones at Verizon does not attain the goals outlined in the plan, her boss will start to ask questions. Imagine that after investigation, Jones's boss discovers that Jones has been playing a lot of golf and not putting much time in at work. Jones may be replaced by someone who has a greater appetite for work. Alternatively, Jones may have been working hard but simply lacked the resources required to execute the plan in the specified time. In this case Jones's boss might try to get her more resources. The point is that plans are living documents that can be, and often are, adjusted as new information arrives.

■ // The Benefits and Pitfalls of Planning

Having reviewed the nature of planning, we can now discuss its benefits and pitfalls. The benefits are implicit in much of the discussion so far:

1. Planning gives direction and purpose to an organization; it is a mechanism for deciding the goals of the organization.

2. Planning is the process by which management allocates scarce resources, including capital and people, to different activities.

3. Planning drives operating budgets—strategic, operations, and unit plans determine financial budgets for the coming year.

4. Planning assigns roles and responsibilities to individuals and units within the organization.

5. Planning enables managers to better control the organization.

Thus planning is unambiguously a central task of management. Without planning an organization would be chaotic, drifting like a ship without propulsion. Academic research seems to support this view. A study that analyzed the results of 26 previously published studies came to the conclusion that on average, strategic planning has a positive impact on company performance.[22] Another study of strategic planning in 656 firms found that formal planning methodologies are part of a good strategy formulation process, even in rapidly changing environments.[23]

■ AOL and Time Warner: Planning Failure.

Despite these obvious benefits, however, planning has a bad name in some circles. Managers often groan when they are told it is time for another round of strategic planning. Some management theorists assert that the best strategies arise in the absence of planning, and that planning can limit creativity and freedom of action.[24] Moreover, there are some striking cases of organizations that pursued failed strategies despite having gone through comprehensive planning exercises.

For example, in 2000 AOL and Time Warner executed what was then the largest merger in history, valued at $166 billion. The strategic plan for the new organization, AOL–Time Warner, called for Time Warner to distribute digital versions of its magazines, such as *Fortune,* through AOL and for AOL to benefit from Time Warner's extensive cable TV operations, offering broadband versions of AOL via Time Warner cable. Managers stated that their goal for the merged company was to increase earnings at 25 percent per year compounded. It didn't work. Within three years AOL–Time Warner had taken a massive $60 billion charge against earnings to write down the value of "goodwill" associated with AOL's assets; AOL's subscriber and revenue growth had stalled; the stock price had fallen by over 80 percent; and all of the top managers associated with the merger had resigned. The new CEO, Richard Parsons, in an admission that the plan had failed, stated that the new goal was to grow earnings by 8–12 percent per year.[25]

The Best Laid Plans   Time Warner CEO Gerald Levin and AOL CEO Steve Case celebrate the completion of the largest merger in business history. Within two years their plan for the new company was in tatters, grounded on the hard rocks of market realities.

© Getty Images.

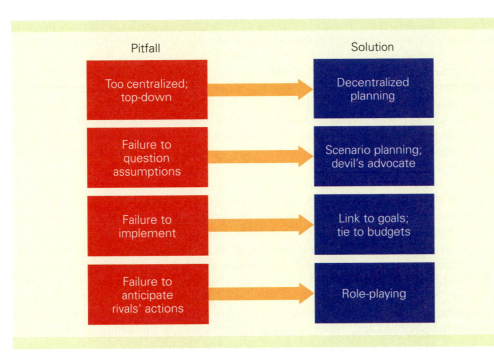

FIGURE 5.5

Countering the Pitfalls of Planning

// THE PITFALLS OF PLANNING

Why do plans sometimes fail to produce the desired results? What goes wrong with carefully made plans such as the postmerger plans for AOL and Time Warner? There are several pitfalls managers can fall victim to when they are planning (see Figure 5.5).

Too Centralized and Top-Down Some planning systems are too centralized and top-down. As a result, planners make decisions that do not take market realities into account. This can become a problem when the planners are far removed from daily operations—when they lack the knowledge that comes from a close relationship with the market. For example, General Electric used to be known for its highly centralized strategic planning process. At one time planning was touted as a strength of General Electric. However, corporate planners often drew up plans that made no sense to business unit and operating managers. In one famous example, corporate planners analyzed demographic data, found out that family size was shrinking, and told GE's appliance unit to start making smaller refrigerators. They did; but the smaller appliances did not sell. The reason was that even though family size was shrinking, houses were getting larger; people had more room for refrigerators, and they preferred to buy big refrigerators that they could keep fully stocked. The planners got it wrong because they were removed from the business and failed to understand and take customer preferences into account.[26]

Good ideas about business and operations strategy are not the preserve of top management; they can and often do emerge from lower down within an organization. Indeed, management scholars have often declared that good ideas can take root almost anywhere within an organization, even at the lowest levels, and that rather than imposing all strategy from the top, good planning systems should give lower-level employees an opportunity to suggest, lobby for, and pursue strategies that might benefit the organization.[27]

Failure to Question Assumptions All plans are based on assumptions about the future. Sometimes those assumptions are wrong, even when the plans are first made. Other times the assumptions may have initially been reasonable, but unanticipated changes may have invalidated them. In either case the result is that the plans are no longer valid, and unless management recognizes this in a timely manner and makes adjustments, the plans will fail to produce the desired results.[28] For example, in the early 1980s oil prices reached record highs of $35 a barrel following supply reductions by the OPEC cartel. Oil refiners like Exxon then made investment plans

■ GE: The problem with centralized planning.

■ Exxon: Problems with planning.

based on the assumption that prices would continue to rise, hitting over $50 a barrel by the mid-1980s. For Exxon those plans included massive investments in shale oil deposits that would not be profitable unless oil prices stayed over $30 a barrel. As it turned out, the key assumption about oil prices was wrong. By the mid-1980s oil prices had fallen to less than $15 a barrel as new supplies came from Alaska and the North Sea; and oil prices stayed low for the next 15 years, making Exxon's investment worthless. Ironically this experience so hurt companies like Exxon that when oil prices climbed again in the early 2000s, they initially held off on making the investments in exploration required to increase supply. The assumption that the 1980s oil boom and bust was about to repeat itself in the early 2000s made them more cautious than they perhaps should have been.

Failure to Implement Plans often fail because they are not put into action. One of the standard quips about strategic planning is that after a planning exercise has been completed, the planning books stay on the shelf, gathering dust, never to be opened again.[29] One reason plans are not put into action is that it is difficult to do so, particularly if the plan calls for a departure from the regular way of doing business or requires a substantial change in organizational practices. As we will see when we consider organizational change in Chapter 18, effectively managing change is one of the most difficult tasks that can confront a manager; managers often pull back when facing the turmoil associated with change efforts, so the planned change does not occur. A few years ago this author acted as a consultant for a strategic planning process at a city-owned electric utility. The planning process was successful in that the top managers, after extensive consultation with employees, committed themselves to major strategic changes in the utility that would significantly lower costs and enhance service. However, attempts to enact the plan led to protests from unionized employees, who objected to the planned reorganization of the utility, fearing that it might jeopardize their job security. The unions lobbied the city government, and the mayor, who did not appreciate the negative publicity, replaced the CEO of the utility with a city bureaucrat who maintained the status quo. The message to managers from that event was clear: Don't rock the boat! The strategic plan was never implemented and is now gathering dust on a shelf somewhere.

Failure to Anticipate Rivals' Actions Plans can fail because managers do not consider what rivals are doing. The planners proceed as if the organization has no rivals, and they make investments based on plans without considering how the value of those investments will be affected by rivals' actions. This was a problem in the case of many dot-com companies in the late 1990s and early 2000s. Following the success of early dot-com enterprises such as AOL, Amazon, Yahoo, and eBay, hundreds of companies entered the dot-com arena. Many of these companies had a business model based on advertising revenues. The problem was that each company assumed that it would capture significant advertising revenues; but with many other companies chasing the same advertising dollars, there simply was not enough business to go around, and most of these companies failed. Had these enterprises looked at what their rivals were doing, they might have been more cautious about their investment plans, and the results might not have been so bad.

// IMPROVING PLANNING

Dealing with the pitfalls just discussed requires that managers take a number of steps (see Figure 5.5). To guard against the problems associated with centralized, top-down planning, managers need to ensure that responsibility for planning is decentralized to the appropriate level and that a broad constituency of employees has an opportunity to participate in the planning process. An important

You know, I'm still bummed I didn't name myself e-rob.com and go public in the 90's. Coulda been huge, man.

© Streeter/Cartoon Stock.

principle of good planning is that *those who have primary responsibility for putting a plan into action should also participate in formulating the plan.* Thus, for example, manufacturing managers should be involved in a planning process that looks at how manufacturing processes might be reorganized to drive down unit costs, and marketing managers should help formulate a plan that calls for the repositioning of a company's product offering in the marketplace.

As for opening up the planning process to a broad constituency of employees, here organizations can and do use a variety of mechanisms. At Google, for example, employees are asked to spend 20 percent of their time working on something that interests them away from their main jobs. Companywide, a full 10 percent of employee time at Google is spent dreaming up new projects. Although most of these projects never become products, some do—such as Google Maps, Google mail, Google Earth, and Google books (a controversial service that lets users search inside published books).[30] General Electric has a process known as "work out" in which lower-level managers and other employees spend three days at a retreat, without their boss, formulating ideas to improve the performance of their business unit. They then suggest their ideas to their boss, who has to decide on the spot which ideas to pursue. This process has empowered employees, has made them feel as if they have a role in determining the plans of their unit, and has produced many ideas that improved performance at General Electric.[31]

■ Google: Decentralized strategy making.

To try to ensure that plans are not based on unrealistic assumptions and to account for uncertainty about the future, managers can use scenario planning methods. As discussed earlier, scenario planning methods force managers to think about what they would do under different assumptions about the future. One of the great advantages of the scenario method is that it is not based on a single assumption about the future. In addition, managers can use an independent "devil's advocate" to question plans and their underlying assumptions, exposing any flaws or weak assumptions (we discuss this in more detail in the next section).[32] Beyond such approaches, senior managers need the courage to walk away from plans that are no longer working because of unanticipated events and to push the organization in a new direction if that is called for. One of the classic examples of this occurred in 1995 when Microsoft's Bill Gates responded to the unanticipated emergence of the World Wide Web based on the Hyper Text Markup Language (HTML) by abandoning Microsoft's established strategy for the Internet, which was based on a version of MSN that used proprietary software. Instead he stated that Microsoft would incorporate HTML language into all of its products, making them Web enabled.

■ Microsoft: Changing strategic plans.

To make sure plans are implemented, managers need to follow the steps of the planning model to their conclusion—drafting action plans, identifying who is responsible for putting the plans into effect, tying budgets to plans, and holding managers accountable for reaching goals. The hard truth is that plans will not work unless they are linked to goals that matter and are tied to operating budgets. Unfortunately, in many organizations the planning exercise is decoupled from the budget process and from performance reviews, which implies that the plans have no teeth.

Finally, managers need to consider how rivals will respond to their plans. One technique for doing this is to engage in strategic role-playing, where groups within the organization take on the role of competing enterprises and state how they would counter the plans of the organization. This technique is a standard feature of Microsoft's regular strategy conferences. At those conferences, groups assigned to take the position of Microsoft rivals draft plans to "beat Microsoft." The idea is to generate insights into what the strategy of rivals might be and how they might respond to actions by Microsoft.

■ // Decision Making

The strategic planning system we have reviewed in this chapter is an example of a rational decision-making model. In essence, strategic planning is a formal process for making important decisions about strategies, tactics, and operations. More generally, making decisions is a major component of a manager's job. Strategic planning systems are a subset of what is often referred to as the *classic rational model of decision making.*

FIGURE 5.6

The Rational Decision-Making Model

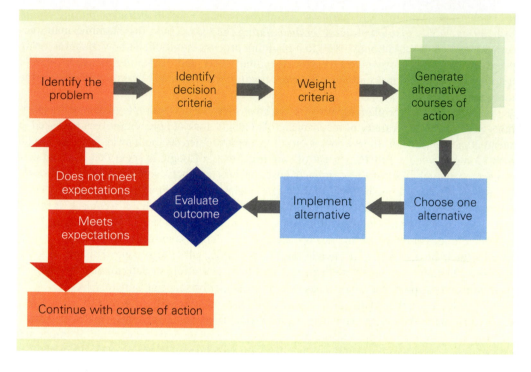

// THE RATIONAL DECISION-MAKING MODEL

The rational decision-making model has a number of discrete steps (see Figure 5.6). First, managers have to identify the problem to be solved by a decision. Problems often arise when there is a gap between the desired state and the current state. For example, if a firm is not attaining its goals for profitability and growth, the gap signifies a problem. Second, managers must identify *decision criteria,* which are the standards used to guide judgments about which course of action to pursue. Imagine, for example, that a manager has to decide what model of car to purchase for a company fleet. The decision criteria might include cost, fuel efficiency, reliability, performance, and styling. Third, managers need to *weight* the criteria by their importance. The weighting should be driven by the overall goals of the organization. Thus for an organization that is trying to reduce costs, a manager choosing cars for a company fleet would probably weight fuel efficiency higher than styling or power. Fourth, managers need to generate alternative courses of action. In the example used here, this would mean specifying the different models of car that fall into the feasible set. Fifth, managers need to compare the alternatives against the weighted criteria, and choose one alternative. Sixth, they should implement that choice (for example, issue a purchase order to buy cars). Finally, after a suitable period they should always evaluate the outcome and decide whether the choice was a good one. If the outcome does not meet expectations, this constitutes a problem that triggers another round of decision making.

// BOUNDED RATIONALITY AND SATISFICING

The rational decision-making model is reasonable except for one problems: The implicit assumption that human decision makers are rational is not valid. This point was made forcibly by Nobel Prize winner Herbert Simon.[33] According to Simon, human beings are not rational calculating machines. Our rationality is bounded by our own limited cognitive capabilities. **Bounded rationality** refers to limits in our ability to formulate complex problems, to gather and process the information necessary for solving those problems, and thus to solve those problems in a rational way.[34] Due to the constraints of bounded rationality, we tend not to optimize, as assumed by the rational decision-making model. Rather we **satisfice**, aiming for a satisfactory level of a particular performance variable, rather than its theoretical maximum.

bounded rationality

Limits in human ability to formulate complex problems, to gather and process the information necessary for solving those problems, and thus to solve those problems in a rational way.

satisfice

Aiming for a satisfactory level of a particular performance variable rather than its theoretical maximum.

For example, instead of trying to maximize profits, the theory of bounded rationality argues that managers will try to attain a satisfactory level of profits.

Satisficing (settling for a good enough solution to a problem) occurs not only because of bounded rationality, but also because of the prohibitive costs of collecting all the information required to identify the optimal solution to a problem—and often because some of the required information is unavailable. For example, identifying the optimal strategy for gaining market share from competitors may require information about consumer preferences; consumer responses to changes in key product variables such as price, quality, and styling; the cost structure, current and future product offerings, and strategy of rivals; and future demand conditions. Much of this information is costly to gather (data about consumer preferences and responses), private (the cost structure and future product offerings of rivals), and unpredictable (future demand conditions), so managers tend to collect a limited amount of publicly available information and make satisficing decisions based on that.

// DECISION-MAKING HEURISTICS AND COGNITIVE BIASES

Cognitive psychologists argue that when making decisions, due to bounded rationality we tend to fall back on **decision heuristics**, or simple rules of thumb. Decision heuristics can be useful, because they help us make sense out of complex and uncertain situations. An example of a decision-making heuristic is the so-called **80–20 rule**, which states that 80 percent of the consequences of a phenomenon stem from 20 percent of the causes.[35] A common formulation of the 80–20 rule states that 80 percent of a firm's sales are derived from 20 percent of its products, or that 20 percent of the customers account for 80 percent of sales. Another common formulation often voiced in software companies is that 20 percent of the software programmers produce 80 percent of the code. It is also claimed that 20 percent of criminals produce 80 percent of all crimes, 20 percent of motorists are responsible for 80 percent of accidents, and so on.[36] Managers often use the 80–20 rule to make resource allocation decisions, for example, by focusing sales and service efforts on the 20 percent of customers who are responsible for 80 percent of revenues. Although the 80–20 rule might be verified through empirical measurement, often it is not. People just assume it is true—and there lies the problem: The rule does not always hold. The assumption may be invalid, and decisions made on the basis of this heuristic might be flawed.

Generalizing from this, cognitive psychologists say that as useful as heuristics might be, their application can cause severe and systematic errors in the decision-making process.[37] **Cognitive biases** are decision-making errors that we are all prone to making and that have been repeatedly verified in laboratory settings or controlled experiments with human decision makers. Due to the operation of these biases, managers with good information may still make bad decisions.

A common cognitive bias is known as the **prior hypothesis bias**, which refers to the fact that decision makers who have strong prior beliefs about the relationship between two variables tend to make decisions on the basis of these beliefs, even when presented with evidence that their beliefs are wrong. Moreover, they tend to seek and use information that is consistent with their prior beliefs while ignoring information that contradicts these beliefs. To put this bias in a strategic context, it suggests that a CEO who thinks a certain strategy makes sense might continue to pursue that strategy, despite evidence that it is inappropriate or failing.

Another well-known cognitive bias, **escalating commitment**, occurs when decision makers, having already committed significant resources to a project, commit even more resources if they receive feedback that the project is failing.[38] This may be an irrational response; a more logical response might be to abandon the project and move on. Feelings of personal responsibility for a project, along with a desire to recoup their losses, can induce decision makers to stick with a project despite evidence that it is failing.

A third bias, **reasoning by analogy**, involves the use of simple analogies to make sense out of complex problems. The problem with this heuristic is that the analogy may not

decision heuristics
Simple rules of thumb.

80–20 rule
A heuristic stating that 80 percent of the consequences of a phenomenon stem from 20 percent of the causes.

cognitive biases
Decision-making errors that we are all prone to making and that have been repeatedly verified in laboratory settings or controlled experiments with human decision makers.

prior hypothesis bias
Decision makers who have strong prior beliefs about the relationship between two variables tend to make decisions on the basis of these beliefs, even when presented with evidence that their beliefs are wrong.

escalating commitment
Arises when decision makers, having already committed significant resources to a project, commit even more resources if they receive feedback that the project is failing.

reasoning by analogy
The use of simple analogies to make sense out of complex problems.

representativeness

Generalizing from a small sample or even a single vivid anecdote.

■ Dot-com boom and bust.

illusion of control

The tendency to overestimate one's ability to control events.

availability error

Arises from our predisposition to estimate the probability of an outcome based on how easy the outcome is to imagine.

be valid. A fourth bias, **representativeness**, is rooted in the tendency to generalize from a small sample or even a single vivid anecdote. This bias violates the statistical law of large numbers, which says that it is inappropriate to generalize from a small sample, let alone from a single case. In many respects the dot-com boom of the late 1990s was based on reasoning by analogy and representativeness. Prospective entrepreneurs saw some of the early dot-com companies such as Amazon and Yahoo! achieve rapid success, at least judged by some metrics. Reasoning by analogy from a small sample, they assumed that any dot-com could achieve similar success. Many investors reached similar conclusions. The result was a massive wave of start-ups that jumped onto the Internet in an attempt to capitalize on the perceived opportunities. That the vast majority of these companies subsequently went bankrupt is testament to the fact that the analogy was wrong, and the success of the small sample of early entrants was no guarantee that other dot-coms would succeed.

Another cognitive bias, known as the **illusion of control**, is the tendency to overestimate one's ability to control events. General or top managers seem to be particularly prone to this bias: Having risen to the top of an organization, they tend to be overconfident about their ability to succeed. According to Richard Roll, such overconfidence leads to what he has termed the *hubris hypothesis* of takeovers.[39] Roll asserts that top managers are typically overconfident about their abilities to create value by acquiring another company. So, they end up making poor acquisition decisions, often paying far too much for the companies they acquire. Servicing the debt taken on to finance such an acquisition makes it all but impossible to make money from the acquisition (the acquisition of Time Warner by AOL, discussed earlier, is a good example of management hubris).

The **availability error** is yet another common bias. The availability error arises from our predisposition to estimate the probability of an outcome based on how easy the outcome is to imagine. For example, more people seem to fear a plane crash than a car accident, and yet statistically people are far more likely to be killed in a car on the way to the airport than in a

Time Warner CEO Gerald Levin and AOL CEO Steve Chase after their merger.
© Chris Wattie/Reuters/Corbis.

plane crash. They overweight the probability of a plane crash because the outcome is easier to imagine and because plane crashes are more vivid events than car crashes, which affect only small numbers of people at a time. As a result of the availability error, managers might allocate resources to a project, with an easily visualized outcome rather than one that might have a higher return.

Finally, the way a problem or decision is framed can result in the **framing bias**.[40] In a classic illustration of framing bias, Tversky and Kahneman give the example of what they call the Asian disease problem.[41] They asked participants in an experiment to imagine that the United States is preparing for the outbreak of an unusual disease from Asia that is expected to kill 600 people. Two programs to combat the disease have been developed. One group of participants was told that the consequences of the programs were as follows:

- Program A: 200 people will be saved.
- Program B: There is a one-third probability that 600 people will be saved and a two-thirds probability that no one will be saved.

When the consequences were presented this way, 72 percent of participants preferred program A. A second group of participants was given the follow choice:

- Program C: 400 people will die.
- Program D: There is a one-third probability that no one will die and a two-thirds probability that 600 people will die.

When the consequences were presented this way, 78 percent of the participants preferred program D. However, programs A and C are the same, as are programs B and D! The point, of course, is that the preferences were shaped by how the problems were framed.

The wrong frames can have significant negative implications for a company. A good example concerns Encyclopedia Britannica, which thought it was in the book business until it found out it was really in the knowledge and information business, which had gone digital. The company's sales reportedly peaked at around $620 million in 1989 and then fell off sharply as CD-ROM and then Internet-based digital encyclopedias, such as Encarta, took away market share. Today, after a close brush with bankruptcy, Encyclopedia Britannica survives as a Web-based business, but it attracts far less traffic than Wikipedia, the dominant online encyclopedia.

> **framing bias**
> Bias arising from how a problem or decision is framed.

■ Encyclopedia Britannica: Framing bias.

// PROSPECT THEORY

Prospect theory, which was developed by psychologists Daniel Kahneman and Amos Tversky, is a widely cited model that gives an example of how the cognitive biases arising from simple heuristics can influence managerial decision making.[42] Prospect theory has been used to explain the observation that people seem to make decisions that are inconsistent with the rational model. Prospect theory suggests that individuals assign different subjective values to losses and gains of equal magnitude that result from a decision (see Figure 5.7). According to this theory, when evaluating the potential gains and losses associated with a course of action, people start by establishing a reference point or anchor. The reference point is usually the current situation. Thus if a firm is currently making a return on invested capital of 10 percent, this might be the reference point for a decision that affects this measure of profitability. However, as just noted when we discussed the framing bias, the reference point can be influenced by how a problem or decision is framed. Prospect theory predicts that decision makers will subjectively overweight the value of potential losses and underweight the value of potential gains relative to their objective, or monetary, value. Put differently, decision makers are *loss averse*—they avoid actions that have a potential negative outcome.

An interesting implication of prospect theory is that if decision makers have incurred significant losses in the past, they become distressed (they assign a subjectively high negative value to those losses); this shifts their reference point, and they tend to make riskier decisions than would otherwise have been the case. In other words, loss averse decision makers try to recoup losses by taking bigger risks—paradoxically they become risk seekers. This explains a

FIGURE 5.7

Prospect Theory

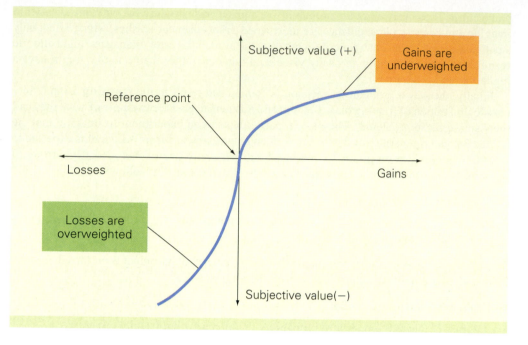

well-documented tendency for gamblers who are losing to place progressively riskier bets. Similarly, investors in the stock market who have lost significant money have been observed trying to recoup their losses by investing in more speculative stocks.[43] For a managerial example, look no further than Enron, the now-bankrupt energy trading company, where the response to mounting losses was increasing pursuit of the risky strategy of trying to hide those losses by shifting them into off–balance sheet entities and engaging in illegal trades to inflate profits.[44] Had the reference point for Enron been more positive, it seems unlikely that the managers would have taken these risks. Note that prospect theory also explains the phenomenon of escalating commitment we discussed earlier.[45]

// GROUPTHINK

Because most decisions are made by groups, the group context within which decisions are made is an important variable in determining whether cognitive biases will adversely affect the strategic decision-making processes. Psychologist Irvin Janis asserts that many groups are characterized by a process known as *groupthink* and as a result make poor strategic decisions.[46] **Groupthink** occurs when a group of decision makers embarks on a course of action without questioning underlying assumptions. Typically a group coalesces around a person or policy. It ignores or filters out information that can be used to question the policy, develops after-the-fact rationalizations for its decisions, and pushes out of the group members who question the policy. Commitment to mission or goals becomes based on an emotional rather than an objective assessment of the "correct" course of action. The consequence can be poor decisions.

It has been said that groupthink may help to explain why organizations often make poor decisions in spite of sophisticated planning processes. Janis traces many historical fiascoes to defective policy making by government leaders who received social support from their in-group of advisers. For example, he suggests that President John F. Kennedy's inner circle suffered from groupthink when the members of this group supported the decision to launch the Bay of Pigs invasion of Cuba in 1961, even though available information showed that it would be an unsuccessful venture (which it was). Similarly, Janis argues that the decision to escalate the commitment of military forces to Vietnam by the Johnson administration and increase the bombing of North Vietnam, despite the availability of data showing that this probably would not help win the war, was the result of groupthink. Indeed, when a member of the in-group of decision makers, Defense Secretary Robert McNamara, started to express doubts about this

groupthink

Arises when a group of decision makers embarks on a course of action without questioning underlying assumptions.

policy, he was reportedly asked to leave by the president and resigned. However, despite the emotional appeals of such anecdotes, academic researchers have not found strong evidence in support of groupthink.[47]

// IMPROVING DECISION MAKING

The existence of bounded rationality, cognitive biases, and groupthink raises the issue of how to bring critical information into the decision mechanism so that the decisions of managers are more realistic, objective, and based on thorough evaluation of the available data. Scenario planning can be a useful technique for counteracting cognitive biases: The approach forces managers to think through the implications of different assumptions about the future. As such, it can be an antidote to hubris and the prior hypothesis bias. Two other techniques known to counteract groupthink and cognitive biases are devil's advocacy and dialectic inquiry.[48] **Devil's advocacy** requires the generation of both a plan and a critical analysis of the plan. One member of the decision-making group acts as the devil's advocate. The purpose of the devil's advocate is to question assumptions underlying a decision and to highlight all the reasons that might make the proposal unacceptable. In this way decision makers can be made aware of the possible perils of recommended courses of action. **Dialectic inquiry** is more complex: It requires the generation of a plan (a thesis) and a counterplan (an antithesis) that reflect *plausible but conflicting* courses of action.[49] Managers listen to a debate between advocates of the plan and counterplan and then decide which plan will lead to higher performance. The purpose of the debate is to reveal problems with definitions, recommended courses of action, and assumptions of both plans. As a result of this exercise, managers can form a new and more encompassing conceptualization of the problem, which becomes the final plan (a synthesis). Dialectic inquiry can promote thinking strategically.

Another technique for countering cognitive biases championed by Daniel Kahneman (of prospect theory fame) is known as the outside view.[50] The **outside view** requires planners to identify a reference class of analogous past strategic initiatives, determine whether those initiatives succeeded or failed, and evaluate the project at hand against those prior initiatives. According to Kahneman, this technique is particularly useful for countering biases such as the illusion of control (hubris), reasoning by analogy, and representativeness. Thus, for example, when considering a potential acquisition planners should look at the track record of acquisitions made by other enterprises (the reference class), determine if they succeeded or failed, and objectively evaluate the potential acquisition against that reference class. Kahneman asserts that such a "reality check" against a large sample of prior events tends to constrain the inherent optimism of planners and produce more realistic assessments and plans.

Finally, decision makers are more likely to run into problems of bounded rationality, and resort to simple decision-making heuristics, when they have too much information to process.[51] A solution to this problem is to reduce the amount of information that managers have to process, giving them more time to focus on critical issues, by delegating routine decision-making responsibilities to subordinates. We return to this issue in Chapter 8 when we discuss internal organization structure.

devil's advocacy
The generation of both a plan and a critical analysis of the plan by a devil's advocate.

dialectic inquiry
The generation of a plan (a thesis) and a counterplan (an antithesis) that reflect plausible but conflicting courses of action.

outside view
Identifying a reference class of analogous past strategic initiatives, determining whether those initiatives succeeded or failed, and evaluating a project at hand against those prior initiatives.

IN CONCLUSION \ WHY DOES IT MATTER?

Why should students studying management care about planning and decision making? Planning is one of the central activities of managers, who devote a lot of time and energy to formulating and then implementing plans; it is crucial that managers plan well because the evidence suggests that whereas good planning can improve the performance of an organization, bad planning may be as damaging as no planning at all. Without planning, the organization can lack purpose, and there may be no agreement about its strategy. Without planning, different parts of the organization may pull in different directions, there may be a lack of synchronicity between actions, and different units may pursue inconsistent strategies. Without planning, resources may be allocated in a haphazard fashion, with no link between strategy and budgets. Finally, there may be a lack of control in the enterprise: By allowing managers to compare performance against goals, planning becomes a crucial link in the process of controlling the organization.

At the same time it is wise to keep the limitations of planning in mind. Planning does not guarantee perfect strategy formulation. Good ideas can emerge in the absence of planning: Much of what organizations do is not planned but rather is a response to unanticipated circumstances. However, if such responses are something other than a quick tactical move, they may subsequently be incorporated into the plans of the enterprise. Thus although Microsoft did not plan for the emergence of a World Wide Web based on HTML, when it did emerge Microsoft quickly made plans based on that new reality. So although planning does not have a monopoly on the generation of good ideas, and plans can be made obsolete by unforeseen events, coordinated action is still needed to exploit good ideas and respond to unforeseen events.

In addition, much of a manager's work involves making decisions. Planning is nothing more than a formal process for making decisions. As we have seen, decision makers suffer from bounded rationality and tend to fall back on simple heuristics when making complex decisions. In turn, these heuristics can give rise to cognitive biases. Even the best-designed decision-making systems will fail to produce the desired results if managers let cognitive biases skew their decisions. Thus managers should use techniques that have been shown to minimize the likelihood that cognitive biases and groupthink will contaminate the decision-making process. These techniques include scenario planning, devil's advocacy, dialectic inquiry, and taking an outside view.

MANAGEMENT CHALLENGES

1. "In high-technology industries, where things are moving quickly, it is impossible to plan, so don't bother!" Is this statement reasonable?

2. What decision-making biases help explain why many acquisitions fail to create value for the acquiring company? What should managers do to guard against these biases?

3. What role can a lower-level manager play in his or her company's strategic planning process? What might occur if lower-level managers have no input into the strategic planning process of the organization?

4. How are planning systems also a control device?

5. Microsoft describes its mission as follows: "At Microsoft, we work to help people and businesses throughout the world realize their full potential. This is our mission. Everything we do reflects this mission and the values that make it possible." Is this a customer-oriented mission statement? How might this mission influence product development decisions within Microsoft?

MANAGEMENT PORTFOLIO

FOR THE ORGANIZATION YOU HAVE CHOSEN TO FOLLOW:

1. Find out as much as you can about the mission, vision, values, and major goals of the organization.

2. Evaluate the firm's mission, vision, values, and goals. What are the positive aspects of these statements? Is there anything you would criticize?

3. Do you think the firm is living up to its mission, vision, values, and goals? What evidence do you have to support your conclusion?

4. Can you find any evidence that managers at the organization might have made any significant strategic errors over the last decade? If they have, what role did poor planning, a lack of planning, or decision-making traps play in these errors?

CLOSING CASE   BOOM AND BUST IN TELECOMMUNICATIONS

In 1997 Michael O'Dell, the chief scientist at WorldCom, which owned the largest network of "Internet backbone" fiber optic cable in the world, stated that data traffic over the Internet was doubling every hundred days. This implied a growth rate of over 1,000 percent a year. O'Dell went on to say that there was not enough fiber optic capacity to go around, and that "demand will far outstrip supply for the foreseeable future."

Electrified by this potential opportunity, a number of companies rushed into the business. These firms included Level 3 Communications, 360 Networks, Global Crossing, Qwest Communications, WorldCom, Williams Communications Group, Genuity Inc., and XO Communications. In all cases the strategic plans were remarkably similar: Raise lots of capital, build massive fiber optic networks that straddled the nation (or even the globe), cut prices, and get ready for the rush of business. Managers at these companies believed that surging demand would soon catch up with capacity, resulting in a profit bonanza for those that had the foresight to build out their networks. It was a gold rush, and the first into the field would stake the best claims.

However, there were dissenting voices. As early as October 1998 an Internet researcher at AT&T Labs named Andrew Odlyzko published a paper that debunked the assumption that demand for Internet traffic was growing at 1,000 percent a year. Odlyzko's careful analysis concluded that growth was much slower—only 100 percent a year! Although still large, that growth rate was not nearly large enough to fill the massive flood of fiber optic capacity that was entering the market. Moreover, Odlyzko noted that new technologies were increasing the amount of data that could be sent down existing fibers,

reducing the need for new fiber. But with investment money flooding into the market, few paid any attention to him. WorldCom was still using the 1,000 percent figure as late as September 2000.

As it turned out, Odlyzko was right. Capacity rapidly outstripped demand, and by late 2002 less than 3 percent of the fiber that had been laid in the ground was actually being used! While prices slumped, the surge in volume that managers had bet on did not materialize. Unable to service the debt they had taken on to build out their networks, company after company tumbled into bankruptcy—including WorldCom, 360 Networks, XO Communications, and Global Crossing. Level 3 and Qwest survived, but their stock prices had fallen by 90 percent, and both companies were saddled with massive debts.[52]

CASE DISCUSSION QUESTIONS

1. Why did the strategic plans adopted by companies like Level 3, Global Crossing, and 360 Networks fail?

2. The managers who ran these companies were smart, successful individuals, as were many of the investors who put money into these businesses. How could so many smart people have been so wrong?

3. What specific decision-making biases do you think were at work in this industry during the late 1990s and early 2000s?

4. What could the managers running these companies have done differently that might have led to a different outcome?

ENDNOTES

1. Sources: "Intel's Right Hand Turn," *The Economist*, May 14, 2005, p. 67; C. Edwards, "Getting Intel Back on the Inside Track," *BusinessWeek*, November 29, 2004, p. 39; C. Edwards, "Shaking Up Intel's Insides," *BusinessWeek*, January 31, 2005, p. 35; B. Snyder Bulik, "Intel's New Strategy Demands a New Partner," *Advertising Age*, March 14, 2005, pp. 4–5.

2. J. Hallinan, "3M's Next Chief Plans to Fortify Results with Discipline He Learned at GE Unit," *The Wall Street Journal*, December 6, 2000, p. B17; 3M Investor Meeting, September 30, 2003, archived at http://www.corporate-ir.net/ireye/ir_site.zhtml?ticker=MMM&script=2100.

3. W.T. Coombs, *Ongoing Crisis Communication: Planning, Managing, and Responding* (Thousand Oaks, CA: Sage Publications, 1999).

4. J. Greenwald, "September 11th Attacks Show Value of Planning for a Crisis," *Business Insurance*, January 7, 2002, p. 17.

5. Coombs. *Ongoing Crisis Communication: Planning, Managing, and Responding*.

6. H. Courtney, J. Kirkland, and P. Viguerie, "Strategy under Uncertainty," *Harvard Business Review* 75 (November–December 1997), pp. 66–79.

7. P.J.H. Schoemaker, "Multiple Scenario Development: Its Conceptual and Behavioral Foundation," *Strategic Management Journal* 14 (1993), pp. 193–213.

8. P. Schoemaker, P.J.H. van der Heijden, and A.J.M. Cornelius, "Integrating Scenarios into Strategic Planning at Royal Dutch Shell," *Planning Review* 20, no. 3 (1992), pp. 41–47; I. Wylie, "There Is No Alternative to…" *Fast Company,* July 2002, pp. 106–11.

9. "The Next Big Surprise: Scenario Planning," *The Economist,* October 13, 2001, p. 71.

10. K.R. Andrews, *The Concept of Corporate Strategy* (Homewood, IL: Dow Jones Irwin, 1971); H.I. Ansoff, *Corporate Strategy* (New York: McGraw-Hill, 1965); C.W. Hofer and D. Schendel, *Strategy Formulation: Analytical Concepts* (St. Paul, MN: West, 1978). Also see P.J. Brews and M.R. Hunt, "Learning to Plan and Planning to Learn," *Strategic Management Journal* 20 (1999), pp. 889–913; R.W. Grant, "Planning in a Turbulent Environment," *Strategic Management Journal* 24 (2003), pp. 491–517.

11. http://www.kodak.com/US/en/corp/careers/why/valuesmission.jhtml.

12. D.F. Abell, *Defining the Business: The Starting Point of Strategic Planning* (Englewood Cliffs, NJ: Prentice-Hall, 1980).

13. See G. Hamel and C.K. Prahalad, "Strategic Intent," *Harvard Business Review* (May–June 1989), p. 64.

14. J.C. Collins and J.I. Porras, "Building Your Company's Vision," *Harvard Business Review,* September–October 1996, pp. 65–77.

15. http://www.nucor.com/.

16. M.D. Richards, *Setting Strategic Goals and Objectives* (St. Paul, MN: West, 1986).

17. E.A. Locke, G.P. Latham, and M. Erez, "The Determinants of Goal Commitment," *Academy of Management Review* 13 (1988), pp. 23–39.

18. R.E. Hoskisson, M.A. Hitt, and C.W.L. Hill, "Managerial Incentives and Investment in R&D in Large Multiproduct Firms," *Organization Science* 3 (1993), pp. 325–41.

19. R.H. Hayes and W.J. Abernathy, "Managing Our Way to Economic Decline," *Harvard Business Review,* July–August 1980, pp. 67–77.

20. R.S. Kaplan and D.P. Norton, *The Strategy Focused Organization: How Balanced Scorecard Companies Thrive in the New Business Environment* (Boston: Harvard Business School Press, 2001).

21. Sources: A. Latour and C. Nuzum, "Verizon Profit Soars Fivefold on Wireless Growth," *The Wall Street Journal,* July 28, 2004, p. A3; S. Woolley, "Do You Fear Me Now?" *Forbes,* November 10, 2003, pp. 78–80; A.Z. Cuneo, "Call Verizon Victorious," *Advertising Age,* March 5, 2004, pp. 3–5.

22. C.C. Miller and L.B. Cardinal, "Strategic Planning and Firm Performance: A Synthesis of More Than Two Decades of Research," *Academy of Management Journal* 37 (1994), pp. 1649–65. Also see P.R. Rogers, A. Miller, and W.Q. Judge, "Using Information Processing Theory to Understand Planning/Performance Relationships in the Context of Strategy," *Strategic Management Journal* 20 (1999), pp. 567–77.

23. Brews and Hunt, "Learning to Plan and Planning to Learn."

24. H. Mintzberg, "Patterns in Strategy Formulation," *Management Science* 24 (1978), pp. 934–48.

25. C.J. Loomis, "AOL Time Warner's New Math," *Fortune,* February 4, 2002, pp. 98–103.

26. *GE's Two-Decade Transformation: Jack Welch's Leadership* (Harvard Business School Case 9-399-150, 1999).

27. For details, see R.A. Burgelman, "Intraorganizational Ecology of Strategy Making and Organizational Adaptation: Theory and Field Research," *Organization Science* 2 (1991), pp. 239–62; Mintzberg, "Patterns in Strategy Formulation"; S.L. Hart, "An Integrative Framework for Strategy Making Processes," *Academy of Management Review* 17 (1992), pp. 327–51; G. Hamel, "Strategy as Revolution," *Harvard Business Review* 74 (July–August 1996), pp. 69–83; Grant, "Planning in a Turbulent Environment."

28. This is the premise of those who advocate that complexity and chaos theory should be applied to strategic planning. See S. Brown and K.M. Eisenhardt, "The Art of Continuous Change: Linking Complexity Theory and Time Based Evolution in Relentlessly Shifting Organizations," *Administrative Science Quarterly* 29 (1997), pp. 1–34; and R. Stacey and D. Parker, *Chaos, Management, and Economics* (London: Institute for Economic Affairs, 1994). See also Courtney, Kirkland, and Viguerie, "Strategy under Uncertainty."

29. As a consultant, the author has come across this many times.

30. Q. Hardy, "Google Thinks Small," *Forbes,* November 14, 2005, pp. 198–202.

31. *GE's Two-Decade Transformation: Jack Welch's Leadership* (Harvard Business School Case 9-399-150, 1999).

32. D. Lovallo and D. Kahneman, "Delusions of Success: How Optimism Undermines Executives' Decisions," *Harvard Business Review* 81 (July 2003), pp. 56–67; J.S. Hammond, R.L. Keeny, and H. Raiffa, "The Hidden Traps in Decision Making," *Harvard Business Review* 76 (September–October 1998), pp. 25–34.

33. H. Simon, *Administrative Behavior* (New York: McGraw-Hill, 1957).

34. G. Girgenzer and R. Selten, *Bounded Rationality* (Cambridge, MA: MIT Press, 2001); D. Kahneman, "Maps of Bounded Rationality: Psychology for Behavioral Economics," *American Economic Review* 93 (2003), pp. 1449–75. Also see M.H. Bazerman, *Judgment in Managerial Decision Making,* 6th ed. (New York: Wiley, 2006).

35. R. Koch, *The 80–20 Principle* (New York, Doubleday, 1996).

36. Koch, *The 80–20 Principle.*

37. The original statement of this phenomenon was made by A. Tversky and D. Kahneman, "Judgment under Uncertainty: Heuristics and Biases," *Science* 185 (1974), pp. 1124–31. Also see Lovallo and Kahneman, "Delusions of Success: How Optimism Undermines Executives' Decisions"; Hammond, Keeny, and Raiffa, "The Hidden Traps in Decision Making"; and Bazerman, *Judgment in Managerial Decision Making.*

38. B.M. Staw, "The Escalation of Commitment to a Course of Action," *Academy of Management Review* 6 (1981), pp. 577–87.

39. R. Roll, "The Hubris Hypotheses of Corporate Takeovers," *Journal of Business* 59 (1986), pp. 197–216.

40. A. Tversky and D. Kahneman, "The Framing of Decisions and the Psychology of Choice," *Science* 211 (1981), pp. 453–58.

41. Tversky and Kahneman, "The Framing of Decisions and the Psychology of Choice."

42. D. Kahneman and A. Tversky, "Prospect Theory: An Analysis of Decision under Risk," *Econometrica,* 47 (1979), pp. 263–92.

43. M. Myagkov and C.R. Plott, "Exchange Economies and Loss Exposure: Experiments in Exploring Prospect Theory," *American Economic Review* 87 (1997), pp. 810–29.

44. B. McLean and P. Elkind, *The Smartest Guys in the Room* (New York: Penguin, 2003).

45. G. Whyte, "Escalating Commitment to a Course of Action: A Reinterpretation," *Academy of Management Review* 11 (1986), pp. 311–22.

46. I.L. Janis, *Victims of Groupthink,* 2nd ed. (Boston: Houghton Mifflin, 1982). For an alternative view, see S.R. Fuller and R.J. Aldag, "Organizational Tonypandy: Lessons from a Quarter Century of the Groupthink Phenomenon," *Organizational Behavior and Human Decision Processes* 73 (1998), pp. 163–84.

47. Fuller and Aldag, "Organizational Tonypandy: Lessons from a Quarter Century of the Groupthink Phenomenon."

48. See R.O. Mason, "A Dialectic Approach to Strategic Planning," *Management Science* 13 (1969), pp. 403–14; R.A. Cosier and J.C. Aplin, "A Critical View of Dialectic Inquiry in Strategic Planning," *Strategic Management Journal* 1 (1980), pp. 343–56; and I.I. Mintroff and R.O. Mason, "Structuring III—Structured Policy Issues: Further Explorations in a Methodology for Messy Problems," *Strategic Management Journal* 1 (1980), pp. 331–42.

49. Mason, "A Dialectic Approach," pp. 403–14.

50. Lovallo and Kahneman, "Delusions of Success: How Optimism Undermines Executives' Decisions."

51. C.W.L. Hill and R.E. Hoskisson, "Strategy and Structure in the Multiproduct Firm," *Academy of Management Review* 12 (1986), pp. 331–41.

52. Sources: Y.J. Dreazn, "Behind the Fiber Glut," *The Wall Street Journal,* September 26, 2002, p. B1; R. Blumenstein, "Overbuilt Web: How the Fiber Barons Plunged the Nation into a Telecom Glut," *The Wall Street Journal,* June 18, 2001, p. A1; D.K. Berman, "Level 3 Finds a Way to Fight Telecom Crash," *The Wall Street Journal,* November 19, 2002, p. C1; Level 3 10K reports, 2002 and 2003.

6

STRATEGY

Wal-Mart is the largest business enterprise on the planet. The company has over 5,000 stores, sales of over $300 billion, and 1.8 million employees. Established in 1962 by the legendary Sam Walton, Wal-Mart made its name by selling general merchandise at everyday low prices. For years Wal-Mart has been more profitable than competitors such as Target and Kmart. The company achieved this by pursuing strategies that lowered its costs, which enabled Wal-Mart to offer low prices and still make healthy profits.[1] To lower costs, Sam Walton's stores were self-service rather than full-service operations, which reduced the number of employees and thus labor costs. The design of the stores was basic, which further reduced costs. Because the early Wal-Mart stores were based in small Southern towns, Sam Walton found it difficult to get suppliers to deliver directly to his stores inexpensively. So he built the first of many Wal-Mart distribution centers. Each distribution center supplied stores within a 300-mile radius. Wal-Mart could now purchase inventory from suppliers in larger lots, storing it at the distribution centers. In return for larger orders, the suppliers lowered prices, which further shrank Wal-Mart's cost structure.

Over the years Walton and his successors also invested in information systems to track what was being sold in the stores daily. Wal-Mart was one of the first retailers in the country to require that all products sold in its stores have bar codes and was the first to install bar code scanners in all checkout stands and link the checkout stands to a centralized computer system. Information gathered by these systems let Wal-Mart manage its inventory more efficiently than rivals. As a result, the company carried less inventory, reducing the amount of space it had to devote to storage and the amount of capital tied up in inventory sitting in distribution centers or stores, all of which took further costs out of Wal-Mart's operations.

strategy
An action managers take
to attain a goal of an
organization.

■ Wal-Mart: Low-cost
strategy.

The story of Wal-Mart illustrates how the strategies of an enterprise can enable it to gain a competitive advantage over its rivals. In the last chapter we looked at the planning systems managers use to select strategies. In this chapter we discuss the different strategies managers can choose from. A **strategy** is an action managers take to attain a goal of an organization. In Wal-Mart's case the strategies were directed toward lowering costs. Wal-Mart's emphasis on low cost is an example of what we call a *business-level strategy,* which is the basic theme a company emphasizes to compete effectively with its rivals. However, many of the strategies that have enabled Wal-Mart to lower its costs were undertaken at the operating level of the company. This brings us to a key message of this chapter: *Business-level strategy is implemented through operations and organization.* For Wal-Mart's managers deciding to pursue a low-cost strategy was the easy part. Putting that strategy into effect was hard work and required a set of actions at the operating level—essentially *operating strategies.* As we will see, executing strategy also requires putting the right *organization* in place.

By the early 1990s Wal-Mart had been so successful at driving down costs that it had become the largest retailer in the United States. But now Sam Walton's successor as CEO, David Glass, faced another problem: Wal-Mart's growth opportunities in the United States were limited. What could the company do to continue growing? The answer Glass came up with was twofold. First, Wal-Mart increased the size of its stores so it could start selling groceries in addition to general merchandise. Wal-Mart reasoned that its state-of-the-art distribution and information systems would let the company lower the costs of selling groceries just as it had cut the costs of selling general merchandise. Second, Wal-Mart decided to start expanding internationally. As a result, by 2005 some 26 percent of Wal-Mart's sales came from groceries, and 17 percent of sales were generated from nine countries outside the United States.

Wal-Mart's diversification into the grocery business and international expansion are both examples of *corporate-level strategy,* which is primarily concerned with deciding which businesses and national markets a firm should be competing in. Until the early 1990s Wal-Mart's business was general merchandise retailing, and it operated in one national market, the United States. Since then it has entered the grocery business and nine additional markets, including Mexico, Germany, and the United Kingdom. Wal-Mart, in short, has pursued the corporate-level strategies of diversification and international expansion.

In this chapter we discuss both business-level strategy and corporate strategy. We show what must be done if a firm is to establish a competitive advantage over rivals. We also discuss how a competitive advantage is necessary for a firm to attain its performance goals. We begin by looking at the nature of those performance goals and the concept of competitive advantage. Then we examine the different strategic options managers can choose from.

■ // Superior Performance and Competitive Advantage

The overriding goal of most organizations is superior performance. For the business firm, superior performance has a clear meaning: It is the ability to generate high profitability and increase profits over time (see Figure 6.1).[2] A central task of managers is to pursue strategies that enable their firm to attain superior performance, measured by profitability and profit growth. This is easier said than done! A principal reason is that firms must compete against rivals for scarce resources. Wal-Mart's success is exemplary precisely because it has been able to outperform rivals such as Kmart and Target over the long haul.

In general, a business firm is more likely to attain high profitability and solid profit growth if it can outperform its rivals in the marketplace—if it can stay ahead in the race for consumer dollars. When a firm outperforms its rivals, we say that it has a **competitive advantage**. At the most basic level, competitive advantage comes from two sources: (1) the ability of the firm to *lower costs* relative to rivals and (2) the ability to *differentiate* its product offering from that of rivals.[3] As we will see shortly, the business-level strategies a firm can pursue are aimed at lowering costs and better differentiating its products.

competitive advantage
Advantage obtained when a
firm outperforms its rivals.

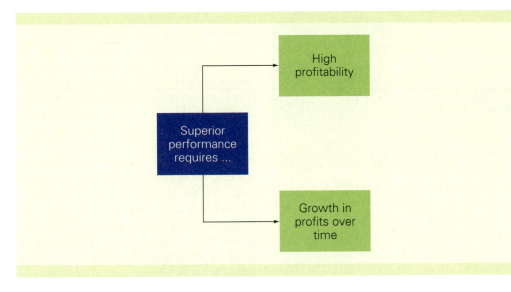

FIGURE 6.1
Superior Performance

If a firm has lower costs than its rivals, other things being equal, it will outperform them. It can charge the same price as its rivals and be more profitable. Alternatively, it might use its low costs to charge less, gain market share, and increase its profits faster than rivals. Or it can do some combination of these two things. Dell Computer, for example, has a competitive advantage over rivals due to its lower cost structure. It has used this low cost structure to cut prices for personal computers, gain market share, and increase its profits faster than rivals. Moreover, due to its low cost structure, Dell can still make good profits at low price points where its rivals lose money.

■ Dell: Low-cost strategy.

If a firm has successfully differentiated its products from those of rivals by attributes such as superior design, quality, reliability, after-sales service, and so on, it should also be able to outperform its rivals. It can charge more than rivals but still register significant sales and earn high profits. Alternatively, it can charge a similar price as less differentiated rivals but use the superior appeal of its products to gain market share and increase its profits faster than rivals. Or it can do some combination of these two things. The high-end department store retailer Nordstrom, for example, has differentiated its product offering from that of rivals by the quality of its merchandise and by its superior in-store customer service. This differentiation has let Nordstrom charge more than rivals while capturing more demand and growing its profits faster than rivals over time.

In general, when a firm has a competitive advantage it derives from one or more distinctive competencies. A **distinctive competency** is a unique strength that rivals lack (we discussed the sources of unique strengths in Chapter 2). For example, Dell Computer has a unique strength in using the Internet to coordinate a globally dispersed supply chain to such an extent that the firm holds only two days of inventory at its assembly plants. Because inventory is a major source of costs in the personal computer business, and most of Dell's rivals operate with as much as 30 days of inventory on hand, Dell's distinctive competency in supply chain management helps explain the firm's low cost structure.[4] Nordstrom, in contrast, has a distinctive competency in customer service. Nordstrom's salespeople are the best in the industry at respectfully helping customers purchase clothes that make them look good. Because customer service gives Nordstrom a differential advantage, it can charge higher prices than rivals for the same basic merchandise.

distinctive competency

A unique strength that rivals lack.

■ Dell and Nordstrom: Distinctive competency.

When a firm outperforms its rivals for a long time, we say that it has a sustainable competitive advantage. A **sustainable competitive advantage** arises from a distinctive competency that rivals cannot easily match or imitate.[5] For example, rivals find it hard to copy Dell's distinctive competency in supply chain management. Dell's strength here is based on the ability to take orders that flow into its Web site from customers and communicate those instantly via the Internet to its suppliers, wherever in the world they might be located. Rivals like Hewlett-Packard would like to do the same thing, but they cannot because unlike Dell, which sells directly to consumers via its Web site, Hewlett-Packard sells mostly through retailers. Thus Hewlett-Packard lacks the real-time information about sales that Dell has, and thus HP cannot execute supply chain

sustainable competitive advantage

A distinctive competency that rivals cannot easily match or imitate.

barrier to imitation
Factors that make it difficult for a firm to imitate the competitive position of a rival.

■ Microsoft: Barriers to imitation.

You Won't Find This at Wal-Mart
A Nordstrom shoe salesperson helps a customer find the perfect fit. Superior customer service is one way Nordstrom differentiates itself from rivals. Nordstrom even has "personal shoppers"—dedicated salespeople assigned to important customers. In contrast, Wal-Mart is a self-service store.
© Mark Richards/Photo Edit.

management techniques based on access to such information.

A distinctive competency is difficult for rivals to match or imitate when it is protected from copying by a **barrier to imitation**. Barriers to imitation include intellectual property rights (such as patents, trademarks, and copyrights) and processes that are embedded deep within a firm and not easy for rivals to see or copy.[6] For example, a barrier to imitation that makes it difficult for rivals to create products similar to Microsoft Office, the company's suite of productivity programs, is the copyright Microsoft has on the computer code that makes up the Office programs, which rivals cannot directly copy without breaking copyright law. Similarly, 3M has a distinctive competency in innovation that has enabled the company to generate 30 percent of its sales from differentiated products introduced within the last five years. Rivals find this competency difficult to imitate because it is based on *processes* for generating new product ideas and taking those ideas from conception through market introduction. These processes are embedded deep within the organization and not easy to observe. There is, in other words, no code book or book of blueprints a rival can purchase to learn how to operate like 3M.

Legacy constraints can also make it difficult for rivals to imitate a firm's distinctive competency. **Legacy constraints** arise from prior investments in a particular way of doing business that are difficult to change and limit a firm's ability to imitate a successful rival. Hewlett-Packard, for example, has invested in reaching consumers for personal computers through retail channels. This is a legacy constraint that makes it difficult for Hewlett-Packard to adopt quickly the direct selling model that Dell uses—that would require HP to walk away from long-established relationships with retailers. If HP were to do that, it would undoubtedly lose significant sales in the short run as it transitioned its business from selling through retailers to selling direct.

In sum, to achieve superior performance, a firm must have a competitive advantage, which allows a firm to achieve lower costs than rivals and better differentiate its product offering. A competitive advantage is typically based on one or more distinctive competencies or unique strengths that the firm has relative to rivals (see Figure 6.2). That competitive advantage will

legacy constraints
Prior investments in a particular way of doing business that are difficult to change and limit a firm's ability to imitate a successful rival.

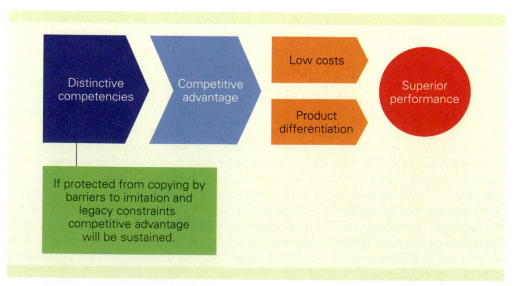

FIGURE 6.2
Competitive Advantage

be more sustainable if it is difficult for rivals to copy or imitate the firm's distinctive competencies. Barriers to imitation and legacy constraints are important factors that make it difficult for rivals to copy a firm's distinctive competencies.

For managers, the key task is to figure out what they must do to build a distinctive competency in one or more activities to gain a competitive advantage over rivals. Moreover, it is clearly preferable that competency be difficult for rivals to imitate due to barriers to imitation and rivals' legacy constraints. In such circumstances the firm's advantage will be more sustainable. Indeed, without barriers to imitation or legacy constraints rivals will quickly copy any new products or processes that managers develop, and any competitive advantage that derives from those products or processes will be transitory.

▮ // Business-Level Strategy

To build a sustainable competitive advantage managers need a good grasp of business-level strategy. A firm's **business-level strategy** is the basic theme that a company emphasizes to compete effectively with rivals in an industry. A firm's business-level strategy encompasses three related choices: the competitive theme that managers emphasize, how to segment the market within an industry, and which segments to serve.

// COMPETITIVE THEME: DIFFERENTIATION OR LOW COST?

Basic business-level strategy is concerned with making the choice between low cost and differentiation. We have already noted that these are two distinct ways of gaining a competitive advantage. So basic are these two strategic orientations that Michael Porter, who wrote one of the classic books on competitive strategy, has referred to them as "generic strategies."[7]

Low-Cost Strategy A **low-cost strategy** is concerned with giving consumers value for money and focusing managerial energy and attention on doing everything possible to lower the costs of the organization. Wal-Mart, Dell Inc., and Southwest Airlines are all examples of firms that have pursued a low-cost strategy. All three enterprises focus on offering basic goods and services at a reasonable price, and they try to produce those goods and services as efficiently as possible. Thus Wal-Mart's stores have minimal fixtures and fittings, are self-service rather than full-service, and sell merchandise at a discounted price. Unlike its rivals, Dell does not invest heavily in R&D to produce leading-edge computers. Rather, it sells good machines at a discounted price. Similarly, Southwest Airlines provides its customers with minimal in-flight service in an attempt to lower costs and thus support inexpensive ticket prices.

The successful pursuit of a low-cost strategy lets a firm charge less than its rivals and still make profits. Moreover, firms that charge lower prices might also be able to gain market share—as Dell, Wal-Mart, and Southwest Airlines have all done—which allows them to realize **economies of scale** (cost advantages derived from a large sales volume) and reap further cost reductions. Thus firms that successfully pursue a low-cost strategy can set up a value cycle similar to that illustrated in Figure 6.3, which lets them consolidate their cost advantage over time.

Differentiation Strategy A **differentiation strategy** is concerned with increasing the value of a product offering in the eyes of consumers. A product can be differentiated by superior reliability (it breaks down less often or not at all), better design, superior functions and features, better point-of-sale service, better after-sales service and support, better branding, and so on. Thus a Rolex watch is differentiated from a Timex watch by superior design, functions, features, and reliability; a Toyota car is differentiated from a General Motors car by superior reliability (new Toyota cars have fewer defects than new GM cars); Nordstrom differentiates itself from Wal-Mart by the quality of its products (such as Armani suits), numerous in-store sales personnel that can help even the most fashion-challenged individual dress well, and a store design that creates a luxurious shopping atmosphere.

business-level strategy
Strategy concerned with deciding how a firm should compete in the industries in which it has elected to participate.

low-cost strategy
Focusing managerial energy and attention on doing everything possible to lower the costs of the organization.

economies of scale
Cost advantages derived from a large sales volume.

differentiation strategy
Increasing the value of a product offering in the eyes of consumers.

■ Nordstrom: Differentiation.

■ Starbucks: Differentiation.

Cost Cutters   By relentlessly taking steps to lower costs Chairman Michael Dell and CEO Kevin Rollins have made Dell Inc. the most profitable enterprise in the personal computer industry. In the early 2000s Dell took advantage of its low-cost position to launch a price war and gain market share from its rivals.

If consumers value a differentiated product offering over that sold by rivals, a differentiation strategy will give the firm a competitive advantage so it can capture more consumer demand. For example, Starbucks has successfully differentiated its product offering from that of rivals such as Tully's by the excellent quality of its coffee-based drinks; the quick, efficient, and friendly service its baristas offer customers; the comfortable atmosphere created by the design of its stores; and its strong brand image. This differentiation has given Starbucks more of the market for coffee-based drinks.

Having differentiated their product, the issue facing managers is how best to translate the competitive advantage that comes from successful differentiation into sustained high profitability and profit growth. Complicating the issue is the fact that differentiation often (but not always) raises the cost structure of the firm. It costs Starbucks quite a lot, for example, to purchase, roast, and brew premium coffee, to train its baristas, and to furnish its stores.

One option managers have is to raise prices to reflect the differentiated nature of the product offering and cover any increase in costs (see Figure 6.4). This is an option that many pursue. It can by itself enhance profitability so long as prices increase more than costs. For example, the Four Seasons chain has luxurious hotels. It costs a lot to provide that luxury, but Four Seasons also charges high prices for its rooms, and the firm is profitable as a result.

However, greater profitability and profit growth can also come from the increased demand associated with successful differentiation, which allows the firm to use its assets more efficiently and thereby simultaneously realize lower costs from scale economies.

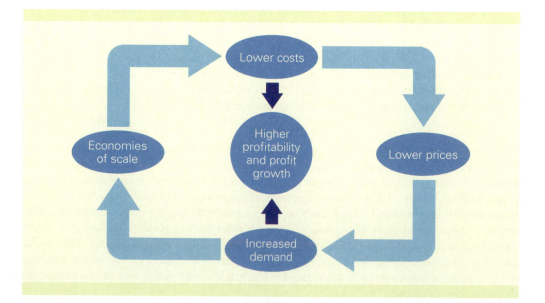

FIGURE 6.3

The Low-Cost Value Cycle

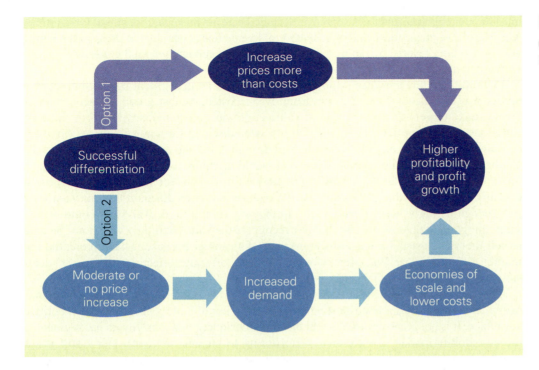

FIGURE 6.4

Options for Exploiting Differentiation

This leads to another option: The successful differentiator can also hold prices constant (or increase prices only slightly), sell more, and boost profitability through scale economies (see Figure 6.4).[8] Thus successful differentiation by Starbucks raises the volume of traffic in each Starbucks store, thereby increasing the productivity of employees in the store (they are always busy) and the productivity of the capital invested in the store itself. So each store realizes scale economies from greater volume, which lowers the average costs at each store. Spread that across the 6,000 stores that Starbucks operates, and you have potentially huge cost savings that translate into higher profitability. Add this to the enhanced demand that comes from successful differentiation, which in the case of Starbucks enables the firm not only to sell more from each store but also to open more stores, and profit growth will also accelerate.

// SEGMENTING THE MARKET

Markets are characterized by different types of consumers. Some are wealthy, some are not; some are old, some are young; some are influenced by popular culture, some never watch TV; some care deeply about status symbols, other do not; some place a high value on luxury, some on value for money. Markets can be segmented by a variety of factors, common examples being the income, demographics, preferences, and tastes of consumers. Moreover, different enterprises can segment the same market in different ways, and various approaches might be reasonable. Take the retail market for apparel: Wal-Mart's clothing department targets lower-income, value-conscious consumers looking for basic clothing; Chico's targets value-conscious, middle-income and middle-aged women with an eye for fashion; Abercrombie & Fitch targets the casual fashion-conscious youth market; Brooks Brothers targets middle- and upper-income male business executives with a taste for stylish formal business attire; Eddie Bauer targets middle- and upper-income consumers who are looking for stylish casual clothing with an outdoor theme; Victoria's Secret targets…well, never mind! These different approaches all represent different ways of segmenting the market—by value preferences, income, age, tastes, and so on.

There is no single best way of segmenting a market; but in terms of attaining a competitive advantage, some approaches to segmentation make more sense. At a minimum, a segment must have enough demand to be served profitably. There are no apparel retailers, for example, who target a segment consisting of sedentary old white males who like to dress in the baggy athletic clothing favored by rap musicians; there are not enough potential consumers in that segment to make it profitable to serve.

Beyond this commonsense notion, there may be value in segmenting the market in a unique way that distinguishes the firm from rivals. Costco, the fast-growing discount warehouse store, targets relatively affluent value-conscious consumers. We tend to think of warehouse stores as offering merchandise at a deep discount from normal prices (they are pursuing a low-cost strategy). Costco indeed does that; but the merchandise the firm sells can be high-end, from Polo brand shirts that would normally retail for $70, which Costco might offer for $40, to $40,000 diamond rings that Costco sells for $25,000. As one Costco executive told this author, "We can offer Polo shirts at a deep discount and our customer will recognize the value and snap them up, buying 10 at a time. Wal-Mart could do the same thing, and their customers wouldn't recognize the value, and they would not be able to sell them."[9] Costco attracts a different type of customer because it has segmented the market differently than Wal-Mart. Costco's product offering reflects its managers' decisions about how best to segment the market.

Generalizing from the Costco example, segmenting the market in a unique but economically viable way can be a good starting point in the quest to build a sustainable competitive advantage. It is not necessary to segment the market uniquely, however. Toyota has segmented the automobile market conventionally (according to income and age), but it still has a competitive advantage. When segmenting the market, managers must have a clear idea of the consumers they are trying to serve, what the needs of those consumers are, and how the business is going to serve those needs.

// CHOOSING SEGMENTS TO SERVE

Having decided how to segment the market, managers must decide which segments to serve. Some enterprises focus on a few segments or just one. Others serve a broad range of segments. In the automobile industry, Toyota has brands that address the entire market: Scion for budget-constrained, young, entry-level buyers; Toyota for the middle market; and Lexus for the luxury end of the market. In each of these segments Toyota pursues a differentiation strategy; it tries to differentiate itself from rivals in the segment by the excellent reliability and high perceived quality of its offerings. In contrast, Porsche focuses exclusively on the top of the market, targeting wealthy middle-aged male consumers who have a passion for the speed, power, and engineering excellence associated with its range of sports cars. Porsche is clearly pursuing a differentiation strategy with regard to these segments, although it emphasizes a different type of differentiation than Toyota. When managers decide to serve a limited number of segments, or just one segment, we say that they are pursuing a **focus strategy**. When they decide to serve the entire market, they are pursuing a **broad market strategy**.

// SEGMENTATION AND STRATEGY

We have suggested that there are three dimensions to business-level strategy: the competitive theme managers emphasize (low cost or differentiation), the way they choose to segment the market, and the segments they serve. Taken together, these dimensions allow a variety of different ways to compete in an industry. Figure 6.5 summarizes two of these dimensions—competitive theme and segments served. Also included in Figure 6.5 are some illustrative examples chosen from the U.S. retail industry.

Broad low-cost and broad differentiation strategies aim to serve many segments in an industry and strive for either a low-cost or a differentiated position. Focused low-cost and focused differentiation strategies focus on one or a few specific segments and strive to attain a low-cost or differentiation position *relative to that segment.* However, Figure 6.5 does not capture the full richness of business-level strategy. Various businesses may segment the

■ Costco: Market segmentation.

focus strategy
Serving a limited number of segments.

broad market strategy
Serving the entire market.

FIGURE 6.5

Types of Business-Level
Strategy

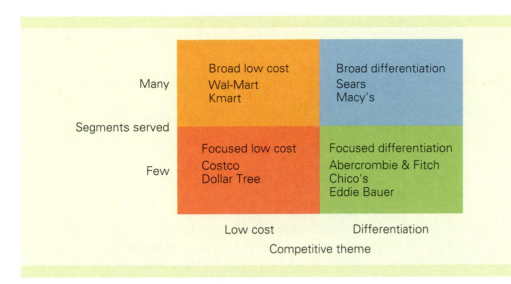

market differently and focus on disparate segments. Although Costco and Dollar Tree are both shown as focused low-cost businesses in the retail industry, they compete in very different spaces. All of the merchandise in a Dollar Tree store is priced at a dollar or less. Dollar Tree sells a lot of small household items at deep discounts to low-income consumers. In contrast, as already noted, Costco sells higher-end items at a deep discount to middle- and high-income value-conscious consumers. Costco customers do not usually enter Dollar Tree stores and vice versa.

// THE LOW COST–DIFFERENTIATION FRONTIER

So far we have suggested that low-cost positions and differentiated positions are two different ways of gaining competitive advantage. The enterprise that is striving for the lowest costs does everything it can to cut costs out of its operations, whereas the enterprise striving for differentiation necessarily has to bear higher costs to achieve that differentiation. Put simply, a firm cannot simultaneously be Wal-Mart and Nordstrom, Porsche and Kia, or Rolex and Timex. Managers must choose between these basic ways of attaining competitive advantage.

However, presenting the choice between differentiation and low costs in these terms is something of a simplification. In practice, the strategic issue facing managers is what position to choose on a continuum that is anchored at one end by very low costs and at the other by a very high level of differentiation. To understand this issue, look at Figure 6.6. Its convex curve illustrates what is known as an *efficiency frontier*.[10] The efficiency frontier shows all the different positions a firm can adopt with regard to differentiation and low cost assuming that its internal operations are configured efficiently to support a particular position. (Note that the horizontal axis in Figure 6.6 is reverse scaled—moving along the axis to the right implies lower costs.) For an enterprise to reach the efficiency frontier—to have a competitive advantage and achieve superior performance—it must have unique strengths or distinctive competencies that rivals inside the frontier lack and that enable it to operate efficiently.

The efficiency frontier has a convex shape because of *diminishing returns*: When a firm already has significant differentiation built into its product offering, increasing differentiation by a relatively small amount requires significant additional costs. The converse also holds: When a firm already has a low cost structure, it has to give up a lot of differentiation in its product offering to get additional cost reductions.

The efficiency frontier shown in Figure 6.6 is for the U.S. retail apparel business (Wal-Mart sells more than apparel, but that need not concern us here). As you can see, Nordstrom and Wal-Mart are both shown on the frontier, implying that both organizations have configured their internal operations efficiently. However, they have adopted different

FIGURE 6.6

The Efficiency Frontier
in Retail Apparel

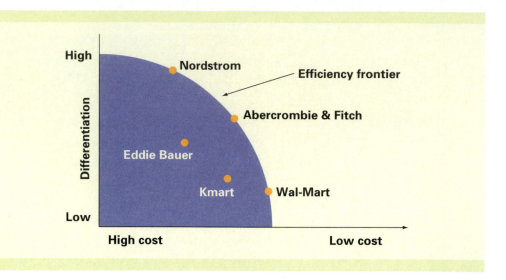

strategic positions. Nordstrom has high differentiation and high costs (it is pursuing a differentiation strategy), whereas Wal-Mart has low costs and low differentiation (it is pursuing a low-cost strategy). These are not the only viable positions in the industry. We have also shown Abercrombie & Fitch on the frontier. Abercrombie & Fitch offers higher-quality apparel than Wal-Mart, sold in a more appealing store format; but its offering is nowhere near as differentiated as that of Nordstrom, and it is positioned between Wal-Mart and Nordstrom. This midlevel position, offering moderate differentiation at a higher cost than Wal-Mart, makes sense because there is a large enough segment of consumers that demand this kind of offering.

Often multiple positions on the low cost–differentiation continuum are viable in the sense that they have enough demand to support an offering. The strategic task for managers is to identify a viable position in the industry and then configure the enterprise's internal operations as efficiently as possible, to enable the firm to reach the frontier. Not all firms can do this. Only firms that can get to the frontier have a competitive advantage.

Not all positions on an industry's efficiency frontier are equally as attractive. At some positions there may not be sufficient demand to support a product offering. At other positions too many competitors may be going after the same consumers (the competitive space might be too crowded), and the resulting competition might drive prices down below levels that are acceptable.

In Figure 6.6 Kmart is shown inside the frontier. Kmart is trying to position itself in the same space as Wal-Mart, but its internal operations are not efficient. Indeed, the company was operating under bankruptcy protection in the early 2000s (it is now out of bankruptcy). Also shown in Figure 6.6 is the Redmond, Washington–based clothing retailer Eddie Bauer, which is owned by Spiegel. Like Kmart, Eddie Bauer is not currently run efficiently relative to its rivals, and its parent company is operating under bankruptcy protection.

value innovation

Using innovation to offer more value at a lower cost than competitors

■ Dell: Value innovation.

Value Innovation The efficiency frontier in an industry is not static; it is continually being pushed outward by the efforts of managers to improve their firms' performance.[11] The companies that push out the efficiency frontier can offer more value to their customers (through enhanced differentiation) at lower cost than their rivals—a process sometimes referred to as *value innovation*.[12] Dell Computer has achieved value innovation in the personal computer industry (see Figure 6.7). In the 1980s when other computer firms were selling through retailers, Michael Dell pioneered the practice of selling direct. By the mid-1990s Dell was selling over the Internet, and today 85 percent of its home PCs are sold this way. A great advantage of this strategy for customers is that they can customize their PCs, mixing and matching components to get just what they want. Thus by adopting a direct selling business model, Dell differentiated itself from competitors, offering its customers more value.

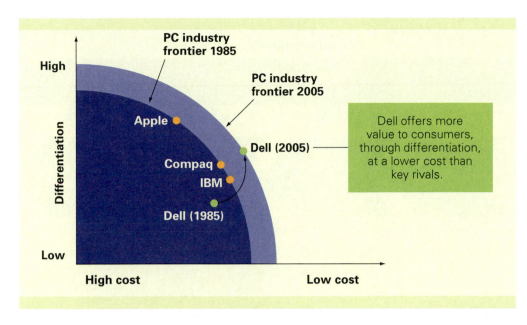

FIGURE 6.7

Pushing Out the Efficiency Frontier through Value Innovation

The direct selling strategy has also had far-reaching implications for Dell's costs. Because it sells direct, Dell can build to order. Unlike competitors, it does not have to fill a retail channel with inventory. Moreover, Dell can use the Internet to feed real-time information about order flow to its suppliers so they have up-to-the-minute information about demand trends for the components they produce, along with volume expectations for the upcoming 4–12 weeks. Dell's suppliers use this information to adjust their own production schedules, manufacturing just enough components for Dell's needs and shipping them by the most appropriate mode to arrive just in time for production. Dell's ultimate goal is to drive all inventories out of the supply chain apart from those actually in transit between suppliers and Dell, effectively replacing inventory with information. Although it has not yet achieved this goal, it has driven down inventory to the lowest level in the industry. Dell has about two days of inventory on hand, compared to 20–30 at competitors such as Hewlett-Packard and Gateway. This is a major source of competitive advantage in the computer industry, where component costs account for 75 percent of revenues and the value of components falls by 1 percent per week due to rapid obsolescence. Thus by pioneering online selling of PCs, and by using information systems to coordinate its supply chain, Dell Computer has attained new levels of operational efficiency.

In essence, Dell has built new distinctive competencies, and in doing so has pushed out the efficiency frontier in the personal computer industry. Dell now offers more differentiation (the ability to customize a PC when placing an order on the Web) at lower cost than its rivals can offer. In industry after industry this is how competition proceeds: Firms compete by developing superior competencies that enable them to push out the efficiency frontier, stranding rivals at a competitive disadvantage. It follows that a central strategic task of managers is to look for ways of improving operating efficiency and enhancing value through differentiation in order to take the enterprise to a new level of excellence.

▮ // Implementing Business-Level Strategy

We have just seen that reaching the efficiency frontier in an industry, given managers' choice of strategic position, requires efficient operations. Moreover, in the long run sustaining a competitive advantage requires managers to continually improve operational efficiency, thereby pushing out the efficiency frontier and staying ahead of rivals in a race that has no end. To grasp this we need to dig a little deeper into the nature of operations and consider how operational excellence can help an enterprise build distinctive competencies and thus lower costs or better differentiate its product offering. We return to operational strategy in Chapter 7, when we discuss some of these issues in more depth.

FIGURE 6.8

The Value Chain

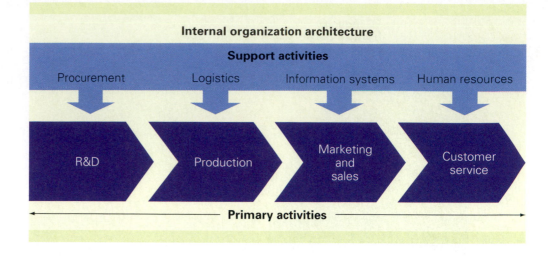

// CONFIGURING THE VALUE CHAIN

The operations of a firm can be thought of as a value chain composed of a series of distinct activities including production, marketing and sales, logistics, R&D, human resources, information systems, and the firm's infrastructure. We can categorize these activities, or operations, as *primary activities* and *support activities* (see Figure 6.8).[13] We use the term *value chain* because each activity adds value to the product offering. These operations are embedded within the internal organization architecture of a firm, which includes the organization structure, controls, incentives, culture, and people of the enterprise. Organization architecture provides the context within which operations take place.

primary activities

Activities having to do with the design, creation, and delivery of the product; its marketing; and its support and after-sale service.

Primary Activities Primary activities have to do with the design, creation, and delivery of the product; its marketing; and its support and after-sale service. Following normal practice, in the value chain illustrated in Figure 6.8 the primary activities are divided into four functions: research and development, production, marketing and sales, and customer service.

Research and development (R&D) is concerned with the design of products and production processes. Although we think of R&D as being associated with the design of physical products and production processes in manufacturing enterprises, many service companies also undertake R&D. Banks compete with each other by developing new financial products and new ways of delivering those products to customers. Online banking and smart debit cards are two examples of new product development in the banking industry. Through superior product design, R&D can increase the functionality of products, which makes them more attractive to consumers (increasing differentiation). Alternatively, R&D may result in more efficient production processes, thereby cutting production costs. Either way, the R&D function can help create a competitive advantage.

Production creates a good or service. For physical products, when we talk about production we generally mean manufacturing. Thus we can talk about the production of an automobile. For services such as banking or health care, production typically occurs when the service is delivered to the customer (such as when a bank originates a loan for a customer). For a retailer such as Wal-Mart, production includes selecting the merchandise, stocking the store, and ringing up sales at cash registers. Production can help a firm create competitive advantage through efficiency or greater differentiation.

The marketing and sales functions can help a firm attain a differentiated or low-cost position in several ways. Through brand positioning and advertising, marketing can affect consumers' perceptions of how differentiated a firm's product offering is. If consumers have a favorable impression of a firm's products, the firm can charge more or expand sales volume. For example, Ford produces a high-value version of its Ford Expedition SUV. Sold as the

Lincoln Navigator and priced around $10,000 higher, the Navigator has the same body, engine, chassis, and design as the Expedition. But through skilled advertising and marketing, supported by some fairly minor feature changes (such as more accessories and the addition of a Lincoln-style engine grille and nameplate), Ford has fostered the perception that the Navigator is a luxury SUV. This marketing strategy has increased the perceived differentiation of the Navigator relative to the Expedition, and Ford can charge a higher price for the car.

Marketing and sales can also create value by discovering consumer needs and communicating them back to the R&D function of the company, which can then design products that better match those needs. For example, the allocation of research budgets at Pfizer, the world's largest pharmaceutical company, is determined by the marketing function's assessment of the potential market size associated with solving unmet medical needs. Thus Pfizer is currently directing significant funds to R&D efforts aimed at finding treatments for Alzheimer's disease, principally because marketing has identified the treatment of Alzheimer's as a major unmet medical need.

The role of a firm's service activity is to provide after-sale service and support. This function can create a perception of superior differentiation in the minds of consumers by solving customer problems and supporting customers after they have purchased the product. Caterpillar, the U.S.-based manufacturer of heavy earth-moving equipment, can get spare parts to any point in the world within 24 hours, thereby minimizing the amount of downtime its customers have to suffer if their Caterpillar equipment malfunctions. This is an extremely valuable capability in an industry where downtime is expensive. It has helped increase the value that customers associate with Caterpillar products and thus the price that Caterpillar can charge.

No Downtime   Caterpillar can get spare parts to anywhere in the world in 24 hours.

Reprinted Courtesy of Caterpillar Inc.

■ Pfizer: Creating value through R & D.

Support Activities   The support activities of the value chain provide inputs that allow the primary activities to occur (see Figure 6.8). In terms of attaining competitive advantage, they can be as important, if not more important, than the primary activities of the firm. The procurement function is responsible for purchasing inputs to the production process, including raw materials, partly finished products, and in the case of retailers, items for resale. Procurement can lower costs by getting the best deals and by leveraging buying power to lower the price paid for inputs. Procurement can also help increase differentiation by purchasing higher-quality inputs. The logistics function controls the transmission of physical materials through the value chain, from procurement through production and into distribution. The efficiency with which this is carried out can significantly reduce costs. As noted earlier, logistics is a major source of Wal-Mart's competitive advantage.

The human resources function can help create competitive advantage in a number of ways. It ensures that the company has the right mix of skilled people to perform its value creation activities effectively. Wal-Mart, for example, uses local managers to run Wal-Mart's stores and logistics operations in countries outside the United States. The thinking behind this is that local managers will have a better feel for the tastes and preferences of local customers than expatriate managers from the United States. Insofar as this improves the fit between Wal-Mart's merchandising and local tastes, it should result in higher sales. The human resources function also ensures that people are adequately trained, motivated, and compensated to perform their value creation tasks.

Information systems are the electronic systems for managing inventory, tracking sales, pricing products, selling products, dealing with customer service inquiries, and so on.

support activities
Activities that provide inputs that allow the primary activities to occur.

■ Wal-Mart: Human resources.

Information systems, when coupled with the communications features of the Internet, can alter the efficiency and effectiveness with which a firm manages other activities in the value chain. Again, Wal-Mart's competitive advantage is based largely on its pioneering use of information systems to track store sales. This tracking capability means that Wal-Mart is almost never caught with too much or too little of a certain item. This reduces Wal-Mart's need to hold extensive buffer inventory, which reduces inventory costs, and makes sure that Wal-Mart never has to hold sales to unload excess inventory, keeping prices from having to be reduced.

Organization Architecture As already noted, the operations of the firm are embedded within the internal organization architecture of the enterprise, which includes the organization structure, incentives, control systems, people, and culture of the firm. In a real sense strategy is implemented through organization architecture. Because organization architecture is so important to strategy implementation and the attainment of competitive advantage, we discuss it in depth in Part 3 of this book. For now note that if a firm is to attain competitive advantage, its organization architecture must support its operations and enable it to successfully implement its strategy.

■ Wal-Mart: Organization structure.

For example, if a firm is trying to become a low-cost industry player, it should have an organization architecture that focuses the attention of everyone within the enterprise on the need to drive down costs. Thus Wal-Mart operates with a very flat organization structure (there are few layers between the head office and individual stores). Unlike most other large national retailers, the company has no regional offices. It sees regional offices as an additional cost, so it has cut them out, preferring to manage the entire U.S. operations from its headquarters in Arkansas. Wal-Mart also has an organizational culture that emphasizes the need to contain costs. An important norm at Wal-Mart is that when senior managers travel from headquarters to visit stores, they should share hotel rooms and stay in budget hotels to save costs. Another norm is that they should return from each trip with enough ideas to cover the cost of the trip. These norms are designed to emphasize the importance of controlling costs. In other words, the organization architecture of Wal-Mart supports the company's strategy, which is to drive down costs, and its operations, which again are geared toward maximizing efficiency.

// COMPETITIVE ADVANTAGE AND STRATEGIC FIT

If a business enterprise is to attain superior performance, its business-level strategy (as captured by its desired strategic position on the efficiency frontier) must make sense given industry conditions (for example, there must be sufficient demand to support that strategic choice). Operations must be configured in a way that supports the strategy, and the internal organization architecture must support the operations and strategy of the firm. In other words, as illustrated in Figure 6.9, industry conditions, strategy, operations, and organization must all be consistent with each other, or *fit* each other, for competitive advantage to be attained and superior performance to occur. Moreover, the operations and organization of the firm must give it a distinctive competency in one or more activities of the value chain. Without unique and valuable skills, a firm will not be able to outperform rivals.

The issue of strategic fit is actually more complex than illustrated in Figure 6.9. The firm can influence industry conditions through its choice of strategy. For example, by launching a price war in their industry, a firm's managers can make the industry conditions they face more hostile, and that might require a fundamental change of strategy. Alternatively, through their choice of strategy managers can reduce the intensity of competition in their industry, making it more favorable. In addition, shifts in market conditions caused by new technologies, government action such as deregulation, demographics, or social trends can mean that the strategy of the firm no longer fits the industry. In such circumstances the firm must change its strategy, operations, and organization to fit the new reality. This can be an extraordinarily difficult challenge. We discuss the management of change in depth in Chapter 18.

FIGURE 6.9
Strategic Fit

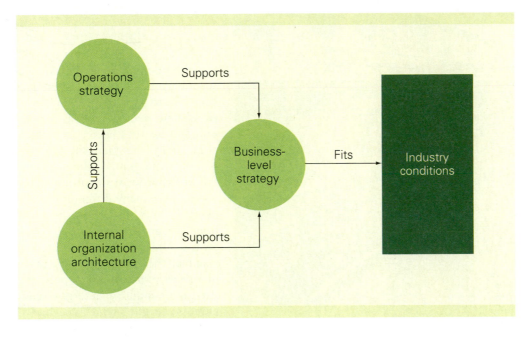

■ // Competitive Tactics

The **competitive tactics** of an enterprise are actions that managers take to try to outmaneuver rivals in the marketplace.[14] Whereas the business-level *strategy* of an enterprise represents its basic competitive theme and tends to be pursued for a long time, *tactics* are individual actions taken to gain advantage over rivals or even to inhibit rivals from emerging in the first place, thereby making it easier to attain competitive advantage. Competitive tactics can be short-term maneuvers or longer-term actions, but they are always about gaining a better market position relative to actual or potential rivals. Tactics include decisions about pricing and product offerings. We review some here to give you an idea of what tactics encompass.

competitive tactics
Actions that managers take to try to outmaneuver rivals in the market.

// TACTICAL PRICING DECISIONS

Managers can make a number of different tactical pricing decisions. Launching a *price war* to gain share from competitors is one example of a tactical pricing decision. This is what Dell Computer did in 2000–2001 when it took advantage of its low cost structure to drive down the prices of personal computers and gain share from its major rivals. A variant of this tactic is *price signaling,* such as cutting prices when new competitors enter the market to send a signal to potential rivals that they will have a tough fight if they wish to gain share. When discount airlines such as Jet Blue started to expand into profitable routes served by American Airlines, American responded by slashing prices. Not only did this make it more difficult for Jet Blue to gain a foothold; it also sent a signal to other discount airlines that American would not give up its market share easily. American's hope, of course, was that such actions would deter future entry.

Another common tactical pricing decision is *razor and razor blade pricing,* so called because it was pioneered by razor manufacturer Gillette. Gillette's idea was to price razors low (at cost) to sell them to consumers, then make money from the sale of blades, which were priced high. Today Hewlett-Packard uses this tactic in the market for ink jet printers and supplies. HP prices its ink jet printers low (some can be purchased for under $100) and makes little profit on these sales. However, the company charges a high price for ink cartridges for the printers (often over $30) and makes high profit margins on these. The strategy works because once consumers have purchased the ink jet printers they are tied into those products by high switching costs (the cost of buying a printer from another company) and so are likely to continue buying HP ink cartridges.

■ Gillette: Razor and blade pricing.

Product Proliferation   Walk into a supermarket and you will see dozens of different varieties of cereal; yet the industry is dominated by just four firms—Kellogg, General Mills, Post, and Quaker. Each manufacturer has proliferated its brands to occupy as much shelf space as it can, thereby shutting out competitors and creating an entry barrier.

© McGraw-Hill Companies, Inc./Gary He, photographer.

// TACTICAL PRODUCT DECISIONS

As with pricing, managers can pursue a wide range of tactical product decisions to gain an advantage over rivals. One tactic, known as *product proliferation,* has been successfully pursued by the manufacturers of laundry detergent. Walk down the aisle of your local supermarket and you will see many different laundry detergent brands. Most of these brands are produced by just two firms, Unilever and Procter & Gamble. They produce a wide range of different brands to supply any variant of laundry detergent consumers might wish to buy— powdered detergent, liquid detergent, colorfast detergent, detergent with fabric softener, and so on—and thus occupy all of the shelf space in a supermarket, limiting the opportunities for market entry by new rivals. Thus product proliferation is an entry-deterring tactic; and to the extent that it has been successful, Unilever and Procter & Gamble can charge higher prices than would otherwise be the case, which improves their performance. A similar strategy has been pursued by manufacturers in the cereal industry.

Another common product strategy is known as *bundling.* The idea behind a bundling strategy is to tie together a set of related products and charge a single price for them, which is marginally lower than the price of each product when sold separately. This can appeal to consumers, who wish to pay only a single bill and deal with a single provider, and it can raise demand far beyond what could be attained if the firm sold each item separately. The cable company Comcast is currently pursuing this strategy. In addition to cable TV, Comcast now uses its cable into the home to provide high-speed Internet access via a cable modem, video on demand, digital video recording capabilities, and long-distance telephone service. By bundling these services together Comcast hopes to be able to gain market share and revenues from rivals that sell just one of these services.

■ Comcast: Product bundling.

■ // Corporate-Level Strategy

corporate-level strategy

Strategy concerned with deciding which industries a firm should compete in and how the firm should enter or exit industries.

So far we have been discussing strategy at the business level. Now it is time to consider **corporate-level strategy**, which is concerned with deciding what businesses and national markets an enterprise should participate in. The business options are to focus on a single business; vertically integrate into adjacent businesses, forming a supply chain from raw materials to consumers; and diversify into other businesses. The national market options are to focus on the firm's home market or expand internationally. Corporate-level strategy also encompasses decisions about *how* to enter new businesses and markets—whether through acquisitions and mergers or by establishing new ventures. As always, the goal of management in pursuing these strategies is to boost the overall performance of the enterprise measured by profitability and profit growth.

// FOCUS ON A SINGLE BUSINESS

Focusing on a single business makes sense if a firm is growing rapidly, consuming all available capital resources and the time and energy of its managers. Almost all enterprises start out focusing on a single industry. So long as that business continues to grow, they are often advised to continue doing so. Expanding into other businesses becomes an option when the growth rate in the core business is decelerating, as can occur when the market the firm serves is saturated and overall industry growth has slowed down.

The strategic question managers must answer then is whether to enter new businesses or simply return the cash generated by the existing business to shareholders in the form of higher dividend payouts. This was the question managers at Microsoft were contemplating in 2004. The growth rate in the company's core software business had slowed down due to maturation of the personal computer market, but the company was generating huge cash flows (by mid-2004 it had some $64 billion in cash). Microsoft's managers had to decide whether to use that cash to fund additional diversification efforts (such as the company's move into the video game businesses with Xbox) or to return it to shareholders. Because they could not find enough profitable opportunities outside their existing business, they chose to return over $30 billion to shareholders in a huge special dividend payout. Basically Microsoft's managers were saying that they could not see opportunities for profitably redeploying those funds to other businesses, so they decided to let investors enjoy the fruits of their ownership of the company. Sometimes, however, managers may see opportunities for boosting the overall performance of a firm by vertically integrating into adjacent activities, diversifying into new businesses, or expanding internationally to enter new markets.

// VERTICAL INTEGRATION

■ Apple: Vertical integration.

Vertical integration involves moving *upstream* into businesses that supply inputs to the firm's core business or *downstream* into businesses that use the outputs of the firm's core business. An example of upstream vertical integration would be for Dell Computer to enter the memory chip business, making the memory chips that go into its personal computers (currently Dell purchases these chips from independent suppliers). An example of downstream vertical integration is the 2001 decision by Apple Computer to enter the retail business with its Apple Store. The stores sell Apple products and third-party products, and as of 2006 there were close to 150 of these stores.

> **vertical integration**
> Moving upstream into businesses that supply inputs to a firm's core business or downstream into businesses that use the outputs of the firm's core business.

Vertical integration makes sense if it improves the competitive position of the firm's core business. For this to be so, *vertical integration must enable the firm's core business either to lower its costs or to better differentiate its product offering.* Apple's entry into retailing, for example, is designed to provide better point-of-sales service to customers wishing to purchase an Apple product than can be had from independent stores. By helping to raise the overall level of differentiation associated with Apple's offering, the strategy is designed to strengthen Apple's competitive position.

Vertical Integration In 2001 Apple decided to start opening its own stores to sell Apple products, including Apple computers and iPods. This is an example of downstream vertical integration.

AP Photo/Mark Lennihan.

Although vertical integration might look good on paper, many enterprises that have vertically integrated upstream have found themselves locked into high-cost businesses that detract from their competitive advantage. A common problem is that in-house suppliers lack a strong incentive to drive down costs because they have a guaranteed buyer for their products—their own firm. As a result, over time in-house suppliers can become less efficient, making vertical integration a liability rather than an asset. General Motors, for example, was until recently highly vertically integrated, making many of the components that go into GM cars. Unfortunately for GM, high labor costs in its unionized in-house supply operations raised input costs above those enjoyed by rivals like Toyota, putting GM at a competitive disadvantage. In the late 1990s GM rectified this situation by selling its in-house suppliers, effectively *deintegrating*. This strategic action gave GM greater freedom to purchase components from independent suppliers that had a lower cost structure and could offer GM lower prices.

// DIVERSIFICATION

diversification

Entry into new business areas.

related diversification

Diversification into a business related to the existing business activities of an enterprise by distinct similarities in one or more activities in the value chain.

unrelated diversification

Diversification into a business not related to the existing business activities of an enterprise by distinct similarities in one or more activities in the value chain.

■ General Electric: Unrelated diversification.

economies of scope

Cost reductions associated with sharing resources across businesses.

■ Procter & Gamble Economies of scope.

The strategy of **diversification** involves entry into new business areas. Microsoft's entry into the video game business with its Xbox offering is an example of diversification, as is General Electric's move into network broadcasting with the acquisition of NBC. The Microsoft case is an example of what is called **related diversification**: The new business is related to the existing business activities of the enterprise by distinct similarities in one or more activities in the value chain. The video game business is a software-based business, so Microsoft could use its established software engineering skills to develop both an operating system for the Xbox (which is actually based on Windows) and the video games themselves. The General Electric case is an example of **unrelated diversification**: The new business, NBC, was *not* related to the existing activities of the enterprise by similar value chain activities.[15]

As with vertical integration, the key to successful diversification is that it should increase the performance of one or more businesses beyond what could be achieved if each enterprise were an independent business in its own right.[16] If this does not happen, there is no value to different businesses being part of the same organization.

Leveraging Core Competencies   One way in which diversified enterprises boost the performance of their constituent units is by leveraging valuable core competencies and applying them to a new line of business. Thus Microsoft used its valuable skills in software engineering to enter the video game business with Xbox. The aim here is to create a competitive advantage in the new business activity by leveraging the competencies that enabled the original business activity to gain a competitive advantage. A good example of a firm that has done this consistently for decades is 3M, which among other things leveraged its skills in adhesives, originally developed to hold the grit on sandpaper, to create new businesses. These new businesses have included masking tape, medical tape, and the ubiquitous Post-it notes.

Economies of Scope   Another way of improving performance through diversification is to realize what are called **economies of scope**, which are the cost reductions associated with sharing resources across businesses.[17] Firms that can share resources across businesses have to invest proportionally less in the shared resource than companies that cannot share. For example, Procter & Gamble makes both disposable diapers and paper towels. Both of these paper-based products are valued for their ability to absorb liquid without disintegrating. Because both products need the same attribute—absorbency—Procter & Gamble can share the R&D costs associated with producing an absorbent paper-based product across the two businesses. Similarly, because both products are sold to the same customer set (supermarkets), P&G can use the same sales force to sell both products. In contrast, competitors that make just paper towels or just disposable diapers cannot achieve the same economies and will have to invest more in both R&D and maintaining a sales force. The net result is that other things being equal, P&G will have lower expenses and higher profitability than firms that lack the ability to share resources.

Superior Internal Governance A final way in which diversification can improve the performance of the enterprise is through superior internal governance skills.[18] *Internal governance skills* are the ability of senior managers to elicit high levels of performance from the constituent businesses of a diversified enterprise. Senior managers can do this via organization architecture that creates incentives for the managers and employees running the businesses to work productively; by selecting highly skilled managers to run the constituent businesses; by coaching those managers, helping them to upgrade their managerial skills; by helping them to diagnose problems within their businesses and identify ways of improving performance; and by pushing managers to search for ways to improve the performance of their units.

Jack Welch, the longtime CEO of General Electric, was a master at internal governance. Welch said he spent 70 percent of his time on people issues and that his greatest contribution to General Electric was finding and coaching great managers and pushing those managers to improve the performance of their units and share best practices across businesses.

Diversification Failures Although diversification can improve the profitability and profit growth of an enterprise, the opposite can also be the case. There are many examples of diversification efforts that failed. In some cases these diversification efforts involved the acquisition of an established business in another industry, as opposed to organic expansion like that of 3M or Microsoft's entry into the video game business. There are several problems with such diversification.[19] First, there is evidence that acquiring enterprises pay too much for the companies they acquire (they overvalue them). Second, acquiring firms often let acquired businesses continue to operate as stand-alone enterprises. Managers of the acquiring firm take no action to transfer core competencies, realize economies of scope, or improve performance through the application of superior governance skills. When no steps are taken to improve the performance of the acquired business, it is hardly surprising that the diversification move fails to improve performance.

Finally, even when proactive efforts are made to improve the performance of the newly acquired business, many unexpected problems can stymie attempts to do this. Often these problems stem from differences in organization architecture and cultures. After an acquisition, many acquired businesses experience high management turnover, possibly because their employees do not like the acquiring company's way of doing things.[20] Evidence suggests that the loss of management talent and expertise in the acquired enterprise can materially harm the performance of the acquired unit.[21]

// INTERNATIONAL EXPANSION

International expansion is the final corporate strategy we consider here. International expansion can be a good way to increase the performance of a firm. Historically managers have turned their attention to international expansion after their business has become established in its home market. More recently, however, with the emergence of global markets managers are starting to think about international expansion even at an early point in the development of their enterprise. Nowadays even some small enterprises have a global presence. We reviewed the reasons for expanding internationally in Chapter 3. Here we note briefly that international expansion can enlarge the market for a firm's products, thereby boosting profit growth; enable a firm to realize *scale economies* from serving a large global market, which can lower unit costs and boost profitability; enable a firm to realize *location economies* and increase profitability by basing different business activities where they can be performed most efficiently; and boost both profitability and profit growth by transferring skills between different national subsidiaries, a process known as *global learning*.

---

internal governance skills
The ability of senior managers to elicit high levels of performance from the constituent businesses of a diversified enterprise.

IN CONCLUSION   WHY DOES IT MATTER?

All organizations have to compete with rivals to obtain scarce resources and achieve their performance goals. For sustained high performance, an organization needs a competitive advantage over its rivals. A competitive advantage does not happen by accident. Gaining and sustaining a competitive advantage over the long haul requires managers to craft and then implement strategies that result in a fit between the products of the enterprise and competitive conditions in the markets in which the enterprise participates. Without the correct set of strategies at the corporate, business, operating, and organizational levels, performance will suffer, the enterprise will go into decline, and the job security, career prospects, and reputations of its managers will suffer. By the same token, successful careers are enjoyed by managers who establish a reputation for being able to craft and then effectively implement strategies.

Designing and implementing strategy is not the sole preserve of top managers. Although top managers may guide the strategy-making process, the strategies crafted and implemented by operating managers also play a key role in strategic success. It is crucially important, therefore, that even the lowest-level managers in an organization have a good grasp of strategy and understand their role in the process of building and sustaining a competitive advantage.

An interesting example was referred to several times in this chapter: Microsoft's entry into the video game business with its Xbox offering. The Xbox was not the result of a grand strategic vision crafted by Chairman Bill Gates and CEO Steve Balmer; it was the result of the actions of four engineers and their manager, who developed a prototype of the Xbox by their own initiative and on their own time, and then successfully lobbied Gates and Balmer to devote resources to the commercialization of the product. To be able to pull off this kind of initiative, managers, whatever their level, must be able to articulate what the strategy should be. They cannot do that unless they understand the basics of strategy as laid out in this chapter.

Even if they are not pushing strategic initiatives, newly hired junior managers can still be surprised by how rapidly they are drawn into the strategy-making vortex of an enterprise. This is certainly true at Microsoft, where management interns have recounted, sometimes with a sense of wonder in their eyes at the possibilities, how they found themselves in a strategy session where their team was trying to articulate and defend the competitive strategy for its product offering to Bill Gates or Steve Balmer. "What a rush," one noted as he recounted the experience; "here I was, not even graduated yet, and I had to answer this blizzard of questions from Bill Gates, who was just ripping into our plan. Amazingly, at the end of the session, he told us to go ahead!"[22] The ability of this intern to hold his own in the strategy conversation was due to the fact that he understood what strategy was about, what was required to gain and sustain competitive advantage, and how to articulate that. This is a skill that managers must have if they are to be successful.

MANAGEMENT CHALLENGES

1. "The only goal of strategy is to maximize the profitability of the enterprise." Is this statement correct?

2. How would you characterize the business-level strategies of the following enterprises in the airline industry: Jet Blue, Maxjet (www.maxjet.com), and United Airlines? Can you plot the position that each enterprise aspires to on the efficiency frontier in the industry?

3. "Success in strategy is 10 percent inspiration and 90 percent perspiration." In the context of the material discussed in this chapter, what does this statement mean?

4. Visit the Web site of the Boeing Corporation and familiarize yourself with the different activities of the organization. Then answer the following questions:

   a. What is the business-level strategy of Boeing's commercial jet aircraft business?

   b. What tactics is Boeing pursuing to raise entry barriers into the commercial jet aircraft business?

   c. What is the corporate-level strategy of Boeing? How might this strategy help the company increase the profitability of the entire enterprise?

5. Compare and contrast Toyota and General Motors. (You might want to visit the Web sites of both companies and review their financial performance using the data found at the Yahoo finance site, finance.yahoo.com.) Which company is on the efficiency frontier in the automobile industry, and which company is inside the frontier? How important are the following in explaining the differences between the two companies?

   a. Business-level strategy.

   b. Operating strategy.

   c. Corporate strategy.

   d. Competitive tactics.

MANAGEMENT PORTFOLIO

FOR THE ORGANIZATION YOU HAVE CHOSEN TO FOLLOW:

1. What is the business-level strategy of this firm? (For a multibusiness firm, focus on the largest business unit.)

2. Plot the position to which the firm aspires on the efficiency frontier. Also plot its actual position if that is different. If you think the firm is positioned inside the frontier, state why. If you think it is on the frontier, how did it get there?

3. What is the corporate-level strategy of the firm? In your opinion, does this strategy create additional value, boosting the profitability of the enterprise, or is it destroying value and lowering profitability? How did you reach your conclusion?

CLOSING CASE   GOOGLE'S QUEST FOR COMPETITIVE ADVANTAGE

In 1996 two computer science PhD students at Stanford University, Sergey Brin and Larry Page, were wondering how they could sort through the massive amount of information that was starting to appear on the Web to find specific and useful information on a topic. Although there were several different technologies, or search engines, available to search the Web for information, none of them seemed particularly useful to Brin and Page because they failed to distinguish between useful and trivial Web sites. Brin and Page decided to build a search engine that not only would examine the words on Web pages and then index them as other search engines did, but also would look at how and where these words were being used and at the number of other Web sites linked to a page.

The goal was to have the search engine return a list of Web pages with the most useful appearing at the top.

The first version of their search engine, which relied on a proprietary algorithm developed by Brin and Page, was known as BackRub. BackRub soon created a buzz among other computer science students at Stanford; but it was the encouragement of a former Stanford student, David Filo, one of the founders of Yahoo!, that persuaded Brin and Page to start their own company.

By December 1998 the beta version of Google's search engine had been up and running on the Web for months, answering over 10,000 search queries a day. From that point on growth was exponential. By December 2000 Google's index included more than 1.3 billion Web pages, and the company was answering some 60 million search queries a day. By 2004 the number of Web pages indexed by Google exceeded 4 billion, and the search engine was handling more than 300 million queries a day. Google's technology quickly became pervasive. Soon most major Web portals were using Google's search engine technology, including Yahoo! and AOL. Estimates suggested that in 2003 some 75 percent of Internet searches were made using Google. What was most impressive about Google, however, was that unlike many other dot-com businesses of the 1990s, Google found a way to make money. In 2003 the company made $967 million in revenues and $105 million in net profits. In 2004 revenues surged to $3.19 billion and net income to $399 million.

Google Guys   From small beginnings in 1996, Sergey Brin and Larry Page have built one of the largest and most profitable online enterprises in the world, Google.

Courtesy of Google Inc.

To make money Google sells to advertisers the words that people put in when they search for something on the Web. This means that whoever bids the most for a particular term, say digital cameras, gets their link put at the top of a Google-generated list. Google distinguishes between independent search results and those that are paid for by listing "sponsored links" on its page. However, sponsors do not pay Google unless a user clicks through to them from a Google-generated link.

To determine the price to charge advertisers for a term, Google uses an automated bidding process known as a *Vickery second price auction*. Under this bidding methodology, winning bidders pay only one cent more than the bidder below them. Thus if there are three bids for the term "digital cameras"—say $1 a click, $0.50 a click, and $0.25 a click—the winner will pay $0.51 a click to Google.

In August 2004 Google went public, raising over $1.5 billion. With no debt and flush with cash, the company looked set to build on its lead in the search engine business. However, competitors were not sitting on the sidelines. In 2003 Yahoo! purchased a rival search engine company, Overture Services, for some $1.6 billion. In February 2004

Yahoo! replaced Google as the search engine on its site with a proprietary search engine based on Overture's technology. Microsoft too seems to have its sights set on Google. Microsoft is reportedly working on its own search engine technology, which it plans to integrate with its software, including Microsoft Office and Longhorn, the next version of the Windows operating system (due for release in 2007).

CASE DISCUSSION QUESTIONS

1. What business-level strategy is Google pursuing?

2. What value does Google create for customers and advertisers? How does this value translate into superior performance, measured by profitability and profit growth?

3. What are the sources of Google's competitive advantage? How secure are these advantages from imitation by competitors? What must Google do to keep the competitors at bay?

4. Do competitors such as Yahoo! and Microsoft potentially have assets and capabilities that give them an advantage over Google in the search engine business?[23]

ENDNOTES

1. Sources: "How Big Can It Grow?" *The Economist,* April 17, 2004, pp. 74–78; "Trial by Checkout," *The Economist,* June 26, 2004, pp. 74–76.

2. T. Copeland, T. Koller, and J. Murrin, *Valuation: Measuring and Managing the Value of Companies* (New York: Wiley, 2000).

3. M.E. Porter, *Competitive Advantage* (New York: Free Press, 1985); and M.E. Porter, *Competitive Strategy* (New York: Free Press, 1980).

4. S. Scherreik, "How Efficient Is That Company?" *BusinessWeek,* December 23, 2003, pp. 94–95.

5. B. Barney, "Company Resources and Sustained Competitive Advantage," *Journal of Management* 17 (1991), pp. 99–120.

6. R. Reed and R.J. DeFillippi, "Causal Ambiguity, Barriers to Imitation, and Sustainable Competitive Advantage," *Academy of Management Review* 15 (1990), pp. 88–102.

7. Porter, *Competitive Strategy.*

8. C.W.L. Hill, "Differentiation versus Low Cost or Differentiation and Low Cost: A Contingency Framework," *Academy of Management Review* 13 (1988), pp. 401–12.

9. This was a comment made by an executive MBA student of Charles Hill, who held a relatively senior position at Costco.

10. M.E. Porter, "What Is Strategy?" *Harvard Business Review,* February 1, 2000.

11. See W.C. Kim and R. Maugborgne, *Blue Ocean Strategy* (Boston: Harvard Business School Press, 2005).

12. Kim and Maugborgne, *Blue Ocean Strategy.*

13. Porter, *Competitive Advantage.*

14. Game theory is the tool most often used to think about the different tactics an enterprise can pursue. See A.K. Dixit and B.J. Nalebuff, *Thinking Strategically* (London: W.W. Norton, 1991). Also see A.M. Brandenburger and B.J. Nalebuff, "The Right Game: Using Game Theory to Shape Strategy," *Harvard Business Review,* July–August 1995, pp. 59–71; D.M. Kreps, *Game Theory and Economic Modeling* (Oxford: Oxford University Press, 1990).

15. The distinction between different types of diversification goes back to R.P. Rumelt, *Strategy, Structure, and Economic Performance* (Cambridge, MA: Harvard Business School Press, 1974).

16. C.W.L. Hill, "The Role of Headquarters in the Multidivisional Firm," in *Fundamental Issues in Strategy Research,* ed. R. Rumelt, D.J. Teece, and D. Schendel (Cambridge, MA: Harvard Business School Press, 1994), pp. 297–321.

17. D.J. Teece, "Economies of Scope and the Scope of the Enterprise," *Journal of Economic Behavior and Organization* 3 (1980), pp. 223–47. For recent empirical work on this topic, see C.H. St. John and J.S. Harrison, "Manufacturing-Based Relatedness, Synergy, and Coordination," *Strategic Management Journal* 20 (1999), pp. 129–45.

18. See, for example, Jones and Hill, "A Transaction Cost Analysis," *Strategic Management Journal* 9, (1988), pp. 159–72; Williamson, *Markets and Hierarchies* (New York: Free Press), pp. 132–75; and Hill, "The Role of Headquarters in the Multidivisional Firm."

19. One of the classic studies was by D.J. Ravenscraft and F.M. Scherer, *Mergers, Selloffs, and Economic Efficiency* (Washington, DC: Brookings Institution, 1987).

20. See J.P. Walsh, "Top Management Turnover Following Mergers and Acquisitions," *Strategic Management Journal* 9 (1988), pp. 173–83.

21. See A.A. Cannella and D.C. Hambrick, "Executive Departure and Acquisition Performance," *Strategic Management Journal* 14 (1993), pp. 137–52.

22. The intern was an MBA student of Charles Hill.

23. Sources: Google S1 form, filed with the SEC; "Spiders in the Web," *The Economist,* May 15, 2004, pp. 14–16; "The Weakness of Google," *The Economist,* May 1, 2004, pp. 67–68; B. Elgin, "Google's Success Is Spurring Competitors to Take Search Technology to the Next Level," *BusinessWeek*, May 17, 2004, pp. 46–47;. Google 10K form, 2004.

7

MANAGING OPERATIONS

LEARNING OBJECTIVES

After Reading This Chapter You Should Be Able to:

1. Explain how operational excellence can lead to competitive advantage.

2. Describe different operating strategies managers can pursue.

3. Explain the role of operations in an enterprise.

4. Outline how the design of production systems and strategies for asset utilization, improving product quality, managing inventory, managing supply chains, and developing products can all improve the efficiency of an organization.

5. Describe methodologies for improving operating processes, and explain how improvements in processes over time can lead to competitive advantage.

/ / / / / / / / / /

After years of poor financial performance, managers at Mount Carmel Health, a health care provider in Ohio, decided to implement a six sigma program (explained later in this chapter) to improve their operating efficiency. One of the first projects focused on a simple and common problem among health care providers: timely and accurate reimbursement of costs. Mount Carmel discovered that it was writing off large amounts of potential revenue from Medicare HMO plans as uncollectible because the charges were denied by Medicare administrators. Mount Carmel had low expectations for this business anyway, so its managers had never analyzed why the write-offs were so high. Careful analysis as part of a six sigma project discovered that a significant portion of the denials were due to the incorrect coding of reports submitted to Medicare. If the reports were coded correctly—that is, if fewer errors were made in the production of forms—the six sigma team estimated that annual income would be some $300,000 higher, so they devised improved processes for coding the forms to reduce the error rate. The result was that net income rose by over $800,000! It appeared that improving the coding process for this one parameter improved the reporting of many other parameters and led to a reimbursement rate much higher than anticipated. By 2004 Mount Carmel had over 400 six sigma quality improvement projects either completed or ongoing. The organization estimates that since it launched the process in July 2000, it has reduced costs by some $71 million.[1]

The case of Mount Carmel Health illustrates the impact that efficient operations management can have on the performance of an enterprise. The six sigma process is an example of a specific operating strategy. In previous chapters we learned that operating strategies are the actions managers take at the operating level to support their business-level strategy and reach the efficiency frontier in their industry. In this chapter we examine the various operating strategies managers can pursue. By **operations** we mean the different activities involved in creating an organization's products and services. **Operations managers** manage these activities. The typical responsibilities of operations managers include the management of production systems, product quality, inventory systems, supply chains, and product and process development. By managing operations efficiently and effectively, managers can lower the costs of their organization and increase the differentiation of its products, thereby reaching the efficiency frontier in their industry.

Many of the operating strategies and methodologies we discuss here are just as important for service enterprises as for manufacturing enterprises. Sometimes people erroneously assume that operations management tools are not applicable to service organizations, and that service organizations have their own unique character. Although there may be differences in details and emphasis, fundamentally all businesses handle the same issues whether their product is a physical good or a service. The quality of production processes and of the end product is an issue of great importance for both manufacturing and service enterprises. Improving productivity is a key concern in both manufacturing and service organizations. Like manufacturing enterprises, service enterprises also have to configure their production systems, manage inventory, and design products. In this chapter we show by examples how the techniques we discuss apply to both manufacturing and service enterprises.

operations
The different activities involved in creating an organization's products and services.

operations managers
People who manage operations.

■ // Productivity and Efficiency

productivity
The output produced by a given input.

In the last chapter we noted that managers strive to reach the efficiency frontier in their industry and that doing so requires operational excellence. The key determinant of efficiency in most organizations is the productivity of two key inputs, labor and capital. **Productivity** can be defined as the output produced by a given input:

$$\text{Productivity} = \text{Output/Input}$$

productivity of labor
Unit output divided by some measure of labor inputs.

■ Productivity in the automobile industry.

The **productivity of labor** is typically measured by unit output divided by some measure of labor input, such as hours worked or number of employees. For example, managers in automobile companies often look at the number of employee hours needed to build a car. In 2004 it took Toyota 20.6 employee hours to build a car in its United States assembly operations. This compares to 23.6 hours at General Motors, 25.4 hours at Ford, and 26.0 hours at Daimler Chrysler.[2] Thus we can conclude that Toyota had higher labor productivity than its three rivals and should therefore have lower costs and greater profitability, which indeed seems to have been the case. In 2004 Toyota made more profit than the other three companies combined.

productivity of capital
Sales divided by the total capital (money) invested in a business.

■ Wal-Mart and Target: Capital productivity.

The **productivity of capital** is usually measured by sales divided by the total capital (money) invested in a business. Often referred to as *capital turnover,* this measure tells managers how many dollars of sales are produced for every dollar of capital invested in the business.[3] In 2005, for example, Wal-Mart's capital turnover ratio was 4.16, meaning that every dollar Wal-Mart invested in its stores, distribution centers, information systems, and inventory generated $4.16 of sales. By way of comparison, Target had a capital turnover ratio of just 1.86, which implies that Target was less productive than Wal-Mart in its use of capital and thus would probably have a higher cost structure and higher profitability. This was the case in 2005, when Wal-Mart's profitability, measured by its return on invested capital, was 14.5 percent compared to 11.5 percent at Target.[4]

The key point is that *the productivity rates of labor and capital are major determinants of efficiency and thus the cost structure of an enterprise.* The task facing managers is to improve labor and capital productivity over time, thereby lowering costs and boosting performance. Doing so is important irrespective of whether the business-level strategy of the firm is one of low costs or differentiation. Even the differentiated firm has to configure its operations as efficiently as possible, given the constraints imposed by its choice of strategic position, if it is to reach the efficiency frontier in its industry.

The operating strategies we consider in the rest of this chapter *all* improve the productivity of labor and capital and thus the competitive position of a business. For example, by reducing labor time wasted building defective products that subsequently have to be repaired or scrapped, quality enhancement methodologies such as six sigma improve labor productivity. By managing inventories more efficiently, operating strategies can reduce the amount of capital tied up in inventory, thereby improving capital productivity.

■ // Configuring the Production System

The **production system** of an organization refers to how the flow of work is configured. Production can be configured in a number of different ways, depending on the nature of the product, consumer requirements, and available production technologies. Traditionally production systems have been categorized into one of four main categories: job shop, batch production, assembly line, or continuous flow. We will look at each system, and how the systems differ with regard to productivity and costs, before discussing the rise of new production technologies and their role in facilitating what is known as mass customization.

// TRADITIONAL PRODUCTION SYSTEMS

Job shop systems are used when items are ordered individually and tend to be unique to the requirements of a particular customer. Many small manufacturing operations are organized on a job shop basis—a high-end cabinetmaker, for example, may produce specialized cabinets designed for individual homes. Service businesses can also use job shop systems. For example, each job undertaken by a management consulting firm may differ depending on the needs of the client, requiring the firm to develop a different product for each client. Higher-end restaurants also use job shop systems, producing individual items to order from a menu and customizing the orders depending on customer requests.

Small batch production systems are used when customers order in small batches, but when each order is different. The cabinetmaking firm, for example, may be able to produce in small batches if it serves builders who construct 100 houses a year using the same floor plan. The cabinetmaker may then make 100 cabinets for a particular type of house before altering the equipment to process a different order.

Assembly-line production systems are used to mass-produce large volumes of a standardized product. First popularized by Henry Ford in the 1920s to produce the Model T Ford, assembly-line technology is widely used today. Assembly lines involve breaking down a production process into discrete steps and assigning employees to different work stations on a continually moving line where they perform specialized tasks. Automobile manufacturers use assembly-line systems to mass-produce specific car models; Dell uses assembly-line systems to mass-produce personal computers; and food manufacturers use assembly lines to produce packaged food. Service enterprises also use assembly-line processes: McDonald's restaurants use an assembly-line methodology to make Big Macs, doctors may use an assembly-line methodology to perform certain procedures (laser-based eye surgery, for example), and a bank may use assembly-line systems to process mortgage loan applications in a highly standardized fashion.

production system
How the flow of work is configured.

job shop
Production systems used when items are ordered individually.

small batch
Production systems used when customers order in small batches but when each order is different.

assembly-line production
Systems used to mass-produce large volumes of a standardized product.

Every Product Is Unique A high-end cabinetmaker at work. Cabinets like these are made using a job shop process.
Courtesy of Mick Harper/Blue Sky Woodworks, LLC, Corrales, NM

continuous flow production

Production systems that continuously produce a standardized output that flows out of the system.

Finally, **continuous flow production** systems continuously produce a standardized output that flows out of the system. Oil refineries are a good example: They take crude oil as an input and refine that oil to produce a continuous output of gasoline and other oil-based liquid products. Many continuous flow systems cannot be easily shut down; they tend to operate around the clock, continuously producing a highly standardized output.

// PRODUCTION SYSTEMS, FLEXIBILITY, AND COSTS

Production systems differ in the degree to which their output is standardized, their flexibility, and their costs (see Figure 7.1). Job shop and small batch systems are more flexible than assembly-line and continuous flow systems; they have to be because their outputs are less standardized. They pay a penalty for this flexibility, however, in the form of higher costs. In general, enterprises that use job shop and small batch systems will charge higher prices to recoup their costs. In terms of the framework introduced in the last chapter, small batch and job shop systems tend to be used to produce a differentiated product offering that is customized to individual customer requirements. Firms using such systems charge high prices to cover the costs of producing a differentiated output.

Assembly-line and continuous flow systems mass-produce or continuously produce a standardized output, and by doing so they can reduce costs in two ways: economies of scale and learning effects. **Economies of scale** are the cost advantages derived from large-volume production. One source of scale economies is the ability to spread the fixed costs associated with tooling a factory to make a product over a large volume of production. Thus although it might cost Intel $5 billion to build a facility to mass-produce microprocessors, that fixed cost can be spread over 100 million microprocessors, driving down the cost of each unit. Similarly, automobile companies spread the fixed costs associated with tooling an assembly line to produce a specific car model over a large output—perhaps as much as a million units over five years—thereby lowering the costs of each car.

Another source of economies of scale is the ability of companies producing in large volumes to achieve a greater division of labor and specialization. Specialization is said to have a favorable impact on productivity, mainly because it enables employees to become skilled at performing a particular task. The classic example of such economies is Ford's Model T car. By

economies of scale

Cost advantages derived from large-volume production.

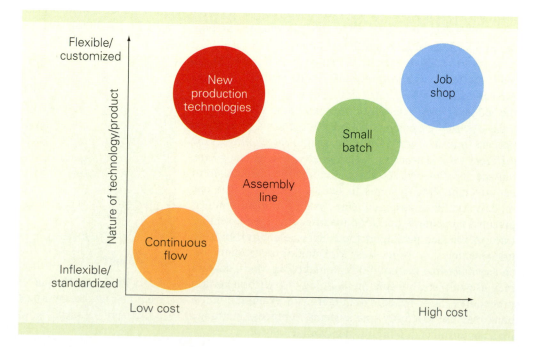

FIGURE 7.1

Production Systems—Costs and Flexibility

introducing assembly-line mass production techniques, Ford achieved greater division of labor (splitting assembly into small, repeatable tasks) and specialization, which boosted employee productivity. Ford was also able to spread the fixed costs of developing a car and setting up production machinery over a large volume of output. As a result of these economies, the cost of manufacturing a car at Ford fell from $3,000 to less than $900 (in 1958 dollars).

Learning effects are cost savings that come from learning by doing. For example, workers learn by repetition how best to carry out a task. In general, labor productivity increases over time and unit costs fall as individuals learn the most efficient way to perform a particular task. Equally important, managers in new production facilities learns over time how to run the new operation more efficiently. Hence production costs decline because of increasing labor productivity and management efficiency due to learning. Learning effects were first documented in the aircraft industry during World War II when military aircraft were first being mass-produced on Boeing's assembly lines.[5] It was observed that each time *cumulative* production of a particular aircraft model was doubled, unit costs fell to 80 percent of their previous level (that is, the fourth aircraft cost 80 percent as much as the second to assemble,

You Can Have It in Any Color You Want, So Long as It's Black!   The grandfather of all assembly lines—Ford's Model T assembly line. Introduced in 1913, the Model T assembly line cut the cost of building a car by two-thirds.

From the collections of Ford Motor Company

the eight cost 80 percent as much as the fourth, and so on). Further study found the reason: Over time employees found ways to work smarter, made fewer mistakes, and wasted less time, all of which boosted labor productivity.

Learning effects are just as important in service industries as in manufacturing. One famous study of learning in the context of the health care industry found that more experienced medical providers posted significantly lower mortality rates for a number of common surgical procedures, suggesting that learning effects are at work in surgery.[6] The authors of this study used the evidence to argue for establishing regional referral centers for the provision of highly specialized medical care. These centers would perform many specific surgical procedures (such as heart surgery), replacing local facilities with lower volumes and presumably higher mortality rates.

Another study found strong evidence of learning effects in a financial institution. The study looked at a newly established document processing unit with 100 staff and found that over time documents were processed much more rapidly as the staff learned the process. Overall the study concluded that unit costs fell with every doubling of the cumulative number of documents processed since the unit was established.[7]

The implication is that standardization of work processes associated with assembly-line and continuous flow production leads to higher productivity and lower costs (due to scale and learning effects). Indeed, this was the original impetus behind Henry Ford's famous application of assembly-line technology to automobile production. By moving to an assembly line Ford helped to lower the cost of making cars by realizing economies of scale and learning effects. He was then able to lower prices and expand the market, creating the first mass market for an automobile with his Model T. In what is now regarded as a classic statement regarding the connection between mass production and product standardization, Ford said that consumers could have the Model T in any color they wanted, "so long as it was black."

In sum, assembly-line and continuous flow processes allow enterprises to substantially lower costs and thus prices, but a penalty is paid in the lack of product variety—which reduces differentiation. Thus these systems are most often adopted by organizations that are trying to adopt a low-cost strategy rather than a differentiated position in their industry. McDonald's, for example, applied the assembly-line philosophy to the production of fast food, which is highly

learning effects
Cost savings that come from learning by doing.

■ Learning effects at Boeing.

Learning Environment   A modern aircraft assembly line. Learning effects are important in aircraft assembly.

© Louie Psihoyos/Corbis

■ Mass customization at Toyota.

standardized. This lowered costs and let McDonald's lower prices and increase demand for its product in a classic example of the low-cost value circle (see Chapter 6).

// NEW PRODUCTION TECHNOLOGIES: MASS CUSTOMIZATION

The last few decades have seen increasing attention devoted to the development of new production technologies that are designed to break the well-established relationship between product customization and higher costs (see Figure 7.1). Many of these new technologies are rooted in the observation that a major source of increased costs associated with greater customization is the *setup* costs required to produce small batches of output. It costs a lot to retool an automobile assembly line to produce a new model, so automobile companies prefer to produce fewer models. But what if the time to retool a factory or to set up machinery could be dramatically reduced? Wouldn't that make mass production of a customized final product economical?

In the automobile industry this insight was first pursued by a remarkable engineer, Ohno Taiichi, who worked at Toyota.[8] Beginning in the mid-1950s Ohno began to think about ways to produce auto body parts in small numbers. At that time it could take a full day to set up the equipment to stamp out a particular body part—say a right door panel. As a consequence, auto companies found it economical to stamp out 20–30 days of inventory at a time and warehouse it until it was needed. Ohno thought this was wasteful: It costs money to store inventory, including the capital tied up in the warehouses and the inventory itself. If machines could be set up quickly, the company would need to produce enough inventory for only a day or so; inventory holding costs would fall; and the productivity of capital would rise, as would Toyota's profitability. Moreover, Ohno understood that if equipment setup times could be reduced, Toyota could also produce a greater variety of cars without a cost penalty.

Ohno and his engineers began to experiment with a number of techniques to speed up the time it took to change the dies in stamping equipment. These included using rollers to move dies in and out of position along with a number of simple mechanized adjustment mechanisms to fine-tune the settings. These techniques were relatively easy to master, so Ohno directed production workers to perform the die changes themselves. This in itself reduced the need for specialists and eliminated the idle time that workers previously had enjoyed while waiting for the dies to be changed, which boosted labor productivity. Through a process of trial and error, Ohno succeeded in reducing the time required to change dies on stamping equipment from a full day to 15 minutes by 1962 and to as little as three minutes by 1971. This meant that Toyota needed to produce only enough inventories for its immediate needs, and costs fell sharply.

In essence, Ohno Taiichi had invented a **flexible production technology**. Flexible production technologies are a set of methodologies that allow enterprises to produce a wider range of end products from a given production system without incurring a cost penalty.[9] They run the gamut from computer-controlled machine tools grouped into cells of four to six machines, to lower-tech solutions such as those first developed by Ohno and his team, which were based on pulleys and levers.

The automobile industry is among those now rapidly adopting the latest generation of computer-controlled flexible manufacturing technologies, which make intensive use of robotics. Ford is introducing such equipment into its automotive plants around the world, and it hopes to have 75 percent of its production built on flexible assembly lines by 2010. If

flexible production technology

A set of methodologies that allows enterprises to produce a wider range of end products from a given production system without incurring a cost penalty.

successful, Ford's investments in flexible factories could reduce annual costs by some $2 billion a year.[10] The cost savings come from two main sources: the reduced downtime associated with changing a line to produce a different model, and the lower inventory holding costs when products can be produced in small batches. Ford spent $400 million modernizing an 80-year-old assembly plant in Chicago. Prior to the investment, the plant could produce only a single model. Now it can produce eight models from two different chassis.

Increasingly flexible production technologies are allowing **mass customization**, which is the ability to customize the final output of a product to individual customer requirements without suffering a cost penalty.[11] Mass customization can enable an enterprise to (1) better differentiate its product offering, which pays dividends in the form of higher prices or greater demand, and (2) garner significant cost savings from reductions in inventory holding costs.

One industry that is starting to see the beginnings of a move toward mass customization is apparel, where both man-ufacturers and retailers are experimenting with this approach. Years ago almost all clothing was made to individual order by a tailor (a job shop production method). Then along came the 20th century and techniques for mass production, mass marketing, and mass selling. Production in the industry shifted toward larger volume and less variety based on standardized sizes. The benefits in terms of production cost reductions were enormous, but the customer did not always win. Offsetting lower prices was the difficulty of finding clothes that fit as well as tailored clothes once did. People have an amazing variety of shapes and sizes; but shirts often come in just four sizes: small, medium, large, and extra large! It is estimated that the current sizing categories in clothing fit only about one-third of the population. The rest of us wear clothes with less than ideal fit.

The mass production system has drawbacks for apparel manufacturers and retailers too. Year after year, apparel firms find themselves saddled with billions of dollars in excess inventory that is either thrown away or put on sale because retailers had too many items of the wrong size and color. To try to solve this problem, clothing retailers have been experimenting with mass customization techniques. One success story is Lands' End.

To purchase customized clothes from Lands' End, the customer provides information on the Lands' End Web site by answering a series of 15 questions (for pants) or 25 questions (for shirts) covering everything from waist to inseam. The process takes about 20 minutes the first time through, but once the information is saved by Lands' End it can be quickly accessed for repeat purchases. The customer information is then analyzed by an algorithm that pinpoints a person's body dimensions by running these data points against a huge database of typical sizes to create a unique, customized pattern. The analysis is done automatically by a computer, which then transmits the order to one of five contract manufacturing plants in the United States and elsewhere that cut and sew the garments and ship the finished products directly to customers.

Today customization is available for most categories of Lands' End clothing. Some 40 percent of its online shoppers choose a customized garment over the standard-sized equivalent when they have the choice. Even though prices for customized clothes are at least $20 higher and they take about three to four weeks to arrive, customized clothing reportedly accounts for a rapidly growing percentage of Lands' End's $500 million online business. Lands' End states that its profit margins are roughly the same for customized clothes as regular clothes, but the reductions in inventories that come from matching demand to supply account for additional cost savings. Moreover, customers who customize appear to be more loyal, with reordering rates that are 34 percent higher than those of buyers of standard-sized clothing.[12]

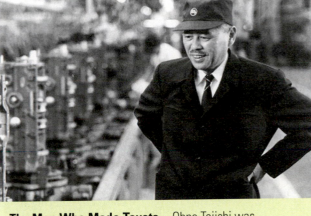

The Man Who Made Toyota Ohno Taiichi was responsible for the development of Toyota's revolutionary lean production system, which reduced the cost of building an automobile and represented the biggest advance in the industry since Henry Ford introduced the assembly line.

Courtesy of Toyota Motor Sales, USA, Inc.

mass customization
The ability to customize the final output of a product to individual customer requirements without suffering a cost penalty.

■ Mass customization at Lands' End.

// OPTIMIZING WORK FLOW: PROCESS REENGINEERING AND PROCESS INNOVATION

One key to improving productivity is to make sure the flow of work within a production system is configured optimally. Process evaluation and reengineering are tools commonly used to achieve this.[13] The goal is to analyze the flow of work in an organization, looking for possible causes of low productivity, and to streamline that flow if possible so work is performed more efficiently, thereby lowering costs.

The technique most enterprises use to analyze their work processes is a *model cell,* which is a fully functioning microcosm of an entire work process. The technique allows managers to conduct experiments and smooth out kinks while working toward an optimal design of work flow. Only when a design is perfected is the new process rolled out across the entire organization.

Most reengineering projects involve several basic principles.[14] One is physically placing adjacent processes near one another, which can accelerate work flow. A health insurance company found that its ability to process claims was slow because the employees who received the claims were located on a different floor from those who processed the claims, and it could take more than a day for files to shuttle from one floor to another. The company quickened the work flow simply by placing receivers and processors next to each other.

A second principle is to standardize procedures at each step in the work flow, which makes it easier for replacement workers to fill in for an absent individual. A third principle is to eliminating *loop backs* in which work returns to a previous stage for further processing. Loop backs are a major source of low productivity. For example, in product development projects loop backs can occur when a product is passed from R&D to manufacturing, only to be sent back to R&D when the manufacturing personnel find out that as designed, the product cannot be manufactured economically. The redesign soaks up time and money. If manufacturing and R&D work together on product design, products can be designed with manufacturing in mind.

A fourth principle is to balance work loads across different stages in a process to make sure there are no bottlenecks and no stage has insufficient work. A fifth principle is to separate nonroutine complex tasks and pass them to specialists so the flow of routine work is not slowed down by the need to deal with a complex transaction. Anybody who has stood in line at a bank while a single teller handles a complex transaction can understand the importance of this principle. Many banks have improved their speed of serving customers by having a specialist customer service representative, rather than a teller, handle complex tasks. A sixth principle is to share the results of improvements in performance so that all can see the benefits of the reengineered processes.

By adopting such principles many enterprises have been able to dramatically improve their flow of work and thus their productivity and costs. Moreover, by analyzing their work flow, managers have often come up with ways to take entire steps out of their organizations' work processes. The resulting process innovations have enhanced the efficiency of these organizations.

For an example, consider Wal-Mart's management of inventories. In general, inventories are shipped from suppliers to a Wal-Mart distribution center, where they are stored and shipped when needed to a Wal-Mart store (see Figure 7.2). At the distribution center this process involved six steps: unloading the contents of an incoming truck, scanning bar codes on the inventory with a handheld scanner, storing the inventory inside the distribution center, retrieving the inventory, scanning it again, and reloading it on a departing truck. In the early 1990s Wal-Mart realized that if it could coordinate the flow of trucks so that incoming trucks from suppliers arrived shortly before trucks were scheduled to depart to stores, it could take one step out of the process by simply moving inventory directly from an incoming truck to an outgoing truck parked in an adjacent dock (Figure 7.2). The technique Wal-Mart developed to do this is called *cross-docking.* Cross-docking reduced the need to store and retrieve inventory. This process improve-

A Radio Frequency Identification (RFID) tag can be attached to an object to be tracked.

Courtesy of Barcoding Inc.

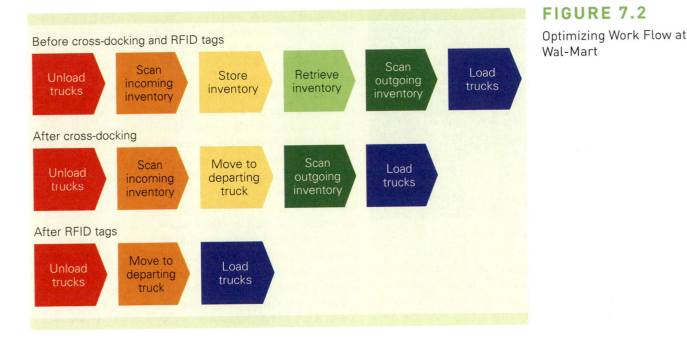

FIGURE 7.2

Optimizing Work Flow at
Wal-Mart

ment increased labor productivity and reduced the size required for a distribution center (less inventory needed to be stored), which reduced capital requirements. It also increased the efficiency of inventory management (inventory spent less time sitting in a distribution center—it got to the stores quicker, where it could be sold). Although not all inventory can be cross-docked, over 40 percent of Wal-Mart's inventories are now handled through cross-docking, substantially reducing Wal-Mart's cost structure.

In 2005 Wal-Mart started to eliminate two more steps in the process—those involving the scanning of inventory. Wal-Mart required suppliers to place radio frequency identification (RFID) tags on all pallets of inventory. The tags emit a radio signal that is picked up by a receiver connected to Wal-Mart's information systems. By eliminating the need to manually scan inventory, the RFID tags take two more steps out of the process of inventory sorting, thereby boosting labor productivity and further reducing costs.

Process innovations such as those developed by Wal-Mart push out the efficiency frontier and enable a business to stay ahead of its rivals in the quest to establish a sustainable competitive advantage. Many companies currently recognized as having a competitive advantage in their industry, such as Wal-Mart, Dell, Southwest Airlines, Toyota, and Nucor Steel, got there because they were, and continue to be, process innovators.

■ Process optimization at Wal-Mart.

// Asset Utilization

Almost all organizations have significant physical assets. For a retailer these include its stores, distribution warehouses, and delivery trucks; for a hospital they include the hospital building itself; for an automobile manufacturer they include its assembly plants and the equipment therein; a bank's assets include the space devoted to branches; restaurant assets include the space devoted to customer seating and the kitchen equipment; and an airline's assets include aircraft. Assets do not come free—a business needs capital to own or lease them. **Asset utilization** refers to the extent to which assets are "working," generating income for the organization. If operating managers can find ways to utilize their physical assets more intensively, they can increase the productivity of the firm's capital, thus lowering the cost structure of the organization and boosting its profitability.

Consider a restaurant: One task for the restaurant owner is to utilize her tables as intensively as possible to generate more sales for every dollar of capital invested in the restaurant. A key

asset utilization

The extent to which assets are "working," generating income for the organization.

Can We Do This in Less Than 15 Minutes? Aircraft don't make money when they are sitting on the ground. Southwest Airlines ground crews can turn around aircraft in 15 minutes, which increases productivity through better asset utilization.

Courtesy of Southwest Airlines

to utilizing these assets is to turn the tables over more frequently. If the tables are just used once a night, sales will be much lower than if tables are turned over two or three times a night. How can the restaurant owner maximize table turnover?

First, it is important for the restaurant owner to *optimize capacity,* balancing seating capacity with expected demand. If the restaurant is too big for the local market, asset utilization and capital productivity will be low, and costs will be high. Assuming that capacity is optimized, asset utilization can be further enhanced by the *efficient operation* of the restaurant (which in this case means quick customer service and cleaning of tables). By reducing the time people spend at their tables and the time tables wait to be cleaned (*turnaround time*), quick service and cleaning allow the tables to be used more often. Another important method is *scheduling* when people are seated, primarily through a good reservation system that coordinates reservations with how long it takes customers to eat a meal, so that new customers are scheduled to arrive just as a table is being cleared. Some busy restaurants in New York have taken scheduling further by telling customers that they have only a certain amount of time at the table (perhaps two hours). By efficiently scheduling the serving of meals, clearing of tables, and reservations, some fashionable restaurants in New York can use their tables three times a night, dramatically increasing their asset utilization and capital productivity.

Another example of asset utilization can be seen in the airline industry. The key to asset utilization in the airline industry is to have aircraft fly as often as possible (they don't generate money when they are on the ground) and as full as possible. Again, the issue is one of optimizing capacity and scheduling, coupled with efficient operations on the ground to turn around flights as quickly as possible. Airlines try to match their capacity on a route (say Denver to Seattle) with demand. They also schedule flights to match demand and try to minimize the time a plane has to spend on the ground not just through scheduling but also by training ground crews to turn around planes as quickly as possible, thereby reducing the amount of time the assets are not working. At Southwest airlines, for example, ground crews can turn around an airplane in just 15 minutes, which keeps Southwest's planes in the air more often.

As suggested by these examples, asset utilization is often influenced by three closely related variables: optimizing capacity, scheduling, and quick turnaround to intensify utilization of the asset (see Figure 7.3). These three variables are not independent of each other. Efficient scheduling can reduce the amount of capacity a business needs, as can quick turnaround time. Managers must predict and manage demand as well as possible, invest in the appropriate level of capacity for expected demand, and try to reduce the amount of capacity needed by efficient scheduling and minimizing turnaround time. Operations managers use complex algorithms to predict demand flows and optimize scheduling. In a manufacturing setting, flexible technologies are used to create quick turnaround (by reducing setup times for a machine).

Changing prices to make sure capacity is fully utilized is also often an option (see Figure 7.3). Businesses that take orders electronically have a particularly good view of real-time order flows and can use real-time pricing algorithms to set the best prices to match demand and supply. Airlines are infamous for adjusting prices, often by the minute, to try to fully utilize their capacity.[15] Railroads too now use dynamic pricing algorithms to make sure their rolling stock is fully utilized. Dell Computer uses dynamic pricing to optimize capacity utilization in its assembly operations. Dell will alter the prices for specific models and components (sometimes daily) to keep its factories humming at optimal capacity and to better manage inventory.

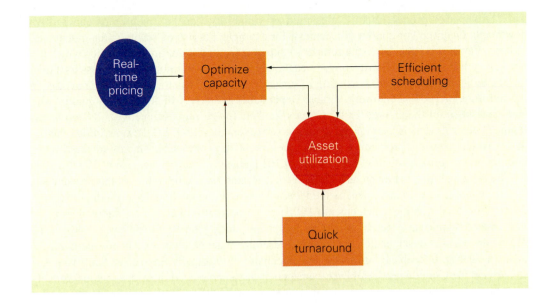

FIGURE 7.3

Increasing Asset Utilization

// Quality Management

An important aspect of product quality is product reliability. A product is said to be *reliable* when it consistently does the job it was designed for, does it well, and rarely, if ever, breaks down. Quality management methodologies try to eliminate *defects* in the process of producing a good or service, thereby producing a more reliable end product. Product reliability can be a huge source of cost savings for several reasons (see Figure 7.4). First, if defects are reduced, time and materials are not wasted building products that later have to be scrapped or reworked. Second, if products perform as advertised, the firm will save on warranty costs. Beyond this, if a firm's products are viewed by customers as more reliable than those of competitors, this can be a source of differentiation and lead to superior pricing, greater demand, or some combination of the two. When demand grows due to a superior reputation for quality, the firm can realize greater scale economies, which lowers costs.

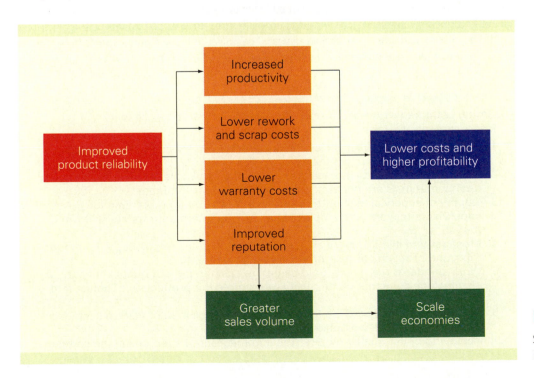

FIGURE 7.4

Superior Product Reliability and Costs

■ Quality at Toyota.

Thus superior product quality, measured by reliability, can be a source of competitive advantage. Over the last quarter of a century, for example, the rise of Toyota in the global auto industry has in part been due to the company's superior reputation for product quality, which has been an enduring source of differentiation enabling it to charge premium prices across its model range *and* gain market share. According to surveys Toyota still has the best quality rankings in the industry. In 2004 J.D. Power's Vehicle Dependability Study, which measures quality after cars have been on the market for three years, ranked Toyota number one with 207 problems reported per 100 vehicles, compared to an industry average of 269. J.D. Power's Initial Quality Study, which measures problems reported in the first 90 days after sale, similarly ranked Toyota number one in terms of quality, with a score of 101 against an industry average of 119.[16]

The principal tool that many managers now use to increase the reliability of their products is the *six sigma* quality improvement methodology. The six sigma methodology is a direct descendent of the total quality management (TQM) philosophy that was widely adopted, first by Japanese companies and then by American companies, during the 1980s and early 1990s.[17] The TQM concept was developed by a number of American management consultants, including W. Edwards Deming, Joseph Juran, and A. V. Feigenbaum.[18] Originally these consultants won few converts in the United States. However, managers in Japan embraced their ideas enthusiastically and even named their premier annual prize for manufacturing excellence after Deming. See Table 7.1 for Deming's steps that should be part of any quality improvement program.

It took the rise of Japan to the top rank of economic powers in the 1980s to alert Western business to the importance of the TQM concept. Since then quality improvement methodologies have spread rapidly throughout Western industry. The six sigma methodology that was the focus of the opening case is widely used today. The term *sigma* comes from the Greek letter that statisticians use to represent a standard deviation from a mean: The higher the number of sigma, the fewer the errors. A six sigma production process would be 99.99966 percent accurate, creating just 3.4 defects per million units. Although it is almost impossible for a company to achieve such a low defect rate, the idea behind a six sigma program is to strive toward that goal.

The six sigma methodology is based on what is known as DMAIC, which stands for **d**efine, **m**easure, **a**nalyze, **i**mprove, and **c**ontrol.[19] With DMAIC a problem is first defined and quantified; then measurement data are collected to bound and clarify the problem; analytical tools are deployed to trace the problem to its root cause; a solution to the root cause is identified and implemented; and finally the ongoing operations are subject to ongoing control to prevent a recurrence. Six sigma projects are performed by teams that are led by "black belts," who are specially trained six sigma experts. Projects normally take three to six months, and a black belt should be able to lead four to six projects a year. The power of the six sigma approach lies in the disciplined methodology it provides for structuring, analyzing, and solving business problems.

Deming identified a number of steps that should be part of any quality improvement program:

1. A company should have a clear business model to specify where it is going and how it is going to get there.
2. Management should embrace the philosophy that mistakes, defects, and poor-quality materials are not acceptable and should be eliminated.
3. Quality of supervision should be improved by allowing more time for supervisors to work with employees and giving them appropriate skills for the job.
4. Management should create an environment in which employees will not fear reporting problems or recommending improvements.
5. Work standards not only should be defined as numbers or quotas but should also include some notion of quality to promote the production of defect-free output.
6. Management is responsible for training employees in new skills to keep pace with changes in the workplace.
7. Achieving better quality requires the commitment of everyone in the company.

TABLE 7.1

Deming's Quality Improvement Steps

Six sigma is a logical problem-solving methodology that in many ways is akin to detective work. Often six sigma analysis can turn up surprising root causes for a specific problem. In one such case a pharmaceutical company was experiencing rapid growth in demand for a new drug, but the drug's manufacturing line had low yields. Management thought the problem lay in poor-quality raw material from a supplier. However, six sigma analysis uncovered the real cause of the problem: variation in the temperature in different parts of the production plant. Adjusting the air conditioning system to make sure the entire plant operated at the same standard temperature improved yields by 60 percent and saved the company more than $17 million a year. Moreover, the improved yield let the company postpone a $500 million investment in another production facility.[20]

Despite many examples of success, quality improvement practices are not universally accepted. A study by the American Quality Foundation found that only 20 percent of U.S. companies regularly review the consequences of quality performance, compared with 70 percent of Japanese companies.[21] Another study, this one by Arthur D. Little, of 500 American companies using TQM found that only 36 percent believed that TQM was increasing their competitiveness.[22] A prime reason for this, according to the study, was that many companies did not fully understand or embrace the TQM concept. They were looking for a quick fix, whereas implementing a quality improvement program is a long-term commitment.

■ // **Managing Inventory**

Inventories are material inputs into a production process and the finished products that an organization holds in anticipation of future sales. Although many organizations have to hold inventories, they tend to be a major cost driver in manufacturing and retailing organizations. For manufacturing enterprises, inventories take three basic forms: inventories of inputs into a production process, inventories of work in progress, and inventories of finished goods. For an automobile manufacturer, inventories of inputs include the component parts it must buy from suppliers to make its cars; inventories of work in progress include partly assembled automobiles that are still progressing through the automobile plant; and inventories of finished goods include unsold cars sitting on dealers' lots. For a retailer, inventories include the stock of unsold goods sitting in storage or on store shelves.

The most obvious component of inventory-driven costs is **inventory holding costs**. which include both the capital cost of money tied up in inventory and the cost of the warehouse space required to store inventory. In addition, other costs are associated with holding excess inventory. For example, in the personal computer industry the prices of components can drop significantly over the space of a few months. If a manufacturer purchases too much inventory of a memory chip, and the price subsequently drops by 40 percent before most of that inventory is used, *component devaluation costs* will be associated with having purchased too much product too soon. Similarly, if a manufacturer produces too much of a particular computer model and has to reduce prices to shift unsold inventory, a *price reduction cost* must be borne (this is the difference between the planned price and the actual price). In the case of excess production, some products might also be returned to the manufacturer from the retailer because they were not sold (*return costs*), and the firm might have to write off the value of some finished goods that have become obsolete (*obsolescence costs*). But there are also costs associated with having too little inventory. The inability to make goods due to shortages of component parts and finished products creates *stockout costs*, which are the opportunity costs associated with lost business.

The total *inventory-driven costs* of an enterprise are thus the sum of holding costs, component devaluation costs, price reduction costs, return costs, obsolescence costs, and stockout costs. The actual magnitude of inventory-driven costs will vary depending on the nature of the business, but they can constitute a significant percentage of the overall cost structure of an enterprise. One study of Hewlett-Packard, for example, found that before it adopted inventory reduction programs, the total inventory-driven costs in its mobile computer division amounted to 18.7 percent of revenue (the study did not measure stockout costs).[23]

Given the importance of inventory-driven costs as a component of the overall cost structure of an enterprise, managers often devote considerable attention to formulating and implementing

inventory holding costs
The capital cost of money tied up in inventory and the cost of the warehouse space required to store inventory.

■ Dell Computer: Inventory turnover.

Asset or Liability? Inventory sitting on shelves in a warehouse can be expensive. Just-in-time inventory management systems are designed to minimize inventory and reduce inventory holding costs. The goal is to get rid of warehouses like these.

© Stock Trek/Getty Images

just in time
Inventory that enters a production process just in time to be used.

inventory turnover
The speed with which inventory is replaced.

strategies for reducing the amount of inventory an organization has to hold. One goal often embraced is to have inventory arrive **just in time** to enter a production process or be placed on a store shelf for sale. The success of managers at doing this can be assessed by **inventory turnover**, which is normally measured by the number of days it takes to totally replace inventory. Different businesses will turn over inventory at different rates. Wal-Mart, which is one of the most efficient retailers when it comes to inventory management, turns over its inventory every 45 days. Dell, which is the most efficient company in the personal computer industry, turns over its inventory every two days! At Dell the mantra is to "replace inventory with information," meaning that the only inventory Dell wants is that in transit between suppliers and Dell's assembly operations.

The bottom line is that if inventory can be turned over more often, inventory-driven costs will be significantly reduced. The business will have less capital tied up in inventory, it will need less space to store inventory, and it will be far less likely to suffer other inventory-driven costs. As a result, its profitability should be significantly higher. Indeed, superior management of inventory is widely recognized as a principle source of competitive advantage at both Wal-Mart and Dell and a major reason why both of those enterprises are on the efficiency frontier in their respective industries. So how can managers increase inventory turnover and reduce inventory-driven costs?

// ECONOMIC ORDER QUANTITY AND SETUP TIME

One starting point of inventory analysis is to determine how much inventory should be held. A widely used algorithm, called *economic order quantity* (EOQ), helps managers to do this. EOQ is defined as follows:

$$EOQ = \sqrt{(2 \times D \times FC)/(VC \times K)}$$

where:

$$D = \text{Annual demand}$$
$$FC = \text{Fixed costs of producing/procuring inventory}$$
$$VC = \text{Variable costs of inventory}$$
$$K = \text{Inventory holding costs}$$

For illustration, suppose the manager of an automobile assembly plant has to decide how many right door panels to order from the body stamping shop at a time. The factory produces 200,000 cars a year, so total annual demand for the door panels is 200,000. The fixed cost of setting up equipment in the stamping shop to produce the panels is $10,000, and the variable cost of each panel is $50. The inventory holding costs (the costs associated with the capital tied up in the inventory and the cost of warehousing) are 20 percent of the variable costs. Then

$$EOQ = \sqrt{(2 \times 200,000 \times 10,000)/(50 \times 0.20)} = 20,000$$

This algorithm tells the manager that the economical batch size is 20,000 units (see Table 7.2). The factory consumes 200,000 right door panels a year, so she will have to reorder 10 times a year (200,000 divided by 20,000). Because there are 365 days in a year, she

EOQ	Annual Demand	Fixed Costs	Variable Costs	Holding Costs	Inventory Turnover (days)	Inventory Holding Costs
20,000	200,000	$ 10,000	50	20%	36.5	$ 100,000
15,492	200,000	$ 6,000	50	20%	28.3	$ 77,460
8,944	200,000	$ 2,000	50	20%	16.3	$ 44,721
6,325	200,000	$ 1,000	50	20%	11.5	$ 31,623
2,000	200,000	$ 100	50	20%	3.7	$ 10,000
632	200,000	$ 10	50	20%	1.2	$ 3,162

should reorder every 36.5 days (365 divided by 10). In other words, under this ordering system the inventory would turn over every 36.5 days.

We can also use the algorithm to calculate the cost of holding the inventory, which is the holding costs, K, times the variable cost, VC, times half of the EOQ. (We are assuming that the inventory is depleted at a steady rate and the new inventory arrives just as the inventory in storage is depleted, so that the average inventory in storage is half of the EOQ.) Thus the inventory holding costs are

$$\text{Inventory holding costs} = K \times VC \times \tfrac{1}{2}(EOQ)$$
$$= 20\% \times \$50 \times \tfrac{1}{2}(20,000 \text{ units})$$
$$= \$100,000$$

So far so good! However, if the goal of the firm is to maximize profitability, the manager should see the $100,000 in inventory holding costs as something to be reduced. This was exactly the issue that confronted Ohno Taiichi, the engineer at Toyota who pioneered the development of flexible production systems in the company. Ohno's solution was to reduce the fixed costs of setting up equipment to produce inventory (FC). As can be seen from Table 7.2, which shows the EOQ and inventory holding costs using different assumptions regarding fixed costs, the impact of this can be quite dramatic. If the fixed cost can be reduced from $10,000 to just $1,000, for example, the EOQ falls to 6,325 units, and inventory holding costs decline to $31,623. As discussed earlier, at Toyota Ohno and his team reduced setup times (which drive fixed costs) from a day down to minutes. The effect was to boost inventory turnover and reduce inventory holding costs. The last row in Table 7.2 is a good analogy for what Ohno achieved by his development of flexible manufacturing technology: The fixed costs associated with setting up machinery were reduced to almost zero (just $10 in our example), EOQ batch size fell to about a day's worth of inventory, and holding costs became trivial ($3,162 in our example). As a result, Toyota's profitability increased.

// JUST-IN-TIME INVENTORY SYSTEMS

By pioneering attempts to reduce setup times, Ohno not only invented a flexible manufacturing technology, but also created the concept of just-in-time inventory. When the fixed costs associated with setting up equipment to produce a component part can be reduced to almost zero, the parts can be produced economically in very small batches and enter the production process almost immediately—in essence, just in time for them to be used. To coordinate the flow of materials within Toyota, Ohno developed another process innovation known as the *kanban system*. Under the kanban system, component parts were delivered to the assembly line in containers. As each container was emptied, it was sent back to the previous step in the manufacturing process. This became the signal to make more parts.

At Toyota the just-in-time system was originally developed in-house, but over time it was also extended to embrace most of the company's suppliers. Toyota helped its suppliers adopt flexible manufacturing technologies and the kanban system. Many of these suppliers located

■ Toyota: Just-in-time inventory.

their plants adjacent to Toyota's assembly operations to reduce the amount of inventory in transit as much as possible. By doing this Toyota was able to extend the gains from in-house inventory reductions to its entire supply chain, which reduced the costs it had to pay for component parts from suppliers and therefore its overall cost structure.

Toyota's just-in-time model has now been replicated in many organizations and, as at Toyota, has often been extended to even those with globally dispersed supply chains. In a 21st-century variant of the kanban system, Dell Computer electronically shares information regarding the orders it receives through its Web site on a real-time basis with its suppliers. This helps Dell's suppliers optimize their own production schedules and inventory, producing just what Dell needs. The flow of parts in transit, whether via ship, plane, or truck, is tightly controlled and synchronized so parts arrive at Dell's assembly plants just in time to enter the manufacturing process.

■ Dell Computer: Just-in-time inventory.

As at Dell, modern information systems and flexible manufacturing technologies have made it easier for other organizations to adopt just-in-time inventory systems. Flexible technologies mean that more goods can now be economically produced in smaller lot sizes. Bar code scanning of inventory, along with Internet-enabled data links between a firm, its suppliers, and transportation providers shipping inventory, have made it possible to tightly control the flow of inventory, which reduces inventory-driven costs.

Just-in-time systems are also important for retailers. If inventory arrives at a store just in time to be placed on the shelf for sale, the store does not have to devote space to holding inventory (reducing inventory holding costs), which means more space can be devoted to displaying goods for sale. Moreover, just-in-time delivery of goods means the retailer is less likely to be left with inventory that it cannot sell or has to mark down, thereby avoiding price reduction and obsolescence costs.

A final tangible benefit associated with just-in-time systems is that defective parts show up in the production process soon after they have been made. This makes it easier to identify and fix the source of the defect than if the parts had been stored in a warehouse for an extended period. In effect, just-in-time inventory systems help managers improve product quality by eliminating defects from the production process.

buffer stocks
Inventories held for some unexpected contingency.

The biggest drawback with just-in-time systems is that they eliminate inventory buffers. **Buffer stocks** of inventory are inventories held for some unexpected contingency—for example, if the equipment in a supplier's plant breaks down and has to be replaced. If no buffer stock is held in reserve, the entire assembly operation could stop while the firm waited for its supplier to fix equipment. As insurance against such contingencies, some organizations keep buffer stocks of inventory on hand—perhaps a few days' more supply than they need. Of course doing so raises inventory-driven costs. Managers in some organizations, such as Dell, have decided to operate without such buffer stocks. This means that from time to time, when unanticipated events occur, they may have to scramble to solve a sudden shortage of inventory. This happened to Dell twice in the early 2000s: once after the terrorist attacks on the United States on September 11, 2001, and once during the outbreak of the SARS virus in China during 2003. Although the total shutdown of ports and airports in the aftermath of September 11 hurt Dell, it was able to adapt to the slowdown of supplies from China by reconfiguring its supply chain, pulling supplies from ships and flying them directly to the United States.

// BUILD TO ORDER AND INVENTORY

build-to-stock
Stocking a distribution channel in the anticipation that a customer will purchase those products.

A final way of reducing inventory-driven costs is to move from a build-to-stock business model toward a build-to-order business model. In a **build-to-stock** model, a business makes products to stock the distribution channel in the anticipation that customers will purchase those products. Thus General Motors builds cars to stock dealers' lots, Hewlett-Packard builds personal computers to stock the shelves of electronic retailers, and Levi makes jeans to stock the racks of clothing retailers. In a **build-to-order** model a firm takes an order first and then builds the product. When Lands' End sells customized shirts and pants over the Internet, it is adopting a build-to-order strategy—as does Dell when it

build-to-order
Taking an order first, and then building the product.

takes customer orders for personal computers over the Internet, or Boeing when it takes orders to build commercial jet aircraft.

Build-to-order systems have two big advantages over build-to-stock systems. First, because the company knows exactly how much of an item it will sell in advance of production, it can order just enough parts for orders in hand. Second, a build-to-order system eliminates the problems associated with building too large or too small an inventory of finished products. Thus the firm does not have to mark down products to shift unsold inventory and does not suffer stockout costs. Under a build-to-order system the firm does not have to guess what demand will be, so it can closely align supply and demand and reduce its inventory-driven costs.

With these advantages, you might wonder why all firms don't build to order. There are several reasons. First, building to order normally implies smaller production lots, which may drive up costs, particularly for products where mass production is still the best manufacturing method (such as making toothpaste). Second, consumers may not want to order individual items, instead preferring to walk into a store and purchase what they want (nobody wants to place a special order for toothpaste). Third, it generally takes a while to build products to order, and consumers may not want to wait. (Who wants to wait two weeks for toothpaste to be delivered?)

Finally, legacy considerations may make it difficult for a business to move from a build-to-stock to a build-to-order business model. For example, Hewlett-Packard (HP) would love to run its personal computer business entirely on a build-to-order basis, as Dell does, basing production on orders coming in over the company Web site. However, HP has a vast network of dealers that currently sell its products. If HP shifted to a Web-based build-to-order system overnight, its sales would probably slump because the increase in Web sales would not likely offset the decline in sales through traditional retail channels. Interestingly, HP is starting to move toward a build-to-order model and now sells personal computers via the Web; but

■ Hewlett-Packard: Build to order.

Build Your Own Car   Toyota is moving to a build-to-order system for its cars.

Courtesy of Toyota Motor Sales, USA, Inc.

it still distributes the vast majority of its personal computer products through traditional channels.

As with HP, many manufacturing enterprises, particularly those that make large durable products, are trying to move toward a build-to-order business model, or at least increase the proportion of their sales that come this way. The rise of flexible manufacturing systems, with their implications for mass customization, has made build-to-order systems more economical. Several automobile companies are experimenting with a build-to-order approach in an attempt to eliminate the problems that arise from inventory overstocking or understocking. Nissan has calculated that if it could move to a build-to-order system with a short cycle time, it could reduce costs by as much as $3,600 a vehicle.[24] In Germany, BMW now builds 60 percent of its cars to order, but the delivery time can be as long as two months. Toyota, too, is trying to build more cars to order. In late 2004 the automaker claimed that it was building about 11 percent of the cars it sold in the United States to order, with a build time of just 14 days.[25]

■ // Supply Chain Management and Information Systems

supply chain

The chain of suppliers that provides raw materials, partly finished products, or finished products to an organization.

The **supply chain** of an organization is the vertically integrated chain of suppliers that provides raw materials, partly finished products, or finished products to an organization. Wal-Mart's supply chain, for example, includes all organizations that supply the products it sells in its stores. Similarly, Dell's supply chain includes all enterprises that make the component parts for its assembly operations.

The central task in supply chain management is to synchronize the flow of products from suppliers, through transportation networks, to the firm, and then out to the firm's customers, so that inventory is minimized and capacity utilization is optimized. One way in which managers try to improve supply chain coordination is to have suppliers locate close to their own operations. Many of Toyota's suppliers, for example, locate their plants next to Toyota's assembly operations, making it easier to implement just-in-time inventory systems. However, in today's global economy, this is not always desirable. Many suppliers have moved production facilities to low-cost locations such as China, Malaysia, or Mexico to take advantage of low labor costs. Indeed, the demands of a firm for lower-priced inputs may force them to do this. Thus many of Wal-Mart's suppliers have established production facilities in China to better serve the giant retailer's demands for lower prices.

As a result of such trends, in recent decades the supply chains of many enterprises have stretched out geographically. Coordinating such globally dispersed supply chains is a major challenge for operations managers.

Fortunately Web-based information systems give operating managers tight control over such dispersed supply chains. By tracking component parts through a supply chain, information systems let a firm optimize its production scheduling according to when components are expected to arrive. By locating component parts in the supply chain precisely, good information systems allow a firm to accelerate production when needed by pulling key components out of the regular supply chain and having them flown to the manufacturing plant.

Firms increasingly use *electronic data interchange* (EDI) to coordinate the flow of materials into manufacturing, through manufacturing, and out to customers. EDI systems require computer links between a firm, its suppliers, and its shippers. Sometimes customers also are integrated into the system (as in Dell's build-to-order system). These electronic links are used to place orders with suppliers, register parts leaving a supplier, track them as they travel toward a manufacturing plant, and register their arrival. Suppliers typically also use an EDI link to send invoices to the purchasing firm. One consequence of an EDI system is that suppliers, shippers, and the purchasing firm can communicate with each other with no time delay, which increases the flexibility and responsiveness of the whole supply system. A second consequence is that much of the paperwork between suppliers, shippers, and the purchasing firm is eliminated.

Before the emergence of the Internet as a major communication medium, firms and their suppliers normally had to purchase expensive proprietary software solutions to implement

EDI systems. The ubiquity of the Internet and the availability of Web-based applications have made most of these proprietary solutions obsolete. Less expensive Web-based systems that are much easier to install and manage now dominate the market for supply chain management software. These Web-based systems are rapidly transforming the management of supply chains, allowing even small firms to achieve a much better balance between supply and demand, thereby reducing the inventory in their systems and reaping the associated productivity benefits. With increasing numbers of firms adopting these systems, those that don't may find themselves at a significant competitive disadvantage.

■ // Product Development and Productivity

The creation and commercialization of new products form a central mission in many organizations. Indeed, without a powerful new product development engine, many businesses would ultimately go into decline as their products are made obsolete by the advances of others. Computer companies, wireless phone companies, and consumer electronics concerns must regularly produce smaller, better, cheaper, faster new products—or lose market share. Automobile companies have to develop new models and update their old ones—or lose share. Pharmaceutical companies have to develop new drugs to replace those that come off patent and go generic, or their growth will falter. Frozen food companies must produce better food that contains superior ingredients, tastes good, and can be prepared easily—or lose share to competitors. Breakfast cereal companies have to develop new brands to increase their market share, as Kellogg's has recently done with its new varieties of Special K that contain freeze-dried fruit. Nor is it just manufacturing companies that must develop new products. For example, one way that financial institutions compete is by developing new financial products that they can use to attract business, as Merrill Lynch did in the early 1990s when it created the first cash management accounts that combined a traditional brokerage account with the features of a checking account to give customers greater financial flexibility. In short, creating new and better products is how many firms differentiate their offerings from those of competitors and gain competitive advantage.

■ Product development at Kellogg's.

Product development is so important for so many businesses that we devote a significant part of Chapter 18 to discussing the product development process and what managers can do to manage that process effectively and efficiently. Here we note that if a firm wishes to increase productivity and reach the efficiency frontier in its industry, it must design products that can be manufactured easily.

Design for manufacturing is a philosophy that tries to increase productivity by designing products that are easy to manufacture. For example, by cutting the number of parts that make up a product, R&D can dramatically decrease the required assembly time, which translates into higher employee productivity, lower costs, and higher profitability. After Texas Instruments redesigned an infrared sighting mechanism that it supplies to the Pentagon, it had reduced the number of parts from 47 to 12, the number of assembly steps from 56 to 13, the time spent fabricating metal from 757 minutes to 219 minutes per unit, and unit assembly time from 129 minutes to 20 minutes. The result was a substantial decline in production costs. In another recent example, Toyota took a close look at the grip handles mounted above the doors inside most cars. By working closely with suppliers Toyota managed to reduce the number of parts in these handles from 34 to 5, which cut procurement costs by 40 percent and reduced installation time from 12 seconds to 3 seconds.[26]

Design for manufacturing requires close coordination between the production and R&D functions of the company. R&D and production personnel have to work *concurrently* on product design issues so that production issues are foremost in the minds of product development engineers when they design new products. The creation of cross-functional teams that contain production and R&D personnel who work jointly on design problems is a popular way of achieving this. We discuss the management of cross-functional product development teams in more detail in Chapter 18.

design for manufacturing
Trying to increase productivity by designing products that are easy to manufacture.

IN CONCLUSION WHY DOES IT MATTER?

As we have seen, managing operations is a central task of an organization. The skilled and effective management of operations can increase productivity and lower costs, enabling a firm to outperform rivals and reach the efficiency frontier in its industry. The competitive advantage of many enterprises is based on their superior operating capabilities—their ability to achieve operating excellence—which in turn is the result of hard work by managers at the operating level.

By configuring the firm's production system, adopting flexible production technologies, and pioneering process innovations, operating managers can lower costs. Productivity can be further enhanced by taking actions to make sure the physical assets of an organization are fully utilized by, for example, optimizing capacity investments, production scheduling, and turnaround time. Quality improvement methodologies such as six sigma and various techniques for inventory management can lower costs even further, as can the efficient management of supply chains and designing products that are easy to manufacture.

Effective operations management can also help a firm better differentiate its product offering. Mass customization, which is made possible by modern flexible production technologies, can increase customer loyalty and repeat purchases. Customers keep coming back because they can get products that are perfect for their particular needs. Efficient management of inventory, by making sure the firm does not suffer stockouts, also keeps customers coming back to an organization because they can be confident the firm will have the products they are looking for in stock. And finally, by boosting product reliability, quality improvement methodologies such as six sigma increase the quality that consumers ascribe to the firm's product offering—and therefore its ability to differentiate that offering from that of rivals.

In short, effective operations management is clearly key to establishing competitive advantage. Moreover, improving the efficiency of operations over time is how a firm stays ahead of rivals and sustains its competitive advantage.

MANAGEMENT CHALLENGES

1. "Inventory is the enemy of efficiency." Discuss this statement. Is it always true?

2. What are the key drivers of operating efficiency in the supermarket business? (Think about this the next time you visit a supermarket.) What operating strategies should managers at supermarkets pursue to reach the efficiency frontier in their industry?

3. How important is the utilization of physical assets in driving down costs in the steel industry, the airline industry, and the computer software industry? What accounts for the differences in importance across these industries?

4. What are the benefits of having a globally dispersed supply chain? What are the risks? How can information systems enhance the benefits and reduce the risks?

5. How might a build-to-order strategy, if successfully implemented, change the economics of the automobile industry? What is required at the operating level for such a strategy to work?

MANAGEMENT PORTFOLIO

FOR THE ORGANIZATION YOU HAVE CHOSEN TO FOLLOW:

1. Is this firm efficiently run at the operating level? What is your evidence? (*Hint:* One way of getting at this is comparing the firm against its competitors.)

2. Are there any ways in which the firm might be able to improve its operating efficiency? If so, what operating strategies could it pursue, and how might they enhance the competitiveness of the enterprise?

3. If the firm is a manufacturing enterprise, could the firm implement a build-to-order strategy? What would be the benefits of doing so? What would it have to do to deliver on that strategy? (If the firm already has a build-to-order strategy, outline the benefits and state how it implemented that strategy).

4. If the firm is a service enterprise, is its product offering standardized or customized to individual customers or customer groups? Are there benefits to increasing product customization? What operating process would have to be put in place to do that?

CLOSING CASE   IMPROVING PRODUCTIVITY IN THE AUTO INDUSTRY

In 2004 Detroit's big three car makers—GM, Ford, and Daimler Chrysler—accounted for only 58.6 percent of vehicles sold in the United States, the lowest level ever, down from 76.7 percent in 1984. For most of the last decade strong sales of sports utility vehicles, in which Detroit dominates, have held overall market share losses in check; but now foreign producers such as Toyota, Honda, and Kia are going after that segment too, creating huge potential problems for Detroit.

The American automobile makers have responded by trying to reinvigorate their passenger car business, coming out with a host of new designs and cutting the costs of developing and producing those cars. The old rule of thumb in the industry was that it took four years and cost $1 billion to design a new car and tool a factory to produce it. To recoup these costs, Detroit would typically sell a car for seven years before developing a new design. Unfortunately for the American producers, the Japanese have shortened the life cycle of a typical vehicle to five years; and by lowering development and tooling costs, they have been able to make good money on their car models.

Now the American producers are trying to strike back. Typical is Ford, which has reduced its product development time by a quarter since the late 1990s and continues to reduce development time by 10 percent per year. Ford now designs almost a third of its models in less than 30 months. One reason for this progress has been the increase in communication among designers at Ford. Ford designers used to work in different teams and did not share enough knowledge about parts and platform design. Now teams get together to see how they can share the design work.

Moreover, design teams are trying to use the same parts in a wider variety of car models, and where appropriate use parts from old models in new cars. Detroit auto designers used to boast that new models were completely redesigned from the floor up with all new parts. Now that is seen as costly and time-consuming. At General Motors, for example, the goal is now to reuse 40–60 percent of parts from one car generation to the next, thereby reducing design time and tooling costs. At Ford the number of parts has been slashed. For example, Ford engineers now choose from just 4 steering wheels instead of contemplating 14 different designs.

Another important trend has been to reduce the number of platforms used for car models. This is something Japanese producers have long done. Honda, for example, builds its Odyssey minivan and Pilot and Acura MDX SUVs on the same platform and has added a pickup truck to the mix. Currently Chrysler bases its vehicle fleet on 13 distinct platforms. The company is trying to bring this down to just four platforms, reducing the product development budget from $42 billion to $30 billion in the process. Ford and General Motors have similar aims. The platform for GM's new small car offering, the Pontiac Solstice, will also be used for its new Saturn coupe and perhaps one more GM car. As GM develops its next generation Chevy Silverado and GMC Sierra pickups, it plans to reuse much of the existing platform, cutting development costs in half to nearly $3 billion. Over the next eight years Ford plans to use its Mazda 6 sedan platform (Ford owns Mazda) as the basis for 10 new vehicles. The idea, according to Ford's head of operations, is to engineer it once and use it often.

Along with these changes in design philosophy, the Detroit companies are retooling their factories to reduce costs and make them capable of producing several car models from the same line. By doing so they hope to reduce the breakeven point for a new car model. GM's Solstice, for example, is forecast to sell around 25,000 units a year—too few to recoup fixed costs under the old design and build philosophy. But GM has cut design costs (by using a common platform and parts) and tooling costs (by investing in flexible manufacturing technologies that can produce multiple designs based on the Solstice platform from the same basic line). GM has also worked hard to get unions to agree to changes in inflexible work rules. Assembly-line workers now perform several different jobs, which reduces waste and boosts productivity. Similarly, Ford hopes to have 75 percent of its production built on flexible assembly lines by 2010; if successful, its investments in flexible factories could reduce annual costs by some $2 billion a year.

The big problem with the new vision coming out of Detroit, as critics see it, is that not much is new about it.

The techniques being talked about will reduce development time and tooling costs; but Japanese automakers have been pursuing the same techniques for years. The critics fear that Detroit is chasing a moving target, and when they arrive in the promised land it will be too late because their global competitors will already have taken competition to the next level.[27]

CASE DISCUSSION QUESTIONS

1. How have lower development and tooling costs given Japanese auto manufacturers an advantage in the marketplace?

2. What steps are the Detroit automobile makers taking to reduce product development time and tooling costs? If they are successful, what are the implications of these initiatives for the number of car models they can sell and breakeven volumes for individual models? Will these initiatives benefit Detroit's customers? How?

3. The Japanese producers have for years used many of the methodologies now being introduced in Detroit. Why do you think it has taken the Detroit automakers so long to respond to their foreign competitors?

4. If the Detroit companies successfully implement their new operating strategies, do you think it will give them a competitive advantage in the marketplace?

ENDNOTES

1. Sources: I.R. Lazarus and K. Butler, "The Promise of Six Sigma," *Managed Healthcare Executive,* October 2001, pp. 22–26; D. Scalise, "Six Sigma, the Quest for Quality," *Hospitals and Health Networks,* December 2001, pp. 41–44; S.F. Gale, "Building Frameworks for Six Sigma Success," *Workforce,* May 2003, pp. 64–69; J. Goedert, "Crunching Data: The Key to Six Sigma Success," *Health Data Management,* April 2004, pp. 44–48.

2. Data reported in J. Palmer, "Can Anyone Stop Toyota," *Barron's,* September 13, 2004, pp. 25–29.

3. T. Copeland, T. Koller, and J. Murrin, *Valuation: Measuring and Managing the Value of Companies* (New York: Wiley, 1996). Also see S.F. Jablonsky and N.P. Barsky, *The Manager's Guide to Financial Statement Analysis* (New York: Wiley, 2001).

4. Figures computed by the author from Value Line data.

5. A.A. Alchian, "Reliability of Progress Curves in Airframe Production," *Econometrica* 31 (1963), pp. 679–93.

6. H. Luft, J. Bunker, and A. Enthoven, "Should Operations Be Regionalized?" *New England Journal of Medicine* 301 (1979), pp. 1364–69.

7. S. Chambers and R. Johnston, "Experience Curves in Services," *International Journal of Operations and Production Management* 20 (2000), pp. 842–60.

8. M.A. Cusumano, *The Japanese Automobile Industry*; (Boston, MA: Harvard University Press, 1989); O. Taiichi, *Toyota Production System* (Cambridge, MA: Productivity Press, 1990; Japanese edition, 1978); J.P. Womack, D.T. Jones, and D. Roos, *The Machine That Changed the World* (New York: Macmillan, 1990).

9. See P. Nemetz and L. Fry, "Flexible Manufacturing Organizations: Implications for Strategy Formulation," *Academy of Management Review* 13 (1988), pp. 627–38; N. Greenwood, *Implementing Flexible Manufacturing Systems*

(New York: Halstead Press, 1986); Womack, Jones, and Roos, *The Machine That Changed the World*; R. Parthasarthy and S.P. Seith, "The Impact of Flexible Automation on Business Strategy and Organizational Structure," *Academy of Management Review* 17 (1992), pp. 86–111; J.H. Gilmore and B.J. Pine II, "The Four Faces of Mass Customization," *Harvard Business Review,* January–February 1997, pp. 91–101.

10. J. Muller, "The Little Car That Could," *Forbes,* December 8, 2003, p. 82; "The Year of the Car," *The Economist,* January 3, 2004, p. 47.

11. B.J. Pine, *Mass Customization: The New Frontier in Business Competition* (Boston: Harvard Business School Press, 1993); S. Kotha, "Mass Customization: Implementing the Emerging Paradigm for Competitive Advantage," *Strategic Management Journal* 16 (1995), pp. 21–42; Gilmore and Pine, "The Four Faces of Mass Customization."

12. Sources: J. Schlosser, "Cashing In on the New World of Me," *Fortune,* December 13, 2004, pp. 244–49; V.S. Borland, "Global Technology in the Twenty-First Century," *Textile World,* January 2003, pp. 42–56; www.landsend.com.

13. M. Hammer, "Deep Change: How Operational Innovation Can Transform Your Company," *Harvard Business Review,* April 2004, pp. 84–94.

14. C.K. Swank, "The Lean Service Machine," *Harvard Business Review,* October 2003, pp. 123–32.

15. D. Bertsimas and S. de Boer, "Dynamic Pricing and Inventory Control for Multiple Products," *Journal of Revenue and Pricing Management,* January 2005, pp. 303–30.

16. J.D. Power press release, April 28, 2004, "Korean Branded Vehicles Overtake Europeans and Domestics in Initial Quality"; J.D. Power press release, June 29, 2004, "Toyota Motor Sales Capture Top Corporate Rankings in Vehicle Dependability."

17. See the articles published in the special issue of the *Academy of Management Review on Total Quality Management* 19, no. 3 (1994). The following article provides a good overview of many of the issues involved from an academic perspective: J.W. Dean and D.E. Bowen, "Management Theory and Total Quality," *Academy of Management Review* 19 (1994), pp. 392–418. Also see T.C. Powell, "Total Quality Management as Competitive Advantage," *Strategic Management Journal* 16 (1995), pp. 15–37.

18. For general background information, see "How to Build Quality," *Economist,* September 23, 1989, pp. 91–92; A. Gabor, *The Man Who Discovered Quality* (New York: Penguin, 1990); and P.B. Crosby, *Quality Is Free* (New York: Mentor, 1980).

19. M. Hammer, "Process Management and the Future of Six Sigma," *MIT Sloan Management Review,* Winter 2002, pp. 26–32.

20. Hammer, "Process Management and the Future of Six Sigma."

21. J. Bowles, "Is American Management Really Committed to Quality?" *Management Review,* April 1992, pp. 42–46.

22. O. Port and G. Smith, "Quality," *BusinessWeek,* November 30, 1992, pp. 66–75. See also "The Straining of Quality," *Economist,* January 14, 1995, pp. 55–56.

23. G. Callioni et al., "Inventory Driven Costs," *Harvard Business Review,* March 2005.

24. "Fighting Back (A Survey of the Car Industry)," *The Economist,* September 4, 2004, pp. 14–16.

25. R. Rosmarin, "Your Custom Car Is Ready at Toyota," *Business 2.0,* October 2004, pp. 150–51.

26. B. Bremner and C. Dawson, "Can Anything Stop Toyota?" *BusinessWeek,* November 17, 2003, pp. 114–17.

27. Sources: D. Welch and K. Kerwin, "Detroit Tries It the Japanese Way," *Business Week,* January 26, 2004, p. 76; A. Taylor, "Detroit Buffs Up," *Fortune,* February 9, 2004, pp. 90–94; Muller, "The Little Car That Could"; "The Year of the Car," *The Economist.*

8

ORGANIZING

HOW
COLD STEEL
⊣ CAN CREATE ⊢
BURNING LOYALTY.

The success of our company rests solely on the shoulders of our employees. Not because we put it there, but because they did. You see, we do everything we can to enhance our company culture. That's why we put into place a pay for performance plan that rewards the highest producers. Why we have a no-layoff practice. Why we help our employees put their kids through college. And why we treat each person the way we want to be treated. It's no wonder people here don't see this as just another business, but as their business. **It's Our Nature**

⊣ *Visit www.nucor.com to learn more.* ⊢

Pay for Performance Is in Our Nature Managers at Nucor Steel believe that the competitive advantage of the company is rooted in its flat decentralized structure, pay for performance systems, and organizational culture—all aspects of its organization architecture.

Courtesy of Nucor Corporation

Nucor Corporation, a manufacturer of steel and steel products, is something of a phenomenon. In an industry characterized by shrinking demand, excess capacity, tough pricing, and persistent losses that have driven some of the most venerable steelmakers in the United States into bankruptcy, Nucor has made good money and grown its sales and profits steadily for over 30 years. Today Nucor is both the largest steelmaker in the United States and the most profitable. How did the firm get to be this way? Part of the answer is that Nucor was an early investor in minimill technology, a small-scale steelmaking technology that uses electric arc furnaces to smelt scrap steel. However, Nucor is hardly alone in this; many other steelmaking enterprises use minimill technology. What distinguishes Nucor is its *organization architecture*—including a flat organization structure, a tradition of decentralizing decision making to the lowest level possible, controls and incentive pay systems that reward the workforce for hitting productivity goals, an egalitarian culture characterized by gain sharing, and an employee base selected for its ability to thrive within this environment. Collectively these elements of Nucor's organization architecture combine to foster very high employee productivity, which lowers Nucor's cost structure and helps the company to record strong profits while its rivals struggle.

In Chapter 6 we noted that strategy is implemented through the organization architecture of a firm. High performance requires that a firm's strategy be supported by the right operations and the right organization architecture. In Chapter 7 we reviewed operations strategy. In the next four chapters we zero in on organization, and we discuss how managers can shape the architecture of their organization to successfully implement the firm's strategy and reach the efficiency frontier in their industry. Nucor is an example of a firm that has done just this. Nucor has pursued a low-cost strategy. To make that strategy work, managers at Nucor designed an organization architecture that has helped raise productivity and lower costs. In this chapter we give a general overview of organization architecture and then focus on an important element of architecture, organization structure. In subsequent chapters we look at control and incentive systems, organizational culture, and developing and managing teams within the context of a specific organization architecture.

organization architecture

The totality of a firm's organization, including formal organization structure, control systems, incentive systems, organizational culture, and people.

▪ // Organization Architecture

The term **organization architecture** refers to the totality of a firm's organization, including formal organization structure, control systems, incentive systems, organizational culture, and people.[1] Figure 8.1 illustrates these different elements. By **organization structure** we mean three things: the location of decision-making responsibilities in the firm (centralized or decentralized); the formal division of the organization into subunits such as functions, product divisions, and national operations; and the establishment of integrating mechanisms to coordinate the activities of subunits (such as cross-functional teams).

Controls are the metrics used to measure the performance of subunits and judge how well managers are running those subunits. **Incentives** are the devices used to encourage desired employee behavior. Incentives are closely tied to performance metrics. For example, the incentives of a manager in charge of General Electric's lighting business might be linked to the performance of that division. We will take a close look at controls and incentives in Chapter 9.

Organizational culture refers to the values and assumptions that are shared among the employees of an organization. Just as societies have cultures, so do organizations. Organizations are societies of individuals who come together to perform collective tasks. They have their own distinctive patterns of culture and subculture.[2] As we will see when we return to this issue in Chapter 10, organizational culture can have a profound impact on how

organization structure

The location of decision-making responsibilities in the firm, the formal division of the organization into subunits, and the establishment of integrating mechanisms to coordinate the activities of subunits.

controls

Metrics used to measure the performance of subunits and to judge how well managers are running those subunits.

incentives

Devices used to encourage desired employee behavior.

organizational culture

Values and assumptions that are shared among the employees of an organization.

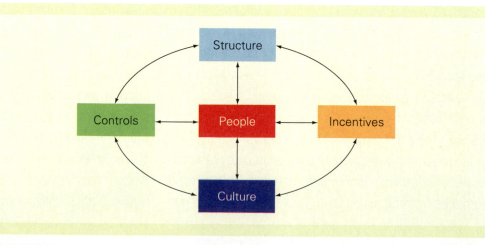

FIGURE 8.1   Organization Architecture

a firm performs. Finally, by **people** we mean not just the employees of the organization, but also the strategy used to recruit, compensate, motivate, and retain those individuals and the type of people they are in terms of their skills, values, and orientation—in other words, their human capital (we discuss the people aspects of organization later in the book).

As illustrated by the arrows in Figure 8.1, the various components of organization architecture are not independent of each other: Each component shapes the others. An obvious example is the strategy regarding people. This can be used proactively to hire individuals whose internal values are consistent with those the firm wishes to emphasize in its organizational culture. The people component of architecture can be used to reinforce the prevailing culture of the organization.

If a business enterprise to going to attain a competitive advantage and maximize its performance, it must pay close attention to achieving internal consistency between the various components of its architecture, and the architecture must support the strategy and operations of the firm. For illustration, let's return to the example of Nucor Corporation. As noted earlier, Nucor operates in a very tough industry that has been characterized by decades of sluggish demand, excess capacity, and price competition. Whereas many U.S. steelmakers have gone bankrupt in the last decade, Nucor's performance has been exemplary. Between 1994 and 2005 sales revenues grew from $2.9 billion to $12.7 billion; earnings per share increased from $1.30 to $8.26; and the company's profitability, measured by ROIC, has averaged around 13.5 percent. How did Nucor achieve this strong performance in such a hostile environment?

The short answer is that Nucor has the lowest operating costs in the industry due to the successful implementation of a low-cost strategy. What is particularly interesting is how its organization architecture helped Nucor attain this position. Nucor is a minimill: It uses electric arc furnaces to smelt scrap steel. It has some 25 steelmaking plants, each of which is organized as a stand-alone division. There are only three management layers in each plant—a divisional general manager, a department manager, and a supervisor. The divisional general manager reports directly to Nucor's small head office. The workforce in each plant is organized into 20–30 person self-managing teams that are responsible for an entire work process and that can schedule work and develop process improvements. Each plant has about 300 employees. Thus Nucor has a very flat organization, which lowers costs, and a high level of decentralization.

From a control perspective, each plant is assigned a profitability target, and each work group a productivity goal. Due to the decentralized nature of the organization, the plant managers and work groups are responsible for their own performance, which is quite visible. This makes accountability and control relatively easy. Senior managers monitor performance against goals, intervening only when goals are not met. These control systems are linked to aggressive performance-based incentive pay systems. Nucor's philosophy is to tie pay closely to performance. Employees in the work groups are paid weekly performance bonuses based on their ability to meet and exceed productivity goals. Although Nucor's base pay is lower than the steel industry average, the bonuses can total 80–150 percent of an employee's base pay, making take-home pay significantly above the average. To get bonuses, however, employees have to work productively, which lowers Nucor's costs and helps make the firm competitive. Similar incentive plans are in place for department managers and general managers. The bonus pay of general managers is linked to that of Nucor as a whole. As a result, if employees within a division find ways to improve production processes over time (which their incentives encourage them to do), lowering the costs of the division, the general manager has an incentive to quickly share these with other divisions because that will boost the performance of Nucor as a whole and hence his or her bonus pay. Thus the bonus pay system creates an incentive for sharing knowledge across divisions.

Nucor's pay-for-performance systems and high levels of decentralization are not for everybody. Nucor's managers realize that self-reliant, goal-oriented individuals will do best in its organization, so its human resource professionals try to hire individuals that have this particular profile (they give prospective employees psychometric tests to identify their personality profiles).

people
The employees of an organization, the strategy used to recruit, compensate, motivate, and retain those individuals, and the type of people they are in terms of their skills, values, and orientation.

■ Organization architecture at Nucor.

Nucor's culture is focused on cost minimization, commitment to employees, and an egalitarian ethos. The culture of the organization was largely shaped by the former CEO, Ken Iverson. Iverson engaged in significant symbolic behavior that sent strong signals to all employees that cost containment was important. Iverson drove an old car, had a low base salary (much of his pay was performance linked), answered his own phone, flew in coach class, stayed in inexpensive hotels when traveling, and would walk rather than take a taxi if that was possible. At the head office there are no assigned parking spaces and no executive dining room (the dining room is a delicatessen across the road from the head office). Nucor operates with an "open book" philosophy, so all employees know how their work groups, divisions, and the company are doing. Nucor has had a long-standing commitment to all employees that when demand turns down in this cyclical industry, no one will be laid off. Instead employees work fewer hours, and managers take cuts in their base pay! The culture shaped by these actions creates an atmosphere within which employees recognize the importance of cost containment and are motivated to reduce costs because the organization is committed to its employees.

In sum, Nucor's flat decentralized organization structure, simple but powerful control systems, aggressive pay-for-performance systems, hiring practices, and organizational culture combine to create an organization architecture that encourages employees to work in a productive manner (which lowers the cost structure of Nucor) and to discover and share ways of improving work process to attain higher productivity (thereby pushing out the efficiency frontier in the industry). Organization architecture, in other words, is a key to Nucor's competitive advantage.

As the Nucor example illustrates, organization architecture is the bedrock upon which efficient operations and effective strategy implementation are built. However, the organization that works for Nucor might not make sense for a business that is pursuing a different strategy in a different industry. A retail business like Nordstrom, for example, which competes through differentiation (in Nordstrom's case superior in-store customer service), may need a different type of organization architecture. A crucial task of managers, therefore, is to design an organization architecture that makes sense for the market in which an enterprise competes and the basic strategic positioning it is trying to achieve. The start of this process is to design the correct organization structure.

// Designing Structure: Vertical Differentiation

vertical differentiation

The location of decision-making responsibilities within a structure.

horizontal differentiation

The formal division of the organization into subunits.

integrating mechanisms

Mechanisms for coordinating subunits.

Organization structure can be thought of in terms of three dimensions:

1. **Vertical differentiation**, which refers to the location of decision-making responsibilities within a structure (that is, centralization or decentralization) and also to the number of layers in a hierarchy (that is, whether the organizational structure is tall or flat).

2. **Horizontal differentiation**, which refers to the formal division of the organization into subunits.

3. The establishment of **integrating mechanisms**, which are mechanisms for coordinating subunits.

We discuss these dimensions next.

// CENTRALIZATION AND DECENTRALIZATION

A firm's vertical differentiation determines where in its hierarchy the decision-making power is concentrated.[3] Are production and marketing decisions centralized in the offices of upper-level managers, or are they decentralized to lower-level managers? Where does the responsibility for R&D decisions lie? Are important strategic and financial decisions pushed down to operating units, or are they concentrated in the hands of top managers?

There are arguments for both centralization and decentralization. **Centralization** is the concentration of decision-making authority at a high level in a management hierarchy. **Decentralization** vests decision-making authority in lower-level managers or other employees.

Arguments for Centralization There are four main arguments for centralization. First, centralization can facilitate coordination. Consider a firm that manufactures components in California and performs final assembly in Seattle. These activities may need to be coordinated to ensure a smooth flow of components to the assembly operation. This might be achieved by centralizing production scheduling at the firm's head office. In another example, Microsoft recently reduced the number of divisions in its organization from six to three, thereby centralizing decision making in fewer senior managers, in an attempt at greater coordination. Microsoft felt that having six divisions in the company led to confused sales, marketing, and product development efforts and that greater centralization was required to harmonize efforts.[4]

Second, centralization can help ensure that decisions are consistent with organizational objectives. When decisions are decentralized to lower-level managers, those managers may make decisions at variance with top managers' goals. Centralization of important decisions minimizes the chance of this occurring. Major strategic decisions, for example, are often centralized to make sure the entire organization is pulling in the same direction. In this sense centralization is a way of controlling the organization.

Third, centralization can avoid duplication of activities by various subunits within the organization. For example, many firms centralize their R&D functions at one or two locations. Similarly, production activities may be centralized at key locations to eliminate duplication, attain economies of scale, and lower costs. The same may also be true of purchasing decisions. Wal-Mart, for example, has centralized all purchasing decisions at its headquarters in Arkansas. By wielding its enormous bargaining power, purchasing managers at the head office can drive down the costs Wal-Mart pays for the goods it sells in its stores. It then passes on those savings to consumers in the form of lower prices, which lets the company grow its market share and profits.

Fourth, by concentrating power and authority in one individual or a management team, centralization can give top-level managers the means to bring about needed major organizational changes. Often firms seeking to transform their organizations centralize power and authority in a key individual (or group) who then sets the new strategic direction for the firm and redraws organization architecture. Once the new strategy and architecture have been decided on, however, greater decentralization of decision making normally follows. Put differently, *temporary* centralization of decision-making power is often an important step in organizational change.

Arguments for Decentralization There are five main arguments for decentralization. First, top management can become overburdened when decision-making authority is centralized. Centralization increases the amount of information senior managers have to process. As a result of information overload, managers might suffer the constraints imposed by bounded rationality.[5] The cognitive biases discussed in Chapter 5 are more likely to occur when managers are stretched too thin, have too much information to process, experience the constraints imposed by bounded rationality, and rely on simple heuristics to make complex decisions. Decentralization gives top management time to focus on critical issues by delegating more routine issues to lower-level managers and reducing the amount of information top managers have to process, making them less vulnerable to cognitive biases.

Second, motivational research favors decentralization. Behavioral scientists have long argued that people are willing to give more to their jobs when they have a greater degree of individual freedom and control over their work. The idea behind employee empowerment is that if you give employees more responsibility for their jobs they will work harder, which increases productivity and reduces costs.

centralization
The concentration of decision-making authority at a high level in a management hierarchy.

decentralization
Vesting decision-making authority in lower-level managers or other employees.

■ Wal-Mart: Centralization.

FIGURE 8.2

Decentralization and Control

Third, decentralization permits greater flexibility—more rapid response to environmental changes. In a centralized firm the need to refer decisions up the hierarchy for approval can significantly slow decision making and inhibit the ability of the firm to adapt to rapid environmental changes.[6] This can put the firm at a competitive disadvantage. Managers deal with this by decentralizing decisions to lower levels within the organization. Thus at Wal-Mart, although purchasing decisions are centralized so the firm can realize economies of scale in purchasing, routine pricing and stocking decisions are decentralized to individual store managers, who set prices and choose the products to stock depending on local conditions. This enables store managers to respond quickly to changes in their local environment, such as a drop in local demand or actions by a local competitor.

Fourth, decentralization can result in better decisions. In a decentralized structure, decisions are made closer to the spot by individuals who (presumably) have better information than managers several levels up a hierarchy. It might make little sense for the CEO of Procter & Gamble to make marketing decisions for the detergent business in Germany because he or she is unlikely to have the relevant expertise and information. Instead those decisions are decentralized to local marketing managers, who are more in tune with the German market.

Fifth, decentralization can increase control (see Figure 8.2). Decentralization can establish relatively autonomous, self-contained subunits within an organization. An **autonomous subunit** has all the resources and decision-making power required to run its operation daily. Managers of autonomous subunits can be held accountable for subunit performance. The more responsibility subunit managers have for decisions that impact subunit performance, the fewer excuses they have for poor performance and the more accountable they are. Thus by giving store managers the ability to set prices and make stocking decisions, Wal-Mart's top managers can hold local store managers accountable for the performance of their stores, and this increases the ability of top managers to control the organization. Just as centralization is one way of maintaining control in an organization, decentralization is another. We return to this issue in Chapter 9 when we discuss control systems.

The Choice between Decentralization and Centralization The choice between centralization and decentralization is not absolute. Frequently it makes sense to centralize some decisions and decentralize others, depending on the type of decision and the firm's strategy. We have already noted, for example, how Wal-Mart has centralized purchasing decisions but decentralized pricing and stocking decisions. Similarly, Microsoft performs major development activities for its Windows operating system at its Redmond corporate campus, but the company has decentralized responsibility for marketing and sales to local managers in each country and region where it does business. Although the choice between centralization and decentralization depends on the circumstances being considered, a few important generalizations can be made.

autonomous subunit

A unit that has all the resources and decision-making power required to run its operation daily.

First, decisions regarding overall firm strategy, major financial expenditures, financial objectives, and legal issues are centralized at the senior management level in most organizations. Operating decisions, such as those relating to production, marketing, R&D, and human resource management, may or may not be centralized depending on the firm's strategy and conditions in the external environment.

Second, when the realization of economies of scale is an important factor, there tends to be greater centralization. Thus purchasing and manufacturing decisions are often centralized in an attempt to eliminate duplication and realize

Local Adaptation. Unilever decentralizes to local subsidiaries decisions about packaging and marketing of its food products.

© AP Photo/Fabian Bimmer   © AP Photo/Joerg Sarbach

scale economies. In contrast, sales decisions tend to be more decentralized because economies of scale are less of a consideration here.

Third, when local adaptation is important, decentralization is typically favored. Thus when there are substantial differences between conditions in local markets, marketing and sales decisions are often decentralized to local marketing and sales managers. Many multinational consumer products firms, such as Unilever, centralize decisions about manufacturing and purchasing to realize scale economies, but decentralize marketing and sales decisions to local brand managers in different countries because competitive conditions differ from country to country and local adaptation is required.[7]

■ Decentralization at Google.

Finally, decentralization is favored in environments that are characterized by high uncertainty and rapid change. When competitive conditions in a firm's market are changing rapidly, with new technologies and competitors emerging and conditions changing in ways that are difficult to anticipate, centralization, because it slows down decision making, can put the firm at a competitive disadvantage. This is why many high-technology firms operate with a greater degree of decentralization than firms operating in more stable and predictable environments.[8] At Google, for example, lower-level employees are given explicit permission to develop new business ideas and the right to lobby top managers for the funds to develop those ideas. Such decentralization of strategy making would not be found in firms operating in a more stable and predictable environment, such as the automobile industry.

A vivid example of the costs of making the wrong choice between centralization and decentralization occurred in 2005, when the Federal Emergency Management Agency (FEMA) had to respond to the devastating impact of Hurricane Katrina on New Orleans. The hurricane flooded much of New Orleans and resulted in a mandatory evacuation of the city. FEMA, the federal agency responsible for disaster response, was widely criticized for being very slow to help the hundreds of thousands of mostly poor people who had been made homeless. For several days while thousands of homeless people huddled in the New Orleans Superdome, lacking food and adequate sanitary facilities, FEMA was nowhere to be seen. Later analysis revealed that one reason for FEMA's slow response was that the once autonomous agency had been placed under the direct supervision of the Department of Homeland Security after September 11, 2001. FEMA officials apparently felt that they had to discuss relief efforts with their superiors before proceeding. This cost the agency crucial hours in the early part of the disaster, which significantly slowed its response and meant that the relief effort was less effective than it might have been.[9]

■ FEMA: The costs of being too centralized.

The Consequence of a Slow Response   Victims of Hurricane Katrina are ferried from their flooded homes in New Orleans. FEMA's slow response to Katrina was in part due to FEMA's lack of autonomy within the Department of Homeland Security.

© AP Photo/Eric Gay

// TALL VERSUS FLAT HIERARCHIES

tall hierarchies

Organizations with many layers of management.

flat hierarchies

Organizations with few layers of management.

A second aspect of vertical differentiation refers to the number of levels in an organization's hierarchy. **Tall hierarchies** have many layers of management; **flat hierarchies** have few layers (see Figure 8.3). Most firms start out small, often with only one or at most two layers in the hierarchy. As they grow, however, managers find that there is a limit to the amount of information they can process and the control they can exert over daily operations. To avoid being stretched too thin and losing control, they tend to add layers to the management hierarchy, hiring more managers and delegating some decision-making authority to them. In other words, as an organization gets larger it tends to become taller. In addition, as organizations grow they often start to undertake more activities—expanding their product lines, diversifying into adjacent activities, vertically integrating, or expanding into new regional or national markets. This too creates problems of coordination and control, and once again these are often solved by adding layers to the management hierarchy.

For example, consider the history of a business founded by the father of this chapter's author. The business was a small factory that made wood products for the construction industry, such as doors, window frames, and stairs. Initially the factory had just one manager, who was also the CEO (the author's father), and 10 employees. At this point the CEO performed multiple functions—managing employees, planning production, going on sales calls, doing the books, purchasing lumber, and so on. The firm was soon successful and business grew, so the CEO hired more employees. Soon he was too busy to perform all the tasks he had been doing. At this point he hired help—a factory manager to supervise employees and plan production, a sales manager and three other salespeople to seek business, an accounts manager to manage the books, and a purchasing manager to buy lumber. This freed the CEO to concentrate on bigger strategic issues. In effect, the CEO added another layer to the management hierarchy to cope with growth.

The process did not stop here. Over time the CEO decided to enter other businesses that were related to the wood products industry, including home building, a brickmaking business, and a construction equipment rental company. With more businesses to manage the CEO found that he was once again stretched, so he created four divisions: the wood products factory, the home builder, the brick factory, and the equipment rental company. To run each division he appointed a general manager. The CEO then managed the general managers and focused his attention on issues that cut across businesses, while the general managers manage

FIGURE 8.3

Tall versus Flat
Hierarchies

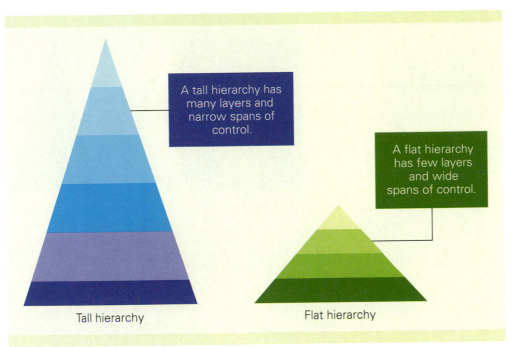

people within their businesses. In effect the CEO added a third layer to the management hierarchy. To better manage growth and diversification of the firm, he made the hierarchy taller.

As this example illustrates, growth in the number of layers in a hierarchy is driven by the size of an organization and the number of different activities it undertakes. Adding more levels in the hierarchy is a response to the problems of control that mount when a manager has too much work. How many layers are added is also partly determined by the span of control managers can effectively handle.

Span of Control The term **span of control** refers to the number of direct reports a manager has. At one time it was thought that the optimal span of control was only about six subordinates.[10] The argument was that a manager responsible for more than six subordinates would soon lose track of what was going on. Now we recognize that the relationship is not this simple. The number of direct reports a manager can handle depends on the nature of the work being supervised, how visible the performance of subordinates is, and the extent of decentralization within the organization. Generally if the work being performed by subordinates is routine, if the performance of subordinates is visible and easy to measure, and if the subordinates are empowered to make many decisions by themselves, managers can operate with a wide span of control. How wide is the subject of some debate, but it seems that good managers can effectively handle as many as 20 direct reports if the circumstances are right.

In sum, as organizations grow and undertake more activities, the management hierarchy tends to become taller. How tall depends on the span of control that is feasible, which in turn depends on the nature of the work, the visibility of subordinate performance, and the extent of decentralization within the organization. Note that managers can influence the visibility of subunit performance and the extent of decentralization through organization design, thereby limiting the impact of organization size and diversity on the size of a management hierarchy (see Figure 8.4). This is significant because we know that although adding layers to an organization can reduce the workload of higher-level managers and attenuate control loss, tall hierarchies have their own problems.

Problems in Tall Hierarchies Several problems can occur in tall hierarchies that may result in lower organizational efficiency and effectiveness. First, there is a tendency for

span of control
The number of direct
reports a manager has.

FIGURE 8.4

Number of Levels
in a Hierarchy

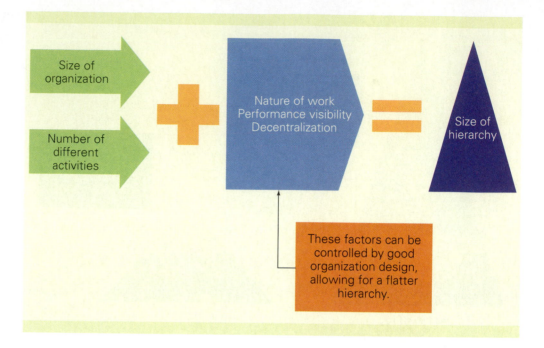

information to get *accidentally distorted* as it passes through layers in a hierarchy. The phenomenon is familiar to anyone who has played the game "telephone." In this game players sit in a circle; somebody whispers a message to the next person, who then whispers the message to the next person, and so on around the circle. By the time the message has been transmitted by a number of people, it becomes distorted and the meaning starts to change (this can have amusing consequences, which of course is the point of the game). Human beings are not good at transmitting information; they tend to embellish or miss data, which distorts the information. In a management context, if crucial information has to pass through many layers in a tall hierarchy before it reaches decision makers, it may get distorted in the process. So decisions may be based on inaccurate information, and poor performance may result.

There is also the problem of *deliberate distortion* by midlevel managers who are trying to curry favor with their superiors or pursue some agenda of their own. For example, the manager of a division might suppress bad information and exaggerate good information in an attempt to window-dress the performance of his or her unit to higher-level managers and win their approval. By doing so the manager may get access to more resources, earn performance bonuses, or avoid sanctions for poor performance. Other things being equal, the more layers there are in a hierarchy, the more opportunities there are for people to deliberately distort information. To the extent that information is distorted, senior managers will make decisions on the basis of inaccurate information, which can result in poor performance. Economists refer to the loss of efficiency that arises from deliberate information distortion for personal gain within an organization as **influence costs**, and they argue that influence costs can be a major source of low productivity.[11]

A third problem with tall hierarchies is that they are expensive. The salaries and benefits of multiple layers of midlevel managers can add up to significant overhead, which can increase the cost structure of the firm; unless there is a commensurate benefit, a tall hierarchy can put a firm at a competitive disadvantage. A final problem concerns the inherent inertia associated with a tall hierarchy. As we will see in Chapter 18 when we discuss change, organizations are inherently inert—they are difficult to change. One cause of inertia in organization is that to protect their turf and perhaps their jobs, managers often argue for the maintenance of the status quo. In tall hierarchies there is more turf (more centers of power and influence) and thus more voices arguing against change. Thus tall hierarchies tend to be slower to change.

influence costs

The loss of efficiency caused by deliberate information distortion for personal gain within an organization.

Delayering: Reducing the Size of a Hierarchy Given the disadvantages associated with tall hierarchies, many firms attempt to limit the size of the management hierarchy. During the last 15 years or so, **delayering** to reduce the number of levels in a management hierarchy has become a standard component of many attempts to boost firms' performance.[12] Delayering is based on the assumption that when times are good, firms tend to expand their management hierarchies beyond the point of efficiency. The bureaucratic inefficiencies associated with a tall hierarchy become evident only when the competitive environment becomes tougher, at which time managers seek to delayer the organization. Delayering, and simultaneously widening spans of control, is also seen as a way of enforcing greater decentralization within an organization and reaping the associated efficiency gains.

The King of Delayering During his tenure as CEO of General Electric, Jack Welch cut the number of layers in the management hierarchy from nine to five, instituting wide spans of control.

© Najlah Feanny/Corbis SABA

The process of delayering was a standard feature of Jack Welch's tenure at General Electric, during which he laid off 150,000 people, reduced the number of layers in the hierarchy from nine to five, and simultaneously increased General Electric's profits and revenues. Welch believed that GE had become too top-heavy during the tenure of his successors. A key element of his strategy was to transform General Electric into a leaner and faster-moving organization—which required delayering. Welch himself had a wide span of control, with some 20 subordinates reporting directly to him, including the heads of GE's 15 top businesses. Similarly, Jeffery Immelt, the head of GE's medical systems business under Welch, had 21 direct reports (Immelt replaced Welch as CEO).[13]

Delayering has also been prompted by the realization that large firms can function with relatively flat structures if their organization architecture is designed correctly. Nucor, for example, has only four layers in its hierarchy, yet it is the largest steelmaker in the United States. As at Nucor, achieving a flat hierarchy requires decentralization of responsibility for many decisions to lower-level managers who run autonomous self-contained units (in Nucor's case, individual steel plants). If these units are managed on an arm's-length basis, with top management intervening in subunit operations only when performance goals are not met, the top managers can handle a wide span of control, which makes a flat organization feasible. Nucor, for example, has 25 divisions. The general manager of each reports directly to the CEO, which implies that the CEO has a very wide span of control (probably close to 30 if other corporate executives such as the COO are included).

Although performance benefits are often associated with moving to a flat structure, the process of delayering is not an easy one; and research shows that delayering can cause significant stress and poor morale among managers if the process is not handled correctly.[14] Jack Welch believed that the key to successful delayering is to move fast (thereby eliminating lingering uncertainty among managers concerning their job security) and to reward and promote managers who thrive within the new structure, thereby indicating the management style that will be favored.

delayering
Reducing the number of layers in a hierarchy.

■ Delayering at General Electric.

■ // Designing Structure: Horizontal Differentiation

As we have seen, vertical differentiation is concerned with the location of decision-making responsibilities within an organization. In contrast, horizontal differentiation is concerned with how to divide the organization into subunits. We look at four different types of structure here: functional, multidivisional, geographic, and matrix.

// FUNCTIONAL STRUCTURE

functional structure
A structure that follows the obvious division of labor within the firm, with different functions focusing on different tasks.

Most firms begin with no formal structure and are run by a single entrepreneur or a small team of individuals. As they grow, the demands of management become too great for an individual or small team to handle. At this point the organization is split into functions that typically represent different aspects of the firm's value chain. In other words, in a **functional structure** the structure of the organization follows the obvious division of labor within the firm, with different functions focusing on different tasks. Thus there might be a production function, an R&D function, a marketing function, a sales function, and so on (see Figure 8.5). These functions are typically overseen by a top manager, such as the CEO, or a small top management team.

Functions themselves can be and often are subdivided into subunits. Further horizontal differentiation within functions is typically on the basis of similar tasks and processes. Within the manufacturing facilities of Toyota, for example, the workforce is grouped into teams, and each team is responsible for a discrete activity or task, such as the production of a major component that goes into an automobile. At Nucor too the workforce is grouped into teams, with each team taking on responsibility for a particular step in the steelmaking process. These teams may have significant decision-making responsibility, be held accountable for their performance, and have their pay and bonuses tied to teamwide goals.

A functional structure can work well for a firm that is active in a single line of business and focuses on a single geographic area. But problems can develop once the firm expands into different businesses or geographies. Consider first what happens when a firm expands into different business lines. The Dutch multinational Philips NV, for example, began making electric lights, but diversification took the company into consumer electronics (visual and audio equipment), industrial electronics (integrated circuits and other electronic components), and medical systems (MRI scanners and ultrasound systems). In such circumstances a functional structure can be clumsy. Problems of coordination and control arise when different business areas are managed within the framework of a functional structure.[15]

It becomes difficult to identify the profitability of each distinct business—and thus to assess whether a business is performing well or poorly—when the activities of businesses are scattered across various functions. Moreover, because no individual or management team is responsible for the performance of each business, there is a lack of accountability within the organization, and this too can result in poor control. As for coordination, when the different

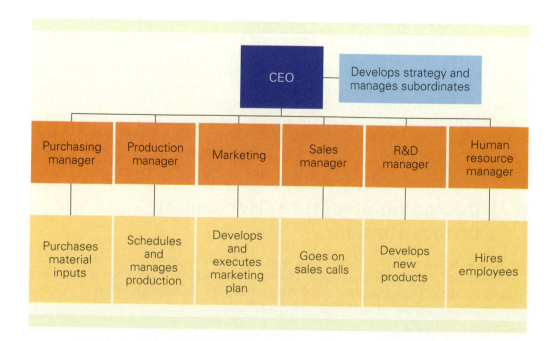

FIGURE 8.5
A Typical Functional Structure

activities that constitute a business are embedded in different functions, such as production and marketing, that are simultaneously managing other businesses, it can be difficult to achieve the tight coordination between functions needed to effectively run a business. Moreover, it is difficult to run a functional department that is supervising the value creation activities of several business areas.

// MULTIDIVISIONAL STRUCTURE

The problems we have just discussed were first recognized in the 1920s by one of the pioneers of American management thinking, Alfred Sloan, who at the time was CEO of General Motors, then the largest company in the world.[16] Under Sloan GM had diversified into several businesses. In addition to making cars under several distinct brands, it made trucks, airplane engines, and refrigerators. After struggling to run these different businesses within the framework of a functional structure, Sloan realized that a fundamentally different structure was required. His solution, which has since become the classic way to organize a multibusiness enterprise, was to adopt a multidivisional structure (see Figure 8.6).

In a **multidivisional structure** the firm is divided into different product divisions, each of which is responsible for a distinct business area. Thus Philips created product divisions for lighting, consumer electronics, industrial electronics, and medical systems. Each division is set up as a self-contained, largely autonomous entity with its own functions. Responsibility for operating decisions and business-level strategy is typically decentralized to the divisions, which are then held accountable for their performance. Headquarters is responsible for the overall strategic development of the firm (corporate-level strategy), for the control of the various divisions, for allocating capital between divisions, for supervising and coaching the managers who run each division, and for transferring valuable skills between divisions.

The product divisions are generally left alone to run their daily operations so long as they hit performance targets, which are typically negotiated annually between the head office and divisional management. Head office management, however, will often help divisional managers think through their strategies. Thus while Jack Welch at GE did not develop strategy for the various businesses within GE's portfolio (that was decentralized to divisional managers), he did probe the thinking of divisional managers about their strategies. In addition, Welch devoted a lot of effort to getting managers to share best practices across divisions. For example, Welch was a driving force in getting different divisions at GE to adopt the six sigma process improvement methodology (see Chapter 7 for details).

■ Multinational structure at Philips NV.

multidivisional structure

A structure in which a firm is divided into different divisions, each of which is responsible for a distinct business area.

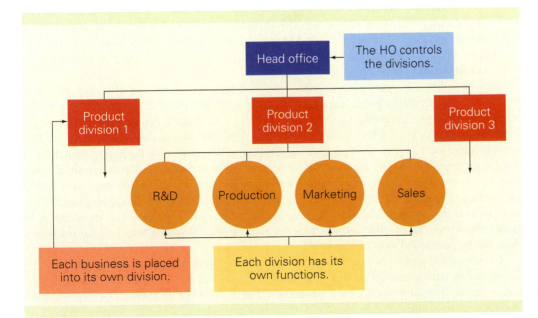

FIGURE 8.6

A Multidivisional Structure

Structural Engineer   Alfred Sloan, the longtime CEO of General Motors, was the first to introduce a multidivisional structure. Sloan later wrote about his management experiences in a famous autobiography, *My Years at General Motors*, which is still widely read today. Bill Gates has described Sloan's book as the most important management book ever written.

© Bettmann/Corbis

geographic structure

A structure in which a firm is divided into different units on the basis of geography.

One of the great virtues claimed for the multidivisional structure is that it creates an internal environment that gets divisional managers to focus on efficiency.[17] Because each division is a self-contained entity, its performance is highly visible. The high level of responsibility and accountability implies that divisional managers have few alibis for poor performance. This motivates them to focus on improving efficiency. Base pay, bonuses, and promotional opportunities for divisional managers can be tied to how well the divisions do. Capital is also allocated by top management between the competing divisions depending on how effectively top managers think the division managers can invest that capital. The desire for capital to grow their businesses, and for pay increases and bonuses, creates further incentives for divisional managers to focus on improving the competitive positions of the businesses under their control.

On the other hand, if the head office puts too much pressure on divisional managers to improve performance, this can result in some of the worst practices of management. These can include cutting necessary investments in plant, equipment, and R&D to boost short-term performance, even though such actions can damage the long-term competitive position of the enterprise.[18] To guard against this possibility, head office managers need to develop a good understanding of each division, set performance goals that are attainable, and have staff who can regularly audit the accounts and operations of divisions to ensure that each division is not being managed for short-term results or in a way that destroys its long-term competitiveness.

// GEOGRAPHIC STRUCTURE

Some firms first grow not by expanding into different businesses through diversification, but by expanding into other geographic regions—either within their home countries or (increasingly in today's global economy) into other national markets. For firms that are active in multiple regions with a single business, the structural solution to managing growth is to adopt a geographic structure. In a **geographic structure** the main subunits of the organization are geographic areas, such as regions within a country, countries, or multicountry regions.

Figure 8.7 illustrates a form of geographic structure found in some international businesses.[19] Under this structure the firm is divided into geographic areas. An area may be a country (if the market is large enough) or a group of countries. Each area division tends to be a self-contained, largely autonomous entity. Each may have its own set of functions (such as its own production, marketing, R&D, and human resource functions). Operations authority and strategic decisions relating to each of these activities may be decentralized to each area, with headquarters retaining authority for the overall strategic direction of the firm and financial control.

This structure facilitates responsiveness to local market conditions. Because decision-making responsibilities are decentralized, each area can customize product offerings, marketing strategy, and business strategy to the local conditions. As we saw in Chapter 3, there are significant differences in cultures and business systems across nations, so this approach has some appeal. On the other hand, this structure also encourages fragmentation of the organization into highly autonomous entities, which can make it difficult to transfer core skills between areas. Moreover, because each geographic region has its own production facilities, duplication inhibits the realization of economies of scale that could be gained if the firm served the entire world market from a single favorable location. The duplication of functions across regions also implies that the firm is not placing different functions where they can be performed most efficiently.[20]

To solve these problems, many international businesses operate with a hybrid geographic–functional structure, similar to that illustrated in Figure 8.8. In this structure functions like R&D, purchasing, and production are centralized at the optimal locations. The world is then divided into geographic regions for local marketing and sales.

FIGURE 8.7
Geographic Structure

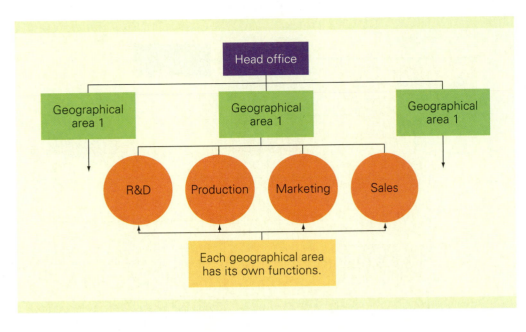

A geographic structure, or a hybrid geographic–functional structure, can become unwieldy when a firm is engaged in several different businesses. Under such circumstances each geographic area might itself be divided into different product divisions—one for each business—with functions appearing underneath the divisions. This was the structure Unilever used to operate with. Although this structure had the advantage of allowing Unilever to customize its product offering and marketing strategy from country to country, the duplication of manufacturing facilities drove up costs. By the late 1990s this structure was no longer tenable, and in 2000 Unilever established two worldwide product divisions: one to manage its foods business (packaged foods) and one to manage its home products business (shampoos, detergents). The division heads were responsible for the worldwide profitability of the businesses under their control.

Under this new structure Unilever consolidated its manufacturing in fewer facilities, each located where costs were favorable. Those facilities served regional or global markets, letting the company realize economies of scale and drive down costs. R&D was also centralized at the

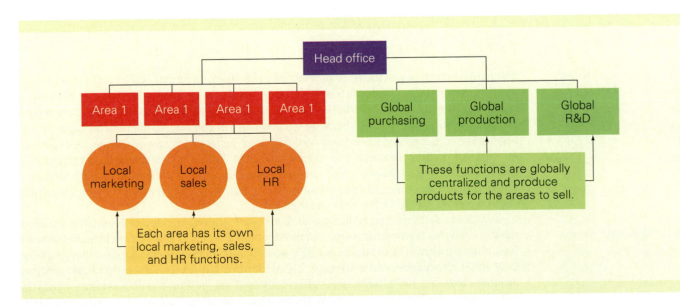

FIGURE 8.8 Hybrid Geographic–Functional Structure

FIGURE 8.9

Unilever's Structure

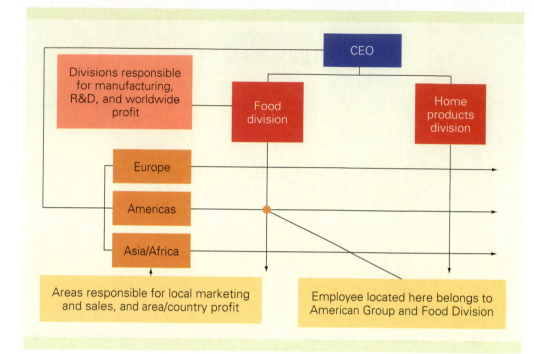

divisional level. However, Unilever still felt that it needed to customize aspects of its sales and marketing strategy, as well as product packaging, to account for country differences in tastes, preferences, distribution systems, and the like. To solve this dilemma, Unilever has kept elements of its geographic structure in place, with the head of each geographic area maintaining responsibility for profitability in the area under his or her control, and country managers within each region being given responsibility for local marketing and sales (and held accountable for performance in that country). Unilever's structure as of 2005, which is illustrated in Figure 8.9, is an attempt to solve conflicting demands on the organization while maintaining the best features of a multidivisional structure and a geographic structure.[21] Unilever is hardly alone is struggling with such a dilemma; many other firms do as well. One solution to such organizational dilemmas is to adopt a matrix structure, which is in effect how Unilever is now operating. As we will see next, however, matrix structures also have problems.

// MATRIX STRUCTURE

matrix structure

An organization with two overlapping hierarchies.

The matrix structure is sometimes adopted when no single structural design seems to solve all of a firm's problems. With a **matrix structure**, managers try to combine two different organizing philosophies in a single design. Unilever, for example, saw benefits to being organized both on the basis of divisions (enabling the company to consolidate manufacturing facilities and realize economies of scales) and on the basis of geographic areas (enabling the company to respond to different national and regional markets). The firm's senior managers want all of these benefits, so they have adopted a matrix structure with two overlapping hierarchies: one on the basis of business and one on the basis of area. This means that a lower-level manager might have two bosses—divisional and regional.

In addition to diversified multinational firms like Unilever, high-technology firms based in rapidly changing environments sometimes adopt a matrix structure.[22] In such cases the need for a matrix is driven by the desire for tight coordination between different functions, particularly R&D, production, and marketing. Tight coordination is required so that R&D designs products that can be manufactured efficiently and are designed with customer needs in mind—both of which increase the probability of successful product commercialization. Tight coordination between R&D, manufacturing, and marketing has also been shown to result in

■ Structure at Unilever.

FIGURE 8.10

Matrix Structure in a
High-Tech Firm

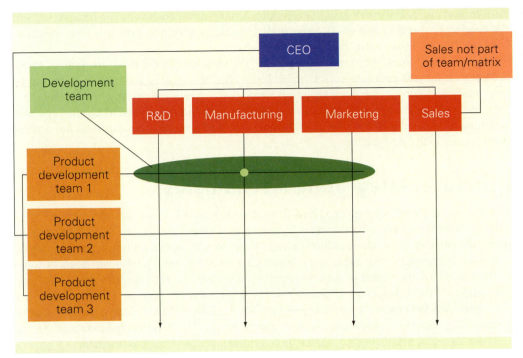

faster product development, which can help a firm gain an advantage over its rivals.[23] As illustrated in Figure 8.10, in such an organization an employee may belong to two subunits within the firm. For example, a manager might be a member of both the manufacturing function and a product development team.

A matrix structure looks nice on paper, but the reality can be different. Unless this structure is managed carefully it may not work well.[24] In practice a matrix can be clumsy and bureaucratic. It can require so many meetings that it is difficult to get any work done. The dual hierarchy structure can lead to conflict and perpetual power struggles between the different sides of the hierarchy. In one high-technology firm, for example, the manufacturing manager was reluctant to staff a product development team with his best people because he felt that would distract them from their functional work. As a result, the product development teams did not work as well as they might.

To make matters worse, it can prove difficult to ascertain accountability in a matrix structure. When all critical decisions are the product of negotiation between different hierarchies, one side can always blame the other when things go wrong. As a manager in one high-tech matrix structure said to the author when reflecting on a failed product launch, "Had the engineering (R&D) group provided our development team with decent resources, we would have gotten that product out on time, and it would have been successful." For his part, the head of the engineering group stated, "We did everything we could to help them succeed, but the project was not well managed. They kept changing their requests for engineering skills, which was very disruptive." Such finger-pointing can compromise accountability, enhance conflict, and make senior management lose control over the organization.

However, there is also evidence that properly managed matrix structures can work.[25] Among other things, making a matrix work requires clear lines of responsibility. Normally this means that one side of the matrix must be given the primary role while the other is given a support role. In a high-tech firm, for example, the product development teams might be given the primary role because getting good products to market as quickly as possible is key to competitive success. In a diversified multinational firm like Unilever, the divisions might be given the primary role because they are responsible for manufacturing costs and product development, while the geographic areas take on the support role. Clear goals should be well prioritized so that when conflicts occur, which is inevitable, the goals help to indicate what is most important. In Unilever's case, for example, driving down costs is an important goal, and the need to first satisfy this goal can be used as a decision rule to help solve any conflicts between the division and area hierarchies in the matrix.

Despite such steps, managing within a matrix structure is difficult. In light of these problems, managers have sometimes tried to build "flexible" matrix structures based more on enterprisewide management knowledge networks, and a shared culture and vision, than on a rigid hierarchical arrangement. Within such companies the informal structure plays a greater role than the formal structure. We discuss this issue when we consider informal integrating mechanisms in the next section.

// Designing Structure: Integrating Mechanisms

In the previous section we explained how firms divide themselves into subunits. Now we need to examine some means of coordinating those subunits. One way of achieving coordination is through centralization. If the coordination task is complex, however, centralization may not be effective. Higher-level managers responsible for achieving coordination can soon become overwhelmed by the volume of work required to coordinate the activities of various subunits, particularly if the subunits are large, diverse, or geographically dispersed. When this is the case, managers look toward integrating mechanisms, both formal and informal, to help achieve coordination. Here we introduce the various integrating mechanisms managers use and discuss how the choice of integrating mechanism is determined by the strategy of the firm.

// FORMAL INTEGRATING MECHANISMS

The formal integrating mechanisms used to coordinate subunits vary in complexity from simple direct contact and liaison roles, to teams, to a matrix structure (see Figure 8.11). In general, the greater the need for coordination between subunits, the more complex formal integrating mechanisms need to be.[26]

Direct contact between subunit managers is the simplest integrating mechanism: Managers of the various subunits just contact each other whenever they have a common

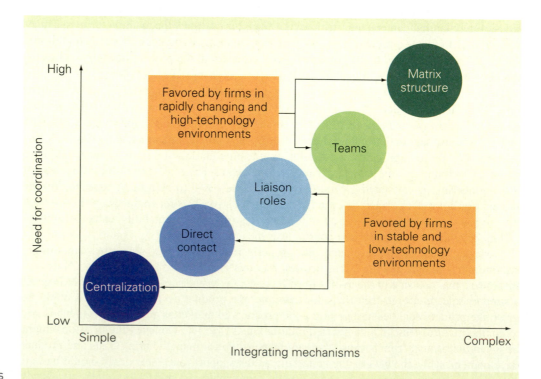

FIGURE 8.11

Integrating Mechanisms

concern. Direct contact may not be effective, however, if managers have differing orientations that impede coordination. Managers of various subunits may have different orientations partly because they have different tasks. For example, production managers are typically concerned with production issues such as capacity utilization, cost control, and quality control, whereas marketing managers are concerned with marketing issues such as pricing, promotions, distribution, and market share. These differences can inhibit communication between managers, who may not "speak the same language." Managers can also become entrenched in "functional silos," which can lead to a lack of respect between subunits and inhibit the communication required to achieve cooperation and coordination. For these reasons, direct contact may not be sufficient to achieve coordination between subunits when the need for integration is high.

Liaison roles are a bit more complex than direct contact. As the need for coordination between subunits increases, integration can be improved by assigning a person in each subunit to coordinate with another subunit. Through these roles, the people involved establish a permanent relationship. This helps attenuate any impediments to coordination.

Teamwork   This cross-functional product development team is working on the design of interior trim for heavy-duty trucks. Cross-functional product development teams are widely used in firms that compete through product innovation. The teams represent the best way of achieving tight coordination between different functions.

© Digital Vision

When the need for coordination is greater still, firms use temporary or permanent teams composed of individuals from the subunits that need to achieve coordination. Teams often coordinate product development efforts, but they can be useful when any aspect of operations or strategy requires the cooperation of multiple subunits. Product development teams are typically composed of personnel from R&D, production, and marketing. The resulting coordination aids the development of products that are tailored to consumer needs and that can be produced at a reasonable cost (through design for manufacturing).

When the need for integration is very high, firms may institute a matrix structure, in which all roles are viewed as integrating roles. This structure is designed to maximize integration among subunits. As discussed earlier, common matrix organizations include structures based on functions and product development teams, as in high-technology firms (see Figure 8.10), or on divisions and geographic areas, as in diversified multinational enterprises (see Figure 8.9). However, as we have already noted, matrix structures can bog down in a bureaucratic tangle that creates as many problems as it solves. If not well managed, matrix structures can become bureaucratic, inflexible, and characterized by conflict rather than the hoped-for cooperation. For such a structure to work it needs to be somewhat flexible and to be supported by informal integrating mechanisms.[27]

// INFORMAL INTEGRATING MECHANISMS: KNOWLEDGE NETWORKS

In attempting to alleviate or avoid the problems associated with formal integrating mechanisms in general and matrix structures in particular, firms with a high need for integration have been experimenting with an informal integrating mechanism: knowledge networks supported by an organizational culture that values teamwork and cross-unit cooperation.[28] A **knowledge network** is a network for transmitting information within an organization that is based not on formal organization structure, but on informal contacts between managers within an enterprise and on distributed information systems.[29] The great strength of such a network is that it can be a nonbureaucratic conduit for knowledge flows within an enterprise.[30] For a network to exist, managers at different locations within the organization must be

knowledge network
A network for transmitting information within an organization based on informal contacts between managers within an enterprise and on distributed information systems.

FIGURE 8.12

A Knowledge Network

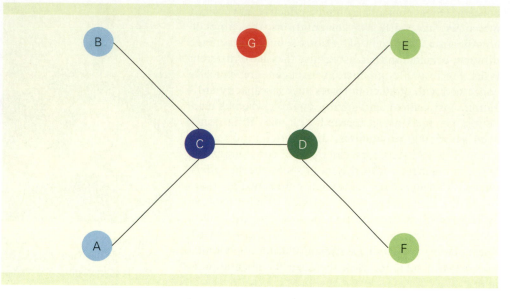

linked to each other at least indirectly. For example, Figure 8.12 shows the simple network relationships between seven managers within a complex multinational firm. Managers A, B, and C all know each other personally, as do Managers D, E, and F. Although Manager B does not know Manager F personally, they are linked through common acquaintances (Managers C and D). Thus Managers A through F are all part of the network. Manager G is not.

Imagine Manager B, a marketing manager in Spain, needs to know the solution to a technical problem to better serve an important European customer. Manager F, an R&D manager in the United States, has the solution to Manager B's problem. Manager B mentions her problem to all of her contacts, including Manager C, and asks if they know anyone who might be able to provide a solution. Manager C asks Manager D, who tells Manager F, who then calls Manager B with the solution. In this way coordination is achieved informally through the network rather than by formal integrating mechanisms such as teams or a matrix structure.

For such a network to function effectively it must embrace as many managers as possible. For example, if Manager G had a problem similar to Manager B's, he would not be able to use the informal network to find a solution; he would have to resort to more formal mechanisms. Establishing firmwide knowledge networks is difficult. Although network enthusiasts speak of networks as the "glue" that binds complex organizations together, it is unclear how successful firms have been at building companywide networks. Techniques that establish knowledge networks include information systems, management development policies, and conferences.

Firms are using distributed computer and telecommunications information systems to provide the foundation for informal knowledge networks.[31] Electronic mail, videoconferencing, high-bandwidth data systems, and Web-based search engines make it much easier for managers scattered over the globe to get to know each other, to identify contacts that might help solve a particular problem, and to publicize and share best practices within the organization. Wal-Mart, for example, uses its intranet to communicate ideas about merchandizing strategy between stores located in different countries.

Firms are also using management development programs to build informal networks. Tactics include rotating managers through various subunits regularly so they build their own informal network and using management education programs to bring managers of subunits together so they can become acquainted. In addition, some science-based firms use internal conferences to establish contact between people in different units of the organization. At 3M regular multidisciplinary conferences gather scientists from different business units and get them talking to each other. Apart from the benefits of direct interaction in the conference setting, after the conference the scientists may continue to share ideas, increasing knowledge flow within the organization. 3M has many stories of product ideas that were the result of such

■ Knowledge network at 3M.

knowledge flow—including the ubiquitous Post-it note, whose inventor, Art Fry, first learned about its adhesive from a colleague working in another division of 3M, Spencer Silver, who had spent several years shopping his adhesive around 3M.[32]

Knowledge networks by themselves may not be sufficient to achieve coordination if subunit managers pursue subgoals that are at variance with firmwide goals. For a knowledge network to function properly (and also for a formal matrix structure to work) managers must share a strong commitment to the same goals. To appreciate the nature of the problem, consider again the case of Managers B and F. As before, Manager F hears about Manager B's problem through the network. However, solving Manager B's problem would require Manager F to devote considerable time to the task. If this would divert Manager F away from regular tasks—and the pursuit of subgoals that differ from those of Manager B—he may be unwilling to do it. Thus Manager F may not call Manager B, and the informal network would fail to solve Manager B's problem.

Post-It Note Man   Art Fry, the inventor of the Post-it note, first learned about the adhesive that he would later use on Post-it notes through 3M's internal knowledge network.

To eliminate this flaw, organization managers must adhere to a common set of norms and values that override differing subunit orientations.[33] In other words, the firm must have a strong organizational culture that promotes teamwork and cooperation. When this is the case, a manager is willing and able to set aside the interests of his own subunit when doing so benefits the firm as a whole. If Managers B and F are committed to the same organizational norms and value systems, and if these organizational norms and values place the interests of the firm as a whole above the interests of any individual subunit, Manager F should be willing to cooperate with Manager B on solving her subunit's problems. We look at what managers can do to promote a strong organizational culture in Chapter 10.

// STRATEGY, COORDINATION, AND INTEGRATING MECHANISMS

All enterprises need coordination between subunits, whether those subunits are functions, businesses, or geographic areas. However, the degree of coordination required and the integrating mechanisms used vary depending on the strategy of the firm. Consider first enterprises that are active in just one business. In the single-business enterprise, the need for coordination between functions is greater in firms that are competing through product innovation.[34] As we discussed earlier, such organizations need to coordinate the R&D, manufacturing, and marketing functions of the firm to ensure that new products are developed in a timely manner, are designed to be efficiently manufactured, and match consumer demands. We saw that a matrix structure is one way of achieving such coordination. Another more common solution is to form temporary teams to oversee the development and introduction of a new product. Once the new product has been introduced, the team is disbanded and employees return to their usual functions or move to another team.

There is also a high need for coordination in firms that face an uncertain and highly turbulent competitive environment, where rapid adaptation to changing market conditions is required for survival.[35] In such cases there is a need to make sure the different functions of the firm are all pulling in the same direction so that the firm's response to a changing environment is coherent and embraces the entire organization. Temporary teams are often used to effect such coordination. For example, in the mid-1990s the World Wide Web, which is based on a computer language known as HTML, emerged with stunning speed and in a way that was anticipated by very few managers. The rise of the WWW produced a profound change in the environment facing computer software firms, such as Microsoft, where managers quickly realized that they needed to shift their strategy, make their products Web enabled, and position the marketing and sales activities of the firm to compete in this new landscape. At Microsoft the entire company quickly embraced the WWW, and all products were soon Web enabled. Making this shift required tight coordination between different software engineering groups, such as those working on the software code for Windows, Office, and MSN, so that all of the products not only were Web enabled but also worked seamlessly with each other. Microsoft achieved this by forming cross-functional teams. In addition to formal integrating mechanisms, firms with a high need for coordination between subunits, such as those based in turbulent high-technology environments, would do well to foster informal knowledge networks to facilitate greater coordination between subunits.

In contrast, if a firm is based in a stable environment characterized by little or no change, and if developing new products is not a central aspect of the firm's business strategy, the need for coordination between functions may be lower. In such cases a firm may be able to function with minimal integrating mechanisms, such as direct contact or simple liaison roles. These mechanisms, coupled with a strong culture that encourages employees to share the same goals and to cooperate with each other for the benefit of the entire organization, may be all that is required to achieve coordination between functions.

For multibusiness firms organized into product divisions, the need for coordination varies with the type of diversification strategy managers are pursuing.[36] In particular, if a firm has diversified into related businesses and is trying to realize economies of scope by sharing inputs across product divisions, or is trying to boost profitability by leveraging valuable core competencies across product divisions, it will need integrating mechanisms to coordinate product division activities. (See Chapter 6 for details of diversification strategies.) Liaison roles, temporary teams, and permanent teams can all be used to ensure such coordination. On the other hand, if top management is focusing primarily on boosting profitability through superior governance, and if each division is managed on a stand-alone basis with no attempt to leverage competencies or realize economies of scope, the firm may well operate well with minimal or no integrating mechanisms between divisions.

IN CONCLUSION WHY DOES IT MATTER?

There are numerous reasons why managers should care about the structure of their organization. Structure is the way in which work is allocated in an organization. Structure clarifies who is responsible and accountable for tasks within an organization. The accountability derived from structure is an important aspect of control in an organization. For example, the head of a product division is responsible and accountable for the performance of that division. The head office will exercise control by setting goals for the division, monitoring its performance, rewarding divisional managers for attaining or exceeding those goals, and holding the head of the division accountable if the goals are not met. Similarly, the head of a function (such as manufacturing) or a cross-functional team (such as a product development team) is responsible and accountable for the tasks of that subunit, and controls should be linked to how well that unit reaches its goals. Structure, in other words, is more than a way of allocating tasks; it is also an important means through which managers control the organization. Without the right structure, it may be impossible to exercise effective control over the operations of an enterprise.

Moreover, strategy is implemented in part through organization structure. If the structure of the firm does not match its strategy, the result can be poor performance. A diversified firm that operates with a functional structure will probably perform poorly, as will a high-tech firm based in a rapidly changing environment that does not use cross-functional teams. Structure must match strategy for superior performance. Managers need to get structure right if they are to successfully implement the strategy of their firm and attain competitive advantage. But structure is just one aspect of organization architecture. Structure must be aligned with control systems, incentives, organizational culture, and people for strategy to be successfully implemented. In the next few chapters we look at these other elements of an organization's architecture.

MANAGEMENT CHALLENGES

1. Successful organizations tend to increase the number of layers in their management hierarchy. Why do you think this happens? Is this a good thing? What can be done to limit hierarchical growth?

2. Explain the links among structure, decentralization, responsibility, accountability, and control.

3. Accountability is often compromised within a matrix organization. Why?

4. Under what circumstances might a large, diversified enterprise want to centralize at the corporate head office decisions regarding (a) purchasing and (b) human resource policies?

5. Even though Microsoft is a global corporation, it has centralized much of its R&D activities at its Redmond headquarters. Why do you think this is the case? Can you see any downside to this approach?

MANAGEMENT PORTFOLIO

FOR THE ORGANIZATION YOU HAVE CHOSEN TO FOLLOW:

1. Describe the basic organization structure of the enterprise.

2. Does the structure match the strategy of the enterprise? If it does, explain how. If it does not, explain why not, and outline what should be changed to bring strategy and structure into alignment.

3. Does the organization have a tall or flat management hierarchy? Is the number of levels in the hierarchy appropriate?

4. What is the span of control of the CEO? In your judgment is this span too narrow, too wide, or just right?

5. What decisions within this organization are centralized at the head office? What decisions are decentralized to subunits? Does the approach toward centralization and decentralization make sense?

CLOSING CASE   DOW CHEMICAL

A handful of major players compete head-to-head around the world in the chemical industry. These companies are Dow Chemical and Du Pont of the United States, Great Britain's ICI, and the German trio of BASF, Hoechst AG, and Bayer. The barriers to the free flow of chemical products between nations largely disappeared in the 1970s. This, along with the commodity nature of most bulk chemicals and a severe recession in the early 1980s, ushered in a prolonged period of intense price competition. In such an environment, the company that wins the competitive race is the one with the lowest costs. Dow Chemical was long among the cost leaders.

For years Dow's managers insisted that part of the credit belonged to its "matrix" organization. Dow's organizational matrix had three interacting elements: functions (such as R&D, manufacturing, and marketing), businesses (like ethylene, plastics, and pharmaceuticals), and geography (for example, Spain, Germany, and Brazil). Managers' job titles incorporated all three elements (plastics marketing manager for Spain), and most managers reported to at least two bosses. The plastics marketing manager in Spain might report to both the head of the worldwide plastics business and the head of the Spanish operations. The intent of the matrix was to make Dow operations responsive to both local market needs and corporate objectives. Thus the plastics business might be charged with minimizing Dow's global plastics production costs, while the Spanish operation might determine how best to sell plastics in the Spanish market.

When Dow introduced this structure, the results were less than promising: Multiple reporting channels led to confusion and conflict. The many bosses created an unwieldy bureaucracy. The overlapping responsibilities resulted in turf battles and a lack of accountability. Area managers disagreed with managers overseeing business sectors about which plants should be built where. In short, the structure didn't work. Instead of abandoning the structure, however, Dow decided to see if it could be made more flexible.

Dow's decision to keep its matrix structure was prompted by its move into the pharmaceuticals industry. The company realized that the pharmaceuticals business is very different from the bulk chemicals business. In bulk chemicals, the big returns come from achieving economies of scale in production. This dictates establishing large plants in key locations from which regional or global markets can be served. But in pharmaceuticals, regulatory and marketing requirements for drugs vary so much from country to country that local needs are far more important than reducing manufacturing costs through scale economies. A high degree of local responsiveness is essential. Dow realized its pharmaceutical business would never thrive if it were managed by the same priorities as its mainstream chemical operations.

Accordingly, instead of abandoning its matrix, Dow decided to make it more flexible to better accommodate the different businesses, each with its own priorities, within a single management system. A small team of senior executives at headquarters helped set the priorities for each type of business. After priorities were identified for each business sector, one of the three elements of the matrix—function, business, or geographic area—was given primary authority in decision making. Which element took the lead varied according to the type of decision and the market or location in which the company was competing. Such flexibility required that all employees understand what was occurring in the rest of the matrix. Although this may seem confusing, for years Dow claimed this flexible system worked well and credited much of its success to the quality of the decisions it facilitated.

By the mid-1990s, however, Dow had refocused its business on the chemicals industry, divesting itself of its pharmaceutical activities where the company's performance had been unsatisfactory. Reflecting the change in corporate strategy, in 1995 Dow decided to abandon its matrix structure in favor of a more streamlined structure based on global product divisions. The matrix structure was just too complex and costly to manage in the intense competitive environment of the time, particularly given the company's renewed focus on its commodity chemicals where competitive advantage often went to the low-cost producer. As Dow's then-CEO put it in a 1999 interview, "We were an organization that was matrixed and depended on teamwork, but there was no one in charge. When things went well, we didn't know whom to reward; and when things went poorly, we didn't know whom to blame. So we created a global divisional structure and cut out layers of management. There used to be eleven layers of management between me and the lowest-level employees; now there are five."[37]

CASE DISCUSSION QUESTIONS

1. Why did Dow Chemical first adopt a matrix structure? What benefits did it hope to derive from this structure?

2. What problems emerged with this structure? How did Dow try to deal with them? In retrospect, do you think those solutions were effective?

3. Why did Dow change its structure again in the mid-1990s? What was Dow trying to achieve this time? Do you think the current structure makes sense given the industry in which Dow operates and the strategy of the firm? Why?

ENDNOTES

1. D. Naidler, M. Gerstein, and R. Shaw, *Organization Architecture* (San Francisco: Jossey-Bass, 1992).

2. G. Morgan, *Images of Organization* (Beverly Hills, CA: Sage Publications, 1986).

3. The material in this section draws on J. Child, *Organizations* (London: Harper & Row, 1984). Recent work addressing the issue includes J.R. Baum and S. Wally, "Strategic Decision Speed and Firm Performance," *Strategic Management Journal* 24 (2003), pp. 1107–20; and D.I. Jung and B.J. Avolio, "Effects of Leadership Style and Followers' Cultural Orientation on Performance in Groups and Individual Task Conditions," *Academy of Management Journal* 42 (1999), pp. 208–18.

4. J. McCarthy and E. Montalbano, "Microsoft Reshuffles the Deck," *InfoWorld* 27 (September 26, 2005), pp. 12–13.

5. This is a key tenet of the information processing view of organizations. See J. Galbraith, *Designing Complex Organizations* (Reading, MA: Addison-Wesley, 1972).

6. J. Kim and R.M. Burton, "The Effects of Uncertainty and Decentralization on Project Team Performance," *Computational & Mathematical Organization Theory* 8 (2002), pp. 365–84.

7. J. Birkinshaw, N. Hood, and S. Jonsson, "Building Firm Specific Advantages in Multinational Corporations: The Role of Subsidiary Initiatives," *Strategic Management Journal* 19 (1998), pp. 221–41.

8. K.M. Eisenhardt, "Making Fast Strategic Decisions in High Velocity Environments," *Academy of Management Journal* 32 (1989), pp. 543–75.

9. "When Government Fails—Katrina's Aftermath," *The Economist,* September 2005, p. 25.

10. G.P. Hattrup and B.H. Kleiner, "How to Establish a Proper Span of Control for Managers," *Industrial Management* 35 (1993), pp. 28–30.

11. The classic statement was made by P. Milgrom and J. Roberts, "Bargaining Costs, Influence Costs, and the Organization of Economic Activity," in *Perspectives in*

Positive Political Economy, ed. J.E. Alt and K.A. Shepsle (Cambridge: Cambridge University Press, 1990). Also see R. Inderst, H.M. Muller, and K. Warneryd, "Influence Costs and Hierarchy," *Economics of Governance* 6 (2005), pp. 177–98.

12. C.R. Littler, R. Wiesner, and R. Dunford, "The Dynamics of Delayering," *Journal of Management Studies* 40 (2003), pp. 225–40.

13. J.A. Byrne, "Jack: A Close Look at How America's #1 Manager Runs GE," *BusinessWeek,* June 8, 1998, pp. 90–100. Also see GE's Two-Decade Transformation *(Harvard Business School* Case #9-399-150).

14. L. Worrall and C. Cooper, "Managers, Hierarchies, and Perceptions," *Journal of Managerial Psychology* 19 (2004), pp. 41–55.

15. A.D. Chandler, *Strategy and Structure: Chapters in the History of the Industrial Enterprise* (Cambridge, MA: MIT Press, 1962). Also see O.E. Williamson, *Markets and Hierarchies: Analysis and Anti-Trust Implications* (New York: Free Press, 1975).

16. A.P. Sloan, *My Years at General Motors* (New York: Bantum Books, 1996). This book was originally published in 1963.

17. C.W.L. Hill, M.A. Hitt, and R.E. Hoskisson, "Cooperative versus Competitive Structures in Related and Unrelated Firms," *Organization Science* 45 (1992), pp. 501–21; Williamson, *Markets and Hierarchies: Analysis and Anti-Trust Implications.*

18. C.W.L. Hill, M.A. Hitt, and R.E. Hoskisson, "Declining U.S. Competitiveness: Reflections on a Crisis," *Academy of Management Executive* 2 (1988), pp. 51–60.

19. J.M. Stopford and L.T. Wells, *Strategy and Structure of the Multinational Enterprise* (New York: Basic Books, 1972).

20. C.A. Bartlett and S. Ghoshal, *Managing across Borders* (Boston: Harvard Business School Press, 1989); S.M. Davis, "Managing and Organizing Multinational Corporations," in *Transnational Management,* ed. C.A. Bartlett and S. Ghoshal (Homewood, IL: Richard D. Irwin, 1992). Also see J. Wolf and W.G. Egelhoff, "A Reexamination and Extension of International Strategy–Structure Theory," *Strategic Management Journal* 23 (2002), pp. 181–89.

21. "Unilever's Restructuring Makes Us Like P&G," *Marketing Week,* February 24, 2005, pp. 8–9; Unilever's Q4 2004 Roadshow Presentation archived at http://www.unilever.com/resources/downloadlibrary.asp.

22. P.R Lawrence and J. Lorsch, *Organization and Environment* (Boston: Harvard University Press, 1967).

23. K.B. Clark and S.C. Wheelwright, *Managing New Product and Process Development* (New York: Free Press, 1993); M.A. Schilling and C.W.L. Hill, "Managing the New Product Development Process," *Academy of Management Executive* 12, no. 3 (August 1998), pp. 67–81; S.L. Brown and K.M. Eisenhardt, "Product Development: Past Research, Present Findings, and Future Directions," *Academy of Management Review* 20 (1995), pp. 343–78.

24. L.R. Burns, and D.R. Whorley, "Adoption and Abandonment of Matrix Management Programs: Effects of Organizational Characteristics and Interorganizational Networks," *Academy of Management Journal,* February 1993, pp. 106–38; C.A. Bartlett, and S. Ghoshal, "Matrix Management: Not a Structure, a Frame of Mind," *Harvard Business Review,* July–August 1990, pp. 138–45.

25. S. Thomas and L.S. D'Annunizo, "Challenges and Strategies of Matrix Organizations," *HR Human Resource Planning* 28 (2005), pp. 39–49.

26. See Galbraith, *Designing Complex Organizations.*

27. M. Goold and A. Campbell, "Structured Networks: Toward the Well-Designed Matrix," *Long Range Planning,* October 2003, pp. 427–60.

28. Bartlett and Ghoshal, *Managing across Borders;* F.V. Guterl, "Goodbye, Old Matrix," *Business Month,* February 1989, pp. 32–38; I. Bjorkman, W. Barner-Rasussen, and L. Li, "Managing Knowledge Transfer in MNCs: The Impact of Headquarters Control Mechanisms," *Journal of International Business* 35 (2004), pp. 443–60.

29. M.S. Granovetter, "The Strength of Weak Ties," *American Journal of Sociology* 78 (1973), pp. 1360–80.

30. A.K. Gupta and V.J. Govindarajan, "Knowledge Flows within Multinational Corporations," *Strategic Management Journal* 21, no. 4 (2000), pp. 473–96; V.J. Govindarajan and A.K.Gupta, *The Quest for Global Dominance* (San Francisco: Jossey-Bass, 2001); U. Andersson, M. Forsgren, and U. Holm, "The Strategic Impact of External Networks: Subsidiary Performance and Competence Development in the Multinational Corporation," *Strategic Management Journal* 23 (2002), pp. 979–96.

31. For examples, see W.H. Davidow and M.S. Malone, *The Virtual Corporation* (New York: Harper Collins, 1992).

32. 3M, *A Century of Innovation: The 3M Story* (3M, 2002). Available at http://www.3m.com/about3m/century/index.jhtml.

33. W.G. Ouchi, "Markets, Bureaucracies, and Clans," *Administrative Science Quarterly* 25 (1980), pp. 129–44.

34. D. Miller, "Relating Porter's Business Strategies to Environment and Structure," *Academy of Management Journal* 31 (1988), pp. 280–308.

35. Lawrence and Lorsch, *Organization and Environment.*

36. Hill, Hitt, and Hoskisson, "Cooperative versus Competitive Structures in Related and Unrelated Firms."

37. Sources: "Dow Draws Its Matrix Again, and Again, and Again," *The Economist,* August 5, 1989, pp. 55–56; Anonymous, "Dow Goes for Global Structure," *Chemical Marketing Reporter,* December 11, 1995, pp. 4–5; R.M. Hodgetts, "Dow Chemical CEO William Stavropoulos on Structure and Decision Making," *Academy of Management Executive* 13 (November 1999), pp. 29–35.

9

CONTROL SYSTEMS

NORDSTROM

Inventory Controller. By focusing its control systems on inventory, Nordstrom was able to increase its inventory turnover and profits.

© Getty Images

In 2001 Nordstrom, the venerable high-end department store, was facing some challenges. Despite industry-leading sales per square foot, profits had fallen short of the company's goals for three years in a row and were down some 35 percent from 1999. The problem: Poor inventory controls meant that Nordstrom had either too much merchandise that was in low demand or too little of the merchandise consumers wanted. The failure to have popular items in stock meant Nordstrom was losing high-margin sales. To correct this problem, Nordstrom revamped its inventory control systems. The company invested heavily in information technology to track its inventory on a real-time basis. It also built electronic links with suppliers to show what was selling at Nordstrom and what the reorder pattern would be. The goal was to stock only what consumers demanded by having inventories delivered to stores as needed. To measure the success of this program, Nordstrom focused on two metrics—inventory turnover and the average inventory per square foot of selling space. In 2001 the company was turning over its inventory 3.73 times a year, and on average throughout the year had $60 of inventory for every square foot of selling space in a store. By 2004, as a result of better inventory controls, inventory was turning over 4.51 times a year, and the company held $52.46 of inventory for every square foot of selling space. Due to improved operating efficiency, net profits surged from $125 million in 2001 to $406 million in 2004.[1]

■ Control systems at Nordstrom.

A critical task of managers is to control the activities of their organization. As we noted in Chapter 8, controls are an integral part of an enterprise's organization architecture. Controls are necessary to make sure an organization is operating efficiently and in a manner consistent with its intended strategy. Without adequate controls, control loss occurs and the organization's performance will suffer. This was clearly the case at Nordstrom in the early 2000s. A lack of adequate systems to track inventory meant that Nordstrom lost control over what was stocked in its stores. This translated into higher costs and lower profits. To rectify this problem and regain control, Nordstrom had to put an inventory control system in place. In this chapter we look in detail at control systems. We begin by reviewing basic control systems and the various ways in which managers control their organizations.

■ // Control Systems

control

The process through which managers regulate the activities of individuals and units.

standard

A performance requirement that the organization is meant to attain on an ongoing basis.

subgoal

An objective that, if achieved, helps an organization attain or exceed its major goals.

Within organizations, **control** can be viewed as the process through which managers regulate the activities of individuals and units so they are consistent with the goals and standards of the organization.[2] As we noted earlier in the book, a goal is a desired future state that an organization attempts to realize (see Chapter 5). A **standard** is a performance requirement the organization is meant to attain on an ongoing basis. As we will see, there are several different ways in which managers can regulate the activities of individuals and units so they remain consistent with organization goals and standards. Before considering these, however, we need to review the workings of a typical control system. As illustrated in Figure 9.1, this system has five main elements: establishing goals and standards, measuring performance, comparing performance against goals and standards, taking corrective action, and providing reinforcement.[3]

// ESTABLISHING GOALS AND STANDARDS

Most organizations operate with a hierarchy of goals. In the case of a business enterprise, the major goals at the top of the hierarchy are normally expressed in terms of profitability and profit growth (see Chapter 6). These goals are typically translated into subgoals that can be applied to individuals and units within the organization. A **subgoal** is an objective that helps the organization attain or exceed its major goals. As with major goals, subgoals should be precise and measurable, address important issues, be challenging but realistic, and specify a time period.

FIGURE 9.1

A Typical Control System

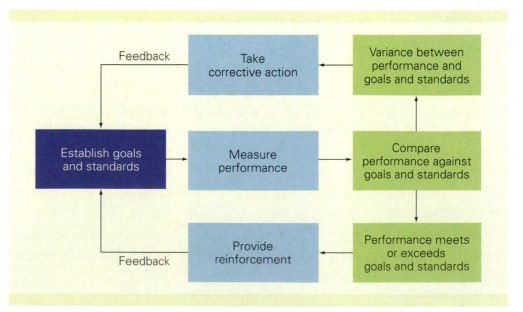

To illustrate what we mean by a goal hierarchy, suppose Nordstrom decides to achieve a 15 percent return on invested capital (ROIC) in the coming year. This is the company's major profitability goal. One way of doing this is to reduce the amount of capital needed to generate a dollar's worth of sales—perhaps by reducing the amount of capital tied up in inventory. How does the company do that? By turning over inventory more rapidly! Thus Nordstrom might operate with a subgoal of turning over inventory five times in the next year. If it reaches that subgoal, which is precise, measurable, and challenging and must be achieved within a prespecified period, the company's profitability, measured by ROIC, will increase.

Dell Computer is a good example of a company that adopts a hierarchical approach to goal setting and performance measurement. According to Michael Dell, in an effort to boost performance in the mid-1990s Dell introduced a companywide approach to educate everyone about the importance of boosting profitability as measured by return on invested capital. "We explained specifically how everyone could contribute (to higher ROIC) by reducing cycle times, eliminating scrap and waste, selling more, forecasting accurately, scaling operations effectively, increasing inventory turns, collecting accounts receivable efficiently, and doing things right the first time."[4] Dell went further: It made goals relating to these items the core of the company's control and incentive compensation systems.

Standards are similar to goals in that they too are objectives; but standards tend to be things the organization is expected to achieve as a part of its routine operations rather than a challenging goal it is striving to attain. For example, an organization might operate with a standard that vendors should be paid within 30 days of submitting an invoice, customer inquiries should be answered within 24 hours, all employees should have a formal performance review and be given written feedback once a year, safety checks should be performed on production equipment every six months, or employees should fly coach on business trips.

A key element in the control process is generating the right goals, subgoals, and standards. Managers need to choose goals and standards carefully in case they generate the wrong kind of behavior. There is an old saying: "You get what you measure." If you choose the wrong goals and standards, you will get the wrong behavior. A few years ago a placement agency decided to evaluate and reward its staff based on how many job seekers they sent to job interviews. This productivity measure seemed to produce the desired results—over the next few months more job seekers got interviews. However, after a while the numbers started to drop off alarmingly. When managers looked into the issue, they found that several prospective employers would no longer interview people referred to them by the placement agency. In an effort to hit their numbers, staff members had been sending people to interview for jobs for which they were not qualified. This had damaged the reputation of the placement agency among prospective employers and reduced business for the agency—the opposite of what managers had been trying to achieve. Managers subsequently changed the measure to reflect the number of job seekers who were actually hired.

A similar example occurred in the customer service call center of a large organization. In an attempt to raise the productivity of call center staff, managers instituted a standard that customer complaints should be resolved within 5 minutes. What happened (predictably perhaps) was that call center staff would cut off customers 4 minutes and 58 seconds into a call, whether the customer problem had been resolved or not! This behavior damaged the company's reputation for service quality.[5]

Another important consideration when choosing goals is to make sure the right goals are assigned to the right individuals and units. A classic mistake is to assign a goal to people who lack the responsibilities and resources required

Hammer It In! American automobile companies discovered that because assembly-line workers were not given goals relating to quality, they did not pay attention to quality when building a car. It took the rise of high-quality Japanese manufacturers to persuade American companies to give quality goals to workers on an assembly line.

© Getty Images

to attain it while not assigning the goal to those who do. In traditional automobile assembly operations, for example, quality goals were assigned to the quality assurance department, which checked finished automobiles for defects when they came off an assembly line. This might seem logical, but it didn't work well. The defects were normally built into cars upstream in the manufacturing process, and the quality assurance department could not improve the manufacturing process. Moreover, the people who made the mistakes (the assembly-line employees) were not given quality goals—rather they were assessed on volume output goals, such as the number of employee hours it took to build a car. Because they were not measured on quality, they had no incentive to pay attention to quality issues, and defect rates remained high. This problem was fixed only when automobile companies started to make assembly-line workers responsible for product quality.[6]

// MEASURING PERFORMANCE

Once goals, subgoals, and standards have been established, performance must be measured against the criteria specified. This is not as easy as it sounds. Information systems have to be put in place to collect the required data; and the data must be compiled into usable form and transmitted to the appropriate people in the organization. Reports summarizing actual performance might be tabulated daily, weekly, monthly, quarterly, or annually. Wal-Mart, for example, produces weekly reports summarizing the performance of every store across a range of key measures such as profits and inventory turnover. Moreover, some performance metrics, such as store sales, are reported daily. Achieving such comprehensive and timely reporting requires significant investments in information technology. Thus for Nordstrom to measure inventory turnover, bar codes have to be placed on all merchandise, which is scanned when it enters a store and scanned again when it is sold. The data are loaded onto a central computer that tracks inventory at all Nordstrom stores, and inventory data are communicated to managers and suppliers. To implement such a system, Nordstrom had to invest in computer technology and scanners.

With the massive advances in computing power that have occurred over the last three decades, managers have seemingly infinite quantitative information at their disposal. As advantageous as this is, there is danger in relying too much on quantitative data. Performance measurement has a soft element; the data might not tell the full story. It is in the interests of managers to leave their desks, visit the field, and try to see behind the numbers. For example, for years Wal-Mart's data showed that individual stores were hitting profit goals. In the early 2000s, however, a blizzard of lawsuits alleged that some store employees had been pressured to work overtime for no extra pay. Apparently some store managers were hitting their performance goals by resorting to behaviors that were not sanctioned by the company and in fact explicitly violated both the law and the values of the organization. Such behavior could not be detected simply by reviewing quantitative data.[7]

// COMPARING PERFORMANCE AGAINST GOALS AND STANDARDS

The next step in the control process is to compare actual performance against goals and standards. If performance is in line with goals or standards, that is good. However, managers need to make sure the reported performance is being achieved in a manner consistent with the values of the organization. If reported performance falls short of goals and standards, managers need to find the reason for the variance. This typically requires collecting more information, much of which might be qualitative data gleaned from face-to-face meetings and detailed probing. The same is true if reported performance exceeds goals or standards. Managers must find the reasons for such favorable variance, and doing so requires collecting more information.

For example, a hobby game company noted that sales of a new game were falling significantly behind sales goals in the United States while exceeding goals in Europe.[8] To examine these variances, managers met with distributors and retailers to see what was occurring. The U.S. distributor was in financial difficulty and had cut back on its sales force without informing the company: It was not promoting the game to retailers. In contrast, in Europe the major distributor had adopted an aggressive posture, setting up retail displays where potential customers could play the game before purchasing it. This strategy proved successful. Apparently the game was so unusual that customers were initially put off; but once they played it, many former skeptics became enthusiastic customers. Thus by collecting additional qualitative data, managers found the reason for the variances from goals.

// TAKING CORRECTIVE ACTION

Variances from goals and standards require that managers take corrective action. When actual performance easily exceeds a goal, corrective action might include raising the goal. When actual performance falls short of a goal, depending on what further investigation reveals, managers might change strategy, operations, or personnel. After Nordstrom failed to hit its profit goals for three years running, the board of directors fired the CEO and replaced him with a member of the founding family, Blake Nordstrom, who at the time was only 39 years old. Blake Nordstrom led the charge to improve the operating efficiency of the company. His first action was to visit the stores and talk to employees to discover what was going wrong. His actions included putting another family member, James Nordstrom, in charge of revamping Nordstrom's inventory management system (which he successfully executed).

■ Nordstrom: Taking corrective action.

Radical change is not always the appropriate response when an organization fails to reach a major goal. Investigation might reveal that the original goal was too aggressive, or that changes in market conditions outside the control of management accounted for the poor performance. In such cases the response to a shortfall might be to adjust the goal downward.

In the case of the hobby game company just discussed, after discovering the reason for the variance managers terminated the relationship with the U.S. distributor and hired a small sales force to visit retailers. In addition, the company adopted the strategy that had proved so successful in Europe—setting up displays in retail stores so potential customers could play the game. In Europe, managers raised the sales goals.

// PROVIDING REINFORCEMENT

If the goals and standards are met or exceeded, managers need to provide timely positive reinforcement to those responsible—congratulations for a job well done, awards, pay increases, bonuses, or enhanced career prospects. Providing positive reinforcement is just as important an aspect of a control system as taking corrective action. Behavioral scientists have long known that positive reinforcement increases the probability that those being acknowledged will continue to pursue such behavior in the

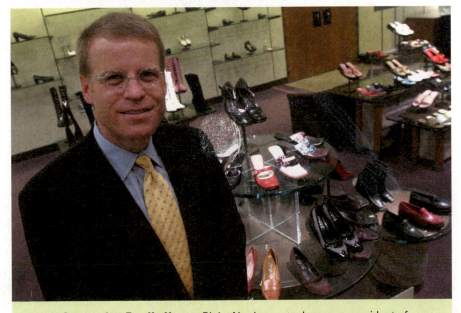

Fourth-Generation Family Hero   Blake Nordstrom took over as president of Nordstrom after the company failed to hit its performance goals for several years. A fourth-generation member of the founding family, he decided to revamp the company's inventory management system.

© Deseret Morning News

future.[9] Without positive reinforcement, people become discouraged, feel underappreciated, may not be willing to work as hard, and might look for other employment opportunities where they are better appreciated.

■ // Methods of Control

Now that we have a clear idea of how a control system works, we can look at the different ways in which managers can regulate the activities of individuals and units so that they are consistent with organization goals and standards. Here we review six main ways of achieving control: personal controls, bureaucratic controls, output controls, cultural controls, control through incentives, and market controls.[10]

// PERSONAL CONTROLS

personal control

Making sure through personal inspection and direct supervision that individuals and units behave in a way that is consistent with the goals of an organization.

As the name suggests, **personal control** is control by personal contact with and direct supervision of subordinates. Personal control consists of making sure through personal inspection and direct supervision that individuals and units behave in a way that is consistent with the goals of the organization. Personal control can be very subjective, with the manager assessing how well subordinates are performing by observing and interpreting their behavior. As a philosophy for control within an organization, personal control tends to be found primarily in small firms where the activities of a few people might be regulated through direct oversight. By its nature personal control tends to be associated with the centralization of power and authority in a key manager, who is often the owner of the small business. Personal control may work best when this key manager is a charismatic individual who can command the personal allegiance of subordinates.

Personal control has serious limitations. For one thing, excessive supervision can be demotivating. Employees may resent being closely supervised and may perform better with a greater degree of personal freedom. Moreover, the subjective nature of personal control can create a lack of objectivity and procedural justice in the performance review process. Subordinates may feel that favoritism, personal likes and dislikes, and individual idiosyncrasies are as important in performance reviews as actual performance. Personal control is also costly in that managers must devote considerable time and attention to direct supervision of subordinates, which takes their attention away from other important issues. The real problem with personal control, however, is that it starts to break down as an organization grows in size and complexity. As this occurs, the key manager has no choice but to decentralize decision making to others within the hierarchy if the enterprise is to continue growing. Doing so effectively requires the adoption of different control philosophies.

However, even in large organizations some limited personal control is still used, although typically as an adjunct to other control methods. For example, while relying on objective metrics to monitor performance, the CEO may also use personal control to shape the behavior of his or her immediate subordinates. In turn, these managers may use personal control in addition to other control methods to influence the behavior of their subordinates, and so on down through the organization. Jack Welch, the longtime CEO of General Electric, had regular one-on-one meetings with the heads of all of GE's major businesses.[11] He used these meetings to probe the managers about the strategy, structure, and financial performance of their operations and to communicate to his subordinates the importance of certain key values. In doing so he exercised some personal control over these managers and undoubtedly over the strategies they favored. At the same

Can I Take a Look at That?   Close supervision is required for personal control.

© Ryan McVay/Getty Images

time, managers like Welch also give their subordinates considerable autonomy, reviewing their performance by looking at objective measures such as the performance of the units under their control.

// BUREAUCRATIC CONTROLS

The great German sociologist Max Weber was the first to describe the nature of bureaucratic controls.[12] Writing in the early 20th century, Weber described how bureaucratic organizations emerged as a rational and efficient response to the problems of organizing large-scale economic and social activity. According to Weber, bureaucracies are goal-oriented organizations characterized by hierarchical management systems and extensive division of labor into specialized tasks. Weber saw control within a bureaucracy as being achieved by impersonal written rules and standardized procedures. Advancement within such organizations, according to Weber, was based on the ability of an individual to perform well against predetermined standards.

Following Weber, **bureaucratic control** is typically defined as control through a formal system of written rules and procedures.[13] Bureaucratic control methods rely primarily on prescribing what individuals and units can and cannot do—that is, on establishing bureaucratic standards. At the University of Washington, for example, a bureaucratic standard specifies that faculty members can perform no more than one day a week of outside work. Other standards articulate the steps to be taken when hiring and promoting faculty, purchasing computer equipment for faculty, and so on.

> **bureaucratic control**
> Control through a formal system of written rules and procedures.

Almost all large organizations use some bureaucratic controls. Familiar examples are budgetary controls and controls over capital spending. Budgets are essentially a set of rules for allocating an organization's financial resources. A subunit's budget specifies with some precision how much the unit may spend and how that spending should be allocated across different areas. Senior managers in an organization use budgets to control the behavior of subunits. For example, an R&D budget might specify how much an R&D unit can spend on product development in the coming year. R&D managers know that if they spend too much on one project, they will have less to spend on others; so they modify their behavior to stay within the budget. Most budgets are set by negotiation between headquarters and subunit managers. Headquarters managers can encourage the growth of certain subunits and restrict the growth of others by manipulating their budgets.

Similarly, capital spending rules might require senior managers to approve any capital expenditure by a subunit that exceeds a certain amount. (A budget lets headquarters specify the total amount a subunit can spend in a given year, whereas capital spending rules give headquarters additional control over how that money is spent.) Headquarters can be expected to deny approval for capital spending requests that are at variance with the overall goals of the enterprise and to approve those that are congruent with enterprise objectives.

As you should realize by now, although the term *bureaucratic* often has negative connotations, in fact bureaucratic control methods can be useful in organizations. They allow managers to decentralize decision making within the constraints specified by formal rules and procedures. However, too great a reliance on bureaucratic rules can lead to problems. Excessively formal rules and procedures can be stifling, limiting the ability of individuals and units to respond in a flexible way to specific circumstances. This can sour performance and sap the motivation of those who value individual freedom and initiative. As such, extensive bureaucratic control methods are not well suited to organizations facing dynamic, rapidly changing environments or to organizations that employ skilled individuals who value autonomy. The costs of monitoring the performance of individuals and units to make sure they comply with bureaucratic rules can also be significant and may outweigh the benefits of establishing extensive rules and standards.

Bureaucratic standards can also lead to unintended consequences if people try to find ways around rules that they think are unreasonable. An interesting and controversial case is forced school busing in the United States. In the 1970s school districts around America started to bus children to schools outside their immediate neighborhoods to achieve a better racial mix. This well-intentioned bureaucratic rule was designed to speed racial integration in a society characterized by significant racial discrimination. Unfortunately the rule had unintended

Social Engineering   Forced school busing was a well-intentioned effort to speed up racial integration in the United States. Unfortunately, like many bureaucratic rules, it had unintended consequences—in this case "white flight" to the suburbs.

© Comstock/Picture Quest

consequences. Parents of all races objected to their children being bused to distant schools. In many large cities where forced busing was practiced, white families with children responded by fleeing to suburbs where there were few minorities and busing was not practiced, or by sending their children to expensive private schools within the city. As a result, rather than advancing racial integration, busing had the opposite effect. For example, in Seattle the percentage of white students in city schools dropped from 60 percent to 41 percent over the 20 years of forced busing.[14] In the 1990s most school districts ended forced busing.

// OUTPUT CONTROLS

Output controls can be used when managers can identify tasks that are complete in themselves in the sense of having a measurable output or criterion of overall achievement that is visible.[15] For example, the overall achievement of an automobile factory might be measured by the number of employee hours required to build a car (a measure of productivity) and the number of defects found per 100 cars produced by the factory (a measure of quality). Similarly, Nordstrom measures the overall achievement of the unit responsible for inventory management by the number of inventory turns per year, and FedEx measures the performance of each of its local stations in its express delivery network by the percentage of packages delivered before 10:30 a.m. In a multibusiness company such as GE or 3M, senior management might measure the output of a product division in terms of that division's profitability and profit growth.

When complete tasks can be identified, **output controls** are goals set for units or individuals to achieve; performance is monitored against those goals. Unit managers' performance is then judged by their ability to achieve the goals.[16] If goals are met or exceeded, unit managers will be rewarded (an act of reinforcement). If goals are not met, senior managers will normally intervene to find out why and take appropriate corrective action. Thus, as in a classic control system, control is achieved by comparing actual performance against targets, providing reinforcement, and intervening selectively to take corrective action.

■ FedEx: Use of output controls.

output controls

Setting goals for units or individuals to achieve and monitoring performance against those goals.

The goals assigned to units depend on their role in the firm. Self-contained product divisions are typically given goals for profitability and profit growth. Functions are more likely to be given goals related to their particular activity. Thus R&D will be given product development goals, production will be given productivity and quality goals, marketing will be given market share goals, and so on.

As with budgets, output goals are normally established through negotiation between units and senior managers at headquarters. Generally headquarters tries to set goals that are challenging but realistic so unit managers are forced to look for ways to improve their operations—but not so pressured that they will resort to dysfunctional behavior. Output controls foster a system of "management by exception" in that so long as units meet their goals, unit managers are granted considerable autonomy. If a unit fails to attain its goals, however, headquarters managers are likely to ask questions. If they don't get satisfactory answers, they are likely to intervene in a unit, perhaps by replacing managers and looking for ways to improve efficiency.

The great virtue of output controls is that they facilitate decentralization and give individual managers within units much greater autonomy than either personal controls or bureaucratic controls. This autonomy lets managers within a unit configure their work environment to match the particular contingencies they face, rather than having a work environment imposed from above. Thus output controls are useful when units have to respond rapidly to changes in the markets they serve. Output controls also involve less extensive monitoring than either bureaucratic or personal controls. Senior managers can achieve control by comparing actual performance against targets and intervening selectively. As such, output controls reduce the workload on senior executives and allow them to manage a larger and more diverse organization with relative ease. Thus many large multiproduct and multinational enterprises rely heavily on output controls in their various product divisions and foreign subsidiaries.

Like personal and bureaucratic controls, output controls have limitations. First, as noted earlier when we discussed control systems, senior managers need to look behind the numbers to make sure unit managers are achieving goals in a way that is consistent with the values of the organization. Second, as also noted earlier, managers need to choose the right output criteria to measure lest they encourage dysfunctional behavior.

Third, output controls do not always work well if there are extensive interdependencies between units.[17] The performance of a unit may be ambiguous if it is based on cooperation with other units. To illustrate this problem, consider the case of a diversified enterprise—PDN Inc.—that has three product divisions making three different products: paper towels, disposable diapers, and napkins (see Figure 9.2a). Initially the head office places each product into a self-contained product division, each with its own functions, and assigns each division a profitability target. At this point the output controls work well. However, all three divisions sell to the same customers, supermarkets. Imagine that these customers don't want to deal with three different sales forces from the same company, so they pressure PDN Inc. to consolidate its sales force. PDN responds by creating a fourth division that is responsible for marketing and selling the three products to supermarkets (Figure 9.2b). The three product divisions are still assigned profitability goals, whereas the marketing and sales division is evaluated on the basis of sales growth.

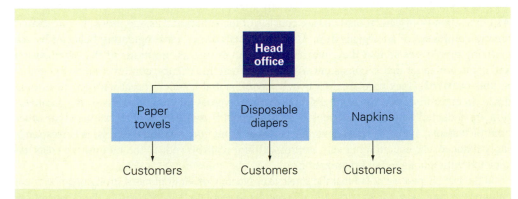

FIGURE 9.2A

PDN Inc. before Reorganization

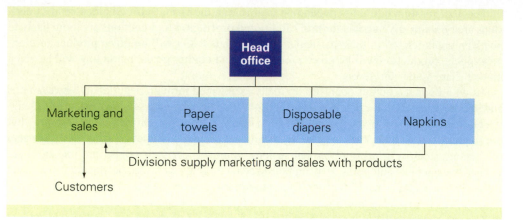

Divisions supply marketing and sales with products

Customers

All this seems reasonable; but now consider what occurs if the disposable diaper business fails to reach its profitability target for the year, and the marketing division misses its sales target for diapers. Top management asks the head of the diaper division to explain why this has occurred. He replies, "It's not my fault; my division executed well, but the guys in the marketing division screwed up. I gave them a great product, and they didn't sell it well." Next the top managers ask the head of the marketing division what the problem was. She says, "My people did everything expected of them and more, but we were dealt a poor hand. The diaper division produced a poor-quality product that cost too much, and try as we might we could not sell enough to hit our sales goal."

The interdependence between the diaper division and the marketing division has created performance ambiguity. **Performance ambiguity** occurs when it is difficult to identify the cause of poor (or strong) performance—that is, when the link between cause and effect is ambiguous. Performance ambiguity means senior managers cannot effectively control the division simply by relying on obvious output controls. They have to discover the true causes of poor or strong performance. In this case, because the statements from the two divisional executives contradict each other, top managers have no choice but to audit the operations of both divisions, collecting more information, to determine the true cause of the poor performance. This of course can be done, but doing so increases the costs of controlling the organization. Thus, in general, interdependence between units within an organization can create performance ambiguities that make output controls more difficult to interpret. Resolving these ambiguities requires managers to collect more information, which places more demands on top management and raises the monitoring costs associated with output controls. It also increases the possibility that managers will become overloaded with information, run into the constraints implied by bounded rationality, and fall back on simple heuristics when making decisions, which can lead to cognitive biases (see Chapter 5).

// CULTURAL CONTROL

As noted already, organizational culture consists of the values and assumptions that are shared among employees of an organization. **Cultural control** involves regulating behavior by socializing employees so that they internalize the values and assumptions of the organization and act in a manner that is consistent with them. When this occurs, employees tend to engage in **self-control**—they regulate their own behavior so that it is congruent with organizational goals. In enterprises with a strong culture where the values and assumptions of the organization are accepted by most employees and self-control is widely practiced, the need for other control systems, and particularly extensive personal and bureaucratic controls, is correspondingly reduced. By encouraging self-control, cultural controls reduce the monitoring costs associated with managing an organization.

In the last chapter we noted that the steelmaker Nucor Corporation has a strong organizational culture. We could say Nucor uses cultural controls to regulate behavior within the organization.

---

performance ambiguity

A situation that occurs when the link between cause and effect is ambiguous.

cultural control

Regulating behavior by socializing employees so that they internalize the values and assumptions of an organization and act in a manner that is consistent with them.

self-control

Occurs when employees regulate their own behavior so that it is congruent with organizational goals.

Nucor is not alone. Microsoft, for example, has a very strong culture that was set by the company's founder, Bill Gates. Gates always placed a high value on technical brilliance, competitiveness, and a willingness to work long hours, something that he himself did (as did Steve Ballmer, the current CEO). Gates and Ballmer hired people who shared these characteristics and then led by example. As a result, today Microsoft remains a company where technical brilliance and competitiveness are highly valued and where people work long hours—not because any bureaucratic rules tell them to do so, and not because supervisors explicitly require them to do so, but because new employees are socialized into these norms by their coworkers, who themselves were thus socialized in the past. At Microsoft cultural control has reduced the need for bureaucratic and personal controls. The company can trust people to work hard and to behave in a very competitive manner because this is such a pervasive aspect of the culture.

Grrrrrr...Let Me at Them!
Microsoft CEO Steve Ballmer embodies the hard-driving, competitive culture of the company. Because employees are so well socialized into this culture, the company does not have to use other controls to encourage competitive behavior.
© Reuters/Corbis

Although cultural control can mitigate the need for other controls, thereby reducing monitoring costs, it is not universally beneficial. Cultural control can have dysfunctional aspects too. The hard-driving, competitive aspect of Microsoft's culture was arguably a contributing factor in the antitrust violations of which the company was accused in the 1990s (the U.S. Justice Department, which brought the antitrust case against Microsoft in the United States, used as evidence internal e-mail messages at Microsoft in which one senior manager stated that Microsoft would "cut off a competitor's air supply"). Moreover, Microsoft's culture of working long hours clearly has a downside: Many good employees have burned out and left the company. The company is aware of this; and as its workforce has aged and started families, it has tried to become more accommodating, stressing that output is more important than hours worked. However, culture is difficult to change, and therein lies the problem: If cultural controls need to be changed, it may not be easy to do so.

■ Culture at Microsoft.

// CONTROL THROUGH INCENTIVES

Incentives are devices used to encourage and reward appropriate employee behavior. Many employees receive incentives in the form of annual bonus pay. Incentives are usually closely tied to the performance metrics used for output controls. For example, targets linked to profitability might be set to measure the performance of a subunit, such as a product division. To create positive incentives for employees to work hard to exceed those targets, they may be given a share of any profits above those targeted. If a subunit has set a goal of a 15 percent return on invested capital and it actually achieves a 20 percent return, unit employees may be given a share in the profits generated in excess of the 15 percent target in the form of bonus pay.

incentives
Devices used to encourage and reward appropriate employee behavior.

The idea is that giving employees incentives to work productively cuts the need for other control mechanisms. Control through incentives is designed to facilitate *self-control*—employees regulate their own behavior in a manner consistent with organizational goals to maximize their chance of earning incentive-based pay. Although paying out bonuses and the like costs the organization money, well-designed incentives typically pay for themselves. That is, the increase in performance due to incentives more than offsets the incentives' costs.

The type of incentive used may vary depending on the employees and their tasks. Incentives for employees working on the factory floor will probably differ from the ones for senior managers. The incentives used must match the type of work performed. The employees on the factory floor of a manufacturing plant may be broken into teams of 20 to 30

Parenting Incentives.   This onsite day care facility for employees provides positive incentives for parents to continue working full time after they have had a child. Abbott Labs, IKEA, and Microsoft are just some of the companies that offer onsite day care facilities to their employees.

© AP Photo/Ann Heisenfelt

individuals, and they may have their bonus pay tied to the ability of their team to reach or exceed targets for output and product quality. In contrast, the senior managers of the plant may be rewarded according to metrics linked to the output of the entire operation. The basic principle is to make sure the incentive scheme for an individual employee is linked to an output target over which he or she has some control. Individual employees on the factory floor may not be able to influence the performance of the entire operation, but they can influence the performance of their team, so incentive pay is tied to output at this level.

When incentives are tied to team performance they have the added benefit of encouraging cooperation between team members and fostering a degree of peer control. **Peer control** occurs when employees pressure others within their team or work group to perform up to or in excess of the expectations of the organization.[18] Thus if the incentive pay of a 20-person team is linked to team output, team members can be expected to pressure those in the team who are perceived as slacking off, urging them to pick up the pace and make an equal contribution to team effort. Strong peer control reduces the need for direct supervision of a team and can facilitate attempts to move toward a flatter management hierarchy.

peer control

Occurs when employees pressure others within their team or work group to perform up to or in excess of the expectations of the organization.

■ Blockbuster: Excess compensation?

In sum, incentives can reinforce output controls, induce employees to practice self-control, increase peer control, and lower the need for other control mechanisms. Like all other control methods discussed here, control through incentives has limitations. Because incentives are typically linked to the metrics used in output controls, the points made about output controls also apply here. Specifically, managers need to make sure incentives are not tied to output metrics that result in unintended consequences or dysfunctional behavior. Moreover, incentive systems have been abused in some firms, with senior managers being awarded incentive contracts that set the performance bar so low that they earn significant bonus pay, irrespective of whether there is a substantial improvement in the performance of the organization. In 2004, for example, the CEO of Blockbuster Inc. earned $56.8 million in pay and bonuses (an increase of 541 percent over 2003) in a year when the operating income of Blockbuster fell 50 percent and its share price declined by 47 percent! In part this was achieved because the board of directors replaced 4.3 million of his stock options—which were worthless because the exercise price for them was significantly above the current stock price—with an outright grant of 1.6 million shares of stock as a "retention measure." Incentives like these seem to reward senior managers for mediocre performance or worse, and as such they are not worthy of being called incentives. As an aside, it is worth noting that due to massive boosts in incentive pay, in 2004 the average CEO of an American public company earned 400 times what the average hourly worker took home, up from 42 times since 1980. Looking at these figures, many commentators have argued that senior managers have benefited from an abuse of incentive pay and are reaping huge gains at the expense of other employees and shareholders.[19]

// MARKET CONTROLS

market controls

Regulating the behavior of individuals and units within an enterprise by setting up an internal market for some valuable resource such as capital.

Market controls involve regulating the behavior of individuals and units within an enterprise by setting up an *internal market* for some valuable resource such as capital.[20] Market controls are usually found within diversified enterprises organized into product divisions, where the head office might act as an internal investment bank, allocating capital funds between the competing claims of the different product divisions based on an assessment of their likely future performance. Within this internal market, all cash generated by the divisions is viewed as belonging to the head office. The divisions then have to compete for access to the capital resources controlled by the head office. Because they need that capital to grow their divisions, the assumption is that this internal competition will drive divisional managers to look for ways to improve the efficiency of their units. One of the first companies in the world to establish an internal capital market was the Japanese electronics manufacturer Matsushita (best known for its Panasonic brand name), which introduced such systems in the 1930s.[21]

In addition, in some enterprises divisions compete for the right to develop and sell new products. Again, Matsushita has a long history of letting different divisions develop similar new products, then assigning overall responsibility for producing and selling the product to the division that seems to be furthest along in the commercialization process. Although some people might view such duplication of product development effort as wasteful, Matsushita's legendary founder, Konosuke Matsushita, believed that the creation of an internal market for the right to commercialize technology drove divisional managers to maximize the efficiency of product development efforts within their unit. Similarly, within Samsung, the Korean electronics company, senior managers often set up two teams within different units to develop new products such as memory chips. The purpose of the internal competition between the teams is to accelerate the product development process, with the winning team earning significant accolades and bonuses.[22]

Industrial Samurai Konosuke Matsushita, the legendary founder of Japan's Matsushita, which is best known for its Panasonic brand name, believed that fostering internal competition between divisions for the right to develop new products and for access to capital created incentives for divisional managers to run their units efficiently.

Courtesy of Panasonic

The main problem with market controls is that fostering internal competition between divisions for capital and the right to develop new products can make it difficult to establish cooperation between divisions for mutual gain.[23] If two different divisions are racing against each other to develop similar new products and are competing against each other for limited capital resources, they may be unwilling to share technological know-how with each other, perhaps to the detriment of the entire corporation. Companies like Samsung deal with this problem by using integrating mechanisms, such as the liaison role, and assigning the responsibility for leveraging technological know-how across divisions to key individuals.

■ Controls at Matsushita.

// SUMMARY

To recap, managers can use six different control methods to regulate the behavior of individuals and units within their organization: personal controls, bureaucratic controls, output controls, cultural controls, incentive controls, and market controls. In practice, few managers rely on just one control method. Most organizations mix methods to achieve control. Some personal controls might be used to manage relationships with direct reports; bureaucratic controls are frequently used to set standards for budgets and capital spending; output controls are used for relatively self-contained units that produce a measurable output; and incentives may also be tied to the metrics used for output controls. Both cultural and incentive controls can induce employees to regulate their own behavior in a manner that is consistent with the goals of the organization, and market controls might help allocate capital resources between competing divisions within diversified enterprises. Each control method has advantages and disadvantages. As we will see in the next section, the choice between different methods has to be made in light of prevailing circumstances.

■ // Matching Controls to Strategy and Structure

Although organizations typically use most of the control methods discussed here, the precise mix of controls tends to vary with the size, strategy, and organization structure of the enterprise. As organizations grow they tend to rely less on personal controls and more on other methods. Beyond this generalization, we need to consider how controls vary with the strategy and structure of an enterprise. Here we look at different controls first in single-business enterprises and then in multibusiness enterprises.

// CONTROLS IN THE SINGLE BUSINESS

In the last chapter we noted that the organization structure of a single business depends on the strategy it is pursuing and the environment in which it is based. Specifically, firms in stable environments with little product innovation tend to operate with functional structures and use simple integrating mechanisms, such as direct contact and liaison roles, to achieve coordination between functions. In contrast, firms in dynamic and uncertain environments, such as those characterized by rapid technological change, tend to operate with functional structures and achieve tight coordination with more complex integrating mechanisms such as temporary or permanent cross-functional teams or matrix structures. How might the controls that managers use vary across such enterprises?

Functional Structure with Low Integration Consider first a firm with a functional structure and no integrating mechanisms between functions beyond direct contact and simple liaison roles. The environment facing the firm is stable, so the need for integration is minimal. Within such a firm, bureaucratic controls in the form of budgets are used to allocate financial resources to each function and to control spending. Output controls assess how well each function is performing. Different functions are assigned different output targets, depending on their specific tasks. The procurement function might be assigned an output target based on procurement costs as a percentage of sales; the manufacturing function might be given productivity and product quality targets such as output per employee and defects per thousand products; the logistics function might have an inventory turnover target; the marketing and sales function might be given sales growth and market share goals; and the success of the service function might be measured by the time it takes to resolve a customer problem. To the extent that each function hits these targets, the overall performance of the firm will improve and its profitability will increase.

Output controls might also be pushed further down within functions. Thus the manufacturing process might be subdivided into discrete tasks, each of which has a measurable output. Employee teams might be formed and empowered to take ownership of each discrete task. Each team will be assigned an output target. To the extent that functions can be divided into teams and output controls applied to those teams, this will facilitate decentralization within the organization, wider spans of control (because it is relatively easy to control a team by monitoring its outputs), and a flatter organization structure.

Within such a structure, the CEO will control the heads of the functions. They in turn will exercise control over units or teams within their functions. There may also be some degree of personal control within the structure, with the CEO using personal supervision to influence the behavior of functional heads, who in turn will do the same for their direct reports. Incentives will be tied to output targets. Thus the incentive pay of the head of manufacturing might be linked to the attainment of predetermined productivity and quality targets for the manufacturing function; the incentive pay of the head of logistics might be linked to increases in inventory turnover; and so on. Incentives might also be pushed further down within the organization, with members of teams within functions being rewarded on the basis of the ability of their teams to reach or exceed targets. A portion of the incentive pay for managers (and perhaps all employees) might also be tied to the overall performance of the enterprise to encourage cooperation and knowledge sharing within the organization.

Finally, such an enterprise can have strong cultural controls, which may reduce the need for personal controls and bureaucratic rules. Individuals might be trusted to behave in the desired manner because they accept the prevailing culture. Thus cultural controls might allow the firm to operate with a flatter organization structure and wider spans of control and generally increase the effectiveness of output controls and incentives.

Functional Structure with High Integration A functional structure with high integration presents managers with a more complex control problem. The problem is particularly severe if the firm adopts a matrix structure. As noted in the last chapter, such a structure might be adopted by a firm based in a dynamic environment where competition centers on product development. Within such an enterprise bureaucratic controls will again be used for financial budgets, and output controls will be applied both to the different functions and to cross-functional product development teams. Thus a team might be assigned output targets covering development time, production costs of the new product, and the features the product should incorporate. For functional managers, incentive controls might be linked to output targets for their functions, whereas for the members of a product development team, incentives will be tied to team performance.

Extreme Incentives   Yahoo! CEO Terry Semel agreed to cut his salary to just $1 a year, and take all of his compensation tied to the performance of Yahoo's stock price.

© Rick Wilking/Reuters/Corbis

The problem with such an arrangement is that the performance of the product development team depends on support from the various functions, including people and information from manufacturing, marketing, and R&D. Consequently, significant performance ambiguity might complicate the process of using output controls to assess the performance of a product development team. The failure of a product development team to achieve output targets might be due to the poor performance of team members, but it could just as well be due to the failure of functional personnel to support the team. Identifying the cause of performance variations requires senior managers to collect more information (much of it subjective), which increases the time and energy they must devote to the control process, diverts their attention from other issues, and increases the costs of monitoring and controlling the organization. Other things being equal, this reduces the span of control senior managers can handle, suggesting the need for a taller hierarchy—which as we saw in the last chapter creates additional problems.

Performance ambiguity raises the question of whether there is a better solution to the control problem. One step is to make sure the incentives of all key personnel are aligned. The classic way of doing this is to tie incentives to a higher level of organization performance. Thus, in addition to being rewarded for the performance of their functions, functional heads might also be rewarded for the overall performance of the firm. Insofar as the success of product development teams increases firm performance, this gives functional heads an incentive to make sure the product development teams receive adequate support. In addition, strong cultural controls can help establish companywide norms and values emphasizing the importance of cooperation between functions and teams for their mutual benefit.

// CONTROLS IN DIVERSIFIED FIRMS

In the last chapter we discussed how diversified enterprises are organized into a structure based on product divisions. In a classic multidivisional structure, each business is placed into its own division with its own functions as a self-contained entity. The role of the head office is to control divisions, determine the overall strategic direction of the enterprise, and allocate capital resources between the different divisions to maximize the economic performance of the enterprise.

In Chapter 6 we saw three ways in which diversified firms might try to improve the performance of their constituent units: leveraging core competencies across divisions, sharing resources across divisions to realize economies of scope, and superior internal governance.

Controls in the Diversified Firm with Low Integration In firms that focus primarily on boosting performance through superior internal governance, the need for integration between divisions is low. These firms are not trying to share resources or leverage core competencies across divisions, so there is no need for complex integrating mechanisms, such as cross-divisional teams, to coordinate the activities of different divisions. In these enterprises the head office typically controls the divisions in four main ways.[24]

First, bureaucratic controls regulate the financial budgets and capital spending of the divisions. Typically each division must have its financial budgets approved for the coming year by the head office. In addition, any capital expenditures in excess of a certain amount have to be approved by the head office. Thus, for example, any item of spending by a division in excess of $50,000 might have to be approved by the head office.

Second, the head office will use output controls, assigning each division output targets that are normally based on measurable financial criteria such as the profitability, profit growth, and cash flow of each division. Typically targets for the coming year are set by negotiation between divisional heads and senior managers at the head office. So long as the divisions hit their targets, they are left alone to run their operations. If performance falls short of targets, however, top managers will normally audit the affairs of a division to discover why this occurred, taking corrective action if necessary by changing strategy or personnel.

Third, incentive controls will be used, with the incentives for divisional managers tied to the financial performance of their divisions. Thus to earn pay bonuses, divisional managers will have to achieve or exceed the performance targets previously negotiated between the head office and the divisions. To make sure divisional managers do not try to "talk down" their performance targets for the year, making it easy for them to earn bonuses, the head office will normally benchmark a product division against its competitors, take a close look at industry conditions, and use this information to establish performance targets that are challenging but attainable.

Fourth, the head office will use market controls to allocate capital resources between different divisions.[25] As noted earlier, in multidivisional enterprises the cash generated by product divisions is normally viewed as belonging to the head office, which functions as an internal investment bank, reallocating cash flows between the competing claims of different divisions based on an assessment of likely future performance. The competition between divisions for access to capital creates further incentives for divisional managers to run their operations efficiently and effectively. In addition, as at Matsushita, the head office might use market controls to allocate rights to develop and commercialize new products between divisions.

Within divisions, the control systems used will be those found within single-business enterprises. Head office managers might also use personal controls to influence the behavior of divisional heads. In particular, the CEO might exercise control over divisional heads by meeting with them and probing for richer feedback about operations.

Controls in the Diversified Firm with High Integration The control problem is more complex in diversified firms that are trying not only to improve performance through superior internal governance but also to leverage core competencies across product divisions and realize economies of scope. 3M is an example of such an enterprise. 3M is a diversified enterprise with multiple product divisions. The company devotes a lot of effort to leveraging core technology across divisions (and as we saw in Chapter 8, one way in which the company does this is by establishing internal knowledge networks). In addition, the company tries to realize economies of scope, particularly in the areas of marketing, sales, and distribution with a marketing and sales group that sells the products of several 3M divisions. In this sense 3M has an organization structure that is similar in some respects to PDN Inc. (see Figure 9.2b). More generally, when a multidivisional enterprise tries to improve performance through economies of scope and via the leveraging of core competencies across divisions, the need for integration between divisions is high.

■ Controls at 3M.

In such organizations top managers use the standard repertoire of control mechanisms discussed in the last section. However, they also have to address two control problems that are not found in multidivisional firms with no cooperation and integration between divisions. First, they have to find a control mechanism that induces divisions to cooperate with each other for mutual gain. Second, they need to handle the performance ambiguities that arise when divisions are tightly coupled, sharing resources and performance results.

The solution to both problems is in essence the same as that for single-business firms with high integration between functions. Specifically, the firm needs to adopt incentive controls for divisional managers that are linked to higher-level performance—in this case the performance of the entire enterprise. Improving the performance of the entire firm requires cooperation between divisions; such incentive controls should facilitate that cooperation. In addition, strong cultural controls can create values and norms that emphasize the importance of cooperation between divisions for mutual gain. At 3M, for example, there is a long-established cultural norm that while products belong to the divisions, the technology underlying those products belongs to the entire company. Thus the surgical tape business might use adhesive technology developed by the office supplies business.

Despite such solutions to control problems, top managers in firms with tightly integrated divisions have to cope with greater performance ambiguities than top managers in less complex multidivisional organizations. Integration between various product divisions means that it is hard for top managers to judge the performance of each division merely by monitoring objective output criteria. To get a true picture of performance and achieve adequate controls, they probably have to spend more time auditing the operating divisions and talking to divisional managers to get a more qualitative picture of performance. Other things being equal, this might limit the span of control they can effectively handle—and thus the scope of the enterprise.[26]

■ // Choosing Control Metrics: The Balanced Scorecard

An important issue confronting managers, particularly with regard to output and incentive controls, is deciding what metrics to use for a firm's control systems. Historically many firms have relied on financial metrics, such as profitability, profit growth, and cash flow. Such metrics are important and should always be used in a business enterprise; but several commentators have argued that overreliance on a narrow set of financial metrics to control an organization can have negative consequences.[27] Most notably, in an attempt to improve current financial performance managers might pursue actions that boost short-term profitability at the expense of long-term competitiveness and profits. The problem with such an approach, for example, is that a lack of investment in equipment and products can significantly hurt the firm down the road.

One approach to this problem is to use what is known as **the balanced scorecard**. Robert Kaplan and David Norton, who developed the balanced scorecard, suggest that managers use a number of different financial and operational metrics to track performance and control an organization.[28] In addition to traditional financial measures, which they refer to as the *financial perspective,* they suggest that managers use metrics related to how customers see the organization (the *customer perspective*), what the organization must excel at (the *operational*

the balanced scorecard

A control approach that suggests managers use several different financial and operational metrics to track performance and control an organization.

perspective), and the ability of the organization to learn and improve its offerings and processes over time (the *innovation perspective*).

The precise metric used to capture each of these perspectives will vary from business to business depending on the strategy of the enterprise, the nature of its production process, and the industry in which it is based. Obviously a retailer like Wal-Mart or Costco would use different operational measures from a software company like Microsoft or a manufacturing company such as General Motors. Examples of the kinds of metrics managers might use are given in Figure 9.3, which summarizes some of the measures for a balanced scorecard used by a high-tech medical equipment company that the author consulted for. This company wished to differentiate itself from competitors by being able to fill customer orders quickly (many of its competitors operated with long backlogs) and offering industry-leading after-sale service and support. Thus for the customer perspective, it chose to measure the time from order to delivery and the time taken to solve customer service problems. From the operational perspective the strategic objective was to be an efficient, high-quality manufacturer of medical equipment; thus managers selected a series of operational metrics including unit costs, inventory turnover, and defect rates in manufacturing to track operating efficiency. For the innovation perspective, the company was based in an industry where technology was advancing rapidly and timely new product development was crucial for long-term success. Managers tracked success along this dimension by the percentage of sales generated from

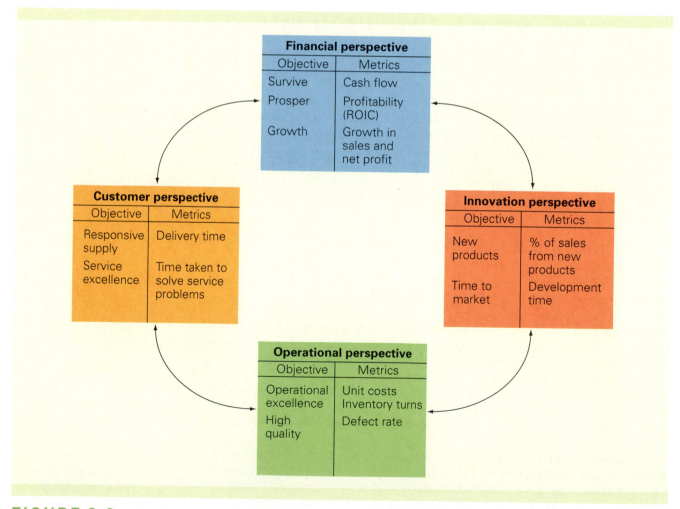

FIGURE 9.3   The Balanced Scorecard

new products introduced in the last three years and by the time it took to develop a new product. With regard to the *financial perspective,* the company wished to survive, prosper, and grow, so it chose a fairly standard set of financial metrics, including cash flow measures, a profitability measure (return on invested capital or ROIC), and growth measures.

Kaplan and Norton's contention is that the balanced scorecard is akin to the dials and indicators in an airplane cockpit. It gives managers a fast but comprehensive view of the business that balances financial measures with operational, customer-centered, and innovation measures; and it gives a better view of the overall health of the business than relying on just financial measures. Implementing the balanced scorecard approach requires managers to identify which individuals and units within the organization should be responsible for achieving which metrics, linking output controls and incentives to those metrics. Thus manufacturing managers might be given the responsibility for achieving the unit cost, inventory turn, and defect rate goals detailed in Figure 9.3. They might also be given responsibility for goals related to delivery time because that is largely within the control of manufacturing. Customer service managers might be responsible for goals related to the time taken to solve customer service problems; reducing product development time might be a responsibility shared by marketing, manufacturing, and R&D managers because all three functions must work together closely to develop products quickly.

■ Backchannel control at Starbucks.

■ Backchannel control at Southwest.

■ // Backchannel Control Methods

backchannel
An informal channel through which managers can collect important information.

The control methods discussed so far in this chapter all rely for their execution on formal reporting channels within an organization. In addition to these formal systems, managers often use backchannel methods to collect additional qualitative information that gives them another view of how the organization is performing, adds richness to the data collected through formal channels, and enables them to achieve greater control. A **backchannel** is an informal channel via which managers can collect important information. To establish a backchannel, managers have to develop a network of contacts within the organization that gives an honest picture of how the organization is performing.

At Starbucks, for example, the first thing CEO Jim Donald does every morning is call 5 to10 stores to talk to the managers and other employees there and get a sense of how their stores are performing. Donald also stops at a local Starbucks every morning on the way to work to buy his morning coffee. This has allowed him to get to know individual employees there well. Donald finds these informal contacts a useful source of information about how the company is performing.[29]

Managers often buy products from their own organization, interacting with it as customers, to see how well it is treating this crucial constituency. Some senior managers work alongside lower-level employees—partly to build a network of contacts and partly to understand how the organization is performing at that level. Herb Kelleher, the charismatic founder and former CEO of Southwest Airlines, would often help airline attendants on Southwest flights, distributing refreshments and talking to customers. One frequent flyer on Southwest Airlines reported sitting next to Kelleher three times in 10 years. Each time Kelleher asked him and others nearby how Southwest Airlines was doing in a number of areas, looking for trends and spotting inconsistencies.[30]

Herb Kelleher, the founder and Executive Chairman of Southwest Airlines, pictured here on a Harley-Davidson motorcycle given to him by his pilots, is enjoying the company's chili cook-off. Organizational events such as these help build the organization's culture.

Courtesy Southwest Airlines

IN CONCLUSION   WHY DOES IT MATTER?

It is difficult to overemphasize the importance of the material covered in this chapter for managers. Control is a fundamental task of management. Without adequate control systems in place, an organization can drift from its goals and will not attain a satisfactory level of performance. Without adequate control systems in place, managers will not know how well the organization is actually operating, what is working and what is broken, or whether employees are complying with critical standards.

It is not enough, however, just to put any old control systems in place: Managers must put the *right* systems in place. As we have seen in this chapter, the wrong systems can have unintended consequences. They can produce dysfunctional behavior, stifle employee initiative with too much bureaucracy, and inhibit needed cooperation. Managers can choose a number of different metrics and control methods; the best choice depends on the strategy of the firm and its organization structure. Strategy, structure, and controls must be matched. A business operating in a stable environment may require very different control systems from a dynamic enterprise based in a rapidly changing environment. Deciding which methods are best, and what criteria to use to judge the performance of the organization, is one of the most challenging tasks of management—and one of the most critical.

MANAGEMENT CHALLENGES

1. "As the name suggests, bureaucratic control systems are demotivating and should be avoided at all costs." Do you agree with this statement?

2. Why might cooperation between two units in an organization to achieve a common goal lead to performance ambiguities? What can managers do to overcome these ambiguities?

3. What are the benefits of using market controls within an organization? What are the potential costs? When do you think it makes most sense to establish market controls?

4. Why might it pay managers to develop backchannel control methods? Can you see any drawbacks of such methods?

5. For a long time in Britain, the National Health Service paid dentists for each filling they installed. What might be the unintended consequences of this system? Can you think of a better system?

MANAGEMENT PORTFOLIO

FOR THE ORGANIZATION YOU HAVE CHOSEN TO FOLLOW:

1. Try to discover all you can about the main methods top managers use to control the organization.

2. Do these control methods make sense given the structure and strategy of the enterprise? How?

3. Would you suggest any change in control methods for the organization? If so, what?

CLOSING CASE   LINCOLN ELECTRIC

Lincoln Electric is one of the leading companies in the global market for arc welding equipment. This is a cost-competitive business in which consumers are price sensitive. Lincoln's success has been based on extremely high levels of employee productivity. The company attributes its productivity to a strong organizational culture and an incentive scheme based on piecework. Lincoln's organizational culture dates back to James Lincoln, who in 1907 joined the company his brother had established a few years earlier. Lincoln had a strong respect for the ability of the individual and believed that, correctly motivated, ordinary people could achieve extraordinary performance. He emphasized that the company should be a meritocracy where people were rewarded for their individual effort. Strongly egalitarian, Lincoln removed barriers to communication between workers and managers, practicing an open-door policy. He made sure that all who worked for the company were treated equally; for example, everyone ate in the same cafeteria, there were no reserved parking places for managers, and so on. Lincoln also believed that any productivity gains should be shared with consumers in the form of lower prices, with employees in the form of higher pay, and with shareholders in the form of higher dividends.

The organizational culture that grew out of James Lincoln's beliefs was reinforced by the company's incentive system. Production workers receive no base salary but are paid according to the number of pieces they produce. The piecework rates at the company enable an employee working at a normal pace to earn an income equivalent to the average wage for manufacturing workers in the area where a factory is based. Workers are responsible for the quality of their output and must repair any defects spotted by quality inspectors before the pieces are included in the piecework calculation. Since 1934 production workers have been awarded semiannual bonuses based on merit ratings. These ratings are based on objective criteria (such as an employee's level and quality of output) and subjective criteria (such as an employee's attitudes toward cooperation and his or her dependability). These systems give Lincoln's employees an incentive to work hard and to generate innovations that boost productivity—doing so influences

Productivity Beaters!   The pay of employees at Lincoln Electric is tied closely to productivity targets. So successful have these incentive systems been that the company has the highest productivity in its industry, along with the lowest cost structure.

Courtesy of the Lincoln Electric Company

their level of pay. Lincoln's factory workers have been able to earn a base pay that often exceeds the average manufacturing wage in the area by more than 50 percent, and they also receive bonuses that in good years can double their base pay. Despite high employee compensation, the workers are so productive that Lincoln has a lower cost structure than its competitors.[31]

CASE DISCUSSION QUESTIONS

1. What kind of control systems does Lincoln Electric rely on to generate high employee productivity?

2. Can you think of any possible unintended consequences of an incentive pay system based on piecework? How does Lincoln guard against these unintended consequences?

3. Do Lincoln's control systems match the strategy of the enterprise? How?

ENDNOTES

1. J. Batsell, "Cost Cutting, Inventory Control Help Boost Nordstrom's Quarterly Profit," *Knight Ridder Tribune News*, February 22, 2002, p. 1; Nordstrom's 2004 10K statement.

2. J. Child, *Organization: A Guide to Problems and Practice* (Harper & Row: London, 1984).

3. S.G. Green and M.A. Welsh, "Cybernetics and Dependence: Reframing the Control Concept," *Academy of Management Review* 13, no. 2 (1988), pp. 287–301.

4. M. Dell, *Direct from Dell: Strategies That Revolutionized an Industry* (New York: Harper Collins, 1999), p. 135.

5. A. Neely et al., "Dysfunctional Performance through Dysfunctional Measures," *Cost Management* 17, no. 5 (2003), pp. 41-46.

6. J.P. Womack, D.T. Jones, and D. Roos, *The Machine That Changed the World* (New York: Macmillan, 1990).

7. C.R. Gentry, "Off the Clock," *Chain Store Age*, February 2003, pp. 33–36.

8. The author serves on the advisory board of the company.

9. For a recent summary, see D.M. Wiegand and E.S. Geller, "Connecting Positive Psychology and Organization Behavior Management," *Journal of Organization Behavior Management* 24, no. 12 (2004–2005), pp. 3–20.

10. See J. Child, "Strategies of Control and Organization Behavior," *Administrative Science Quarterly* 18 (1973), pp. 1–17; K. Eisenhardt, "Control: Organizational and Economic Approaches," *Management Science* 31 (1985), pp. 134–49; S.A. Snell, "Control Theory in Human Resource Management," *Academy of Management Review* 35 (1992), pp. 292–328; W.G. Ouchi, "The Transmission of Control through Organizational Hierarchy," *Administrative Science Quarterly* 21 (1978), pp. 173–92.

11. J. Welsh and J. Byrne, *Jack: Straight from the Gut* (Warner Books: New York, 2001).

12. M. Weber, *Economy and Society,* trans. and ed. G. Roth and C. Wittich (New York: Bedminster Press, 1968/1921).

13. Child, *Organization: A Guide to Problems and Practice.*

14. R. Teichroeb, "End to Forced Busing Creates New Problems for Seattle's Schools," *Seattle Post Intelligencer*, June 3, 1999, Web edition.

15. Child, *Organization: A Guide to Problems and Practice.*

16. C.W.L. Hill, M.E. Hitt, and R.E. Hoskisson, "Cooperative versus Competitive Structures in Related and Unrelated Diversified Firms," *Organization Science* 3 (1992), pp. 501–21.

17. J.D. Thompson, *Organizations in Action* (New York: McGraw-Hill, 1967).

18. Peer control has long been argued to be a characteristic of many Japanese organizations. See M. Aoki, *Information, Incentives, and Bargaining in the Japanese Economy* (Cambridge: Cambridge University Press, 1988).

19. L. Lavelle, "A Payday for Performance," *BusinessWeek*, April 18, 2005, pp. 78–81.

20. O.E. Wiliamson, *The Economic Institutions of Capitalism* (New York: Free Press, 1985).

21. C. Bartlett, *Philips versus Matsushita: A New Century, a New Round.* (Harvard Business School Case # 9-302-049, 2005).

22. L. Kim, "The Dynamics of Samsung's Technological Learning in Semiconductors," *California Management Review* 39, no. 3 (1997), pp. 86–101.

23. Hill, Hitt, and Hoskisson, "Cooperative versus Competitive Structures in Related and Unrelated Diversified Firms."

24. Hill, Hitt, and Hoskisson, "Cooperative versus Competitive Structures in Related and Unrelated Diversified Firms."

25. C.W.L. Hill, "The Role of Corporate Headquarters in the Multidivisional Firm," in *Fundamental Issues in Strategy Research*, ed. R. Rumelt, D.J.Teece, and D. Schendel (Cambridge, MA: Harvard Business School Press, 1994), pp. 297–321.

26. C.W.L. Hill and R.E. Hoskisson, "Strategy and Structure in the Multiproduct Firm," *Academy of Management Review* 12 (1988), pp. 331–41.

27. C.W.L. Hill, M.A. Hitt, and R.E. Hoskisson, "Declining U.S. Competitiveness: Reflections on Crisis," *Academy of Management Executive* 2 (1988), pp. 51–60.

28. R.S. Kaplan and D.P. Norton, *The Balanced Scorecard: Translating Strategy into Action* (Boston: Harvard Business School Press, 1996).

29. Comments were made by Jim Donald at a presentation to University of Washington MBA students.

30. B. McConnell and J. Huba, *Creating Customer Evangelists* (Chicago: Dearborn Trade Publishing, 2003).

31. Sources: J. O'Connell, *Lincoln Electric: Venturing Abroad* (Harvard Business School Case # 9-398-095, April 1998); and www.lincolnelectric.com.

NOTES

10

ORGANIZATIONAL
CULTURE

LEARNING OBJECTIVES

After Reading This Chapter You Should Be Able to:

1 Describe the elements of organizational culture.

2 Discuss the importance of organizational subcultures.

3 List four categories of artifacts through which corporate culture is deciphered.

4 Discuss the conditions under which cultural strength improves corporate performance.

5 Identify four strategies to change and strengthen an organization's culture.

6 Compare and contrast four strategies for merging organizational cultures.

Dell Inc.'s sales slumped and its stock price dived when the dot-com bubble burst a few years ago. The downturn also revealed that Dell's corporate culture was too focused on financial performance. "In the dot-com boom, a lot of people got very wealthy, and we had a company culture that was (focused on) the stock price," says Dell CEO Kevin Rollins. Employees even had stock tickers as screen savers. So when the stock price tanked, so did morale. An internal survey of Dell employees also found that more than 50 percent of them would quit if offered a similar job elsewhere.

This lack of loyalty was due not just to the stock-focused culture; it was also due to the fact that Dell's culture was so obsessed with work efficiency and winning business that employee well-being often took a backseat in most decisions. "We have folks who get great business results, but they break too much glass along the way," admits Michael George, Dell's chief marketing officer. "They're not collaborative with their colleagues." A related concern was the ethical consequences of a company with a stock-focused culture. Enron, another Texas-based firm, had just gone bankrupt because its pathological focus on stock value led to illegal accounting practices. Rollins wanted to steer Dell away from that risk.[1]

Rollins was convinced that Dell's culture had to be adjusted, but is it possible to change organizational culture? And if so, how could Rollins and other managers alter the existing culture? Equally important, what culture should guide Dell employees into the future?

Managers at Dell and most other companies are paying a lot of attention these days to organizational culture. This chapter looks at the meaning and management of organizational culture as it addresses the questions that faced Dell's managers. It begins by describing the concept of organizational culture and identifying ways to determine its particular characteristics—its cultural content—in your company. Next we consider the importance of organizational culture to an organization's success. This is followed by a discussion of whether the content and strength of organizational culture can be altered and, if so, how managers can bring about the required cultural changes. The final section of this chapter examines corporate culture issues when two companies are merged or when one is acquired by the other.

■ // What Is Organizational Culture?

organizational culture

The values and assumptions shared within an organization.

The concept of organizational culture has been around for decades and started to gain popularity beyond academic circles in the 1980s. Today it seems that most corporate leaders actively think about their company's culture daily or weekly. Certainly it is on the minds of Kevin Rollins and Michael Dell at Dell Inc. What is this abstract thing we call **organizational culture**? As we noted in Chapter 2, it consists of the values and assumptions shared within an organization.[2] Organizational culture directs everyone in the organization toward the "right way" of doing things. It frames and shapes the decisions that managers and other employees should make and the actions they should take. As this definition states, organizational culture consists of two main components: shared values and assumptions. Figure 10.1 illustrates how these shared values and assumptions relate to each other and are associated with artifacts, which we discuss later in this chapter.

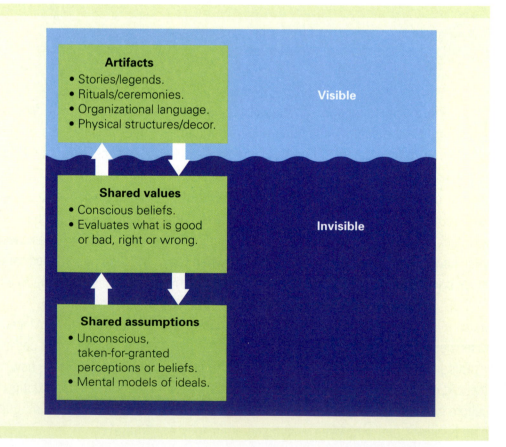

FIGURE 10.1

Organizational Culture Assumptions, Values, and Artifacts

Source: Based on information in E.H. Schein, *Organizational Culture and Leadership: A Dynamic View* (San Francisco: Jossey-Bass, 1985).

// SHARED VALUES

Values, which were introduced in Chapter 1, are stable, evaluative beliefs that guide our preferences for outcomes or courses of action in a variety of situations.[3] They are conscious perceptions about what is good or bad, right or wrong. Values tell us to what we "ought" to do. They
serve as a moral compass that directs our motivation and potentially our decisions and actions
(Figure 10.2). Everyone has values because they partly define who we are as individuals and as
members of groups with similar values. People organize the dozens of values into a hierarchy or
value system. Some people value security and tradition; others give these values a much lower
priority. Instead they might give top priority to the values of excitement and challenge.

Security, tradition, excitement, challenge, and dozens of other values exist within
individuals. Yet values also exist as a component of organizational culture in the form of
shared values. Shared values are values that people within the organization or work unit have
in common and place near the top of their hierarchy of values.[4] At Dell, employees place a
high priority on winning, meaning that they value performance and achievement more than,
say, security or tradition.

It has become trendy for leaders to determine and publicly announce their company's shared
values. Yahoo!, the online portal company, is no exception. Its Web site proudly says that six
values represent its corporate DNA or "what makes it tick": excellence, innovation, customer
fixation, teamwork, community, and fun. Do these values really represent the content of Yahoo!'s
culture? Maybe, but what companies say they value isn't necessarily what they actually value.

■ Yahoo's DNA.

The key distinction managers need to consider is whether they are referring to espoused
values or enacted values.[5] *Espoused values* represent the values people say they use and, in
many cases, think they use even if they don't. Values are socially desirable, so people create a
positive public image by claiming to believe in values that others expect them to embrace. For
instance, one large international corporation hung signs around its headquarters proclaiming
that its culture embraced "trust"; yet the same company required all employees to be searched
whenever they entered or exited the building. Furthermore, even if the company's dozen or so
top executives embrace these values, they are not necessarily the values held by most people
throughout the organization. *Enacted values,* on the other hand, represent the values people
actually rely on to guide their decisions and actions. These values in use are apparent by
watching people in action. An organization's culture consists of these enacted values, not
espoused values.[6]

1	Ranking of corporate culture (tied with employee benefits) among list of job applicant inquiries during interviews, as reported by *Fortune* 1,000 executives.
1	Ranking of corporate culture among reasons why 147 employed U.S. executives surveyed by ExecuNet want to change jobs.
2	Ranking of "good fit with company culture" among factors 1,000 hiring managers look for when evaluating college graduates for employment (number one factor was relevant experience).
3	Ranking of corporate culture as a factor influencing American MBA students in their decision to accept or reject a job offer (top two factors were compensation package and challenging role).
36	Percentage of Finnish university students who say the best employers have a strong culture.
36	Percentage of employers who list corporate culture as one of the benefits of working at their company.

FIGURE 10.2   How Important Is Corporate Culture?

Sources: "As Employment Market Improves," ExecuNet press release, December 1, 2005; "More Jobs and
Higher Salaries in Store," CareerBuilder press release, April 5, 2006; Universum Communications,
American MBA Survey, 2005; Universum Communications, Graduate Survey, Finnish Edition, 2005;
Robert Half International, Office of the Future 2005 study.

// SHARED ASSUMPTIONS

The deepest element of organizational culture (some experts believe it is really the essence of culture) is the shared assumptions that people carry around in their heads. *Assumptions* are unconscious perceptions or beliefs that have worked so well in the past that they are considered the correct way to think and act toward problems and opportunities. These assumptions are so deep that they are taken for granted—they are so obviously good and right for the company that no one really thinks about or questions them. For many decades Hewlett-Packard's culture was so deeply embedded that no one really questioned its underlying assumptions. The California-based technology company's legendary culture, known as "the H-P Way," revered innovation, employee well-being, and collegial teamwork. It was a role model for cultures in other Silicon Valley companies.

The opening vignette to this chapter provides another example of how strong organizational cultures operate at a level of unconscious assumptions. Dell's focus on winning the competition game had been so successful over the years that no one questioned it. Even when Dell's executives realized that the company's winning culture had changed into one that focused too much on the company's stock price, they didn't try to disturb the underlying emphasis on winning. "It's not that we didn't have a culture with the qualities that drive business success," explains Paul McKinnon, Dell's vice president of human resources. "We were performance-driven, cost-driven, built on speed, very low on politics. We just aspired to do better.… What would a new winning culture look like here at Dell?"[7]

■ Procter & Gamble's cultural resistance.

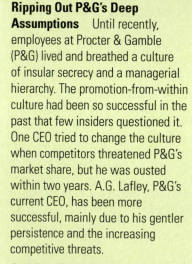

Ripping Out P&G's Deep Assumptions Until recently, employees at Procter & Gamble (P&G) lived and breathed a culture of insular secrecy and a managerial hierarchy. The promotion-from-within culture had been so successful in the past that few insiders questioned it. One CEO tried to change the culture when competitors threatened P&G's market share, but he was ousted within two years. A.G. Lafley, P&G's current CEO, has been more successful, mainly due to his gentler persistence and the increasing competitive threats.

© AP Photo/Elise Amendola

Along with being the deepest part of organizational culture, shared assumptions are the most difficult to change. Consider the corporate culture of Procter & Gamble. Until a few years ago employees at the consumer goods company lived and breathed a culture of insular secrecy and a managerial hierarchy. Top positions were filled through promotions; rarely would anyone consider hiring an outsider to fill a management role. Anyone who left P&G was considered a traitor, never to be welcomed back. New hires were quickly "Procterized"; they completely embraced the culture or left the company. P&G's culture had been so successful for so long that it would be ridiculous to question it. This culture remained intact even when P&G lost market share during the late 1990s to more customer-focused competitors. P&G's chief executive at the time tried to change the culture, complaining that he would "like to have an organization where there are rebels." The CEO underestimated the depth of shared assumptions. After pushing through culture changes for two years, he was replaced. His successor, A.G. Lafley, was more successful by taking a gentler but equally persistent approach to making employees aware that P&G's old culture was dysfunctional.[8]

// CONTENT OF ORGANIZATIONAL CULTURE

■ Contrasting cultures of SAS Institute and Wal-Mart.

Organizations differ in their cultural content—that is, the relative ordering of values and assumptions. Spend some time at SAS Institute and you will soon discover that the world's largest privately held software company has one of the most employee-friendly cultures on the planet. Located on a 200-acre campus in Cary, North Carolina, SAS supports employee well-being with free on-site medical care, unlimited sick days, heavily subsidized day care, ski trips, personal trainers, inexpensive gourmet cafeterias, and tai chi classes. Unlike other software companies, SAS encourages its employees to stick to a 35-hour workweek.[9] In contrast, visit Wal-Mart's headquarters in Bentonville, Arkansas, and you will find a workplace that almost screams frugality and efficiency. The world's largest retailer has a spartan waiting room for suppliers. Visitors pay for their own soft drinks and coffee. In each of the building's inexpensive cubicles, employees sit at inexpensive desks finding ways to squeeze more efficiencies and lower costs out of suppliers as well as their own work processes.[10]

How many corporate cultural values are there? Some writers and consultants have attempted to classify organizational cultures into several categories. One of these models claims that there are seven corporate cultures in the world: attention to detail, outcome orientation, people orientation, team orientation, aggressiveness, stability, and innovation and risk taking. Another organizational culture model identifies eight cultures organized around a circle, indicating that some cultures are opposite to each other. A rules-oriented culture is opposite to an innovation culture; an internally focused culture is opposed to an externally focused culture; a controlling culture is opposite to a flexible culture; and a goal-oriented culture is opposite to a supportive culture.[11]

Managers like to use these organizational culture models because they are handy templates when figuring out what kind of culture they currently have and what kind of culture they want to develop. Although they probably clarify the messy business of sorting out organizational values, these models oversimplify the diversity of cultural values in organizations. The fact is, there are dozens of individual values, so there are likely as many organizational values. Thus managers need to be wary of models that reduce the variety of organizational cultures into a few simple categories with catchy labels. By relying on these models, managers could possibly form an impression of their culture that is not sufficiently accurate or precise.

// ORGANIZATIONAL SUBCULTURES

When discussing organizational culture, we are actually referring to the *dominant culture:* the values and assumptions shared most widely by people throughout the organization. However, organizations also have *subcultures* located throughout their various divisions, geographic regions, and occupational groups.[12] Some subcultures enhance the dominant culture by espousing parallel assumptions, values, and beliefs. For instance, some teams or departments within Dell probably feel more strongly about customer service than about winning. Both are important, so the subculture's values are compatible; but the priorities of values are somewhat different.

Other subcultures are called *countercultures* because they directly oppose the organization's core values. Procter & Gamble's clubby hierarchical culture was likely opposed by a few small teams or work units, whose members protected themselves from the dominant culture and were able to nurture a culture of creativity and innovation within their little niches. These contrarians are typically tolerated if small enough or far enough away from headquarters.

Subcultures (particularly countercultures) potentially create conflict and dissent among employees, but they also serve two important functions.[13] First, they maintain the organization's standards of performance and ethical behavior. Employees who hold countercultural values are an important source of surveillance and critique over the dominant order. They encourage constructive conflict and more creative thinking about how the organization should interact with its environment. By preventing employees from blindly following one set of values, subcultures help the organization to abide by society's ethical values.

The second function of subcultures is that they are the spawning grounds for emerging values that keep the firm aligned with the needs of customers, suppliers, society, and other stakeholders. Companies eventually need to replace their dominant values with ones that are more appropriate for the changing environment. If subcultures are suppressed, the organization may take longer to discover and adopt values aligned with the emerging environment.

■ // Deciphering an Organization's Culture

artifacts
The observable symbols and signs of an organization's culture.

We can't directly see an organization's shared values and assumptions. Instead, as Figure 10.1 illustrated earlier, organizational culture needs to be deciphered through **artifacts**. Artifacts are the observable symbols and signs of an organization's culture, such as the way visitors are greeted, the physical layout, and how employees are rewarded.[14] Some experts suggest that artifacts are the essence of corporate culture, whereas others view artifacts as symbols or indicators of culture. Either way, artifacts are important because they represent the best source of information about a company's culture. Discovering an organization's culture is much like an anthropological investigation of a new society. It involves observing workplace behavior, listening for unique language in everyday conversations, studying written documents, and interviewing staff about corporate stories. As we will learn later, artifacts are also important because they reinforce and potentially support changes to an organization's culture.

■ Mayo Clinic's cultural expedition.

The Mayo Clinic recognized the importance of deciphering its organizational culture through artifacts. The medical center has a well-established culture at its original clinic in Rochester, Minnesota, but maintaining that culture in its expanding operations in Florida and Arizona has been challenging. "We were struggling with growing pains [and] we didn't want to lose the culture, [so] we were looking at how to keep the heritage alive," explains Matt McElrath, Mayo Clinic human resources director in Arizona. The Mayo Clinic retained anthropologist Linda Catlin to decipher Mayo's culture and identify ways to reinforce it at the two newer sites. Catlin shadowed employees and posed as a patient to observe what happens in waiting rooms. "She did countless interviews, joined physicians on patient visits, and even spent time in the operating room," says McElrath. At the end of her six-week cultural expedition, Catlin submitted a report outlining Mayo's culture and how its satellite operations varied from that culture. The Mayo Clinic adopted all of Catlin's 11 recommendations, such as requiring all new physicians at the three sites to attend an orientation in Rochester where they learn about Mayo's history and values.[15]

Mayo Clinic's Cultural Expedition   The Mayo Clinic hired an anthropologist to help decipher its organizational culture and find ways to transfer that culture from its original center in Rochester, Minnesota, to its expanding operations in Florida and Arizona. The anthropologist's six-week expedition included shadowing employees and posing as a patient to observe what happens in waiting rooms.

Courtesy of Mayo Clinic

Kevin Rollins hadn't conducted a full anthropological expedition when he concluded that Dell's culture was amiss, but he did use artifacts to identify some cultural content. Rollins noticed that employees talked about the company's stock value more often than do people in other firms. He observed that many employees used a stock market ticker as a screen saver on their computer monitors. And when the stock price crashed from $58 to $16 per share, Rollins saw the effect on morale and turnover intentions.

■ Dell searches for its culture.

After this initial diagnosis, Dell engaged a consulting firm to more formally analyze the company's culture.[16] The process, consisting of a lengthy questionnaire completed by all employees, confirmed that Dell has a culture that values winning and operational excellence (efficiency and speed). The results also confirmed Rollins's worry that Dell's relentless pursuit of growth and efficiency was sometimes hurting employee well-being. "[The] surveys showed that certain sales leaders were routinely rewarded and promoted despite trampling on the feelings of their team members," recalls Michael George, Dell's chief marketing officer. "New hires complained that they had been thrown into the most challenging position of their lives with little support or backup from superiors."

Surveys can reveal some information about a company's culture, but managers should not rely on that information alone to understand the company's culture. Several organizational culture experts have warned that culture is too deep and there are too many varieties of cultural values to be adequately captured in a pencil-and-paper questionnaire. Instead they recommend a combination of surveys and painstaking assessment of many artifacts.[17] Four broad categories of artifacts are organizational stories and legends, rituals and ceremonies, language, and physical structures and symbols.

// ORGANIZATIONAL STORIES AND LEGENDS

Many years ago Southwest Airlines introduced an ad campaign with the phrase "Just Plane Smart." Unknowingly the Dallas-based airline had infringed on the "Plane Smart" slogan at Stevens Aviation, an aviation sales and maintenance company in Greensville, South Carolina. Rather than paying buckets of money to lawyers, Stevens chairman Kurt Herwald and Southwest CEO Herb Kelleher decided to settle the dispute with an old-fashioned arm-wrestling match at a run-down wrestling stadium in Dallas. A boisterous crowd watched the "Malice in Dallas" event as "Smokin" Herb Kelleher and "Kurtsey" Herwald battled their designates and then each other. When Kelleher lost the final round to Herwald, he jested (while being carried off on a stretcher) that his defeat was due to a cold and the strain of walking up a flight of stairs. Stevens Aviation later decided to let Southwest Airlines continue to use its ad campaign, and both companies donated funds from the event to charities.[18]

■ Southwest Airlines' cultural legend.

Malice in Dallas is a legend that almost every Southwest employee knows by heart. It is a tale that communicates one of the maverick airline's core values—that having fun is part of doing business. Stories and legends about past corporate incidents serve as powerful social prescriptions of the way things should (or should not) be done. They also provide human realism to corporate expectations, individual performance standards, and assumptions about ideal behaviors and decisions.

Not all stories and legends are positive. Some are communicated to demonstrate what is wrong with the dominant corporate culture. Some time ago General Motors (GM) was known for its strong hierarchical culture, in which employees were expected to respect the position and power of their higher-ups. Employees who rejected the automaker's dominant culture liked to tell how dozens of GM people would arrive at the airport to meet a senior executive. An executive's status was symbolized by the number of vehicles leaving the airport with the executive; but critics told this story to illustrate the decadence and time wasted in serving GM's leaders rather than other stakeholders.[19]

■ General Motors' countercultural story.

Stories are important artifacts because they personalize the culture and generate emotions that help people remember lessons within these stories. Stories have the greatest effect at communicating corporate culture when they describe real people, are assumed to be true, and are remembered by employees throughout the organization. Stories are also prescriptive—they advise people what to do or not to do.[20]

■ BMW's fast-moving culture.

// RITUALS AND CEREMONIES

Rituals are the programmed routines of daily organizational life that dramatize an organization's culture. They include how visitors are greeted, how often senior executives visit subordinates, how people communicate with each other, how much time employees take for lunch, and so on. BMW is well known for its fast-paced culture, which is soon apparent quite literally in how quickly employees walk around the German carmaker's offices. "When you move through the corridors and hallways of other companies' buildings, people kind of crawl—they walk slowly," says BMW board of management chair Helmut Panke. "But BMW people tend to move faster."[21] **Ceremonies** are more formal artifacts than rituals. Ceremonies are planned activities conducted specifically for the benefit of an audience, such as publicly rewarding (or punishing) employees or celebrating the launch of a new product or newly won contract.

rituals
The programmed routines of daily organizational life that dramatize the organization's culture.

ceremonies
Planned activities conducted specifically for the benefit of an audience.

// ORGANIZATIONAL LANGUAGE

The language of the workplace speaks volumes about the company's culture. How employees address coworkers, describe customers, express anger, and greet stakeholders are all verbal symbols of cultural values. Employees at The Container Store compliment each other about "being Gumby," meaning that they are being as flexible as the well-known green toy—going outside their regular jobs to help a customer or another employee. (A human-sized Gumby is displayed at the retailer's headquarters.)[22] Language also highlights values held by organizational subcultures. For instance, consultants working at Whirlpool kept hearing employees talk about the appliance company's "PowerPoint culture." This phrase, which names Microsoft's presentation software, is a critique of Whirlpool's hierarchical culture in which communication is one-way (from executives to employees).[23]

// PHYSICAL STRUCTURES AND DÉCOR

■ Oakely's fortress culture.

The size, shape, location, and age of buildings might suggest the company's emphasis on teamwork, environmental friendliness, flexibility, or any other set of values. An extreme example is the "interplanetary headquarters" of Oakley Inc. The ultra-hip eyewear and clothing company built a vaultlike structure in Foothill Ranch, California, complete with towering metallic walls studded with oversize bolts, to represent its secretive and protective culture. Ejection seats from a B-52 bomber furnish the waiting area. A full-size torpedo lies in a rack behind the receptionist's armored desk. Overall, the building symbolizes a highly protective culture in which employees believe they are at war with the competition. "We've always had a fortress mentality," says an Oakley executive. "What we make is gold, and people will do anything to get it, so we protect it."[24]

Even if the building doesn't make much of a statement, there is a treasure trove of physical artifacts inside. Desks, chairs, office space, and wall hangings (or lack of them) are just a few of the items that might convey cultural meaning. Each of these artifacts alone might not say much, but enough of them together make the company's culture easier to decipher. Consider Chandler Chicco Agency's (CCA's) offices in Manhattan's meatpacking district. The creative advertising agency is a cubicle-free and status-free zone. Desks are arranged in clusters where senior staffers

Oakley's Fortress Culture   Oakely Inc.'s bunkerlike headquarters in Foothill Ranch, California, symbolizes a culture that is highly protective of its product inventions. The company's *Physics Elevated to an Art Form* approach to product design is enforced by more than 545 worldwide patents.

Courtesy of Oakley, Inc.

share the same space and similar responsibilities as those who joined the company a week ago. These artifacts suggest that CCA has an egalitarian and possibly frugal culture.[25]

■ // Is Organizational Culture Important?

Why would executives at Dell Inc. and other companies want to tamper with their culture? Does corporate culture really make a difference? The answer, in a word, is yes. Various studies indicate that companies with strong cultures are more likely to be successful, but only under a particular set of conditions.[26] The explanation of how organizational culture influences corporate prosperity and employee well-being has a few twists and turns, which we walk through in this section.

To begin, the effect of organizational culture depends partly on its strength. Corporate culture *strength* refers to how widely and deeply employees hold the company's dominant values and assumptions. In a strong organizational culture, most employees across all subunits hold the dominant values. These values are also institutionalized through well-established artifacts, thereby making it difficult for those values to change. Furthermore, strong cultures tend to be long-lasting; some can be traced back to the beliefs and values established by the company's founder. In contrast, companies have weak cultures when the dominant values are short-lived and held mainly by a few people at the top of the organization. A strong corporate culture potentially increases the company's success by serving three important functions:

1. *Control system:* In Chapter 2 we briefly noted that organizational culture influences what managers and employees can and can't do. And in Chapter 9 we noted that culture is a deeply embedded form of social control that influences employee decisions and behavior.[27] As a control system, culture is pervasive and operates unconsciously. You might think of it as an automatic pilot, directing employees in ways that are consistent with organizational expectations.

2. *Social glue:* Organizational culture is the "social glue" that bonds people together and makes them feel part of the organizational experience.[28] Employees are motivated to internalize the organization's dominant culture because it fulfills their need for social identity. This social glue is increasingly important as a way to attract new staff and retain top performers.

3. *Sense making:* Organizational culture assists the sense-making process.[29] It helps employees understand what goes on and why things happen in the company. Corporate culture also makes it easier for them to understand what is expected of them and to interact with other employees who know the culture and believe in it.

// ORGANIZATIONAL CULTURE STRENGTH AND FIT

Strong cultures are *potentially* good for business, as we just explained, but studies have found only a modestly positive relationship between culture strength and success.[30] Why the weak relationship? One reason is that a strong culture increases organizational performance only when the cultural content is appropriate for the organization's environment (see Figure 10.3). Recall from a few pages back that culture *content* refers to the relative ordering of values and assumptions. Trouble occurs when the relative ordering of cultural values is misaligned with the firm's environment. This lack of fit causes employees to make decisions and engage in behaviors that are inconsistent with the company's best interests. Strong cultures create a greater risk because culture strength indicates that a greater number of employees will be guided by those values and assumptions.

The corporate landscape is dotted with companies that suffered performance setbacks because their culture became dangerously misaligned with the external environment. Home Depot is a recent example. Founded in 1978, America's second largest retailer (Wal-Mart

■ Home Depot's cultural re-alignment.

FIGURE 10.3

Organizational Culture
and Performance

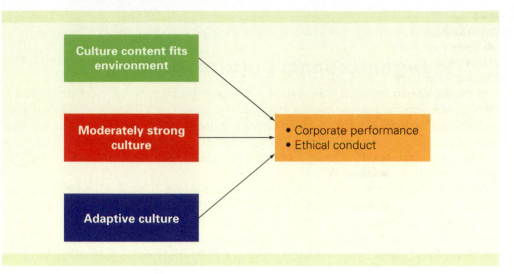

is number one) grew and prospered through a culture of "entrepreneurial high-spiritedness," a passionate commitment to customers, and an aversion to bureaucracy. But when competition set in, Home Depot's freewheeling culture became a liability. The company was an inefficient hodgepodge of fiefdoms representing different regions that practically ignored the head office. Each region even had its own supplier agreements, whereas one companywide agreement would have significantly increased Home Depot's purchasing power. The company needed a culture that emphasized more structure and efficiency to squeeze out unnecessary costs. Leading this transformation was former GE executive Robert Nardelli. Over the past five years Nardelli has introduced a much more efficiency-focused, performance-oriented culture, similar to GE's famous culture. Nardelli faced considerable resistance, but Home Depot's culture is changing. "He saved the company," claims Home Depot cofounder Ken Langone.[31]

Kevin Rollins also started to notice a lack of cultural fit at Dell Inc. As noted in the opening vignette to this chapter, the stock-focused culture hurt employee morale and possibly performance whenever the stock dipped. The intense winning orientation further undermined employee loyalty when Dell, poised to double in size over the next few years, couldn't afford to lose valuable talent. Although the existing culture was generally effective for driving Dell's performance, it needed adjustment.

"We wanted our culture to be as rich and as well-defined as our operational model," says Rollins. "And so we also launched the concept of the Soul of Dell." To add substance and commitment to the "Soul of Dell," employees were asked what they would expect to see in a great place to work. That feedback, along with results from the cultural audit survey, became the foundation of five values: customer-focused, team-oriented, direct relationships, global citizenship, and a passion for winning. Rollins says this culture partly exists today and partly is a goal to which the company aspires. "I would like our employees to say, 'That's what I believe in, that's what the company believes in, and that's why I'm proud to be at Dell.'"[32]

CORPORATE CULTS AND SUPPRESSING DISSENT A second reason why companies with strong cultures aren't necessarily more effective is that they become corporate cults that lock decision makers into mental models and blind them to new opportunities or unique problems. Thus strong cultures might cause decision makers to overlook or incorrectly define subtle misalignments between the organization's activities and the changing environment. Several bankrupt steel manufacturers apparently suffered from this problem. "It was 100 years of integrated culture," recalls Mittal Steel vice president John Mang III, who worked at one of the now-bankrupt firms for three decades. "People in the organization are inbreds, including myself. You grew up in the culture; you didn't see anything else. … It is a culture from within, so you have these rose-colored glasses that everything's fine."[33]

A third consideration is that very strong cultures tend to suppress dissenting subcultural values. As we noted earlier, subcultures encourage constructive conflict, which improves creative thinking and offers some level of ethical vigilance over the dominant culture. In the long run, a subculture's nascent values could become important dominant values as the environment changes. Strong cultures suppress subcultures, thereby undermining these benefits.

// ADAPTIVE CULTURES

So far we have learned that strong cultures are more effective when the cultural values are aligned with the organization's environment. Also, no corporate culture should be so strong that it blinds employees to alternative viewpoints or completely suppresses dissenting subcultures. Research from various sources adds one more recommendation to this list— namely that organizations are more likely to succeed when they have an adaptive culture.[34] An **adaptive culture** exists when employees focus on the changing needs of customers and other stakeholders and support initiatives to keep pace with these changes. Adaptive cultures have an external focus, and employees assume responsibility for the organization's performance. As a result, they are proactive and quick. Employees seek opportunities rather than waiting for them to arrive. They act quickly to learn through discovery rather than engaging in "paralysis by analysis."

Organizational culture experts are starting to piece together the elements of adaptive cultures.[35] First and foremost, adaptive cultures have an external focus. Employees hold a common mental model that change is both necessary and inevitable to keep pace with a dynamic external environment. Second, employees in adaptive cultures pay as much attention to organizational processes as they do to organizational goals. They continuously improve internal processes (production, customer service, and so on) to serve external stakeholders. Third, employees in adaptive cultures have a strong sense of ownership. They assume responsibility for the organization's performance. In other words, they believe "It's our job" rather than "It's not my job." Fourth, adaptive cultures are proactive and quick. Employees seek out opportunities, rather than wait for them to arrive. They act quickly to learn through discovery rather than engage in "paralysis by analysis."

Home Depot's Cultural Realignment   Home Depot became one of the fastest-growing and most successful retailers in history, thanks to its freewheeling entrepreneurial culture. But this culture became a liability when competition set in, requiring a more cost-conscious and performance-oriented mindset. CEO Robert Nardelli was hired to transform Home Depot's culture for better alignment with its environment.

© Michael Newman/PhotoEdit

adaptive culture
An organizational culture in which employees focus on the changing needs of customers and other stakeholders and support initiatives to keep pace with these changes.

// ORGANIZATIONAL CULTURE AND BUSINESS ETHICS

An organization's culture influences more than just the bottom line; it can also potentially influence its ethical conduct. This makes sense because good behavior is driven by ethical values. An organization can guide the conduct of its employees by embedding ethical values in its dominant culture. Dell executives saw this connection when they developed the "soul of Dell" initiative. CEO Kevin Rollins was concerned that the obsession with profits and stock price among many Dell employees increased the risk of unethical conduct. Such a focus on stock price led Enron, the Texas-based energy company, and Worldcom, the Louisiana-based telecommunications giant, into bankruptcy.

■ Dell's ethical culture.

Citibank's Culture Pushes Ethical Boundaries   In just six years Citibank Japan's business increased tenfold and delivered profits that outscored all other private banks in the company's huge network. Unfortunately much of this success was due to unethical dealing. Citigroup chief executive Charles Prince, shown here with a colleague bowing at a Tokyo news conference in apology for the violations, admits that Citigroup's culture had been too numbers-focused.

Yuriko Nakao/Reuters/Corbis

■ Citibank's culture pushes ethical boundaries.

So Dell's new set of cultural values include clear linkages to ethical conduct. Its "direct relationships" value includes "behaving ethically in every interaction and in every aspect of how we conduct business." Its "global citizenship" value refers to participating responsibly in the global marketplace. When discussing the company's passion for winning, Rollins emphasizes that it is really about "winning with integrity." All of these principles are connected to the company's code of conduct, called "the higher standard."[36]

Unfortunately it seems that companies make headlines every day for failing to incorporate ethics into their culture. Citibank illustrates this in its serious ethical lapse in Japan. In just six years Citibank Japan's business increased tenfold and delivered profits that outscored all other private banks in the company's huge network. Unfortunately the Japanese government's financial watchdog recently concluded that Citibank Japan's culture supported "a law-evading sales system," citing infractions ranging from grossly overcharging clients to helping them falsify profit and manipulate stock. With 83 infractions, Citigroup was told to close some of its Japanese operations. "It's our fault, because all we talk about is delivering the numbers. We've done this forever," admits Citigroup chief executive Charles Prince. Prince fired several top executives in Tokyo and New York and is now on a mission to change Citibank's culture. He has a major challenge ahead of him. Dow Jones news service reports that Citigroup's culture has an "established reputation for pushing the limits of acceptable banking behavior."[37]

■ // How to Change and Strengthen Organizational Culture

Can managers change an organization's culture? Yes, but it isn't easy, it rarely occurs quickly, and often the culture ends up changing managers. Remember that culture is deeply embedded in the collective mindset. Employees don't just value some things more than others; they don't even question why they believe something is the right thing to do. Artifacts further reinforce that cultural system of beliefs. The shared assumptions of an organization's culture are so well established that employees rely on them to make decisions and engage in behavior without consciously questioning them. Indeed, when outsiders critique those culturally congruent decisions and actions, employees often respond with disbelief that anyone would doubt such logical courses of action.

Many executives have been driven out of organizations because they tried to change the organizations' culture. One casualty, as we mentioned earlier in this chapter, was a Procter & Gamble CEO who lasted only two years because he tried to deculturize an intransigent "Proc-terized" workforce too quickly and forcefully. Carly Fiorina, the former CEO of Hewlett-Packard (HP), is another example.[38] The California-based technology company's legendary culture, known as "the HP Way," revered innovation, employee well-being, and collegial teamwork. It was a role model for cultures in other Silicon Valley companies. But HP started to lose ground to Dell, Compaq, and other competitors who were responding with more agility and efficiency to customer demands. Furthermore, an internal assessment revealed that HP's culture had shifted. "The HP Way has been misinterpreted and twisted as a gentle bureaucracy of entitlement instead of a performance-based meritocracy," said Fiorina soon after becoming Hewlett-Packard's CEO.

■ Defeated by "the HP Way."   As HP's first CEO hired from outside the company, Fiorina's task was to alter the HP Way so the company would become more competitive. She launched "the Rules of the Garage," a set of cultural values having symbolic reference to the Palo Alto garage where founders William Hewlett and David Packard started the company in 1939. Fiorina reinforced these performance-focused values with a customer-driven bonus system and organizational structure. Her biggest initiative was acquiring Compaq, a fast-paced and aggressive competitor from Texas. The merger was intended to inject "a little of Compaq's DNA into the HP Way, especially speed and agility," said a Compaq executive who later took an executive position at HP.

Hewlett-Packard's acquisition of Compaq seems to have had some effect on the HP culture—but at a cost. Both board members from the founding families (Hewlett and Packard) quit over the changed culture; HP lost its status as one of the top 10 best places to work in America (it isn't even on the top 100 today); and Fiorina was ousted as CEO. On the surface, Hewlett-Packard's board lost confidence in Fiorina because she failed to raise the company's profitability and achieve related targets. But sources say that Fiorina also tried to change more of the HP Way than was necessary, which battered employee loyalty, productivity, and ultimately profitability. "A little of the HP Way would probably work pretty well right now," says Quantum CEO and former HP executive Richard E. Belluzzo soon after Fiorina was fired. "The strength of HP has always been its culture and its people."

The lesson here is that changing an organization's culture can be a manager's greatest challenge. At the same time, as we noted earlier, organizational culture can be a powerful influence on the company's success. So how can managers change and strengthen organizational culture? Over the next few pages we highlight four strategies that have had some success. This list, outlined in Figure 10.4, is not exhaustive; but each activity seems to work well under the right circumstances.

// ACTIONS OF FOUNDERS AND LEADERS

An organization's culture begins with its founders and leaders. Founders set the tone, emphasizing what is most important and what should receive a lower priority. They are often visionaries who provide a powerful role model for others to follow. Experts suggest that the company's culture sometimes reflects the founder's personality, and this cultural imprint often remains with the organization for decades. Dell Inc. has a winning culture because Michael Dell is a high achiever. The HP Way culture emphasizes collegiality and employee well-being because the company's founders were outgoing and benevolent.

Founders establish an organization's culture, but they and subsequent CEOs can sometimes reshape that culture. A legendary example is Zhang Ruimin's corporate culture transformation

■ Changing Haier Group's culture.

FIGURE 10.4

Strategies to Change and Strengthen Organizational Culture

Actions of founders and leaders
- Symbolize the new culture (or need for one) through memorable events.
- Model the new culture through subtle decisions and actions.

Culturally consistent rewards
- Reward employees for culturally consistent behaviors.
- Reward managers who help employees understand the culture.

Changing and strengthening organizational culture

Selecting and socializing employees
- Hire people whose values are consistent with the culture.
- Inform and indoctrinate new staff about what the culture means.

Aligning artifacts
- Share stories supporting the culture.
- Celebrate goals/milestones to support the culture.
- Inhabit buildings that reflect the culture.

Hammering Out a New Culture   Soon after his arrival as CEO two decades ago, Zhang Ruimin was so incensed by the poor quality of the products built at Haier Group's factory in Qingdao that he picked up a sledgehammer and, with employees watching, smashed several washing machines. Zhang's dramatic behavior symbolized the need to replace the entitlement culture with one that values quality and performance. Today Haier Group is a model of modern efficiency.

© AP Photo/Katsumi Kasahara

of Haier Group, the Chinese state-owned appliance manufacturer. Soon after his arrival as CEO two decades ago, Zhang was so incensed by the poor quality of the products built at Haier Group's factory in Qingdao that he picked up a sledgehammer and, with employees watching, smashed several washing machines. Zhang's dramatic behavior symbolized the need for radical change, including replacing the entitlement culture with one that values quality and performance. Today Haier Group is a model of modern efficiency. Visitors to Qingdao's shop floor will find the legendary sledgehammer displayed in a glass case, reminding everyone of how Haier Group's culture has changed.[39]

■ IBM's culture tries a new shirt.

Zhang's actions illustrate that leaders play an important symbolic role in organizational culture change. Fortunately there are ways other than smashing products with a sledgehammer to communicate the need for cultural change. For example, when Louis Gerstner was brought in to turn around troubled IBM in the early 1990s, he showed up on the first day wearing a blue shirt. What's so symbolic about the incoming CEO wearing a blue shirt? Quite a lot at IBM, where every male employee wore a neatly starched white shirt. (Several decades earlier IBM founder Thomas Watson had disapproved of anyone wearing shirts that weren't white.) Gerstner's blue shirt attire wasn't accidental. It was a deliberate signal that he intended to break the technology firm's bureaucratic follow-mindless-rules culture. The message was so powerful that IBM was buzzing for weeks about how the new CEO dared to wear a blue shirt in IBM's hallowed halls. Three months later IBM staffers everywhere were wearing blue shirts, so Gerstner sometimes reverted to wearing white shirts! He also made the point to everyone that IBM employees are not evaluated by the colors of their shirts. Instead they should wear attire appropriate for the occasion and will be rewarded for their performance.[40]

The leader's symbolic words and actions are sometimes highlighted in ceremonial events (such as Zhang's sledgehammer); but they are equally important in more mundane ways, such as how meetings are conducted, where the manager locates his or her office, and who gets on the manager's schedule and for how long. Employees watch managers at all levels of the organization to determine how serious they are about changing the culture and how that culture translates into behavior. Thus anything managers say or do that is consistent with the desired culture will potentially lead the organization toward that culture.[41]

■ Dell's leaders practice the new culture.

Founder Michael Dell and CEO Kevin Rollins relied on symbolic events to begin the process of reshaping Dell's culture. A 360-degree feedback report (in which employees evaluate their superiors) concluded that Dell was impersonal and emotionally detached, while Rollins was considered autocratic and antagonistic. So in front of the top management team, Dell and Rollins candidly told everyone about their 360 results. Dell acknowledged that he was intensely shy and would work toward creating a more open and collegial workplace. "I've got some things to work on," he admitted. Dell taped this self-admission and later showed it to several thousand Dell managers across the country. "It didn't feel good," recalls Rollins about the event, "but what we realized was, if we wanted the organization to improve and to admit failure, we'd have to set the example. And we did."[42]

// ALIGNING ARTIFACTS

Artifacts represent more than just the visible indicators of a company's culture. They are also mechanisms that keep the culture in place. Thus by altering these artifacts—or creating new ones—managers can potentially adjust organizational culture. Stories and legends represent a type of artifact that can help to reshape an organization's culture. Leaders can play an active role in creating memorable events that later become stories. For instance, earlier we described the executive meeting in which Michael Dell and Kevin Rollins acknowledged their limitations and goal to change their style. This event is more than symbolic evidence of the leaders' dedication to a new culture; it has become a story that Dell employees around the world know about and retell to newcomers when they join the company. Leaders also play an important storytelling role by seeking out employee experiences compatible with the desired culture and telling others about those incidents.

Rituals and ceremonies can also be altered to fit the new cultural mandate. If managers want to instill more open communication, they might keep their office doors open or move completely out of their offices into open space. To discourage bureaucracy, some executives have hosted ceremonies in which all employees watch as volumes of policy manuals are burned. Some firms have also introduced unusual (and perhaps questionable) ceremonies to engender a more performance-oriented culture. For instance, Brown & Brown Inc., one of the largest independent insurance companies in the United States, held an event at one of its annual sales meetings that would shake the nerves of any poor performer. Managers of the worst-performing divisions were led to a podium by employees dressed as medieval executioners while a funeral dirge played over loudspeakers. These managers had to explain to an audience of 1,000 salespeople why they failed to meet their annual goals. "It does sound a bit harsh, but that's the culture," says Brown & Brown's chief executive. "This is not a warm and fuzzy world."[43]

Earlier we observed that buildings and décor are artifacts of an organization's culture. At the same time some leaders are moving into offices that reflect what they want the company's culture to become. National Australia Bank's (NAB) National@Docklands, a low-rise campuslike building in Melbourne's docklands area, is an example. The building's open design and colorful décor symbolize a more open, egalitarian, and creative culture, compared to the closed hierarchical culture that NAB executives are trying to shed. The docklands building project was initiated when executives realized that MLC, a financial services firm that NAB had acquired a few years earlier, was able to change its culture after moving into its funky headquarters in Sydney. "There's no doubt that MLC has moved its culture over the last few years to a more open and transparent style which is a good example for the rest of the group to follow," admits an NAB executive.[44]

■ Brown & Brown's performance culture.

■ National Australia Bank's more open culture.

// INTRODUCING CULTURALLY CONSISTENT REWARDS

Reward systems are artifacts that often have a powerful influence on steering an organization's culture—so much so that we describe them here as a separate culture change strategy.[45] One of Robert Nardelli's first steps to change Home Depot's culture was to introduce precise measures of corporate performance and drill managers with weekly performance objectives around those metrics. The previous hodgepodge of subjective performance reviews was replaced with one centralized fact-based system to evaluate store managers and weed out poor performers. Nardelli instituted quarterly business review meetings in which objective measures of revenue, margins, inventory turns, cash flow, and other measures were analyzed across stores and regions. A two-hour weekly conference call became a ritual in which Home Depot's top executives were held accountable for the previous week's goals. All of these actions reinforced a more disciplined (and centralized), performance-oriented culture, which eventually replaced Home Depot's freewheeling, entrepreneurial culture.[46]

Kevin Rollins and Michael Dell applied a similar strategy to adjust Dell's culture. But whereas Nardelli used performance-based rewards to reinforce a performance-oriented culture, Dell introduced a system that rewarded managers for creating a better place to work. Specifically, while half of the bonus Dell managers receive is still based on reaching or beating sales targets, the other half is now determined from employee ratings of their bosses in quarterly surveys. "We now pay our managers against how their employees vote on them in terms of their management capability," explains Rollins. The first few years proved painful because some managers with over-the-top sales performance had a large part of their bonus pulled because of low scores on the employee ratings.[47]

■ Using rewards to shift Home Depot's culture.

// SELECTING AND SOCIALIZING EMPLOYEES

■ Bristol-Myers's cultural misfit.

People at Bristol-Myers noticed that executives hired from the outside weren't as successful as those promoted from within. Within a year many quit or were fired. Managers looked closely at the problem and arrived at the following conclusion: "What came through was that those who left were uncomfortable in our culture or violated some core area of our value system," says a Bristol-Myers executive. From this discovery, Bristol-Myers assessed its culture—it's team-oriented, consistent with the firm's research and development roots. Now applicants are carefully screened to ensure they have compatible values.[48]

Bristol-Myers and a flock of other organizations strengthen and sometimes reshape their corporate cultures by hiring people with values and assumptions similar to those cultures. They realize that a good fit of personal and organizational values makes it easier for employees to adopt the corporate culture. A good person–organization fit also improves job satisfaction and organizational loyalty because new hires with values compatible to the corporate culture adjust more quickly to the organization.[49] For instance, Robert Nardelli's transformation of Home Depot's culture was aided by hiring many former GE managers who already embraced a performance-oriented culture. He also encouraged employment of former military personnel, partly because they tend to support a more structured and disciplined approach to doing business.

Job applicants also pay attention to corporate culture during the hiring process. They realize that as employees, they must feel comfortable with the company's values, not just the job duties and hours of work. Thus job applicants tend to look at corporate culture artifacts when deciding whether to join a particular organization. By diagnosing the company's dominant culture, they are more likely to determine whether its values are compatible with their own.

organizational socialization

The process by which individuals learn the values, expected behaviors, and social knowledge necessary to assume their roles in an organization.

Along with selecting people with compatible values, companies maintain strong cultures through the process of **organizational socialization**: the process by which individuals learn the values, expected behaviors, and social knowledge necessary to assume their roles in the organization.[50] If the company's dominant values are communicated, job candidates and new hires are more likely to internalize these values quickly and deeply.

Selection and socialization were issues that Dell had to address when changing its culture. Management realized that the company's skyrocketing stock price during the late 1990s was attracting people who mainly valued financial gain. "The dark side of the [dot-com boom] was the possibility that we had attracted a lot of people who thought they would get rich. And if they all of a sudden thought they wouldn't get rich, then they'd wonder what they're doing here," says Michael Dell.[51] Today the company carefully interviews and tests job applicants to see how their values align with the company's culture.

Dell also tells job applicants about its culture before they receive job offers. For example, applicants at Dell's new computer assembly plant in Winston-Salem, North Carolina, are invited to a special information session where they learn about the company and the jobs offered. "We will discuss the Soul of Dell, give them a realistic job preview, and give them the opportunity to complete a job application," explains Dell's human resource manager for the plant. "It will be a chance to determine the mutual interest between the candidates and Dell."[52]

■ // Managing Organizational Culture during Mergers

Along with changing and strengthening an organization's culture, managers need to keep a watchful eye on culture throughout the process of mergers and acquisitions. The corporate world is littered with mergers that failed or had a difficult gestation because of clashing organizational cultures. Various studies report that between 60 and 75 percent of all mergers fail to return a positive investment (Figure 10.5). Often corporate leaders are so focused on the financial or marketing logistics of a merger that they forget to audit their respective corporate cultures.[53]

■ Culture clash of AOL and Time Warner.

The marriage of AOL Time Warner is one of the most spectacular recent examples. In theory, the world's largest merger offered huge opportunities for converging AOL's dominance in Internet services with Time Warner's deep knowledge and assets in traditional media.

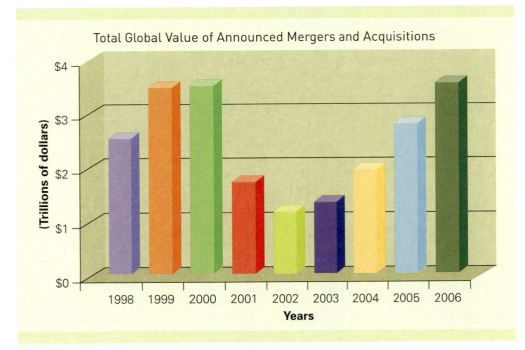

FIGURE 10.5

Merger Mania

Source: Thomson Financial, *Mergers & Acquisitions Review* (quarterly newsletter), various quarters.

Instead the two corporate cultures mixed as well as oil and water. AOL's culture valued youthful, high-flying, quick deal making. People were rewarded with stock options. Time Warner, on the other hand, had a buttoned-down, hierarchical, systematic culture. Executives were older, and the reward was a decent retirement package (affectionately known as the "golden rubber band" because people who left invariably returned later in their careers for the retirement benefits).[54]

Organizational leaders can minimize such cultural collisions and fulfill their duty of due diligence by conducting a bicultural audit.[55] A **bicultural audit** diagnoses cultural relations between companies and determines the extent to which cultural clashes will likely occur. The bicultural audit process begins by identifying cultural differences between the merging companies. Next the bicultural audit data are analyzed to determine which differences between the two firms will result in conflict and which cultural values provide common ground on which to build a cultural foundation in the merged organization. The final stage involves identifying strategies and preparing action plans to bridge the two organizations' cultures.

bicultural audit
The practice of diagnosing cultural relations between companies and determining the extent to which cultural clashes will likely occur.

// STRATEGIES TO MERGE DIFFERENT ORGANIZATIONAL CULTURES

In some cases a bicultural audit results in a decision to end merger talks because the two cultures are too different to merge effectively. However, even with substantially different cultures, two companies may form a workable union if they apply the appropriate merger strategy. The four main strategies for merging different corporate cultures are assimilation, deculturation, integration, and separation (see Figure 10.6).[56]

Assimilation Assimilation occurs when employees at the acquired company willingly embrace the cultural values of the acquiring organization. Corporate cultural clashes are less likely to occur with this strategy because the acquired company often has a weak, dysfunctional culture, whereas the acquiring company's culture is strong and aligned with the external environment. Research in Motion (RIM), the company that makes Blackberry wireless devices, applies the assimilation strategy by deliberately acquiring only small start-up firms. "Small companies...don't have cultural issues," says RIM co-CEO Jim Balsillie, adding that they are typically absorbed into RIM's culture with little fuss or attention.[57]

Merger Strategy	Description	Works Best When:
Assimilation	Acquired company embraces acquiring firm's culture.	Acquired firm has a weak culture.
Deculturation	Acquiring firm imposes its culture on unwilling acquired firm.	Rarely works—may be necessary only when acquired firm's culture doesn't work but employees don't realize it.
Integration	Combining two or more cultures into a new composite culture.	Existing cultures can be improved.
Separation	Merging companies remain distinct entities with minimal exchange of culture or organizational practices.	Firms operate successfully in different businesses requiring different cultures.

FIGURE 10.6   Strategies for Merging Different Organizational Cultures

Source: Based on ideas in A.R. Malekazedeh and A. Nahavandi, "Making Mergers Work by Managing Cultures," *Journal of Business Strategy,* May–June 1990, pp. 55–57; K.W. Smith, "A Brand-New Culture for the Merged Firm," *Mergers and Acquisitions* 35 (June 2000), pp. 45–50.

Deculturation Assimilation is rare. Employees usually resist organizational change, particularly when they are asked to throw away organizational values that were similar to their personal values. Instead acquiring companies often apply a *deculturation* strategy by imposing their culture and business practices on the acquired organization. They strip away artifacts and reward systems that support the old culture. People who cannot adopt the acquiring company's culture are often terminated. Deculturation may be necessary when the acquired firm's culture doesn't work but employees aren't convinced of this. However, this strategy is difficult to apply effectively because the acquired firm's employees resist the cultural intrusions from the buying firm, thereby delaying or undermining the merger process.

Integration A third strategy is to combine the cultures into a new composite culture that preserves the best features of the previous cultures. Integration is slow and potentially risky because many forces preserve the existing cultures. Still, this strategy should be considered when acquired companies have relatively weak cultures or when their cultures include several overlapping values. Integration also works best when people realize that their existing cultures are ineffective and are therefore motivated to adopt a new set of dominant values.

Lockheed Martin provides a good example of the cultural integration strategy. The aerospace giant was created in the mid-1990s from the merger of 16 companies. Some of these firms had previously been accused of unethical conduct in government procurement contracts. When these diverse cultures were integrated, senior executives wanted to be sure that the emerging culture emphasized ethical conduct. To accomplish this, they adopted six core values that represented both the company's culture and its ethical standards: honesty, integrity, respect, trust, responsibility, and citizenship.[58]

Separation A separation strategy occurs when the merging companies agree to remain distinct entities with minimal exchange of culture or organizational practices. This strategy is most appropriate when merging companies are in unrelated industries or operate in different countries: The most appropriate cultural values tend to differ by industry and national culture. However, this separation strategy doesn't usually last long because executives in the acquiring firm have difficulty keeping their hands off the acquired firm. According to one survey, only 15 percent of acquiring firms leave the acquired organization as a stand-alone unit.[59]

One recent situation in which the separation strategy was applied is Cisco Systems' acquisition of Linksys. Cisco Systems, the California-based Internet equipment maker, has acquired approximately 90 companies over the past two decades, most of them small, privately held start-up firms with technical expertise in high-growth niches compatible with Cisco's own products. For most acquisitions Cisco assimilates the smaller firms into its own culture. Linksys, the home wireless network company, was an exception. Linksys employs 400 people and was just a few years younger than Cisco. Furthermore, unlike Cisco, Linksys had developed a low-cost business with mass-market retail channels. To avoid disrupting its success, Linksys was kept separate from Cisco. Cisco executives were so concerned that Linksys should retain its existing culture that a "filtering team" was formed to prevent Cisco's culture or its leaders from taking over the smaller enterprise. So far the separation strategy has worked. Linksys continues to thrive in a competitive low-cost market even though it is wholly owned by Cisco, which focuses on the high-end network business.[60]

Marriage of Cultural Separation Cisco Systems has acquired dozens of smaller companies and typically assimilates them into Cisco's culture. However, Cisco applied a separation strategy when it acquired Linksys, because its cost efficiency–oriented culture was more compatible with the highly competitive home wireless network market.

© AP Photo/Paul Sakuma

■ Cultural separation of Cisco Systems and Linksys.

IN CONCLUSION   WHY DOES IT MATTER?

Why does organizational culture matter to managers? Because management is about getting things done through others, and culture is a form of control that guides employee behavior in the accomplishment of organizational tasks. To perform their jobs well, managers need to understand what cultural values and assumptions dominate their company, and adjust that culture if it is not aligned with strategy and environment. They can do the former by acting as anthropologists—observing artifacts that signify the culture in subtle ways, such as how employees greet each other, how the building directs social interaction, what milestones or events get celebrated, where executives are located, what people say about the company's history, and so on.

Reading the organization's culture isn't easy, particularly for managers who have worked for the organization for many years. But even more challenging is the task of changing that culture. Cultural values and assumptions are so deeply embedded that employees don't think about or question them. The process of changing organizational culture, on the other hand, not only requires staff members to consciously understand and question the existing culture but also requires them to abandon those values and assumptions in favor of others. Too often managers discover that the embedded culture is stronger than their capacity to bring about the required changes.

Managers also need to pay attention to organizational culture in mergers and acquisitions because cultural clashes are one of the most common reasons why these corporate marriages fail. As with changing their own culture, managers must understand the content of the two cultures, determine their compatibility, identify the extent to which one or both are compatible with the merged company's strategy and environment, and then apply the most appropriate cultural merger strategy. Overall, organizational culture may lurk under the radar screen, but it is a powerful force in organizations. As we discovered in Chapter 9, culture is a significant control system in organizational settings.

MANAGEMENT CHALLENGES

1. Identify a well-known company with a strong organizational culture. Does the content of that culture work effectively for the organization? What changes in the external environment might occur that would make the company's current culture a poor fit?

2. Some people suggest that the most effective organizations have the strongest cultures. What do we mean by the "strength" of organizational culture, and what possible problems are there with a strong organizational culture?

3. In each of the following categories, identify at least two artifacts you have observed in an organization where you currently work or have been employed in the past: (a) organizational stories and legends, (b) rituals and ceremonies, (c) language, (d) physical structures and décor.

4. Acme Inc. is planning to acquire Beta Inc., which operates in a different industry. Acme's culture is entrepreneurial and fast-paced, whereas Beta employees value slow, deliberate decision making by consensus. Which merger strategy would you recommend to minimize culture shock when Acme acquires Beta? Explain your answer.

5. Suppose you are asked by senior officers of a city government to identify ways to reinforce a new culture of teamwork and collaboration. The senior executive group clearly supports these values, but it wants everyone in the organization to embrace them. Identify four types of activities that would strengthen these cultural values.

MANAGEMENT PORTFOLIO

FOR THE ORGANIZATION YOU HAVE CHOSEN TO FOLLOW:

1. Scan through the company's Web site to find any explicit statements made about the company's culture. Does the company explain how long it has held these cultural values or how they were formed? To whom are these "espoused" values directed on the Web site? Prospective employees? Customers?

2. Look through a recent company annual report and search for recent news stories about the company (from either Internet searches or full-text newspaper sources available through your college library's online portal). Are these stories generally consistent with or contrary to the company's "espoused" culture (what it says it values)?

CLOSING CASE　　SCHWAB ACQUIRES U.S. TRUST

During the peak of the dot-com boom, Charles Schwab & Co. CEO David Pottruck was convinced that as investors became wealthier they would migrate from the San Francisco–based discount broker to full-service firms that offered more personalized service. So Schwab paid top dollar to acquire U.S. Trust, a high-brow New York–based private bank that served only clients with at least $10 million to invest.

Schwab customers who grew wealthy would be shunted over to U.S. Trust for more personalized service.

While negotiating the takeover, U.S. Trust executives expressed concern about possible differences in the corporate cultures of the two firms. Schwab's culture values rapid change, cost-cutting frugality, process efficiency, and egalitarianism. Schwab employees see themselves as nimble nonconformists who empowered millions of people through low-cost Internet-based stock trading. In contrast, U.S. Trust was an exclusive club that was slow to adopt technology and preferred to admit new clients through referrals from existing clients. Clients were pampered by "wealth advisers" who earned huge bonuses and worked in an environment that reeked of luxury.

In light of the cultural differences, Schwab agreed to leave U.S. Trust as a separate entity. This separation strategy didn't last long. Within a year Schwab cut U.S. Trust's lucrative bonuses and tied annual rewards to Schwab's financial performance. U.S. Trust executives were pushed to cut costs and set more aggressive goals. Schwab even tried to acculturate several hundred U.S. Trust employees with a board game that used a giant mat showing hills, streams, and a mountain with founder Charles Schwab's face carved into the side. U.S. Trust staff complained that the game was demeaning—particularly wearing smocks over their high-priced suits as they played the role of investors.

In meetings immediately following the acquisition, U.S. Trust executives winced when their counterparts at Schwab frequently used the term *customers*. They reminded Schwab's staff that U.S. Trust has *clients*. This reflects the long-term, deep relationships that U.S. Trust staff members have with their clients, compared with the more impersonal connection between Schwab's staff and their customers. U.S. Trust advisers also resisted Schwab's referrals of newly minted millionaires in blue jeans. "We were flabbergasted," said one Schwab board member about the cultural clash. "Some of the U.S. Trust officers simply refused to accept our referrals."

When the depth of cultural intransigence became apparent, Pottruck replaced U.S. Trust's CEO with Schwab executive Alan Weber. Weber later insisted that "there is no culture clash" because Schwab "never tried to change the nature of the organization." Meanwhile, sources say that more than 300 U.S. Trust wealth advisers have defected to competitors since the acquisition, taking many valued clients with them. Pottruck's strategy also backfired; apparently most of Schwab's customers still wanted cheap trades as they became wealthier.

Three years after acquiring U.S. Trust, Pottruck lost his job as Schwab CEO, in part because of the acquisition's failure. Observers say the U.S. Trust acquisition is now worth less than half of its original purchase price. "Here are two first-class companies, but structural and cultural problems keep the combination from the kind of success they expected," explains a financial adviser in Florida.[61]

CASE DISCUSSION QUESTIONS

1. Diagnose the culture of the two companies. What values did each company seem to prize? Identify artifacts reflecting those values. Explain why those respective cultures did (or did not) suit the environments in which the two firms operated.

2. What merger strategy did Charles Schwab & Co. apply when acquiring U.S. Trust? Was this the best strategy under the circumstances? Why or why not? If not, justify another merger strategy for this situation.

ENDNOTES

1. "Ringing in the Changes at Dell," *New Zealand Management,* October 2004, p. 11; "On the Record: Kevin Rollins," *San Francisco Chronicle,* July 18, 2004, p. J1; L.M. Fisher, "How Dell Got Soul," strategy+business 2004, pp. 1–14; A. Schatz, "Dell Reboots Morale of Its Workers," *Austin American-Statesman,* February 16, 2004, p. E1.

2. A. Williams, P. Dobson, and M. Walters, *Changing Culture: New Organizational Approaches* (London: Institute of Personnel Management, 1989); E.H. Schein, "What Is Culture?" in *Reframing Organizational Culture,* ed. P.J. Frost et al. (Newbury Park, CA: Sage, 1991), pp. 243–53.

3. B.M. Meglino and E.C. Ravlin, "Individual Values in Organizations: Concepts, Controversies, and Research," *Journal of Management* 24, no. 3 (1998), pp. 351–89; B.R. Agle and C.B. Caldwell, "Understanding Research on Values in Business," *Business and Society* 38, no. 3 (September 1999), pp. 326–87; S. Hitlin and J.A. Pilavin, "Values: Reviving a Dormant Concept," *Annual Review of Sociology* 30 (2004), pp. 359–93.

4. N.M. Ashkanasy, "The Case for Culture," in *Debating Organization,* ed. R. Westwood and S. Clegg (Malden, MA: Blackwell, 2003), pp. 300–10.

5. B. Kabanoff and J. Daly, "Espoused Values in Organisations," *Australian Journal of Management* 27, special issue (2002), pp. 89–104; P. Babcock, "Is Your Company Two-Faced?" *HRMagazine,* January 2004, pp. 42–47.

6. Edgar Schein's original model suggested that organizational culture consists of espoused values. But others have subsequently pointed out that enacted values are a more logical part of culture because enacted values are consistent with other elements of the model—namely shared assumptions on one side and

artifacts on the other. See D. Denison, "Organizational Culture: Can It Be a Key Lever for Driving Organizational Change?" in *International Handbook of Culture and Climate,* ed. C. Cooper, S. Cartwright, and P.C. Earley (New York: John Wiley & Sons, 2000).

7. Fisher, "How Dell Got Soul," p. 6.

8. T. Parker-Pope, "New CEO Preaches Rebellion for P&G's 'Cult,'" *The Wall Street Journal,* December 11, 1998; K. Brooker and J. Schlosser, "The Un-CEO," *Fortune,* September 16, 2002, pp. 88–93.

9. M. Fan, "Cary, N.C., Software Firm Posts Steady Growth without IPO," *San Jose Mercury News,* July 29, 2001; B. Darrow, "James Goodnight, Founder and CEO, SAS Institute," *Computer Reseller News,* December 12, 2005, p. 23.

10. A. D'Innocenzio, "Wal-Mart's Town Becomes New Address for Corporate America," *Associated Press,* September 19, 2003; J. Useem, "One Nation under Wal-Mart," *Fortune,* March 3, 2003, pp. 65–78.

11. J.J. van Muijen, "Organizational Culture," in *A Handbook of Work and Organizational Psychology: Organizational Psychology,* 2nd ed., ed. P.J.D. Drenth, H. Thierry, and C.J. de Wolff (East Sussex, UK: Psychology Press, 1998), pp. 113–32.

12. J.S. Ott, *The Organizational Culture Perspective* (Pacific Grove, CA: Brooks/Cole, 1989), pp. 45–47; S. Sackmann, "Culture and Subcultures: An Analysis of Organizational Knowledge," *Administrative Science Quarterly* 37 (1992), pp. 140–61.

13. A. Sinclair, "Approaches to Organizational Culture and Ethics," *Journal of Business Ethics* 12 (1993); A. Boisnier and J. Chatman, "The Role of Subcultures in Agile Organizations," in *Leading and Managing People in Dynamic Organizations,*

ed. R. Petersen and E. Mannix (Mahwah, NJ: Lawrence Erlbaum Associates, 2003), pp. 87–112.

14. Ott, *The Organizational Culture Perspective,* Chapter 2; J.S. Pederson and J.S. Sorensen, *Organizational Cultures in Theory and Practice* (Aldershot, England: Gower, 1989), pp. 27–29; M.O. Jones, *Studying Organizational Symbolism: What, How, Why?* (Thousand Oaks, CA: Sage, 1996).

15. M. Doehrman, "Anthropologists-Deep in the Corporate Bush," *Daily Record* (Kansas City, MO), July 19, 2005, p. 1.

16. Fisher, "How Dell Got Soul," pp. 9–10.

17. E.H. Schein, "Organizational Culture," *American Psychologist,* February 1990, pp. 109-19; A. Furnham and B. Gunter, "Corporate Culture: Definition, Diagnosis, and Change," *International Review of Industrial and Organizational Psychology* 8 (1993), pp. 233-61; E.H. Schein, *The Corporate Culture Survival Guide* (San Francisco: Jossey-Bass, 1999), Chapter 4; J. Martin, *Organizational Culture: Mapping the Terrain* (Thousand Oaks, CA: Sage, 2002), Chapter 7.

18. K. Frieberg and J. Frieberg, *Nuts!* (New York: Bantam Doubleday Dell, 1998).

19. J.Z. DeLorean, *On a Clear Day You Can See General Motors* (Grosse Pointe, MI: Wright Enterprises, 1979).

20. A.L. Wilkins, "Organizational Stories as Symbols Which Control the Organization," in *Organizational Symbolism,* ed. L.R. Pondy et al. (Greenwich, CT: JAI Press, 1984), pp. 81–92; R. Zemke, "Storytelling: Back to a Basic," *Training* 27 (March 1990), pp. 44–50; J.C. Meyer, "Tell Me a Story: Eliciting Organizational Values from Narratives," *Communication Quarterly* 43 (1995), pp. 210–24; W. Swap et al., "Using Mentoring and Storytelling to Transfer Knowledge in the Workplace," *Journal of Management Information Systems* 18 (Summer 2001), pp. 95–114.

21. "The Ultimate Chairman," *Business Times Singapore,* September 3, 2005.

22. D. Roth, "My Job at The Container Store," *Fortune,* January 10, 2000, pp. 74–78.

23. R.E. Quinn and N.T. Snyder, "Advance Change Theory: Culture Change at Whirlpool Corporation," in *The Leader's Change Handbook,* ed. J.A. Conger, G.M. Spreitzer, and E.E. Lawler III (San Francisco: Jossey-Bass, 1999), pp. 162–93.

24. P. Roberts, "The Empire Strikes Back," *Fast Company,* no. 22 (February–March 1999), pp. 122–31. Some details are also found at www.oakley.com and america-hurrah.com/Oakley/Entry.htm.

25. B. Herskovits, "Chandler and Chicco Thrive on Their Differences," *PR Week* (U.S.), July 11, 2005, p. 11.

26. T.E. Deal and A.A. Kennedy, *Corporate Cultures* (Reading, MA: Addison-Wesley, 1982); J.B. Barney, "Organizational Culture: Can It Be a Source of Sustained Competitive Advantage?" *Academy of Management Review* 11 (1986), pp. 656–65; C. Siehl and J. Martin, "Organizational Culture: A Key to Financial Performance?" in *Organizational Climate and Culture,* ed. B. Schneider (San Francisco: Jossey-Bass, 1990), pp. 241-81; C.P.M. Wilderom, U. Glunk, and R. Maslowski, "Organizational Culture as a Predictor of Organizational Performance," in *Handbook of Organizational Culture and Climate,* ed. N.M. Ashkanasy, C.P.M. Wilderom, and M.F. Peterson (Thousand Oaks, CA: Sage, 2000), pp. 193–210; A. Carmeli and A. Tishler, "The Relationships between Intangible Organizational Elements and Organizational Performance," *Strategic Management Journal* 25 (2004), pp. 1257–78.

27. C.A. O'Reilly and J.A. Chatman, "Culture as Social Control: Corporations, Cults, and Commitment," *Research in Organizational Behavior* 18 (1996), pp. 157-200; J.C. Helms Mills and A.J. Mills, "Rules, Sensemaking, Formative Contexts, and Discourse in the Gendering of Organizational Culture," in *International Handbook of Organizational Climate and Culture,* ed. N. Ashkanasy, C. Wilderom, and M. Peterson (Thousand Oaks, CA: Sage, 2000), pp. 55–70; J.A. Chatman and S.E. Cha, "Leading by Leveraging Culture," *California Management Review* 45 (Summer 2003), pp. 20–34.

28. M. Alvesson, *Understanding Organizational Culture* (London: Sage, 2002), Chapter 2.

29. M.R. Louis, "Surprise and Sensemaking: What Newcomers Experience in Entering Unfamiliar Organizational Settings," *Administrative Science Quarterly* 25 (1980), pp. 226–51; S.G. Harris, "Organizational Culture and Individual Sensemaking: A Schema-Based Perspective," *Organization Science* 5 (1994), pp. 309–21.

30. D.R. Denison, *Corporate Culture and Organizational Effectiveness* (New York: Wiley, 1990); G.G. Gordon and N. DiTomasco, "Predicting Corporate Performance from Organizational Culture," *Journal of Management Studies* 29 (1992), pp. 783–98; J.P. Kotter and J.L. Heskett, *Corporate Culture and Performance* (New York: Free Press, 1992).

31. D. Howell, "Nardelli Nears Five-Year Mark with Riveting Record," *DSN Retailing Today,* May 9, 2005, pp. 1, 38; R. Charan, "Home Depot's Blueprint for Culture Change," *Harvard Business Review,* April 2006, pp. 61-70; R. DeGross, "Five Years of Change: Home Depot's Results Mixed under Nardelli," *Atlanta Journal-Constitution,* January 1, 2006, p. F1.

32. L. Tischler, "Can Kevin Rollins Find the Soul of Dell?" *Fast Company,* November 2002, pp. 110–14; K. James, "Finding Dell's Soul," *Business Times Singapore,* October 9, 2004; "Soul of Dell" (Dell Inc., 2006), www.dell.com (accessed January 25, 2006).

33. A. Holeck, "Griffith, Ind., Native Takes Over as Steel Plant Manager," *The Times* (Munster, IN), May 24, 2003.

34. Kotter and Heskett, *Corporate Culture and Performance*; D.R. Denison and A.K. Mishra, "Toward a Theory of Organizational Culture and Effectiveness," *Organization Science* 6, no. 2 (March–April 1995), pp. 204–23; J.P. Kotter, "Cultures and Coalitions," *Executive Excellence* 15 (March 1998), pp. 14–15.

35. The features of adaptive cultures are described in W.F. Joyce, *Megachange: How Today's Leading Companies Have Transformed Their Workforces* (New York: Free Press, 1999).

36. A. Maitland and K. Rollins, "The Two-in-a-Box World of Dell," *Financial Times* (London), March 20, 2003, p. 14.

37. "Japanese Officials Order Citibank to Halt Some Operations," *Dow Jones Business News,* September 17, 2004; "Citigroup CEO Prince Holds Press Conference in Japan," *Business Wire* (Tokyo), October 25, 2004; A. Morse, "Citigroup Extends Apology to Japan," *The Wall Street Journal,* October 26, 2004, p. A3; M. Pacelle, M. Fackler, and A. Morse, "Mission Control," *The Wall Street Journal,* December 22, 2004, p. A1.

38. B. Pimentel, "Losing Their Way?" *San Francisco Chronicle,* September 6, 2001; P. Burrows, *Backfire: Carly Fiorina's High-Stakes Battle for the Soul of Hewlett-Packard* (New York: John Wiley & Sons, 2003); C. Swett, "HP Seems to Have Digested Compaq," *Sacramento Bee* (California), May 13, 2003, p. D1; P. Burrows, "The HP Way out of a Morass," *BusinessWeek Online,* February 14, 2005; D. Gillmor, "Getting Back the HP Way," *Computerworld,* March 7, 2005, pp. 24–25.

39. "Emerging Market Corporates," *The Banker,* July 1, 2003; G. Chellam, "Haier Story a Smash-Hit," *New Zealand Herald,* September 20, 2003; D.J. Lynch, "CEO Pushes China's Haier as Global Brand," *USA Today,* January 3, 2003, p. 1B.

40. "Big Blue Is Finally Living Up to Its Name," *Charleston Daily Mail,* February 9, 1995, p. 5H.

41. E.H. Schein, "The Role of the Founder in Creating Organizational Culture," *Organizational Dynamics* 12, no. 1 (Summer 1983), pp. 13–28.

42. A. Park and P. Burrows, "What You Don't Know about Dell," *BusinessWeek,* November 3, 2003, p. 76; James, "Finding Dell's Soul," p. 6.

43. M. Cooke, "Humiliation as Motivator?" *Meetings & Conventions* 36 (July 2001), p. 26; G. Groeller, "Eat or Be Eaten Ethic Boosts Bottom Line," *Orlando Sentinel,* April 30, 2001, p. 16.

44. J. Hewett, "Office Politics," *Australian Financial Review,* September 27, 2003, p. 29.

45. J. Kerr and J.W. Slocum Jr., "Managing Corporate Culture through Reward Systems," *Academy of Management Executive* 1 (May 1987), pp. 99–107; K.R. Thompson and F. Luthans, "Organizational Culture: A Behavioral Perspective," in *Organizational Climate and Culture,* ed. B. Schneider (San Francisco: Jossey-Bass, 1990), pp. 319–44.

46. Howell, "Nardelli Nears Five-Year Mark with Riveting Record"; Charan, "Home Depot's Blueprint for Culture Change"; DeGross, "Five Years of Change: Home Depot's Results Mixed under Nardelli"; B. Grow, D. Brady, and M. Arndt, "Renovating Home Depot," *BusinessWeek,* March 6, 2006, pp. 50–57.

47. "On the Record: Kevin Rollins"; Fisher, "How Dell Got Soul."

48. C. Daniels, "Does This Man Need a Shrink?" *Fortune,* February 5, 2001, pp. 205–8.

49. Chatman and Cha, "Leading by Leveraging Culture"; A.E.M. Van Vianen, "Person-Organization Fit: The Match between Newcomers' and Recruiters' Preferences for Organizational Cultures," *Personnel Psychology* 53 (Spring 2000), pp. 113-49; C.A. O'Reilly III, J. Chatman, and D.F. Caldwell, "People and Organizational Culture: A Profile Comparison Approach to Assessing Person-Organization Fit," *Academy of Management Journal* 34 (1991), pp. 487–516.

50. J. Van Maanen, "Breaking In: Socialization to Work," in *Handbook of Work, Organization, and Society,* ed. R. Dubin (Chicago: Rand McNally, 1976).

51. Fisher, "How Dell Got Soul," p. 6.

52. R. Craver, "Dell Thinning Out List of Job Candidates," *Winston-Salem Journal,* April 23, 2005.

53. Schein, *The Corporate Culture Survival Guide,* Chapter 8; M.L. Marks, "Mixed Signals," *Across the Board,* May 2000, pp. 21-26; J.P. Daly, R.W. Pouder, and B. Kabanoff, "The Effects of Initial Differences in Firms' Espoused Values on Their Postmerger Performance," *Journal of Applied Behavioral Science* 40, no. 3 (September 2004, pp. 323–43). The merger failure rates are cited in G. Costa, "More to Mergers Than Just Doing the Deal," *Sydney Morning Herald,* January 8, 2004; J. Kirby, "The Trouble with Mergers," *Canadian Business,* February 16–29, 2004, p. 64.

54. A. Klein, "A Merger Taken AO-Ill," *Washington Post,* October 21, 2002, p. E1; A. Klein, *Stealing Time: Steve Case, Jerry Levin, and the Collapse of AOL Time Warner* (New York: Simon & Shuster, 2003).

55. C.A. Schorg, C.A. Raiborn, and M.F. Massoud, "Using a 'Cultural Audit' to Pick M&A Winners," *Journal of Corporate Accounting & Finance,* May–June 2004, pp. 47-55.

56. A.R. Malekazedeh and A. Nahavandi, "Making Mergers Work by Managing Cultures," *Journal of Business Strategy,* May–June 1990, pp. 55–57; K.W. Smith, "A Brand-New Culture for the Merged Firm," *Mergers and Acquisitions* 35 (June 2000), pp. 45–50.

57. T. Hamilton, "RIM on a Roll," *Toronto Star,* February 22, 2004, p. C01.

58. J. Davidson, "The Business of Ethics," *Working Woman,* February 1998, pp. 68–71.

59. Hewitt Associates, "Mergers and Acquisitions May Be Driven by Business Strategy—but Often Stumble over People and Culture Issues," PR Newswire news release (Lincolnshire, IL: August 3, 1998).

60. I. Mount, "Be Fast Be Frugal Be Right," *Inc* 26, no. 1 (January 2004), pp. 64–70; S. Anthony and C. Christensen, "Mind over Merger," *Optimize,* February 2005, pp. 22–27.

61. F. Vogelstein and E. Florian, "Can Schwab Get Its Mojo Back?" *Fortune,* September 17, 2001, p. 93; B. Morris, "When Bad Things Happen to Good Companies," *Fortune,* December 8, 2003, 78; S. Craig and K. Brown, "Schwab Ousts Pottruck as CEO," *The Wall Street Journal,* July 21, 2004, p. A1; R. Frank, "U.S. Trust Feels Effects of Switch," *The Wall Street Journal,* July 21, 2004, p. A8; R. Frank and S. Craig, "White-Shoe Shuffle," *The Wall Street Journal,* September 15, 2004, p. A1; C. Harrington, "Made in Heaven? Watching the Watchovia-Tanager Union," *Accounting Today,* December 20, 2004, p. 18; J. Kador, "Cultures in Conflict," *Registered Rep.,* October 2004, p. 43.

11

DEVELOPING
HIGH-PERFORMANCE TEAMS

When John MacKay cofounded Whole Foods Market in 1980, he adopted one of the central recommendations from the then-popular Japanese management books: Successful companies rely on teams more than individuals. Although the Austin, Texas, food retailer has grown from a single supermarket employing 19 people to 181 stores employing 40,000 people in three countries, Whole Foods remains true to its team-based structure.

Every Whole Foods store is divided into about 10 teams, such as the prepared foods team, the cashier/front end team, and the seafood team. Teams are "self-directed" because team members make decisions about their work units with minimal interference from management. Each team is responsible for managing inventory, labor productivity, and gross margins. Team members make many product placement decisions—a sharp contrast to the centralized purchasing decisions in most grocery chains.

Whole Foods teams also decide whether new hires get to remain as permanent team members. After a recruit is temporarily employed for 30 to 45 days, team members vote on whether the individual should become a permanent member; at least two-thirds must vote in favor for the recruit to join the team permanently. Team members take these hiring decisions seriously because their monthly bonuses are based on team performance. Every four weeks the company calculates each team's performance against goals and cost efficiencies. When the team finds ways to work more effectively, the unused budget is divided among them. This team bonus can add up to hundreds of extra dollars in each paycheck.[1]

Several factors explain why Whole Foods Market has become a retail success story and one of the best places to work in America, but the company's focus on teams is clearly one of those factors. Many other companies in various sectors of the economy have also adopted the team approach. Many banks and brokerage firms have shifted toward team-based work to better satisfy complex client needs. SANS Fibres, the South African manufacturer of synthetic fiber and polyester polymers, relies on the team approach to eliminate waste, maximize manufacturing flow, minimize inventories, and meet customer requirements. International Steel Group's (ISG) Cleveland plant rose from the ashes of bankruptcy and quickly became profitable in part because it formed teams in which employees share duties and help others across departments. "It wasn't the traditional one job for one person," says ISG executive John Mang III. "It was a team."[2]

teams

Groups of people who interact and influence each other, are mutually accountable for achieving common goals associated with organizational objectives, and perceive themselves as a social entity within an organization.

Teams are groups of people who interact and influence each other, are mutually accountable for achieving common goals associated with organizational objectives, and perceive themselves as a social entity within an organization.[3] This definition has a few important components worth repeating. First, all teams exist to fulfill some purpose, such as assembling a product, providing a service, designing a new manufacturing facility, or making an important decision. Second, team members are held together by their interdependence and need for collaboration to achieve common goals. All teams require some form of communication so members can coordinate and share common objectives. Third, team members influence each other, although some members are more influential than others regarding the team's goals and activities. Finally, a team exists when its members perceive themselves to be a team.

This chapter begins by examining the reasons why organizations rely on teams, why people join informal groups in organizational settings, and why teams aren't always necessary or beneficial in work processes. Several types of teams are described, including the increasing prevalence of self-directed teams and virtual teams. A large segment of this chapter examines a model of team effectiveness, which includes team and organizational environment, team design, and the team processes of development, norms, roles, cohesiveness, and trust. Next we identify the foundations of conflict in teams. We close this chapter by discussing ways to manage conflict.

■ // Why Rely on Teams?

■ Teamwork drives Burberry's success.

In the first chapter of this book we described how Rose Marie Bravo engineered the remarkable turnaround of Burberry, the London fashion house. When asked how this former head of Saks Fifth Avenue achieved Burberry's transformation, Bravo highlighted the fact that teams, not individuals, are at the core of successful companies, and that a manager's job is to leverage the power of those teams. "One of the things I think people overlook is the quality of the team," says Bravo. "It isn't one person, and it isn't two people. It is a whole group of people—a team that works cohesively toward a goal—that makes something happen or not."[4]

Bravo's observation that teams are important is reflected in a major survey of human resource professionals, which recently concluded, "Teams are now an integral part of workplace management." Figure 11.1 summarizes a few more interesting numbers, illustrating the importance of team work. Why are companies paying so much attention to teams? The answer to this question has a long history, dating back to research on British coal mining in the 1940s and the Japanese economic miracle of the 1970s.[5] These early studies and a huge volume of investigations since have revealed that under the right conditions, teams make better decisions, develop better products and services, and create a more engaged workforce compared with employees working alone.[6]

Under the right circumstances, teams are generally more successful than individuals working alone at identifying problems, developing alternatives, and choosing from those alternatives. Similarly, team members can quickly share information and coordinate tasks, whereas these processes are slower and prone to more errors in traditional departments led by supervisors. Teams typically provide superior customer service because they provide more breadth of knowledge and expertise to customers than individual "stars" can offer.

80   Average percentage of production workforce who work in self-directed teams in top-ranked North American manufacturing firms (averaged across the past five years of survey results)

11.5   Average number of members in self-directed teams in top-ranked North American manufacturing firms

86   Percentage of Canadian executives who view effective teamwork as "very critical" to the success of their organization.

31   Percentage of Canadian executives who rated their own company's teamwork as "very efficient."

25   Percentage of organizations in the United Kingdom with team-based bonus and incentive plans.

FIGURE 11.1   Teamwork: Some Key Numbers

Sources: "Canadian Businesses Failing to Meet the Information Sharing Needs of Employees," Microsoft Canada press release, October 21, 2003; Chartered Institute of Personnel & Development, Reward Management 2006 Survey; T. Purdum, "Teaming, Take 2," *Industry Week*, May 2005, 41–44.

Consider Celestica's experience with teamwork at its manufacturing plant in Monterrey, Mexico.[7] The electronics equipment manufacturer formed a "lean team" of five core members, who learned about lean manufacturing practices such as reducing time, space, and movement. Lean manufacturing practices are related to the quality management principles that you learned about in Chapter 7. The lean team brainstormed with workstation operators to identify and eliminate non–value-added activities. Another team was set up to revamp the manufacturing line so it would be more responsive to small batch production. The team videotaped the entire process and measured how long it took to complete each step. "We looked at each process and what tools were used," recalls Christy Mitchell, Celestica's customer-focused team director. "We looked at floor plans and the amount of time it took to go from one station to the next. We looked at everything."

■ Celestica's lean teams.

After teams had identified and implemented changes, the Monterrey plant cut lead time from almost a week to less than two days, production changeover time from four hours to 30 minutes, the distance employees walked from 1,173 feet to just 358 feet, and scrap levels by 66 percent. It also won the prestigious Shingo Prize for these achievements. Celestica has since extended its lean journey to other plants around the world. Hundreds of intensive quality improvement investigations of production facilities (called "kaizen blitzes") have been completed by dozens of production teams, cutting costs by approximately $200 million in one year.

// WHY PEOPLE BELONG TO INFORMAL GROUPS

Although most of our attention in this chapter is on formal teams, employees also belong to informal groups. All teams are groups, but many groups do not satisfy our definition of teams. Groups include people assembled together whether or not they have any interdependence or organizationally focused objective. The friends you meet for lunch are an *informal group* but wouldn't be called a team because they have little or no task interdependence (each person could just as easily eat lunch alone) and no organizationally mandated purpose (which is why they are "informal"). Instead they exist primarily for the benefit of their members. Although the terms are used interchangeably, *teams* has largely replaced *groups* in the business language referring to employees who work together to complete tasks.[8]

One reason why informal groups exist is that they fulfill the innate drive to bond. People invest considerable time and effort forming and maintaining relationships without any special circumstances or motives beyond the need for affiliation. We define ourselves by our group affiliations, which motivates us to be associated with work teams or informal groups that are viewed favorably by others. We are also motivated to become members of groups that are similar to ourselves because this reinforces our self-perception.[9]

A second reason why people join informal groups is that these groups accomplish personal goals that cannot be achieved by individuals working alone. For example, employees will sometimes form a group to oppose organizational changes because they have more power when banded together than when complaining separately. A third explanation for informal groups is that in stressful situations we are comforted by the mere presence of other people and are therefore motivated to be near them. This is evident when employees mingle more often after hearing rumors that the company might be sold.

■ // The Trouble with Teams

process losses

Resources (including time and energy) expended toward team development and maintenance rather than tasks.

We outlined the benefits of teams, but managers also need to keep in mind that teams aren't always needed.[10] Some tasks are performed just as easily by one person as by a group. Even if teams are somewhat useful, they tend to require more care and feeding than individuals working alone. These costs are known as **process losses**—resources (including time and energy) expended toward team development and maintenance rather than tasks.[11]

Another issue is that teams require the right environment to flourish. Many managers forget this point by putting people in teams without changing anything else. As will be described more fully later in this chapter, teams require appropriate rewards, communication systems, team leadership, and other conditions. Without these, the shift to a team structure could be a waste of time and a huge frustration for those involved. Overall, though, managers need to determine whether changing these environmental conditions to improve teamwork will cost more than benefits for the overall organization.[12]

// SOCIAL LOAFING

social loafing

Occurs when people exert less effort (and usually perform at a lower level) when working in groups than when working alone.

Perhaps the best-known limitation of teams is the risk of productivity loss due to **social loafing**. Social loafing occurs when people exert less effort (and usually perform at a lower level) when working in groups than when working alone.[13] A few management scholars question whether social loafing is common, but students can certainly report many instances of this problem in their team projects!

Social loafing is most likely to occur in large teams where individual output is difficult to identify. This particularly includes situations in which team members work alone toward a common output pool. Under these conditions employees aren't as worried that their performance will be noticed. Therefore, one way to minimize social loafing is to make each team member's contribution more noticeable, such as by reducing the size of the team or measuring each team member's performance. Social loafing is also less likely to occur when the task is interesting because individuals have a higher intrinsic motivation to perform their duties. Social loafing is less common when the group's objective is important, possibly because individuals experience more pressure from other team members to perform well. Finally, social loafing occurs less frequently among members who value group membership and believe in working toward group objectives.[14]

■ // Types of Teams

There are many types of teams in organizational settings, most of which are summarized in Figure 11.2. Some employees work in *departmental teams,* such as the accounting and finance departments, where a supervisor coordinates the work flow. Traditional manufacturing and service operations organize employees into *production teams,* which produce a common product or service or make ongoing decisions. *Advisory teams* provide recommendations to decision makers. *Task forces* also make recommendations, but they are usually temporary and focused on a specific issue. *Skunkworks* are unusual teams that exist in some

FIGURE 11.2

Types of Formal Teams
in Organizations

Team Type	Description
Departmental teams	Employees have similar or complementary skills and are located in the same unit of a functional structure; such teams usually feature minimal task interdependence because each person works with employees in other departments.
Production/service/leadership teams	Typically multiskilled (having diverse competencies) team members collectively produce a common product or service or make ongoing decisions; production/service teams typically have an assembly-line type of interdependence, whereas leadership teams tend to have tight interactive (reciprocal) interdependence.
Self-directed teams	Similar to production/service teams except (1) they produce an entire product or subassembly that has low interdependence with other work units, and (2) they have very high autonomy (they usually control inputs, flow, and outputs with no supervision).
Advisory teams	These entities, such as committees, advisory councils, work councils, and review panels, provide recommendations to decision makers; they may be temporary but are often permanent, some with frequent rotation of members.
Task force (project) teams	These are usually multiskilled, temporary entities whose assignment is to solve a problem, realize an opportunity, or develop a product or service.
Skunkworks	These multiskilled entities are usually located away from the organization and are relatively free of its hierarchy; such teams are often initiated by an entrepreneurial team leader *(innovation champion)* who borrows people and resources *(bootlegging)* to create a product or develop a service.
Virtual teams	Members of these formal teams operate across space, time, and organizational boundaries and are linked through information technologies to achieve organizational tasks; they may be temporary task forces or permanent service teams.

companies; they are relatively free from the corporate hierarchy and are usually located away from the company's physical operations to create a product or develop a service. Two other types of teams that exist in many other organizations are self-directed teams and virtual teams. These team structures are becoming so important that we look at each of them in more detail next.

// SELF-DIRECTED TEAMS

self-directed teams

Teams organized around work processes that complete an entire piece of work requiring several interdependent tasks and have substantial autonomy over the execution of those tasks.

Whole Foods Market organizes its employees not just into teams, but into **self-directed teams**. Self-directed teams are similar to production/service teams in that team members typically have diverse competencies and are organized around a common product or service, but they differ from traditional production/service teams in several ways.[15] First, self-directed teams complete an entire piece of work, whether it's a product, a service, or part of a larger product or service. Team members at Whole Foods are responsible for the entire processes in their areas, such as food preparation, display, inventory, and some purchasing.

Second, the team—not supervisors—assigns tasks that individual team members perform. In other words, the team plans, organizes, and controls work activities with little or no direct involvement of someone with higher formal authority. Harley-Davidson has taken this high-autonomy approach to such an extreme that there are no supervisors at all at its assembly plant near Kansas City, Missouri. Instead self-directed teams of 8 to 15 employees make most daily decisions through consensus. An umbrella group, representing teams and management, makes plantwide decisions. "There's a lot of work being done to empower the workforce," says Karl Eberle, vice president and general manager of Harley-Davidson's Kansas City operations. "But there are very few examples of where they've taken the workforce to run the factory. And that's what we've done."[16]

Motorcycle Teams
Surrounded by tall prairie grass, Harley-Davidson's assembly plant near Kansas City, Missouri, exemplifies an organization that relies on self-directed teams. In fact, the facility has no supervisors. Instead self-directed teams of 8 to 15 employees make most daily decisions through consensus. An umbrella group, representing teams and management, makes plantwide decisions.
© AP Photo/Orlin Wagner

Third, self-directed teams control most work inputs, flow, and output. At Whole Foods, for instance, some self-directed teams work directly with suppliers, and all are responsible for their work processes and interacting directly with customers on the output side. Fourth, self-directed teams are responsible for correcting work flow problems as they occur. In other words, the teams maintain their own quality and logistical control. Fifth, self-directed teams receive team-level feedback and rewards. This recognizes and reinforces the fact that the team—not individual employees—is responsible for the work, although team members may also receive individual feedback and rewards.

Surveys estimate that somewhere between one-third and two-thirds of the medium-sized and large organizations in the United States use self-directed team structures for part of their operations. In addition, almost all of the top-rated manufacturing firms rely on these teams.[17] This popularity is consistent with research indicating that self-directed teams potentially increase both productivity and job satisfaction. For instance, one study found that car dealership service shops that organized employees into self-directed teams were significantly more profitable than shops where employees worked without a team structure. Another reported that both short and long-term measures of customer satisfaction increased after street cleaners in a German city were organized into self-directed teams.[18]

Success Factors for Self-Directed Teams If self-directed teams are so wonderful, why doesn't every organization have them? Self-directed teams probably would add value in most organizations, but they are not easy to put in place. In addition to managing the team dynamics described later in this chapter, corporate leaders need to ensure the following:[19]

1. *Responsible for an entire work process:* Self-directed teams work best when they are responsible for making an entire product, providing a service, or otherwise completing an entire work process. For instance, the seafood team at a Whole Foods store would be responsible for the entire process of ordering, preparing, and serving food items in this

area of the store. This organization around a work process keeps each team sufficiently independent that it can change its work process and content without interfering with, or having interference from, other work units. It also gives employees a sense of interdependence and cohesiveness by working toward a common goal.[20]

2. *Sufficient autonomy:* Self-directed teams should have sufficient freedom from management control to organize and coordinate work. This autonomy allows self-directed teams to respond more quickly and effectively to client and stakeholder demands. It also motivates team members through feelings of empowerment. Many high-performance teams have failed because managers were reluctant to hand over some of their power or employees did not feel comfortable with their increased responsibilities.

3. *Technology-supported team dynamics:* Self-directed teams are successful when technology is implemented in a way that supports coordination and communication among team members and increases job enrichment.[21] Too often management calls a group of employees a "team"; yet the work layout, assembly-line structure, and other technologies isolate employees from each other. For example, automakers have referred to groups of employees along an assembly line as teams, but assembly-line technology does not lend itself to effective team dynamics because team members at one end rarely see coworkers at the other end of the line.

// VIRTUAL TEAMS

PricewaterhouseCoopers (PwC) employs 190 training professionals in 70 offices across the United States. These professionals, along with many more consultants and academics who provide employee development services, routinely form virtual teams for new projects. "Virtual teaming is the norm for us," says Peter Nicolas, a PwC learning solutions manager in Florham Park, New Jersey.[22]

PricewaterhouseCoopers makes better use of its human capital by creating **virtual teams**. Virtual teams are teams whose members operate across space, time, and organizational boundaries and are linked through information technologies to achieve organizational tasks.[23] Virtual teams differ from traditional teams in two ways: (1) They are not usually colocated (they do not work in the same physical area), and (2) due to their lack of colocation, members of virtual teams depend primarily on information technologies rather than face-to-face interaction to communicate and coordinate their work efforts.

Virtual teams are one of the most significant developments in organizations over the past decade. "Virtual teams are now a reality," says Frank Waltmann, head of learning at pharmaceuticals company Novartis. One reason for their popularity is that the Internet, intranets, instant messaging, virtual whiteboards, and other technologies have made it easier than ever before to communicate and coordinate with people at a distance.[24] The shift from production-based to knowledge-based work is a second reason why virtual teamwork is feasible. It isn't yet possible to make a product when team members are located elsewhere, but most of us now make decisions and create ideas. Information technologies allow people to exchange this knowledge work, such as software code, product development plans, and ideas for strategic decisions.

Information technologies and knowledge-based work make virtual teams possible, but knowledge management and globalization are two reasons why they are increasingly necessary. Virtual teams represent a natural part of the knowledge management process because they encourage employees to share and use knowledge when geography limits more direct forms of collaboration. Globalization makes virtual teams increasingly necessary because employees are spread around the planet rather than around one city. Thus global businesses depend on virtual teamwork to leverage their human capital.[25]

Invensys PLC is a case in point. A few years ago the British process and control engineering firm became a global leader by merging companies with offices in several countries. To make the best use of this far-reaching talent, the company introduced information technologies whereby employees could participate in specialized projects at a moment's

virtual teams
Teams whose members operate across space, time, and organizational boundaries and are linked through information technologies to achieve organizational tasks.

24-Hour Virtual Team Service Invensys PLC is a global leader in process and control engineering with offices in several countries. To make the best use of this far-reaching talent, the company introduced information technologies whereby employees could participate in specialized projects at a moment's notice without travel.

© Getty Images

notice without flying around the world. "Our development projects operate in a virtual mode and [gather] people from multiple sites based on project needs," explains Joe Ayers, a manager at Invensys's process simulation unit in Lake Forest, California. "It is common for projects to utilize developers from three different time zones in a 'follow the sun' development mode."[26]

Success Factors for Virtual Teams Virtual teams have all the challenges of traditional teams as well as the vagaries of distance and time. Information technology plays a critical role for virtual teams to exist and work more effectively, but so far no technology completely solves the distance problem. Fortunately management researchers have been keenly interested in virtual teams, and their studies are now revealing ways to improve virtual team effectiveness. Here are three of the clearest recommendations:[27]

- *Virtual team competencies:* Virtual team members require competencies beyond those needed in traditional teams. They should have the ability to communicate easily through technology, strong self-leadership skills to motivate and guide their behavior without peers or bosses nearby, and higher emotional intelligence so they can decipher the feelings of teammates from e-mail and other limited communication media. "On a call, I use subtle listening," explains Karim Ladak, a Procter & Gamble executive whose virtual team members live in at least six cities around the world. "I listen for a quiver or a pause. And even then I know that I can very quickly miss something."[28]

- *Flexible information technologies:* Researchers have found that corporate leaders like to impose technology on virtual teams rather than letting them adopt technology that suits their needs. The best situation occurs when virtual teams have a toolkit of communication vehicles (e-mail, virtual white boards, video conferencing, and so on), which gain and lose importance over different parts of the project.

- *Occasional face-to-face interaction:* This may seem contrary to the entire notion of virtual teams, but so far no technology has replaced face-to-face interaction for high-level bonding and mutual understanding. This direct interaction is particularly valuable when virtual teams form. For instance, when IBM recently formed a virtual team to build an electronic customer access system for Shell, employees from both firms began with an "all hands" face-to-face gathering to assist the team development process. The two firms also made a rule that the dispersed team members should have face-to-face contact at least once every six weeks throughout the project. Without this, "after about five or six weeks we found some of that communication would start to break down," says Sharon Hartung, the IBM comanager for the project.[29]

∎ // A Model of Team Effectiveness

Most U.S. manufacturing firms organize employees into production teams but, as revealed in a recent survey (see Figure 11.3), most managers in these firms believe the effectiveness of these teams is still far from ideal. Why are some teams effective while others fail? This question has challenged organizational researchers for some time, and as you might expect, numerous models of team effectiveness have been proposed over the years.[30] Figure 11.4 presents a model of team effectiveness that pulls together most existing literature about team effectiveness; we'll examine this model closely over the next several pages.

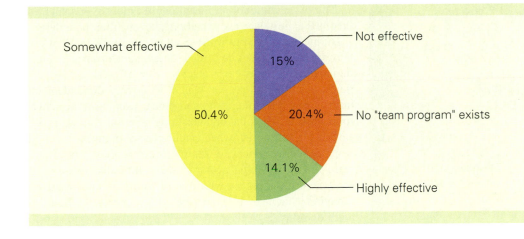

FIGURE 11.3

How Effective Are Teams in U.S. Manufacturing Firms?

Source: Data from the 2004 Industry Week/MPI Census of Manufacturers survey, cited in T. Purdum, "Teaming, Take 2," *Industry Week*, May 2005, 41–44.

Let's begin by clarifying the meaning of *team effectiveness*. **Team effectiveness** refers to how the team affects the organization, individual team members, and the team's existence.[31] First, effective teams achieve their objectives relating to the organization or other system in which the group operates. Second, team effectiveness relates to the satisfaction and well-being of its members. People join groups to fulfill their personal needs, so effectiveness is partly measured by this need fulfillment. Third, team effectiveness relates to the team's ability to survive. It must be able to maintain the commitment of its members, particularly during the turbulence of the team's development. Without this commitment, people may leave and the team can fall apart. This element of team effectiveness also includes the ability to secure sufficient resources and find a benevolent environment in which to operate.

team effectiveness
The team's effect on the organization, individual team members, and the team's existence.

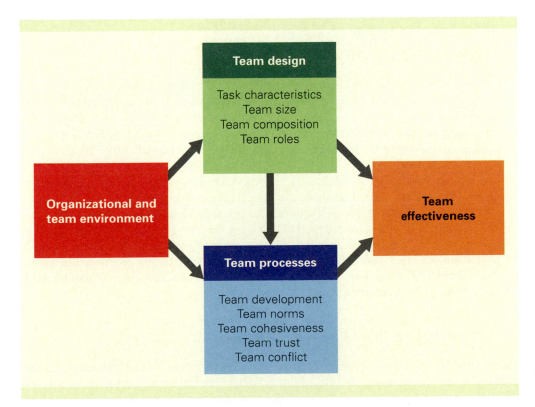

FIGURE 11.4

Team Effectiveness Model

Medrad Sees the U in Team   Medrad, Inc., found that one of the best ways to support teams was by replacing the straight assembly line with a clustered production arrangement in which members of each team work more closely in U-shaped work cells. The new physical arrangement improved team performance by helping team members observe and assist each other.

Courtesy of Medrad, Inc., USA

The organizational and team environment represents all factors that influence teams and exist beyond their boundaries. Team members tend to work together more effectively when they are at least partly rewarded for team performance. Communication systems can influence team effectiveness—particularly in virtual teams, which are highly dependent on information technologies to coordinate work. Another environmental factor is the organizational structure; as we noted earlier, teams flourish when employees are organized around work processes because this increases interaction among team members. High-performance teams also depend on organizational leaders who provide support and strategic direction while team members focus on operational efficiency and flexibility.[32]

Along with these conditions, the physical layout of the team's workspace can make a difference. Medrad, Inc., the Indianola, Pennsylvania, medical device manufacturer, redesigned the production process from straight-line assembly to clustered structures in which members of each team now work more closely in U-shaped work cells. A successful trial confirmed that the U-shaped cell physical arrangement improved team performance by enhancing the ability of team members to observe and assist each other.[33]

■ // Team Design Features

Along with setting up a compatible environment, managers need to carefully design the team itself, including task characteristics, team size, team composition, and team roles.

// TASK CHARACTERISTICS

Experts are still figuring out the best types of work for teams. Some evidence says that teams are more effective when their tasks are well structured because a clear structure makes it easier to coordinate work among several people. But other research indicates that teams flourish on more complex tasks because the complexity motivates them to work together as a team.[34] Task structure and task complexity aren't opposites, but it can be difficult to find complex work that is well structured.

One task characteristic that is definitely important for teams is **task interdependence**: the extent to which team members must share common inputs to their individual tasks, need to interact while performing their work, or receive outcomes (such as rewards) that are partly determined by the performance of others. The higher the level of task interdependence, the greater the need for teams rather than individuals working alone. Employees tend to be more motivated and satisfied working in teams when their tasks are highly interdependent—but only when team members have the same job goals, such as serving the same clients or collectively assembling the same product.[35]

task interdependence
The extent to which team members must share common inputs to their individual tasks, need to interact while performing their work, or receive outcomes (such as rewards) that are partly determined by the performance of others.

// TEAM SIZE

The most effective teams have the right number of members. One popular (but untested) rule is that the optimal team size is somewhere between five and seven people. In reality the optimal team size depends on a few things. We know that larger teams are typically less effective because members consume more time and effort coordinating their roles and resolving differences. A somewhat extreme example is Whole Foods' 140-person cashier team in New York City's Columbus Circle. A team this large is too difficult to coordinate, and team members lack cohesiveness; so Whole Foods divides the group into a dozen or so smaller teams. All cashiers meet as one massive group every month to discuss production issues, but the subteams work more effectively daily.[36]

Although companies usually need to break up large teams, they also run into trouble when teams are too small to accomplish their objectives. The general rule is that teams should be large enough to provide the necessary competencies and perspectives to perform the work, yet small enough to maintain efficient coordination and meaningful involvement of each member.

■ "Hewlett-Packard picks team players.

// TEAM COMPOSITION

When Hewlett-Packard hires new talent, it doesn't look for just technical skills and knowledge. The high-tech computer manufacturer also looks for job applicants who fit into a team environment. "It's important for candidates to prove to us that they can work well with others," explains business development manager Bill Avey. "We're looking for people who value the different perspectives that each individual brings to a team." Avey describes how Hewlett-Packard recruiters will ask applicants to recall a time they worked in a group to solve a problem. "Successful candidates tend to show how they got differences out in the open and reached a resolution as a team," says Avey.[37]

Hewlett-Packard has a strong team orientation, so it carefully selects people with the necessary motivation and competencies for teamwork. Whole Foods is equally serious about hiring team members who can work together. As the opening vignette to this chapter described, new hires are approved for permanent employment by teammates, not by managers. The reason for the teams' involvement in hiring is that teams require members who are motivated to work together rather than alone, abide by the teams' rules of conduct, and support the teams' goals. Effective team members also possess valuable skills and knowledge for the team's objectives and can work well with others. Notably, research suggests that high-performing team members demonstrate more cooperative behavior toward others and generally have better awareness of others' needs and views.[38]

Another important dimension of team composition is diversity.[39] Teams whose members have diverse knowledge, skills, and perspectives are generally more effective in situations involving complex problems requiring innovative solutions. One reason is that people from different backgrounds see a problem or opportunity from different perspectives. A second reason is that they usually have a broader knowledge base. A third reason favoring teams with diverse members is that they provide better representation of the teams' constituents, such as other departments or clients from similarly diverse backgrounds. However, diverse employees take longer to become a high-performing team and tend to experience more conflict that can potentially sever alliances of team members into subgroups. For this reason it is sometimes better to form a team of like-minded and skilled people when diverse knowledge is not required and the team has little time to develop.

// TEAM ROLES

Every work team and informal group has various roles necessary to assist the team's task and maintain its smooth functioning. A **role** is a set of behaviors that people are expected to perform because they hold certain positions in a team and organization.[40] Some roles help the team achieve its goals; other roles maintain relationships so the team survives and team members fulfill their needs. Many team roles are formally assigned to specific people, but several are taken informally based on each team member's personality, values, and expertise. These role preferences are usually worked out during the storming stage of team development (discussed in the next section). However, in a dynamic environment team members often need to assume various roles temporarily as the need arises.[41]

role

A set of behaviors that people are expected to perform because they hold certain positions in a team and organization.

FIGURE 11.5

Belbin's Team Roles

Sources: R.M. Belbin, *Team Roles at Work* (Oxford, UK: Butterworth-Heinemann, 1993); www.belbin.com. Reprinted with permission from Belbin Associates.

Role Title	Contributions	Allowable Weaknesses
Plant	Creative, imaginative, and unorthodox; solves difficult problems.	Ignores details; too preoccupied to communicate effectively.
Resource investigator	Extroverted, enthusiastic, and communicative; explores opportunities; develops contacts.	Overly optimistic; loses interest once initial enthusiasm has passed.
Coordinator	Mature, confident, a good chairperson; clarifies goals, promotes decision making, delegates well.	Can be seen as manipulative; delegates personal work.
Shaper	Challenging, dynamic, thrives on pressure; has the drive and courage to overcome obstacles.	Can provoke others; hurts people's feelings.
Monitor/evaluator	Sober, strategic, and discerning; sees all options; judges accurately.	Lacks drive and ability to inspire others; overly critical.
Teamworker	Cooperative, mild, perceptive, and diplomatic; listens, builds, averts friction, calms the waters.	Indecisive in crunch situations; can be easily influenced.
Implementer	Disciplined, reliable, conservative, and efficient; turns ideas into practical actions.	Somewhat inflexible; slow to respond to new possibilities.
Completer/finisher	Painstaking, conscientious, and anxious; searches out errors and omissions; delivers on time.	Inclined to worry unduly; reluctant to delegate; can be a nitpicker.
Specialist	Single-minded, self-starting, and dedicated; provides knowledge and skills in rare supply.	Contributes on only a narrow front; dwells on technicalities; overlooks the big picture.

One of the most popular models of team roles is Belbin's team role theory, shown in Figure 11.5.[42] The model identifies nine team roles that are related to specific personality characteristics. People have a natural preference for one role or another, although they can adjust to a secondary role. Belbin's model emphasizes that all nine roles must be engaged for optimal team performance. Moreover, certain team roles should dominate over others at various stages of the team's project or activities. For example, shapers and coordinators are key figures when the team is identifying its needs, whereas completers and implementers are most important during the follow-through stage of the team's project.

■ // Team Processes

Up to this point we have looked at two sets of elements in the team effectiveness model: (1) organizational and team environment and (2) team design. The third set of team effectiveness elements, collectively known as *team processes,* includes team development, norms, cohesiveness, trust, and conflict management. These represent evolving dynamics that the team shapes and reshapes over time.

// TEAM DEVELOPMENT

A few years ago the National Transportation Safety Board (NTSB) studied the circumstances under which airplane cockpit crews were most likely to have accidents and related problems. What they discovered was startling: 73 percent of all incidents took place on the crew's first day, and 44 percent occurred on the crew's very first flight together. This isn't an isolated example. NASA studied fatigue of pilots after returning from multiple-day trips. Fatigued pilots made more errors in the NASA flight simulator, as one would expect. But the NASA researchers didn't expect the discovery that fatigued crews who had worked together made fewer errors than did rested crews who had not yet flown together.[43]

The NTSB and NASA studies reveal that team members must resolve several issues and pass through several stages of development before emerging as an effective work unit. They must get to know each other, understand their respective roles, discover appropriate and inappropriate behaviors, and learn how to coordinate their work or social activities. The longer team members work together, the better they develop common mental models, mutual understanding, and effective performance routines to complete the work.

The five-stage model of team development, shown in Figure 11.6, provides a general outline of how teams evolve by forming, storming, norming, performing, and eventually adjourning.[44] The model shows teams progressing from one stage to the next in an orderly fashion, but the dashed lines illustrate that they might also fall back to an earlier stage of development as new members join or other conditions disrupt the team's maturity.

■ NASA and NTSB discover power of team development.

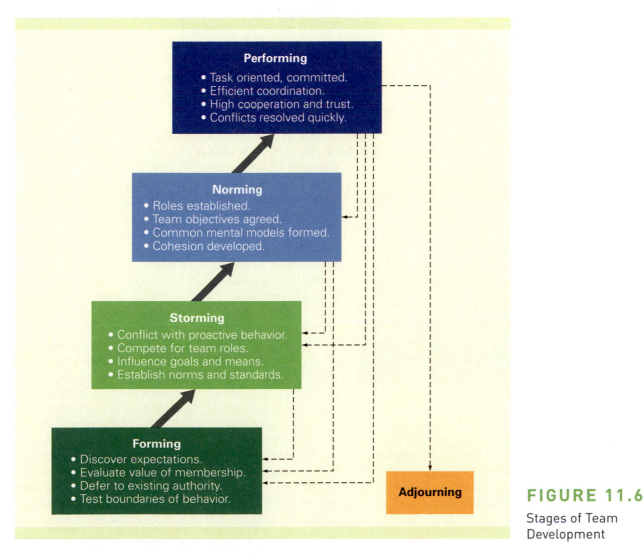

FIGURE 11.6

Stages of Team Development

1. *Forming:* The first stage of team development is a period of testing and orientation in which members learn about each other and evaluate the benefits and costs of continued membership. People tend to be polite during this stage and will defer to the existing authority of a formal or informal leader, who must provide an initial set of rules and structures for interaction. Members try to find out what is expected of them and how they will fit into the team.

2. *Storming:* The storming stage is marked by interpersonal conflict as members become more proactive and compete for various team roles. Coalitions may form to influence the team's goals and means of goal attainment. Members try to establish norms of appropriate behavior and performance standards. This is a tenuous stage in the team's development, particularly when the leader is autocratic and lacks the necessary conflict management skills.

3. *Norming:* During the norming stage, the team develops its first real sense of cohesion as roles are established and a consensus forms around group objectives. Members have developed relatively similar mental models, so they have common expectations and assumptions about how the team's goals should be accomplished. They have developed a common team-based mental model that allows them to interact more efficiently so they can move into the next stage, performing.[45]

4. *Performing:* The team becomes more task-oriented in the performing stage. Team members have learned to coordinate and resolve conflicts more efficiently. Further coordination improvements must occasionally be addressed, but the greater emphasis is on task accomplishment. In high-performance teams, members are highly cooperative, have a high level of trust in each other, are committed to group objectives, and identify with the team.

5. *Adjourning:* Most work teams and informal groups eventually end. During this stage, members shift their attention away from task orientation to a socioemotional focus as they realize that their relationship is ending.

The team development model is a useful framework for thinking about how teams develop. In fact, a recent study found that it fits nicely with student recollections of their experiences with work on team projects for class assignments.[46] You have probably experienced initial politeness and uncertainty, followed by subtle or not-so-subtle conflicts as fellow students spar for particular roles or squabble over the best way to complete the project. Some student teams work together long enough to experience norming and possibly performing, particularly if students have collaborated on previous assignments.

The team development model is also nicely illustrated in Blue Angels training. The U.S. Navy's aerial demonstration team needs to complete its maneuvers with nearly perfect timing, and this requires team development to the performing stage. Although highly experienced before joining the squad, the pilots put in long hours of practice to reach the pinnacle of team development. The F/A-18A Hornets are well spaced apart during the first few practices, but the team gradually tightens up the formation over the 10-week training program until the fighter jets are at times only 18 inches apart. "I know exactly what [the lead] jet is going to do, and when," says Lt. Cdr. John Saccomando, who flies the Number 2 position. "It takes a while to build that confidence." Team development is also sped up through candid debriefings after every practice. "We close the door, and there's no rank," says Saccomando, who is expected to offer frank feedback to commanding officer and flight leader Cdr. Stephen R. Foley. Foley points out that the

Sky-High Team Development   Reaching the performing stage of team development isn't just a goal for the Blue Angels; it's an absolute necessity to ensure that the U.S. Navy's aerial demonstration team completes its maneuvers with nearly perfect timing. Although highly experienced before joining the squad, the pilots put in long hours of practice to reach the pinnacle of team development.[47]

© Guy Motil/Corbis

safety and success of the Blue Angels depend on how well the team development process works. "The team concept is what makes [everything] here click," Foley emphasizes.[48]

Although the team development model is a useful gauge of this team process, it is not a perfect representation. For instance, it does not show that some teams remain in a particular stage longer than others or that team development is a continuous process. As membership changes and new conditions emerge, teams cycle back to earlier stages in the developmental process to regain the equilibrium or balance lost by the changes (as shown by the dashed lines in Figure 11.6).

Speeding Up Team Development through Team Building Before Milton Elementary School in Milton, Delaware, opened its doors for the first time, school principal Sheila Baumgardner took her new teaching and support staff to Arlington Echo Outdoor Education Center in Millersville, Maryland, for three days of team building. "The idea behind that is to develop teamwork skills since I'm bringing teachers together from buildings all over the district," Baumgardner explains. Along with walking in the woods and sharing meals together, staff spent time developing school support programs. "Our main purpose is to develop teamwork skills—camaraderie—to facilitate communication once the school year begins," she says.[49]

Sheila Baumgardner sped up the team development process through **team building**—any formal activity intended to improve the development and functioning of a work team.[50] Some team-building activities also improve other team processes (such as team norms and cohesiveness). Team building is sometimes applied to newly established teams, such as Milton Elementary School, because team members are at the earliest stages of team development. However, it is more common among existing teams that have regressed to earlier stages of team development. Team building is therefore most appropriate when a team experiences high membership turnover or members have lost sight of their respective roles and team objectives.

Some team-building interventions clarify the team's performance goals, increase the team's motivation to accomplish these goals, and establish a mechanism for systematic feedback on the team's goal performance. Others clarify roles by having team members reconstruct their perceptions of their roles as well as the role expectations they have of other team members. Popular interventions such as wilderness team activities, paintball wars, and obstacle course challenges are used in team building as ways to increase trust and interpersonal bonding. "If two colleagues hold the rope for you while you're climbing 10 meters up, that is truly team-building," explains Jan Antwerpes, a partner in a German communications consulting firm. "It also shows your colleagues that you care for them."[51]

// TEAM NORMS

Have you ever noticed how employees in one branch office will be absent from work during inclement weather or any sign of cold symptoms, whereas their counterparts in another office practically have to be ordered to stay home when sick or discouraged from coming to work during bad weather? These differences are partly due to **norms**—the informal rules and shared expectations that groups establish to regulate the behavior of their members. Norms apply only to behavior, not to private thoughts or feelings. Moreover, norms exist only for behaviors that are important to the team.[52]

Norms guide how team members deal with clients, how they share resources, whether they are willing to be absent from work, and many other behaviors in organizational life. Some norms ensure that employees support organizational goals, whereas other norms might conflict with organizational objectives. For example, studies report that employee absenteeism from work is influenced by absence norms in the workplace, not just the individual's health or job satisfaction.[53]

One reason employees conform to team norms is peer pressure. Coworkers might grimace if we are late for a meeting or make sarcastic comments if we don't have our part of the project completed on time. Norms are also directly reinforced through praise from

■ Team building at Milton Elementary School.

team building
Any formal activity intended to improve the development and functioning of a work team.

norms
The informal rules and shared expectations that groups establish to regulate the behavior of their members.

high-status members, more access to valued resources, or other rewards available to the team. For the most part, however, team members conform to prevailing norms without direct reinforcement or punishment because they identify with the group. The more a team member identifies with the group, the more he or she is motivated to avoid negative sanctions from that group.[54]

How Team Norms Develop   Norms develop as soon as teams form because people need to anticipate or predict how others will act. Even subtle events during the team's formation, such as how team members initially greet each other and where they sit in the first meetings, can initiate norms that are later difficult to change. Norms also form as team members discover behaviors that help them function more effectively (such as the need to respond quickly to e-mail). In particular, a critical event in the team's history can trigger formation of a norm or sharpen a previously vague one. A third influence on team norms is the past experiences and values that members bring to the team. If members of a new team value work–life balance, norms are likely to develop that discourage long hours and work overload.[55]

Preventing and Changing Dysfunctional Team Norms   Team norms often become deeply anchored, so the best way to avoid norms that undermine organizational success or employee well-being is to establish desirable norms when teams are first formed. As was just mentioned, norms form from the values that people bring to the team; so one strategy is to select people with appropriate values. If organizational leaders want their teams to have strong safety norms, they should hire people who already value safety.

Another strategy is to clearly state desirable norms as soon as teams are created. For instance, when Four Seasons Hotels & Resorts opens a new hotel, it forms a 35-person task force consisting of staff from other Four Seasons hotels. The task force "Four Seasonizes" the new recruits by training them and watching for behaviors and decisions that are inconsistent with the Four Seasons way of doing things. "The task force helps establish norms [in the new hotel]," explains a Four Seasons manager who has served on these task forces.[56]

The suggestions so far refer to new teams; how can organizational leaders maintain desirable norms in older teams? One way, which The Container Store has practiced for many years, is to frequently discuss the team's norms. One of the first and last tasks of the day is for staff to gather for the "huddle," where they learn about the day's sales target, review the store's vision, and discuss issues related to the store's vision. Generally huddle sessions were introduced to educate employees, create a team environment, and reinforce norms that the company wants to instill in employees. "The spirit was to keep people on the same page," explains Garrett Boone, cofounder and chair of the Dallas-based seller of customized storage products.[57]

■ Four Seasons Hotels & Resorts shapes team norms.

Huddles Reinforce Team Norms   At The Container Store in White Plains, New York, floor leader Scott Buhler (shown in photo) starts the morning huddle by declaring the day's sales target. Then he asks the group about the store's vision and today's product tip. The Container Store institutionalized huddle sessions to educate employees, create a team environment, and reinforce norms that the company wants to instill in employees.

© Stuart Bayer/*The Journal News*

Team-based reward systems can also strengthen desired norms and weaken counterproductive norms. However, one classic study reported that some employees in a pajama factory were able to process up to 100 units per hour and thereby earn more money, but they all chose to abide by the group norm of 50 units per hour. Only after the team was disbanded did the strong performers working alone increase their performance to 100 units per hour.[58] Finally, if dysfunctional norms are deeply ingrained and the previous solutions don't work, it may be necessary to disband the group and replace it with people having more favorable norms. Managers should seize the opportunity to introduce performance-oriented norms when the new team is formed, selecting members who will bring desirable norms to the group.

// TEAM COHESIVENESS

Team cohesiveness—the degree of attraction people feel toward a team and their motivation to remain members—is considered an important factor in a team's success.[59] Employees feel cohesiveness when they believe the team will help them achieve their personal goals, fulfill their need for affiliation or status, or provide social support during times of crisis or trouble. Cohesiveness is an emotional experience, not just a calculation of whether to stay or leave the team. It exists when team members make the team part of their social identity. Cohesiveness is the glue or esprit de corps that holds the group together and ensures that its members fulfill their obligations.

Several factors influence team cohesiveness: member similarity, team size, member interaction, difficult entry, team success, and external competition or challenges. For the most part these factors reflect the individual's social identity with the group and beliefs about how team membership will fulfill personal needs.

Member Similarity Earlier in this chapter we learned that highly diverse teams potentially tend to experience more conflict, leading to factious subgroups and higher turnover among team members. Although this suggests that diverse teams are less cohesive than homogeneous teams, not all forms of diversity have this negative effect. For example, teams consisting of people from different job groups seem to gel together just as well as teams of people from the same job.[60]

Team Size Smaller teams tend to be more cohesive than larger teams because it is easier for a few people to agree on goals and coordinate work activities. The smallest teams aren't always the most cohesive, however. Small teams are less cohesive when they lack enough members to perform the required tasks. Thus team cohesiveness is potentially greatest when teams are as small as possible, yet large enough to accomplish the required tasks.

Member Interaction Teams tend to be more cohesive when team members interact with each other fairly regularly. This occurs when team members perform highly interdependent tasks and work in the same physical area.

Somewhat Difficult Entry Teams tend to be more cohesive when entry to the team is restricted. The more elite the team, the more prestige it confers on its members, and the more they tend to value their membership in the unit. Existing team members are also more willing to welcome and support new members after they have "passed the test," possibly because they have shared the same entry experience.[61]

Team Success Cohesiveness increases with the team's level of success because people feel more connected to teams that fulfill their goals. Furthermore, individuals are more likely to attach their social identity to successful teams than to those with a string of failures.

External Competition and Challenges Team cohesiveness tends to increase when members face external competition or a challenging objective that is valued. Under these conditions, employees value the team's ability to overcome the threat or competition if they can't solve the problem individually. They also value their membership as a form of social support. However, severe external threats can undermine team cohesiveness when the resulting stress undermines the team's ability to function well.[62] For example, staff members at Lighthouse Publishing are a highly cohesive team because they excel in a ferociously competitive environment. "Lighthouse staff members [have] kept us independent in the face of stiff competition

team cohesiveness
The degree of attraction people feel toward a team and their motivation to remain members.

Storm-Proof Cohesiveness Staff members at Lighthouse Publishing in Bridgewater, Nova Scotia, Canada, are a highly cohesive team because they excel in a ferociously competitive environment. They have also overcome numerous internal challenges, such as getting their weekly newspaper, the *Bridgewater Bulletin*, published on time after the printing machinery broke down. "Lighthouse succeeds because of its multitalented, highly dedicated team of employees," says company president Lynn Hennigar. "It's a team that embraces change."

Courtesy of Lighthouse Publishing. Photo by Robert Hirtle.

and corporate takeovers," says Lynn Hennigar, president of the small newspaper publisher in Bridgewater, Nova Scotia, Canada. Cohesiveness is also strengthened by internal challenges, such as when staff scrambled to get the paper out on time after the machinery broke down. This cohesion partly explains why Lighthouse recently earned more than two dozen awards and its weekly newspaper, the *Bridgewater Bulletin,* has been judged as one of the top five in its class across Canada.[63]

Consequences of Team Cohesiveness Every team must have some minimal level of cohesiveness to maintain its existence. People who belong to high-cohesion teams are motivated to maintain their membership and to help the team perform effectively. Compared to low-cohesion teams, high-cohesion team members spend more time together, share information more frequently, and are more satisfied with each other. They provide each other with better social support in stressful situations.[64]

Members of high-cohesion teams are generally more sensitive to each other's needs and develop better interpersonal relationships, thereby reducing dysfunctional conflict. When conflict does arise, members tend to resolve these differences swiftly and effectively. For example, one study reported that cohesive recreational ice hockey teams engaged in more constructive conflict—that is, team members tried to resolve their differences cooperatively— whereas less cohesive teams engaged in more combative conflict.[65]

With better cooperation and more conformity to norms, high-cohesion teams usually perform better than low-cohesion teams. This is true only when team norms are compatible with organizational values and objectives, however. Cohesiveness motivates employees to perform at a level more consistent with group norms, so when team norms conflict with the organization's success (such as when norms support high absenteeism or acting unethically), high cohesion will reduce team performance.[66]

// TEAM TRUST

trust

A psychological state comprising the intention to accept vulnerability based on positive expectations of the intent or behavior of another person.

Any relationship—including the relationship among team members—depends on a certain degree of trust.[67] **Trust** is a psychological state comprising the intention to accept vulnerability based on positive expectations of the intent or behavior of another person. A high level of trust occurs when others affect you in situations where you are at risk, but you believe they will not harm you. Trust includes both your beliefs and conscious feelings about the relationship with other team members. In other words, a person both logically evaluates the situation as trustworthy and feels that it is trustworthy.[68] Trust can also be understood in terms of the foundation of that trust. From this perspective, people trust others based on three foundations: calculus, knowledge, and identification (see Figure 11.7).

Calculus-based trust represents a logical calculation that other team members will act appropriately because they face sanctions if their actions violate reasonable expectations. Each party believes that the other will deliver on its promises because punishments will be administered if they fail.[69] In class projects, students have at least a calculus-based level of trust that their teammates will complete their part of the assignment because the instructor might fail those who do not make any contribution.

Predictability of another team member's behavior is the foundation for *knowledge-based trust.* The more we understand others and can predict what they will do in the future, the more we trust them, up to a moderate level. Even if we don't agree with a particular team member's actions, his or her consistency generates some level of trust. Knowledge-based trust also relates to confidence in the other person's ability or competence. People trust others based on their known or perceived expertise, such as when they trust a physician.[70]

This third and highest foundation of trust, called *identification-based trust,* is based on mutual understanding and emotional bonds among team members. Identification occurs when team members think like, feel like, and act like each other. High-performance teams exhibit this level of trust because they share the same values and mental models. Identification-based trust is connected to the concept of social identity; the more you define yourself in terms of membership in the team, the more trust you have in that team.[71]

FIGURE 11.7

Three Foundations of
Trust in Teams

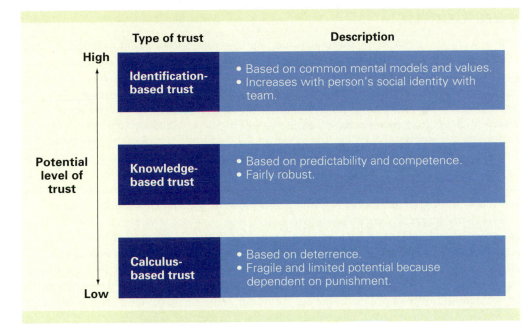

A Hierarchy of Team Trust These three foundations of trust can be arranged in a hierarchy. Calculus-based trust offers the lowest potential level of trust and is easily broken by a violation of expectations. Generally calculus-based trust alone cannot sustain a team's relationship because it relies on deterrence. Relationships don't become strong when based only on the threat of punishment if one party fails to deliver on its promises. Knowledge-based trust offers a higher potential level of trust and is more stable because it develops over time. Suppose that another member of your virtual team submitted documentation to you on schedule in the past, but it arrived late this time. Knowledge-based trust might be dented, but not broken, in this incident. Through knowledge-based trust you "know" that the late delivery is probably an exception because it deviates from the coworker's past actions.

Identification-based trust is potentially the strongest and most robust of all three. The individual's self-image is based partly on membership in the team and he or she believes their values highly overlap, so any transgressions by other team members are quickly forgiven. People are more reluctant to acknowledge a violation of this high-level trust because it strikes at their self-image.

Dynamics of Team Trust A common misconception is that team members build trust from a low level when they first join a team. Yet studies suggest that people typically join a virtual or conventional team with a moderate or high level—not a low level—of trust in their new coworkers. The main explanation for the initially high trust (called *swift trust*) in organizational settings is that people usually believe their teammates are reasonably competent (knowledge-based trust), and they tend to develop some degree of social identity with the team (identification-based trust). Even when working with strangers, most of us display some level of trust, if only because it supports our self-image of being a nice person.[72]

However, trust is fragile in new relationships because it is based on assumptions rather than experience. Consequently recent studies report that trust tends to decrease rather than increase over time. In other words, new team members experience trust violations, which pushes their trust to a lower level. Employees who join the team with identification-based trust tend to drop back to knowledge-based or perhaps calculus-based trust. Declining trust is particularly challenging in virtual teams because communication among team members is an important condition for sustaining trust. Equally important, employees become less forgiving and less cooperative toward others as their level of trust decreases, which undermines team and organizational effectiveness.[73]

▪ // **Managing Team Conflict**

▪ Managing conflict at Armstrong Worldwide.

A few years ago Armstrong Worldwide, Inc., put together a team of information systems employees and outside consultants to select and install a new client–server network. Before long team members at the flooring and building materials company were engaging in several heated disagreements. The consultants preferred working 12-hour days, Monday through Thursday, then flying home on Friday. This didn't sit well with Armstrong's people, who lived nearby and therefore favored a traditional schedule. A second dispute centered on who was in charge. Armstrong's executives decided that the consultants should lead the project, but this meant that Armstrong's people were stuck with whatever system and configuration the consultants decided. A third source of tension was that some information systems employees were worried about losing their jobs to the outside consultants. "[These conflicts] created a large amount of stress and some turnover for us," recalls Armstrong's information systems development manager.[74]

conflict

A process in which one party perceives that its interests are being opposed or negatively affected by another party.

The client–server network installation team at Armstrong Worldwide experienced the wrath of dysfunctional conflict and its consequences. **Conflict** is a process in which one party perceives that its interests are being opposed or negatively affected by another party.[75] Armstrong's information systems employees experienced conflict with the consultants (and with Armstrong's own managers) because they believed the consultants were deliberately or incidentally opposing their interests, including hours of work, long-term technology obligations, and job security. Notice that conflict is a perception, which means that it begins long before observable disagreements. Thus managers need to look for subtle signs of conflict perceptions to prevent dysfunctional behaviors that may follow.

// TASK VERSUS RELATIONSHIP CONFLICT

A few decades ago management experts warned that conflict was bad and that effective managers prevented conflict from developing. They observed that conflict resulted in the same problems that Armstrong Worldwide experienced, including stress, turnover, lack of information sharing, and nonproductive behavior toward others. The more intense the conflict, the lower the team's performance and satisfaction. More recently management writers have adopted the view that conflict is good to a certain degree. They have developed an elegant upside-down U-shaped model showing that team performance is highest when managers encourage moderate levels of conflict (the top of the upside-down U). This advice is based on evidence that some level of conflict motivates team members to more thoroughly debate and analyze problems and opportunities. Conflict-motivated debate brings out new ideas and improves everyone's understanding of the issue, which then produces better decisions and team performance, particularly for ambiguous tasks.

Unfortunately the "moderate conflict is good" advice isn't quite correct, either. To understand the influence of conflict on team effectiveness, we need to distinguish between task-related conflict and relationship conflict. *Task-related conflict* (also called *constructive conflict*) occurs when team members perceive that the conflict is in the task or problem rather than in each other. Team members view the problem as something "out there" that needs to be resolved, and the employees are merely messengers in this discussion. In contrast, *relationship conflict* occurs when team members view differences as personal attacks that threaten their self-esteem and resources. The conflicting parties view others (their attitudes, biases, and decisions) as the source of conflict.

Consider the different conflict perspectives adopted by Bob Goodenow and Ted Saskin, the former and current leaders of the National Hockey League Players' Association. For 15 years Goodenow took an uncompromising approach that rewarded players handsomely, but critics say it also generated relationship conflict with NHL team owners. That relationship conflict may have been a factor in the cancellation of an entire hockey season a few years ago. When the owners canceled the season, Goodenow didn't mince words, saying that the players "never had a real negotiating partner." Goodenow stepped down when players agreed to the NHL owners' request to cap team salaries. Goodenow was replaced by Ted Saskin, who has taken a more conciliatory and task-oriented approach to the conflict. "We've got to be able to work more cooperatively (with the NHL) in the future," Saskin announced on the day he took over.

NHL board of governors chair Harley Hotchkiss thinks Saskin's approach to resolving differences is good for the sport's future. "I will say nothing bad about Bob Goodenow," insists Hotchkiss. "I just think that in any business you need a spirit of cooperation to move forward, and I think Ted Saskin will handle that well."[76]

Minimizing Relationship Conflict The "moderate conflict is good" advice assumes that relationship conflict can remain low as task-related conflict increases up to some midpoint. Unfortunately it isn't that simple. Relationship conflict flares up in some teams even when members experience low levels of task-related conflict. Other teams can have high levels of task-related conflict without developing perceptible levels of relationship conflict. The best advice for managers is to encourage task-related conflict and apply the following four strategies to suppress relationship conflict:[77]

Stick-Handling NHL Conflict   Bob Goodenow (left in photo), who led the National Hockey League Players' Association over the past 15 years, has been called the Darth Vader of hockey. His never-give-in style rewarded players handsomely but may have generated relationship conflict with NHL team owners. Goodenow stepped down after a yearlong NHL strike and was replaced by Ted Saskin (right in photo), who has taken a more conciliatory and task-oriented approach to the conflict.

© AP Photo/Adrian Wyld, CP

- *Emotional intelligence:* Relationship conflict is less likely to occur, or is less likely to escalate, when team members have high levels of emotional intelligence. Team members have high emotional intelligence when they are aware of their own and others' emotions, and when they are able to manage emotions in themselves and others. Employees with high emotional intelligence can better regulate their emotions during debate, which reduces the risk of escalating perceptions of interpersonal hostility.

- *Cohesive team:* Relationship conflict is suppressed when the conflict occurs within a highly cohesive team. The longer people work together, get to know each other, and develop mutual trust, the more latitude they give each other to show emotions without being personally offended. Members of cohesive teams are also motivated to remain with the team, which motivates them to avoid escalating relationship conflict during otherwise emotionally turbulent discussions.

- *Supportive team norms:* Various team norms can hold relationship conflict at bay during constructive debate. When team norms encourage openness, for instance, team members learn to appreciate honest dialogue without personally reacting to any emotional display during the disagreements. Other norms might discourage team members from displaying negative emotions toward coworkers.

- *Problem-solving conflict management style:* Whether relationship conflict emerges from constructive debate depends to some extent on the interpersonal conflict management style used by those participating in the conflict. Specifically, team members who take a problem-solving approach are less likely to trigger strong emotions compared with those who assertively force their preferences on others. These and other conflict management styles are discussed next.

// INTERPERSONAL CONFLICT MANAGEMENT STYLES

Sometimes team members approach conflict with a winner-take-all attitude that views the other party as a competitor. Or they might try to resolve the conflict with the perception that everyone can come out ahead through creative problem solving. The conflict literature identifies five interpersonal conflict management styles, each with a unique degree of

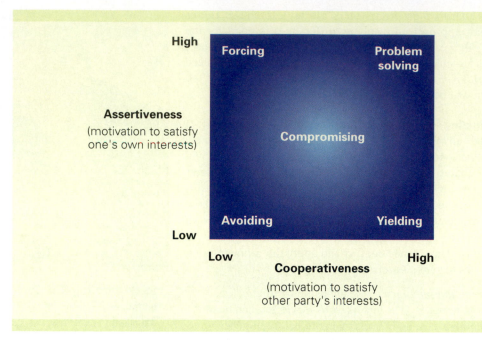

FIGURE 11.8   Interpersonal Conflict Management Styles

Source: Adapted from C.K.W. de Dreu, A. Evers, B. Beersma, E.S. Kluwer, and A. Nauta, "A Theory-Based Measure of Conflict Management Strategies in the Workplace," *Journal of Organizational Behavior* 22 (2001), pp. 645–68. For earlier variations of this model, see T.L. Ruble and K. Thomas, "Support for a Two-Dimensional Model of Conflict Behavior," *Organizational Behavior and Human Performance* 16 (1976), p. 145.

cooperativeness and assertiveness (see Figure 11.8).[78] No single style is best in every situation. However, as we mentioned, some styles are more likely than others to transform task-related conflict into relationship conflict.

- *Problem solving:* Problem solving tries to find a mutually beneficial solution for both parties. Information sharing is an important feature of this style because both parties collaborate to identify common ground and potential solutions that satisfy both (or all) of them. This style is often preferred because it minimizes the risk of relationship conflict. However, it won't work well if team members lack trust and the sides have perfectly opposing interests.

- *Avoiding:* Avoiding tries to smooth over or avoid conflict situations altogether. It represents a low concern for both self and the other party. For example, some employees will rearrange their work areas or tasks to minimize interaction with certain coworkers.[79] This style works best when the problem has already generated relationship conflict and the issue is not worth fighting over.

- *Forcing:* Forcing tries to win the conflict at the other's expense. This style relies on assertive influence tactics. The forcing style creates a high risk of relationship conflict, but it may be necessary when the dispute requires a quick solution or the opposing party's views are unethical.

- *Yielding:* Yielding involves giving in completely to the other side's wishes, or at least cooperating with little or no attention to your own interests. This style may be necessary when the opponent has substantially more power or the issue is not as important to you as to the other party. In the long run, however, yielding may produce more conflict because it raises the other party's expectations of an easy win in disputes.

- *Compromising:* Compromising involves actively searching for a middle ground between the interests of the two parties. This style may be best when there is little hope for mutual gain through problem solving, both parties have equal power, and both are under time pressure to settle their differences. However, compromising tends to overlook creative solutions such as those discovered when using the problem-solving style.

// STRUCTURAL SOLUTIONS TO TEAM CONFLICT

So far we have looked at the interpersonal side of team conflict. But when conflict escalates or continues without resolution, managers need to identify the structural causes of that conflict and apply corresponding solutions. One of the most common structural causes of conflict is incompatible goals. Consider the disagreement described earlier between Armstrong Worldwide employees and the external consultants over work schedule preferences. The employees wanted a well-spaced balance of work and leisure, whereas the external consultants wanted a large chunk of work so they could fly back home for a longer weekend.

There is no easy solution to goal incompatibility, but one idea is to emphasize superordinate goals to both groups. **Superordinate goals** are common objectives held by conflicting parties that are more important than the departmental or individual goals on which the conflict is based. By increasing commitment to corporatewide goals, employees place less emphasis on, and therefore feel less conflict with, coworkers regarding competing individual or departmental-level goals.

A second source of team conflict is the different beliefs, backgrounds, and values that employees bring to the group. Your values shape your preferences and motivation, so people with different values tend to prefer different choices and have different motivations. Earlier we noted that diverse values and backgrounds improve team effectiveness, so reducing this diversity isn't usually the best solution to conflict. Instead managers need to find ways for employees to understand each other's differences—in other words, to increase empathy among team members.

Task interdependence is a third reason why conflict exists. The more tightly interconnected your work is with other people's work, the more likely your actions are to interfere with their goals. And because a team is partly defined by the interdependence of its members, conflict is going to occur. If conflict gets out of hand, managers might look at ways to reduce the intensity of interdependence. For instance, rather than have two people perform highly interdependent services for a customer, it may be better for each employee to provide both services.

Finally, conflict often results from ambiguity over rules and responsibilities. Look back at the Armstrong Worldwide conflict again. Armstrong's employees and the external consultants lacked clear guidelines over work hours and (at first) leadership responsibilities, which motivated them to act competitively toward each other. Eventually Armstrong executives doused the conflict by clarifying these duties and expectations. They also set up an advisory group to make further rules if employees and consultants developed future disputes.

> **superordinate goals**
> Common objectives held by conflicting parties that are more important than the departmental or individual goals on which the conflict is based.

IN CONCLUSION   WHY DOES IT MATTER?

What's so important about managing teams? The answer is this: Teams can make a significant difference in how well the organization serves its clients, provides creative ideas, and keeps the workforce engaged toward higher performance. Under the right circumstances, employees also fulfill their drive to bond through teamwork. At the same time, managers need to recognize the conditions where teams are valuable and where they merely increase the cost of production or aggravation to everyone involved in the team.

Managing teamwork also matters because teams do not always work well without help from management. In fact, there are probably as many team failures as successes in organizations because managers sometimes wrongly assume that teams can operate effectively without management guidance and intervention. This is obviously a false assumption. As we learned in this chapter, teams thrive under the right conditions and with the right team characteristics. Companies need high-performing managers to put these potentially high-performing teams together.

Although high-performance teams can do much to manage their own processes, managers are always needed to facilitate and offer constructive feedback. For instance, members of even the highest-performance teams are sometimes reluctant to correct behavior problems of a fellow teammate; they welcome involvement from managers to assist. Similarly, managers occasionally need to step forward to point out when the team needs some intensive team building or when a simmering conflict is dragging down the team's performance and camaraderie. Thus although high-performance teams rely less on managers for day-to-day decisions, they will continue to depend on them to maintain a team-friendly work environment and help steer the team when members don't realize they are heading for shoals.

MANAGEMENT CHALLENGES

1. This chapter identifies three success factors for effective self-directed teams. Explain why these factors might influence the effectiveness of these teams.

2. Suppose the instructor for this course assigned you to a project team consisting of three other students who are currently taking similar courses in Ireland, India, and Brazil. All students speak English and have similar expertise in the topic. Use your knowledge of virtual teams to discuss the problems your team might face, compared with a team of local students who can meet face-to-face.

3. Diversity is a double-edged sword for team dynamics. Discuss the benefits of team diversity as well as the problems this diversity potentially creates.

4. You have been put in charge of a cross-functional task force that will develop enhanced Internet banking services for retail customers. The team includes representatives from marketing, information services, customer service, and accounting, all of whom will move to the same location at headquarters for three months. Describe the behaviors you might observe during each stage of the team's development.

5. Some firms have turned to volunteering as a form of team building, whereby a group of employees spends a day working together on a community project, often outside their expertise. In what ways might volunteering be an effective team building activity?

6. To what extent would team cohesiveness improve the performance of crew members in the NASA space shuttle program?

7. The chief executive officer of Creative Toys, Inc., has read about cooperation in Japanese companies and wants to bring this same philosophy to the company. The goal is to avoid all conflict so that employees will work cooperatively and be happier at Creative Toys. Discuss the merits and limitations of the CEO's policy.

MANAGEMENT PORTFOLIO

FOR THE ORGANIZATION YOU HAVE CHOSEN TO FOLLOW:

1. Review the basic structure you described in Chapter 8 for the organization you are studying. To what extent does that structure organize people into teams?

2. Does this organization group employees into self-directed teams? Describe the structure and responsibilities of those teams.

3. Virtual teams are more common in some companies and industries than in others. To what extent does the company you are studying rely on virtual teams, and in what areas of the organization? Why do these virtual teams exist here rather than elsewhere in the organization?

4. What conflicts in this organization have come to the public's knowledge? What caused those conflicts? How would you resolve them?

CLOSING CASE   THE SHIPPING INDUSTRY ACCOUNTING TEAM

For the past five years I have been working at McKay, Sanderson, and Smith Associates, a midsized accounting firm in Boston that specializes in commercial accounting and audits. My particular specialty is accounting practices for shipping companies, ranging from small fishing fleets to a couple of the big firms with ships along the East Coast.

About 18 months ago McKay, Sanderson, and Smith Associates became part of a large merger involving two other accounting firms. These firms have offices in Miami, Seattle, Baton Rouge, and Los Angeles. Although the other two accounting firms were much larger than McKay, all three firms agreed to avoid centralizing the business around one office in Los Angeles. Instead the new firm—called Goldberg, Choo, and McKay Associates—would rely on teams across the country to "leverage the synergies of our collective knowledge" (an often-cited statement from the managing partner soon after the merger).

The merger affected me a year ago when my boss (a senior partner and vice president of the merger firm) announced that I would be working more closely with three people from the other two firms to become the firm's new shipping industry accounting team. The other team members were Elias in Miami, Susan in Seattle, and Brad in Los Angeles. I had met Elias briefly at a meeting in New York City during the merger, but I had never met Susan or Brad although I knew they were shipping accounting professionals at the other firms.

Initially the shipping team activities involved e-mailing each other about new contracts and prospective clients. Later we were asked to submit joint monthly reports on accounting statements and issues. Normally I submitted my own monthly reports that summarized activities involving my own clients. Coordinating the monthly report with three other people took much more time, particularly because different accounting documentation procedures across the three firms were still being resolved. It took numerous e-mail messages and a few telephone calls to work out a reasonable monthly report style.

During this aggravating process, it became apparent—(to me at least) that this "team" business was costing me more time than it was worth. Moreover, Brad in Los Angeles didn't have a clue about how to communicate with the rest of us. He rarely replied to e-mail. Instead he often used the telephone voice mail system, which resulted in lots of telephone tag. Brad arrives at work at 9:30 a.m. in Los Angeles (and is often late!), which is early afternoon in Boston. I typically have a flexible work schedule from 7:30 a.m. to 3:30 p.m. so I can chauffeur my kids after school to sports and music lessons. So Brad and I have a window of less than three hours to share information.

The biggest nuisance with the shipping specialist accounting team started two weeks ago when the firm asked the four of us to develop a new strategy for attracting more shipping firm business. This new strategic plan is a messy business. Somehow we have to share our thoughts on various approaches, agree on a new plan, and write a unified submission to the managing partner. Already the project is taking most of my time just writing and responding to e-mail and talking in conference calls (which none of us did much before the team formed).

Susan and Brad have already had two or three misunderstandings via e-mail about their different perspectives on delicate matters in the strategic plan. The worst of these disagreements required a conference call with all of us to resolve. Except for the most basic matters, it seems that we can't understand each other, let alone agree on key issues. I have come to the conclusion that I would never want Brad to work in my Boston office (thank goodness he's on the other side of the country). Although Elias and I seem to agree on most points, the overall team can't form a common vision or strategy. I don't know how Elias, Susan, or Brad feel, but I would be quite happy to work somewhere that did not require any of these long-distance team headaches.

CASE DISCUSSION QUESTIONS

1. What type of team was formed here? Was it necessary, in your opinion?

2. Use the team effectiveness model to identify the strengths and weaknesses of this team's environment, design, and processes.

3. Assuming that these four people must continue to work as a team, recommend ways to improve the team's effectiveness.

ENDNOTES

1. C. Fishman, "The Anarchist's Cookbook," *Fast Company,* July 2004, p. 70; J. Mackay, "Open Book Company," *Newsweek,* November 28, 2005, p. 42; A. Kimball-Stanley, "Bucking the Trend in Benefits," *Providence Journal* (Rhode Island), May 14, 2006, p. H01; K. Zimbalist, "Green Giant," *Time,* April 24, 2006, p. 24.

2. E. Hart, "Manager of the Year: John Mang," *Iron & Steelmaker,* June 2003, pp. 5–7; P. Haw, "Learning from Lean Principles," *Business Day,* July 7, 2003, p. 7.

3. M.E. Shaw, Group Dynamics, 3rd ed. (New York: McGraw-Hill, 1981), p. 8; S.A. Mohrman, S.G. Cohen, and A.M. Mohrman Jr., *Designing Team-Based Organizations: New Forms for Knowledge Work* (San Francisco: Jossey-Bass, 1995), pp. 39–40; E. Sundstrom, "The Challenges of Supporting Work Team Effectiveness," in *Supporting Work Team Effectiveness,* ed. E. Sundstrom and associates (San Francisco: Jossey-Bass, 1999), pp. 6–9.

4. S. Beatty, "Bass Talk: Plotting Plaid's Future," *The Wall Street Journal,* September 9, 2004, p. B1.

5. M. Moldaschl and W. Weber, "The 'Three Waves' of Industrial Group Work: Historical Reflections on Current Research on Group Work," *Human Relations* 51 (March 1998), pp. 347–88. The survey quotation is found in J.N. Choi, "External Activities and Team Effectiveness: Review and Theoretical Development," *Small Group Research* 33 (April 2002), pp. 181–208. Several popular books in the 1980s encouraged teamwork based on the Japanese economic miracle. These books included W. Ouchi, *Theory Z: How American Management Can Meet the Japanese Challenge* (Reading, MA: Addison-Wesley, 1981); and R.T. Pascale and A.G. Athos, *Art of Japanese Management* (New York: Simon and Schuster, 1982).

6. C.R. Emery and L.D. Fredenhall, "The Effect of Teams on Firm Profitability and Customer Satisfaction," *Journal of Service Research* 4 (February 2002), pp. 217–29; G.S. Van der Vegt and O. Janssen, "Joint Impact of Interdependence and Group Diversity on Innovation," *Journal of Management* 29 (2003), pp. 729–51.

7. B. Jorgensen, "Look before You Leap," *Electronic Business* 30, no. 12 (2004), pp. 35–36; J. Baljko, "The Lean Journey," *Electronics Supply & Manufacturing,* June 2005; C. Mitchell and M. Moreno, "Lean Manufacturing—a Case Study," *Surface Mount Technology Magazine,* May 2005, pp. 59–61.

8. R.A. Guzzo and M.W. Dickson, "Teams in Organizations: Recent Research on Performance and Effectiveness," *Annual Review of Psychology* 47 (1996), pp. 307–38; D.A. Nadler, "From Ritual to Real Work: The Board as a Team," *Directors and Boards* 22 (Summer 1998), pp. 28–31; L.R. Offerman and R.K. Spiros, "The Science and Practice of Team Development: Improving the Link," *Academy of Management* Journal 44 (April 2001), pp. 376–92.

9. B.D. Pierce and R. White, "The Evolution of Social Structure: Why Biology Matters," *Academy of Management Review* 24 (October 1999), pp. 843–53; M.A. Hogg et al., "The Social Identity Perspective: Intergroup Relations, Self-Conception, and Small Groups," *Small Group Research* 35, no. 3 (June 2004), pp. 246–76; J.R. Spoor and J.R. Kelly, "The Evolutionary Significance of Affect in Groups: Communication and Group Bonding," *Group Processes & Intergroup Relations* 7, no. 4 (2004), pp. 398–412; M. Van Vugt and C.M. Hart, "Social Identity as Social Glue: The Origins of Group Loyalty," *Journal of Personality and Social Psychology* 86, no. 4 (2004), pp. 585–98.

10. "The Trouble with Teams," *Economist,* January 14, 1995, p. 6; H. Robbins and M. Finley, *Why Teams Don't Work* (Princeton, NJ: Peterson's/Pacesetters, 1995), Chapter 20; E.A. Locke et al., "The Importance of the Individual in an Age of Groupism," in *Groups at Work: Theory and Research,* ed. M.E. Turner (Mahwah, NJ: Lawrence Erbaum Associates, 2001), pp. 501–28; N.J. Allen and T.D. Hecht, "The 'Romance of Teams': Toward an Understanding of Its Psychological Underpinnings and Implications," *Journal of Occupational and Organizational Psychology* 77 (2004), pp. 439–61.

11. I.D. Steiner, *Group Process and Productivity* (New York: Academic Press, 1972); N.L. Kerr and S.R. Tindale, "Group Performance and Decision Making," *Annual Review of Psychology* 55 (2004), pp. 623–55.

12. R. Cross, "Looking before You Leap: Assessing the Jump to Teams in Knowledge-Based Work," *Business Horizons,* September 2000; Q.R. Skrabec Jr., "The Myth of Teams," *Industrial Management,* September–October 2002, pp. 25–27.

13. S.J. Karau and K.D. Williams, "Social Loafing: A Meta-Analytic Review and Theoretical Integration," *Journal of Personality and Social Psychology* 65 (1993), pp. 681–706; R.C. Liden et al., "Social Loafing: A Field Investigation," *Journal of Management* 30 (2004), pp. 285–304.

14. M. Erez and A. Somech, "Is Group Productivity Loss the Rule or the Exception? Effects of Culture and Group-Based Motivation," *Academy of Management Journal* 39 (1996), pp. 1513–37; Kerr and Tindale, "Group Performance and Decision Making."

15. S.A. Mohrman, S.G. Cohen, and J. Mohrman, A.M., *Designing Team-Based Organizations: New Forms for Knowledge Work* (San Francisco: Jossey-Bass, 1995); D.E. Yeatts and C. Hyten, *High-Performing Self-Managed Work Teams: A Comparison of Theory and Practice* (Thousand Oaks, CA: Sage, 1998); E.E. Lawler, *Organizing for High Performance* (San Francisco: Jossey-Bass, 2001); R.J. Torraco, "Work Design Theory: A Review and Critique with Implications for Human Resource Development," *Human Resource Development Quarterly* 16, no. 1 (Spring 2005), pp. 85–109.

16. C. Eberting, "The Harley Mystique Comes to Kansas City," *Kansas City Star,* January 6, 1998, p. A1; D. Fields, "Harley Teams Shoot for Better Bike," *Akron Beacon Journal,* June 15, 1998; J. Singer and S. Duvall, "High-Performance Partnering by Self-Managed Teams in Manufacturing," *Engineering Management Journal* 12 (December 2000), pp. 9–15; P.A. Chansler, P.M. Swamidass, and C. Cammann, "Self-Managing Work Teams: An Empirical Study of Group Cohesiveness in 'Natural Work Groups' at a Harley-Davidson Motor Company Plant," *Small Group Research* 34 (February 2003), pp. 101–20.

17. P. Panchak, "Production Workers Can Be Your Competitive Edge," *Industry Week,* October 2004, p. 11; S.K. Muthusamy, J.V. Wheeler, and B.L. Simmons, "Self-Managing Work Teams: Enhancing Organizational Innovativeness," *Organization Development Journal* 23, no. 3 (Fall 2005), pp. 53–66.

18. C.R. Emery and L.D. Fredendall, "The Effect of Teams on Firm Profitability and Customer Satisfaction," *Journal of Service Research* 4 (February 2002), pp. 217–29; A. Krause and H. Dunckel, "Work Design and Customer Satisfaction: Effects of the Implementation of Semi-Autonomous Group Work on Customer Satisfaction Considering Employee Satisfaction and Group Performance (translated abstract)," *Zeitschrift fur Arbeits-und Organisationspsychologie* 47, no. 4 (2003), pp. 182–93; H. van Mierlo et al., "Self-Managing Teamwork and Psychological Well-Being: Review of a Multilevel Research Domain," *Group & Organization Management* 30, no. 2 (April 2005), pp. 211–35.

19. M. Moldaschl and W.G. Weber, "The 'Three Waves' of Industrial Group Work: Historical Reflections on Current Research on Group Work," *Human Relations* 51 (March 1998), pp. 259–87; W. Niepce and E. Molleman, "Work Design Issues in Lean Production from Sociotechnical System Perspective: Neo-Taylorism or the Next Step in Sociotechnical Design?" *Human Relations* 51, no. 3 (March 1998), pp. 259–87.

20. E. Ulich and W.G. Weber, "Dimensions, Criteria, and Evaluation of Work Group Autonomy," in *Handbook of Work Group Psychology,* ed. M.A. West (Chichester, UK: John Wiley and Sons, 1996), pp. 247–82.

21. K.P. Carson and G.L. Stewart, "Job Analysis and the Sociotechnical Approach to Quality: A Critical Examination," *Journal of Quality Management* 1 (1996), pp. 49–65; C.C. Manz and G.L. Stewart, "Attaining Flexible Stability by Integrating Total Quality Management and Socio-Technical Systems Theory," *Organization Science* 8 (1997), pp. 59–70.

22. J. Gordon, "Do Your Virtual Teams Deliver Only Virtual Performance?" *Training,* June 2005, pp. 20–24.

23. J. Lipnack and J. Stamps, *Virtual Teams: People Working across Boundaries with Technology* (New York: John Wiley and Sons, 2001); B.S. Bell and W.J. Kozlowski, "A Typology of Virtual Teams: Implications for Effective Leadership," *Group & Organization Management* 27 (March 2002), pp. 14–49; G. Hertel, S. Geister, and U. Konradt, "Managing Virtual Teams: A Review of Current Empirical Research," *Human Resource Management Review* 15 (2005), pp. 69–95.

24. G. Gilder, *Telecosm: How Infinite Bandwidth Will Revolutionize Our World* (New York: Free Press, 2001); L.L. Martins, L.L. Gilson, and M.T. Maynard, "Virtual Teams: What Do We Know and Where Do We Go from Here?" *Journal of Management* 30, no. 6 (2004), pp. 805–35. The Novartis quotation is from S. Murray, "Pros and Cons of Technology: The Corporate Agenda: Managing Virtual Teams," *Financial Times* (London), May 27, 2002, p. 6.

25. J.S. Lureya and M.S. Raisinghani, "An Empirical Study of Best Practices in Virtual Teams," *Information & Management* 38 (2001), pp. 523–44; Y.L. Doz, J.F.P. Santos, and P.J. Williamson, "The Metanational Advantage," *Optimize,* May 2002, p. 45ff.

26. D. Robb, "Global Workgroups," *Computerworld,* August 15, 2005, pp. 37–38.

27. D. Robey, H.M. Khoo, and C. Powers, "Situated Learning in Cross-Functional Virtual Teams," *Technical Communication,* February 2000, pp. 51–66; Martins, Gilson, and Maynard, "Virtual Teams"; Hertel, Geister, and Konradt, "Managing Virtual Teams."

28. S. Prashad, "Building Trust Tricky for 'Virtual' Teams," *Toronto Star,* October 23, 2003, p. K06.

29. G.Buckler, "Staking One for the Team," *Computing Canada*, October 22, 2004, p. 16.

30. M.A. West, C.S. Borrill, and K.L. Unsworth, "Team Effectiveness in Organizations," *International Review of Industrial and Organizational Psychology* 13 (1998), pp. 1–48; R. Forrester and A.B. Drexler, "A Model for Team-Based Organization Performance," *Academy of Management Executive* 13 (August 1999), pp. 36–49; J.E. McGrath, H. Arrow, and J.L. Berdahl, "The Study of Groups: Past, Present, and Future," *Personality & Social Psychology Review* 4, no. 1 (2000), pp. 95–105; M.A. Marks, J.E. Mathieu, and S.J. Zaccaro, "A Temporally Based Framework and Taxonomy of Team Processes," *Academy of Management Review* 26, no. 3 (July 2001), pp. 356–76.

31. G.P. Shea and R.A. Guzzo, "Group Effectiveness: What Really Matters?" *Sloan Management Review* 27 (1987), pp. 33–46; J.R. Hackman et al., "Team Effectiveness in Theory and in Practice," in *Industrial and Organizational Psychology: Linking Theory with Practice,* ed. C.L. Cooper and E.A. Locke (Oxford, UK: Blackwell, 2000), pp. 109–29.

32. These and other environmental conditions for effective teams are discussed in R. Wageman, "Case Study: Critical Success Factors for Creating Superb Self-Managing Teams at Xerox," *Compensation and Benefits Review* 29 (September–October 1997), pp. 31–41; Sundstrom, "The Challenges of Supporting Work Team Effectiveness"; Choi, "External Activities and Team Effectiveness: Review and Theoretical Development"; T.L. Doolen, M.E. Hacker, and E.M. Van Aken, "The Impact of Organizational Context on Work Team Effectiveness: A Study of Production Teams," *IEEE Transactions on Engineering Management* 50, no. 3 (August 2003), pp. 285–96; S.D. Dionne et al., "Transformational Leadership and Team Performance," *Journal of Organizational Change Management* 17, no. 2 (2004), pp. 177–93.

33. L. Adams, "Medrad Works and Wins as a Team," *Quality Magazine,* October 2004, p. 42; "Lean Manufacturing Increases Productivity, Decreases Cycle Time," *Industrial Equipment News,* October 2005.

34. M.A. Campion, E.M. Papper, and G.J. Medsker, "Relations between Work Team Characteristics and Effectiveness: A Replication and Extension," *Personnel Psychology* 49 (1996), pp. 429–52; D.C. Man and S.S.K. Lam, "The Effects of Job Complexity and Autonomy on Cohesiveness in Collectivistic and Individualistic Work Groups: A Cross-Cultural Analysis," *Journal of Organizational Behavior* 24 (2003), pp. 979–1001.

35. R. Wageman, "Interdependence and Group Effectiveness," *Administrative Science Quarterly* 40 (1995), pp. 145–80; G.S. Van der Vegt, J.M. Emans, and E. Van de Vliert, "Patterns of Interdependence in Work Teams: A Two-Level Investigation of the Relations with Job and Team Satisfaction," *Personnel Psychology* 54 (Spring 2001), pp. 51–69; R. Wageman, "The Meaning of Interdependence," in *Groups at Work: Theory and Research,* ed. M.E. Turner (Mahwah, NJ: Lawrence Erlbaum Associates, 2001), pp. 197–217.

36. Fishman, "The Anarchist's Cookbook."

37. S.E. Nedleman, "Recruiters Reveal Their Top Interview Questions," *Financial News Online,* February 16, 2005.

38. M.R. Barrick et al., "Relating Member Ability and Personality to Work-Team Processes and Team Effectiveness," *Journal of Applied Psychology* 83 (1998), pp. 377–91; S. Sonnentag, "Excellent Performance: The Role of Communication and Cooperation Processes," *Applied Psychology: An International Review* 49 (2000), pp. 483–97.

39. D. van Knippenberg, C.K.W. De Dreu, and A.C. Homan, "Work Group Diversity and Group Performance: An Integrative Model and Research Agenda," *Journal of Applied Psychology* 89, no. 6 (2004), pp. 1008–22; D.C. Lau and J.K. Murnighan, "Interactions within Groups and Subgroups: The Effects of Demographic Faultlines," *Academy of Management Journal* 48, no. 4 (August 2005), pp. 645–59.

40. A.P. Hare, "Types of Roles in Small Groups: A Bit of History and a Current Perspective," *Small Group Research* 25 (1994), pp. 443–48.

41. S.H.N. Leung, J.W.K. Chan, and W.B. Lee, "The Dynamic Team Role Behavior: The Approaches of Investigation," *Team Performance Management* 9 (2003), pp. 84–90.

42. R.M. Belbin, *Team Roles at Work* (Oxford, UK: Butterworth-Heinemann, 1993).

43. The NTSB and NASA studies are summarized in J.R. Hackman, "New Rules for Team Building," *Optimize,* July 2002, pp. 50–62.

44. B.W. Tuckman and M.A.C. Jensen, "Stages of Small-Group Development Revisited," *Group and Organization Studies* 2 (1977), pp. 419–42; B.W. Tuckman, "Developmental Sequence in Small Groups," *Group Facilitation*, Spring 2001, pp. 66–81.

45. J.E. Mathieu and G.F. Goodwin, "The Influence of Shared Mental Models on Team Process and Performance," *Journal of Applied Psychology* 85 (April 2000), pp. 273–84; J. Langan-Fox and J. Anglim, "Mental Models, Team Mental Models, and Performance: Process, Development, and Future Directions," *Human Factors and Ergonomics in Manufacturing* 14, no. 4 (2004), pp. 331–52.

46. D.L. Miller, "The Stages of Group Development: A Retrospective Study of Dynamic Team Processes," *Canadian Journal of Administrative Sciences* 20, no. 2 (2003), pp. 121–34.

47. Scott, "Blue Angels."

48. W.B. Scott, "Blue Angels," *Aviation Week & Space Technology,* March 21, 2005, pp. 50–57.

49. A.G. Dawson, "Administrators Settle into New Digs," *Delaware Coast Press,* July 16, 2003.

50. W.G. Dyer, *Team Building: Current Issues and New Alternatives,* 3rd ed. (Reading, MA: Addison-Wesley, 1995); C.A. Beatty and B.A. Barker, *Building Smart Teams: Roadmap to High Performance* (Thousand Oaks, CA: Sage Publications, 2004).

51. "German Businesswoman Demands End to Fun at Work," *Reuters,* July 9, 2003.

52. D.C. Feldman, "The Development and Enforcement of Group Norms," *Academy of Management Review* 9 (1984), pp. 47–53; E. Fehr and U. Fischbacher, "Social Norms and Human Cooperation," *Trends in Cognitive Sciences* 8, no. 4 (2004), pp. 185–90.

53. G. Johns, "Absenteeism Estimates by Employees and Managers: Divergent Perspectives and Self-Serving Perceptions," *Journal of Applied Psychology* 79 (1994), pp. 229–39.

54. N. Ellemers and F. Rink, "Identity in Work Groups: The Beneficial and Detrimental Consequences of Multiple Identities and Group Norms for Collaboration and Group Performance," *Advances in Group Processes* 22 (2005), pp. 1–41.

55. J.J. Dose and R.J. Klimoski, "The Diversity of Diversity: Work Values Effects on Formative Team Processes," *Human Resource Management Review* 9, no. 1 (Spring 1999), pp. 83–108.

56. R. Hallowell, D. Bowen, and C.-I. Knoop, "Four Seasons Goes to Paris," *Academy of Management Executive* 16, no. 4 (November 2002), pp. 7–24.

57. L. Grant, "Container Store's Workers Huddle Up to Help You Out," *USA Today,* April 30, 2002, p. B1; S.F. Gale, "Swanky Dinners, Trips, and Everyday Praise Are Part of the Container Store's Culture," *Workforce Management,* August 2003, pp. 80–82.

58. L. Coch and J. French, J.R.P., "Overcoming Resistance to Change," *Human Relations* 1 (1948), pp. 512–32.

59. C.R. Evans and K.L. Dion, "Group Cohesion and Performance: A Meta-Analysis," *Small Group Research* 22 (1991), pp. 175–86; B. Mullen and C. Copper, "The Relation between Group Cohesiveness and Performance: An Integration," *Psychological Bulletin* 115 (1994), pp. 210–27; A.V. Carron et al., "Cohesion and Performance in Sport: A Meta-Analysis," *Journal of Sport and Exercise Psychology* 24 (2002), pp. 168–88; D.J. Beal et al., "Cohesion and Performance in Groups: A Meta-Analytic Clarification of Construct Relations," *Journal of Applied Psychology* 88, no. 6 (2003), pp. 989–1004.

60. S.S. Webber and L.M. Donahue, "Impact of Highly and Less Job-Related Diversity on Work Group Cohesion and Performance: A Meta-Analysis," *Journal of Management* 27, no. 2 (2001), pp. 141–62.

61. E. Aronson and J. Mills, "The Effects of Severity of Initiation on Liking for a Group," *Journal of Abnormal and Social Psychology* 59 (1959), pp. 177–81; H.F.M. Lodewijkx, M. Van Zomeren, and J. Syroit, "The Anticipation of a Severe Initiation-Gender Differences in Effects on Affiliation Tendency and Group Attraction," *Small Group Research* 36, no. 2 (April 2005), pp. 237–62.

62. M. Rempel and R.J. Fisher, "Perceived Threat, Cohesion, and Group Problem Solving in Intergroup Conflict," *International Journal of Conflict Management* 8 (1997), pp. 216–34; M.E. Turner and T. Horvitz, "The Dilemma of Threat: Group Effectiveness and Ineffectiveness under Adversity," in *Groups at Work: Theory and Research,* ed. M.E. Turner (Mahwah, NJ: Lawrence Erlbaum Associates, 2001), pp. 445–70.

63. F. Piccolo, "Brownie Points," *Atlantic Business,* October–November 2004, p. 22.

64. W. Piper et al., "Cohesion as a Basic Bond in Groups," *Human Relations* 36 (1983), pp. 93–108; C.A. O'Reilly, D.E. Caldwell, and W.P. Barnett, "Work Group Demography, Social Integration, and Turnover," *Administrative Science Quarterly* 34 (1989), pp. 21–37.

65. P. Sullivan, J. and D.L. Feltz, "The Relationship between Intrateam Conflict and Cohesion within Hockey Teams," *Small Group Research* 32 (June 2001), pp. 34–55.

66. C. Langfred, "Is Group Cohesiveness a Double-Edged Sword? An Investigation of the Effects of Cohesiveness on Performance," *Small Group Research* 29 (1998), pp. 124–43; K.L. Gammage, A.V. Carron, and P.A. Estabrooks, "Team Cohesion and Individual Productivity: The Influence of the Norm for Productivity and the Identifiability of Individual Effort," *Small Group Research* 32 (February 2001), pp. 3–18.

67. S.L. Robinson, "Trust and Breach of the Psychological Contract," *Administrative Science Quarterly* 41 (1996), pp. 574–99; D.M. Rousseau et al., "Not So Different after All: A Cross-Discipline View of Trust," *Academy of Management Review* 23 (1998), pp. 393–404; D.L. Duarte and N.T. Snyder, *Mastering Virtual Teams: Strategies, Tools, and Techniques That Succeed,* 2nd ed. (San Francisco: Jossey-Bass, 2000), pp. 139–55.

68. D.J. McAllister, "Affect- and Cognition-Based Trust as Foundations for Interpersonal Cooperation in Organizations," *Academy of Management Journal* 38, no. 1 (February 1995), pp. 24–59; M. Williams, "In Whom We Trust: Group Membership as an Affective Context for Trust Development," *Academy of Management Review* 26, no. 3 (July 2001), pp. 377–96.

69. O.E. Williamson, "Calculativeness, Trust, and Economic Organization," *Journal of Law and Economics* 36, no. 1 (1993), pp. 453–86.

70. E.M. Whitener et al., "Managers as Initiators of Trust: An Exchange Relationship Framework for Understanding Managerial Trustworthy Behavior," *Academy of Management Review* 23 (July 1998), pp. 513–30; J.M. Kouzes and B.Z. Posner, *The Leadership Challenge,* 3rd ed. (San Francisco: Jossey-Bass, 2002), Chapter 2; T. Simons, "Behavioral Integrity: The Perceived Alignment between Managers' Words and Deeds as a Research Focus," *Organization Science* 13, no. 1 (January–February 2002), pp. 18–35.

71. Hogg et al., "The Social Identity Perspective."

72. S.L. Jarvenpaa and D.E. Leidner, "Communication and Trust in Global Virtual Teams," *Organization Science* 10 (1999), pp. 791–815; M.M. Pillutla, D. Malhotra, and J. Keith Murnighan, "Attributions of Trust and the Calculus of Reciprocity," *Journal of Experimental Social Psychology* 39, no. 5 (2003), pp. 448–55.

73. K.T. Dirks and D.L. Ferrin, "The Role of Trust in Organizations," *Organization Science* 12, no. 4 (July–August 2004), pp. 450–67.

74. E. Horwitt, "Knowledge, Knowledge, Who's Got the Knowledge," *Computerworld,* April 8, 1996, pp. 80–84.

75. J.A. Wall and R.R. Callister, "Conflict and Its Management," *Journal of Management* 21 (1995), pp. 515–58; M.A. Rahim, "Toward a Theory of Managing Organizational Conflict," *International Journal of Conflict Management* 13, no. 3 (2002), pp. 206–35.

76. "The NHL Cancels the Season," *CBC Sports Online,* February 16, 2004; D. Cox, "Goodenow's Downfall," *Toronto Star,* July 29, 2005, p. A1; A. Maki, "NHLPA's New Leader Is a Peacemaker, Not a Warrior," *Globe & Mail,* July 29, 2005, p. S1; M. Spector, "Players: He Is Your Father," *National Post,* July 29, 2005, p. B8.

77. J. Yang and K.W. Mossholder, "Decoupling Task and Relationship Conflict: The Role of Intergroup Emotional Processing," *Journal of Organizational Behavior* 25 (2004), pp. 589–605.

78. C.K.W. De Dreu et al., "A Theory-Based Measure of Conflict Management Strategies in the Workplace," *Journal of Organizational Behavior* 22 (2001), pp. 645–68.

79. K. Jelin, "A Multimethod Examination of the Benefits and Detriments of Intragroup Conflict," *Administrative Science Quarterly* 40 (1995), pp. 245–82.

12

STAFFING AND DEVELOPING A DIVERSE WORKFORCE

LEARNING OBJECTIVES

After Reading This Chapter You Should Be Able to:

1. Outline the human resource staffing process.

2. Explain how human resource staffing is connected to corporate strategic planning.

3. Describe the steps followed in human resource planning.

4. Discuss the importance of diversity in organizational settings.

5. Explain the value of the employer brand in recruitment.

6. Identify ways to improve the validity of employment interviews.

7. Describe several selection methods for hiring employees.

8. Outline training methods and what managers should do to maximize their effectiveness.

Google has a problem that other companies wouldn't mind having. The California-based company that created the world's most popular search engine needs to hire at least 10 people in the United States every day to keep up with its blistering growth. That's 70 or more people each week—more than 3,650 people each year. Google is also growing quickly in India and many other countries. Google's managers have many initiatives in development, ranging from wireless Internet access to online retailing, so they need people to achieve those objectives. "Can we hire the quality and quantity of people we want to? No," admitted cofounder Sergey Brin to several hundred investment analysts. "We're underinvesting in our business because of the limitations of hiring."

Even though the limitations of hiring are dragging its business growth, Google wants to remain fussy about who it hires. Alan Eustace, one of Google's vice presidents of engineering, explains that one top-notch engineer is worth "300 times or more than the average." He suggests that Google would rather lose an entire incoming class of engineering graduates than one exceptional technologist. Google's war for talent is made all the more challenging because most technology companies are currently hiring while the applicant pool seems to be shrinking. "We're working hard to get [talent], but other companies across Silicon Valley are doing that as well," says Google's staffing director. The tech wreck of 2000 also had a devastating effect as thousands of people left the area and industry following massive layoffs. The problem now is how Google's managers can keep up with their staffing requirements.[1]

FIGURE 12.1

Human Resource
Staffing Process

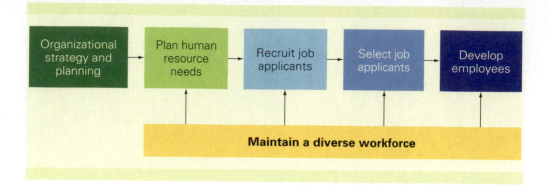

Economists point out that companies depend on land, labor, and capital to stay in business. Certainly some firms fail because they undercapitalize (they lack sufficient financial and material resources), and many still require land on which to manufacture products or provide services. But these days it is really labor—the people hired to work toward organizational goals—that determines an organization's survival and competitive advantage. This priority of human capital is particularly true in knowledge industries such as Google's high-technology software businesses. Google and other companies depend on employees to discover the next product breakthrough, to provide a higher level of service than competitors, and ultimately to secure the land and capital needed to sustain the organization. It's little wonder, then, why we emphasized in Chapter 1 that developing employees—including hiring, training, mentoring, and rewarding them—is one of the cornerstones of effective management. Yet as management guru Peter Drucker has noted, only about one in three selection and promotion decisions is more than minimally effective.[2]

This chapter travels through the staffing and development process shown in Figure 12.1. We begin by describing the five steps in human resource planning and noting issues with contingent work. Next we look at workforce diversity and its importance for organizations. The third section takes us through the recruitment process, including the importance of employer branding, internal versus external recruitment, various types of recruitment channels, and the role of recruitment in maintaining a diverse workforce. Then we describe various selection practices, consider the role of selection in diversity, and examine how organizational and applicant conflicts interfere with the staffing process. The final section of this chapter looks at employee development, including two methods of training needs analysis, several training methods, and ways in which managers can support the training process.

// Human Resource Planning: Translating Strategy into Staffing Requirements

■ HR planning at Conroe Independent School District.

human resource (HR) planning

The process of ensuring that the organization has the right kinds of people in the right places at the right time.

Conroe Independent School District is growing by leaps and bounds. Enrollment at the Texan school district increased from just under 35,000 in 2000 to 42,000 in 2005. By 2012 the district estimates that it will serve more than 52,000 students.[3] Aside from the challenges of figuring out how many schools to build and where to put them, Conroe's managers must determine how many teachers and other staff with specific capabilities to hire each school year. In other words, Conroe's managers rely on various forms of **human resource (HR) planning**—the process of ensuring that the organization has the right kinds of people in the right places at the right time.[4]

HR planning is vital because it puts the right number of people with the right qualifications in place to achieve the organization's strategic objectives in the most cost-effective and humane way. To illustrate the importance of HR planning, imagine if Conroe's school board didn't plan for its future human resource needs. The school board might not hire enough teachers, resulting in overcrowded classrooms. Or if they hired too many teachers and other staff,

Conroe's managers would face the difficult task of laying people off. HR planning extends beyond numbers of people; it also tries to ensure that the organization has people with the required qualifications. For instance, HR planning minimizes the risk that Conroe's school board has too many science teachers and not enough technical trades teachers.

HR planning is equally important for new strategic initiatives. When Verizon Communications, Inc., recently won the cable franchise in Hillsborough County (Tampa), Florida, its managers estimated that the telecommunications giant needed to hire 450 cable technicians in addition to the 1,500 it already employed in the counties surrounding Tampa Bay.[5] By predicting the required number of qualified technicians, Verizon was able to quickly activate a recruitment and selection process and set up facilities to orient and train these new recruits. If Verizon hadn't anticipated this number in advance, it would not have been as responsive when the contract was awarded.

HR planning occurs in many ways—some relevant to large companies, others more relevant to small businesses. However, all HR planning generally follows the five steps shown in Figure 12.2 and discussed next: (1) Conduct a job analysis, (2) estimate the demand for people in the future, (3) document the current human resource supply, (4) estimate the future internal human resource supply, and (5) estimate the future external human resource supply.

// STEP 1: CONDUCT JOB ANALYSIS

Traditionally HR planning begins with **job analysis**—the systematic investigation and documentation of duties performed, tools and equipment involved, conditions surrounding work, and competencies required by job incumbents to perform the work.[6] This analysis typically results in a *job description,* which is a written statement of this information. Even Google, which grew quickly from a hobby at Stanford University in the late 1990s, writes job descriptions for many positions. This documentation also includes the list of required competencies for the job (called a *job specification*). Job analysis allows managers to categorize work so HR planning can identify needs more specifically. For instance, Conroe Independent School District would have job descriptions for teachers, principals, and various support staff. Job analysis also ensures that all required duties are assigned to people in specific jobs.

An increasing number of companies have reduced their reliance on job descriptions because the boundaries of job duties have become blurred as companies depend more on multiskilled teams than individuals to perform work.[7] Job descriptions can still be created in flexible firms, but the descriptions are necessarily more generic rather than precisely relevant to a specific job. Still, job analysis remains a legal requirement to minimize the risk of job discrimination.

> **job analysis**
> The systematic investigation and documentation of duties performed, tools and equipment involved, conditions surrounding work, and competencies required by job incumbents to perform the work.

// STEP 2: ESTIMATE HUMAN RESOURCE DEMAND

The second step in HR planning is to predict how many people with what competencies are required at some point in the future. As you can imagine, this prediction is not an exact science. It typically relies on organizational strategy, operational plans, and estimates of future demand for

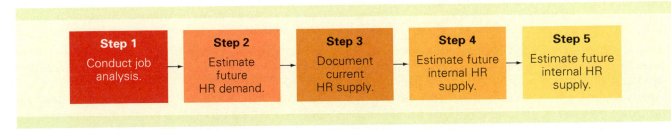

| **Step 1** | **Step 2** | **Step 3** | **Step 4** | **Step 5** |
| Conduct job analysis. | Estimate future HR demand. | Document current HR supply. | Estimate future internal HR supply. | Estimate future internal HR supply. |

FIGURE 12.2   Human Resource Planning Process

the organization's products or services. Verizon would estimate the number of cable technicians to hire in Hillsborough County based either on the number of miles of cable that must be installed and maintained or on the number of customers projected for that area for the next few years. At Conroe Independent School District and most other school districts, managers likely estimate future demand for teachers based on expected student enrollments and the ideal student–teacher ratio. If student enrollments are expected to grow by 1,000 students next year and the ideal ratio is 20 students per teacher, Conroe needs to employ 50 more teachers.

Of course Conroe will require different types of teachers, so this macro-level estimate needs to be supplemented with a micro-level prediction. For a micro-level estimate, managers examine the operational plans within their work units and estimate the number of people required to execute those plans. This information is judgmental but is closer to the ground, so it can pick up subtle requirements overlooked by the macro-level predictions. It tends to be better than macro estimates at taking into account specific capabilities, such as how many teachers are required with a background in science, who speak Spanish fluently, or have completed training in special education programs.

// STEP 3: DOCUMENT CURRENT HUMAN RESOURCE SUPPLY

Projecting future demand is only part of the forecasting process. Another part is to estimate how many staff will still be employed by the organization at future dates. This estimate begins by examining the stock of employees—how many people are currently employed in each job group with specific competencies. Managers might simply document the number of employees in various positions as well as their credentials and competencies. However, most large organizations have sophisticated human resource information systems that track details about every employee and provide more precise estimates of future supply.

Dofasco Keeps Its HR Planning Irons in the Fire Dofasco, Inc., estimates that more of its managers will retire over the next few years than it normally promotes and trains. To ensure that the supply of managers matches demand, the successful Canadian steelmaker is taking a micro-level approach to estimating future internal human resource supply. It is identifying specific employees three or four levels below the managers who have leadership potential. This helps the company estimate how many people will have management capabilities in the future.

Courtesy of Dofasco.

// STEP 4: ESTIMATE FUTURE INTERNAL HUMAN RESOURCE SUPPLY

The next step in human resource planning is to estimate how many current employees will be in various jobs within the organization at some future date. This prediction of future internal human resource supply can occur at a macro level, micro level, or combination of both levels. At the macro level, managers use estimates of past flows of people through and out of the organization. Conroe Independent School District can predict how many current teachers will be employed next year by looking at how many quit, retire, or otherwise leave the organization in a typical year. At the micro level, managers predict and plan for replacement of specific individuals based on their knowledge of those people. The principal and other managers at each school would have some information about which staff members are likely to quit, go on maternity or medical leave, or retire next year. This micro-level approach offers more precise information than the macro-level approach about what skills are required next year.

Dofasco, Inc., uses both the macro- and micro-level approaches to estimate its future supply of managers. At a macro-level analysis, it has figured out that more managers will retire over the next few years than it normally promotes and trains during that time. "It takes about 15 years to develop a good manager," says Dave Santi, human resource manager at the successful Canadian steelmaker. "We just have to figure out a way to do it in seven or eight." At the micro level, Dofasco searches for employees three or four levels below the manager and identifies those with leadership potential. "We are trying to find out as much as we can about an individual's qualities as early as possible," says Santi. In fact, Dofasco begins its leadership competencies search at campus interviews with prospective employees. "We are looking for leadership qualities right from day one," Santi explains. "It is not just the highest marks that get you into the company."[8]

// STEP 5: ESTIMATE FUTURE EXTERNAL HUMAN RESOURCE SUPPLY

Employees quit, retire, and move into different jobs, so invariably managers depend on the external labor market for new recruits. But can the external supply deliver the human capital the company needs? Most managers today would loudly complain NO! There is a "war for talent" due to retiring baby boomers, rapidly changing technologies, and a host of other factors. Google's staffing dilemma, which we introduced at the beginning of this chapter, is due in part to the dot-com meltdown a few years ago, which dramatically shrank Silicon Valley's pool of high-tech talent. Even so, Google's pickings were easier a couple of years ago when other high-tech firms were in a holding pattern. Today it seems that every company is battling over a limited number of applicants. One recent survey of 33,000 employers in 23 countries reported that 40 percent are struggling to find enough qualified job candidates.[9]

Given every company's dependence on the external labor market, managers must do all they can to anticipate and adjust their strategies and plans to estimates of the future human resource supply. Here's a recent example: Eastern Europe experienced low birthrates during the early 1990s, which will soon result in a significant drop in the number of young people graduating from high school. Managers at Anhalt Elektro Motor Works anticipated this problem during their human resource planning process a few years ago. The 165-employee specialty engine maker in Dessau, Germany, has since adjusted its staffing activities by hiring more workers over 50 years old. "Companies that still think they can just keep hiring young people out of school will very soon be in for a shock," says Anhalt Elektro CEO Reiner Storch.[10]

■ Anhalt Elektro solves Germany's skills shortage with age.

// RELYING ON THE CONTINGENT WORKFORCE

The five-step HR planning process is somewhat simplified because it assumes that everyone is a permanent employee. Yet over the past two decades, companies have dramatically increased their reliance on **contingent work**. Contingent work includes any job in which the individual does not have an explicit or implicit contract for long-term employment, or one in which the minimum hours of work can vary in a nonsystematic way. Many contingent workers are employees with temporary, fixed-term contracts with a company. Others are contractors assigned to specific projects who also work at other organizations. A third group includes people employed by temporary staffing agencies or contracting companies who work all of the time at a client's offices as if they are employees. By some estimates, more than 15 percent of the U.S. workforce is employed in a contingent work arrangement. Experts predict that the percentage of the workforce in contingent work will continue to increase.[11]

Contingent work has become more common because it gives companies greater flexibility in human resource planning.[12] It is easier to increase or decrease the size of the workforce through contingent work contracts rather than by hiring and firing permanent employees. Organizations also respond faster to market demands by temporarily contracting skilled people than by retraining current staff in the new skills. Consultants and other skilled contractors bring valuable knowledge to the organization that is immediately applied and shared with others.[13] Another reason for the increasing reliance on contingent work is that many organizations offer fewer employer-paid benefits and lower wages to contingent workers than to permanent staff. Some employers also reduce administrative costs

contingent work
Any work arrangement in which the individual does not have an explicit or implicit contract for long-term employment, or one in which the minimum hours of work can vary in a nonsystematic way.

by outsourcing and leasing back noncore employees from a large professional company specializing in that field (such as information technology services).[14]

Although contingent work seems to reduce payroll costs and increase flexibility around human resource demand, it also creates several potential problems.[15] One concern is that contingent workers potentially have less loyalty and motivation to work for the organization because their employment is temporary or their allegiance is to the agency that actually employs them.[16] Another concern is that both contingent and permanent employees who work side-by-side may feel uncomfortable or sense injustice because permanent staff have significantly better work arrangements.[17] A third issue is that some contingent workers have less training and work experience, which leads to lower-quality products or services and higher accident rates.[18]

■ // Staffing a Diverse Workforce

As we learned in the opening paragraphs to this chapter, Google is putting a lot of effort into hiring more people so it can offer new products and services and, more generally, fulfill its strategic mandate. Yet Google's recruitment binge also includes the objective of maintaining a diverse workforce. One consultant helped Google find more female engineers by tracking down all women who graduated from the top 50 universities in the world with a graduate degree in physics, math, or computer science. The consultant then personally telephoned thousands of these women to assess their interest in a job with Google.[19]

Evaluating Diversity Maturity Lockheed Martin, which has made workforce diversity a corporate strategy, uses a diversity maturity model to evaluate each of its business units on how well they have implemented the company's diversity principles.

Courtesy of Lockheed Martin.

Lockheed Martin, which has made workforce diversity a corporate strategy, also emphasizes recruitment of specific groups. However, the aerospace company goes further by evaluating each of its business units on how well they have implemented the company's diversity principles. Units ranked at Level 1 in Lockheed Martin's "diversity maturity model" do nothing to promote diversity. Level 2 units have recruitment and mentoring programs in place, mainly aimed at hiring college and university students with diverse backgrounds. Work units ranked at Level 3 have a comprehensive staffing strategy with a full talent pipeline; employees know their training and career options; and teams are built around diverse skills and knowledge. Level 4 units extend the diversity pipeline to employees moving into leadership positions; also, these units ensure that knowledge flows from veterans to new hires. Work units with the highest ranking (Level 5) in Lockheed Martin's diversity maturity model have an inclusive workforce approach to recruitment. They also have industry-leading staff development, a mentoring process that is "embedded in the culture," and a diverse workforce that provides a competitive advantage in winning business.[20]

// SURFACE-LEVEL AND DEEP-LEVEL DIVERSITY

workforce diversity
Differences in the demographic, cultural, and personal characteristics of employees.

Google and Lockheed Martin are model employers that reflect the increasing diversity of people living in the United States as well as in many other countries. **Workforce diversity** refers to differences in the demographic, cultural, and personal characteristics of employees. Diversity occurs when organizations adopt an *inclusive corporate culture*—that is, they respect each employee's uniqueness and view this individuality as a source of sustained competitive advantage.[21] Workforce diversity takes many forms. **Surface-level diversity** includes observable demographic or physiological differences in people, such as their race, ethnicity, gender, age, and physical disabilities. This is the most obvious form of diversity, and it has changed considerably in the United States over the past few decades.

surface-level diversity
Observable demographic or physiological differences in people, such as their race, ethnicity, gender, age, and physical disabilities.

People with non-Caucasian or Hispanic origin represent one-third of the American population, and this proportion is projected to increase substantially over the next few decades. The Hispanic population recently replaced African Americans as the second largest ethnic group. Within the next 50 years one in four Americans will be Hispanic, 14 percent will be African American, and 8 percent will be of Asian descent. By 2060 non-Hispanic Caucasians will be a minority.[22] Meanwhile, women now account for nearly half of the paid workforce in the United States—more than double the participation rate a few decades ago. Gender-based shifts continue to occur within many occupations. For example, the percentage of women enrolled in medical schools has jumped from 9 percent in 1970 to almost 50 percent today.[23]

Surface-level diversity receives the most attention because it is the most obvious and easiest to measure. However, managers also need to consider **deep-level diversity**, representing differences in the psychological characteristics of employees, including personalities, beliefs, values, and attitudes.[24] We can't directly see deep-level diversity, but it is evident in a person's decisions, statements, and actions. This deep-level diversity is derived to some extent from surface-level diversity and demographic characteristics that lie just below the surface. Religion and geographic location, for example, influence a person's personal values. Education and work experience shape a person's beliefs and attitudes on a variety of issues. An individual's personal wealth (income), parental status, and other factors influence personal needs and preferences.

One illustration of deep-level diversity is the different attitudes and expectations held by employees across generational cohorts.[25] *Baby boomers*—people born between 1946 and 1964—seem to expect and desire more job security and are often intent on improving their economic and social status. In contrast, *Generation-X* employees—those born between 1965 and 1979—expect less job security and are motivated more by workplace flexibility, the opportunity to learn (particularly new technology), and working in an egalitarian and "fun" organization. Meanwhile some observers suggest that *Generation-Y* employees (those born after 1979) are noticeably self-confident, optimistic, multitasking, and more independent than even Gen-X coworkers. These statements certainly don't apply to everyone in each cohort, but they reflect the fact that different generations have different values and expectations.

deep-level diversity

Differences in the psychological characteristics of employees, including personalities, beliefs, values, and attitudes.

// IS DIVERSITY IMPORTANT?

Although companies have been under pressure for several decades to improve workforce diversity, many have made this issue a top priority. Figure 12.3 lists the top 30 companies in America for diversity. Why do these and other companies actively develop a more diverse workforce? The most widely held explanation is that diversity makes good business sense.[26]

1. Verizon Communications/Wireless*
2. Consolidated Edison Co. of New York*
3. The Coca-Cola Co.*
4. Health Care Service Corp.
5. HBO
6. PricewaterhouseCoopers
7. Turner Broadcasting
8. Abbott
9. BellSouth*
10. Blue Cross and Blue Shield of Florida
11. JPMorgan Chase
12. Comerica*
13. HSBC
14. Sodexho
15. Cingular Wireless
16. Colgate-Palmolive
17. Wells Fargo
18. PepsiCo*
19. Sempra Energy
20. Macy's/Bloomingdale's
21. Wachovia*
22. Marriott International*
23. Allstate
24. Ernst & Young
25. Bank of America*
26. IKON Office Solutions
27. Citigroup*
28. SunTrust Banks
29. Toyota North America*
30. American Express*

FIGURE 12.3

America's Top 30 Companies for Diversity

* Indicates company is also ranked in Black Enterprise Top 40 Companies for Diversity

Sources: Ranking is from the 2006 DiversityInc Top 50 Companies for Diversity, April 17, 2006. Black Enterprise list (noted with asterisk) is from "Black Enterprise Announces the 40 Best Companies for Diversity," Black Enterprise news release, June 12, 2006.

In fact, 70 percent of the 140 leading organizations in the United Kingdom say that diversity initiatives are primarily driven by the competitive advantage that diversity offers. "Achieving excellence in diversity is one of the marks of a truly world-class company," suggests Barclays Group chief executive Matt Barrett. "Diversity is not a 'nice to have' but a significant part of an answer to our business challenges."

In support of this view, studies have found that companies with the highest representation of women on their top management teams experienced significantly better financial performance than firms with the lowest representation of women. Other research reports that teams with some forms of diversity (particularly occupational diversity) make better decisions about complex problems than do teams whose members have similar backgrounds. Diversity also makes sense when we recognize that companies lacking diversity are restricting access to the complete pool of talent in the workforce. By employing mostly white men in top management positions, for example, an organization loses a wealth of knowledge, skills, and perspectives that people with other demographic backgrounds can offer. "When there are a variety of different ideas from different people, you find linkages where significant innovation occurs," says Deborah Dagit, executive director of the Diversity & Work Environment at pharmaceutical company Merck & Co. "Where you have groups of people who think similarly, there is only incremental change."[27]

■ Leveraging diversity at Southern California Gas Co. and MONY Group.

Anecdotal evidence also suggests that a diverse workforce is more likely to understand and respond to the needs of equally diverse customers. For example, many Vietnamese customers insisted that Southern California Gas Co. field staff remove their steel-toed work boots when entering the customer's home, yet doing so would violate safety regulations. Some of the gas company's Vietnamese employees found a solution: Customers would be satisfied if employees wore paper booties over the boots. Here's another example: Executives at MONY Group discovered that none of the New York insurance firm's employees who served the Hispanic market were Hispanic. But the executives received a bigger surprise when they started hiring more Hispanic employees to market these products. "Once we started hiring and recruiting people from those ethnic markets, we found that our products did not relate to these people at all," says MONY CEO Michael Roth. So Roth asked employees to revamp MONY's products and marketing efforts so they would be more appealing to Hispanic clients.[28]

Although workforce diversity is a sound business proposition, it is also a double-edged sword. In fact, several experts suggest that the benefits of diversity are subtle and contingent on a number of factors. The general conclusion is that most forms of diversity offer both advantages and disadvantages.[29] As we noted in Chapter 11, diverse employees usually take longer to become a high-performing team. Diversity is a source of conflict, which can lead to lack of information sharing and, in extreme cases, morale problems and higher turnover. In sum, diversity can make a difference to the organization's reputation and bottom line, but we still need to untangle what types of diversity make a difference and under what circumstances their benefits surpass the problems.

Diversity as an Ethical and Legal Imperative Whether or not diversity is a business advantage, managers need to make it a priority because surface-level diversity is a moral and legal imperative. Ethically, companies that offer an inclusive workplace are, in essence, making fair and just decisions regarding employment, promotions, rewards, and so on. Fairness is a well-established influence on employee loyalty and satisfaction. "Diversity is about fairness; we use the term *inclusive meritocracy*," says Ann M. Limberg, president of Bank of America New Jersey. "What it does for our workforce is build trust and assures that individual differences are valued."[30] This perception of fairness extends to the organization's public reputation. Verizon Communications is a good example. Minorities make up 30 percent of Verizon's workforce of 200,000 and 18 percent of top management positions. Women represent 43 percent of its workforce and 32 percent of top management. This inclusive culture has made Verizon the top company in America for diversity (see Figure 12.3); the company has also won awards from numerous organizations representing Hispanics, African Americans, gays and lesbians, people with disabilities, and other groups.[31]

Equal Pay Act of 1963	Protects men and women who perform substantially equal work in the same establishment from sex-based wage discrimination.
Civil Rights Act of 1964	Prohibits employment discrimination based on race, color, religion, sex, or national origin.
Age Discrimination in Employment Act of 1967	Protects individuals who are 40 years of age or older.
Americans with Disabilities Act of 1990	Prohibit employment discrimination against qualified individuals with disabilities in the private sector and in state and local governments.
Rehabilitation Act of 1973	Prohibits discrimination against qualified individuals with disabilities who work in the federal government.
Civil Rights Act of 1991	Provides monetary damages in cases of intentional employment discrimination.
Family/Medical Leave Act of 1993	Grants employees up to a total of 12 workweeks of unpaid job-protected leave during any 12-month period for the birth and care of the newborn child, adoption or foster care needs, care for an immediate family member with a serious health condition, or to take medical leave due to a serious health condition.

FIGURE 12.4   U.S. Federal Equal Employment Opportunity Laws

Sources: Equal Employment Opportunity Commission, "Federal Equal Employment Opportunity (EEO) Laws" (www.eeoc.gov); U.S. Department of Labor, The Family and Medical Leave Act of 1993 (http://www.dol.gov/esa/regs/statutes/whd/fmla.htm).

In contrast, firms that fail to represent the diversity of people in the relevant labor force are unfairly discriminating against those who are significantly underrepresented. **Employment discrimination** occurs when some people have a lower probability of being hired, promoted, financially rewarded, or receiving valuable training and development opportunities due to non–job-related demographic characteristics. U.S. federal legislation over the past four decades explicitly prohibits companies from unfairly discriminating against job applicants, employees, and other stakeholders. The most important legislation is listed in Figure 12.4. Basically, these laws and related court cases say that employers must not unfairly disadvantage people based on their age, race, gender, religion, or other factors identified in the legislation. Notice that our definition of workforce diversity and the concept of an inclusive corporate culture extend to forms of diversity beyond these legal categories.

Companies can legally discriminate on the basis of gender or other identifiable categories if they are *bona fide occupational qualifications,* meaning that these characteristics are necessary to perform the job. It's acceptable for a senior citizen home to employ only women for bathing female residents, for example.[32] However, these exceptions are rare and closely monitored by government authorities. For the most part, managers need to carefully consider whether any of their decisions and actions unfairly limit the opportunities and benefits that some employees and job candidates receive compared to others in identifiable groups.

Without due diligence to maintain a diverse workforce, an organization could be forced to pay large settlements and face great embarrassment. This recently occurred at Morgan Stanley, which paid $54 million to female staff members after a court ruled that the investment firm paid them at lower rates and promoted them less often than their male counterparts without justification. A few years earlier, Coca-Cola paid out more than $200 million in racial and gender discrimination lawsuit settlements. Meanwhile the number of age discrimination cases is growing (nearly 18,000 per year) with a median award of $266,000 in recent years.[33] Figure 12.5 identifies the percentage of discrimination charges that individuals have recently filed with the Equal Employment Opportunities Commission.

employment discrimination

Any situation in which some people have a lower probability of being hired, promoted, financially rewarded, or receiving valuable training and development opportunities due to non–job-related demographic characteristics.

FIGURE 12.5

Individual Discrimination Charges Filed with the Equal Employment Opportunity Commission 2005

Note: Numbers exceed 100 percent because individuals often file charges claiming multiple types of discrimination. This chart excludes "retaliation" charges.

Source: Equal Employment Opportunity Commission, Charge Statistics, 2005 (http://www.eeoc.gov/stats/charges.html).

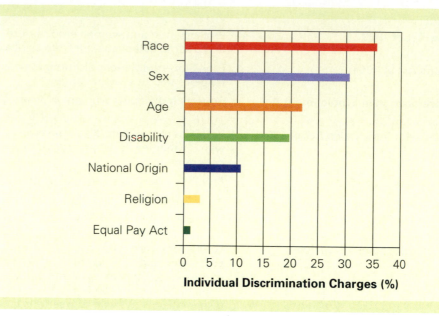

These employment discrimination complaints apply to a host of corporate actions, but they have been most pertinent to the three staffing activities that we describe in the remainder of this chapter: recruitment, selection, and training and development.

▪ // Recruiting Job Applicants

The human resource planning process described earlier estimates the number of people with specific qualifications required in the future to fulfill the organization's strategic objectives. Now it is up to recruitment, selection, and development to attract those people, choose the most suitable applicants, and, where necessary, train them in the required competencies. **Recruitment**, the first of these activities, consists of a set of activities that improves the number and quality of people who apply for employment, as well as the probability that qualified and compatible applicants will accept employment offers. A number of myths about recruitment can cause short- or long-term problems. Here are three of the most common myths:

recruitment

A set of activities that improves the number and quality of people who apply for employment and the probability that qualified and compatible applicants will accept employment offers.

- *Myth #1: Companies should attract as many job applicants as possible.* Large applicant pools can improve the quality of the people hired, but this strategy also creates a few problems. First, it costs more money to recruit more people, so at some point the cost exceeds the value. This problem is compounded as the recruitment activities attract applicants with a poor fit to the job and organization. Second, the company must reject more applicants as more people apply. A high rejection rate may increase the risk of discrimination lawsuits or (at least) the risk of having many rejected applicants with negative feelings toward the company.

- *Myth #2: Companies should focus their recruitment on people with the highest credentials.* On the surface, this assumption makes sense because applicants with the best credentials will generally perform the best. But job performance is only one factor to consider when recruiting and selecting applicants. Particularly during times of low unemployment or high skill shortages, people's desire for employment stability as well as their fit with the organizational culture can be important considerations.

- *Myth #3: Companies should appear as attractive as possible during recruitment.* Glamorizing the job or hiding negative features of the organization is a common ploy to attract more job applicants, but this strategy often backfires. Dissatisfaction, mistrust of management, and turnover can occur as recruits discover that reality is less than what the company advertised.

Overall, recruitment is a process of communicating information to people who would be most suitable to the job and organization. However, achieving this goal begins not with recruitment brochures or campus visits. Instead it begins with the more strategic approach of nurturing the employer brand.

// NURTURING THE EMPLOYER BRAND

Compass Group employs 440,000 people in 96 countries (including 120,000 in the United States) for its food service operations in hotels, company and school cafeterias, and sports complexes. Despite its size and global reach, the British-based company is not well known to prospective applicants. That was a concern for Compass's management because it is an ongoing challenge to find and hire qualified applicants in this industry. To improve its recruiting, Compass held focus groups with more than 1,000 employees in 20 countries to understand employee perceptions of the company's brand image as an employer and what could be done to strengthen that image. Compass developed a new slogan—Great People, Real Opportunities —that captures the importance of employees, and the firm revised its global recruiting to maintain a more consistent message about what Compass Group stands for as an employer. "It's tough to launch a brand until you know what you stand for, but this provided a framework and context," explains Chris Ashcroft, executive vice president of human resources for Compass Group North America in Charlotte, North Carolina.[34]

For Compass Group and almost every other company, an important component of recruitment is the comprehensive process of developing and maintaining an **employer brand**.[35] This term refers to the package of functional, economic, and psychological benefits provided by employment and identified with the company as an employer. It is an organization's reputation as an employer, including people's expectations about working at that company, what the company values (its corporate culture), and how it differentiates itself from other employers in that industry or labor market. Employer branding provides a significant advantage in recruiting and retaining people. It serves the same benefits provided by any product or service brand: a focused clarity that stands out from a confusing array of choices. A brand bundles the complex combination of beliefs and expectations about something into a more simplified image. People immediately recognize GE as a performance-oriented global conglomerate, SAS Institute as an employee-friendly software company, and Apple Computer as an innovative computer company. Each of these brand images gives job applicants a compressed picture of what it might be like to work in those organizations.

> **employer brand**
> The package of functional, economic, and psychological benefits provided by employment and identified with the company as an employer.

To nurture their employer brands, companies must ensure that their reward systems, corporate cultures, and career-development opportunities are consistent with their brand images. Employers' brand images are also heavily influenced by the brand images of their products and services.[36] One study based on personal interviews with more than 35,000 people across 16 countries reported that companies with well-known products or services are much more highly regarded as employers than companies with less well-known brands. Furthermore, firms with a low-price image are perceived less favorably as employers than those whose products or services have an expensive brand image.

For instance, Figure 12.6 lists BMW as one of the top employer brands in America (based on a survey of 37,000 students at 207 universities and colleges). The German automaker has a positive image as an employer because of the reputation of its automobiles. In fact, BMW does no college recruitment, partly because it receives so many applications already. "Great brands attract great people," says one BMW executive.[37]

Compass Finds Its Brand   Compass Group employs 440,000 people worldwide (including 120,000 in the United States), yet the British-based company is not well known to prospective applicants. To improve its recruiting, Compass held focus groups with employees to understand its brand image as an employer and what could be done to strengthen that image.
Courtesy of Compass Group.

FIGURE 12.6

U.S. Undergraduate and MBA Student Rankings of the Top Employer Brands

Sources: Universum Communications, "The American Undergraduate Edition, 2006" (www.universumusa.com/undergraduate.html); Universum Communications, "The American MBA Edition, 2006" (www.universumusa.com/mba.html). Reprinted with permission.

Rank	All Undergraduate Students	MBA Students
1	Walt Disney	McKinsey & Company
2	Google	Google
3	U.S. Department of State	Goldman Sachs
4	Federal Bureau of Investigation	Bain & Company
5	Central Intelligence Agency	Boston Consulting Group
6	Microsoft	Citigroup
7	Apple Computer	Apple Computer
8	Johnson & Johnson	General Electric
9	BMW	Johnson & Johnson
10	Sony	Morgan Stanley

Developing an employer brand requires a comprehensive strategy that begins with becoming aware of the existing image, aligning company culture and practices with the desired differentiating brand image, and communicating that image consistently and meaningfully to the public through various channels. Here are the main activities that support an employer brand:

- *Identify and develop positive differentiating features.* Compass Group, described earlier, followed the first step in employer branding, which is to know the company's competitive advantages as an employer within the industry or labor market and to further develop those differentiating features by ensuring that rewards, culture, training, and other systems are aligned. This process often begins with a survey of current employees about their perceptions of the company. Where cost-effective, firms should also survey targeted applicant groups to determine their perceptions of the employer brand.

- *Raise the company's public profile.* Firms with well-known (and respected) products or services have stronger employer brands. Other companies need to improve their employer brands by more heavily marketing their products and services—particularly directed toward prospective employees rather than just consumers. Experts also suggest that including the company's name in the product or service improves employer brand awareness.

- *Use consistent messages in recruiting and marketing.* The messages communicated to potential employees must be consistently focused around a common image of the company. If a company is at the forefront of innovation and wants to be known for this characteristic, then it must be stated or obvious in college recruitment interviews, brochures, and marketing literature for the company's products and services.

- *Earn third-party recognition.* One reason (of several) why corporate leaders bother to participate in time-consuming awards surveys—as the best employer, the best place for diversity, the best company for women, and so forth—is that favorable rankings from these independent sources improve a company's brand image as an employer.

// INTERNAL VERSUS EXTERNAL RECRUITMENT

Developing and maintaining an employer brand is a significant advantage in the recruitment process, but finding enough people with the right qualifications also requires other strategic decisions and tasks. One of the first decisions is whether to hire outsiders or promote people within the organization. Many firms prefer internal recruitment (communicating job openings only to current employees) because the applicants' qualifications and potential are known from reliable sources within the organization, whereas information about external job candidates might be sketchy or biased. Internal recruiting is also less expensive because the company does not pay for job advertisements or headhunters. These first two benefits lead to a third one: It takes less time to recruit internally than externally. A fourth advantage of internal recruitment is that job applicants are more familiar with the organization, including its practices and culture, whereas external applicants are more likely to experience problems adjusting to the job and organization. Finally, internal recruitment rewards successful employees through promotions to more challenging and usually high-paying jobs.[38]

External recruitment is both necessary and desirable for most entry-level positions as well as in situations where there aren't enough qualified current staff members to fill higher-level positions. Google faces this situation. It has doubled its size over the past two years, so it relies on external recruitment at all levels. The need for external hires also occurs when a company changes its strategy or moves into new fields of knowledge. Again, this shift is occurring at Google, which is expanding into new online services such as online retail and payment systems. These new business strategies require skill sets that are not sufficiently available from current employees.

External recruiting also brings new perspectives, so managers will take this path when they want to change the organization's culture or infuse more creativity. Procter & Gamble (P&G), which was a solid defender of internal recruiting for decades, recently increased its external hiring to shake up the workforce and proliferate new ideas from different perspectives. While the consumer products giant was laying off executives and other staff, it dramatically expanded its design department by hiring an army of creative types from other organizations and pairing them with long-service P&G staff.[39]

// CHOOSING RECRUITING CHANNELS

There are many channels through which job openings are communicated and gain the attention of prospective employees. Internal recruitment typically occurs through job postings. At one time large organizations would distribute to all employees throughout the company a weekly newspaper filled with internal job postings. Today employees usually review job postings through the company's intranet. Internal recruitment also occurs through career planning and referrals from the employee's immediate supervisor.

Employee referrals represent the most common informal method for externally recruiting job applicants. National City Corp. is a case in point. The Cleveland-based financial institution doesn't yet have enough qualified people inside the company to fill the expanding number of broker positions, so it relies on current employees to recruit their friends and acquaintances for these jobs. National City and many other employers prefer this recruitment method because it is inexpensive and because the referring employee tends to provide applicants with more realistic and detailed information than is available through formal recruitment methods. Most (but not all) studies agree that employee referrals offer these benefits.[40]

■ Employee referrals help National City Corp. recruit talent.

Other external recruitment channels include advertisements, campus visits, government and private employment agencies, and executive search firms. Private employment agencies and executive search firms (often called "headhunters") are more expensive. However, they are important sources for professional and senior management job applicants because they tend to screen applicants and actively lure them aware from their current employment.

Online Recruitment (e-Recruitment) The Internet as a medium for recruitment (often called "e-recruitment") has exploded over the past decade.[41] Every day approximately 4 million Americans use the Internet to look for information about jobs. Almost half of all human resource executives responsible for recruiting believe that online job boards are better than traditional recruitment channels at finding job candidates. Most medium-sized and large companies have developed recruitment content on their own Web sites. Google, for example, has details of available jobs in every country, lists the top 10 reasons to work at the company, and provides downloadable videos in which Google staff describe what it's like to work at the Googleplex. Google and other companies also include formal job application processes on these sites; but most firms rely on specialized Internet job boards developed by third parties, such as Monster.com, Careerbuilder.com, and Hotjobs.com.

■ Online recruitment helps Sainsbury and Nike slash costs.

Online recruitment also saves time and money. Recruitment content is uploaded more quickly and at a much lower cost than is possible with newspaper ads or distributed brochures. Applicant details are submitted directly to the human resource system, saving money compared to filing and coding manual application forms. Confirmation of applications and subsequent correspondence typically occur via e-mail, which further saves time and money. Sainsbury, the British supermarket chain, recently slashed its administrative costs by U.S. $8 million by conducting all its recruitment processes online. Nike also recently switched to online recruitment at its European offices, which decreased recruitment costs by more than 50 percent, cut the time to fill vacancies from 62 to 42 days, and reduced the embarrassment of losing job applications that candidates had submitted by mail.[42]

Guerrilla Recruitment   Online recruiting has become a standard practice in many organizations, but it is a passive approach that overlooks many people who might not be thinking about employment at another company. Google uses online recruitment to attract applicants; but to fulfill its rapidly expanding human resource needs, it also relies on *guerrilla recruiting* methods—activities that are proactive, on the ground, and creative. Google has an army of private and in-house recruiters who actively seek out technology stars from around the world. These recruiters increase the number of highly qualified applicants by personally contacting employees working elsewhere who might not otherwise think about working at Google. Campus recruiters also rely on guerrilla tactics, such as inviting visitors with the highest potential to a special meeting the next day with Google's engineers.

Another strategy is to host competitions or sponsor events that offer a parallel benefit of attracting prospective employees. Google recently funded a "Summer of Code" event in which 410 college-level students (out of thousands who submitted proposals) received mentoring support from several partner organizations while writing open-source software code. Google paid a small stipend to mentors at the other organizations and $4,500 to students who completed their projects. The Summer of Code was a form of guerrilla recruiting because it gave Google (and the other mentoring firms) an inside track on high-quality applicants. "It was a way to start a dialogue with people around the world who might not necessarily be looking for a job—but might become a future employee," says Judy Gilbert, Google's staffing program director. Google also hosts an online competition called "Code Jam" in which contestants around the world are challenged to write code to solve specific problems, then find ways to "break" the code that others have written. Winners in the final round of 100 contestants (out of thousands in the first round) receive up to $10,000, trips to the Googleplex (Google headquarters), and job offers.[43]

Google Goes Guerrilla in the War for Talent   Google has a strong employer brand, but it is also becoming well known for its innovative guerrilla recruitment practices. One example was the billboard and subway banners (shown in photo) Google created, luring curious commuters to follow a series of Web sites with math problems. Only those with top-notch math skills could decipher each puzzle, which eventually led to Google's Web site with an invitation to submit a résumé.

© David L. Ryan, The Boston Globe.

Some guerrilla recruiting strategies gain attention in unusual ways. For instance, Google developed a "Google Labs Aptitude Test" (GLAT), posted it on its Web site and in tech magazines, and invited engineers to submit their answers to the 21 questions along with their résumés. "Score high enough, and we'll be in touch," says Google.

Google also posted a cryptic message on a billboard in Silicon Valley and commuter banners at subway stops in Cambridge, Massachusetts, inviting viewers to a Web site named as a 10-digit prime number representing a natural logarithm. Google wasn't mentioned on either the posters or the Web site, but curious problem solvers found more mathematical problems to direct them to other Web sites. Eventually they arrived at a Google Web page asking for their résumés. "One thing we learned while building Google is that it's easier to find what you're looking for if it comes looking for you," said the final Google Web page. "What we're looking for are the best engineers in the world. And here you are!"[44]

// RECRUITMENT AND DIVERSITY

Recruiting methods might disadvantage some groups more than others, which potentially undermines workforce diversity. Online recruiting is fine for most people, but it tends to underrepresent people who are older and who have less access to computer and Internet resources. Employee referrals also suffer from potentially biased recruiting because employees tend to refer people who are similar to them, which can underrepresent minorities and women in the applicant pool. Companies that rely on the top-ranked schools may also discover that they are cutting out a disproportionate number of people in some demographic categories.

To maintain a truly diverse workforce, managers need to seek out people in diverse groups who might not otherwise consider employment with the organization. Verizon Communications maintains a diverse workforce through partnerships with the national Black MBA Association, the National Society of Hispanic MBAs, and the National Association of Asian American Professionals.[45]

// Selecting Job Applicants

Selection is the process of deciding which job applicants will make the most suitable employees. This decision process consists of collecting and verifying details about job candidates, and then using this information to predict who is most suitable to the job and organization. Selection occurs after human resource planning, but it tends to run alongside the recruitment process. Many of Google's employees are recruited through campus fairs, but their first meeting with the recruiter is also the company's first step in the selection process. Recruiters don't just sell the company; they find out more about these students and immediately decide who should receive further attention for recruitment and selection.

There are many types of selection methods, and most companies use two or more of them to identify suitable job applicants. But how do managers know which methods to rely on? To answer this question, we need to consider two things: (1) what constitutes a "suitable" candidate and (2) how well the selection method measures or predicts that suitability. For the most part *suitability* refers to an applicant's job performance or skills and abilities that are required for future performance. However, suitability also refers to how well the employee's values and interpersonal skills fit the organization's culture.[46]

selection
The process of deciding which job applicants will make the most suitable employees.

// RELIABILITY AND VALIDITY OF SELECTION METHODS

The second issue to consider is how well a selection method measures or predicts people's suitability. If a job calls for applicants with strong math skills, then the selection method should measure math skills with a high degree of reliability and validity. **Reliability** refers to how consistently a selection method measures a person's characteristics. If a job applicant's scores on a math test vary considerably over one month, the test probably lacks reliability because math skills don't actually change much over that period. To understand the importance of reliable selection methods, imagine trying to shoot a distant target with a bow and arrows. If your arrows land all over the target, then you have low reliability and will only

reliability
How consistently a selection method measures a person's characteristics.

occasionally hit the bull's-eye. But if your arrows land in the same place (not necessarily the bull's-eye), then you have high reliability and it is just a matter of redirecting your aim somewhat to hit the bull's-eye every time.

Validity, which refers to how well a selection method predicts an applicant's suitability as an employee, is the bull's-eye. A selection method has a high degree of validity if it does a good job of predicting how successful applicants will be on the job, such as their job performance, turnover, loyalty, or other important outcomes. Google believes that education is a highly valid indicator of an applicant's suitability. "We're impressed by the determination and drive it takes to complete the degrees," says Stacy Sullivan, Google's human resources director.[47] Google managers believe (and likely have evidence showing) that education predicts a person's persistence, creativity, and ability to grasp cutting-edge knowledge, all of which are necessary in new product development. They may have also found that employees with higher educational degrees or grades are less likely to be overwhelmed with the work, so they have lower turnover and higher job satisfaction at Google. Work experience might also predict job performance, but Google believes it is less predictive (has lower validity) than education.

Validating everything we use to select job applicants is a huge challenge, but two rules of thumb offer some guidance.[48] The first rule is that past behavior is the best predictor of future behavior. People who provided good customer service in their previous jobs are likely to serve customers well in their next jobs, particularly in similar situations. The second, and somewhat related, rule of thumb is that samples of a person's work are usually better predictors of future behavior and performance than are abstract signs. Past behavior and work simulations are samples because they represent the person's actual behavior. Signs, on the other hand, include more abstract information, such as personality and aptitude tests. People don't complete personality tests as part of their job. Instead the personality test is an abstract sign of how well people perform their jobs.

Figure 12.7 lists the various selection techniques that we will describe over the next few pages. Generally selection methods that represent or are close to being samples or represent

validity

How well a selection method predicts an applicant's suitability as an employee.

Selection Method	Popularity	Validity	Comments
Application forms, résumés, reference checks	High	Moderate	Validity is only as good as information provided, so reference checks should verify application form information.
Work sample tests	Moderate	Moderately high	Excellent application of "sample" rather than "sign" as predictor, but can be expensive (assessment centers) and are not easy to apply to some jobs.
Unstructured employment interview	Very high	Low to moderate	Validity increases with number of interviewers involved and types of questions asked.
Patterned behavior description interview	Moderate	Moderately high	Consistently the most valid interview method for selection, but less popular with applicants and interviewers.
Ability tests	Moderate	Moderate	Knowledge-based tests are close to "samples," but aptitude tests are also closely linked to job-related behavior.
Personality tests	Moderately low	Low to moderate	Increasingly popular (although still low) in selection, but only specific personality traits predict success for specific performance dimensions on specific jobs.

FIGURE 12.7   Popularity and Validity of Selection Methods

past behavior have the highest validity, whereas selection methods that are remote signs tend to have lower validity. This figure also indicates the popularity of each selection method, which refers to how many companies use each method.

// APPLICATION FORMS, RÉSUMÉS, AND REFERENCE CHECKS

Usually the first information received is the applicant's résumé or completed application form. Not long ago, organizing and sorting these documents was a nightmare. Today, thanks to online applications and software that transcribes scanned résumés, it is much easier to use this information to screen out people who lack the minimum education, work experience, or other requirements. A more sophisticated approach is the *weighted application blank,* which statistically identifies information in the application form that best predicts the applicant's suitability.[49]

One glaring problem is that somewhere between 25 and 50 percent of application forms contain false information. Although most of these inaccuracies are minor, there are also many high-profile misrepresentations.[50] For example, a former CEO of Radio Shack, an executive at NASA, a football coach at the University of Notre Dame, and a mayor of Rancho Mirage, California, embellished their educational credentials. Lucent Technologies discovered that a former executive had lied about having a PhD from Stanford University and hid his criminal past involving forgery and embezzlement. Ironically this executive was Lucent's director of recruiting! Many firms conduct *reference checks* to minimize false information in application forms. They contact previous employers, educational institutions, and reference sources listed by the applicant to confirm that information in the application form or résumé is accurate. Reference checks have become difficult because many organizations refuse to answer reference check questions for fear of liability. Fortunately several states now protect companies that provide reference information in good faith. Also, according to recent court cases, companies may be liable for refusing to divulge an applicant's past wrongdoings if the person causes damage in the next workplace.[51]

// WORK SAMPLE TESTS

Work sample tests tend to be a highly valid selection method because they require job candidates to demonstrate their behavior and performance in a real-time situation.[52] Musicians who apply for a job in a symphony orchestra are asked to perform a piece of music. Graphic artists and computer animation specialists might be asked to complete a small piece of work in a few hours during the hiring process. Internships and work-study programs represent another form of work sampling because the employer observes the student's behavior and performance in these temporary roles. The previously mentioned Summer of Code and Code Jam events that Google sponsors provide small samples of work from participants before they even consider applying for a job at the search technology company. Work samples also occur in *assessment centers*, which are a series of simulations that test for managerial potential. One typical assessment center simulation is the in-basket exercise, in which participants indicate how they would dispense with each issue identified in a series of phone and e-mail messages and notes.

Evaluation hiring is an extreme variation of work sampling whereby someone is hired by an employment agency but works at a client company. After a fixed period the client either hires the individual as a permanent employee or sends the person back to the employment agency for work elsewhere. Honda America follows this "try-before-you-buy" strategy. All new production employees are employed by Adecco Employment Services for a two-year training period. Those who remain at the end of the two years are guaranteed an interview for a permanent job with Honda.[53] Although evaluation hiring is one of the best ways to predict employee performance without the encumbrance of actually employing people, it potentially creates the problems of contingent work that we mentioned earlier in this chapter, such as reduced loyalty and perceived unfairness in the employment relationship.

work sample test
A selection method that requires job candidates to demonstrate their behavior and performance in a real-time situation.

■ Honda America's evaluation hiring strategy.

// EMPLOYMENT INTERVIEWS

Managers regard the employment interview as the most important and trustworthy method for selecting job applicants.[54] Rarely is someone hired without a formal meeting in which they are asked questions to determine their suitability for the job and organization. What are managers looking for in employment interviews? They are mainly assessing the applicant's personality traits—particularly responsibility, dependability, initiative, and persistence.[55] Unfortunately studies have found that managers aren't very good at guessing personality characteristics from someone's behavior or statements in an interview setting.

Social skills represent the second most common characteristic that managers look for in employment interviews. In particular, they assess the applicant's interpersonal skills, team focus, and general ability to work with people. Fortunately managers tend to be fairly good at evaluating people's social skills. The reason for this accuracy is that the interview is a sample of the job candidate's behavior, revealing his or her ability to interact with other people. Along with social skills and personality, managers rely on interviews to gather information about the applicant's general mental capability (intelligence) as well as job knowledge and skills.

Although popular, traditional unstructured interviews tend to have low validity. Why? One reason is that the interviews are inconsistent from one applicant to the next, resulting in different hiring standards. An equally troublesome issue is that the questions might not have anything to do with the job duties or predict how well the applicant will perform on the job. A third problem is that interviewers tend to distort the information received during the interview. They ignore or quickly forget information that is contrary to their expectations and tend to seek negative information more than positive information. Perhaps most important, interviewers tend to form an opinion of each job applicant within minutes (or, according to some research, within seconds!).

Improving Employment Interviews Employment interviews are too popular to remove from the selection process, so we need to find ways to make them more useful in selection decisions. One possible solution is to train managers to be aware of interviewer biases. Several studies have concluded that training only minimally improves the validity of employment interviews, but it has at least some benefit over a complete lack of training.[56] Training is important, however, for teaching interviewers what questions they can and cannot ask in interviews. For example, interviewers cannot ask if an applicant is married with young children. Instead, if the job involves frequent travel, applicants might be asked if they can fulfill the required travel obligations.

> **patterned behavior description interview**
>
> A structured employment interview method that asks applicants to recall specific incidents in the past and describe how they handled the situations.

Along with training, companies can improve the validity of interviews by ensuring that they are structured and that the questions are related to job performance. One structure that improves interview validity, called the **patterned behavior description interview**, asks applicants to recall specific incidents in the past and describe how they handled these situations.[57] For example, to determine how well applicants work with coworkers, managers might ask, "Describe a time when a coworker strongly and publicly disagreed with your views on an important decision. What did you do?" To gather enough details, this "stem" question is then followed with several "probe" questions, such as "Can you tell me more about that?" or "What did you do next?"

The U.S. division of DaimlerChrysler recently introduced the patterned behavior description interview to improve the selection process. "Managers whose daytime job is not full-time interviewing wanted a tool they could use quickly, confidently, and easily to make the best hiring decisions," explains Sandy Fiaschetti, a human resource manager at the Auburn Hills, Michigan, automaker. All managers must attend a training program that teaches them how to identify the competencies to assess, how to conduct behavioral interviewing, and how to calculate candidates' scores from the interviews. So far the new interview process seems to work well. "Some managers who thought they knew which candidate they wanted going into the interviews used the tool and reached different conclusions," Fiaschetti says. "[Now] they're using the interview to gather data, not reach conclusions."[58]

Along with training and structured interviews, companies can improve interview validity by using multiple interviewers. In fact, selection decisions based on unstructured interviews with multiple interviewers are just as valid as selection decisions based on a patterned behavior description interview conducted by one interviewer.[59] In some cases applicants are interviewed by a panel whose members later compare notes on their impressions of the candidate. Google's on-site interviews typically include two or more Google staff members, including managers and coworkers. But Google further strengthens the interview results by conducting several interviews. Typically Google applicants receive two or possibly three telephone interviews, which screen out people based on their basic knowledge, qualifications, and thinking ability. Applicants who pass this hurdle can count on spending half a day attending three interviews at Google's headquarters or local offices. Applicants who pass those interviews are invited back (usually the next day) for a final interview.[60]

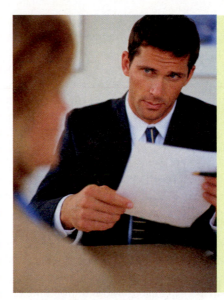

DaimlerChrysler Throttles Up Behavioral Interviewing The U.S. division of DaimlerChrysler introduced patterned behavior description interviewing in which managers ask applicants to recall specific past incidents and describe how they responded to those situations. As a structured format, this interview method allows managers to complete the interview more systematically than the traditional interview.

© Ryan McVay/Getty Images.

// ABILITY AND PERSONALITY TESTS

In addition to application forms, employment interviews, and possibly work samples, many firms require applicants to complete tests that assess either their ability or their personality. Some tests assess the applicant's current knowledge about a particular topic. Others are **aptitude tests**, which measure a person's potential ability, such as general intelligence, perceptual accuracy, mathematical ability, and motor abilities such as finger dexterity. Some of these instruments are paper-and-pencil tests, such as the GMAT, SAT, and MCAT tests required for entry to college programs. Others involve gamelike activities in which applicants move objects quickly in a limited time frame. For example, individuals with superior spatial and mathematical aptitudes tend to excel in architecture. Banyan Air Service, an aircraft maintenance firm in Fort Lauderdale, Florida, gives applicants who lack work experience a mechanical aptitude test to determine their potential as aircraft mechanics. Employment selection researchers have reported that general intelligence is a good predictor of performance in a wide variety of jobs.[61]

Ability tests are signs (rather than samples) of an individual's future performance, but they usually have moderately good validity because of their logical connection to job-specific behavior. In contrast, personality tests measure much more abstract signs. **Personality**, which is described more fully in Chapter 14, is the relatively stable pattern of behaviors and consistent internal states that explains a person's behavioral tendencies.[62] As remote signs of behavior, personality tests aren't the best selection methods. In fact, they were strongly discouraged in the selection process a few decades ago. However, these tests have become more popular over the past decade because several studies report that specific personality traits really do predict specific types of job performance for some jobs. By some estimates, 30 percent of U.S. companies use personality tests to hire and place job applicants or internal recruits.[63]

aptitude test
A selection method that measures a person's potential ability, such as general intelligence and finger dexterity.

personality
The relatively stable pattern of behaviors and consistent internal states that explains a person's behavioral tendencies.

// SELECTION AND DIVERSITY

Throughout the staffing process, managers need to keep an eye on how each activity supports or interferes with the organization's diversity objectives. The greatest concern is whether a selection method has an adverse impact on anyone in a group identified by employment

adverse (or disparate) impact
The effect of a policy or practice that appears neutral but has a significant and unintentional negative influence on one or more protected groups.

affirmative action
Policies and practices to assist members of protected groups that are underrepresented in the organization.

legislation described earlier in this chapter. **Adverse (or disparate) impact** refers to the effect of a policy or practice that appears neutral but has a significant and unintentional negative influence on one or more protected groups.[64] Adverse impact relates to many organizational practices, but it is particularly noticeable in the selection process. Any selection method that creates adverse impact results in fewer job offers to people in some groups compared to other groups even though there is no significant difference in their ability to perform the job. For example, work samples can result in adverse impact because members of some minority groups might have high potential but lack the experience to perform well in a work sample.[65]

Adverse impact is justifiable if the organization can demonstrate that the selection method has high validity. Even so, these companies should consider introducing (or, with government contracts, are required to introduce) affirmative action programs. **Affirmative action** consists of policies and practices to assist members of protected groups that are underrepresented in the organization. These practices might include outreach programs to encourage more people in underrepresented groups to apply. Or they might provide reasonable accommodation, such as by adjusting job content or offering more flexibility so people in disadvantaged groups have a better opportunity to succeed. If a work sample has adverse impact, then companies should instead consider testing the aptitudes of job candidates and giving new hires on-the-job training.

■ // Orienting and Developing Employees

What do employees at Wipro Technologies appreciate most about working at the Indian software giant? Financial rewards and challenging work are certainly on the list, but one of the top benefits is learning. "Wipro provides great learning opportunities," says CEO Vivek Paul. "The core of how employees think about us and value us revolves around training. It simply isn't something we can back off from."[66] After recruiting and selecting employees, companies need to be sure that they have the knowledge and skills needed to perform their jobs and, more generally, work effectively within the organization. At Wipro and probably every other organization these days, employees desire this training as much as managers want them to have it.

// EMPLOYEE ORIENTATION

employee orientation
The organization's systematic process of helping new employees make sense of and adapt to the work context.

■ Laidlaw's realistic job preview.

realistic job preview (RJP)
Giving job applicants a balance of positive and negative information about the job and work context.

The first training that employees should receive is **employee orientation**—the organization's systematic process of helping new employees make sense of and adapt to the work context. In fact, employee orientation should begin *before* the job applicant is hired. It is a process of communicating work-related information beginning with recruiting and continuing through the first few months of employment. Several studies suggest that newcomers adjust better to an organization when they receive a formal orientation program.[67] Even a session lasting a few hours has a significant effect on stress, turnover, and job performance.

One of the first forms of employee orientation should be a **realistic job preview (RJP)**, which occurs during recruitment and selection. In many companies recruiters exaggerate positive features of jobs and neglect to mention their undesirable elements in the hope that the best applicants will get "stuck" on the organization. In contrast, an RJP offers a balance of positive and negative information about the job and work context.[68] Laidlaw, which employs about 1,000 bus drivers on Long Island, shows all job applicants a video of a bus driver's worst day on the job, including a bus full of rowdy kids. This balance helps job applicants decide for themselves whether their skills, needs, and values are compatible with the job and organization. Although RJPs scare away some applicants, they tend to reduce turnover and increase job performance.[69]

After people are hired but before they begin work, orientation takes the form of providing more information about the company and its practices through literature and personal calls or e-mail messages from new coworkers. On the first day of work (when people traditionally, but incorrectly, believe orientation begins), new hires should receive high-priority information, such as the location of key resources and the roles of key people around them. Supervisors and coworkers should demonstrate that the new recruit is a welcome addition to the team, such as by preparing the necessary facilities and symbols of membership (such as a desk with a name plate). Many organizations also support employee orientation with a "buddy system" that assigns newcomers to coworkers for information and social support. Progressive Inc., the Mayfield, Ohio–based insurance firm, relies on current employees to recruit and socialize job applicants. "I think candidates can trust and respect people who already work here," says Jennifer Cohen, Progressive's national employment director. "They get a lot of honest information about the company." [70]

The Bank of Nova Scotia has effectively applied these orientation practices. In particular, the Canadian financial institution takes short-listed job applicants on a tour of the offices where they would actually work. They also meet current employees in the work area, who are quick to show their welcoming support. On the newcomers' first day of work, ScotiaBank assigns buddies to help them adjust to the workplace over the first two years. "We have to make sure, once they are in the door, that they start having a great experience as an employee— and that we haven't overpromised," says Sylvia Chrominska, ScotiaBank's executive vice president of human resources. [71]

■ Bank of Nova Scotia's orientation strategy.

// TRAINING NEEDS ANALYSIS

Training can be expensive, so managers need to identify who needs training, what type of training works best, and when that training is required. These questions are answered by training needs analysis. [72] Figuring out the who–what–when of training usually takes one of two forms: performance gap analysis and organizational analysis.

Performance gap analysis involves diagnosing gaps in employee performance. Suppose one of your employees isn't performing the job as well as he or she should. Does this situation call for training? Possibly, but there can be many explanations for the employee's poor performance, and some of them are corrected through other interventions. [73] One question to ask is whether the employee has performed the job well in the past. If so, has the employee had enough opportunity to practice the skill recently? If not, a training program might consist of practice sessions rather than a full-blown learning process. If the employee does use the skill often, maybe he or she isn't getting meaningful feedback that there is a problem with the results. Along with examining the employee's skills, managers need to consider whether the work environment motivates or discourages good performance. Altogether, this diagnosis works out the cause of the employee's poor performance and determines whether training is required to correct the situation.

Whereas performance gap analysis determines training needs from each employee's behavior and performance, *organizational analysis* takes a top-down view of training needs. Organizational strategy is translated into specific operational plans that cascade down to each department and ultimately every employee. Some employees are affected by strategic initiatives, such as when job duties change or jobs are eliminated. Thus training needs analysis involves anticipating what skills and knowledge employees will require as a result of changes caused by the organizational strategy and operational plans. Notice that organizational analysis links back to the human resource planning process described at the beginning of this chapter. By estimating future demand and supply in the context of the organization's objectives, managers can decipher who needs what training and when they will require it.

// TRAINING METHODS

Suppose you are a manager at a retail financial institution (such as a bank branch) and want to improve the skills and knowledge of customer service staff. What type of training would you provide? There are many varieties of training, so managers need to consider the advantages and limitations of each. The right choice is important because training makes a difference in the financial services industry. "The difference between [a client accepting or rejecting your product] is proper training," explains banking consultant Kenneth Kehrer. "Training could be the difference between keeping a customer for life or watching them walk out the door." One financial services company that is moving forward on the training front is Allstate. The company recently rolled out a training program for bank staff that includes self-assessments, interactive discussion materials, role-playing activities, video demonstrations, and goal setting.[74]

Figure 12.8 highlights seven categories that represent most types of training methods in the workplace. Lectures, readings, and discussion sessions are adequate learning methods for transferring factual or persuasive knowledge. Audiovisual materials have similar learning outcomes, although their graphic display of conditions potentially offers higher persuasiveness and recall of factual knowledge. Visual material is also effective for behavior modeling, which offers some transfer of tacit knowledge. Computer-based training has become very popular because it is cost-effective and allows trainees to learn on their own time, often anywhere. Most computer-based training transfers explicit knowledge and may improve some thinking (cognitive) skills.

Coaching and mentoring provide one-on-one information, encouragement, and feedback to trainees from the supervisor or coworkers. This training method can be very effective for

Training Method	Description	Learning Outcomes
Lectures, readings, discussions	Receiving factual or persuasive information from presenter(s), documentation, and/or other trainees.	Transfers explicit knowledge; changes attitudes.
Audiovisual materials	Watching or listening to information or (for visual media) observing behavior or detailed situations.	Audio transfers explicit knowledge; video transfers both explicit and tacit knowledge through role modeling.
Computer-based training	Learning through interaction with a Web site, CD-ROM, DVD, or related technology, usually without trainers present; increasingly incorporates audiovisual materials.	Develops knowledge and some cognitive skill.
Coaching/mentoring	Providing one-on-one feedback and job-related information to improve the trainee's self-awareness and knowledge about job-related skills.	Develops skills, knowledge, and self-confidence through feedback, focused information, and support.
Job rotation	Giving trainees a series of job assignments for fixed periods in different parts of the production process or around the organization.	Develops skills through practice on the job.
Simulations and role-playing	Practicing job-related behaviors in a environment that replicates the work environment or (for role-playing) where the natural work environment is assumed.	Develops skills through practice away from the usual work environment.
Action learning	Investigating (usually in teams) and applying solutions to real and complex organizational problems or opportunities, with immediate relevance to the company.	Develops cognitive skills and knowledge as well as interpersonal skills in the work environment.

FIGURE 12.8   Training Methods and Their Learning Outcomes

developing knowledge and skill as well as self-confidence.[75] It is sometimes a formal activity but often occurs informally with new employees. Job rotation involves moving trainees into different jobs over time so they continuously develop new skills through on-the-job practice. This method usually includes coaching and mentoring from experienced coworkers.

Simulations and role-playing represent various forms of practice away from the actual workplace. Some simulations are very lifelike, such as mock disasters for emergency crews or aircraft cockpit simulators where pilots practice for new aircraft. Role-playing tends to have less workplace "fidelity"; that is, trainees pretend they are in a work situation even though the surrounding environment is a classroom or another place that doesn't look like the natural work setting. Action learning is an increasingly popular training method whereby employees, usually in teams, investigate and apply solutions to a situation that is both real and complex, with immediate relevance to the company.[76] In other words, the task becomes the source of learning.

// SUPPORTING THE TRAINING PROCESS

Along with diagnosing training needs and determining which method of training works best for the training content, managers need to take steps to maximize the learning process. Here are three of the most important issues to consider when introducing a staff training program:[77]

- *Is the trainee ready to learn?* The effectiveness of training depends just as much on the ability and motivation of the employee to learn as it does on the content and instructional methods. Thus managers need to determine whether trainees have the prerequisite knowledge, are sufficiently confident to learn, and believe the training outcomes are valuable.

- *Is the training practice well designed?* One of the most important principles of learning is that active practice is usually more effective than passive learning (such as through observation or lectures). But practice sessions need to be arranged in ways that maximize their effectiveness.[78] One consideration is whether to have one continuous session or to divide the training into several sessions. Learning is usually more effective when the practice is spread out over time rather than experienced all at once. Another issue is whether trainees should practice all of the behaviors at one time or break up the learning content in chunks. Complex content should be divided if feasible.

- *Is the trainee's transfer of learning supported?* Most training requires support to ensure that employees actually use on the job what they learned in a classroom, workshop, or practice area.[79] One strategy, called *relapse prevention,* involves teaching employees to anticipate and overcome obstacles in the workplace that might make it difficult to practice their new skills. This anticipation of barriers seems to reduce those problems when they occur. Another strategy is to teach employees to manage their behavior change. This means that they learn to set goals that use the new skills, find ways to monitor how well they are applying those skills, and reward themselves when performing well with the new skill set.

Lifelike Simulation Training for Emergency Response Crews   Physicians Jonathan Sherbino and Ivy Chong (far right) prepare to amputate the leg of Wesley Bagshaw, who is pinned by a fallen beam in this collapsed building. "If we don't do this, you're going to die," says Sherbino in response to Bagshaw's anguished protests. Fortunately for Bagshaw, the bone saw cuts through a pig's leg rather than his own. The entire incident was a mock disaster to help train the Heavy Urban Search And Rescue (HUSAR) team in Toronto, Canada. For four hours HUSAR crews located victims with dogs and search equipment at this Toronto Fire Services special operations training site, secured the structure, treated Bagshaw and 15 other "victims," and extricated them to a mock hospital at a nearby community college. In all, over 300 HUSAR and Greater Toronto area medical professionals were involved. "People from the hospitals love these exercises because they get to try out all the ideas they have and no one is (adversely) affected," explains one of the event's organizers. "It was definitely a lot more realistic than anything we've done in the past."[80]

© Michael Stuparyk/*Toronto Star.*

IN CONCLUSION WHY DOES IT MATTER?

Anyone who wants to run a successful business needs the right number of people with the right skills, knowledge, and values to accomplish the organization's objectives. But as Google engineering vice president Alan Eustace pointed out at the beginning of this chapter, the most important thing is to attract and hire the right people in the first place rather than try to dramatically improve them after they're on the payroll. Training is important—and necessary—for most employees at various times in their careers; but even the most expensive training can't replace the value of having the right people.

In this chapter we outlined staffing as a continuous process from human resource planning to recruiting to selecting to developing. These are cornerstones of effective management—so much so that we have split them off as a separate category of managing. (The traditional management categories bury these activities under "Leading.") This process of staffing and developing people is so important, in fact, that the most successful corporate leaders believe it should consume most of their time. The reasoning is that hiring and developing the best employees makes it easier for leaders to do their jobs in the long run.

Even if managers are aware of the importance of human resource planning, recruiting, selection, and development, many fall into the various traps that exist within these practices. Human resource planning can degenerate into paralysis by analysis at one extreme or wishful thinking on the other. Recruitment practices often become sales jobs that inflate newcomers' expectations, which crash into frustration with or disrespect for the employer. Selection practices such as traditional interviews are notorious for lulling managers into false confidence that they have a special gift for picking the right candidates when, in fact, the best choices didn't get job offers. Employee development can also be a house of cards, where managers expend huge budgets on training programs with uncertain returns. Overall, staffing and developing isn't just the cornerstone of effective management; it is its testing ground.

MANAGEMENT CHALLENGES

1. As the manager responsible for staffing at XYZ Manufacturing, you face a major challenge over the next five years. According to employment records, approximately 40 of the 200 production employees will be entering their 60s. Although there is no formal retirement age in this firm, production staff usually retire before age 65 because they are eligible for full retirement pensions by then. Furthermore, you have noticed that local colleges are graduating fewer tradespeople in these jobs than they did a decade ago. What can you do to resolve this problem?

2. WestCrude, a large oil company, has just decided that its core competency is in exploring and drilling for oil deposits, and the firm will outsource most of its support services (human resources, information systems). This will result in a large contingent workforce in these functions. What issues should WestCrude consider before moving to a contingent workforce?

3. Google is exceptionally diverse with respect to representation in ethnicity, race, and gender. But some critics point out that the Internet search engine company has an unusually young workforce. What problems, if any, might Google experience with this lack of age diversity? If Google wanted to increase its age diversity, what should it do, and what complications might result from these actions?

4. In your opinion, which colleges and universities around the country have strong employer brands—that is, have widely known and well-regarded packages of functional, economic, and psychological benefits for employees? Why do you think these schools have strong employer brands whereas others do not? Is the development of employer branding different for colleges than for, say, consumer goods companies?

5. Google and a number of other organizations use "guerrilla recruitment" to attract job applicants. What characteristics of guerrilla recruiting activities make them effective, yet different from other forms of recruitment? What other guerrilla recruitment tactics do you know about?

6. Suppose your organization wants to recruit and hire several marketing specialists across the country. What selection method(s) would be most effective at identifying the most suitable applicants?

MANAGEMENT PORTFOLIO

FOR THE ORGANIZATION YOU HAVE CHOSEN TO FOLLOW:

1. Based on available information, does it appear that the company will have a sufficient supply of staff in various job groups over the next five years? Why or why not? What environmental conditions, if any, make it easier or more difficult for this company to estimate its future supply of and demand for employees?

2. To what extent does this organization actively create and maintain a diverse workforce? Does the company Web site, annual report, or other literature suggest why this organization wants a diverse workforce? What else could or should this company do to improve its diversity?

3. How strong and favorable is the employer brand of this company? If you were hired as an employer brand consultant, what would you recommend to strengthen this company's image as an employer?

4. To what extent does this organization provide employee training? Do its training programs seem to be above or below average for this industry? Thinking about production or service jobs, what training methods seem to be most widely used in this organization?

CLOSING CASE   REBRANDING McJOBS

As with most fast-food restaurant chains, McDonald's needs more people to fill jobs in its vast empire. Yet McDonald's executives are finding that recruiting is a tough sell. The industry is taking a beating from an increasingly health-conscious society and the popular film *Supersize Me*. Equally troublesome is a further decline in the already dreary image of employment in a fast-food restaurant. It doesn't help that *McJob*, a slang term closely connected to McDonald's, was recently added to both *Merriam-Webster's Collegiate Dictionary* and the *Oxford English Dictionary* as a legitimate concept meaning a low-paying, low-prestige,

dead-end, mindless service job in which the employee's work is highly regulated.

McDonald's has tried to shore up its employment image in recent years by improving wages and adding some employee benefits. A few years ago it created the "I'm loving it" campaign, which took aim at a positive image of the golden arches for employees as well as customers. The campaign had some effect, but McDonald's executives realized that a focused effort was needed to battle the McJob image.

Now McDonald's is fighting back with a "My First" campaign to show the public—and prospective job applicants—that working at McDonald's is a way to start their careers and develop valuable life skills. The campaign's centerpiece is a television commercial showing successful people from around the world whose first job was at the fast-food restaurant. "Working at McDonald's really helped lay the foundation for my career," says ten-time Olympic track and field medalist and former McDonald's crew member Carl Lewis, who is featured in the TV ad. "It was the place where I learned the true meaning of excelling in a fast-paced environment and what it means to operate as part of a team."

Richard Floersch, McDonald's executive vice president of human resources, claims that the company's top management has deep talent, but the campaign should help to retain current staff and hire new people further down the hierarchy. "It's a very strong message about how when you start at McDonald's, the opportunities are limitless," says Floersch. Even the McDonald's application form vividly communicates this message by showing a group of culturally diverse smiling employees and the caption "At McDonald's You Can Go Anywhere!"

McDonald's has also distributed media kits in several countries with factoids debunking the McJobs myth. The American documentation points out that McDonald's CEO Jim Skinner began his career working the restaurant's front lines, as did 40 percent of the top 50 members of the world-wide management team, 70 percent of all restaurant managers, and 40 percent of all owner/operators. "People do come in with a 'job' mentality, but after three months or so, they become evangelists because of the leadership and community spirit that exists in stores," says David Fairhurst, the vice president for people at McDonald's in the United Kingdom. "For many, it's not just a job, but a career."

McDonald's also hopes the new campaign will raise employee pride and loyalty, which would motivate the 1.6 million staff members to recruit more friends and acquaintances through word of mouth. "If each employee tells just five people something cool about working at McDonald's, the net effect is huge," explains McDonald's global chief marketing officer. So far the campaign is having the desired effect. The company's measure of employee pride has increased by 14 percent, loyalty scores are up by 6 percent, and 90-day employee turnover for hourly staff has dropped by 5 percent.

But McDonald's isn't betting entirely on its new campaign to attract enough new employees. For many years it has been an innovator in recruiting retirees and people with disabilities. The most recent innovation at McDonald's UK, called the Family Contract, allows wives, husbands, grandparents, and children over the age of 16 to swap shifts without notifying management. The arrangement extends to cohabiting partners and same-sex partners. The Family Contract is potentially a recruiting tool because family members can now share the same job and take responsibility for scheduling which family member takes each shift.

Even with these campaigns and human resource changes, some senior McDonald's executives acknowledge that the entry-level positions are not a "lifestyle" job. "Most of the workers we have are students—it's a complementary job," says Denis Hennequin, the Paris-based executive vice president for McDonald's Europe.[81]

CASE DISCUSSION QUESTIONS

1. Discuss McDonald's current situation from a human resource planning perspective.

2. Is McDonald's taking the best approach to improving its employer brand? Why or why not? If you were in charge of developing the McDonald's employer brand, what would you do differently?

3. Would "guerrilla" recruiting tactics help McDonald's attract more applicants? Why or why not? If so, what tactics might be effective?

ENDNOTES

1. "Google Expansion Is Being Held Back by Hiring Process," *The Wall Street Journal,* February 10, 2005, p. B5; C. Hymowitz, "Busy Executives Fail to Give Recruiting Attention It Deserves," *The Wall Street Journal,* November 21, 2005, p. B1; V. Kopytoff, "How Google Woos the Best and Brightest," *San Francisco Chronicle,* December 18, 2005, p. A1; P.-W. Tam and K.J. Delaney, "Talent Search: Google's Growth Helps Ignite Silicon Valley Hiring Frenzy," *The Wall Street Journal,* November 23, 2005, p. A1.

2. P. Drucker, *Peter Drucker on the Profession of Management* (Boston: Harvard Business School Press, 1998).

3. R.C. Lee, "Keeping Up with Growth," *Houston Chronicle,* August 17, 2005, p. 3.

4. S.E. Jackson and R.S. Schuler, "Human Resource Planning," *American Psychologist* 45, no. 2 (1990), pp. 223–39.

5. R. Mullins, "Verizon Goes to Great Lengths," *Tampa Tribune,* February 7, 2006, p. 1.

6. M.T. Brannick and E.L. Levine, *Job Analysis: Methods, Research, and Applications for Human Resource Management in the New Millennium* (Thousand Oaks, CA: Sage, 2002).

7. Committee on Techniques for the Enhancement of Human Performance: Occupational Analysis. Commission on Behavioral and Social Sciences and Education. National Research Council, *The Changing Nature of Work: Implications for Occupational Analysis* (Washington, DC: National Academy Press, 1999).

8. D. Brown, "Success Begins in the Middle," *Canadian HR Reporter,* June 2, 2003, p. 1.

9. N.R. Lockwood, "Workplace Diversity: Leveraging the Power of Difference for Competitive Advantage," *HRMagazine,* June 2005, pp. A1–A10.

10. S. Theil, "The New Old Age," *Newsweek,* January 30, 2006.

11. D.G. Gallagher, "Contingent Work Contracts: Practice and Theory," in *The New World of Work: Challenges and Opportunities,* ed. C.L. Cooper and R.J. Burke (Oxford: Blackwell, 2002), pp. 115–36; K. Barker and K. Christensen (eds.),

Contingent Work: American Employment in Transition (Ithaca, NY: ILR Press, 1998); A.E. Polivka, "Contingent and Alternative Work Arrangements, Defined," *Monthly Labor Review* 119 (October 1996), pp. 3–10; S. Nollen and H. Axel, *Managing Contingent Workers* (New York: AMACOM, 1996), pp. 4–9.

12. J. Walsh and S. Deery, "Understanding the Peripheral Workforce: Evidence from the Service Sector," *Human Resource Management Journal* 9 (1999), pp. 50–63; C. von Hippel, S.L. Mangum, D.B. Greenberger, R.L. Heneman, and J.D. Skoglind, "Temporary Employment: Can Organizations and Employees Both Win?" *Academy of Management Executive* 11 (February 1997), pp. 93–104.

13. S.F. Matusik and C.W.L. Hill, "The Utilization of Contingent Work, Knowledge Creation, and Competitive Advantage," *Academy of Management Review* 23 (October 1998), pp. 680–97.

14. J. Larson, "Temps Are Here to Stay," *American Demographics* 18 (February 1996), pp. 26–30.

15. J. Pfeffer, *New Directions in Organizational Theory* (New York: Oxford University Press, 1997), pp. 18–20.

16. K.M. Beard and J.R. Edwards, "Employees at Risk: Contingent Work and the Psychological Experience of Contingent Workers," in *Trends in Organizational Behavior,* vol. 2, ed. C.L. Cooper and D.M. Rousseau (Chichester, UK: Wiley, 1995), pp. 109–26.

17. Beard and Edwards, "Employees at Risk," *Trends in Organizational Behavior,* vol. 2, pp. 118–19.

18. Y-S. Park and R.J. Butler, "The Safety Costs of Contingent Work: Evidence from Minnesota," *Journal of Labor Research* 22 (Fall 2001), pp. 831–49; D.M. Rousseau and C. Libuser, "Contingent Workers in High Risk Environments," *California Management Review* 39 (Winter 1997), pp. 103–23.

19. Tam and Delaney, "Talent Search."

20. "A Firm's Self-Evaluation," *Washington Post,* May 1, 2006, p. D09.

21. S.E. Jackson, A. Joshi, and N.L. Erhardt, "Recent Research on Team and Organizational Diversity: SWOT Analysis and Implications," *Journal of Management* 29, no. 6 (2003), pp. 801–30; Lockwood, "Workplace Diversity: Leveraging the Power of Difference for Competitive Advantage."

22. M.F. Riche, "America's Diversity and Growth: Signposts for the 21st Century," *Population Bulletin,* June 2000, pp. 3–43; U.S. Census Bureau, *Statistical Abstract of the United States: 2004–2005* (Washington: U.S. Census Bureau, May 2005).

23. Association of American Medical Colleges, "Table 1: Women Applicants, Enrollees-Selected Years 1949–1950 through 2002–2003" (July 14, 2003), http://www.aamc.org/members/wim/statistics/stats03/start.htm (accessed June 20, 2005); U.S. Census Bureau, *Statistical Abstract of the United States: 2004–2005* (Table no. 570), p. 371.

24. D.A. Harrison et al., "Time, Teams, and Task Performance: Changing Effects of Surface- and Deep-Level Diversity on Group Functioning," *Academy of Management Journal* 45, no. 5 (2002), pp. 1029–46.

25. R. Zemke, C. Raines, and B. Filipczak, *Generations at Work: Managing the Clash of Veterans, Boomers, Xers, and Nexters in Your Workplace* (New York: Amacom, 2000); M.R. Muetzel, *They're Not Aloof, Just Generation X* (Shreveport, LA: Steel Bay, 2003); S.H. Applebaum, M. Serena, and B.T. Shapiro, "Generation X and the Boomers: Organizational Myths and Literary Realities," *Management Research News* 27, no. 11/12 (2004), pp. 1–28.

26. O.C. Richard, "Racial Diversity, Business Strategy, and Firm Performance: A Resource-Based View," *Academy of Management Journal* 43 (2000), pp. 164–77; Q. Reade, "Diversity Helps to Deliver Better Business Benefits," *Personnel Today,* June 18, 2002, p. 2; Catalyst, *The Bottom Line: Connecting Corporate Performance and Gender Diversity* (New York: Catalyst, 2004); Lockwood, "Workplace Diversity: Leveraging the Power of Difference for Competitive Advantage."

27. A. Birritteri, "Realizing the Benefits of an All-Inclusive Employee Base," *New Jersey Business,* November 2005, p. 36.

28. J. Pellet, "Driving Diversity," *Chief Executive,* May 2004, p. 48; Sempra Energy, "Case History: Putting Diversity to Work" (San Diego, CA: Sempra Energy, 2005), www.sempra.com/diversity.htm (accessed June 21, 2005).

29. R.J. Ely and D.A. Thomas, "Cultural Diversity at Work: The Effects of Diversity Perspectives on Work Group Processes and Outcomes," *Administrative Science Quarterly* 46 (June 2001), pp. 229–73; T. Kochan et al., "The Effects of Diversity on Business Performance: Report of the Diversity Research Network," *Human Resource Management* 42, no. 1 (2003), pp. 3–21; D. van Knippenberg and S.A. Haslam, "Realizing the Diversity Dividend: Exploring the Subtle Interplay between Identity, Ideology, and Reality," *in Social Identity at Work: Developing*

Theory for Organizational Practice, ed. S.A. Haslam et al. (New York: Taylor and Francis, 2003), pp. 61–80; D. van Knippenberg, C.K.W. De Dreu, and A.C. Homan, "Work Group Diversity and Group Performance: An Integrative Model and Research Agenda," *Journal of Applied Psychology* 89, no. 6 (2004), pp. 1008–22; E. Molleman, "Diversity in Demographic Characteristics, Abilities, and Personality Traits: Do Faultlines Affect Team Functioning?" *Group Decision and Negotiation* 14, no. 3 (2005), pp. 173–93.

30. Birritteri, "Workplace Diversity: Realizing the Benefits of an All-Inclusive Employee Base."

31. Verizon, *Making Connections: Verizon Corporate Responsibility Report 2004* (New York: Verizon, December 2004); P. Goffney, "Champions of Diversity: The Path to Corporate Enlightenment," *Essence,* May 2005, pp. 149–57.

32. M.J. Frank, "Justifiable Discrimination in the News and Entertainment Industries: Does Title VII Need a Race or Color BFOQ?" *University of San Francisco Law Review* 35, no. 3 (Spring 2001), pp. 473–525.

33. S. Hirsh, "Morgan Stanley Settles Sex Discrimination Case," *Cincinnati Post,* July 13, 2004, p. C7; "Task Force: Coke Making 'Notable' Diversity Progress," *Associated Press Newswires,* December 15, 2005; G. Griffin, "The Big Kiss-Off," *Denver Post,* January 29, 2006, p. K01.

34. E. Silverman, "Making Your Mark," *Human Resource Executive,* November 4, 2004.

35. T. Gibbon, "Employer Branding: The Last Legal Advantage in Winning the War for Talent," in *On Staffing: Advice and Perspectives from HR Leaders,* ed. N.C. Burkholder, P.J. Edwards Sr., and L. Sartain (Hoboken, NJ: John Wiley & Sons, 2004), pp. 35–47; *Your Employer Brand: The Key to Employee Engagement* (Milwaukee, WI: VersantWorks, May 21, 2005); S. Barrow and R. Mosley, *The Employer Brand: Bringing the Best of Brand Management to People at Work* (Hoboken, NJ: John Wiley & Sons, 2005).

36. Gibbon, "Employer Branding: The Last Legal Advantage in Winning the War for Talent."

37. "The Top 20 Workplaces," *Unlimited* (New Zealand), March 2005, pp. 52–53; "In Search of the Ideal Employer," *The Economist,* August 20, 2005, p. 49.

38. J.A. Breaugh, *Recruitment: Science and Practice* (Boston: PWS-Kent, 1992), pp. 28–34.

39. B. Nussbaum, "Get Creative! How to Build Creative Companies," *BusinessWeek,* August 1, 2005, p. 60.

40. J.A. Breaugh and M. Starke, "Research on Employee Recruitment: So Many Studies, So Many Remaining Questions," *Journal of Management* 26, no. 3 (2000), pp. 405–34; J.A. Breaugh et al., "The Relationship of Recruiting Sources and Pre-Hire Outcomes: Examination of Yield Ratios and Applicant Quality," *Journal of Applied Social Psychology* 33, no. 11 (November 2003), pp. 2267–87; M.E. Taber and W. Hendricks, "The Effect of Workplace Gender and Race Demographic Composition on Hiring through Employee Referrals," *Human Resource Development Quarterly* 14, no. 3 (2003), pp. 303–19; A. Singer, "Cleveland Bank 'Rocks' with Retail Investments," www.bisanet.org (2004; accessed August 16, 2005).

41. C. Smith, "Finding The 'Right People' Just Got Easier," *Franchising World* 37, no. 11 (November 2005), pp. 46–48.

42. "Sainsbury's Goes Online to Cut Recruitment Bill by £4m a Year," *Personnel Today,* November 29, 2005, p. 2; "Nike's Successful e-Recruitment," *Strategic HR Review,* March–April 2005, p. 4.

43. Google, "Google Code Jam 2005" (Mountain View, CA: 2005), http://www.google.com/codejam/ (accessed March 1, 2006); Hymowitz, "Busy Executives Fail to Give Recruiting Attention It Deserves"; S.M. Kerner, "What I Did at Google's Summer of Code," *Internetnews.com,* September 9, 2005; J. Puliyenthuruthel, "How Google Searches—for Talent," *BusinessWeek,* April 11, 2005.

44. "Google Entices Job Searchers with Math Puzzle," *NPR,* September 14, 2004; S. Kuchinskas, "Are You Google Employee Material?" *Internetnews.com,* October 1, 2004; S. Olsen, "Google Recruits Eggheads with Mystery Billboard," *Cnet News.com,* July 9, 2004.

45. Birritteri, "Workplace Diversity."

46. D.S. Chapman et al., "Applicant Attraction to Organizations and Job Choice: A Meta-Analytic Review of the Correlates of Recruiting Outcomes," *Journal of Applied Psychology* 90, no. 5 (September 2005), pp. 928–44.

47. K.J. Dunham, "Career Journal: The Jungle," *The Wall Street Journal,* October 14, 2003, p. B12.

48. P.F. Wernimont and J.P. Campbell, "Signs, Samples, and Criteria," *Journal of Applied Psychology* 52, no. 5 (October 1968), pp. 372–76.

49. L.F. Schoenfeldt, "From Dust Bowl Empiricism to Rational Constructs in Biographical Data," *Human Resource Management Review* 9, no. 2 (1999), pp. 147–67; M.R. Barrick and R.D. Zimmerman, "Reducing Voluntary, Avoidable Turnover through Selection," *Journal of Applied Psychology* 90, no. 1 (2005), pp. 159–66; J.H. Browne, S.H. Wamock, and N.J. Boykin, "Predicting Success of Police Officer Applicants Using Weighted Application Blanks," *Journal of American Academy of Business* 6, no. 1 (March 2005), pp. 26–31.

50. S.L. McShane, "Applicant Misrepresentations in Résumés and Interviews in Canada," *Labor Law Journal,* January 1994, pp. 15–24; J. Jaucius, "Internet Guru's Credentials a True Work of Fiction," *Ottawa Citizen,* June 12, 2001; S. Romero and M. Richtel, "Second Chance," *The New York Times,* March 5, 2001, p. C1; "Up to 40 Percent of U.S. Workers Pad Their Résumés," *Agence France Presse* (Washington, DC), February 22, 2006; P. Sabatini, "Fibs on Résumés Commonplace," *Pittsburgh Post-Gazette,* February 24, 2006.

51. P.J. Taylor, "Dimensionality and Validity of a Structured Telephone Reference Check Procedure," *Personnel Psychology* 57, no. 3 (Autumn 2004), pp. 745–71; "More Than 70 Percent of HR Professionals Say Reference Checking Is Effective in Identifying Poor Performers," *PR Newswire* (Alexandria, VA), February 3, 2005; P. Snitzer, "'Speak No Evil' Is a Risky Policy," *Modern Healthcare,* December 5, 2005, p. 23.

52. M. Callinan and I.T. Robertson, "Work Sample Testing," *International Journal of Selection and Assessment* 8, no. 4 (2000), pp. 248–60; P.L. Roth, "A Meta-Analysis of Work Sample Test Validity: Updating and Integrating Some Classic Literature," *Personnel Psychology* 58, no. 4 (2005), pp. 1009–37.

53. T. Matthews, "Ohio-Area Companies Turn to 'Evaluation Hiring' to Pick Best Employees," *Columbus Dispatch,* May 13, 2005.

54. G.H. Harel, A. Arditi-Vogel, and T. Janz, "Comparing the Validity and Utility of Behavior Description Interview versus Assessment Center Ratings," *Journal of Managerial Psychology* 18, no. 1/2 (2003), pp. 94–104.

55. A.I. Huffcutt et al., "Identification and Meta-Analytic Assessment of Psychological Constructs Measured in Employment Interviews," *Journal of Applied Psychology* 86, no. 5 (October 2001), pp. 897–913; P.L. Roth et al., "Personality Saturation in Structured Interviews," *International Journal of Selection and Assessment* 13, no. 4 (2005), pp. 261–73.

56. R.A. Posthuma, F.P. Morgeson, and M.A. Campion, "Beyond Employment Interview Validity: A Comprehensive Narrative Review of Recent Research and Trends over Time," *Personnel Psychology* 55, no. 1 (Spring 2002), pp. 1–80.

57. A.L. Day and S.A. Carroll, "Situational and Patterned Behavior Description Interviews: A Comparison of Their Validity, Correlates, and Perceived Fairness," *Human Performance* 16, no. 1 (2003), pp. 25–47; A.I. Huffcutt et al., "The Impact of Job Complexity and Study Design on Situational and Behavior Description Interview Validity," *International Journal of Selection and Assessment* 12, no. 3 (2004), pp. 262–73.

58. K. Tyler, "Train for Smarter Hiring," *HRMagazine,* May 2005, p. 89.

59. F.L. Schmidt and R.D. Zimmerman, "A Counterintuitive Hypothesis about Employment Interview Validity and Some Supporting Evidence," *Journal of Applied Psychology* 89, no. 3 (2004), p. 553.

60. This information is based on several online forums, including the interviews described on Slashdot. See http://slashdot.org/article.pl?sid=05/01/03/0255205&tid=217.

61. C.-H. Ho, C. Eastman, and R. Catrambone, "An Investigation of 2nd and 3rd Spatial and Mathematical Abilities," *Design Studies* in press, corrected proof; "The Aviation Maintenance Executive Roundtable: The Independents' View," *Aviation Maintenance,* November 15, 2005.

62. B. Reynolds and K. Karraker, "A Big Five Model of Disposition and Situation Interaction: Why a 'Helpful' Person May Not Always Behave Helpfully," *New Ideas in Psychology* 21 (April 2003), pp. 1–13; W. Mischel, "Toward an Integrative Science of the Person," *Annual Review of Psychology* 55 (2004), pp. 1–22.

63. P.G. Irving, "On the Use of Personality Measures in Personnel Selection," *Canadian Psychology* 34 (April 1993), pp. 208–14; R. Winters, "Cull of Personality," *Salt Lake Tribune,* November 14, 2005, p. B8; L.T. Cullen, "SATs for J-O-B-S," *Time,* April 3, 2006, p. 89.

64. "History of Disparate Impact Lawsuits," *IOMA's Human Resource Department Management Report* 5, no. 6 (June 2005), p. 14.

65. P. Bobko, P.L. Roth, and M.A. Buster, "Work Sample Selection Tests and Expected Reduction in Adverse Impact: A Cautionary Note," *International Journal of Selection and Assessment* 13, no. 1 (2005), pp. 1–10.

66. "Wipro: Leadership in the Midst of Rapid Growth," *Knowledge@Wharton,* February 2005.

67. J.D. Kammeyer-Mueller and C.R. Wanberg, "Unwrapping the Organizational Entry Process: Disentangling Multiple Antecedents and Their Pathways to Adjustment," *Journal of Applied Psychology* 88, no. 5 (2003), pp. 779–94.

68. J.A. Breaugh, *Recruitment: Science and Practice* (Boston: PWS-Kent, 1992); J.P. Wanous, *Organizational Entry* (Reading, MA: Addison-Wesley, 1992).

69. J.M. Phillips, "Effects of Realistic Job Previews on Multiple Organizational Outcomes: A Meta-Analysis," *Academy of Management Journal* 41 (December 1998), pp. 673–90; S. Albin, "If You Enjoy Kids and Love to Drive, Have We Got a Job for You," *The New York Times,* September 4, 2005, p. 8.

70. C. Goforth, "Still Recruiting Staff," *Akron Beacon Journal,* July 15, 2001.

71. V. Galt, "Kid-Glove Approach Woos New Grads," *Globe & Mail,* March 9, 2005, p. C1.

72. K.N. Wexley and G.P. Latham, *Developing and Training Human Resources in Organizations,* 2nd ed. (New York: HarperCollins, 1991), Chapter 3.

73. R.F. Mager and P. Pipe, *Analyzing Performance Problems* (Belmont, CA: Lake Publishing, 1984).

74. "New Kehrer Study Finds Training Key to Platform Rep Success," *Business Wire* (Northbrook, IL), November 2, 2004.

75. T. Weiss, *Coaching Competencies and Corporate Leadership* (Boca Raton, FL: St. Lucie Press, 2003).

76. R.W. Revans, *The Origin and Growth of Action Learning* (London: Chartwell Bratt, 1982), pp. 626–27; M.J. Marquardt, *Optimizing the Power of Action Learning: Solving Problems and Building Leaders in Real Time* (Palo Alto, CA: Davies-Black, 2004).

77. Wexley and Latham, *Developing and Training Human Resources in Organizations,* Chapter 4.

78. J.J. Donovan and D.J. Radosevich, "A Meta-Analytic Review of the Distribution of Practice Effect: Now You See It, Now You Don't," *Journal of Applied Psychology* 84, no. 5 (October 1999), pp. 795–805; R. Seabrook, G.D.A. Brown, and J.E. Solity, "Distributed and Massed Practice: From Laboratory to Classroom," *Applied Cognitive Psychology* 19, no. 1 (2005), pp. 107–22.

79. W.L. Richman-Hirsch, "Posttraining Interventions to Enhance Transfer: The Moderating Effects of Work Environments," *Human Resource Development Quarterly* 12, no. 2 (2001), pp. 105–20.

80. I. Teotonio, "Rescuers Pull 'Victims' from Rubble," *Toronto Star,* April 8, 2005, pp. B01, B03.

81. "McDonald's Debuts Advertising on the World of Opportunity under the Golden Arches," McDonald's Corporation news release (Chicago: September 21, 2005); "McDonald's New Ads Tout McJobs," *AFX Asia,* September 22, 2005; A. Chabria, "McDonald's Looks to Boost Staff Pride, Add Top Recruits," *PR Week,* September 26, 2005, p. 5; L. Foster and J. Grant, "McDonald's Woos Its 'Burger Flippers,'" *Financial Times* (London), April 15, 2005, p. 29; D. Thomas, "HR Challenges...I'm Loving It," *Personnel Today,* September 6, 2005, p. w11; J. Arlidge, "McJobs That All the Family Can Share," *Daily Telegraph* (London), January 26, 2006, p. 1.

13

MOTIVATING AND REWARDING
EMPLOYEE PERFORMANCE

ACUITY developed a highly motivated workforce by creating a more supportive and empowering work environment and by linking rewards to performance.
Courtesy of ACUITY.

A decade ago ACUITY (then known as Heritage Mutual) was not a company that inspired employees. Chimes signaled the workday's fixed starting and ending times. Breaks were also fixed and timed. Managers at the Sheboygan, Wisconsin, property and casualty insurer forbade employees from having food or drinks in work areas and discouraged them from placing photos or other personal objects on their desks. Routine audits made sure that employees followed these regimented practices. Managers didn't have much freedom, either, because the CEO was the sole architect of the company's business strategy. The reward system was equally discouraging. Supervisors used a subjective system to rate employees, and those results had little or no influence on the salaries employees received. "It was a very rigid, unfriendly environment,"

says Ben Salzmann, who joined the company as a senior manager during those dark days.

By the time Salzmann was promoted to CEO, ACUITY was in deep trouble. Its revenue per employee was well below the industry average. Employee turnover, which exceeded 25 percent in some years, cost the company more than $10 million annually. But the greatest worry was that ACUITY was losing 17 cents for every dollar it received in insurance premiums. Some of this loss can be recouped through investment returns, but anything more than a 10-cent loss soon leads an insurance company to bankruptcy. Salzmann and his new management team had to figure out how to keep ACUITY in business. How could they build a more engaged workforce that would stay with the company and perform their jobs better?[1]

ACUITY's problems a few years ago were serious, but most companies suffer to some degree from a shortfall of **employee engagement**. Employee engagement refers to employees' emotional and cognitive (rational) motivation, their perceived ability to perform the job, their clear understanding of the organization's vision and their specific role in that vision, and their belief that they have been given the resources to get the job done. Two separate consultant reports estimate that less than a quarter of American employees are highly engaged, approximately 60 percent are disengaged (they are checked out from work—putting in the time but not the energy or passion), and approximately a fifth are "actively disengaged," meaning that they act out their disconnection from work through disruptive behaviors.[2]

Employee engagement has become the catchphrase among managers around the world because it encompasses the four main factors that contribute to employee performance. British retailer Marks & Spencer claims that a 1 percent improvement in the engagement levels of its workforce produces a 2.9 percent increase in sales per square foot. Verizon has estimated that a 1 percent improvement in its employee engagement index produces a 0.5 percent improvement in the telecommunications company's customer satisfaction ratings. Other research estimates that a 5 percent improvement in employee engagement at a 200-person firm will, on average, reduce employee turnover costs by $240,000 and increase profits by $300,000. "True employee engagement is the key to a world-class operation," says Mark Baroni, manager of Owens Corning's plant in Jackson, Tennessee.[3]

So how can managers increase employee engagement? By applying the practices that we'll describe in this chapter and in Chapter 14. Managers make a huge difference in how much employees feel engaged or disengaged, as well as their resulting behavior and performance. Effective managers figure out what motivates employees and align their tasks to those needs. They provide challenging yet fulfilling goals and follow up with constructive, supportive feedback. They align rewards and recognition with employee performance and ensure that those rewards are allocated fairly. They also design jobs in which employees experience fulfillment from the work itself.

Ben Salzmann and other managers at ACUITY applied these strategies, with the result that the insurer is no longer at risk of bankruptcy. On the contrary, its productivity (revenue per employee) has doubled, making it one of the most efficiently run companies in the industry. Rather than losing 17 cents for every dollar received in insurance premiums, ACUITY now earns 10 cents before investment returns. Employee engagement levels have soared, while the turnover rate has plummeted from more than 25 percent to about 2 percent annually. Today ACUITY is not just a survivor; it is a role model as one of the best-performing insurance companies and one of the best places to work in America. In this chapter we'll find out how they accomplished this feat. First we will examine the four factors that influence employee performance.

■ // MARS Model of Individual Behavior and Results

Management buzzwords come and go, but employee engagement will likely be around for a while. Why? Because the definition of employee engagement spells out the four factors that directly influence an employee's voluntary behavior and resulting performance—motivation, ability, role perceptions, and situational factors. These four key ingredients of behavior and performance are diagrammed in the **MARS model**, shown in Figure 13.1. Notice that "MARS" is an acronym representing the four factors in the model's name.[4]

// MOTIVATION

Motivation represents the forces within a person that affect his or her direction, intensity, and persistence of voluntary behavior.[5] *Direction* refers to the path along which people engage their effort. This sense of direction of effort reflects the fact that people have choices about where they put their effort. In other words, motivation is goal-directed, not random. People are motivated to arrive at work on time, finish a project a few hours early, or aim for many other targets. The second element of motivation, called *intensity,* is the amount of effort allocated to the goal. For example, two employees might be motivated to finish their project a few hours early (direction), but only one of them puts forth enough

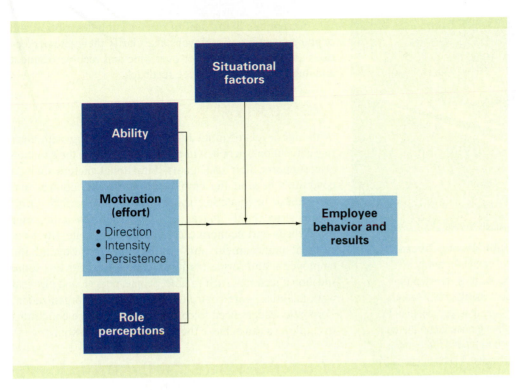

FIGURE 13.1

MARS Model of
Individual Behavior and
Results

effort (intensity) to achieve this goal. In other words, intensity is how much you push your-self to complete the task.

Finally, motivation involves varying levels of *persistence*—that is, continuing the effort for a certain amount of time. Employees sustain their efforts until they reach their goals or give up beforehand. To help remember these three elements of motivation, consider the metaphor of driving a car in which the thrust of the engine is your effort. Direction refers to where you steer the car, intensity is how hard you put your foot down on the gas pedal, and persistence is how long you drive toward that destination.

// ABILITY

Ability consists of both the natural aptitudes and learned capabilities required to successfully complete a task. Ability is an important consideration when hiring job applicants because performing required tasks demands the right knowledge and skills. Ability is also an important factor in employee development. By identifying skill deficiencies, managers can determine which training is required to improve employee performance. In addition to hiring qualified applicants and training employees so they learn the required abilities, managers can improve performance by redesigning the job so employees are given only tasks within their capabilities. AT&T's customer service operations in Dallas took this approach when they realized that many employees were overwhelmed by the increasing variety of products (cable, Internet, HDTV, home theater, and so on). "Our employees just said 'Help! This is way too complex—we're trained on three things and we need help!'" recalls an AT&T executive. The company's solution was to redesign jobs so employees could begin with one area of product knowledge, such as video cable, and then progress to a second knowledge area when the first product is mastered.[6]

■ Person-job matching at AT&T.

// ROLE PERCEPTIONS

Employees who feel engaged in their jobs not only have the necessary motivation and competencies to perform their work but also understand the specific tasks assigned to them, the relative importance of those tasks, and the preferred behaviors to accomplish those tasks. In other words, they have clear *role perceptions*. The most basic way to improve these

Washington Metro Derails with Missing Pieces of MARS   The Metropolitan Area Transit Authority in Washington, D.C., has been plagued by a series of train derailments. According to accident investigation reports, one cause of some derailments was that personnel in the track department failed to maintain lubricants on the tight curves of track; apparently no one reminded them it was part of their job to lubricate the tracks. A second cause of the derailments was that track walkers failed to discover unsafe track because of poor training, lack of time, and low motivation.

© Getty Images.

role perceptions is for staff to receive a job description and ongoing coaching. Employees also clarify their role perceptions as they work together over time and receive frequent and meaningful performance feedback.

// SITUATIONAL FACTORS

With high levels of motivation and ability, along with clear role perceptions, people will perform well only if the situation also supports their task goals. Situational factors include conditions beyond the employee's immediate control that constrain or facilitate his or her behavior and performance.[7] Some situational characteristics—such as consumer preferences and economic conditions—originate from the external environment and consequently are beyond the employee's and organization's control. However, some situational factors—such as time, people, budget, and physical work facilities— are controlled by others in the organization. Corporate leaders need to carefully arrange these conditions so employees can achieve their performance potential.

// USING MARS TO DIAGNOSE EMPLOYEE DISENGAGEMENT

The MARS model is a useful diagnostic tool that should be the starting point for most problems where employee behavior and performance may be a factor. Consider the series of train derailments (eight of them over 20 months) that have recently plagued the Metropolitan Area Transit Authority (Metro) in Washington, D.C.[8] One problem identified in the investigations was that the tracks around the tight curves were not lubricated, so the wheels climbed up the rail and popped off the track. The track department was ordered to lubricate tracks around these bends a few times each year. Yet another derailment occurred less than a year later because key managers in the track department retired or were transferred soon after the initial order, and no one else remembered that it was now part of their job. In this situation employees in the track department seem to be skilled and reasonably motivated, and they possessed the tools and time to perform the work. However, they experienced poor role perceptions: They didn't know that lubricating the track was part of their job.

A second problem related to Metro's three dozen "track walkers"—employees who check the entire track system for unsafe conditions twice each week. Internal audits revealed that many of these people failed to report unsafe tracks because they lacked sufficient training or were covering too much track (eight miles every day) to adequately investigate potential problem spots. Also, one audit suggested that many track walkers were "apathetic"—perhaps not surprising given their routine of walking the same track every week and the fact that their work often goes unnoticed. This information shows that many track walkers score poorly on three of the four elements in the MARS model (and consequently would have low engagement scores). They lack motivation and sufficient resources (too much track to inspect each day), and many of them lack the ability to detect track problems. At least they know what job they are supposed to perform (high role perceptions).

■ // Motivating Employees: A Three-Part Process

Overall, the MARS model provides an excellent diagnostic tool to figure out the primary causes of employee performance problems and the reasons why employees feel disengaged from their work. But MARS is just the first step in the process. Managers need to dig deeper

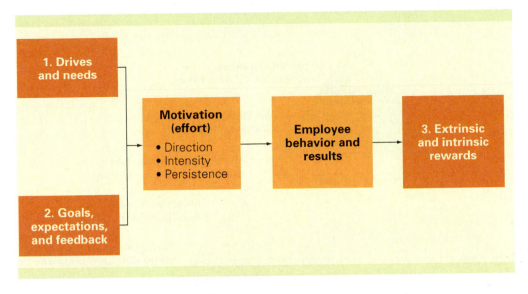

FIGURE 13.2

Three Parts to
Managing Employee
Motivation

into each of the four factors. The previous chapter explained how managers can improve employee ability through selection and training. In the remainder of this chapter we outline ways to manage employee motivation.

How well do managers motivate employees? Not very well, according to a recent survey of 13,000 employees. Only 40 percent of those polled believe that management actually motivates its workers.[9] Motivating people is not as simple as dangling a financial carrot in front of them (even though some companies seem to rely mainly on that motivation strategy). Instead managers need to understand the dynamics of employee motivation as a process consisting of the three critical parts illustrated in Figure 13.2. The first part involves understanding and guiding employee drives and needs; in other words, figuring out what energizes people. The second part is the process in which managers rely on goals, expectations, and feedback to establish the direction of employee effort. The third part of the motivation process is to design both extrinsic and intrinsic rewards that fulfill employee drives and needs, and reinforce behavior that is consistent with organizational objectives.

▪ // Part 1: Managing Motivation through Drives and Needs

Ultimately motivation begins with the employee's own drives and needs. **Drives** are instinctive tendencies to seek particular goals or maintain internal stability. Drives are hardwired in the brain (that is, everyone has the same drives), and they most likely exist to help the species survive.[10] **Needs** are mostly conscious deficiencies that energize or trigger behaviors to satisfy those needs. For the most part we are aware of our needs, whereas drives operate under the surface to generate our emotions and sometimes direct behavior. Needs are produced from our innate drives, but they are also strengthened or weakened through learning and social forces such as culture and childhood upbringing. We will find out how needs and drives relate to each other after introducing the world's most popular motivation theory: Maslow's needs hierarchy.

// MASLOW'S NEEDS HIERARCHY THEORY

Maslow's needs hierarchy theory is probably the one theory in this textbook that almost everyone has heard about. Developed by psychologist Abraham Maslow in the 1940s, the model has been applied in almost every human pursuit, from marketing products to rehabilitating prison inmates. This incredible popularity is rather odd considering that the theory has little research support. So why do we introduce you to Maslow's theory? First, elements of the model are worth noting for motivating employees. Second, most managers

drives
Instinctive tendencies to seek particular goals or maintain internal stability.

needs
Mostly conscious deficiencies that energize or trigger behaviors to satisfy those needs.

Maslow's needs hierarchy theory
A motivation theory of needs arranged in a hierarchy, whereby people are motivated to fulfill a higher need as a lower one becomes gratified.

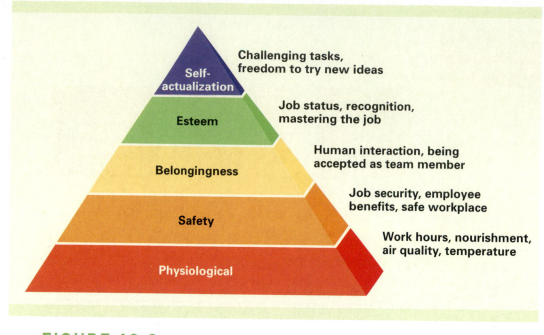

FIGURE 13.3   Maslow's Needs Hierarchy

you meet will mention Maslow's model, so you need to be informed about the theory—and be able to correct your colleagues' misperceptions about it.

Maslow's needs hierarchy organizes dozens of different needs into five basic categories arranged in the hierarchy shown in Figure 13.3.[11] Physiological needs (for food, air, water, shelter, and the like) are at the bottom of the hierarchy. Next are safety needs—the need for a secure and stable environment and the absence of pain, threat, or illness. Belongingness includes the need for love, affection, and interaction with other people. Esteem includes self-esteem through personal achievement as well as social esteem through recognition and respect from others. At the top of the hierarchy is **self-actualization**, which represents the need for self-fulfillment—a sense that one's potential has been realized. In addition to these five, Maslow describes the need to know and need for aesthetic beauty as two needs that do not fit within the hierarchy.

Needs hierarchy theory says that people are motivated by several needs at the same time, but the strongest source is the lowest unsatisfied need. As the person satisfies a lower-level need, the next higher need in the hierarchy becomes the primary motivator and remains so even if never satisfied. Physiological needs are initially the most important, and people are motivated to satisfy them first. As they become gratified, safety needs emerge as the strongest motivator. As safety needs are satisfied, belongingness needs become most important, and so forth. The exception to this need fulfillment process is self-actualization; as people experience self-actualization, they desire more rather than less of this gratification. Thus while the bottom four groups are *deficiency needs* because they become activated when unfulfilled, self-actualization is known as a *growth need* because it continues to develop even when fulfilled.

Limitations of Maslow's Theory   As we warned earlier, the accuracy of Maslow's needs hierarchy theory does not live up to its popularity.[12] The seven categories of needs provide a reasonably good list for most managers to remember, but studies have found that they don't capture all needs. The theory assumes that need priorities shift over months or years, whereas the importance of a particular need likely changes more quickly with the situation. But the most serious limitation of Maslow's needs hierarchy is its assumption that everyone has the same needs hierarchy. Research has revealed that this is a false assumption. People actually have different needs hierarchies tied to their personal values. Needs are conscious

self-actualization

The need for self-fulfillment in reaching one's potential.

deficiencies produced from innate drives but strengthened or weakened through learning and social forces such as culture and childhood upbringing. As a result, some people place belongingness at the pinnacle; others view status as the most important. Furthermore, studies have reported that the general needs hierarchy in some cultures is different from the needs hierarchy in other cultures.[13]

Management Implications of Maslow's Theory Critical parts of Maslow's model may have failed the reality test, but we can take away the following recommendations from Maslow's writing as well as subsequent research on employee needs:

Different Needs Hierarchies?   These UBS Warburg employees in Chicago seem to be enjoying each other's company, suggesting that they are experiencing some fulfillment of their belongingness needs. But do they all have the same needs hierarchy? Maslow's well-known theory claims they do, but evidence now suggests that needs hierarchies vary from one person to the next due to their different value systems. Thus to understand what motivates employees, managers need to understand the values that employees hold dearest.

© Ed Wheeler Photography.

1. *Employees have different needs at different times.* Everyone has a hierarchy of needs, but each person's hierarchy is different. The practical implication is that people value different things at different times. One employee might prefer time off, whereas another might prefer more pay. Managers need to carefully understand the needs of their employees and adjust rewards and other performance outcomes accordingly.

2. *Employees have several interdependent needs, not just one dominant need.* One of Maslow's most important breakthroughs was to emphasize that needs should be understood holistically, not separately. Managers must therefore remember that employees are motivated by a cluster of needs, not just one need. Thus managers must consider the whole person rather than simplistically label each person in terms of one need (for example, Julie wants a social environment, Liam is the status climber).

3. *At some point, most employees want to achieve their full potential (self-actualization).* Throughout his career, Maslow emphasized that people are naturally motivated to reach their potential (self-actualization), and that organizations and societies need to be structured to help people continue and develop this motivation.[14] The recommendation here is that managers must strive for Maslow's vision of enlightened management because the strongest and most sustained motivation tends to occur when employees try to fulfill their need for self-actualization.

4. *Employee needs are influenced by values and norms.* Maslow was one of the first motivation scholars to recognize that higher-order needs are shaped to some extent by the norms and values of the team, organization, and society in which the individual lives. Consequently, managers can adjust employee motivation and effort by reshaping these norms and values. For example, by encouraging more performance-oriented team norms, managers can strengthen team members' self-actualization needs.

These principles guided some of the steps taken by Ben Salzmann and his management team to transform ACUITY into a high-performance organization. The opening story to this chapter described an organization that was oppressive. Salzmann's team removed the chimes, introduced job sharing and flexible work schedules, allowed food and drinks, encouraged a casual dress code, established summer hours (Friday afternoons off), installed a fitness facility, beefed up the company pension plan, added nursing rooms for mothers, brought in occasional lunchtime entertainment (including a Buddy Holly play), and improved communication through town hall meetings with all 800 staff members. They also created a work environment that allowed people to self-actualize by delegating more responsibility. For instance, several committees representing employees throughout the company reviewed and recommended ways to improve the insurer. Maslow probably would have said that ACUITY has become a model of enlightened management.

// LEARNED NEEDS THEORY

Several decades ago psychologist David McClelland expanded on Maslow's idea that need strength is reinforced or weakened by personal values and social influences (culture, norms, and so on). Specifically, McClelland suggested that need strength is reinforced through childhood learning, parental styles, and social norms. He paid attention to three learned needs: achievement, power, and affiliation.[15]

- *Need for achievement (nAch):* People with a strong need for achievement (nAch) want to accomplish reasonably challenging goals through their own efforts. They prefer working alone rather than in teams, and they choose tasks with a moderate degree of risk (neither too easy nor impossible to complete). High nAch people also desire unambiguous feedback and recognition for their success. Successful entrepreneurs tend to have a high nAch.

- *Need for affiliation (nAff):* Need for affiliation (nAff) refers to a desire to seek approval from others, conform to their wishes and expectations, and avoid conflict and confrontation. People with a strong nAff try to project a favorable image of themselves and tend to actively support others and try to smooth out workplace conflicts. Managers must have a relatively low need for affiliation so that their choices and actions are not biased by a personal need for approval.

- *Need for power (nPow):* People with a high need for power (nPow) want to exercise control over others and are concerned about maintaining their leadership positions. Those who enjoy their power to advance personal interests have *personalized power*. Others mainly have a high need for *socialized power* because they desire power as a means to help others. Effective leaders have a high need for socialized rather than personalized power.

McClelland developed training programs that taught participants to increase their need for achievement. Trainees practiced writing achievement-oriented stories and engaged in achievement-oriented behaviors in business games. They also completed a detailed achievement plan for the next two years and formed a reference group with other trainees to maintain their newfound achievement motivation style.[16] Some companies also create a workplace environment that tries to strengthen the need for achievement. Consider General Electric (GE), the conglomerate that operates everything from aircraft engine manufacturing to television programming. Under CEO Jack Welch (and continuing under current CEO Jeffrey Immelt), GE managers have been rewarded for fact-based bottom-line numbers. They are grilled on weekly and monthly results. Routinely the bottom 10 percent of managers are culled, making room for more people who strive for better performance results.[17]

McClelland's learned needs theory repeats the point that a person's needs can be strengthened or weakened with experience (reinforcement) and social influences. The lesson here is that managers can strengthen or weaken employees' need for achievement, power, and affiliation, such as by supporting an achievement-oriented culture, rewarding those who demonstrate achievement orientation, and hiring coworkers who developed a strong achievement orientation in their upbringing.

GE: The Land of Achievement   For more than two decades General Electric has been a company that fuels the need for achievement. The company rigorously monitors manager performance weekly and monthly with fact-based bottom-line numbers. Praise and financial rewards are heaped on the top performers, whereas those in the bottom 10 percent are shown the door if they don't improve.

© AP Photo/Kathy Willens

// FOUR-DRIVE THEORY

Motivation experts have mostly abandoned needs hierarchy theories. However, due to recent breakthrough discoveries in brain research, they are paying close attention to the role of innate drives and how those drives shape human needs through social influences. **Four-drive theory**, which was recently introduced by Harvard Business School professors Paul Lawrence and Nitin Nohria, captures many of these recent discoveries.[18] Earlier we said that drives are instinctive or innate tendencies to seek particular goals or maintain internal stability. Based on their review of existing research, Lawrence and Nohria identified four drives that seem to apply to everyone:

- *Drive to acquire:* This is the drive to seek, take, control, and retain objects and personal experiences. The drive to acquire extends beyond basic food and water; it includes the need for relative status and recognition in society. Thus it is the foundation of competition and the basis of our need for esteem.

- *Drive to bond:* This is the drive to form social relationships and develop mutual caring commitments with others. Research indicates that people invest considerable time and effort in forming and maintaining relationships without any special circumstances or ulterior motives.[19] The drive to bond motivates people to cooperate and consequently is a fundamental ingredient in the success of organizations and the development of societies.

- *Drive to learn:* This is the drive to satisfy our curiosity, to know and understand ourselves and the environment around us. When observing something that is inconsistent with or beyond our current knowledge, we experience a tension that motivates us to close that information gap. The drive to learn is related to the self-actualization need described earlier.

- *Drive to defend:* This drive creates a "fight-or-flight" response in the face of personal danger. The drive to defend goes beyond protecting our physical self. It includes defending our relationships, our acquisitions, and our belief systems. The drive to defend is always reactive—it is triggered by threat. In contrast, the other three drives are always proactive—we actively seek to improve our acquisitions, relationships, and knowledge.

> **four-drive theory**
> A motivation theory based on the innate drives to acquire, bond, learn, and defend that incorporates both emotions and rationality.

All four drives are fixed in our brains through evolution. They are also independent of each other: One drive is not inherently inferior or superior to another drive. Four-drive theory also states that these four drives are a complete set—no other innate drives are excluded from the model. Another key feature is that all of the drives except the drive to defend are proactive, meaning that we regularly try to fulfill them. Thus any notion that a drive is fulfilled is temporary at best.

How do these four drives motivate us? Basically, our brain uses these four drives to quickly evaluate and assign emotions to information received through our senses. Suppose you learn that your boss has been promoted and an outsider has been hired to fill the vacant position. This sort of event likely triggers both the emotions of worry and curiosity. The drive to defend generates your worry about how the new manager will affect your comfortable work routine, whereas the drive to learn generates your curiosity about what the new boss looks and acts like. The key point here is that the four innate drives determine which emotions are triggered in each situation.

Four-drive theory states that neither drives nor the emotions they produce instinctively determine our motivation or behavior. Instead, as Figure 13.4 illustrates, we use our mental skill set—our logic and intelligence—to consciously decide how to sort out and act on the emotional signals generated through our drives. This mental skill set relies on our social norms, personal values, and past experience to decide the best course of action.[20] For instance, you might be curious about your new boss, but social norms prevent you from being too snoopy. You might also be worried about changes the new boss will create, and your past experience motivates you to take specific steps to address that threat.

Where do individual needs fit into this model? Need strength is produced from our drives in the context of our personal values, social norms, and past experience. A person's need for status (esteem) is based on the drive to acquire, but the priority that people give to status depends on their values, as well as the immediate surrounding culture and norms. Some people have a strong need for status because they were raised to value status, and because they currently work in organizations that reward those with higher status. In other words, the strongest needs are determined from a combination of the emotions generated and the person's values, social norms, and past experience.

FIGURE 13.4

Four-Drive Theory of Motivation

Source: Based on information in P.R. Lawrence and N. Nohria, *Driven: How Human Nature Shapes Our Choices* (San Francisco: Jossey-Bass, 2002).

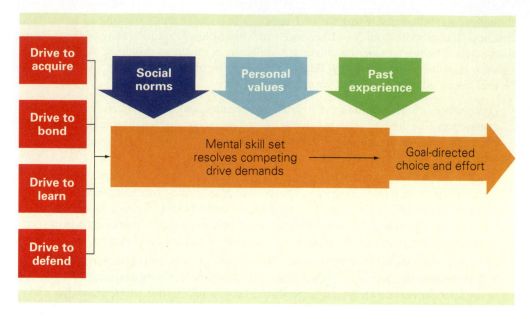

The mental skill set not only prioritizes needs but also translates and channels the experienced emotions into effort and behavior. People have unique values, experiences, and awareness of social norms, which shape how they react to their drive-based emotions. One person might be very forward when curious or defensive, whereas another individual experiencing the same emotions might be more circumspect and diplomatic. Both employees have the same drives and, in this example, experience similar emotions and needs. Yet they are motivated to act differently based on their unique values, experiences, and norm expectations.

Management Implications of Four-Drive Theory Lawrence and Nohria offer managers the following advice to apply four-drive theory: *Ensure that individual jobs and workplaces provide a balanced opportunity to fulfill the drives to acquire, bond, learn, and defend.*[21] There are really two key recommendations here. The first is that everyone in the workplace needs to regularly fulfill all four drives, so companies with highly motivated employees create a workplace where all four drives can be nourished. These firms provide sufficient rewards, learning opportunities, social interaction, and so forth for all employees. ACUITY (the Sheboygan, Wisconsin, insurance firm described at the beginning of this chapter) developed a more motivated workforce by applying this first recommendation. Specifically, it increased opportunities for social interaction (drive to bond), expanded training programs and learning opportunities through employee involvement (drive to learn), introduced a more performance-oriented reward system (drive to acquire), and minimized the previous risks of layoffs (drive to defend) through its increased profitability and growth.

The second recommendation from four-drive theory is that these four drives must be kept in "balance"; that is, organizations should avoid too much or too little opportunity to fulfill one drive at the expense of others. The reason for this advice is that the four drives balance each other. An organization that energizes the drive to acquire (such as through a highly competitive workplace) without the drive to bond may eventually suffer from organizational politics and dysfunctional conflict. Change and novelty in the workplace will aid the drive to learn, but too much will trigger the drive to defend to such an extent that employees become territorial and resistant to change. Creating a workplace that supports the drive to bond can, at extreme levels, undermine the diversity and constructive debate required for effective decision making.

Sony's recent woes seem to illustrate the challenges that occur when all four drives are not in balance. The Japanese company, which led the electronics world a decade ago with its Walkman and Playstation innovations, is now struggling to keep up with competitors. One reason for the current difficulties is Sony's hypercompetitive culture in which engineers are encouraged to outdo each other rather than work together. This competitive culture feeds employees' drive to acquire, but the lack of balance with the drive to bond leads to infighting and information hoarding. For instance, competitive rivalries within Sony delayed the company's launch of a digital music player and online music service to compete against Apple's iPod and iTunes music Web site.[22] Overall, four-drive theory offers potentially valuable understanding of employee motivation as well as ways to maximize that motivation.

Part 2: Managing Motivation through Goals, Expectations, and Feedback

Four-drive theory, learned needs theory, and Maslow's writing collectively help managers to understand and adjust the intensity and persistence of employee effort. People are motivated to a higher degree and a longer time when managers can understand and align employee needs and underlying drives with organizational objectives. But drives and needs represent just the first piece of the motivation puzzle. The second part involves directing that effort through goals, expectations, and feedback. This aspect of motivation is best understood through goal setting and feedback as well as expectancy theory.

Sony's Internal Battles   Sony led the electronics world a decade ago with its Walkman and Playstation innovations, but the firm is now struggling to keep up with competitors. One reason seems to be Sony's hypercompetitive culture in which engineers are encouraged to outdo each other rather than work together. This competitive culture feeds employees' drive to acquire, but the lack of balance with the drive to bond leads to infighting and information hoarding.

© AP Photo/Shizuo Kambayashi.

// GOAL SETTING AND FEEDBACK

One important way that ACUITY, the insurance company described at the beginning of this chapter, dramatically improved employee motivation was by introducing a new performance appraisal system in which employees and their supervisor mutually determine specific, achievable goals for the next six months or year. In addition, under CEO Ben Salzmann's leadership, ACUITY has become highly focused on measurable results. The company closely watches and sets benchmark goals for the all-important combined ratio (claims and expenses against premiums earned), percentage of surplus growth, premium growth rate, employee turnover rate, average premium per agency, and so on.

ACUITY has improved employee motivation through goal setting. **Goal setting** is the process of motivating employees and clarifying their role perceptions by establishing performance objectives. A goal is a desired future state that an organization or person attempts to realize. Goal setting improves role perceptions and consequently clarifies the direction of employee effort. When conducted effectively, goal setting can also increase the intensity and persistence of effort. It achieves this higher level of motivation through employee buy-in and by raising the level of personal goal expectations.

Consider recent events at Speedera Networks (now merged with Akamai). CEO Ajit Gupta announced to all 120 employees in Santa Clara, California, and Bangalore, India, that "if we pull together to achieve our business targets [for the next quarter], then we'll all be on a beach in May." Speedera would cover employee expenses as well as 50 percent of a spouse's or family member's expenses for four days at a Hawaiian resort. Everyone at the Internet applications company worked feverishly toward the company's goals, which included a hefty revenue growth target. Their motivation was further fueled with constant reminders of the Hawaiian trip. "The offices were transformed to look like tropical islands," says Gupta. Staff also received postcards and brochures with tempting images of the resort and its attractions. Much to everyone's delight the company achieved its goals; and Speedera staff from both countries had a memorable bonding experience on the Hawaiian beaches.[23]

goal setting

The process of motivating employees and clarifying their role perceptions by establishing performance objectives.

Beach Goals   Speedera Networks employees moved into high gear when CEO Ajit Gupta announced to all 120 employees in Santa Clara, California, and Bangalore, India, that "if we pull together to achieve our business targets [for the next quarter], then we'll all be on a beach in May." Their motivation was fueled with constant reminders of the Hawaiian trip.

Courtesy of Akamai.

Goal setting provides the critical linkage between the organization's strategic plans and individual motivation. Chapter 5 described how strategic plans are translated into more precise action plans, which include subgoals, responsibilities, time lines, and budgets. These plans are formulated all the way down to each work unit. Managers then translate the units' action plans into specific targets for individuals and teams to achieve.

Translating action plans into goals for individuals and teams involves more than telling them to "do your best."[24] As we described in Chapter 5, goals must be *precise and measurable*; that is, they should specify levels of change over a specific and relatively short time frame, such as "reduce scrap rate by 7 percent over the next six months." Notice that precise goals *specify a time period* in which they should be achieved. Second, managers should limit the number of goals for each employee or team to the *most important objectives*. Third, goals need to be *challenging, yet realistic*. This can be a difficult balancing act. Challenging goals motivate people to put forth more effort and sometimes for a longer time. They also fulfill a person's sense of achievement when the goals are achieved. Yet employees must be committed to the goals.[25] People are less motivated to attempt goals that are too tough.

Finally, goals have little value unless employees *receive associated feedback* about the consequences of their behavior.[26] Feedback lets people know whether they have achieved a goal or are properly directing effort toward it. Feedback is also an essential ingredient in motivation because self-actualization and the need for achievement depend on knowledge of goal attainment.

As with effective goals, feedback works best when it is precise and measurable. It should also be *timely*—available as soon as possible after the behavior or results so employees see a clear association between their actions and the consequences. Feedback should also be *sufficiently frequent*. New employees require more frequent feedback to aid their learning. Some jobs (like those of executives) necessarily have less frequent feedback because the consequences of their actions take longer to materialize than those of, say, a cashier's job. Finally, feedback should be *credible,* such as from people with no vested interest or from reliable monitoring devices.

■ Executive dashboards at Microsoft and Verizon.

Some companies have successfully improved the feedback process through executive dashboards—real-time data shown on an employee's computer screen. Almost half of Microsoft employees use a dashboard to monitor project deadlines, sales, and other metrics. Microsoft CEO Steve Ballmer regularly reviews dashboard results in one-on-one meetings with his seven business leaders. "Every time I go to see Ballmer, it's an expectation that I bring my dashboard with me," says Jeff Raikes, who heads the Microsoft Office division. Verizon CIO Shaygan Kheradpir also appreciates the instant feedback provided by his dashboard, which is a huge plasma screen on the wall of his office. Called the "Wall of Shaygan," the screen displays the status of more than 100 network systems around the country in green, yellow, or red lights. Another part of the screen shows sales, voice portal volumes, call center results, and other business metrics.[27]

Goal setting represents one of the "tried and true" management theories.[28] In partnership with goal setting, feedback also has an excellent reputation for improving employee motivation and performance. At the same time managers sometimes have difficulty putting goal setting into practice.[29] One concern is that goal setting tends to focus employees on a narrow subset of measurable performance indicators while ignoring aspects of job performance that are difficult to measure. A second problem is that when goals are tied to financial rewards, employees are often motivated to set easy goals (while making the boss think they are difficult) so they have a higher probability of receiving the bonus or pay increase.

// EXPECTANCY THEORY OF MOTIVATION

Although goal setting and feedback are powerful tools to motivate employees, they don't really explain why employees are motivated. The **expectancy theory** of motivation provides the missing explanation. Expectancy theory is based on the idea that work effort is directed toward behaviors that people believe will lead to desired outcomes.[30] The theory also predicts the intensity of the person's effort. As illustrated in Figure 13.5, an individual's effort level depends on three factors: effort-to-performance (E-to-P) expectancy, performance-to-outcome (P-to-O) expectancy, and outcome valences (V). Employee motivation is influenced by all three components of the expectancy theory model. If any component weakens, motivation weakens.

- *E-to-P expectancy:* This refers to the individual's perception that his or her effort will result in a particular level of performance. In some situations employees may believe that they can unquestionably accomplish a task (a probability of 1.0). In other situations they expect that even their highest level of effort will not result in the desired performance level (a probability of 0.0). In most cases the E-to-P expectancy falls somewhere between these two extremes.

- *P-to-O expectancy:* This is the perceived probability that a specific behavior or performance level will lead to particular outcomes. In extreme cases employees may believe that accomplishing a particular task (performance) will definitely result in a particular outcome (a probability of 1.0), or they may believe that this outcome will have no effect on successful performance (a probability of 0.0). More often the P-to-O expectancy falls somewhere between these two extremes.

- *Outcome valences:* A valence is the anticipated satisfaction or dissatisfaction that an individual feels toward an outcome. It ranges from negative to positive. (The actual range doesn't matter; it may be from −1 to +1 or from −100 to +100.) An outcome valence represents a person's anticipated satisfaction with the outcome.[31] Outcomes have a positive valence when they are consistent with our values and satisfy our needs; they have a negative valence when they oppose our values and inhibit need fulfillment.

To understand how expectancy theory explains the direction and intensity of employee effort, consider the following situation at ACUITY, the insurance firm described throughout

expectancy theory
A motivation theory based on the idea that work effort is directed toward behaviors that people believe will lead to desired outcomes.

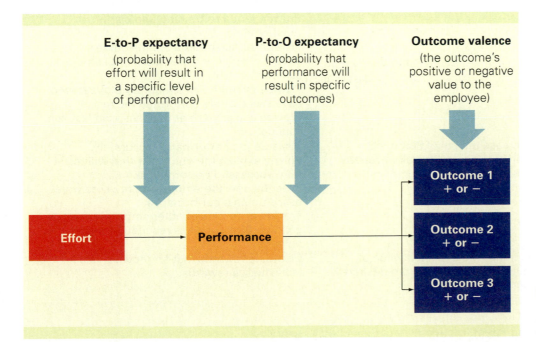

FIGURE 13.5

Expectancy Theory of Motivation

this chapter. Until recently ACUITY distributed sick leave credits for each month that an employee showed up for work but not during months when the person took sick leave. This program was supposed to motivate people to show up for work and to take sick leave only when they were sick, but that's not what happened. Instead many people showed up for work when they were sick; others took lengthy absences in the same month.[32]

The problem with ACUITY's old sick leave plan was that the P-to-O expectancy directed people to avoid sick leave at some times and to take as much as possible at other times. Suppose it's the last day of the month and you wake up with the flu, complete with fever and nausea. You should stay at home to recover and avoid making others sick, but being absent from work today would cost you an entire month of sick leave credit. And given the probability that the illness will last a few more days, you will lose next month's sick leave credit as well. Your solution? Some folks would try to work today to receive this month's sick leave credit. If the illness is just as bad tomorrow, they might take several days off (even when well enough to work) because they have already lost that month's credits anyway! How did ACUITY resolve this problem? It now pays employees when they are sick, trusting them not to abuse this privilege.

Management Implications of Expectancy Theory One of the appealing characteristics of expectancy theory is that it identifies several ways in which managers can increase employee motivation through each of the model's three components (see Figure 13.6).[33]

E-to-P expectancies are influenced by the individual's belief that he or she can successfully complete a task. Some companies increase this can-do attitude by assuring employees that they have the necessary competencies, clear role perceptions, and necessary resources to reach the desired levels of performance. Matching employees to jobs based on their abilities and clearly communicating the tasks required are an important part of this process. Similarly, E-to-P expectancies are learned, so behavioral modeling and supportive feedback (positive reinforcement) typically strengthen employee self-confidence.[34]

Expectancy Theory Component	Objective	Management Implications
E→P expectancies	Increase the belief that employees are capable of performing the job successfully.	• Select people with the required skills and knowledge. • Provide required training and clarify job requirements. • Provide sufficient time and resources. • Assign simpler or fewer tasks until employees can master them. • Provide examples of similar employees who have successfully performed the task. • Provide coaching to employees who lack self-confidence.
P→O expectancies	Increase the belief that good performance will result in certain (valued) outcomes.	• Measure job performance accurately. • Clearly explain the outcomes that will result from successful performance. • Describe how the employee's rewards were based on past performance. • Provide examples of other employees whose good performance has resulted in higher rewards.
Valences of outcomes	Increase the expected value of outcomes resulting from desired performance.	• Distribute rewards that employees value. • Individualize rewards.

FIGURE 13.6 Management Implications of Expectancy Theory

The most obvious ways to improve P-to-O expectancies are to measure employee performance accurately and distribute more valued rewards to those with higher job performance. ACUITY, described at the beginning of this chapter, followed this advice by introducing a more objective performance evaluation system and more closely linking rewards to individual and team performance. P-to-O expectancies are perceptions, so employees should believe that higher performance will result in higher rewards. Having a performance-based reward system is important, but this fact must be communicated. When rewards are distributed, employees should understand how their rewards have been based on past performance. More generally, companies need to regularly communicate the existence of a performance-based reward system through examples, anecdotes, and public ceremonies.

Finally, performance outcomes influence work effort only when they are valued by employees. To improve the valences of outcomes, managers need to individualize rewards so employees who perform well are offered a choice.

■ // Part 3: Managing Motivation through Extrinsic and Intrinsic Rewards

The third part of the motivation puzzle considers what employees receive or experience from their effort and accomplishments. These outcomes can generally be divided into two types: extrinsic rewards and intrinsic rewards. An **extrinsic reward** is anything received from another person that the recipient values and is contingent on his or her behavior or results. Extrinsic rewards include paychecks, performance bonuses, praise, or some other form of recognition. Extrinsic rewards don't occur naturally with the behavior or result; instead someone introduces these rewards. An **intrinsic reward**, on the other hand, is a positive emotional experience resulting directly and naturally from the individual's behavior or results. This would include the enjoyment of learning a new task, a feeling of accomplishment from performing a job well, and a sense of flow or engagement when work is performed smoothly. Notice that these emotions arise naturally from performing the task.

extrinsic reward
Anything received from another person that the recipient values and is contingent on his or her behavior or results.

intrinsic reward
A positive emotional experience resulting directly and naturally from the individual's behavior or results.

■ // Motivating Employees through Extrinsic Rewards

Extrinsic rewards come in many forms, but pay and benefits are clearly at the top of the list. In fact, pay and benefits are ranked as two of the most important features in the employment relationship.[35] The reason for this importance is that a paycheck is more than a form of exchange in the employment relationship. It also conveys status, accomplishment, self-esteem, and power. Financial rewards serve four specific objectives: membership and seniority, job status, competencies, and task performance.

// MEMBERSHIP- AND SENIORITY-BASED REWARDS

Membership- and seniority-based rewards (sometimes called "pay for pulse") represent the largest part of most paychecks. Some employee benefits, such as free or discounted meals in the company cafeteria, remain the same for everyone, whereas others increase with seniority. Many Asian companies distribute a "13th month" bonus that every employee expects to receive each year. These membership- and seniority-based rewards potentially attract job applicants (particularly those who desire predictable income) and reduce turnover. However, they do not directly motivate job performance; on the contrary, they discourage poor performers from seeking work better suited to their abilities. Instead the good performers are lured to better-paying jobs. Some of these rewards are also "golden handcuffs" that can undermine job performance because employees resent being held captive by high pay in a job they dislike.

Since World War II employees in most large Japanese companies have received pay rates and increases determined entirely by their age or seniority, usually topping out at around age 45. Tough times in the 1990s forced many Japanese firms to introduce performance-based pay systems in which annual pay increases varied with the employee's contribution, but some companies have not been happy with the results. Concerned that employees were becoming too stressed over their variable pay rates each year, Tokai Rubber Industries Ltd. recently reintroduced an age-based bonus pay system. "Even during that period [when they can't perform as well as expected], we raise salaries according to their age," says Tokai Rubber president Akira Fujii. Some Japanese firms also pay employees a large bonus for each child born in their families. For example, employees at Daiwa House Industry Co. in Osaka receive U.S. $9,000 every time they have a child.[38]

© Getty Images.

■ Skill-based pay at Marley Cooling Tower Co.

piece rate systems
Systems that reward employees based on the number of units produced.

// JOB STATUS–BASED REWARDS

Almost every organization rewards employees to some extent based on the status of the jobs they occupy. *Job evaluation* is commonly used to rate the worth or status of each job, with higher pay rates going to jobs that require more skill and effort, have more responsibility, and have more difficult working conditions.[36] Organizations that don't rely on job evaluation indirectly reward job status based on surveys estimating what other companies pay specific jobs. A senior engineer typically earns more than, say, a purchasing clerk because the work performed by the engineer is worth more to the organization. It has more value (calculated by a job evaluation system or pay survey), so employees in that job receive more status-based rewards in the organization. People in some higher-status jobs are also rewarded with larger offices, company-paid vehicles, and exclusive dining rooms.

Job status–based rewards create a reward system that employees believe is fair. They also motivate employees to compete for promotions. However, when companies are trying to be more cost-efficient and responsive to the external environment, job status–based rewards potentially do the opposite by encouraging bureaucratic hierarchy. These rewards also reinforce a status mentality, whereas Generation-X and Generation-Y employees expect a more egalitarian workplace. Furthermore, status-based pay potentially motivates employees to compete with each other and to raise the value of their own jobs by exaggerating job duties and hoarding resources.[37]

// COMPETENCY-BASED REWARDS

Many firms have shifted from job status–based rewards to competency reward systems. The National Health Service (NHS) in the United Kingdom is a recent example. Every job in the NHS is now described in terms of its required skills and knowledge. Employees receive annual pay increases through a wide pay band (range from lowest to highest pay for that job) based on how well they meet the job's skill and knowledge requirements.[39] Skill-based pay is a variation of competency-based rewards in which employees are rewarded for the number of skill modules mastered and, consequently, on the number of jobs they can perform. For instance, Marley Cooling Tower Co. in Olathe, Kansas, has about 30 skill modules (skills required for specific jobs) in its production operations. Employees earn the base pay rate for being able to work in one job, but they earn more as they learn other skill modules. Two employees performing the same job would receive different pay rates based on how many skill modules they have mastered. Those who master all 30 modules earn almost three times the base rate because they can perform any job in the production area.[40]

Competency-based rewards improve workforce flexibility by motivating employees to learn a variety of skills and thereby perform a variety of jobs. Product or service quality tends to improve because employees with multiple skills are more likely to understand the work process and know how to improve it. Competency-based rewards also reward employees who continuously learn skills that will keep them employed. One potential problem is that measuring competencies can be subjective, particularly when described as personality traits or personal values. Skill-based pay systems measure specific skills, so they are usually more objective. However, they are expensive because employees spend more time learning new tasks.[41]

// PERFORMANCE-BASED REWARDS

Performance-based rewards have existed since Babylonian days in the 20th century BC, but their popularity has increased dramatically over the past couple of decades.[42] Real estate agents and other salespeople typically earn *commissions*, in which their pay increases with sales volume. **Piece rate systems** reward employees based on the number of units produced. For example, Eurofresh crop workers in Arizona get paid by the volume of tomatoes picked; lawn care employees at The Lawn Mowgul in Dallas, Texas, earn a form of piece rate (called "piece-meal") based on the number of lawns cut.[43] Many employees receive pay increases or bonuses based on a **performance appraisal**. Performance appraisal, which we describe in more detail later, is a systematic process of evaluating an employee's performance.

Increasingly, employees are finding larger parts of their total paychecks determined by team more than individual results. Forward Media, an enterprise software consulting firm in Sydney, Australia, is an example. "We have seen individual incentive programs fail," says James Ward, who cofounded the company with his wife and employs a few dozen people. "We set a group revenue target for each team, then give people a bonus according to the profit their team achieves."[44]

Rather than calculating bonuses from team sales or profit, **gainsharing plans** award bonuses based on cost savings and productivity improvement. John Deere switched to gainsharing a few years ago because its previous individual incentive plan discouraged cooperation and coordination even though jobs were highly interdependent. Under the gainsharing plan, each team at the farm machinery manufacturer has a benchmark work-hour standard to assemble a part, such as an engine or combine attachment. If the team assembles the part in less time, it receives some of the cost savings as a bonus on top of regular wages.[45] As John Deere has learned, gainsharing plans tend to improve team dynamics, knowledge sharing, and pay satisfaction. They also create a reasonably strong link between effort and performance because much of the cost reduction and labor efficiency is within the team's control.

Organizational Rewards Along with individual and team-based rewards, many firms rely on organizational-level rewards to motivate employees. **Profit-sharing plans** calculate bonuses from the previous year's level of corporate profits. ISG employees in Indiana receive checks for each quarter that the steelmaker (part of Mittel Group) earns a profit. The profit-sharing plan is restricted to union members; but ISG's managers receive **stock options** that give them the right to purchase stock from the company at a future date at a predetermined price up to a fixed expiration date. If the stock rises above the predetermined price, employees can buy the stock and reap the windfall. One senior ISG manager had an option to buy stock at $2.76 per share. The manager exercised some of that option when the stock rose to $30, resulting in a hefty bonus that year.[46]

Employee stock ownership plans (ESOPs) encourage employees to buy company stock, usually at a discounted price or with a no-interest loan. Employees are subsequently rewarded through dividends and market appreciation of those investments. Approximately 10 percent of the private sector U.S. workforce participates in an ESOP. Sears Roebuck and UPS are two of the earliest companies to distribute shares to their employees.

A fourth organizational-level reward strategy, which we briefly noted in Chapter 7, is the **balanced scorecard (BSC)**. BSC is a goal-oriented performance measurement system that rewards people (typically executives) for improving performance on a composite of financial, customer, and internal processes, as well as employee factors. The better the measurement improvements across these dimensions, the larger the bonus awarded. For instance, KT (formerly Korea Telecom) relied on BSC to transform the former government-owned telephone company into a more competitive business after privatization. "It guided our employees with clear direction and balanced perspectives," says Song Young-han, KT's executive senior vice president. "By gathering all the employees around BSC, we were able to concentrate our foundation for the performance-oriented organization culture."[47]

How effective are organizational-level rewards? ESOPs, stock options, and balanced scorecards tend to create an "ownership culture" in which employees feel aligned with the organization's success. Balanced scorecards have the added benefit of aligning rewards to several specific measures of organizational performance, but they are potentially more subjective and require a particular corporate culture to be implemented effectively. Profit sharing tends to create less ownership culture, but it has the advantage of automatically adjusting employee compensation with the firm's prosperity, thereby reducing the need for layoffs or negotiated pay reductions during recessions.[48] The main problem with ESOPs, stock options, and profit sharing (less so

performance appraisal
A systematic process of evaluating an employee's performance.

■ Gainsharing at John Deere.

gainsharing plan
A reward system in which team members earn bonuses for reducing costs and increasing labor efficiency in their work process.

profit-sharing plan
A reward system that pays bonuses to employees based on the previous year's level of corporate profits.

stock options
A reward system that gives employees the right to purchase company stock at a future date at a predetermined price.

employee stock ownership plans (ESOPs)
Reward systems that encourage employees to buy company stock.

■ Balanced scorecard at KT in Korea.

balanced scorecard (BSC)
A reward system that pays bonuses for improved results on a composite of financial, customer, internal process, and employee factors.

Yum! Recognition   Yum! Brands, Inc., motivates employees with a peer-recognition program in which employees reward coworkers with Champs cards. Champs is an acronym for the six values at KFC, one of the restaurant chains owned by Yum!. Employees receive the cards for acting consistently with those values, and their names are entered into drawings for small prizes.

© Getty Images.

with balanced scorecards) is that employees often perceive a weak connection between individual effort and corporate profits or the value of company shares. Even in small firms, the company's stock price or profitability is influenced by economic conditions, competition, and other factors beyond the employee's immediate control. This low individual performance-to-outcome expectancy weakens employee motivation.

// NONFINANCIAL REWARDS

Not all extrinsic rewards involve giving employees money. In fact, many firms are discovering that some of the most valued and effective extrinsic rewards don't cost much money at all. "Five to 10 percent of employees leave a company because of money," explains Christopher Owen, CEO of Meriwest Credit Union in San Jose, California. "Most of the time it's because they don't feel they are being recognized." Ed Ariniello, vice president of operations at G.I. Joe's, a sports retailer in Oregon and Washington, goes out of his way to find opportunities to praise employees for a job well done. "I do a lot of walking around patting people on the back," says Ariniello. "When [other managers and I] do that, the employees feel great."[49]

The challenge of recognition is to "catch" employees doing extraordinary things. Keyspan Corporation chairman Bob Catell resolves this by regularly asking managers for lists of "unsung heroes" at the New England gas utility. He calls an employee every week, often spending the first few minutes convincing the listener that it is really him. Approximately one-third of large American firms rely on peer recognition to motivate employees. Among them is Yum! Brands, Inc., the parent company of KFC, Taco Bell, and Pizza Hut. Yum! managers created a system in which employees reward colleagues with "Champs" cards—an acronym for KFC's values (cleanliness, hospitality, and so on).[50]

// IMPROVING PERFORMANCE APPRAISALS

Many extrinsic rewards—particularly individual-level performance-based rewards—have come under attack over the years for discouraging creativity, distancing managers from employees, distracting employees from the meaningfulness of the work itself, and being quick fixes that ignore the true causes of poor performance. Although these issues have kernels of truth under specific circumstances, they do not necessarily mean we should abandon performance-based rewards. On the contrary, the top-performing companies around the world are more likely to pay for performance.[51]

Reward systems do motivate most employees, but only when these systems assign higher rewards to those with higher performance. Unfortunately this simple principle seems to be unusually difficult to apply. In one recent large-scale survey, fewer than half of Malaysian employees said they believe their company rewards high performance or deals appropriately with poor performers. A Gallup survey at an American telecommunications company revealed that management's evaluation of 5,000 customer service employees was unrelated to the performance ratings that customers gave those employees. "Whatever behaviors the managers were evaluating were irrelevant to the customers," concluded Gallup executives. "The managers might as well have been rating the employees' shoe sizes, for all the customers cared."[52]

How can managers more accurately evaluate employee performance? Although appraisals will always have a degree of subjectivity, there are ways to minimize this problem or get around it altogether:

1. *Use more objective measures of performance.* One of the best pieces of advice is simply to rely on more objective indicators of employee performance than performance

appraisals. Some companies have switched from traditional appraisals to output measures such as units delivered or number of people served per hour. Objective measures often occur at the team and organizational level, so companies pay individuals a fixed rate and award bonuses for measures of team performance or organizational profits. This approach gets rid of the performance appraisal altogether, at least for determining financial rewards.

2. *Use anchored performance appraisal instruments.* Where performance appraisals are necessary (that is, if no objective measures are adequate or available), then managers should use anchored appraisal methods. One form of anchor is goal setting, where employees are expected to complete a specific set of objectives before the next appraisal. ACUITY switched from its subjective system of rating employees to a more objective one in which employee performance is evaluated against mutually agreed goals. Compensation that was previously disconnected from supervisor ratings is now tied more closely to goal achievement. The other form of anchoring is to label performance appraisal rating forms with specific examples so raters have a better understanding of what good or average performance means for each dimension of performance.

3. *Use multiple sources of performance information.* An increasingly popular way to improve the accuracy of performance appraisals is through **360-degree feedback.** This process involves receiving information from a full circle of people around the employee, including subordinates, bosses, coworkers, people in other departments (internal clients), and sometimes external clients. Research suggests that 360-degree feedback tends to provide more complete and accurate information than feedback from a supervisor alone. It is particularly useful when the supervisor is unable to observe the employee's behavior or performance throughout the year. Lower-level employees also feel a greater sense of fairness and open communication when they are able to provide upward feedback about their boss's performance. On the downside, 360-degree feedback systems can be time-consuming, produce conflicting and ambiguous information, and encourage politics as employees curry favor from people who will rate them.[53]

> **360-degree feedback**
> Performance feedback received from a full circle of people around an employee.

4. *Use performance appraisal training.* To some degree, performance appraisal accuracy can improve when managers receive various forms of training.[54] Rater error training attempts to reduce perceptual biases by raising awareness of these problems and encouraging raters to avoid them. Performance dimension training attempts to familiarize raters with the meaning of the performance dimensions on the rating instrument. Performance standards training is sometimes called "frame-of-reference" training because it tries to establish a common frame of reference among the raters. This is achieved by presenting samples of job performance along with some indication of the level at which that performance should be rated on the performance evaluation instrument.

The more objective the method of evaluating employee performance, the stronger will be the performance-to-outcome expectancy, which in turn increases employee motivation. More objective rewards also address another important issue: the extent to which employees believe they are being fairly rewarded. Thus our final topic under extrinsic rewards is equity theory.

// REWARDING EMPLOYEES EQUITABLY

Patti Anderson came from a family of Boeing engineers, so she was proud to also work as a manufacturing engineer at the aerospace company's commercial airplane division in Renton, Washington. But that pride evaporated when Anderson discovered that the men in her family earned more than she did at Boeing for performing the same work. "My husband, brother, and dad also performed the same job as me, and each was paid more than me and consistently received higher raises than I," said Anderson in a legal statement. "I know this because I saw their pay stubs."[55]

Patti Anderson's feelings are explained through **equity theory**, which says that feelings of equity or inequity occur when employees compare their own outcome/input ratios to the outcome/input ratios of other people.[56] The outcome/input ratio is the value of the outcomes you receive divided by the value of inputs you provide in the exchange relationship. Anderson probably included her skills and level of responsibility as inputs. Other inputs might include experience, status, performance, personal reputation, and amount of time worked. Outcomes are the things employees receive from the organization in exchange for the inputs. For Anderson, the main outcomes are the paycheck and pay raises. Some other outcomes might be promotions, recognition, or an office with a window.

Equity theory states that we compare our outcome/input ratio with a comparison other.[57] In our example, Anderson compared herself with her male family members and likely other men who worked in the same jobs at Boeing. However, the comparison other may be another person or group of people in the same job, another job, or another organization. Some research suggests that employees frequently collect information on several referents to form a "generalized" comparison other.[58] For the most part, however, the comparison other varies from one person to the next and is not easily identifiable.

Feelings of equity or inequity arise from a comparison of our own outcome/input ratio with the comparison other's ratio. Patti Anderson felt *underreward* inequity because her male counterparts received higher outcomes (pay) for inputs that were comparable to what she contributed at Boeing. Anderson probably would have had feelings of equity if she received the same pay and other outcomes for performing the same work. The third condition, *overreward* inequity, occurs when people realize they are paid more than others with the same inputs (skills, effort, and the like) or when they receive similar outcomes even though they provide lower inputs (such as getting paid the same as someone who is far more skilled and talented than you are).

Watching Executive–Employee Pay Ratios   Over the past few decades many employees have been experiencing feelings of inequity due to the widening pay gap between staff and top management.[59] What is a fair level of pay for corporate executives? Plato (the Greek philosopher) felt that no one in a community should earn more than five times the lowest-paid worker. In the 1970s management guru Peter Drucker suggested that 20 times the lowest worker's earnings was more reasonable. John Pierpont Morgan, who in the 1800s founded the financial giant now called J.P. Morgan Chase, also warned that no CEO should earn more than 20 times an average worker's pay. That advice didn't stop William B. Harrison Jr., the current CEO of J.P. Morgan Chase, from receiving $15 million to $20 million in pay, bonuses, and stock options for each of the past few years. That's more than 700 times the pay of the average employee in the United States!

Costco Wholesale chief executive Jim Sinegal thinks such a large wage gap is blatantly unfair and can lead to long-term employee motivation problems. "Having an individual who is making 100 or 200 or 300 times more than the average person working on the floor is wrong," says Sinegal, who cofounded the Issaquah, Washington, company. With annual salary and bonus of $550,000, Sinegal ranks as one of the lowest-paid executives even though Costco is one of the country's largest retailers and its employees among the highest paid in the industry.[60]

Mind the (Pay) Gap   Costco Wholesale chief executive Jim Sinegal thinks gaps between executive wages and those of their employees are getting out of control and could lead to long-term motivation problems.

Courtesy of Costco Wholesale Corporation.

How Employees Correct Inequity Feelings   What happens when employees feel inequitably rewarded? They experience an emotional tension that motivates them to reduce those inequities. Here are the most common ways in which people try to reduce feelings of inequity:[61]

- *Change inputs:* Employees either perform at a lower level or subtly ask the better-off coworker to do a larger share of the work to justify his or her higher pay or other outcomes.

- *Change outcomes:* Employees might increase their own outcomes by asking for a pay increase or making unauthorized use of company resources. They might reduce the coworker's outcomes by asking the boss to stop giving favorable treatment to the coworker.

- *Change perceptions:* Sometimes employees whisk away feelings of inequity by eventually believing the coworker really is doing more (such as working longer hours) or that the higher outcomes (perhaps a better office) he or she receives really aren't so much better after all.

- *Leave the situation:* Employees have a few ways to remove themselves from the inequitable situation. They might quit or transfer to another job where rewards are more equitably distributed. Those who can't leave might keep away from the office where the coworker is located, take more time off work, or psychologically withdraw from the job (make it less important in their life).

"O.K., if you can't see your way to giving me a pay raise, how about giving Parkerson a pay cut?"

Managing the Reward Process Fairly Equity theory is good at predicting the perceived fairness of pay and other rewards in a variety of situations, particularly if managers get to know their employees' needs (as we discussed in Part 1 of this chapter) and keep communication channels open so employees can complain when they feel decisions are unfair. However, managers also need to pay attention to fairness in the *process* of reward distribution.[62] This process includes the mechanics of deciding how to allocate valued resources (such as paychecks and preferred office space) and in how employees are treated throughout this process.

How do managers improve fairness in the process of distributing rewards and resources?[63] A good place to start is by giving employees "voice" in the process—encouraging them to present their facts and opinions to whoever is allocating the resource. Managers also need to remain unbiased, rely on complete and accurate information, apply existing policies consistently, and listen to the different views held by those affected by the resource allocation decision. Employees are also more likely to feel that decisions are fair if they have the right to appeal the decision to a higher authority. Finally, people usually feel better when managers treat them with respect and give them a full explanation of decisions. If employees believe a decision is unfair, refusing to explain how the decision was made could further inflame those feelings of inequity.

Extrinsic rewards are important, but they aren't the only thing that motivates employees. "High performers don't go for the money," warns William Monahan, CEO of Oakdale, Minnesota–based Imation Corp. "Good people want to be in challenging jobs and see a future where they can get even more responsibilities and challenges." Rafik O. Loutfy, a Xerox research center director, agrees with this assessment. "Our top stars say they want to make an impact—that's the most important thing," he says. "Feeling they are contributing and making a difference is highly motivational for them."[64] In other words, Imation, Xerox, and other companies motivate employees mainly by designing interesting and challenging jobs.

// Motivating Employees through Intrinsic Rewards

Throughout the first half of the 20th century, industry experts and academics spent a lot of time figuring out how to increase employee performance by dividing work into narrower and narrower tasks to the point where employees completed an entire job cycle in less than one minute. To put this in context, assembly-line employees at Chrysler in the United States current have a job cycle of about 64.5 seconds, which means they repeat the same set of tasks about 58 times each hour and about 230 times before they take a meal break.[65]

Why would companies divide work into such tiny bits? One reason is that employees spend less time changing activities because they have fewer tasks to juggle. They also require fewer physical and mental skills to accomplish the assigned work, so less time and resources are needed for training. A third reason is that employees practice their tasks more frequently with shorter work cycles, so jobs are mastered quickly. A fourth reason why work efficiency increases is that employees with specific aptitudes or skills can be matched more precisely to the jobs for which they are best suited.[66]

Narrowing jobs down to short cycle times does have these advantages, to a degree. But this job design strategy can ultimately backfire because it ignores another important fact—namely that tedious jobs don't motivate. Although specialization might improve employee ability, the MARS model described earlier in this chapter points out that employees must also have sufficient motivation to perform their jobs effectively. Thus managers need to design jobs that provide more intrinsic rewards, which as we described earlier are positive emotions resulting directly and naturally from the individual's behavior or results.

// JOB CHARACTERISTICS MODEL

job characteristics model

A job design model that relates the motivational properties of jobs to specific personal and organizational consequences of those properties.

The **job characteristics model** is a useful template for understanding how to improve employee motivation through the job itself.[67] According to the job characteristics model, all jobs have some degree of the five core job dimensions shown in Figure 13.7:

- *Skill variety:* Skill variety refers to the use of different skills and talents to complete a variety of work activities. For example, sales clerks who normally only serve customers might be assigned the additional duties of stocking inventory and changing storefront displays.
- *Task identity:* Task identity is the degree to which a job requires completion of a whole or identifiable piece of work, such as assembling an entire computer modem rather than just soldering in the circuitry.

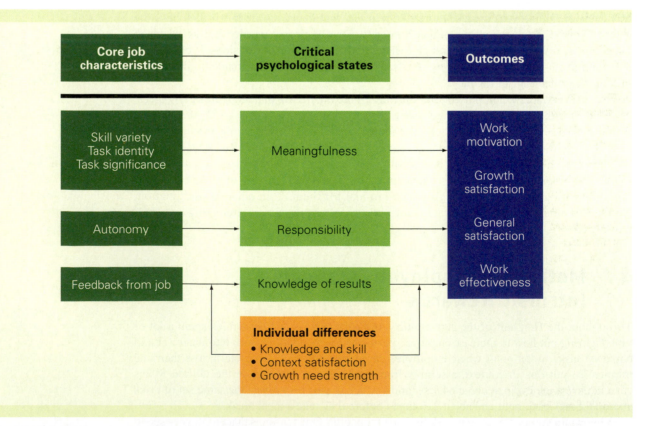

FIGURE 13.7   Job Characteristics Model

- *Task significance:* Task significance is the degree to which the job affects the organization and society.
- *Autonomy:* Jobs with high levels of autonomy provide freedom, independence, and discretion in scheduling work and determining the procedures to be used to complete the work. In autonomous jobs, employees make their own decisions rather than relying on detailed instructions from supervisors or procedure manuals.
- *Job feedback:* Job feedback is the degree to which employees can tell how well they are doing based on direct sensory information from the job itself. Airline pilots can feel how smoothly they land their aircraft; road crews can see how well they have prepared the roadbed and laid the asphalt.

The first three core job dimensions (skill variety, task identity, and task significance) have a combined effect on a psychological state called *experienced meaningfulness*—the belief that one's work is worthwhile or important. Autonomy directly contributes to the feeling of *experienced responsibility*—feeling personally accountable for the outcomes of one's efforts. The third critical psychological state, *knowledge of results,* is derived from job feedback.

The job characteristics model warns that motivation from redesigning jobs increases only when employees have the required skills and knowledge to master the more challenging work. Otherwise job redesign tends to increase stress and reduce job performance. The model also suggests that employees who are unsatisfied with their work context (working conditions, job security) or who have a low growth need strength won't become more motivated, either. However, various studies suggest that employees might be motivated by job design no matter how they feel about their job context or how high or low they score on growth need strength.[68]

// MOTIVATING EMPLOYEES THROUGH JOB ENRICHMENT

The job characteristics model suggests many ways to improve employee motivation, such as by rotating employees through different jobs each day or adding more tasks to one job. But experts agree that the most effective strategy is **job enrichment**: giving employees responsibility for scheduling, coordinating, and planning their own work.[69] One way to increase job enrichment is by combining highly interdependent tasks into one job. By forming natural work units, jobholders have stronger feelings of responsibility for an identifiable body of work. They feel a sense of ownership and therefore tend to increase job quality. Forming natural work units increases task identity and task significance because employees perform a complete product or service and can more readily see how their work affects others.

A second job enrichment strategy, called *establishing client relationships,* involves putting employees in direct contact with their clients rather than using the supervisor as a go-between. By being directly responsible for specific clients, employees have more information and can make decisions affecting those clients.[70] Establishing client relationships also increases task significance because employees see a connection between their work and its consequences for customers.

Forming natural task groups and establishing client relationships are common ways to enrich jobs, but the heart of the job enrichment philosophy is to give employees more autonomy over their work. This basic idea is at the core of a popular concept known as *empowerment.*

// MOTIVATING EMPLOYEES THROUGH EMPOWERMENT

The opening story to this chapter describes the incredible transformation of Wisconsin insurance company ACUITY and the resulting surge in employee motivation. One reason for the increased motivation is that rigid control systems were removed and employees

job enrichment
A job design practice in which employees are given more responsibility for scheduling, coordinating, and planning their own work.

empowerment
A psychological concept represented by four dimensions: self-determination, meaning, competence, and impact of the individual's role in the organization.

The Empowerment of Semco   Most managers like to say they empower their employees, but few can reach the heights of empowerment experienced by employees at Semco Corporation, SA. "Can an organization let people do what they want, when they want, and how they want?" asks Ricardo Semler, CEO of the manufacturing and services conglomerate in Sao Paulo, Brazil. The answer appears to be yes. Organized into small groups of 6 to 10 people, Semco employees choose their objectives every six months, hire their coworkers, work out their budgets, set their own salaries, decide when to come to work, and even elect their own bosses. This may seem radical, but Semler says that the company is "only 50 or 60 percent where we'd like to be." Semler believes that replacing the head office with several satellite offices around Sao Paulo would give employees even more opportunity for empowerment.[74]

Courtesy of Semco, SA.

were invited to actively participate in making decisions that affect the company's strategic and operational direction. In particular, frontline employees and middle managers are rotated through committees that have top managers' full support to actively set direction for technology, customer services, investments, employee relations, and most other issues. As one employee recently noted, "ACUITY treats their employees with respect and also empowers their employees."[71]

ACUITY has created a work environment that makes employees feel empowered. **Empowerment** is a psychological concept represented by four dimensions: self-determination, meaning, competence, and impact of the individual's role in the organization:[72]

- *Self-determination:* Empowered employees feel that they have freedom, independence, and discretion over their work activities.

- *Meaning:* Employees who feel empowered care about their work and believe that what they do is important.

- *Competence:* Empowered people are confident about their ability to perform the work well and have a capacity to grow with new challenges.

- *Impact:* Empowered employees view themselves as active participants in the organization; that is, their decisions and actions influence the company's success.

Chances are that you have heard corporate leaders say they are "empowering" the workforce. What these executives really mean is that they are changing the work environment to support empowerment. To generate beliefs about self-determination, employees must work in jobs with a high degree of autonomy with minimal bureaucratic control. To maintain a sense of meaningfulness, jobs must have high levels of task identity and task significance. And to maintain a sense of self-confidence, jobs must provide sufficient feedback.[73]

Employees also experience more empowerment in organizations where information and other resources are easily accessible, where employee learning is valued, and where reasonable mistakes are viewed as a natural part of the learning process. Furthermore, empowerment requires corporate leaders who trust employees and are willing to take the risks that empowerment creates.[75]

IN CONCLUSION WHY DOES IT MATTER?

There are four cornerstones of employee behavior and performance, and motivation is arguably the most important of these for managers on a daily basis. Two other factors—abilities and situational factors—are fairly stable in the short term, and the third factor—role perceptions—is typically managed within goal setting and related motivational practices. In other words, when it comes to maximizing employee engagement and performance, motivation is vital and probably the dominant factor for managers to consider.

The quest for a motivated and engaged workforce has not been easy, however. Most managers (92 percent of them, according to one major survey) say that motivating employees has become more challenging. Three factors seem to be responsible for this increasing challenge. First, globalization, information technology, corporate restructuring, and other changes have dramatically altered employment relationships. These changes potentially undermine the levels of trust and commitment necessary to energize employees beyond minimal standards. Perhaps this explains why approximately one-fifth of the American workforce is disengaged—retired on the job.[76]

Second, in decades past, companies typically relied on armies of supervisors to closely monitor employee behavior and performance. Even if commitment and trust were low, employees performed their jobs with the boss watching them closely. But most companies have reduced costs by flattening the organizational structure and removing layers of management. Managers now supervise many more employees, so they can't possibly watch for laggards. This is just as well because today's educated workforce resents "command and control" management. Most people enjoy the feeling of being motivated, but this requires the right conditions; so managers need to search for more contemporary ways to motivate staff.

The third challenge is that a new generation of employees has brought different expectations to the workplace. A few years ago various writers disparaged Generation-X and Generation-Y employees as slackers, cynics, whiners, and malcontents. Now we know that the problem wasn't their lack of motivational potential; it was that managers didn't know how to motivate them! It seems that many companies still haven't figured this out: According to one report more than 40 percent of employees aged 25 to 34 sometimes or frequently feel demotivated compared to 30 percent of 35- to 44-year-olds and just 18 percent of 45- to 54-year-olds.[77]

This chapter has described the three foundations of employee motivation: (1) individual drives and needs; (2) goals, expectations, and feedback; and (3) extrinsic and intrinsic rewards. Managers play a central role throughout this process. They try to discover what really drives employees, recognizing that people have complex needs. Then they direct effort from those drives and needs by setting achievable goals, clarifying expectations, and offering constructive feedback along the way. Finally, managers are responsible for configuring financial rewards, providing formal and informal recognition, and designing jobs that exude natural intrinsic rewards. Then, with these three parts well crafted, managers must step back and allow that context to have the intended influence on employee motivation.

MANAGEMENT CHALLENGES

1. An insurance company has high levels of absenteeism among the office staff. The head of office administration believes employees are misusing the company's sick leave benefits, whereas employees say otherwise. Use the MARS model to discuss some possible reason for absenteeism here and how it might be reduced.

2. One of the oldest questions in management is whether money motivates. In your estimation, what is the answer to this question according to Maslow's needs hierarchy?

3. David McClelland suggests that some needs are learned or at least can be strengthened through learning. How might a sales manager use this ability to develop the need for achievement, affiliation, and power in the company's sales force?

4. This chapter outlines ways to increase employee motivation by altering the three components of expectancy theory. Suppose you are the instructor of this class. Use expectancy theory to explain how you would increase student motivation to complete assignments to a high standard and complete readings prior to class.

5. Think back to a recent job you have held or a volunteer task you have performed. In what ways did your boss or task leader use goal setting and feedback to motivate you to complete the work? How might goal setting and feedback be used more effectively in that situation?

6. Several service representatives are upset that a newly hired representative with no previous experience will be paid $3,000 a year above the usual starting salary in the pay range. The department manager explained that the new hire would not accept the entry-level rate, so the company raised the offer by $3,000. All five reps currently earn salaries near the top of the scale ($15,000 higher than the new recruit), although they all started at the minimum starting salary a few years earlier. Use equity theory to explain why the five service representatives feel inequity in this situation.

MANAGEMENT PORTFOLIO

FOR THE ORGANIZATION YOU HAVE CHOSEN TO FOLLOW:

1. Find out what you can (from the Web site, news reports, annual reports, and so on) about the company's practices for motivating and supporting employees. Does the organization sufficiently support each of the drives identified in four-drive theory? Does the organization seem to keep the four drives in balance, in your opinion?

2. Look back at the mission, vision, values, and goals for this organization that you identified in Chapter 5. Now document some of the performance goals this organization would most likely assign to employees in (a) production or service jobs and (b) sales or support jobs.

3. Organizations vary in their emphasis on the four types of rewards: membership/seniority, job status, competencies, and performance. Based on your investigation of this organization, which of these four categories is emphasized the most? Which category seems to receive the least emphasis?

4. Do you think this organization has an empowered workforce relative to other companies in this industry? Why or why not?

CLOSING CASE   BUDDY'S SNACK COMPANY*

Buddy's Snack Company is a family-owned company located in the Rocky Mountains. Buddy Forest started the business in 1951 by selling homemade potato chips out of the back of his pickup truck. Nowadays Buddy's is a $36 million snack food company that is struggling to regain market share lost to Frito-Lay and other fierce competitors. In the early 1980s Buddy passed the business to his son Buddy Jr., who is currently grooming his son Mark to succeed himself as head of the company.

Six months ago Mark joined Buddy's Snacks as a salesperson and after four months was quickly promoted to sales manager. Mark recently graduated from a local university with an MBA in marketing, and Buddy Jr. was hoping Mark would be able to implement strategies that could help turn the company around. One of Mark's initial strategies was to introduce a new sales performance management system. As part of this approach, any salesperson who received a below average performance rating would be required to attend a mandatory coaching session with his or her supervisor.

*Case written by Russell Casey, Clayton State University, and Gloria Thompson, University of Phoenix. Reprinted with permission.

Mark Forest hoped these coaching sessions would motivate his employees to increase their sales. This case describes the reaction of three salespeople who have been required to attend a coaching session because of their low performance over the previous quarter.

LYNDA LEWIS

Lynda is a hard worker who takes pride in her work ethic. She has spent a lot of time reading training material and learning selling techniques, viewing training videos on her own time, and accompanying top salespeople on their calls. Lynda has no problem asking for advice and doing whatever needs to be done to learn the business. Everyone agrees that Lynda has a cheery attitude and is a real "team player," giving the company 150 percent at all times. It has been a tough quarter for Lynda due to the downturn in the economy, but she is doing her best to make sales for the company. Lynda feels that her failure to make quota during this past quarter is due not to lack of effort but just to bad luck in the economy. She is hopeful that things will turn around in the next quarter.

Lynda is upset with Mark about having to attend the coaching session because this is the first time in three years that her sales quota has not been met. Although Lynda is willing to do whatever it takes to be successful, she is concerned that the coaching sessions will be held on a Saturday. Doesn't Mark realize that Lynda has to raise three boys by herself and that weekends are an important time for her family? Because Lynda is a dedicated employee, she will somehow manage to rearrange the family's schedule.

Lynda is now very concerned about how her efforts are being perceived by Mark. After all, she exceeded the sales quota from the previous quarter, yet she did not receive thanks or praise for those efforts. The entire experience has left Lynda unmotivated and questioning her future with the company.

MICHAEL BENJAMIN

Michael is happy to have his job at Buddy's Snack Company, although he really doesn't like sales work that much. Michael accepted this position because he felt that he wouldn't have to work hard and would have a lot of free time during the day. Michael was sent to coaching mainly because his customer satisfaction reports were low; in fact, they were the lowest in the company. Michael tends to give canned presentations and does not listen closely to customers' needs. Consequently he makes numerous errors in new sales orders, which delay shipments and lose business and goodwill for Buddy's Snack Company. Michael doesn't really care because most of his customers do not spend much money, and he doesn't think it is worth his while.

There has been a recent change in the company commission structure. Instead of selling to the warehouse stores and possibly earning a high commission, Michael is now forced to sell to lower-volume convenience stores. In other words, he will have to sell twice as much product to earn the same amount of money. Michael does not think this change in commission is fair, and he feels that the coaching session will be a waste of time. He believes that the other members of the sales team are getting all of the good leads and that is why they are so successful. Michael doesn't socialize with others in the office and attributes others' success and promotions to whom they know in the company rather than the fact that they are hard workers. He feels that no matter how much effort is put into the job, he will never be adequately rewarded.

KYLE SHERBO

For three of the past five years Kyle was the number one salesperson in the division and had hopes of being promoted to sales manager. When Mark joined the company, Kyle worked closely with Buddy Jr. to help Mark learn all facets of the business. Kyle thought this close relationship with Buddy Jr. would ensure his upcoming promotion to the coveted position of sales manager, and he was devastated to learn that Mark received the promotion that he thought was his.

During the past quarter there has been a noticeable change in Kyle's work habits. It has become common for Kyle to be late for appointments or miss them entirely, as well as not returning phone calls or following up on leads. His sales performance has declined dramatically, which resulted in a drastic loss of income. Although Kyle was dedicated and fiercely loyal to Buddy Jr. and the company for many years, he is now looking for other employment. Buddy's Snacks is located in a rural community, which leaves Kyle with limited job opportunities. He was, however, offered a position as a sales manager with a competing company in a larger town, but Kyle's wife refuses to leave the area because of her strong family ties. Kyle is bitter and resentful of his current situation and now faces a mandatory coaching session that will be conducted by Mark.

CASE DISCUSSION QUESTIONS

1. Apply expectancy theory or motivation and equity theory to explain the level of motivation in each of these employees.

2. Apply four-drive theory to explain the motivation of these employees as well as their reactions to the imminent coaching sessions.

ENDNOTES

1. S. Prestegard, "From Heritage to Acuity," *Marketplace Magazine*, March 27, 2001, p. 14; M. Muckian, "Irreverent Heritage," *The Business Journal* (Milwaukee), March 14, 2003, p. A25; R. Romell, "Sharp Focus on Employee Satisfaction Pays Off for ACUITY," *Milwaukee Journal Sentinel*, June 29, 2004, p. 3D; J. Signer, "A Cultural Revolution Transforms ACUITY as an Employer and a Business Partner," *Journal of Organizational Excellence*, Spring 2005, pp. 17–28.

2. "Gallup Study: Feeling Good Matters in the Workplace," *Gallup Management Journal*, January 12, 2006; "Employee Engagement Levels Are Focus of Global Towers Perrin Study," *Tower Perrin Monitor*, January 2006.

3. D. Ulrich and N. Smallwood, *Why the Bottom Line Isn't* (Hoboken, NJ: John Wiley & Sons, 2003), p. 11; "Owens Corning Makes Smart Investments in Employee Training," *The Resource* (Newsletter of Jackson State's Division of Economic and Community Development), Fall 2004, p. 1; P. Kershaw, "Happy Days," *Sydney Morning Herald*, August 23, 2005, p. 6; K. Ockenden, "Inside Story," *Utility Week*, January 28, 2005, p. 26.

4. Also notice that the outcomes of the MARS model are "behavior and results," resulting in the even more memorable acronym MARS BAR. The MARS model is developed from models and writing by several sources, including E.E. Lawler III and L.W. Porter, "Antecedent Attitudes of Effective Managerial Performance," *Organizational Behavior and Human Performance* 2, no. 2 (1967), pp. 122–42; K.F. Kane, "Special Issue: Situational Constraints and Work Performance," *Human Resource Management Review* 3 (Summer 1993), pp. 83–175.

5. C.C. Pinder, *Work Motivation in Organizational Behavior* (Upper Saddle River, NJ: Prentice-Hall, 1998); G.P. Latham and C.C. Pinder, "Work Motivation Theory and Research at the Dawn of the Twenty-First Century," *Annual Review of Psychology* 56 (2005), pp. 485–516.

6. S. Brady, "Deep in the Heart of AT&T Dallas," *Cable World*, October 7, 2002, p. 37.

7. Kane, "Special Issue: Situational Constraints and Work Performance"; S.B. Bacharach and P. Bamberger, "Beyond Situational Constraints: Job Resources Inadequacy and Individual Performance at Work," *Human Resource Management Review* 5, no. 2 (1995), pp. 79-102; G. Johns, "Commentary: In Praise of Context," *Journal of Organizational Behavior* 22 (2001), pp. 31–42.

8. J. Becker and L. Layton, "Safety Warnings Often Ignored at Metro," *Washington Post*, June 6, 2005, p. A01.

9. "Workers' Attitudes toward Leaders Rebounded Strongly between 2002 and 2004, Watson Wyatt Survey Finds," PRNewswire news release (Washington: December 14, 2004).

10. T.V. Sewards and M.A. Sewards, "Fear and Power–Dominance Drive Motivation: Neural Representations and Pathways Mediating Sensory and Mnemonic Inputs, and Outputs to Premotor Structures," *Neuroscience and Biobehavioral Reviews* 26 (2002), pp. 553-79; K.C. Berridge, "Motivation Concepts in Behavioral Neuroscience," *Physiology & Behavior* 81, no. 2 (2004), pp. 179–209.

11. A.H. Maslow, "A Theory of Human Motivation," *Psychological Review* 50 (1943), pp. 370–96; A.H. Maslow, *Motivation and Personality* (New York: Harper & Row, 1954).

12. D.T. Hall and K.E. Nougaim, "An Examination of Maslow's Need Hierarchy in an Organizational Setting," *Organizational Behavior and Human Performance* 3, no. 1 (1968), p. 12; M.A. Wahba and L.G. Bridwell, "Maslow Reconsidered: A Review of Research on the Need Hierarchy Theory," *Organizational Behavior and Human Performance* 15 (1976), pp. 212-40; E.L. Betz, "Two Tests of Maslow's Theory of Need Fulfillment," *Journal of Vocational Behavior* 24, no. 2 (1984), pp. 204–20; P.A. Corning, "Biological Adaptation in Human Societies: A 'Basic Needs' Approach," *Journal of Bioeconomics* 2, no. 1 (2000), pp. 41–86.

13. S. Oishi et al., "Cross-Cultural Variations in Predictors of Life Satisfaction: Perspectives from Needs and Values," *Personality and Social Psychological Bulletin* 25, no. 8 (August 1999), pp. 980–90; J. Kickul, S.W. Lester, and E. Belgio, "Attitudinal and Behavioral Outcomes of Psychological Breach: A Cross Cultural Comparison of the United States and Hong Kong Chinese," *International Journal of Cross Cultural Management* 4, no. 2 (2004), pp. 229–52.

14. R.J. Lowry, *The Journals of A.H. Maslow* (Monterey, CA: Brooks/Cole, 1979); A.H. Maslow, *Maslow on Management* (New York: John Wiley & Sons, 1998).

15. D.C. McClelland, *The Achieving Society* (New York: Van Nostrand Reinhold, 1961); D.C. McClelland and D.H. Burnham, "Power Is the Great Motivator," *Harvard Business Review* 73 (January–February 1995), pp. 126–39; D. Vredenburgh and Y. Brender, "The Hierarchical Abuse of Power in Work Organizations," *Journal of Business Ethics* 17 (September 1998), pp. 1337–47; S. Shane, E.A. Locke, and C.J. Collins, "Entrepreneurial Motivation," *Human Resource Management Review* 13, no. 2 (2003), pp. 257–79.

16. D. Miron and D.C. McClelland, "The Impact of Achievement Motivation Training on Small Business," *California Management Review* 21 (1979), pp. 13–28.

17. D. Brady, "Will Jeff Immelt's New Push Pay Off for GE?" *BusinessWeek*, October 13, 2003, pp. 94-97; B. Morris, "The GE Mystique," Fortune, March 6, 2006, pp. 98–102.

18. P.R. Lawrence and N. Nohria, *Driven: How Human Nature Shapes Our Choices* (San Francisco: Jossey-Bass, 2002).

19. R.E. Baumeister and M.R. Leary, "The Need to Belong: Desire for Interpersonal Attachments as a Fundamental Human Motivation," *Psychological Bulletin* 117 (1995), pp. 497–529.

20. Lawrence and Nohria, *Driven*, pp. 145–47.

21. Lawrence and Nohria, *Driven*, Chapter 11.

22. P. Dvorak, "Out of Tune," *The Wall Street Journal*, June 29, 2005, p. A1.

23. A. Prayag, "All Work and More Play," *Business Line* (The Hindu), June 13, 2005, p. 4; S. Rajagopalan, "Bangalore to Hawaii, an All-Paid Holiday," *Hindustan Times*, May 7, 2005; J.A. Singh, "Hola for Success!" *Business Standard* (India), June 4, 2005.

24. G.P. Latham, "Goal Setting: A Five-Step Approach to Behavior Change," *Organizational Dynamics* 32, no. 3 (2003), pp. 309–18; E.A. Locke and G.P. Latham, *A Theory of Goal Setting and Task Performance* (Englewood Cliffs, NJ: Prentice-Hall, 1990).

25. A. Li and A.B. Butler, "The Effects of Participation in Goal Setting and Goal Rationales on Goal Commitment: An Exploration of Justice Mediators," *Journal of Business and Psychology* 19, no. 1 (Fall 2004), pp. 37–51.

26. M. London, E.M. Mone, and J.C. Scott, "Performance Management and Assessment: Methods for Improved Rater Accuracy and Employee Goal Setting," *Human Resource Management* 43, no. 4 (Winter 2004), pp. 319–36; Latham and Pinder, "Work Motivation Theory and Research at the Dawn of the Twenty-First Century."

27. A. Dragoon, "Sleepless in Manhattan," *CIO*, April 2005, p. 1; S.E. Ante, "Giving the Boss the Big Picture," *BusinessWeek*, February 13, 2006, p. 48.

28. J.B. Miner, "The Rated Importance, Scientific Validity, and Practical Usefulness of Organizational Behavior Theories: A Quantitative Review," *Academy of Management Learning and Education* 2, no. 3 (2003), pp. 250–68. Also see C.C. Pinder, *Work Motivation in Organizational Behavior* (Upper Saddle River, NJ: Prentice-Hall, 1997), p. 384.

29. P.M. Wright, "Goal Setting and Monetary Incentives: Motivational Tools That Can Work Too Well," *Compensation and Benefits Review* 26 (May–June 1994), pp. 41-49; E.A. Locke and G.P. Latham, "Building a Practically Useful Theory of Goal Setting and Task Motivation: A 35-Year Odyssey," *American Psychologist* 57, no. 9 (2002), pp. 705–17.

30. Expectancy theory of motivation in work settings originated in V.H. Vroom, *Work and Motivation* (New York: Wiley, 1964). The version of expectancy theory presented here was developed by Edward Lawler. Lawler's model provides a clearer presentation of the model's three components. P-to-O expectancy is similar to "instrumentality" in Vroom's original expectancy theory model. The difference is that instrumentality is a correlation, whereas P-to-O expectancy is a probability. See J.P. Campbell et al., *Managerial Behavior, Performance, and Effectiveness* (New York: McGraw-Hill, 1970); E.E. Lawler III, *Motivation in Work Organizations* (Monterey, CA: Brooks-Cole, 1973); D.A. Nadler and E.E. Lawler, "Motivation: A Diagnostic Approach," in *Perspectives on Behavior in Organizations*, 2nd, ed., ed. J.R. Hackman, E.E. Lawler III, and L.W. Porter (New York: McGraw-Hill, 1983), pp. 67–78.

31. M. Zeelenberg et al., "Emotional Reactions to the Outcomes of Decisions: The Role of Counterfactual Thought in the Experience of Regret and Disappointment," *Organizational Behavior and Human Decision Processes* 75, no. 2 (1998), pp. 117–41; B.A. Mellers, "Choice and the Relative Pleasure of Consequences," *Psychological Bulletin* 126, no. 6 (November 2000), pp. 910–24; R.P. Bagozzi,

U.M. Dholakia, and S. Basuroy, "How Effortful Decisions Get Enacted: The Motivating Role of Decision Processes, Desires, and Anticipated Emotions," *Journal of Behavioral Decision Making* 16, no. 4 (October 2003), pp. 273–95.

32. Signer, "A Cultural Revolution Transforms ACUITY as an Employer and a Business Partner," p. 21.

33. Nadler and Lawler, "Motivation: A Diagnostic Approach."

34. T. Janz, "Manipulating Subjective Expectancy through Feedback: A Laboratory Study of the Expectancy-Performance Relationship," *Journal of Applied Psychology* 67 (1982), pp. 480–85; K.A. Karl, A.M. O' Leary-Kelly, and J.J. Martoccio, "The Impact of Feedback and Self-Efficacy on Performance in Training," *Journal of Organizational Behavior* 14 (1993), pp. 379–94; R.G. Lord, P.J. Hanges, and E.G. Godfrey, "Integrating Neural Networks into Decision-Making and Motivational Theory: Rethinking Vie Theory," *Canadian Psychology* 44, no. 1 (2003), pp. 21–38.

35. H. Das, "The Four Faces of Pay: An Investigation into How Canadian Managers View Pay," *International Journal of Commerce & Management* 12 (2002), pp. 18–40. For recent ratings of the importance of pay and benefits, see P. Babcock, "Find What Workers Want," *HRMagazine*, April 2005, pp. 50–56.

36. G.T. Milkovich, J.M. Newman, and C. Milkovich, *Compensation* (Burr Ridge, IL: McGraw-Hill/Irwin, 2002), Chapter 5. For a history of job evaluation, see D.M. Figart, "Equal Pay for Equal Work: The Role of Job Evaluation in an Evolving Social Norm," *Journal of Economic Issues* 34 (March 2000), pp. 1–19.

37. E.E. Lawler III, *Rewarding Excellence: Pay Strategies for the New Economy* (San Francisco: Jossey-Bass, 2000), pp. 30–35, 109–19; R. McNabb and K. Whitfield, "Job Evaluation and High Performance Work Practices: Compatible or Conflictual?" *Journal of Management Studies* 38 (March 2001), pp. 293–312.

38. "Seniority Pay System Seeing Revival," *Kyodo News* (Tokyo), March 29, 2004; "More Firms Offering Childbirth Allowances," *Daily Yomiuri* (Tokyo), September 29, 2005, p. 4.

39. "Changing Times in the NHS," *Personnel Today,* December 7, 2004, p. 9.

40. C.T. Crumpley, "Skill-Based Pay Replaces Traditional Ranking," *Kansas City Star,* June 30, 1997, p. B6.

41. E.E. Lawler III, "From Job-Based to Competency-Based Organizations," *Journal of Organizational Behavior* 15 (1994), pp. 3–15; R.L. Heneman, G.E. Ledford Jr., and M.T. Gresham, "The Changing Nature of Work and Its Effects on Compensation Design and Delivery," in *Compensation in Organizations: Current Research and Practice,* ed. S. Rynes and B. Gerhart (San Francisco: Jossey-Bass, 2000), pp. 195–240; B. Murray and B. Gerhart, "Skill-Based Pay and Skill Seeking," *Human Resource Management Review* 10 (August 2000), pp. 271–87; R.J. Long, "Paying for Knowledge: Does It Pay?" *Canadian HR Reporter,* March 28, 2005, pp. 12–13; J.D. Shaw et al., "Success and Survival of Skill-Based Pay Plans," *Journal of Management* 31, no. 1 (February 2005), pp. 28–49.

42. E.B. Peach and D.A. Wren, "Pay for Performance from Antiquity to the 1950s," *Journal of Organizational Behavior Management* (1992), pp. 5–26.

43. J.J. Higuera, "Willcox, Ariz., Greenhouse Tomato Grower, Union Reach Contract Deals," *Arizona Daily Star,* November 21, 2002; L. Spiers, "Piece by Piecemeal," *Lawn & Landscape Magazine,* August 5, 2003.

44. K. Walters, "Dream Team," *Business Review Weekly,* October 13, 2005, p. 92.

45. G.B. Sprinkle and M.G. Williamson, "The Evolution from Taylorism to Employee Gainsharing: A Case Study Examining John Deere's Continuous Improvement Pay Plan," *Issues in Accounting Education* 19, no. 4 (November 2004), pp. 487–503.

46. A. Holecek, "ISG Shares Success—with Everyone," *NWI Times* (Indiana), August 14, 2004.

47. "KT Seeks New Growth Engines," *Korea Herald,* March 2, 2004.

48. J. Chelius and R.S. Smith, "Profit Sharing and Employment Stability," *Industrial and Labor Relations Review* 43 (1990), pp. 256s–73s; S.H. Wagner, C.P. Parkers, and N.D. Christiansen, "Employees That Think and Act Like Owners: Effects of Ownership Beliefs and Behaviors on Organizational Effectiveness," *Personnel Psychology* 56, no. 4 (Winter 2003), pp. 847–71; G. Ledford, M. Lucy, and P. Leblanc, "The Effects of Stock Ownership on Employee Attitudes and Behavior: Evidence from the Rewards at Work Studies," *Perspectives* (Sibson), January 2004; P. Andon, J. Baxter, and H. Mahama, "The Balanced Scorecard: Slogans, Seduction, and State of Play," *Australian Accounting Review* 15, no. 1 (March 2005), pp. 29–38.

49. D. Hopewell, "Credit Union Keeps Productivity up with Friendly Competition," *Silicon Valley/San Jose Business Journal,* December 16, 2002; T.J. Ryan, "Just Rewards," *Sporting Goods Business,* June 2005.

50. D. Creelman, "Interview: Bob Catell & Kenny Moore," *HR.com,* February 2005; E. White, "Praise from Peers Goes a Long Way," *The Wall Street Journal,* December 19, 2005, p. B3.

51. J. Pfeffer, *The Human Equation* (Boston: Harvard Business School Press, 1998); B.N. Pfau and I.T. Kay, *The Human Capital Edge* (New York: McGraw-Hill, 2002). The problems with performance-based pay are discussed in W.C. Hammer, "How to Ruin Motivation with Pay," *Compensation Review* 7, no. 3 (1975), pp 17–27; A. Kohn, *Punished by Rewards* (Boston: Houghton Mifflin, 1993); M. O'Donnell and J. O' Brian, "Performance-Based Pay in the Australian Public Service," *Review of Public Personnel Administration* 20 (Spring 2000), pp. 20–34; M. Beer and M.D. Cannon, "Promise and Peril of Implementing Pay-for-Performance," *Human Resource Management* 43, no. 1 (Spring 2004), pp. 3–48.

52. M. Buckingham and D.O. Clifton, *Now, Discover Your Strengths* (New York: Free Press, 2001); Watson Wyatt, "WorkMalaysia" (Kuala Lumpur: Watson Wyatt, 2004), http://www.watsonwyatt.com/asia-pacific/research/workasia/workmy_keyfindings.asp (accessed December 2, 2005).

53. W.W. Tornow and M. London, *Maximizing the Value of 360-Degree Feedback: A Process for Successful Individual and Organizational Development* (San Francisco: Jossey-Bass, 1998); M.A. Peiperl, "Getting 360 Degree Feedback Right," *Harvard Business Review* 79 (January 2001), pp. 142–47; L.E. Atwater, D.A. Waldman, and J.F. Brett, "Understanding and Optimizing Multisource Feedback," *Human Resource Management Journal* 41 (Summer 2002), pp. 193–208; "Perils & Payoffs of Multi-Rater Feedback Programs," *Pay for Performance Report,* May 2003, p. 1; J.W. Smither, M. London, and R.R. Reilly, "Does Performance Improve Following Multisource Feedback? A Theoretical Model, Meta-Analysis, and Review of Empirical Findings," *Personnel Psychology* 58, no. 1 (2005), pp. 33–66.

54. H.J. Bernardin, C.L. Tyler, and D.S. Wiese, "A Reconsideration of Strategies for Rater Training," in *Research in Personnel and Human Resources Management* (Stamford, CT: JAI Press, 2001), pp. 221–74; D.J. Schleicher et al., "A New Frame for Frame-of-Reference Training: Enhancing the Construct Validity of Assessment Centers," *Journal of Applied Psychology* 87, no. 4 (2002), pp. 735–46.

55. "Boeing Settles Sex Discrimination Suit for up to $73m," *Puget Sound Business Journal,* July 16, 2004; S. Holmes, "A New Black Eye for Boeing?" *BusinessWeek,* April 26, 2004, p. 90; S. Holt, "Boeing Gender-Bias Lawsuit Brings Women's Buried Stories to Surface," *Knight Ridder/Tribune Business* News, July 6, 2004; S. Holt and D. Bowermaster, "Rare Trial Nears: 28,000 Women Accuse Boeing of Gender Bias," *The Seattle Times,* May 14, 2004, p. A1.

56. J.S. Adams, "Toward an Understanding of Inequity," *Journal of Abnormal and Social Psychology* 67 (1963), pp. 422–36; R.T. Mowday, "Equity Theory Predictions of Behavior in Organizations," in *Motivation and Work Behavior,* 5th ed., ed. L.W. Porter and R.M. Steers (New York: McGraw-Hill, 1991), pp. 111–31; R.G. Cropanzano, J. Greenberg, "Progress in Organizational Justice: Tunneling through the Maze," in *International Review of Industrial and Organizational Psychology,* ed. C.L. Cooper and I.T. Robertson (New York: Wiley, 1997), pp. 317–72; L.A. Powell, "Justice Judgments as Complex Psychocultural Constructions: An Equity-Based Heuristic for Mapping Two- and Three-Dimensional Fairness Representations in Perceptual Space," *Journal of Cross-Cultural Psychology* 36, no. 1 (January 2005), pp. 48–73.

57. C.T. Kulik and M.L. Ambrose, "Personal and Situational Determinants of Referent Choice," *Academy of Management Review* 17 (1992), pp. 212–37; G. Blau, "Testing the Effect of Level and Importance of Pay Referents on Pay Level Satisfaction," *Human Relations* 47 (1994), pp. 1251–68.

58. T.P. Summers and A.S. DeNisi, "In Search of Adams' Other: Reexamination of Referents Used in the Evaluation of Pay," *Human Relations* 43 (1990), pp. 497-511.

59. G.S. Crystal, I*n Search of Excess: The Overcompensation of American Executives* (New York: W.W. Norton & Co., 1991).

60. B. Murphy, "Rising Fortunes," *Milwaukee Journal Sentinel,* October 10, 2004, p. 1; S. Greenhouse, "How Costco Became the Anti-Wal-Mart," T*he New York Times,* July 17, 2005, p. BU1.

61. Y. Cohen-Charash and P.E. Spector, "The Role of Justice in Organizations: A Meta-Analysis," *Organizational Behavior and Human Decision Processes* 86 (November 2001), pp. 278–321.

62. Cohen-Charash and Spector, "The Role of Justice in Organizations: A Meta-Analysis"; J.A. Colquitt et al., "Justice at the Millennium: A Meta-Analytic Review of 25 Years of Organizational Justice Research," *Journal of Applied Psychology* 86 (2001), pp. 425–45.

63. J. Greenberg and E.A. Lind, "The Pursuit of Organizational Justice: From Conceptualization to Implication to Application," in *Industrial and Organizational Psychology: Linking Theory with Practice,* ed. C.L. Cooper and E.A. Locke (London: Blackwell, 2000), pp. 72–108. For recent studies of voice and injustice, see K. Roberts and K.S. Markel, "Claiming in the Name of Fairness: Organizational Justice and the Decision to File for Workplace Injury Compensation," *Journal of Occupational Health Psychology* 6 (October 2001), pp. 332–47; J.B. Olson-Buchanan and W.R. Boswell, "The Role of Employee Loyalty and Formality in Voicing Discontent," *Journal of Applied Psychology* 87, no. 6 (2002), pp. 1167–74.

64. "Strong Leaders Make Great Workplaces," *CityBusiness,* August 28, 2000; P.M. Perry, "Holding Your Top Talent," *Research Technology Management* 44 (May 2001), pp. 26–30.

65. P. Siekman, "This Is Not a BMW Plant," *Fortune,* April 18, 2005, p. 208.

66. H. Fayol, *General and Industrial Management,* trans. C. Storrs (London: Pitman, 1949); Lawler III, *Motivation in Work Organizations,* Chapter 7.

67. J.R. Hackman and G. Oldham, *Work Redesign* (Reading, MA: Addison-Wesley, 1980).

68. J.E. Champoux, "A Multivariate Test of the Job Characteristics Theory of Work Motivation," *Journal of Organizational Behavior* 12, no. 5 (September 1991), pp. 431–46; R.B. Tiegs, L.E. Tetrick, and Y. Fried, "Growth Need Strength and Context Satisfactions as Moderators of the Relations of the Job Characteristics Model," *Journal of Management* 18, no. 3 (September 1992), pp. 575–93.

69. J.R. Hackman et al., "A New Strategy for Job Enrichment," *California Management Review* 17, no. 4 (1975), pp. 57–71; R.W. Griffin, *Task Design: An Integrative Approach* (Glenview, IL: Scott Foresman, 1982).

70. Hackman and Oldham, *Work Redesign,* pp. 137-38.

71. Signer, "A Cultural Revolution Transforms ACUITY as an Employer and a Business Partner."

72. This definition is based mostly on G.M. Spreitzer and R.E. Quinn, *"A Company of Leaders: Five Disciplines for Unleashing the Power in Your Workforce"* (2001). However, most elements of this definition appear in other discussions of empowerment. See, for example, R. Forrester, "Empowerment: Rejuvenating a Potent Idea," *Academy of Management Executive* 14 (August 2000), pp. 67–80; W.A. Randolph, "Re-thinking Empowerment: Why Is It So Hard to Achieve?" *Organizational Dynamics* 29 (November 2000), pp. 94–107; S.T. Menon, "Employee Empowerment: An Integrative Psychological Approach," *Applied Psychology: An International Review* 50 (2001), pp. 153–80.

73. B.J. Niehoff et al., "The Influence of Empowerment and Job Enrichment on Employee Loyalty in a Downsizing Environment," *Group and Organization Management* 26 (March 2001), pp. 93–113; J. Yoon, "The Role of Structure and Motivation for Workplace Empowerment: The Case of Korean Employees," *Social Psychology Quarterly* 64 (June 2001), pp. 195–206; T.D. Wall, J.L. Cordery, and C.W. Clegg, "Empowerment, Performance, and Operational Uncertainty: A Theoretical Integration," *Applied Psychology: An International Review* 51 (2002), pp. 146–69.

74. S. Caulkin, "Who's in Charge Here?" *The Observer* (London), April 27, 2003, p. 9; D. Gardner, "A Boss Who's Crazy about His Workers," *Sunday Herald* (Glasgow, Scotland), April 13, 2003, p. 6; S. Moss, "Portrait: 'Idleness Is Good,'" *The Guardian* (London), April 17, 2003, p. 8; R. Semler, *The Seven-Day Weekend* (London: Century, 2003); "Ricardo Semler Set Them Free," *CIO Insight,* April 2004, p. 30.

75. G.M. Spreitzer, "Social Structural Characteristics of Psychological Empowerment," *Academy of Management Journal* 39 (April 1996), pp. 483–504; J. Godard, "High Performance and the Transformation of Work? The Implications of Alternative Work Practices for the Experience and Outcomes of Work," *Industrial & Labor Relations Review* 54 (July 2001), pp. 776–805; P.A. Miller, P. Goddard, and H.K. Spence Laschinger, "Evaluating Physical Therapists' Perception of Empowerment Using Kanter's Theory of Structural Power in Organizations," *Physical Therapy* 81 (December 2001), pp. 1880–88.

76. Business Wire, "Towers Perrin Study Finds, Despite Layoffs and Slow Economy, a New, More Complex Power Game Is Emerging between Employers and Employees," news release (New York: August 30, 2001); Towers Perrin, *Working Today: Understanding What Drives Employee Engagement* (Stamford, CT: 2003).

77. C. Lachnit, "The Young and the Dispirited," *Workforce* 81 (August 2002), p. 18; S.H. Applebaum, M. Serena, and B.T. Shapiro, "Generation X and the Boomers: Organizational Myths and Literary Realities," *Management Research News* 27, no. 11/12 (2004), pp. 1–28. Motivation and needs across generations are also discussed in R. Zemke and B. Filipczak, *Generations at Work: Managing the Clash of Veterans, Boomers, Xers, and Nexters in Your Workplace* (New York: AMACOM, 2000).

14

MANAGING EMPLOYEE ATTITUDES AND WELL-BEING

LEARNING OBJECTIVES

After Reading This Chapter You Should Be Able to:

1 Describe the effect of emotions and attitudes on employee behavior.

2 Identify four ways in which employees respond to job dissatisfaction.

3 Explain how job satisfaction relates to customer service and satisfaction.

4 Distinguish organizational commitment from continuance commitment, including their effects on employee behavior.

5 Discuss ways to strengthen organizational commitment.

6 Describe the stress experience and its consequences.

7 Summarize three common sources of stress in the workplace.

8 List five ways to manage work-related stress.

9 Discuss how managers can help employees improve their work–life balance.

10 Identify the "Big Five" personality dimensions.

11 Explain how personality influences emotions, well-being, job performance, and career satisfaction.

Walk into the offices of CXtec in Syracuse, New York, and you might think employees are in the middle of a birthday party. Around the cubicles are colorful clusters of helium-filled balloons, each representing a small token of the company's appreciation for performing their work effectively. The computer networking equipment company's 300 staff members also enjoy a break room with billiards, foosball, and air hockey. And if employees want a little more enjoyment, the company sponsors miniature golf tournaments in the office, tricycle races around the building, and "CXtec Idol" competitions. Of course all of this fits in with what the company stands for: "Part of our core values is that work is fun," explains Paula Miller, CXtec's director of employee and community relations.

Fun at work? It sounds like an oxymoron. But to attract and motivate valuable talent, companies are finding creative ways to generate positive emotions in the workplace. They are also competing for the distinction of being one of the best places to work. CXtec, for example, is rated as one of the 50 best small and medium-sized companies to work for in America. W.L. Gore & Associates is one of the top five employers in America and has been number one on a similar list in the United Kingdom over the past three years because the manufacturer of fabrics (Gore-Tex), electronics, and industrial and medical products offers employees incredible levels of autonomy (it has no formal bosses).

Ritz-Carlton Hotels in Shanghai, Hong Kong, and Kuala Lumpur have dominated the list of Asia's top eight employers, largely because the firm recognizes employee achievements and offers continuous career development. Vancouver City Savings Credit Union is one the best places to work in Canada because the financial institution helps employees manage workplace stress and is a role model of corporate social responsibility. Pretoria Portland Cement landed the top spot in South Africa after management developed a clearer vision of the company's future and handed more responsibility over to employees to achieve that vision. Danish toolmaker Unimerco is one of the best places to work in Europe, partly because the company distributes earnings each day to its 300 employee–owners. "I look forward to coming to work every morning and every day I go home happy," says a Unimerco employee. "Isn't that the best life you can imagine?"

Wegmans Food Market consistently rates as one of the best employers in America because managers treat employees as the number 1 priority. "It's more of you're not part of a company, you're part of a family," says Katie Southard, who works in customer service at a Wegmans store in Rochester, New York. "You're treated as an individual, not just one of the 350 persons in the store." With happy employees, Wegmans enjoys one of the highest levels of customer loyalty and lowest levels of employee turnover in the industry. Brenda Hidalgo, who works at Wegmans in Buffalo, sums up the positive experience: "I've worked at other places where you wake up and you say 'Ech, I have to go to work,'" she recalls. "Now I love to go to work."[1]

The previous two chapters examined how managers create a high-performance workforce through staffing, training, and motivation practices. These strategies can create a highly engaged, highly skilled workforce focused on organizational objectives. The topics of recruiting, selecting, and training people, which were covered in Chapter 12, affect the individual's ability to perform the assigned work and to have clear role perceptions. The topics discussed in Chapter 13 connect directly to employee motivation. Although both chapters referred to employee attitudes and well-being, these were secondary considerations.

In contrast, this chapter looks at managerial practices that primarily attempt to improve employee emotions, attitudes, and well-being. These are the managerial activities that helped CXtec, W.L. Gore & Associates, Ritz-Carlton, Vancouver City Savings Credit Union, Pretoria Portland Cement, Unimerco, Wegmans, and many other firms to become the best employers in their countries or regions. This chapter begins by describing the role of emotions and attitudes in the workplace, followed by an overview of the two most commonly studied attitudes: job satisfaction and organizational commitment. Next we explore the significance of stress in the workplace, followed by specific strategies to minimize dysfunctional stress.

Each of these topics views employee attitudes and well-being as the goal. Yet as we will point out, these practices also indirectly influence employee engagement, performance, turnover, and other performance-based outcomes. For instance, Vancouver City Savings Credit Union (VanCity) treats its employees well because it is the right thing to do, but CEO David Mowat also points out that the financial institution's people-first philosophy "is central to our business case." If employee attitudes and well-being had no effect on the organization's bottom line, would they still be on management's agenda? The answer is probably yes at VanCity, but many companies treat employees well mainly because of these indirect organizational benefits.

emotions

Physiological, behavioral, and psychological episodes experienced toward an object, person, or event that create a state of readiness.

// Emotions in the Workplace

Emotions have a profound effect on almost everything we do in the workplace.[2] This is a strong statement—one you would rarely find a decade ago in management research or textbooks. For most of its history the field of management assumed that a person's thoughts and actions are governed primarily by conscious reasoning (called *cognitions*). But groundbreaking neuroscience discoveries have revealed that our perceptions, attitudes, decisions, and behavior are influenced by both cognition and emotions, and that the latter often have greater influence. By ignoring the role of emotions, we have limited our ability to understand human behavior in the workplace. Today experts in management, marketing, economics, and many other social sciences are catching up by making emotions a key part of their research and theories.[3]

So what are emotions? **Emotions** are physiological, behavioral, and psychological episodes experienced toward an object, person, or event that create a state of readiness.[4] They are brief events that typically subside or occur in waves lasting a few minutes. Emotions are directed toward someone or something. For example, we experience joy, fear, anger, and other emotional episodes toward tasks, customers, or a software program we are using. This contrasts with *moods,* which are less intense emotional states that are not directed toward anything in particular. Emotions are experiences regulating how our body responds to the environment. When we are happy or bored, our blood pressure, heart rate, facial muscles, voice tone, and other features change. These bodily changes relate to the fact that emotions put us in a state of readiness. Most emotions are experienced unconsciously, but strong emotions make us consciously aware of events that may affect our survival and well-being.[5]

© 1999 Ted Goff

"Biosensors. The whole company knows instantly when I'm displeased."

© Ted Goff

// EMOTIONS, ATTITUDES, AND BEHAVIOR

Emotions influence our thoughts and behavior; but to understand how this works, we also need to know about attitudes. **Attitudes** are clusters of beliefs, assessed feelings, and behavioral intentions toward a person, object, or event.[6] Attitudes are *judgments,* whereas emotions are *experiences.* In other words, attitudes involve conscious logical reasoning, whereas emotions operate as events, often without our awareness. We also experience most emotions briefly, whereas our attitude toward someone or something is more stable over time.

Attitudes include three components: beliefs, feelings, and behavioral intentions. We'll look at each of them using attitude toward mergers as an illustration:

- *Beliefs:* These are established perceptions about the attitude object—what you believe to be true. For example, you might believe that mergers reduce job security for employees in the merged firms. Or you might believe that mergers increase the company's competitiveness in this era of globalization. These beliefs are perceived facts that you acquire from past experience and other forms of learning.

- *Feelings:* Feelings represent your positive or negative evaluations of the attitude object. Some people think mergers are good; others think they are bad. Your like or dislike of mergers represents your assessed feelings toward the attitude object.

- *Behavioral intentions:* These represent your motivation to engage in a particular behavior with respect to the attitude object. You might plan to quit rather than stay with the company during the merger. Alternatively, you might intend to e-mail the company CEO to say that this merger was a good decision.

Now we come to the important part for managers: how emotions and attitudes are connected to each other and to behavior. This process, which is illustrated in Figure 14.1, has two interrelated activities connected to cognition and emotion. On the cognitive side, your feelings

attitudes
Clusters of beliefs, assessed feelings, and behavioral intentions toward a person, object, or event.

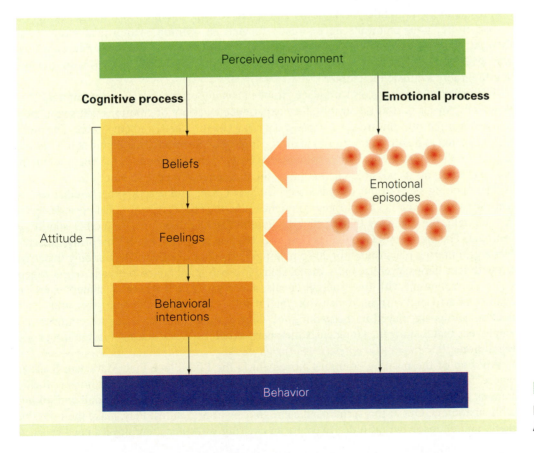

FIGURE 14.1

Model of Emotions, Attitudes, and Behavior

toward someone or something (such as a merger) are shaped by your beliefs about that person or event. If you believe mergers threaten your career development and usually fail to improve organizations' competitiveness, you would likely have negative feelings toward mergers. Next, feelings directly influence behavioral intentions.[7] If you dislike mergers, you might intend to quit or complain to the senior executive team about your company's recently announced merger. Whether you quit or complain depends on your personality, the current situation, and what has worked well for you in the past.

Finally, behavioral intentions are better than feelings or beliefs at predicting a person's behavior. Even so, behavioral intentions do not perfectly predict behavior because they represent only the motivation to act, whereas actual behavior is also caused by the other three factors in the MARS model—ability, role perceptions, and situational factors. You might plan to send an e-mail message to management complaining about the announced merger, but perhaps you never get around to this task due to heavy work obligations. You might intend to quit your job in reaction to the merger but end up staying because you can't find a better job.

How Emotions Influence Attitudes and Behavior   Now that we have outlined the cognitive explanation of how attitudes predict behavior, let's turn to the right side of Figure 14.1, which shows how emotions influence our attitudes and behavior. Essentially we automatically attach emotions to incoming information when it is received through our senses even though we have not consciously thought about it.[8] These are not calculated feelings; they are automatic and unconscious emotional responses based on thin slices of sensory information.

Returning to our previous example, you might experience excitement, worry, nervousness, or happiness upon learning that your company intends to merge with a competitor. The large dots on the right side of Figure 14.1 illustrate these multiple emotional episodes triggered by the merger announcement, subsequent thinking about the merger, discussion with coworkers about the merger, and so on. These emotions are transmitted to the logical reasoning process, where they swirl around and ultimately shape our conscious feelings toward the merger.[9] While you logically figure out whether the proposed merger is a good or bad thing, your emotions have already formed an opinion, which then sways your thoughts. If you experience excitement, delight, comfort, and other positive emotions whenever you think about the merger, these positive emotional episodes will tend to make you favorably evaluate the merger.[10]

■ Google generates positive emotions.

The effect of emotions on workplace attitudes has important management implications. When employees perform their jobs, they experience a variety of emotions that shape their longer-term feelings toward the company, the boss, the job itself, and coworkers. The more they experience positive emotions, the more employees form positive attitudes toward the targets of those emotions. Thus an important role of management is to create as many positive emotions as possible and minimize the incidence of negative emotions.

The opening story of this chapter described how CXtec and several other companies inject more fun at work so employees experience plenty of positive emotional episodes each day. Google, the company that created the ubiquitous search engine, is another sparkling example. The company's Googleplex (headquarters) in Mountain View, California, "resembles a glimmering playground for 20-somethings," says one observer. The building is outfitted with lava lamps, exercise balls, casual sofas, foosball, pool tables, workout rooms, video games, a restaurant with free gourmet meals, and a small pool where swimmers exercise against an artificial current. Beach volleyball matches are held in the courtyard, and roller hockey games are played in the parking lot. Google executives have had to remind some employees that making the Googleplex their permanent residence was against building code regulations.[11]

An icon of the positive emotions movement is the Pike Place Fish Market in Seattle, where fishmongers turned the money-losing, morale-draining business into a world-famous attraction by deciding to have fun at work, such as tossing fish around and joking with customers. Out of this turnaround came four Fish! principles: Play, make their day, be there, and choose your attitude. To create an exciting workplace, employees need to learn how to play, just as the fishmongers toss fish and find other ways to enjoy themselves at work. "Make their day" refers to involving clients and coworkers so they, too, have a positive experience. "Be there" means employees need to be focused (not mentally in several places) and actively engaged to have fun. "Choose your attitude" says that everyone has the power to choose how they feel at work. Although the environment might contribute to malaise, this Fish! principle says that employees ultimately decide how that environment will affect their emotions, attitudes, and behavior.[12]

// COGNITIVE DISSONANCE

Up to this point we have explained how emotions and attitudes influence behavior, yet there are situations in which the opposite occurs. A person's actions sometimes influence his or her attitudes when they are inconsistent with each other. This inconsistency potentially creates an uncomfortable tension, called **cognitive dissonance**, that motivates people to change their attitudes so they are more consistent with the behavior.[13] Everyone experiences some degree of cognitive dissonance from time to time. You remind your staff to show up to work on time, but you arrive late for work a few days later. You teach your children to read class materials long before class, yet you hurriedly scan documents for an important meeting just before the meeting begins.

The extent to which people experience cognitive dissonance tension depends on how much the behavior is public, important, and voluntary.[14] First, there is usually much less tension if no one noticed the inconsistent behavior. You are less likely to experience cognitive dissonance for being late if no one noticed, for instance, whereas dissonance might be quite strong if the employees whom you encouraged a few days earlier to show up to work on time catch you arriving late. The importance of the attitude and behavior is a second factor. You might not feel uncomfortable about being caught arriving late for work if lateness is considered a minor indiscretion in your workplace. A third factor is how much control you have over the behavior. You are more likely to experience cognitive dissonance if you could have avoided being late for work than if the lateness is due to factors beyond your control (such as unusually bad traffic congestion).

When people experience cognitive dissonance, the resulting tension motivates them to realign their attitudes and behavior. Because the behavior has already occurred (and is public, so it can't be denied), the most common way to reduce dissonance is to change the attitude. In our example, if employees notice that you have shown up late for work, you might change your attitude about the importance of arriving at work on time. In the future you might form less of a negative attitude toward people who are late for work, and your new attitude about punctuality might result in less lecturing to employees about this issue.

Now that we have introduced the dynamics of emotions and work attitudes, let's look more closely at two of the most important work attitudes: job satisfaction and organizational commitment.

■ // Job Satisfaction

Job satisfaction, a person's evaluation of his or her job and work context, is probably the most studied attitude in management.[15] It is an *appraisal* of the perceived job characteristics, work environment, and emotional experiences at work. Satisfied employees

Fishing for Positive Emotions   Fishmongers at Pike Place Fish Market in Seattle turned the money-losing, morale-draining business into a world-famous attraction by deciding to have fun at work. Their transformation through positive emotions was so successful that companies around the world now follow the four Fish! principles: Play, make their day, be there, and choose your attitude.

© AP Photo/Elaine Thompson

cognitive dissonance

An uncomfortable tension experienced when behavior is inconsistent with our attitudes.

job satisfaction

A person's evaluation of his or her job and work context.

FIGURE 14.2a

Is Everyone Satisfied? This graph shows the percentage of Americans from 1989 to 2005 who said they were somewhat or very satisfied with their jobs.

Source: Gallup Organization news releases, various years.

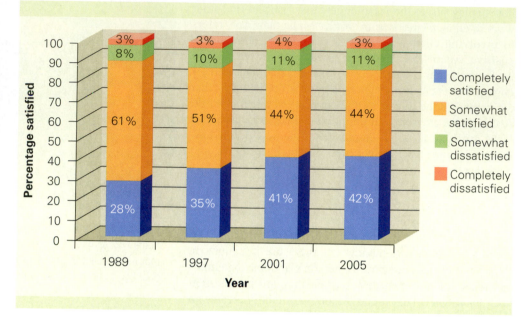

have a favorable evaluation of their job based on their observations and emotional experiences. Job satisfaction is really a collection of attitudes about different aspects of the job and work context. You might like your coworkers but be less satisfied with your workload, for instance.

How satisfied are employees at work? Surveys suggest that more than 85 percent of Americans are satisfied with their jobs, a figure that has remained amazingly consistent over the past two decades (see Figure 14.2a). In fact, the percentage of Americans who say they are "completely satisfied" has actually increased over the years. Around the world, employees in Denmark and India are reportedly the happiest at work. Most studies place Americans in the upper quartile of countries in terms of job satisfaction. In contrast, job satisfaction seems to be quite low among employees in China, South Korea, and Japan, as indicated in Figure 14.2b.[16]

// JOB SATISFACTION AND WORK BEHAVIOR

In the highly competitive fashion industry, Hugo Boss Industries commands an impressive brand image and market share (30 percent for business suits in some markets). The Swiss company's success is due in part to a bonus plan that rewards managers based not just on return on capital and other hard numbers but also on the soft numbers like employee satisfaction.[17] Hugo Boss and many other firms closely monitor employee morale and reward managers who keep morale high because attitudes and well-being affect employee behavior to some degree. A useful template to organize and understand the consequences of job dissatisfaction is the **exit–voice–loyalty–neglect (EVLN) model**. As the name suggests, the EVLN model identifies four ways in which employees respond to dissatisfaction:[18]

exit–voice–loyalty–neglect (EVLN) model

A model that outlines the consequences of job dissatisfaction.

- *Exit* refers to leaving the organization, transferring to another work unit, or at least trying to make these exits. Employee turnover is a well-established outcome of job dissatisfaction, particularly for employees with better job opportunities elsewhere. Conversely, companies whose employees have high job satisfaction report some of their industries' lowest turnover rates. For instance, when asked if she thought about working somewhere else, Vancouver City Savings Credit Union accounts manager Lara Victoria quickly replied, "No, they'd have to push me out. It's worth every minute of it here."[19] An important observation for managers is that exit usually follows specific "shock events,"

FIGURE 14.2b

Is Everyone Satisfied?
(*continued*)

Source: Based on Ipsos-Reid survey of 9,300 employees in 39 countries in the middle of year 2000. See "Ipsos-Reid Global Poll Finds Major Differences in Employee Satisfaction around the World," Ipsos-Reid news release, January 8, 2001. A sample of 22 countries across the range is shown here, including all of the top-scoring countries.

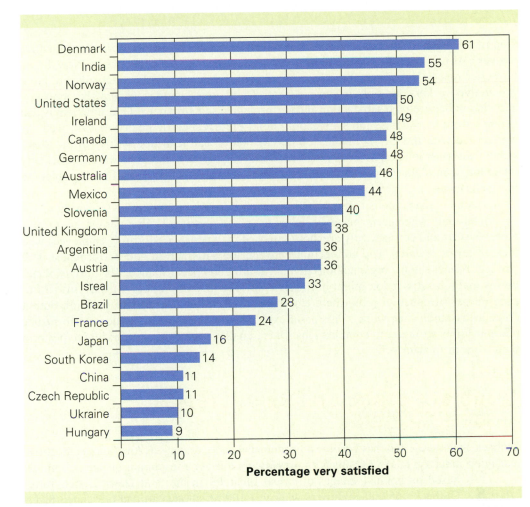

Percentage very satisfied

such as when employees believe their managers treat them unfairly.[20] These shock events generate strong emotions that energize employees to think about and search for alternative employment.

- *Voice* refers to any attempt to change, rather than escape from, a dissatisfying situation. Voice can be a constructive response, such as recommending ways for management to improve the situation; or it can be more confrontational, such as filing formal grievances.[21] In the extreme, some employees might engage in counterproductive behaviors to get attention and force changes in the organization.

- *Loyalty* has been described in different ways. The most widely held view is that "loyalists" are employees who respond to dissatisfaction by patiently waiting—some say they "suffer in silence"—for a problem to work itself out or get resolved by others.[22]

- *Neglect* includes reducing work effort, paying less attention to quality, and increasing absenteeism and lateness. It is generally considered a passive activity that has negative consequences for the organization.

Which of the four EVLN alternatives do employees use? It depends on the person and situation. As we have noted, people's feelings translate into different behavioral intentions based on their past experiences and personal preferences. Also, someone's intention to use the exit, voice, or other response depends on circumstances. With poor job prospects, employees are less likely to use the exit option. Those who identify with the organization are also more likely to use their voices rather than leave. Reactions to job dissatisfaction also depend on people's personal values and personalities.[23]

// JOB SATISFACTION AND PERFORMANCE

One of the oldest beliefs in the business world is that "a happy worker is a productive worker." At one time management experts said that this phrase is inaccurate. Now, based on better research methods, they have concluded that happy workers actually are more productive workers, but only *to some extent.*[24] There are a few reasons why this moderate association between job satisfaction and performance isn't stronger.[25] One argument is that general attitudes (such as job satisfaction) don't predict specific behaviors very well. As we learned with the EVLN model, job dissatisfaction can lead to a variety of outcomes rather than lower job performance (neglect). Some employees continue to work productively while they complain (voice), look for another job (exit), or patiently wait for a problem to be fixed (loyalty).

A second explanation is that job performance leads to job satisfaction (rather than vice versa), but only when performance is linked to valued rewards. Higher performers receive more rewards and consequently are more satisfied than poorly performing employees who receive fewer rewards. The connection between job satisfaction and performance isn't stronger because many organizations do not reward good performance. The third explanation is that job satisfaction might influence employee motivation, but this has little influence on performance in jobs where employees have little control over their job output (such as assembly-line work). This point explains why the job satisfaction–performance relationship is strongest in complex jobs, where employees have more freedom to perform their work or to slack off.

// JOB SATISFACTION AND CUSTOMER SATISFACTION

Outback Steakhouse Inc. has become a phenomenal success story in America's competitive restaurant industry. In 1988 Outback's four partners opened a restaurant in Tampa, Florida, based on popular images of casual lifestyles in the land Down Under. Today Outback's 65,000 employees work in 1,100 restaurants around the United States and Canada. Although the Australian theme launched the company's success, Outback founder and CEO Chris Sullivan says the quality of staff deserves as much credit. Specifically, the company hires energized employees and creates a culture that supports them so they stay with the company and provide excellent service. This service makes customers happy, which brings them back and encourages them to recommend Outback to friends. The result of such customer satisfaction is higher sales, which improve company profits.[26]

Outback Steakhouse is one of many firms where managers believe that customers are happier when employees are happier. "I realized a long time ago that there was a strong correlation between employee satisfaction and customer service," says Gary Pon, CEO of Pinnacol Insurance in Denver. Virgin Group founder Richard Branson echoes this view. "It just seems common sense to me that if you start with a happy, well-motivated workforce, you're much more likely to have happy customers," says Branson. Managers at Wegmans are so convinced that satisfied employees provide better customer service that the Rochester-based grocery chain's motto is "Employees first, customers second."[27]

Management research generally agrees that job satisfaction enhances customer satisfaction.[28] A few years ago Sears Roebuck & Co. calculated that a 5-point improvement in the retail giant's job satisfaction survey scale increases customer satisfaction ratings by 1.3 points, which in turn improves revenue growth by 0.5 percent. Marketing experts have developed the "employee–customer–profit chain" model shown in Figure 14.3, which illustrates how employee satisfaction translates into customer satisfaction and profitability.

Sizzling Satisfaction at Outback Restaurants   The phenomenal success of Outback Restaurants is based on the employee–customer–profit chain model, which says that happy employees produce happy customers, who produce happy shareholders. "Outback's theory of success is that you hire the right people and take care of them," explained founder Chris Sullivan and three colleagues in a recent journal article.

Courtesy of Outback Steakhouse, Inc.

FIGURE 14.3

Employee–Customer–
Profit Chain Model

There are three reasons why happy employees tend to result in happy customers. First, as we have mentioned, job satisfaction is related to employee performance—particularly higher motivation to provide friendly service. This increased effort includes trying to serve customers more effectively. Second, employees are usually in a more positive mood when they feel satisfied with their jobs and working conditions. Employees in a good mood display more naturally friendly service, which most customers interpret as higher-value service. Third, employees with higher job satisfaction are less likely to quit their jobs, so they have better knowledge and skills to serve clients. Lower turnover also gives customers more consistent service. There is some evidence that customers build their loyalty to specific employees, not to the organization, so keeping employee turnover low tends to build customer loyalty.[29]

Before leaving this topic, we should mention that job satisfaction does more than improve work behaviors and customer satisfaction. Job satisfaction is also an ethical issue that influences the organization's reputation in the community. People spend a large portion of their time working in organizations, and many societies now expect companies to provide work environments that are safe and enjoyable. Indeed, employees in several countries closely monitor ratings of the best companies to work for—an indication that employee satisfaction is worth considerable goodwill to employers. This fact is apparent when an organization has low job satisfaction. The company tries to hide this situation, and when morale problems become public, corporate leaders are usually quick to improve employee attitudes.

■ // Organizational Commitment

Along with job satisfaction, managers need to ensure that employees have reasonably high levels of organizational commitment. **Organizational commitment** refers to an employee's emotional attachment to, identification with, and involvement in a particular organization.[30] It is the employee's pride and loyalty toward the organization. Managers need to pay attention to this attitude because loyal employees are less likely to quit their jobs and be absent from work. They also tend to provide better customer service because long-tenure employees have deeper knowledge of work practices, and clients like to do business with the same employees. Employees with greater commitment also have higher work motivation as well as somewhat superior job performance.[31] Notice that we recommended that employees should have "fairly high" levels of organizational commitment. Employees with very high loyalty

organizational commitment

An employee's emotional attachment to, identification with, and involvement in a particular organization.

tend to have high conformity, which results in lower creativity. There are also cases of dedicated employees who have violated laws to defend the organization. However, most companies suffer from too little rather than too much employee loyalty.

// WATCH OUT FOR CONTINUANCE COMMITMENT!

continuance commitment

An employee's calculative attachment to an organization, whereby an employee is motivated to stay only because leaving would be costly.

■ Smith Barney's golden handcuffs.

Organizational commitment is different from **continuance commitment**. Whereas organizational commitment is an emotional bond to the organization, continuance commitment is a calculative attachment.[32] Employees have high continuance commitment when they do not particularly identify with the organization where they work but feel bound to remain there because it would be too costly to quit. In other words, they choose to stay because the calculated (typically financial) value of staying is higher than the value of working somewhere else. You can tell someone has high calculative commitment when she or he says, "I hate this place but can't afford to quit!" This reluctance to quit may be due to the risk of losing a large bonus by leaving early or because the employee is well established in the community.[33]

Unfortunately managers seem to confuse organizational commitment with continuance commitment. Executives often tie employees financially to the organization through low-cost loans, stock options, deferred bonuses, and other "golden handcuffs." For example, several Wall Street brokerage firms boast that fewer than 10 percent of their employees quit each year, but one of the key reasons is that most staff participate in a deferred compensation scheme in which performance bonuses are held back for at least two years. If the employee quits, every penny of the deferred bonus is forfeited. James McCarthy is fighting to get $287,000 that he earned as a broker at Smith Barney, but the company says it can refuse to pay his bonus because he quit his job.[34]

Financial incentives might reduce turnover, but they also increase continuance commitment, not employee loyalty. Research suggests that employees with high levels of continuance commitment have *lower* performance ratings and are *less* likely to engage in organizational citizenship behaviors! Furthermore, unionized employees with high continuance commitment are more likely to use formal grievances, whereas employees with high organizational commitment engage in more constructive problem solving when employee–employer relations sour.[35] Although some level of financial connection may be necessary, employers still need to win employees' hearts (organizational commitment) beyond tying them financially to the organization (continuance commitment).

// BUILDING ORGANIZATIONAL COMMITMENT

There are almost as many ways to build organizational loyalty as topics in this textbook, but the following list is most prominent in the literature:

- *Justice and support:* Employee loyalty is higher in organizations that fulfill their obligations to employees and abide by humanitarian values, such as fairness, courtesy, forgiveness, and moral integrity. These values relate to the recommendation in Chapter 13 that managers need to continually pay attention to the fairness of their decisions, such as the distribution of rewards and resources. The more justice employees perceive, the higher their loyalty to the organization. Similarly, organizations that support employee well-being tend to earn higher levels of loyalty in return.[36]

- *Shared values:* The definition of organizational commitment refers to a person's identification with the organization, and that identification is highest when employees believe their values are congruent with the organization's dominant values (see Chapter 10). Values congruence makes employees feel more comfortable with corporate decisions.[37]

trust

A psychological state comprising the intention to accept vulnerability based on positive expectations of the intent or behavior of another person.

- *Trust:* Chapter 11 introduced the concept of **trust**, which is defined as a psychological state comprising the intention to accept vulnerability based on positive expectations of the intent or behavior of another person.[38] Trust means putting faith in the other person or group. It is also a reciprocal activity: To receive trust, you must demonstrate trust. Employees identify with and feel obliged to work for an organization only when they trust its leaders. This explains why layoffs are one of the greatest blows to employee loyalty: By reducing job security, companies reduce the trust employees have in their employer and the employment relationship.[39]

- *Organizational comprehension:* Organizational commitment is a person's identification with the company, so it makes sense that this attitude is strengthened when employees understand the company, including its past, present, and future. Thus loyalty tends to increase with open and rapid communication to and from corporate leaders, as well as with opportunities to interact with coworkers across the organization. We will discuss organizational communication strategies in Chapter 17.[40]

- *Employee involvement:* Employees feel that they are part of the organization when they contribute to decisions that guide the organization's future. This employee involvement also builds loyalty because giving this power demonstrates the company's trust in its employees.

Organizational commitment and job satisfaction represent two of the most often studied and discussed attitudes in the workplace. Each is linked to emotional episodes and cognitive judgments about the workplace and relationships with the company. Emotions also play an important role in another concept that is on everyone's mind these days: stress. Indeed, managing work-related stress is central to managing employee well-being. Over the next few pages we will examine the stress process, its causes, and, most important, how to improve employee well-being by managing work-related stress.

■ // Work-Related Stress and Its Management

Joe Straitiff realized that his leisure life was in trouble when his boss hung a huge neon sign saying "Open 24 Hours." The former Electronic Arts (EA) software developer also received frequent e-mail messages from the boss to the team, saying that he would see them on the weekend. "You can't work that many hours and remain sane," says Straitiff. "It's just too harsh." Straitiff's complaints were not exaggerations. Two days after joining EA's Los Angeles operations, video programmer Leander Hasty was sucked into a "crunch" period of intense work on *Lord of the Rings: The Battle for Middle Earth.* Soon the entire team was working 13-hour days, seven days per week. Exasperated, Hasty's fiancée, Erin Hoffman, wrote a lengthy diatribe on the Internet describing the dire situation. "The love of my life comes home late at night complaining of a headache that will not go away and a chronically upset stomach," she wrote. Within two days she received more than 1,000 sympathetic messages from people at EA and other video game companies. This flashpoint sparked several lawsuits against EA for unpaid overtime.[41]

Employees at Electronic Arts and many other organizations are experiencing increasing levels of work-related stress. **Stress** is an adaptive response to a situation that is perceived as challenging or threatening to a person's well-being.[42] The stress response is a complex emotion that produces

stress
An adaptive response to a situation that is perceived as challenging or threatening to a person's well-being.

Electronic Stress Electronic Arts (EA), the world's largest independent video game company, has come under pressure to ease the long hours that its employees are expected to work, particularly during "crunch time"—the months just before final release of its products. EA has already settled two lawsuits launched by graphics artists claiming overtime pay. Leander Hasty's financée, Erin Hoffman (both shown here), wrote a lengthy diatribe on the Internet describing the dire situation. Within two days she received more than 1,000 sympathetic messages from people at EA and other video game companies.

© 2002 Richard Koci Hernandez, San Jose Mercury News

FIGURE 14.4
A World Full of Stressed-Out Employees

Sources: T. Haratani, "Job Stress Trends in Japan," in *Job Stress Trends in East Asia (Proceedings of the First East Asia Job Stress Meeting),* ed. A. Tsutsumi (Tokyo: Waseda University, January 8, 2000), pp. 4–10; Canadian Mental Health Association, *The 2001 Canadian Mental Health Survey* (Toronto: Canadian Mental Health Association, 2001); "New Survey: Americans Stressed More Than Ever," *PR Newswire,* June 26, 2003; "Hong Kong People Still Most Stressed in Asia—Survey," *Reuters News,* November 2, 2004; E. Galinsky et al., *Overwork in America: When the Way We Work Becomes Too Much* (New York: Families and Work Institute, March 2005); M. Mandel, "The Real Reasons You're Working So Hard...and What You Can Do about It," *BusinessWeek,* October 3, 2005, p. 60; *Mind, Stress and Mental Health in the Workplace* (London: Mind, May 2005); D. Passmore, "We're All Sick of Work," *Sunday Mail* (Brisbane), November 27, 2005, p. 45.

- 44% of Americans say they are often or very often overworked; 26% experienced this in the previous month.
- 80% of Americans feel too much stress on the job; nearly half indicate that they need help coping with it.
- Approximately one in every four employees in the United Kingdom feels "very or extremely stressed."
- More than 50% of Canadians feel really stressed a few times each week; 9 percent of them feel this way all the time.
- A survey of 4,700 people across Asia reported that one-third were feeling more stress than in the recent past; stress is highest in Taiwan and lowest in Thailand.
- 53% of Australian employees across all occupations feel under pressure a significant amount of the time; one-fifth say they feel exhausted on the job.
- The percentage of Japanese employees who feel "strong worry, anxiety, or stress at work or in daily working life" has increased from 51% in 1982 to almost two-thirds of the population today.

physiological changes to prepare us for "fight or flight"—to defend against a threat or flee from it. Specifically our heart rates and perspiration increase, muscles tighten, and breathing speeds up. Our bodies also move more blood to our brains, release adrenaline and other hormones, fuel our systems by releasing more glucose and fatty acids, activate systems that sharpen our senses, and use resources that would normally go to our immune systems.

We often hear about stress as a negative experience. This is *distress*—physiological, psychological, and behavioral deviation from healthy functioning. However, some level of stress—called *eustress*—is also a necessary part of life because it activates and motivates people to achieve goals, change their environments, and succeed in life's challenges.[43] Our focus will be on the causes and management of distress because it has become a chronic problem in many societies. Figure 14.4 highlights the extent of work-related stress around the world.

// GENERAL ADAPTATION SYNDROME

general adaptation syndrome

A model of the stress experience, consisting of three stages: alarm reaction, resistance, and exhaustion.

The stress experience is a physiological response called the **general adaptation syndrome** that occurs through the three stages shown in Figure 14.5.[44] The *alarm reaction* stage occurs when a threat or challenge activates the physiological stress responses that were just noted. Our energy level and coping effectiveness initially decrease because we have not prepared for the stress. The second stage, *resistance*, activates various biochemical, psychological, and behavioral mechanisms that give us more energy and engage coping mechanisms to overcome or remove the source of stress. To focus energy on the source of the stress, our bodies reduce resources to the immune system during this stage. This explains why we are more likely to catch a cold or other illness when we experience prolonged stress.

People have a limited resistance capacity, and if the stress persists, they will eventually move into the third stage, *exhaustion*. Most of us are able to remove the source of stress or remove ourselves from that source before becoming too exhausted. However, people who frequently reach exhaustion have increased risk of long-term physiological and psychological damage.[45]

// CONSEQUENCES OF DISTRESS

Stress takes its toll on the human body.[46] Many people experience tension headaches, muscle pain, and related problems due to muscle contractions from the stress response. Studies have found that high stress levels also contribute to cardiovascular disease, including heart attacks and strokes. They also produce various psychological consequences, such as job dissatisfaction, moodiness, depression, and lower organizational commitment. Furthermore, various

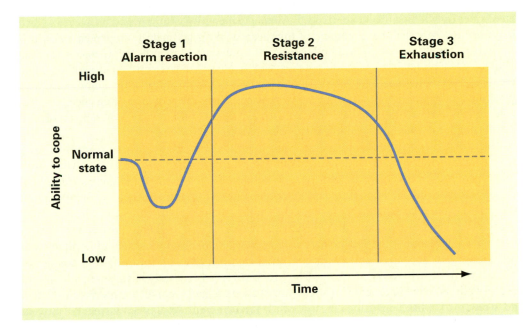

FIGURE 14.5

General Adaptation Syndrome

Source: Adapted from H. Selye, *The Stress of Life* (New York: McGraw-Hill, 1956).

behavioral outcomes have been linked to high or persistent stress, including impaired job performance, poor decision making, and more workplace accidents and aggressive behavior. Most people react to stress through "fight or flight," so increased absenteeism is another outcome because it is a form of flight.[47]

// STRESSORS: THE SOURCES OF STRESS

The general adaptation syndrome describes the stress experience; but to manage work-related stress, we must understand its causes. **Stressors** include any environmental conditions that place a physical or emotional demand on a person.[48] As you might imagine, people face numerous stressors at work. In this section we highlight three of the most prevalent stressors: harassment and incivility, workload, and lack of task control.

Harassment and Incivility For almost seven years Devander Naidu took more abuse from his boss than most of us would experience in a lifetime. The assistant security and fire control manager received ongoing verbal abuse, racial taunts (Naidu is Indo-Fijian), threats of physical violence, swearing, insults to his wife, and lewd behavior from his senior manager responsible for security and fire at News Ltd. (the Australian subsidiary of News Corp., which owns Fox Network). The manager also forced Naidu to perform construction work at his home during work hours. Naidu complained about these incidents to his manager at Group 4 Securitas, the security firm that actually employed him, but the Group 4 manager did little to help, fearing loss of the News Ltd. contract. Over time Naidu developed severe depression and posttraumatic stress disorder as a result of the psychological abuse. The senior manager was sacked after News Ltd.'s internal investigation found sufficient evidence of his behavior problems. (Naidu's situation became known only when News Ltd. investigated claims by female staff that the senior manager had sexually harassed them.) Naidu later sued and won compensation against News Ltd. and Group 4 for their failure to stop the senior manager's harassment.[49]

Devander Naidu experienced extreme and prolonged **psychological harassment**. Psychological harassment includes repeated and hostile or unwanted conduct, verbal comments, actions, or gestures that affect an employee's dignity or psychological or physical integrity and that result in a harmful work environment for the employee. This covers a broad landscape of behaviors—from threats and bullying to subtle yet persistent forms of incivility.[50]

Unfortunately psychological harassment exists to some degree in almost all workplaces, and much of it is caused by managers. One study found that 40 percent of federal court

stressors
Any environmental conditions that place a physical or emotional demand on a person.

■ Psychological harassment at News Ltd.

psychological harassment
Repeated and hostile or unwanted conduct, verbal comments, actions, or gestures that affect an employee's dignity or psychological or physical integrity and that result in a harmful work environment for the employee.

employees in Michigan had experienced workplace incivility within the past five years. Two large surveys reported that 9 percent of European workers and nearly 20 percent of British workers suffered from workplace bullying over the previous 12 months. More than half of the 1,800 lawyers polled in an Australian survey said that they had been bullied or intimidated on the job. Psychological harassment has become such a problem that some European governments explicitly prohibit it in the workplace. When the province of Quebec, Canada, recently passed the first workplace antiharassment legislation in North America, more than 2,500 complaints were received in the first year alone![51]

Sexual harassment is a type of harassment that includes unwelcome conduct of a sexual nature that detrimentally affects the work environment or leads to adverse job-related consequences for its victims. One form of sexual harassment, called *quid pro quo*, includes situations in which a person's employment or job performance is conditional on unwanted sexual relations (for example, a male supervisor threatens to fire a female employee if she does not accept his sexual advances). The second and more common form of sexual harassment, called *hostile work environment*, includes sexual conduct that interferes with an individual's work performance or creates an intimidating, hostile, or offensive working environment. The definition of sexual harassment leads to complications—and interpersonal stress—because men have a narrower interpretation than do women of what constitutes hostile work environment sexual harassment.[52] Sexual harassment sometimes escalates into psychological harassment after the alleged victim complains about the sexual wrongdoing.

Work Overload A half-century ago social scientists predicted that technology would allow employees to enjoy a 15-hour workweek at full pay by 2030. So far it hasn't turned out that way. Americans experience considerable *work overload*—working more hours and more intensely during those hours than they can reasonably cope with. Surveys by the Families and Work Institute report that 44 percent of Americans say they are overworked, up from 28 percent who felt this way three years earlier. This work overload is also the main cause of work–family conflicts because overworked employees have insufficient time to satisfy their nonwork roles of being a parent, spouse, and so forth.[53]

Why do employees work such long hours? One explanation is the combined effects of technology and globalization. "Everyone in this industry is working harder now because of e-mail, wireless access, and globalization," says Christopher Lochhead, chief marketing officer of Mercury Interactive, a California-based consultancy with offices in 35 countries. "You can't even get a rest on the weekend," he says. A second cause, according to a recent study, is that many people are caught up in consumerism; they want to buy more goods and services, which requires more income earned through longer work hours. A third reason, called the "ideal worker norm," is that professionals expect themselves and others to work longer work hours. For many people, toiling away far beyond the normal workweek is a badge of honor—a symbol of their superhuman capacity to perform better than others.

The ideal worker norm is particularly strong in Japan, Korea, China, and other Asian countries, which has led to the increasing incidence of *karoshi*—death from overwork.[54] The Japanese government records 100–200 cases each year, but these include only cases in which family members receive compensation. Experts say the karoshi death toll in Japan is probably closer to 10,000, and that up to 1 million white-collar employees are at risk. According to the Japanese government, employees who work more than 80 hours of overtime per month have a significantly higher risk of karoshi. Currently more than 20 percent of male Japanese employees exceed that level of overtime.[55]

Low Task Control As a private driver for an executive in Jakarta, Eddy knows that traffic jams are a way of life in Indonesia's largest city. "Jakarta is traffic congestion," he complains. "All of the streets in the city are crowded with

---

sexual harassment
A type of harassment that includes unwelcome conduct of a sexual nature that detrimentally affects the work environment or leads to adverse job-related consequences for its victims.

Karoshi Takes Its Toll in Japan Throughout Asia, professionals are working long work hours as a badge of honor. For some, it's a short-lived honor. According to the Japanese government, employees who work more than 80 hours of overtime per month have a significantly higher risk of *karoshi*—death from overwork. Karoshi is also becoming a serious concern in Taiwan and China, where it is called *guolaosi*.

© Getty Images

vehicles. It is impossible to avoid this distressing fact every day." Eddy's boss complains when traffic jams make him late for appointments, which makes matters even more stressful. "Even watching soccer on TV or talking to my wife doesn't get rid of my stress. It's driving me mad."[56]

Eddy and many other people experience stress due to a lack of task control. Along with driving through congested traffic, low task control occurs where the employee's work is paced by a machine, the job involves monitoring equipment, or the work schedule is controlled by someone else. Computers, cell phones, and other technology also increase stress by limiting a person's control of time and privacy.[57]

The extent to which low task control is a stressor increases with the burden of responsibility the employee must carry. Assembly-line workers have little task control, but their stress can also be fairly minimal if their level of responsibility is also low. In contrast, sports coaches are under immense pressure to win games (high responsibility) yet have little control over what happens on the playing field (low task control). Similarly, Eddy (the Jakarta driver) is under pressure to get his employer to a particular destination on time (high responsibility), but he has little control over traffic congestion (low task control).

// MANAGING WORK-RELATED STRESS

Some degree of stress is good (eustress), but for the most part managers need to figure out how to minimize distress among their staff. Most stress management strategies can be organized into the five categories summarized in Figure 14.6: withdraw from the stressor, change stress perceptions, control stress consequences, receive social support, and remove the stressor.

Withdraw from the Stressor One set of strategies for minimizing workplace stress is to permanently or temporarily remove employees from the stressor. Permanent withdrawal occurs when employees are transferred to jobs that better fit their competencies and values. Temporarily withdrawing from stressors involves distancing oneself for a short time (perhaps a few minutes or weeks) from the stressor. Some companies even set up workplace temporary retreats to help employees manage stress. Online marketing firm Brann Baltimore created an Aquarium Room complete with soothing blue lights, blue walls, and bubble columns. The room, which overlooks the National Aquarium in Baltimore, even has a "sandbox" so

Stress Management Strategy	Description	Examples
Withdraw from the stressor.	Temporarily moving away from the source of stress.	Work breaks, days off, vacations, and sabbaticals.
Change stress perceptions.	Improving the employee's beliefs about his or her ability to cope with the stress and its sources.	Increasing employee confidence, providing humor.
Control stress consequences.	Improving the employee's physiological capacity to withstand the effects of stress.	Relaxation and meditation techniques, wellness programs.
Receive social support.	Psychological and informational support from friends, coworkers, managers, and others.	Supportive leadership, social interaction, support groups.
Remove the stressor.	Removing the source of stress from the work environment, or moving employees to jobs with a better fit.	Reassign employees; minimize noise, unsafe conditions, harassment.

FIGURE 14.6 Workplace-Related Stress Management Practices

Singing the Stress Away   Employees at Liggett-Stashower don't have to retreat far from the stresses of work. The Cleveland advertising firm has three theme rooms specially designed for creativity and respite: a bowling room, Zen room, and a karaoke room (shown here) where employees can sing their stress away.

Courtesy of Liggett-Stashower Inc.

employees can dip their bare feet in sand. When employees at Liggett-Stashower Inc. need a short break from the daily stresses of work, they retreat to one of three theme rooms specially designed for creativity and respite. Staff at the Cleveland advertising firm can enter the bowling room and knock down a few pins. Or they might try out the Zen room, which serves as a quiet, relaxing place to think. The third choice is a karaoke room where employees can sing their stress away. "The higher the stress level, the more singing there is going on," says Kristen Flynn, a Liggett art director.[58]

Days off and vacations represent somewhat longer temporary withdrawals from stressful conditions. One study of a police and emergency response service department found that this leisure time significantly improved employees' ability to cope with work-related stress. Paid sabbaticals are offered by several employers, including McDonald's restaurants and accounting firm KPMG. A four-month fully paid sabbatical is mandatory every five years at Ball Janik, a law firm in Portland, Oregon.[59]

Change Stress Perceptions   Employees often experience different levels of stress in the same situation because they have different levels of self-confidence and optimism. Consequently corporate leaders need to find ways to strengthen employees' confidence and self-esteem so that job challenges are not perceived as threatening. A study of newly hired accountants reported that personal goal setting and self-reinforcement can reduce the stress people experience when they enter new work settings.[60] Humor is another way to improve optimism and create positive emotions by taking some psychological weight off the situation.

Control the Consequences of Stress   Coping with workplace stress also involves controlling its consequences. For this reason many companies have fitness centers where employees can keep in shape. Research shows that physical exercise reduces the physiological consequences of stress by helping employees moderate their breathing and heart rates, muscle tension, and stomach acidity.[61] Another way to control the physiological consequences of stress is through relaxation and meditation. For instance, employees at pharmaceutical company AstraZeneca practice a form of meditation called Qi Gong during department meetings and coffee breaks. Research has found that Qi and other forms of meditation ease anxiety, lessen blood pressure and muscle tension, and moderate breathing and heart rates.[62] Along with fitness and relaxation or meditation, many firms have shifted to the broader approach of wellness programs. These programs educate and support employees in better nutrition and fitness, regular sleep, and other good health habits.

Many large employers offer **employee assistance programs (EAPs)**—counseling services that help employees overcome personal or organizational stressors and adopt more effective coping mechanisms. Most EAPs are broad programs that assist employees with any work or personal problems. Family problems often represent the largest percentage of EAP referrals, although this varies with industry and location. For instance, Vancouver City Savings Credit Union, which was described at the beginning of this chapter, received an award from the American Psychological Association for the posttraumatic stress counseling program offered to employees after a robbery.[63] EAPs can be one of the most effective stress management interventions if the counseling helps employees understand stressors, acquire stress management skills, and practice those skills.[64]

Receive Social Support Social support from coworkers, supervisors, family members, friends, and others is generally regarded as one of the more effective stress management practices. Social support refers to a person's interpersonal transactions with others and involves providing either emotional or informational support to buffer the stress experience. Seeking social support is called a "tend and befriend" response to stress, and research suggests that women often follow this route rather than the "fight or flight" alternative mentioned earlier.[65]

Social support reduces stress in at least three ways.[66] First, employees improve their perceptions that they are valued and worthy. This, in turn, increases resilience because they have higher self-esteem and confidence to cope with stressors. Second, social support provides information to help employees interpret, comprehend, and possibly remove stressors. For instance, social support might reduce a new employee's stress if coworkers describe ways to handle difficult customers. Finally, emotional support from others can directly help to buffer the stress experience. This last point reflects the idea that "misery loves company." People seek out and benefit from the emotional support of others when they face threatening situations.[67]

Social support is an important way to cope with stress that everyone can practice by maintaining friendships. This includes helping others when they need a little support in facing life stressors. Managers can strengthen social support by providing opportunities for social interaction among employees as well as their families. They also need to practice a supportive leadership style when employees work under stressful conditions and need this social support. Mentoring relationships with more senior employees may also help junior employees cope with organizational stressors.

Remove the Stressor The stress management strategies described so far may keep employees "stress-fit," but they don't solve the fundamental causes of stress. For this reason some experts argue that the only way companies can effectively manage stress is by removing the stressors that cause unnecessary strain and job burnout. Removing stressors usually begins by identifying areas of high stress and determining their main causes. Managers can also reduce stress by giving employees more control over their work and work environment. They can also ensure that employees are assigned to positions that match their competencies.

Noise and safety risks are stressful, so improving these conditions would also go a long way to minimize stress in the workplace. Workplace harassment can be minimized by carefully selecting employees and having clear guidelines for behavior and feedback to those who violate those standards.[68] Finally, managers must find ways to give employees better **work–life balance**, which refers to minimizing conflict between work and nonwork demands. Work–life balance has become such an important issue that it receives closer attention in the next section.

employee assistance programs (EAPs)
Counseling services that help employees overcome personal or organizational stressors and adopt more effective coping mechanisms.

work–life balance
A state of minimal conflict between work and non-work demands.

// WORK–LIFE BALANCE

One of the top issues facing managers in recent years is how to create a work environment that offers employees work–life balance. Work–life balance was seldom mentioned a couple of decades ago. Most employees assumed that they would put in long hours to ascend the corporate ladder. Asking the boss to accommodate nonwork responsibilities and interests was almost a sign of betrayal.[69] But two-income families, the increasing number of work hours over the past decade, and Gen-X/Gen-Y expectations have made work–life balance a mandatory condition in today's employment relationship. In fact, various surveys report that work–life balance is one of the top factors that job applicants consider when looking for work and one of the most important indicators of career success—far ahead of salary, job responsibility, and other factors.[70]

Managers can support work–life balance in many ways. To begin, they can offer flexible work hours in which employees can arrange to begin and end their workdays earlier or later, depending on their personal needs or preferences. Best Buy has adopted this approach with striking results. Not long ago the Minneapolis-based electronics store chain encouraged a 24/7 work ethos. One manager gave out awards to the employees who turned on the lights in the morning and turned them out at night. Darrell Owens recalls staying at work for three straight days to write a report that was suddenly due. The Best Buy veteran got a bonus and vacation but ended up in hospital. Today Best Buy offers a more flexible work arrangement called ROWE: results-oriented work environment. Employees now work when and where they like to get the job done. They can arrive early or late for work, head home to chauffeur kids for an hour, and then resume work with cell phone or e-mail access. Employees mark on a whiteboard whether they are in the office and, if not, whether they are available by cell phone or e-mail during the day. The ROWE initiative has resulted in lower employee turnover, higher morale and team performance, and much better work–life balance.[71]

Job sharing is another work–life balance initiative in which a position is split between two people. In a typical arrangement two employees work different parts of the week with some overlapping work time in the weekly schedule to coordinate activities.[72] A third strategy is to offer maternity, paternity, and other forms of personal leave so employees have more time and flexibility to raise a family, care for elderly parents, or take advantage of a personal experience. The U.S. Family and Medical Leave Act grants employees up to 12 weeks of unpaid job-protected leave per year for the birth and care of the newborn child. However, almost every other developed nation requires employers to provide paid maternity leave.[73] Volvo is one of the more generous companies in the United States, offering 40 weeks of paid maternity leave.

Telecommuting Along with flexible hours, job sharing, and personal leave, companies are helping employees to experience more work–life balance through *telecommuting* (also called *teleworking*). Telecommuting occurs when employees work at home or a remote site, usually with a computer connection to the office. Consider Karen Dunn Kelley's daily commute. She puts her school-aged children on the bus, feeds breakfast to her 19-month-old before handing him off to a nanny, and then takes a short walk from her house to the office over her garage. Kelley is an executive with Houston-based AIM Management Group, yet the home office where she oversees 40 staff and $75 billion in assets is located in Pittsburgh.[74]

More than a quarter of American employees consider themselves telecommuters, and more than 20 percent work at home at least one day each month. Approximately 10 percent of Canadian and 6 percent of Japanese employees telecommute; the Japanese government wants to increase that figure to 20 percent by 2010 as a way to reduce traffic congestion.[75] Some research suggests that telecommuting potentially lessens employee stress by offering better work–life balance and dramatically trimming time lost through commuting to the office. Under some circumstances it also increases productivity and job satisfaction. Nortel Networks reports that 71 percent

Best Buy Flexes Its Hours   Not long ago (and to some extent still in some departments), Best Buy was a 24/7 culture in which employees were expected to work long hours in the office. Today the Minneapolis-based electronics store chain has adopted a policy giving employees freedom to arrive early or late as long as they get their work done. The change has improved morale, team performance, and work–life balance.

© AP Photo/Chris Carlson

of its U.K. staff members feel more empowered through telecommuting. Others point out that telecommuting reduces the cost of office space and improves the environment by cutting pollution and traffic congestion.[76]

Against these potential benefits, telecommuters face a number of real or potential challenges.[77] Although telecommuting is usually introduced to improve work–life balance, family relations may suffer rather than improve if employees lack sufficient space and resources for a home office. Some studies also report that telecommuting may increase the number of people who work long hours, take time away from family, and increase pressure after normal work hours. Unfulfilled social needs are another common complaint, particularly among telecommuters who rarely visit the office. The bottom line of telecommuting is that it can potentially improve work–life balance, but it still requires management support to ensure that this balance occurs.

■ // Personality Effects on Attitudes and Well-Being

Throughout this chapter we have emphasized that managers make a difference in helping employees feel better at work. Yet to some extent employee attitudes and well-being are also influenced by employees' personalities. **Personality**, which was introduced briefly in Chapter 12, refers to the relatively stable pattern of behaviors and consistent internal states that explains a person's behavioral tendencies. We say that personality explains behavioral *tendencies* because individuals' actions are not perfectly consistent with their personality profiles in every situation. As we explained in Chapter 12, personality is an abstract concept, so it isn't the best information for deciding which job applicants to hire. However, it does influence how people react to their work environments. To understand how personality is connected to attitudes and well-being, we first need to learn about the five main clusters of personality traits.

personality
The relatively stable pattern of behaviors and consistent internal states that explains a person's behavioral tendencies.

// THE BIG FIVE PERSONALITY DIMENSIONS

Since the days of Plato, experts have been trying to develop lists of personality traits. One approach was to catalog the thousands of words in *Roget's Thesaurus* and *Webster's Dictionary* that represented personality traits. Using sophisticated mathematical techniques, these words were clustered into dozens of categories and further shrunk down to five abstract personality dimensions, known as the **Big Five personality dimensions**.[78] These five dimensions, represented by the handy acronym CANOE, are outlined in Figure 14.7 and described here:

Big Five personality dimensions
The five abstract dimensions representing most personality traits: conscientiousness, agreeableness, neuroticism, openness to experience, and extroversion (CANOE).

- *Conscientiousness* refers to people who are careful, dependable, and self-disciplined. Some scholars assert that this dimension also includes the will to achieve. People with low conscientiousness tend to be careless, less thorough, more disorganized, and irresponsible.
- *Agreeableness* includes the traits of being courteous, good-natured, empathetic, and caring. Some scholars prefer the label of "friendly compliance" for this dimension, with its opposite being "hostile noncompliance." People with low agreeableness tend to be uncooperative, short-tempered, and irritable.
- *Neuroticism* characterizes people with high levels of anxiety, hostility, depression, and self-consciousness. In contrast, people with low neuroticism (high emotional stability) are poised, secure, and calm.
- *Openness to experience* is the most complex dimension with the least agreement among scholars. It generally refers to the extent to which people are sensitive, flexible, creative, and curious. Those who score low on this dimension tend to be more resistant to change, less open to new ideas, and more fixed in their ways.
- *Extroversion* characterizes people who are outgoing, talkative, sociable, and assertive. The opposite is *introversion*, which refers to those who are quiet, shy, and cautious.

FIGURE 14.7

Big Five Personality Dimensions

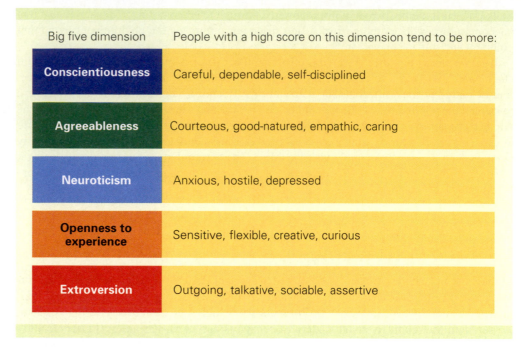

Big five dimension	People with a high score on this dimension tend to be more:
Conscientiousness	Careful, dependable, self-disciplined
Agreeableness	Courteous, good-natured, empathic, caring
Neuroticism	Anxious, hostile, depressed
Openness to experience	Sensitive, flexible, creative, curious
Extroversion	Outgoing, talkative, sociable, assertive

Introverts do not necessarily lack social skills. Rather, they are inclined to direct their interests more to ideas than to social events. Introverts feel comfortable being alone, whereas extroverts do not.

// EFFECTS OF PERSONALITY ON EMOTIONS AND ATTITUDES

Have you ever noticed how some people seem upbeat most of the time while others are almost never happy about anything? To some extent people's emotions are influenced by their personalities, not just by their workplace experiences.[79] Some people have a natural tendency to experience positive emotions. These people have higher levels of extroversion; they are more outgoing, talkative, sociable, and assertive. They also tend to have relatively low levels of neuroticism (high emotional stability); that is, they are more poised, secure, and calm. In contrast, people with high introversion (quietness, shyness, and cautiousness) and neuroticism (anxiety, hostility, depression, and self-consciousness) tend to experience more negative emotions at work and in other environments.

To what extent do these personality traits influence emotions? Some research shows that feelings about work can be predicted two years in advance from personality traits. Studies of twins raised apart conclude that a person's heredity influences emotions and judgments about work. However, other evidence suggests that the actual situation in which people work has a noticeably stronger influence on their attitudes and behavior.[80] Overall it seems that personality traits influence workplace emotions and attitudes, but their effects are not as strong as the work environment.

// EFFECTS OF PERSONALITY ON STRESS AND WELL-BEING

resilience

The capability of individuals to cope successfully in the face of significant change, adversity, or risk.

Because personality affects our moods and emotions, it also influences our stress reactions to the work environment. People who are optimistic, confident, and often experience positive emotions tend to feel less stress.[81] This characteristic refers to an emerging concept known as resilience. **Resilience** is the capability of individuals to cope successfully in the face of significant change, adversity, or risk. Everyone has some resilience; it occurs every time we pull through stressful experiences. However, people with high resilience are better able to maintain equilibrium during stress. They hold their ground, so they don't need to recuperate as much.[82]

Personality is a major influence on the extent to which people have high resilience. Specifically, resilient people are more optimistic; they have more positive outcome expectancies. Optimism produces physiological changes that help the body fight stress, whereas depression and anxiety are known to increase health risks by altering the immune system.[83] Three personality dimensions—neuroticism, extroversion, and conscientiousness—seem to be associated with resilience and optimism. Not surprisingly, highly resilient people have low levels of neuroticism: They experience fewer negative emotions and can better control emotional impulses. Extroverted people tend to be more resilient because they are comfortable in social relationships, and social support is a known coping mechanism. Conscientiousness seems to be associated with resilience because conscientious people demonstrate better problem-solving skills. Problem solving helps people figure out how to remove or minimize sources of stress.[84]

// EFFECTS OF PERSONALITY ON PERFORMANCE

These five personality dimensions affect work-related behavior and job performance to varying degrees.[85] People with high emotional stability tend to work better than others in high-stress situations. Those with high agreeableness tend to handle customer relations and conflict-based situations more effectively. However, conscientiousness has taken center stage as the most valuable personality trait for predicting job performance in almost every job group. Conscientious employees set higher personal goals for themselves, are more motivated, and have higher performance expectations than do employees with low levels of conscientiousness. Highly conscientious employees tend to perform tasks beyond their job description and work better in workplaces that give employees more freedom than in traditional "command and control" workplaces. Employees with high conscientiousness, as well as agreeableness and emotional stability, also tend to provide better customer service.

// EFFECTS OF PERSONALITY ON CAREER SATISFACTION

One fairly successful application of personality knowledge is in the area of vocational choice. Vocational choice is not just about matching your skills with job requirements. It is a complex alignment of personality, values, and competencies with the requirements of work and characteristics of the work environment. You might be very talented at a particular job, but your personality and values must also be aligned with what the job offers. John Holland, a career development scholar, was an early proponent of this notion that career success depends on the degree of congruence between the person and his or her work environment.[87] Holland asserted that people can be classified into different types relating to their personality and that they seek out and are more satisfied in work environments that are congruent with their particular profiles. Thus *congruence* refers to the extent to which someone has the same or similar personality type as the environment in which he or she is working. Some research has found that high congruence leads to better performance, satisfaction, and length of time in a career; other studies are less supportive of the model.[88]

Holland's Six Types Holland's theory classifies both individual personalities and work environments into six categories: realistic, investigative, artistic, social, enterprising, and conventional. Figure 14.8 defines these types of people and work

Finding a Career That Fits the Personality   While working as a Navy diver, Dan Porzio prepared for his next career in financial planning. But he was far from happy in his new field, so he took a job selling cellular phones. Still unhappy, Porzio moved into the investment industry, where he worked for three years. During that time he visited a career counselor and discovered why he lacked interest in his work. "I thought those other jobs were ones that I wanted to do, but I found out I was doing things that didn't jive with my character," Porzio explains. With that knowledge in hand, Porzio found a job that fit his personality as captain of the *Annabelle Lee* riverboat in Richmond, Virginia.[86]

C. Blanchard, *Richmond Times-Dispatch.*

Holland Type	Personality Traits	Work Environment Characteristics	Sample Occupations
Realistic	Practical, shy, materialistic, stable.	Work with hands, machines, or tools; focus on tangible results.	Assembly worker; dry cleaner, mechanical engineer.
Investigative	Analytic, introverted, reserved, curious, precise, independent.	Work involves discovering, collecting, and analyzing; solving problems.	Biologist, dentist, systems analyst.
Artistic	Creative, impulsive, idealistic, intuitive, emotional.	Work involves creation of new products or ideas, typically in an unstructured setting.	Journalist, architect, advertising executive.
Social	Sociable, outgoing, conscientious, need for affiliation.	Work involves serving or helping others; working in teams.	Social worker, nurse, teacher, counselor.
Enterprising	Confident, assertive, energetic, need for power.	Work involves leading others; achieving goals through others in a results-oriented setting.	Salesperson, stockbroker, politician.
Conventional	Dependable, disciplined, orderly, practical, efficient.	Work involves systematic manipulation of data or information.	Accountant, banker, administrator.

FIGURE 14.8   Holland's Six Types of Personalities and Work Environments

Sources: Based on information in D.H. Montross, Z.B. Leibowitz, and C.J. Shinkman, *Real People, Real Jobs* (Palo Alto, CA: Davies-Black, 1995); and J.H. Greenhaus, *Career Management* (Chicago, IL: Dryden, 1987).

environments and suggests sample occupations representing those environments. Few people fall squarely into only one of Holland's classifications. Instead Holland refers to a person's degree of *differentiation*—that is, the extent to which an individual fits into one or several types. A highly differentiated person is aligned with a single category, whereas most people fit into two or more categories.

Because most people fit into more than one personality type, Holland developed a model shaped like a hexagon with each personality type around the points of the model. *Consistency* refers to the extent to which a person is aligned with similar types, which are next to each other in the hexagon (dissimilar types are opposite). For instance, the enterprising and social types are next to each other in Holland's model, so individuals with both enterprising and social personalities have high consistency.

Holland's vocational fit model is far from perfect. For example, the model refers to only a few of the Big Five personality dimensions described earlier, and some "opposing" categories in Holland's hexagon are not really opposite to each other. Still, Holland's model is the dominant model of career counseling today because it explains individual attitudes and behavior to some extent.[89] The main message for managers is that career development isn't just about matching company needs with employee skills. It also about aligning employee personalities and preferences with job characteristics. This person–job matching process produces happier employees. And as we learned throughout this chapter, the resulting positive emotions and attitudes potentially lead to superior job performance, greater customer satisfaction, and other beneficial outcomes for the organization.

IN CONCLUSION   WHY DOES IT MATTER?

Not long ago the concepts presented in Chapters 12 and 13 were the essence of managing employees. The prevailing view was that staffing and motivating employees were the main—or even the only—ways to achieve organizational success. Any manager who takes this view today will be in deep trouble. Employee emotions, attitudes, and well-being are indicators of an ethical imperative. Treating staff with respect, matching their needs with organizational resources, and providing a workplace that minimizes unnecessary stress is simply the right thing to do. Employees are stakeholders, so a second justification is that managing attitudes and well-being is an integral component of corporate social responsibility.

Along with the ethical and corporate social responsibility implications, employee attitudes and well-being influence a company's ability to attract and retain talent. As labor shortages loom and the war for talent heats up, keeping employees happy is an important objective. As we noted in Chapter 12, companies develop a stronger employer brand when they receive awards as great places to work, whereas low morale and high turnover are viewed as evidence of poor treatment of employees. Ultimately a company's public image of how it treats employees can be a decisive factor in the quality of job applicants.

Along with the ethical, corporate social responsibility, and employee retention arguments, employee emotions, attitudes, and well-being are indirectly, but reasonably strongly, associated with job performance and customer satisfaction. Employees won't achieve peak job performance just through the processes of selection, training, and reward management. They also need to have positive work experiences and normal levels of stress. Employees who are satisfied with their jobs generally work more effectively, interact better with coworkers, and serve customers more helpfully and with more positive displays of emotions. The lower turnover rates among satisfied and less stressed employees also increase the quality of talent in the workplace.

MANAGEMENT CHALLENGES

1. After a few months on the job, Susan has experienced several emotional episodes ranging from frustration to joy about the work she has been assigned. Explain how these emotions affect Susan's level of job satisfaction with the work itself.

2. Managers need to pay attention to employee emotions and attitudes, but how can they determine the emotions that people are experiencing on the job?

3. Describe the employee–customer–profit chain model; then identify conditions that might strengthen or weaken the links along that chain. To what extent can managers influence the elements of this model?

4. Although managers are supposed to help minimize workplace stressors such as harassment, they are typically identified as the main contributors to this source of stress. Discuss possible reasons why managers are the main sources of bullying and suggest ways of minimizing this problem.

5. "Happy employees create happy customers." Explain why this statement might be true, and identify conditions in which it might not be true.

6. A senior official of a labor union stated, "All stress management does is help people cope with poor management. [Employers] should really be into stress reduction." Discuss the accuracy of this statement.

MANAGEMENT PORTFOLIO

FOR THE ORGANIZATION YOU HAVE CHOSEN TO FOLLOW:

1. Does this organization win awards or come close to being one of the best places to work in the country? What other information suggests that this organization makes an effort to generate positive emotions for employees?

2. This chapter highlights five ways in which companies can build a more loyal workforce. Evaluate the extent to which this organization fulfills each of these five conditions, and provide evidence to support your evaluation.

3. In your opinion, is this organization a relatively high- or low-stress place to work? Explain your answer. What practices does this organization seem to use to help employees minimize stress?

CLOSING CASE   ROUGH SEAS ON THE LINK650

Professor Suzanne Baxter was preparing for her first class of the semester when Shaun O'Neill knocked lightly on the open door and announced himself: "Hi, Professor, I don't suppose you remember me?" Professor Baxter had large classes, but she did remember that Shaun was a student in her organizational behavior class two years earlier. Shaun had decided to work in the oil industry for a couple of years before returning to school to complete his diploma.

"Welcome back!" Baxter said as she beckoned him into the office. "I heard you were working on an oil rig up in Canada. How was it?"

"Well, Professor," Shaun began, "I had worked two summers in the oil fields and my family's from Canada, so I hoped to get a job on the LINK650. It's that new WestOil drilling rig that arrived with so much fanfare in Newfoundland on Canada's east coast two years ago. The LINK650 was built by LINK Inc. in Texas. A standard practice in this industry is for the rig manufacturer to manage its day-to-day operations, so employees on the LINK650 are managed completely by LINK managers with no involvement from WestOil. We all know that drilling rig jobs are dangerous, but they pay well and offer generous time off. A local newspaper said that nearly a thousand people lined up to complete job applications for the 50 nontechnical positions. I was lucky enough to get one of those jobs.

"Everyone hired on the LINK650 was enthusiastic and proud. We were one of the chosen few and were really pumped up about working on a new rig that had received so much media attention. I was quite impressed with the recruiters—so were several other hires—because they really seemed to be concerned about our welfare out on the plat-

form. I later discovered that the recruiters came from a consulting firm that specializes in hiring people. Come to think of it, we didn't meet a single LINK manager during that process. Maybe things would have been different if some of those LINK supervisors had interviewed us.

"Working on the LINK650 was a real shock even though most of us had some experience working in the oil fields. I'd say that none of the 50 nontechnical people hired was quite prepared for the brutal jobs on the oil rig. We did the dirtiest jobs in the biting cold winds of the North Atlantic. Still, during the first few months most of us wanted to show the company that we were dedicated to getting the job done. A couple of the new hires quit within a few weeks, but most of the people hired with me really got along well—you know, just like the ideas you mentioned in class. We formed a special bond that helped us through the bad weather and grueling work.

"The LINK650 supervisors were another matter. They were tough SOBs who had worked for many years on oil rigs in the Gulf of Mexico or North Sea. They seemed to relish the idea of treating their employees the same way they had been treated before becoming managers. We put up with their abuse for the first few months, but things got worse when the LINK650 was brought into port twice to correct mechanical problems. These setbacks embarrassed LINK's managers, and they put more pressure on the supervisors to get us back on schedule.

"The supervisors started to ignore equipment problems and pushed us to get jobs done more quickly without regard to safety procedures. They routinely shouted obscenities at employees in front of others. A couple of my work mates were fired, and a couple of others quit their jobs. I almost lost my job one day just because my boss thought I was deliberately working slowly. He didn't realize—or care—that the fittings I was connecting were damaged. Several people started finding ways to avoid the supervisors and get as little work done as possible. Many of my coworkers developed back problems. We jokingly called it the 'rigger's backache' because some employees faked their ailment to leave the rig with paid sick leave.

"On top of the lousy supervisors, we were always kept in the dark about the problems on the rig. Supervisors said that they didn't know anything, which was partly true; but they said we shouldn't be so interested in things that didn't concern us. But the rig's problems, as well as its future contract work, were a major concern to crew members who weren't ready to quit. Their job security depended on the rig's production levels and whether WestOil would sign contracts to drill new holes. Given the rig's problems, most of us were concerned that we would be laid off at any time.

"Everything came to a head when Bob MacKenzie was killed because someone secured a hoist improperly. Not sure if it was mentioned in the papers here, but it was big news around this time last year. The Canadian government inquiry concluded that the person responsible wasn't properly trained and that employees were being pushed to finish jobs without safety precautions. Anyway, while the inquiry was going on, several employees decided to call the Seafarers International Union to unionize the rig. It wasn't long before most employees on LINK650 had signed union cards. That really shocked LINK's management and the entire oil industry because it was, I think, just the second time that a rig had ever been unionized in Canada.

"Since then, management has been doing everything in its power to get rid of the union. It sent a 'safety officer' to the rig, although we eventually realized that he was a consultant the company hired to undermine union support. One safety meeting with compulsory attendance of all crew members involved watching a video describing the international union president's association with organized crime. Several managers were sent to special seminars on how to manage a union workforce, although one of the topics was how to break the union. The guys who initiated the organizing drive were either fired or given undesirable jobs. LINK even paid one employee to challenge the union certification vote. The labor board rejected the decertification request because it discovered the company's union-busting tactics. Last month the labor board ordered LINK to negotiate a first contract in good faith.

"So you see, Professor, I joined LINK as an enthusiastic employee and quit last month with no desire to lift a finger for them. It really bothers me because I was always told to do your best, no matter how tough the situation. It's been quite an experience."

CASE DISCUSSION QUESTIONS

1. Use your knowledge of emotions and attitudes to explain why the LINK650 employees were dissatisfied with their work.

2. Identify the various ways in which employees expressed their job dissatisfaction on the LINK650.

3. Shaun O'Neill's commitment to the LINK organization dwindled over his two years of employment. Discuss the factors that affected his organizational commitment.

Source: © Copyright Steven L. McShane. This case is based on actual events, although names and some information have been changed.

ENDNOTES

1. F. Bilovsky, "Wegmans Is Named America's No. 1 Employer," *Democrat & Chronicle* (Rochester, NY), January 11, 2005; D. Furlonger, "Best Company to Work For," *Financial Mail* (South Africa), September 30, 2005, p. 20; J Lee, "Vancity Employees Feel the Difference," *Vancouver Sun*, October 29, 2005, p. E1; W.L. Lee, "Net Value: That Loving Feeling," *The Edge Daily* (Kuala Lumpur), April 25, 2005; T. Knauss, "Small Local Company Is a Happy Place to Work," *Post Standard/Herald-Journal* (Syracuse), March 21, 2006, p. A1; A. Maitland, "Bonds That Keep Workers Happy," *Financial Times* (London), May 18, 2006.

2. C.D. Fisher, "Mood and Emotions While Working: Missing Pieces of Job Satisfaction?" *Journal of Organizational Behavior* 21 (2000), pp. 185–202; M. Pergini and R.P. Bagozzi, "The Role of Desires and Anticipated Emotions in Goal-Directed Behaviors: Broadening and Deepening the Theory of Planned Behavior," *British Journal of Social Psychology* 40 (March 2001), pp. 79–98; J.D. Morris et al., "The Power of Affect: Predicting Intention," *Journal of Advertising Research* 42 (May–June 2002), pp. 7–17.

3. The centrality of emotions in marketing, economics, and sociology is discussed in G. Loewenstein, "Emotions in Economic Theory and Economic Behavior," *American Economic Review* 90, no. 2 (May 2000), pp. 426–32; D.S. Massey, "A Brief History of Human Society: The Origin and Role of Emotion in Social Life," *American Sociological Review* 67 (February 2002), pp. 1–29; J. O'Shaughnessy and N.J. O'Shaughnessy, *The Marketing Power of Emotion* (New York: Oxford University Press, 2003).

4. The definition presented here is constructed from information in the following sources: N.M. Ashkanasy, W.J. Zerbe, and C.E.J. Hartel, "Introduction: Managing Emotions in a Changing Workplace," in *Managing Emotions in the Workplace*, ed. N.M. Ashkanasy, W.J. Zerbe, and C.E.J. Hartel (Armonk, NY: M.E. Sharpe, 2002), pp. 3–18; H.M. Weiss, "Conceptual and Empirical Foundations for the Study of Affect at Work," in *Emotions in the Workplace*, ed. R.G. Lord, R.J. Klimoski, and R. Kanfer (San Francisco: Jossey-Bass, 2002), pp. 20–63. However, the meaning of *emotions* is still being debated. See, for example, M. Cabanac, "What Is Emotion?" *Behavioural Processes* 60 (2002), pp. 69–83.

5. R.B. Zajonc, "Emotions," in *Handbook of Social Psychology*, ed. D.T. Gilbert, S.T. Fiske, and L. Gardner (New York: Oxford University Press, 1998), pp. 591–634.

6. A.H. Eagly and S. Chaiken, *The Psychology of Attitudes* (Orlando, FL: Harcourt Brace Jovanovich, 1993); A.P. Brief, *Attitudes in and around Organizations* (Thousand Oaks, CA: Sage, 1998). There is ongoing debate about whether attitudes represent only feelings or all three components described here. However, those who adopt the single-factor perspective still refer to beliefs as the cognitive

component of attitudes. For example, see I. Ajzen, "Nature and Operation of Attitudes," *Annual Review of Psychology* 52 (2001), pp. 27–58.

7. S.D. Farley and M.F. Stasson, "Relative Influences of Affect and Cognition on Behavior: Are Feelings or Beliefs More Related to Blood Donation Intentions?" *Experimental Psychology* 50, no. 1 (2003), pp. 55–62.

8. J.A. Bargh and M.J. Ferguson, "Beyond Behaviorism: On the Automaticity of Higher Mental Processes," *Psychological Bulletin* 126, no. 6 (2000), pp. 925–45; R.H. Fazio, "On the Automatic Activation of Associated Evaluations: An Overview," *Cognition and Emotion* 15, no. 2 (2001), pp. 115–41; M. Gladwell, *Blink: The Power of Thinking without Thinking* (New York: Little, Brown, 2005).

9. A.R. Damasio, *Descartes' Error: Emotion, Reason, and the Human Brain* (New York: Putnam Sons, 1994); A. Damasio, *The Feeling of What Happens* (New York: Harcourt Brace and Co., 1999); P. Ekman, "Basic Emotions," in *Handbook of Cognition and Emotion*, ed. T. Dalgleish and M. Power (San Francisco: Jossey-Bass, 1999), pp. 45–60; J.E. LeDoux, "Emotion Circuits in the Brain," *Annual Review of Neuroscience* 23 (2000), pp. 155–84; R.J. Dolan, "Emotion, Cognition, and Behavior," *Science* 298, no. 5596 (November 8, 2002), pp. 1191–94.

10. H.M. Weiss and R. Cropanzano, "Affective Events Theory: A Theoretical Discussion of the Structure, Causes, and Consequences of Affective Experiences at Work," *Research in Organizational Behavior* 18 (1996), pp. 1–74.

11. R. Basch, "Doing Well by Doing Good," *Searcher Magazine*, January 2005, pp. 18–28; K. Coughlin, "Goooood Move," *Star-Ledger* (Newark, NJ), June 5, 2005, p. 1.

12. S.C. Lundin, H. Paul, and J. Christensen, *Fish!: A Remarkable Way to Boost Morale and Improve Results* (New York: Hyperion Press, 2000); S.C. Lundin, H. Paul, and J. Christensen, *Fish! Tales: Bite-Sized Stories, Unlimited Possibilities* (New York: Hyperion Press, 2002).

13. L. Festinger, *A Theory of Cognitive Dissonance* (Evanston, IL: Row, Peterson, 1957); A.D. Galinsky, J. Stone, and J. Cooper, "The Reinstatement of Dissonance and Psychological Discomfort Following Failed Affirmation," *European Journal of Social Psychology* 30, no. 1 (2000), pp. 123–47.

14. G.R. Salancik, "Commitment and the Control of Organizational Behavior and Belief," in *New Directions in Organizational Behavior*, ed. B.M. Staw and G.R. Salancik (Chicago: St. Clair, 1977), pp. 1–54.

15. E.A. Locke, "The Nature and Causes of Job Satisfaction," in *Handbook of Industrial and Organizational Psychology*, ed. M. Dunnette (Chicago: Rand McNally, 1976), pp. 1297–1350; H.M. Weiss, "Deconstructing Job Satisfaction: Separating Evaluations, Beliefs, and Affective Experiences," *Human Resource Management Review* no. 12 (2002), pp. 173–94. Some definitions still include emotion as an element of job satisfaction, whereas the definition presented in this book views emotion as a cause of job satisfaction. Also, this definition views job satisfaction as a "collection of attitudes," not several "facets" of job satisfaction.

16. Ipsos-Reid, "Ipsos-Reid Global Poll Finds Major Differences in Employee Satisfaction around the World," news release (Toronto: January 8, 2001). These results are similar to other global satisfaction surveys. See International Survey Research, *Employee Satisfaction in the World's 10 Largest Economies: Globalization or Diversity?* (Chicago: International Survey Research, 2002).

17. T. Lester, "Performance at Hugo Boss," *Executive Briefing (Economist Intelligence Unit)*, May 4, 2006, p. 1.

18. M.J. Withey and W.H. Cooper, "Predicting Exit, Voice, Loyalty, and Neglect," *Administrative Science Quarterly* 34 (1989), pp. 521–39; W.H. Turnley and D.C. Feldman, "The Impact of Psychological Contract Violations on Exit, Voice, Loyalty, and Neglect," *Human Relations* 52 (July 1999), pp. 895–922.

19. B. Morton, "Positive Work Environment Keeps Them Happy, Staffers Say," *Vancouver Sun*, October 5, 2004, p. D1.

20. T.R. Mitchell, B.C. Holtom, and T.W. Lee, "How to Keep Your Best Employees: Developing an Effective Retention Policy," *Academy of Management Executive* 15 (November 2001), pp. 96–108; C.P. Maertz and M.A. Campion, "Profiles of Quitting: Integrating Process and Content Turnover Theory," *Academy of Management Journal* 47, no. 4 (2004), pp. 566–82.

21. A.A. Luchak, "What Kind of Voice Do Loyal Employees Use?" *British Journal of Industrial Relations* 41 (March 2003), pp. 115–34.

22. J.D. Hibbard, N. Kumar, and L.W. Stern, "Examining the Impact of Destructive Acts in Marketing Channel Relationships," *Journal of Marketing Research* 38 (February 2001), pp. 45–61; J. Zhou and J.M. George, "When Job Dissatisfaction Leads to Creativity: Encouraging the Expression of Voice," *Academy of Management Journal* 44 (August 2001), pp. 682–96.

23. M.J. Withey and I.R. Gellatly, "Situational and Dispositional Determinants of Exit, Voice, Loyalty, and Neglect," *Proceedings of the Administrative Sciences Association of Canada, Organizational Behaviour Division*, June 1998; M.J. Withey and I.R. Gellatly, "Exit, Voice, Loyalty, and Neglect: Assessing the Influence of Prior Effectiveness and Personality," *Proceedings of the Administrative Sciences Association of Canada, Organizational Behaviour Division* 20 (1999), pp. 110–19.

24. T.A. Judge et al., "The Job Satisfaction–Job Performance Relationship: A Qualitative and Quantitative Review," *Psychological Bulletin* 127 (2001), pp. 376–407; Saari and Judge, "Employee Attitudes and Job Satisfaction."

25. Judge et al., "The Job Satisfaction–Job Performance Relationship: A Qualitative and Quantitative Review."

26. T. DeCotiis et al., "How Outback Steakhouse Created a Great Place to Work, Have Fun, and Make Money," *Journal of Organizational Excellence* 23, no. 4 (Autumn 2004), pp. 23–33.

27. "The Greatest Briton in Management and Leadership," *Personnel Today*, February 18, 2003, p. 20; T. Monterastelli, "Pinnacol Focuses on Respecting Employees," *Denver Business Journal*, November 19, 2004. The Wegmans motto is mentioned in R. Levering and M. Moskowitz, "The Best 100 Companies to Work For," *Fortune*, January 24, 2005, pp. 90–96.

28. J.I. Heskett, W.E. Sasser, and L.A. Schlesinger, *The Service Profit Chain* (New York: Free Press, 1997); D.J. Koys, "The Effects of Employee Satisfaction, Organizational Citizenship Behavior, and Turnover on Organizational Effectiveness: A Unit-Level, Longitudinal Study," *Personnel Psychology* 54 (April 2001), pp. 101–14; W.-C. Tsai and Y.-M. Huang, "Mechanisms Linking Employee Affective Delivery and Customer Behavioral Intentions," *Journal of Applied Psychology* 87, no. 5 (2002), pp. 1001–08; DeCotiis et al., "How Outback Steakhouse Created a Great Place to Work, Have Fun, and Make Money"; G.A. Gelade and S. Young, "Test of a Service Profit Chain Model in the Retail Banking Sector," *Journal of Occupational & Organizational Psychology* 78 (2005), pp. 1–22. However, some studies have found only a weak relationship between employee attitudes and sales outcomes.

29. P. Guenzi and O. Pelloni, "The Impact of Interpersonal Relationships on Customer Satisfaction and Loyalty to the Service Provider," *International Journal of Service Industry Management* 15, no. 3–4 (2004), pp. 365–84; S.J. Bell, S. Auh, and K. Smalley, "Customer Relationship Dynamics: Service Quality and Customer Loyalty in the Context of Varying Levels of Customer Expertise and Switching Costs," *Journal of the Academy of Marketing Science* 33, no. 2 (Spring 2005), pp. 169–83.

30. R.T. Mowday, L.W. Porter, and R.M. Steers, *Employee Organization Linkages: The Psychology of Commitment, Absenteeism, and Turnover* (New York: Academic Press, 1982).

31. F.F. Reichheld, *The Loyalty Effect* (Boston: Harvard Business School Press, 1996), Chapter 4; J.P. Meyer et al., "Affective, Continuance, and Normative Commitment to the Organization: A Meta-Analysis of Antecedents, Correlates, and Consequences," *Journal of Vocational Behavior* 61 (2002), pp. 20–52; M. Riketta, "Attitudinal Organizational Commitment and Job Performance: A Meta-Analysis," *Journal of Organizational Behavior* 23 (2002), pp. 257–66.

32. J.P. Meyer, "Organizational Commitment," *International Review of Industrial and Organizational Psychology* 12 (1997), pp. 175–228.

33. R.D. Hackett, P. Bycio, and P.A. Hausdorf, "Further Assessments of Meyer and Allen's (1991) Three-Component Model of Organizational Commitment," *Journal of Applied Psychology* 79 (1994), pp. 15–23.

34. J. Churchill, "To the Bitter End," *Registered Rep.*, March 1, 2006, p. 59.

35. J.P. Meyer et al., "Organizational Commitment and Job Performance: It's the Nature of the Commitment That Counts," *Journal of Applied Psychology* 74 (1989), pp. 152–56; A.A. Luchak and I.R. Gellatly, "What Kind of Commitment Does a Final-Earnings Pension Plan Elicit?" *Relations Industrielles* 56 (Spring 2001), pp. 394–417; Z.X. Chen and A.M. Francesco, "The Relationship between the Three Components of Commitment and Employee Performance in China," *Journal of Vocational Behavior* 62, no. 3 (2003), pp. 490–510; D.M. Powell and J.P. Meyer, "Side-Bet Theory and the Three-Component Model of Organizational Commitment," *Journal of Vocational Behavior* 65, no. 1 (2004), pp. 157–77.

36. E.W. Morrison and S.L. Robinson, "When Employees Feel Betrayed: A Model of How Psychological Contract Violation Develops," *Academy of Management Review* 22 (1997), pp. 226–56; J.E. Finegan, "The Impact of Person and Organizational Values on Organizational Commitment," *Journal of Occupational and Organizational Psychology* 73 (June 2000), pp. 149–69.

37. D.M. Cable and T.A. Judge, "Person-Organization Fit, Job Choice Decisions, and Organizational Entry," *Organizational Behavior and Human Decision Processes* 67, no. 3 (1996), pp. 294–311; T.J. Kalliath, A.C. Bluedorn, and M.J. Strube, "A Test of Value Congruence Effects," *Journal of Organizational Behavior* 20, no. 7 (1999), pp. 1175–98; J.W. Westerman and L.A. Cyr, "An Integrative Analysis of Person–Organization Fit Theories," *International Journal of Selection and Assessment* 12, no. 3 (September 2004), pp. 252–61.

38. D.M. Rousseau et al., "Not So Different after All: A Cross-Discipline View of Trust," *Academy of Management Review* 23 (1998), pp. 393–404.

39. S. Ashford, C. Lee, and P. Bobko, "Content, Causes, and Consequences of Job Insecurity: A Theory-Based Measure and Substantive Test," *Academy of Management Journal* 32 (1989), pp. 803–29; C. Hendry and R. Jenkins, "Psychological Contracts and New Deals," *Human Resource Management Journal* 7 (1997), pp. 38–44.

40. T.S. Heffner and J.R. Rentsch, "Organizational Commitment and Social Interaction: A Multiple Constituencies Approach," *Journal of Vocational Behavior* 59 (2001), pp. 471–90.

41. E. Frauenheim, "For Developers, It's Not All Fun and Games," *CNET News.com,* November 18, 2004; A. Pham, "Video Game Programmers Get Little Time to Play," *Houston Chronicle,* November 21, 2004, 6; N. Wong, "Exclusive: Nicole Wong Reveals Identity of EA Spouse," *Mercury News* (San Jose, CA), April 25, 2006.

42. J.C. Quick et al., *Preventive Stress Management in Organizations* (Washington, DC: American Psychological Association, 1997), pp. 3–4; R.S. DeFrank and J.M. Ivancevich, "Stress on the Job: An Executive Update," *Academy of Management Executive* 12 (August 1998), pp. 55–66.

43. Quick et al., *Preventive Stress Management in Organizations,* pp. 5–6; B.L. Simmons and D.L. Nelson, "Eustress at Work: The Relationship between Hope and Health in Hospital Nurses," *Health Care Management Review* 26, no. 4 (October 2001), p. 7ff.

44. H. Selye, *Stress without Distress* (Philadelphia: J.B. Lippincott, 1974).

45. S.E. Taylor, R.L. Repetti, and T. Seeman, "Health Psychology: What Is an Unhealthy Environment and How Does It Get under the Skin?" *Annual Review of Psychology* 48 (1997), pp. 411–47.

46. D. Ganster, M. Fox, and D. Dwyer, "Explaining Employees' Health Care Costs: A Prospective Examination of Stressful Job Demands, Personal Control, and Physiological Reactivity," *Journal of Applied Psychology* 86 (May 2001), pp. 954–64; M. Kivimaki et al., "Work Stress and Risk of Cardiovascular Mortality: Prospective Cohort Study of Industrial Employees," *British Medical Journal* 325 (October 19, 2002), pp. 857–60; A. Rosengren et al., "Association of Psychosocial Risk Factors with Risk of Acute Myocardial Infarction in 11,119 Cases and 13,648 Controls from 52 Countries (the Interheart Study): Case–Control Study," *The Lancet* 364, no. 9438 (September 11, 2004), pp. 953–62.

47. R.C. Kessler, "The Effects of Stressful Life Events on Depression," *Annual Review of Psychology* 48 (1997), pp. 191–214; L. Greenburg and J. Barling, "Predicting Employee Aggression against Coworkers, Subordinates, and Supervisors: The Roles of Person Behaviors and Perceived Workplace Factors," *Journal of Organizational Behavior* 20 (1999), pp. 897–913; M. Jamal and V.V. Baba, "Job Stress and Burnout among Canadian Managers and Nurses: An Empirical Examination," *Canadian Journal of Public Health* 91, no. 6 (November–December 2000), pp. 454–58; L. Tourigny, V.V. Baba, and T.R. Lituchy, "Job Burnout among Airline Employees in Japan: A Study of the Buffering Effects of Absence and Supervisory Support," *International Journal of Cross Cultural Management* 5, no. 1 (April 2005), pp. 67–85.

48. K. Danna and R.W. Griffin, "Health and Well-Being in the Workplace: A Review and Synthesis of the Literature," *Journal of Management,* Spring 1999, pp. 357–84.

49. New South Wales Supreme Court, *Naidu v. Group 4 Securitas Pty Ltd & Anor,* (NSWSC, June 24, 2005).

50. This is a slight variation of the definition in the Quebec antiharassment legislation. See www.cnt.gouv.qc.ca. For related definitions and discussion of workplace incivility, see H. Cowiea et al., "Measuring Workplace Bullying," *Aggression and Violent Behavior* 7 (2002), pp. 33–51; C.M. Pearson and C.L. Porath, "On the Nature, Consequences, and Remedies of Workplace Incivility: No Time for 'Nice'? Think Again," *Academy of Management Executive* 19, no. 1 (February 2005), pp. 7–18.

51. D. Turner, "One in Five Staff 'Bullied' in Past 12 Months," *Financial Times* (London), October 2, 2002, p. 5; A. Garrett, "How to Cure Bullying at Work," *Management Today,* May 2003, p. 80; T. Goldenberg, "Thousands of Workers Intimidated on Job: Study," *Montreal Gazette,* June 11, 2005, p. A9; S. Toomey, "Bullying Alive and Kicking," *The Australian,* July 16, 2005, p. 9.

52. V. Schultz, "Reconceptualizing Sexual Harassment," *Yale Law Journal* 107 (April 1998), pp. 1683–1805; M. Rotundo, D.-H. Nguyen, and P. R. Sackett, "A Meta-Analytic Review of Gender Differences in Perceptions of Sexual Harassment," *Journal of Applied Psychology* 86 (October 2001), pp. 914–22. Several U.S. court cases have discussed these two causes for action, including *Lehman v. Toys 'R' Us Inc.* (1993) 132 N.J. 587; 626 A. (2nd) 445; and *Meritor Savings Bank v. Vinson.* 477 U.S. 57 (1986) (U.S.S.C.).

53. B.K. Hunnicutt, *Kellogg's Six-Hour Day* (Philadelphia: Temple University Press, 1996); E. Galinsky et al., *Overwork in America: When the Way We Work Becomes Too Much* (New York: Families and Work Institute, March 2005); R.G. Netemeyer, J.G. Maxham III, and C. Pullig, "Conflicts in the Work–Family Interface: Links to Job Stress, Customer Service Employee Performance, and Customer Purchase Intent," *Journal of Marketing* 69 (April 2005), pp. 130–45.

54. R. Drago, D. Black, and M. Wooden, *The Persistence of Long Work Hours,* Melbourne Institute Working Paper Series (Melbourne: Melbourne Institute of Applied Economic and Social Research, University of Melbourne, August 2005); R. Konrad, "For Some Techies, an Interminable Workday," *Associated Press Newswires,* May 10, 2005.

55. J. Ryall, "Japan Wakes Up to Fatal Work Ethic," *Scotland on Sunday,* June 15, 2003, p. 22; C.B. Meek, "The Dark Side of Japanese Management in the 1990s: Karoshi and Ijime in the Japanese Workplace," *Journal of Managerial Psychology* 19, no. 3 (2004), pp. 312–31.

56. L. Wahyudi S., "Traffic Congestion Makes Me Crazy," *Jakarta Post,* March 18, 2003. The effect of traffic congestion on stress is reported in G.W. Evans, R.E. Wener, and D. Phillips, "The Morning Rush Hour: Predictability and Commuter Stress," *Environment and Behavior* 34 (July 2002), pp. 521–30.

57. F. Kittel et al., "Job Conditions and Fibrinogen in 14,226 Belgian Workers: The Belstress Study," *European Heart Journal* 23 (2002), pp. 1841–48; S.K. Parker, "Longitudinal Effects of Lean Production on Employee Outcomes and the Mediating Role of Work Characteristics," *Journal of Applied Psychology* 88, no. 4 (2003), pp. 620–34.

58. B. Miller, "Brann Baltimore Marketing Firm's Office Gets a Fun Makeover," *Daily Record,* October 3, 2002.

59. Y. Iwasaki et al., "A Short-Term Longitudinal Analysis of Leisure Coping Used by Police and Emergency Response Service Workers," *Journal of Leisure Research* 34 (July 2002), pp. 311–39; "How Large Firms Make Partner Sabbaticals Both Plausible and Appealing," *Partner's Report for Law Firm Owners,* June 2003, p. 1.

60. M. Waung, "The Effects of Self-Regulatory Coping Orientation on Newcomer Adjustment and Job Survival," *Personnel Psychology* 48 (1995), pp. 633–50; A.M. Saks and B.E. Ashforth, "Proactive Socialization and Behavioral Self-Management," *Journal of Vocational Behavior* 48 (1996), pp. 301–23.

61. W.M. Ensel and N. Lin, "Physical Fitness and the Stress Process," *Journal of Community Psychology* 32, no. 1 (January 2004), pp. 81–101.

62. S. Armour, "Rising Job Stress Could Affect Bottom Line," *USA Today,* July 29, 2003; V.A. Barnes, F.A. Treiber, and M.H. Johnson, "Impact of Transcendental Meditation on Ambulatory Blood Pressure in African-American Adolescents," *American Journal of Hypertension* 17, no. 4 (2004), pp. 366–69; M.S. Lee et al., "Effects of Qi-Training on Anxiety and Plasma Concentrations of Cortisol, ACTH, and Aldosterone: A Randomized Placebo-Controlled Pilot Study," *Stress and Health* 20, no. 5 (2004), pp. 243–48; P. Manikonda et al., "Influence of Non-Pharmacological Treatment (Contemplative Meditation and Breathing Technique) on Stress Induced Hypertension —a Randomized Controlled Study," *American Journal of Hypertension* 18, no. 5, Supplement 1 (2005), pp. A89-A90.

63. J. Newman and D. Grigg, "Vancity's Robbery Intervention Program Wins Award," *Vancouver Sun,* October 16, 2004, p. J3.

64. T. Rotarius, A. Liberman, and J.S. Liberman, "Employee Assistance Programs: A Prevention and Treatment Prescription for Problems in Health Care Organizations," *Health Care Manager* 19 (September 2000), pp. 24–31; J.J.L. van der Klink et al., "The Benefits of Interventions for Work-Related Stress," *American Journal of Public Health* 91 (February 2001), pp. 270–76.

65. S.E. Taylor et al., "Biobehavioral Responses to Stress in Females: Tend-and-Befriend, Not Fight-or-Flight," *Psychological Review* 107, no. 3 (July 2000), pp. 411–29; R. Eisler and D.S. Levine, "Nurture, Nature, and Caring: We Are Not Prisoners of Our Genes," *Brain and Mind* 3 (2002), pp. 9–52.

66. J.S. House, *Work Stress and Social Support* (Reading, MA: Addison-Wesley, 1981).

67. S. Schachter, *The Psychology of Affiliation* (Palo Alto, CA: Stanford University Press: 1959).

68. J.L. Howard, "Workplace Violence in Organizations: An Exploratory Study of Organizational Prevention Techniques," *Employee Responsibilities and Rights Journal* 13 (June 2001), pp. 57–75.

69. W.G. Bennis and R.J. Thomas, *Geeks and Geezers* (Boston: Harvard Business School Press, 2002), pp. 74–79; E.D.Y. Greenblatt, "Work–Life Balance: Wisdom or Whining," *Organizational Dynamics* 31, no. 2 (2002), pp. 177–93.

70. Ipsos-Reid, "What Are Canadians' Top Indicators of Career Success?" Ipsos-Reid news release (Toronto: May 7, 2003); Catalyst, *Beyond a Reasonable Doubt: Building the Business Case for Flexibility* (Toronto: Catalyst, April 2005); "Seventeen Percent of Government Workers Plan to Look for a New Job in 2006, Careerbuilder.Com Survey Finds," *PR Newswire*, February 21, 2006; "Work Loses Out to Family," *The Mirror* (London), March 18, 2006, p. 8; S. Shellenbarger, "Forget Vacation Time, New Grads Want Stability and a Good Retirement Plan," *The Wall Street Journal*, February 16, 2006, p. D1.

71. J. Thottam, "Reworking Work," *Time*, July 25, 2005, pp. 50–53.

72. P. Szuchman, "The Job-Share Advantage," *Working Mother* 25 (May 2002), p. 15.

73. "Driving Ambitions," *Employee Benefits*, September 6, 2002, p. 45. More than 100 countries have paid maternity leave. Among the industrialized countries, only the United States, Australia, and New Zealand do not provide this support. See T. Allard and L. Glendinning, "For Now, Aussie Mums Are Still a World Apart," *Sydney Morning Herald*, August 16, 2001; J. Satterfield, "U.S. Lags Behind Other Nations on Family Leave," *Knoxville News-Sentinel*, May 7, 2001, p. A1. For discussion of the FMLA, see S. Kim, "Toward Understanding Family Leave Policy in Public Organizations: Family Leave Use and Conceptual Framework for the Family Leave Implementation Process," *Public Productivity & Management Review* 22 (September 1998), pp. 71–87.

74. J. Gannon, "The Perfect Commute," *Post-Gazette* (Pittsburgh, PA), April 24, 2003, p. E1.

75. G. Marr, "Home Is Not Where the Office Is," *National Post*, August 6, 2004, p. FP10; Australian Telework Advisory Committee (ATAC), *Telework in Australia: Paper II* (Canberra: Commonwealth of Australia, March 2005); Australian Telework Advisory Committee (ATAC), *Telework-International Developments: Paper III* (Canberra: Commonwealth of Australia, March 2005); D. Bricker and J. Wright, *What Canadians Think about Almost Everything* (Toronto: Doubleday Canada, 2005); J. Cummings, "Masters of a Virtual World," *Network World*, April 25, 2005, pp. 76–77. These estimates exclude employees who bring work home from the office because this practice isn't usually considered virtual work.

76. L. Duxbury and C. Higgins, "Telecommute: A Primer for the Millennium Introduction," in *The New World of Work: Challenges and Opportunities*, ed. C.L. Cooper and R.J. Burke (Oxford: Blackwell, 2002), pp. 157–99; V. Illegems and A. Verbeke, "Telework: What Does It Mean for Management?" *Long Range Planning* 37 (2004), pp. 319–34; S. Raghuram and B. Wiesenfeld, "Work-Nonwork Conflict and Job Stress among Virtual Workers," *Human Resource Management* 43, no. 2–3 (Summer–Fall 2004), pp. 259–77.

77. D.E. Bailey and N.B. Kurland, "A Review of Telework Research: Findings, New Directions, and Lessons for the Study of Modern Work," *Journal of Organizational Behavior* 23 (2002), pp. 383–400; D.W. McCloskey and M. Igbaria, "Does 'Out of Sight' Mean 'Out of Mind'? An Empirical Investigation of the Career Advancement Prospects of Telecommuters," *Information Resources Management Journal* 16 (April–June 2003), pp. 19–34; Sensis, *Sensis® Insights Report: Teleworking* (Melbourne: Sensis, June 2005).

78. This historical review and the trait descriptions in this section are discussed in J.M. Digman, "Personality Structure: Emergence of the Five-Factor Model," *Annual Review of Psychology* 41 (1990), pp. 417–40; M.K. Mount and M.R. Barrick, "The Big Five Personality Dimensions: Implications for Research and Practice in Human Resources Management," *Research in Personnel and Human Resources Management* 13 (1995), pp. 153–200; and R.J. Schneider and L.M. Hough, "Personality and Industrial/Organizational Psychology," *International Review of Industrial and Organizational Psychology* 10 (1995), pp. 75–129.

79. T.A. Judge, E.A. Locke, and C.C. Durham, "The Dispositional Causes of Job Satisfaction: A Core Evaluations Approach," *Research in Organizational Behavior* 19 (1997), pp. 151–88; A.P. Brief and H.M. Weiss, "Organizational Behavior: Affect in the Workplace," *Annual Review of Psychology* 53 (2002), pp. 279–307; D.J. Ozer and V. Benet-Martínez, "Personality and the Prediction of Consequential Outcomes," *Annual Review of Psychology* 57 (2006), pp. 401–21.

80. R.D. Arvey et al., "Genetic Differences on Job Satisfaction and Work Values," *Personality and Individual Differences* 17 (1994), pp. 21–33; J. Schaubroeck, D. C. Ganster, and B. Kemmerer, "Does Trait Affect Promote Job Attitude Stability?" *Journal of Organizational Behavior* 17 (1996), pp. 191–96; C. Dormann and D. Zapf, "Job Satisfaction: A Meta-Analysis of Stabilities," *Journal of Organizational Behavior* 22 (2001), pp. 483–504.

81. S.C. Segerstrom et al., "Optimism Is Associated with Mood, Coping, and Immune Change in Response to Stress," *Journal of Personality & Social Psychology* 74 (June 1998), pp. 1646–55; S.M. Jex et al., "The Impact of Self-Efficacy on Stressor-Strain Relations: Coping Style as an Explanatory Mechanism," *Journal of Applied Psychology* 86 (2001), pp. 401–9.

82. S.S. Luthar, D. Cicchetti, and B. Becker, "The Construct of Resilience: A Critical Evaluation and Guidelines for Future Work," *Child Development* 71, no. 3 (May–June 2000), pp. 543–62; F. Luthans, "The Need for and Meaning of Positive Organizational Behavior," *Journal of Organizational Behavior* 23 (2002), pp. 695–706; G.A. Bonanno, "Loss, Trauma, and Human Resilience: Have We Underestimated the Human Capacity to Thrive after Extremely Aversive Events?" *American Psychologist* 59, no. 1 (2004), pp. 20–28.

83. S.E. Taylor et al., "Psychological Resources, Positive Illusions, and Health," *American Psychologist* 55, no. 1 (January 2000), pp. 99–109.

84. K.M. Connor and J.R.T. Davidson, "Development of a New Resilience Scale: The Connor–Davidson Resilience Scale (CD-RISC)," *Depression and Anxiety* 18, no. 2 (2003), pp. 76–82; M.M. Tugade, B.L. Fredrickson, and L. Feldman Barrett, "Psychological Resilience and Positive Emotional Granularity: Examining the Benefits of Positive Emotions on Coping and Health," *Journal of Personality* 72, no. 6 (2004), p. 1161–90; L. Campbell-Sills, S.L. Cohan, and M.B. Stein, "Relationship of Resilience to Personality, Coping, and Psychiatric Symptoms in Young Adults," *Behaviour Research and Therapy*, in press (2006).

85. T.A. Judge and R. Ilies, "Relationship of Personality to Performance Motivation: A Meta-Analytic Review," *Journal of Applied Psychology* 87, no. 4 (2002), pp. 797–807; A. Witt, L.A. Burke, and M.R. Barrick, "The Interactive Effects of Conscientiousness and Agreeableness on Job Performance," *Journal of Applied Psychology* 87 (February 2002), pp. 164–69.

86. J. Tupponce, "Listening to Those Inner Voices," *Richmond Times-Dispatch*, May 11, 2003, p. S3.

87. J.L. Holland, *Making Vocational Choices: A Theory of Careers* (Englewood Cliffs, NJ: Prentice-Hall, 1973).

88. G.D. Gottfredson and J.L. Holland, "A Longitudinal Test of the Influence of Congruence: Job Satisfaction, Competency Utilization, and Counterproductive Behavior," *Journal of Counseling Psychology* 37 (1990), pp. 389–98; A. Furnham, "Vocational Preference and P–O Fit: Reflections on Holland's Theory of Vocational Choice," *Applied Psychology: An International Review* 50 (2001), pp. 5–29.

89. G.D. Gottfredson, "John L. Holland's Contributions to Vocational Psychology: A Review and Evaluation," *Journal of Vocational Behavior* 55, no. 1 (1999), pp. 15–40.

15

MANAGING THROUGH POWER, INFLUENCE, AND NEGOTIATION

Genentech campus in San Francisco, CA.
© Getty Images

Susan Desmond-Hellmann, president of product development at biotech pioneer Genentech, is regarded as one of the most powerful women in business. For Genentech, 2004 and 2005 were banner years—the company had four new drugs approved by the Federal Drug Administration and positive results from five important clinical trials. Much of the credit for this unprecedented hot streak has been given to Hellmann. Trained as an oncologist, Hellmann joined Genentech in 1995. When Genentech's CEO, Arthur Levinson, wanted the company to move into cancer drugs, Hellmann, one of the few oncologists on staff, was put in charge of the fledgling cancer program. Levinson "promoted her very, very quickly, many times over." He cited her willingness to work 70- to 80-hour weeks and to accept responsibility for success or failure, as well as her good rapport with people. Hellmann oversaw clinical trails for Avastin, Genentech's breakthrough anticancer drug. Although the early trials went well, a large breast cancer trial in 2002 yielded disappointing results. Stock analysts urged Genentech to halt the Avastin program and "stop throwing good money after bad." Hellmann disagreed. After rereading the results of earlier trials, she decided that Avastin held promise in treating colon cancer and urged the company to push on with a large trial for this. In May 2003 Genentech announced positive results from this trial, which showed that the drug slowed tumor growth and prolonged patient survival. Avastin turned out to be the most successful oncology product launch in history, generating $676 million in its first year on the market.

Susan Desmond-Hellmann has accumulated considerable power and influence at Genentech. As head of product development, she bears primary responsibility for drug development, the lifeblood of a biotech company like Genentech. Hellmann's is one of the most important voices in the organization when it comes to deciding how to allocate scarce resources—money and people—between different drug development projects. How did she get to this position? She did it through her expertise, hard work, people skills, willingness to take responsibility for critical decisions, and willingness to make tough calls—such as the decision to go ahead with the Avastin trials in the face of external and internal opposition. These attributes have made Hellmann a very effective manager, someone who can get remarkable things done through other people. That she was shown to be correct in the case of Avastin has only increased her power and influence.[1]

This chapter is about how managers get things done in organizations through the exercise of power and influence and with their negotiating skills. You will recall from Chapter 1 how newly appointed frontline managers must learn how to influence subordinates, peers, and their own bosses.[2] The formal power from hierarchical position is a limited source influence in organizations, and power and influence are often assembled through interpersonal networks of allies. Also in Chapter 1 we discussed how negotiation is a way of life for managers: They are constantly negotiating with others inside and outside the organization to get things done.[3] As we will see, negotiation skills are a vehicle by which managers can translate power into influence over others and achieve their goals. To explore these issues, we start by discussing the sources of power in organizations. Then we look at how managers can use power to exercise influence within an organization. We close with a discussion of what is required to be an effective negotiator.

■ // Power in Organizations

power

The potential of a person, team, or organization to require others to do certain things.

Power derives from the *potential* of a person, team, or organization to require others to do certain things.[4] The stress on the word *potential* is important. People with power may not have to exercise it to get things done. Just the fact that they have power is often sufficient to enable them to influence others to do certain things. The most basic prerequisite of power is that one person or group believes it is dependent on another person or group for something of value.[5] For example, person A has power over person B by controlling something of value that person B needs to achieve his or her goals (see Figure 15.1). You might have power over others by controlling access to resources, information, or even the privilege of being associated with you! Susan Desmond-Hellmann, for example, has power over other researchers in her organization because she controls access to the financial resources they need to fund drug development projects.

countervailing power

Power that subordinates have over their superiors.

Power is not a one-way street; while a manager has power over her subordinates, they in turn can have **countervailing power** over her. A manager needs her employees to work productively, and this gives her employees countervailing power. Subordinates have a number of avenues through which they can exercise countervailing power. For example, they can silently protest what they see as an unjust use of power by working less diligently; they can complain about abuses to their manager's boss; and they can quit and work elsewhere.

Power is often perceptual. People can gain power over others by convincing them that they have something of value. For example, a celebrity probably has power over noncelebrities in her social circle because they might perceive themselves as gaining status by being associated with the celebrity. In such cases perception is reality.

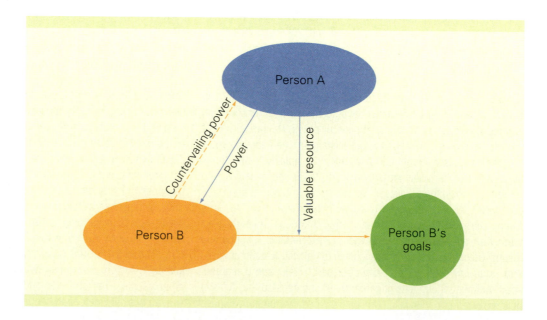

FIGURE 15.1

Power Dependence

Power has received a lot of bad press. In the 19th century Britain's Lord Acton made the famous statement that "power tends to corrupt; absolute power corrupts absolutely." Americans in particular are ambivalent about power and are often reluctant to talk about it. Sociologist Rosabeth Moss Kanter has written, "Power is America's last dirty word. It is easier to talk about money—and much easier to talk about sex—than it is to talk about power. People who have it deny it; people who want it do not want to appear to hunger for it; and people who engage in its machinations do so secretly"[6] Yet, Kanter concludes, power is a critical element in effective managerial behavior. Without power, it is difficult to get things done in organizations. Management author John Kotter makes a similar point. "The overall feeling toward power (in America), which can easily be traced to the nation's very birth, is negative." Yet he too notes that the judicious use of power is important for success in management, noting that "from my own observations, I suspect that a large number of managers—especially the young, well-educated ones—perform significantly below their potential because they have not nurtured and developed the instincts needed to effectively acquire and use power."[7]

Why is power so important to management effectiveness? The answer is that organizations are fundamentally political entities in which different people or units control scarce resources—including money, employee time, and information.[8] To meet her goals, a manager has to recognize that she is dependent on others whose cooperation is needed to get things done. She has to work within the existing distribution of power and accumulate power of her own so she can influence those who control valuable scarce resources needed for the performance of her job. As a frontline manager in Genentech's research organization, for example, Susan Desmond-Hellmann had to persuade her superiors to allocate valuable resources—money, scientists, and lab space—to the cancer project she was overseeing. Over time, by virtue of her hard work, expertise, and engaging people skills, she gained the respect of the CEO, Arthur Levinson, which increased her perceived power in the organization and improved her ability to bargain for resources. She also gained more power through promotions, enabling her to exercise greater control over Genentech's destiny.

Power itself is value-neutral: It is neither good nor bad. What is important is how power is accumulated and used. Power should not be accumulated through unfair or dishonest means or used in an unethical manner. However, power can be accumulated through honest and fair means, and it can be used constructively to do good things in organizations and society in general. Hitler and Gandhi both had power; Hitler used his power to impose terrible suffering on others, whereas Gandhi used his power to liberate an entire nation from British imperial rule. Power did not corrupt Hitler—he was deranged from the start. In contrast, for individuals with a strong ethical foundation such as Gandhi, the accumulation of power may be the only way to achieve ends that are beneficial via means that are not bad. This is not to deny that power does *tend* to corrupt; but that tendency can be held in check if managers have strong personal ethics and if the organizations within which they work promote ethical behavior (see Chapter 4 for details).

Power Tends to Corrupt So said Lord Acton, the 19th-century British historian. Many commentators have misinterpreted Acton's statement, taking it to imply that the possession of power always corrupts the power holder, which is not the case. In reality, the judicious exercise of power is an important skill for managers.

© Bettmann/Corbis

// Sources of Power

If a manager is to accumulate and use power, he or she first has to understand where power comes from. In organizations, power comes from formal position within a hierarchy, from expertise, from control over valuable information, from a network of allies, and from individual attributes.[9] The degree to which these factors confer power on an individual or unit also depends on certain contingencies, including substitutability, centrality, discretion, and visibility (see Figure 15.2).

// FORMAL HIERARCHICAL POSITION

Hierarchical rank within an organization obviously determines power. A CEO has more power than a functional vice president, and a vice president has more power than a frontline manager. Hierarchical power comes from a number of sources: legitimate power, power over rewards and sanctions, and power over the allocation of scarce resources.

FIGURE 15.2

Sources and
Contingencies of Power

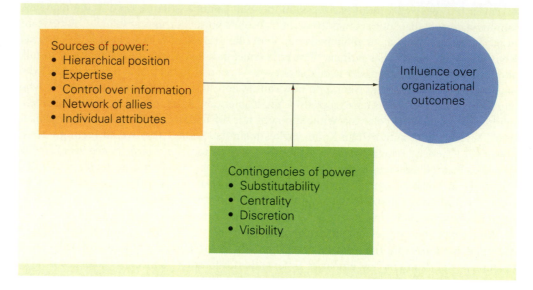

legitimate power

Power deriving from an
implicit agreement that
people higher in a
hierarchy can request
certain behaviors of their
subordinates.

Legitimate Power Legitimate power derives from an implicit agreement among organization members that people higher up in a hierarchy can ask certain behaviors of their subordinates. A frontline manager, for example, can request that employees under his supervision work overtime if conditions warrant. Similarly, a marketing manager at Microsoft will no doubt accept the legitimate power that the CEO, Steve Ballmer, has to send him to meet an important customer in Beijing. For the most part, legitimate power comes not from formal job descriptions, but from the well-understood social norm that those higher up in an organization have the right to direct their subordinates.

However, legitimate power is bounded by laws, formal company rules, and established norms, as well as by managers' need to get subordinates to accept their legitimacy. Laws limit what managers can do. It is illegal, for example, for a manager to instruct a subordinate to alter accounting statements to hide a company's debt from investors. Company rules and norms similarly constrain power. Thus a company may have negotiated certain work agreements with labor unions, and those agreements might restrict the tasks a manager can assign. Similarly, company norms may forbid a manager from telling employees how they should dress. The need for subordinates to accept managers' legitimacy is also a strong factor limiting managerial power. If leaders act outside of what is implicitly accepted by their subordinates as legitimate, subordinates can exercise their countervailing power by refusing to comply, appealing to a higher authority for redress, working slowly, walking away from the job, or staging a strike.

Power over Rewards and Sanctions Hierarchical rank lets managers shape the incentive and control systems within an organization and administer rewards and sanctions. Managers can reward behavior that they deem consistent with company goals and punish those whose performance is below par. Rewards can take the form of pay increases, bonuses, promotions, and other benefits. Punishments include denying the same, and perhaps dismissal.

Like legitimate power, power over rewards and sanctions is often bounded by laws, norms, and a need to maintain legitimacy. Terminated employees can sue managers for unfair dismissal if they believe the managers have overstepped their power. In 2006, for example, three former brokers at Merrill Lynch won a total of $14 million in damages after a court decided that the company had overstepped its power when firing them in the wake of a trading scandal. The brokers had been helping a client to trade mutual funds after a 4 p.m. deadline established by the company; but according to them, Merrill knew what they were doing and applied sanctions only when the government started to investigate the practice. They were, in the words of one, "sacrificial lambs." The court apparently agreed.[10]

■ Overstepping power at Merrill Lynch.

More generally, if the administration of rewards and sanctions is seen as unjust or biased in some way, the administrating managers can lose their legitimacy. To ensure that reward and sanction systems are fair and do not involve bias, favoritism, or coercion, many firms now use 360-degree performance evaluation systems in which subordinates review the performance of their bosses, giving them some countervailing power.

Power over Scarce Resources The allocation of scarce resources can be an important source of hierarchical power. Scarce resources include, but are not limited to, capital, people, plant, equipment, and work space. The CEO of a multibusiness company such as United Technology, for example, derives considerable power from the ability to allocate capital between competing requests of different divisions. Similarly, as head of product development at Genentech, Susan Desmond-Hellmann must allocate scarce scientific and financial resources between drug development projects, which gives her considerable power to shape the drug development pipeline at Genentech.

The power that comes from control over scarce resources has been summarized in what is termed the "new golden rule"—*he who has the gold makes the rules*.[11] Of course it is not that simple. The need to maintain legitimacy and resulting countervailing power remains an important constraint on management action. If Hellmann were to allocate money to projects that had shown poor results in clinical trails, she would soon lose legitimacy among other scientists at Genentech, and that would quickly undermine her power.

// EXPERTISE

Knowledge is power as the saying goes, and this is certainly true in organizations. Expertise in a particular area can give a person considerable power. Susan Desmond-Hellmann started to gain power within Genentech because she was one of the few people with oncology expertise in the organization when Arthur Levinson decided to push the company toward cancer research. In another example, the CFO of WorldCom, Scott Sullivan, wielded enormous personal power in that organization. Sullivan's power came from more than his hierarchical rank. It also came from his expertise in arcane accounting regulations and complex financial transactions. Sullivan was considered a "whiz kid" who had won a prestigious "CFO Excellence Award." Thus when Sullivan asked accounting staff to make questionable entries, they assumed Sullivan had found an innovative—and legal—accounting loophole. Unfortunately Sullivan, along with CEO Bernie Ebbers, was engaging in an $11 billion accounting fraud to inflate WorldCom's earnings and boost the company's stock price (from which Sullivan and Ebbers profited handsomely). When the fraud was uncovered, WorldCom collapsed into bankruptcy. Ebbers and Sullivan ended up in jail.[12]

■ Expert power at WorldCom.

Management writer Peter Drucker has theorized that as our society moves from industry toward a knowledge-based economy, more employees are gaining expert power.[13] In industries from biotechnology to computer software, employee knowledge is becoming the pivotal factor of production. This knowledge is ultimately outside the control of those who manage the company, making them more dependent on powerful expert employees to achieve their corporate objectives.

// CONTROL OVER INFORMATION

It is often said that information is power.[14] This phrase is increasingly relevant in a knowledge-based economy because information is the basis of knowledge. Power, however, derives not so much from information per se as from the ability to control the flow of information within an organization. People who are located at a central node in a communication

Countervailing Power Former WorldCom CEO Scott Sullivan is shown in handcuffs. Sullivan, whose expert power propelled him to the CFO post, ultimately served jail time for abusing that power and helping to mastermind the largest accounting fraud in U.S. history.

© Getty Images

network are in a particularly powerful position. They can act as information gatekeepers, scanning and selectively releasing information in a manner that is consistent with attaining their goals. In the language of politics, they can "spin" the information. They can also use preferential access to information to increase their knowledge and argue more persuasively for policies, programs, or strategies they advocate. Information also helps an organization cope better with change and uncertainty in the external environment, and those who control such information may enjoy significant power.[15] For example, a marketing researcher who understands changes in consumer preferences and future demand trends may be able to leverage that information to gain power and influence within the organization. Information thus confers an advantage to those that have it. Consistent with this view, management researchers have found that centrality in a communication network is positively correlated with an enhanced chance of being promoted, an increase in that person's reputation for power within an organization, and higher pay.[16]

■ Information and Power at SAP.

In an interesting example of the value of centrality, a few years ago SAP, the German business software company, introduced innovative ways for employees to receive the latest company news through their car radios, e-mail newsletters, and intranet sites. SAP employees appreciated this direct communication, but the company's middle managers objected because it undermined their power as the gatekeepers of company information.[17] Previously SAP's middle managers had distributed, regulated, and filtered information throughout the organizational hierarchy. They derived power from this central position, and their power was diminished by the adoption of new methods for information dissemination.

The right to control information flow is a form of legitimate power and is most common in highly bureaucratic firms. The wheel formation in Figure 15.3 depicts this highly centralized control over information flow. In this communication structure, employees depend on the information gatekeeper in the middle of this configuration—such as the middle managers at SAP—to provide the information they require. However, in today's knowledge-based economy the problem facing information gatekeepers is that a centralized information control structure may be incompatible with knowledge management and high-performance work teams. Consequently, SAP and other organizations are encouraging more knowledge sharing by moving toward an all-channel communication structure (see Figure 15.3) in which all employees enjoy relatively equal access to information. This structure democratizes information, allowing

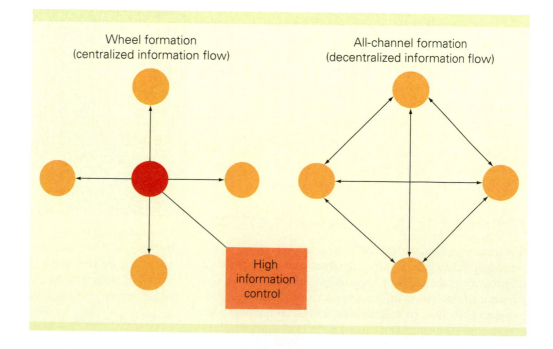

FIGURE 15.3

Power through Information Control

employees and self-directed work teams to make better decisions while reducing the power of information gatekeepers. In its purest form, however, the all-channel network may seem chaotic, so large organizations with bureaucratic cultures tend to slip back into the wheel pattern. The wheel pattern also reemerges because, as we saw at SAP, it confers more power on those who distribute the information.[18]

// NETWORKS OF ALLIES

It is not only *what* you know that matters, it is also *whom* you know. An important source of power in organizations is a network of allies, or supporters, who can help you get things done.[19] You may recall from Chapter 1 how first-year managers discovered that building an interpersonal network was an important prerequisite for mastering the job. Skilled managers put together coalitions of supporters who work collectively to pursue a particular objective, such as the adoption of a strategy or process. A key to building and maintaining a network of allies is *reciprocity*. Put simply, to get somebody to help you, you have to be prepared to help him or her in some way. Reciprocal social exchanges help build and hold together a network of allies.[20]

For example, as a young political staffer, former U.S. President Lyndon Johnson apparently went out of his way to cultivate a network of powerful friends. These included Sam Rayburn, one of the most powerful congressional representatives of the 20th century. Rayburn, a fellow Texan and a bachelor, was a lonely man. The Johnsons frequently invited him to their home. Through his connection with Rayburn, Johnson participated in informal gatherings of powerful figures in Washington, which opened doors for the ambitious young Texan. Johnson also derived power from his association with Rayburn: As a friend of Rayburn, Johnson was not somebody to take lightly.[21]

// INDIVIDUAL ATTRIBUTES

There is no doubt that individual attributes are an important source of personal power (see Figure 15.4). Several attributes have been identified as important for acquiring and holding power in an organization:

1. Energy, endurance, and physical stamina.
2. The ability to focus one's energy and avoid wasted effort.
3. Empathy, which makes it possible to read and understand others.
4. Flexibility, particularly with respect to selecting various means to achieve one's goals.
5. The willingness, when necessary, to engage in conflict and confrontation.
6. Eloquence—the ability to make points in a logical and evocative fashion.
7. Integrity.[22]

Consider again Susan Desmond-Hellmann. In addition to her expertise, her rise within Genentech was in part due to her willingness to work long hours—requiring energy, endurance, and physical stamina. Similarly, the young Lyndon Johnson displayed enormous energy and endurance. He got to work earlier than other congressional staffers, did not stop for lunch, and often worked past eight in the evening.

The ability to discern what is important and focus time and effort on that is another critical skill. In a study of successful general managers, John Kotter found that those who had focused on one industry, and in one company, tended to be more successful.[23]

Empathy—the ability to understand the beliefs, desires, and motives of others—can be a particularly important attribute when it comes to assembling a network of allies. Lyndon Johnson's empathy toward Sam Rayburn allowed him to recruit the older man as a valuable ally. Similarly, the rapport Susan Desmond-Hellmann enjoys with other people is probably due to empathy.

Flexibility is the opposite of stubbornness. Flexibility is the ability to recognize that there are multiple ways to achieve a goal and that if one method is failing, it may be better to try another

FIGURE 15.4

Individual Attributes as Sources of Power

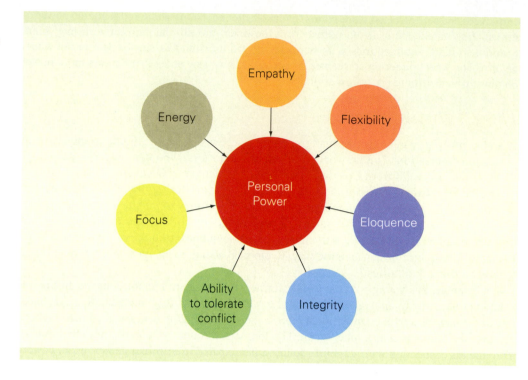

route. Susan Desmond-Hellmann demonstrated flexibility when Genentech's Avastin failed in a late-stage clinical trial for treating breast cancer. After reviewing data, she pushed Avastin ahead in another clinical trial for treating colon cancer, which ultimately produced strong results.

A willingness to engage in conflict when necessary—to be tough—can be an important source of personal power. This does not mean you should be habitually difficult, stubborn, or argumentative. Rather, it implies a need to take a stand on important issues, particularly when the facts are on your side. If you shy away from conflict, you are not likely to get your way; you may be pushed around by individuals who are more assertive; and your power will be diminished. Lyndon Johnson did not avoid conflict when it was necessary; and by signaling to others that he was willing to fight for certain things, Johnson deterred others from moving against him because they feared the consequences.

The ability to communicate in an eloquent fashion is important because it helps make people listen to you—and people who are listened to have power. The expert who mumbles incoherently and does not explain his position in a precise and logical fashion is unlikely to accumulate much power and influence in an organization, no matter how valuable his expertise. Conversely, an eloquent expert can become uniquely powerful. Such people can use their knowledge, and the power of words, to influence the destiny of an organization. The great physicist Richard Feynman was a powerful figure in every organization he was associated with—from Los Alamos, where he worked on the Manhattan Project, to the independent commission looking at the failure of the *Challenger* space shuttle. His power derived not just from his expertise, which was considerable, but also from his eloquent ability to use words to capture the attention of others.[24]

Finally, integrity can be a source of power, particularly when coupled with other sources of power such as expertise. People with integrity gain the respect and trust of others. They build a reputation for being just, reasonable, and incorruptible, which increases their social capital. People with integrity can better build a network of allies, because people are more likely to enter reciprocal exchanges with somebody who has a reputation for integrity. Moreover, the opinions of people who have a reputation for behaving with integrity will be given greater weight than those with a reputation for duplicity, whose opinions may be perceived as self-serving.

The Eloquent Expert Richard Feynman was placed on the commission that looked into the *Challenger* disaster not just because of his expertise, but also because of his eloquence, which had brought him to national attention. As a member of that commission, he famously demonstrated how failure of an O-ring had caused the disaster, and showed how management at NASA had massively underestimated the probability of O-ring failure.

© Time Life Pictures/Getty Images.   © AP Photo/Bruce Weaver

// Contingencies of Power

Imagine that you have expert power by virtue of your ability to forecast and possibly even prevent dramatic changes in the organization's environment. Does this expertise mean that you are influential? Not necessarily! Power is translated into influence over organizational outcomes only under certain conditions. Called the *contingencies of power,* these four conditions are substitutability, centrality, discretion, and visibility.[25] These contingencies are not sources of power; rather they determine the extent to which people can leverage the power they have to make things happen within organizations. You may have lots of expert power, but you will not be able to influence others with this power base if the contingency factors are not in place.

Substitutability refers to the availability of alternatives. Power is strongest when someone has a monopoly over an important resource that has no substitutes. Conversely, power decreases as the number of alternative sources of the critical resource increases. If you are the only person in an organization with expertise on an issue, you will be more powerful than if several other people in your company possess this expertise. Substitutability refers not only to other sources that offer the same resource, but also to substitutes for the resource itself. For instance, the power of labor unions is diminished when companies introduce technologies that replace the need for their union members. At one time a strike by telephone employees would have shut down operations in a telephone company; but computerized systems and other technological innovations that have reduced the need for telephone operators and other personnel let telephone companies continue offering service during labor strikes. Technology can be a substitute for employees and consequently can reduce union power.

Centrality refers to the degree and nature of interdependence between the power holder and others.[26] Public transportation workers have high centrality in cities that rely on public transportation (such as New York) because their actions affect many people quickly. If they go on strike, they can shut down a city. Think about your own centrality for a moment: If you decided not to show up for work or school tomorrow, how many people would be affected, and how much time would pass before they were affected? If you have high centrality, many people in the organization would be affected adversely and immediately by your absence. If you have very low centrality, no one would be affected.

Discretion refers to the freedom to exercise judgment—to make decisions without referring to a specific rule or receiving permission from someone else. Discretion, or autonomy, is another important contingency of power in organizations. Consider the plight of firstline supervisors. It may seem that they have hierarchical power over employees, but this power can be

substitutability
The availability of alternative resources.

centrality
The degree and nature of interdependence between the power holder and others.

discretion
The freedom to exercise judgment—to make decisions without referring to a specific rule or receiving permission from someone else.

curtailed by specific rules. Such lack of discretion reduces the power of supervisors, even though they may have access to some of the power bases described earlier in this chapter. "Middle managers are very much 'piggy-in-the-middle,'" complains a middle manager at Britain's National Health System. "They have little power, only what senior managers give them."[27]

Visibility refers to the extent to which a power holder is known, or visible, to others. People with expert power who are not visible within the organization may not have much influence; they may not be able to leverage their power to influence organizational outcomes. For example, several years ago as a junior copywriter at an advertising agency, Mimi Cook submitted an idea for a potential client to her boss, who then presented it to the agency's founder, Jay Chiat. Chiat was thrilled with the concept, but Cook's boss "never mentioned the idea came from me," recalls Cook. Cook confronted her boss, who claimed the oversight was unintentional. However, when a similar incident occurred a few months later, Cook left the agency for another firm.[28] Cook's problem was that she was not visible within the organization. Cook, who has since progressed to become associate creative director at another ad agency, knows that power does not flow to unknown people in the organization. Those who control valued resources or knowledge can use that power only when others are aware of them, which requires visibility. One way to increase visibility is to take people-oriented jobs and work on projects that require frequent interaction with senior executives. "You can take visibility in steps," advises a pharmaceutical executive. "You can start by making yourself visible in a small group, such as a staff meeting. Then when you're comfortable with that, seek out larger arenas."[29]

visibility

The extent to which a power holder is known, or visible, to others.

■ // Influence

Power gives a person, team, or unit the *opportunity* to exert influence over organizational outcomes. *Influence* is power in action. Exerting influence means using power to shape the attitudes, behavior, and decisions of others within and outside the organization.[30] Here we look at the various steps managers take to accumulate power and influence others to get things done in organizations. We start with a review of influence tactics, and then we discuss the consequences of applying different influence tactics, looking at preferred tactics.

// INFLUENCE TACTICS

Influence tactics are the steps that people can take to exert influence over others in an organization, thereby achieving their goals. If successfully applied, influence tactics can enable even junior managers who lack substantial sources of power to have an impact on the behavior and decisions of others within their organization, including the CEO. They can shape organizational outcomes.

For example, consider the actions of a young software engineer, William Pearson, who was working in the marketing department of discount broker Charles Schwab in the mid-1990s. At the time the World Wide Web was just emerging as a communication platform for the Internet. Pearson quickly saw the transformational power of the Web and realized that it would make obsolete the clunky proprietary software that Schwab's customers were using to access their accounts online. Using the Web as their platform, discount brokers such as E*Trade were growing rapidly and offering their clients the ability to execute trades online—something Schwab's customers could not do. Pearson thought such companies would soon take market share from Schwab unless Schwab also moved its online business to the Web. Try as he might, however, Pearson could not get his supervisor at Schwab interested. Frustrated, he mentioned his ideas to other managers, but they too took no action. The basic problem was that Pearson had no power within the organization. Even though his vision of the future was correct, he could not influence Schwab's strategy.

Then Pearson contacted a former Schwab manager, Anne Hennegar, who now worked as a consultant to the company. He asked Hennegar for help. She suggested meeting with an executive vice president, Tom Seip, who was known for his aversion to Schwab's bureaucracy. Hennegar contacted Seip, who quickly agreed to the meeting and asked if he could include a couple

influence tactics

Steps that people can take to exert influence over others in an organization.

■ Influence tactics at Charles Schwab.

of "friends." When Hennegar and Pearson turned up for the meeting, they were surprised to find that in addition to Seip, CEO Charles Schwab and COO David Pottruck were there. Pearson demonstrated a Web-based interface for what he called E-Schwab to the assembled senior executives. Within an hour Charles Schwab decided to establish a Web-based platform for Schwab that would let customers trade stocks online. Pearson had succeeded in shifting the strategy of Schwab. He had done this by resorting to a classic influence tactic: appeal to a higher authority. He went outside the normal chain of command and appealed to a senior manager with power and influence who was known for his maverick views, Tom Seip.[31]

Appealing to a higher authority is one of several influence tactics. Others include silent authority, assertiveness, network building, exchange, coalition formation, ingratiation, impression management, persuasion, and information control.[32] These influence tactics are *both a way of accumulating more power within an organization, and a way of using the power that a person has to shape organizational outcomes.* Moreover, with the right influence tactics, even people with limited power can have an impact, as William Pearson did at Schwab.

Silent Authority The silent application of authority (what we call **silent authority**) occurs when someone complies with a request because of the requester's legitimate hierarchical power as well as the target person's role expectations. We often refer to this condition as *deference to authority.*[33] This deference occurs when you comply with your boss's request to complete a particular task. If the task is within your job scope and your boss has the right to make this request, then this influence strategy operates without negotiation, threats, persuasion, or other tactics.

Silent authority is often overlooked as an influence strategy. However, it is a common form of influence in many cultures. Japanese culture, for example, teaches that those lower down in a hierarchy should accept the authority of their superiors. Employees comply with supervisor requests without question because they respect the supervisor's higher authority in the organization.[34] Silent authority can also work through role modeling when a manager tries to influence the action of a subordinate by modeling desired behaviors. One study reported that Japanese managers typically influence subordinates by engaging in the behaviors they want employees to mimic.[35]

Assertiveness In contrast to silent authority, **assertiveness** might be called "vocal authority" because it involves actively applying hierarchical power to influence others. Assertiveness includes persistently reminding subordinates of their obligations, frequently checking their work, confronting them, and using threats of sanctions to force compliance. A manager using assertiveness typically applies or threatens to apply punishment if a subordinate does not comply with requests. Explicit or implicit threats range from job loss to losing face by letting down the team. Extreme forms of assertiveness include blackmailing colleagues, such as by threatening to reveal previously unknown failures unless a person complies with your request. As you might imagine, assertiveness is a rather blunt and unappealing influence tactic, and it can backfire, producing resistance from subordinates.

Network Building We have already discussed how networks of allies can be a source of power and help managers get things done within an organization. As an influence tactic, **network building** involves actively seeking out and establishing relationships with people who may prove useful in the future. We have seen how the young Lyndon Johnson went out of his way to build a network that included powerful people, such as Sam Rayburn, who could help him in the future. Active network builders understand the importance of social relationships. They spend time cultivating people who may be useful, such as by going to events where they are likely to encounter others whom they can incorporate into their network. Good network builders recognize and accept that networking is a two-way street and that norms of reciprocity are important in building and maintaining networks. If you want people to help you, you must be prepared to help them in return—you must engage in exchanges. If you do not, you will be seen as selfish, your reputation will suffer, and the network you have built will dissolve.

silent authority
Occurs when someone complies with a request because of role expectations and the requester's legitimate hierarchical power.

assertiveness
Applying hierarchical power to influence others.

network building
Actively seeking and establishing relationships with people who may prove useful in the future.

exchange
The promise of benefits or resources in exchange for another party's compliance with your request.

Exchange As an influence tactic, **exchange** involves the promise of benefits or resources in exchange for another party's compliance with your request. Exchange is often embedded within networks, and this is how people maintain and use the networks they have built to exert influence. Exchange can involve proactively helping someone in the expectation that the favor will be returned or reminding people of past benefits or favors with the expectation that they will now make up for that debt. Clearly the norm of reciprocity is a central and explicit theme in exchange strategies.

Negotiation, which we discuss more fully later in this chapter, is also an integral part of exchange influence tactics. For instance, you might negotiate with your boss for a day off in return for working a less desirable shift at a future date. Here you are using negotiation to agree on the terms of an exchange. Thus you might propose, "If you give me Friday off, I will work the graveyard shift next week."

coalition
A group of people that comes together to cooperate in attaining a certain goal.

Coalition Formation A **coalition** is a group of people that comes together to cooperate in attaining a certain goal. Coalition formation is closely related to network building and exchange. When people lack sufficient power on their own to influence others in the organization, they might form a coalition of allies who support a proposed change. Often that coalition is drawn from a manager's network, and it may be held together by prior exchanges or the expectation of future exchanges (that is, by norms of reciprocity).

A coalition is influential in three ways.[36] First, it pools the power and resources of many people to gain influence. Second, if large enough, the coalition's mere existence can be a source of power by symbolizing the legitimacy of an issue. In other words, a coalition creates a sense that an issue deserves attention because it has broad support. Third, coalitions can create social cohesion among participants who emotionally identify with it. As such, conditions can become potent forces for changes in norms and behaviors. If a coalition has a broad-based membership drawn from various parts of an organization, it can be particularly effective. Other employees are more likely to identify with a broad-based group and consequently accept the coalition's ideas.

■ American Idol: The use of influence tactics.

Rubbish! That is what several American TV networks apparently thought of the idea for the hit TV show *American Idol* when the show's cocreator, Simon Cowell, pitched it to them. It took the clever use of influence tactics to get the Fox network to sign the show.

© Getty Images

Appeal to a Higher Authority Appeal to a higher authority involves trying to exert influence by passing over your immediate superior and appealing to someone higher in the organization. This is a risky but potentially effective influence tactic. As we saw, a frustrated William Pearson adopted this tactic at Schwab. It is risky because your boss may not appreciate being circumvented and could punish you for this. Before you pursue the strategy, therefore, you should be sure you have a strong case and that attempts to influence outcomes through regular hierarchical channels are not working.

An interesting recent example of the value of appealing to a higher authority concerns the TV show *American Idol,* which was based on a hit British TV show, *Pop Idol.* In 2001 the two promoters behind *Pop Idol,* Simon Cowell and Simon Fuller, tried to persuade American TV networks to license a version of the show. They hired Creative Artists Agency (CAA) to help them pitch *Pop Idol* to American TV networks. In meeting after meeting they met silence and blank looks. Executives at ABC and UPN passed. Finally executives at the Fox TV network in Los Angeles showed some interest, but progress toward signing a deal was slow. To push things along, executives from CAA exploited a connection the agency had with Elisabeth Murdoch, daughter of Rupert Murdoch, the founder and CEO of News Corp., which owns Fox. Elisabeth Murdoch runs a News Corp. subsidiary in Britain, the BSkyB satellite channel. She knew how successful *Pop Idol* had been in Britain. When she heard that executives at Fox were dragging their feet, she quickly called her father, urging him to buy the rights. In turn, Rupert Murdoch called the senior Fox executive in Los Angeles and asked how the deal to sign *Pop Idol* was going. He replied, "We're still looking at it." Murdoch shot back, "Don't look at it. *Buy it!* Right now." The show, *American Idol,* went on to become a huge ratings success for Fox. The decision to sign it at Fox, however, was made only after indirect appeal to a higher authority—in this case CEO Rupert Murdoch—through a contact that had been made via networking: his daughter, Elisabeth Murdoch. Managers at CAA had cleverly hit on the right influence tactic.[37]

Ingratiation Appeals to a higher authority, assertiveness, and coalitions are forceful ways to influence other people. At the opposite extreme is a "soft" influence tactic called **ingratiation**, which involves any attempt to increase the extent to which someone likes you.[38] Ingratiation is a useful influence tactic because as a rule, most people prefer to comply with requests from people they know and like. Flattering your boss in front of others, helping coworkers with their work, exhibiting similar attitudes (such as agreeing with your boss's proposal to change company policies), and seeking the other person's counsel (asking for his or her advice) are all examples of ingratiation. Research has shown that collectively, ingratiation behaviors are better than most other forms of influence at predicting career success as measured by performance appraisal feedback, salaries, and promotions.[39]

Psychologically, ingratiation works by increasing the perceived similarity between a person and the target of the ingratiation effort, which causes the target (your boss for example) to form a more favorable opinion of you. However, it is not quite this simple. People who are obvious in their ingratiation efforts risk losing influence because their behaviors may be considered insincere and self-serving. The terms "apple polishing" and "brown-nosing" are applied to those who ingratiate to excess or in ways that suggest selfish motives for the ingratiation. Research confirms that people who engage in high levels of explicit ingratiation are less influential and less likely to be promoted.[40] There is, in other words, an inverted U-shaped relationship between ingratiation efforts and influence (see Figure 15.5). Moderate ingratiation efforts can increase influence, but excessive ingratiation reduces influence. So ingratiation should be subtle and genuine, not obvious and overdone.

Impression Management Ingratiation is part of an influence tactic known as **impression management**, which is the process of actively shaping our public images.[41] These public images might be crafted as being important, vulnerable, threatening, hardworking, rational, critical, or pleasant. For the most part employees routinely engage in pleasant impression management tactics to satisfy the basic norms of social behavior. Thus they may dress in accordance with established norms, ask others how they are doing, express concerns over bad

ingratiation
Attempts to increase the extent to which someone likes you.

impression management
The process of actively shaping one's public image.

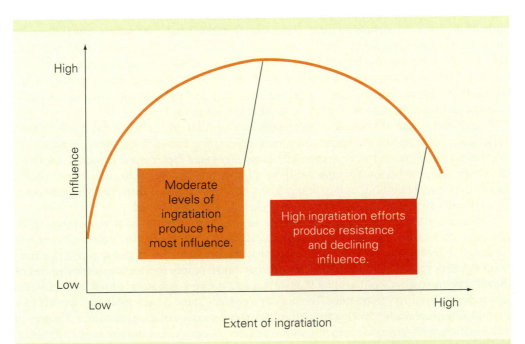

FIGURE 15.5

Ingratiation and Influence

I Have a Dream   Martin Luther King's power to influence the civil rights movement in America came from his ability to shape the attitudes of people through eloquent words that appealed to both reason and emotions.

© AP Photo

■ Joseph Cafasso: Too much impression management.

persuasion

The use of reason through factual evidence and logical arguments.

personal news, offer to help colleagues and customers solve problems, and so on. Impression management is a common strategy for people trying to get ahead in the workplace. An extreme example of impression management occurs when people pad their résumés.

As with ingratiation, employees who use too much impression management tend to be less influential because their behaviors are viewed as insincere.[42] Impression management can also backfire if it involves exaggeration, as in the case of résumé padding. In a recent example, Fox News Channel thought it had found an asset when it hired a gruff, barrel-chested former military man as a consultant to help in its coverage of fighting in Afghanistan. Joseph Cafasso claimed that he had won the Silver Star for bravery, had served in Vietnam, and was part of the secret failed mission to rescue hostages in Iran in 1980. Moreover, Cafasso had an impressive network of contacts in military and political circles that he had built up over the years, including a stint as an organizer for the presidential campaign of Pat Buchanan. However, after more than four months, during which he appeared on Fox News numerous times, he was suddenly dropped from the channel. It had been discovered that his credentials, which people at Fox and elsewhere had taken at face value, were false. Records indicated that his total military experience consisted of 44 days in boot camp in 1976, after which he was honorably discharged as a private, first class![43] Cafasso's fall proves that honesty is best in impression management.

Persuasion   Along with ingratiation, persuasion is one of the most effective influence tactics for career success. The ability to present facts, logical arguments, and emotional appeals to change another person's attitudes and behavior is not just an acceptable way to influence others; in many societies this is a noble art and a quality of effective leaders. The literature on influence tactics has typically described **persuasion** as the use of reason through factual evidence and logical arguments. However, recent studies have begun to adopt a "dual process" perspective in which persuasion is an attempt to influence somebody both by the use of reason and by appeals that evoke an emotional response that leads the listener to identify with the goals of the speaker.[44] The ability to tap into the emotions of others has been shown through history to be a particularly powerful persuasion tactic. Hitler used it, as did Gandhi. President John F. Kennedy encapsulated American foreign policy and evoked an emotional response from the people of Berlin with the phrase "Ich bin ein Berliner," and Martin Luther King moved a nation with his famous "I have a dream" speech. Eloquent words are a source of power and influence not just because they appeal to our rational side, but also because they elicit an emotional response that involves identification with what the speaker is trying to achieve.

The effectiveness of persuasion as an influence tactic depends on characteristics of the persuader, message content, communication medium, and the audience being persuaded.[45] What makes one person more persuasive than another? One factor is the perceived expertise of the speaker. Persuasion attempts are more successful when listeners believe the speaker knows the topic. The ability of the speaker to use eloquent language in an engaging manner is also critically important, as so many great speakers have demonstrated.

Message content can be as important as the messenger is when the issue is important to the audience. Persuasive message content acknowledges several competing points of view and carefully assembles arguments against those that are at variance with the speaker's position. Such an approach elicits more credibility than one that simply ignores competing points of view.[46] The message should also be limited to a few strong arguments, which are repeated a few times but not too frequently. The message content should use emotional appeals (for example, by graphically showing the unfortunate consequences of a bad decision), but only in combination with logical arguments so the audience doesn't feel manipulated. Moreover, emotional appeals directed at a threat should always be accompanied with specific recommendations to overcome the threat. It's not enough, for example, for a manager to state, "This new technology could put us out of business." The manager also needs to show how a project he is proposing could avert this fate. Finally, message content is more persuasive when the audience is warned about opposing arguments. This **inoculation effect** causes listeners to generate counterarguments to the anticipated opposition, which makes any subsequent persuasion attempt by the opposition less effective.[47]

Two other considerations in persuading people are the medium of communication and characteristics of the audience. Generally persuasion works best in face-to-face situations and through other media-rich communication channels. The personal nature of face-to-face communication increases the persuader's credibility, and the richness of this channel provides faster feedback about whether the influence strategy is working. With respect to audience characteristics, it is more difficult to persuade people who have high self-esteem and intelligence, and it is very difficult to change people's attitudes and behaviors if they are strongly connected to their self-images.[48]

Information Control Persuasion typically involves selectively presenting information, whereas information control involves explicitly manipulating others' access to information in order to change their attitudes or behavior. People often trumpet information that presents them in a good light while suppressing information that raises questions about their performance. An example would be the CEO who presents a favorable picture of the company's performance to the board of directors while failing to inform them about negative developments in the business.[49] The problem with this kind of influence tactic is that it can backfire if those who have been denied access to important information discover that they have been deliberately kept in the dark. CEOs, for example, have been fired by boards that discovered they were being misled about the true state of their companies.

// CONSEQUENCES AND CONTINGENCIES

Now that we have reviewed the main tactics used to influence people, you are probably wondering which influence tactics are the most useful. The best way to answer this question is to identify the three ways in which people react when others try to influence them: resistance, compliance, or commitment.[50] **Resistance** occurs when people or work units object to the behavior that somebody with power is requiring of them and refuse to engage in it, argue about it, or try to delay engaging in the behavior. **Compliance** occurs when people comply with a request, but only because they have to, and they exert the minimum level of effort required. They do what they are asked, but that is all. **Commitment** occurs when people identify with the request of somebody trying to influence them and internalize that request, adopting it as their own. Commitment is associated with greater motivation to work toward the ends requested by the influencer. Commitment is thus the strongest consequence of influence and is what the influencer should aim for.

As noted, moderate ingratiation and impression management efforts can produce commitment. However, excessive ingratiation and impression management efforts can produce resistance or at best compliance. Beyond this, in general commitment is more likely when the influencer uses "soft" tactics such as persuasion, network building, and exchange to get things done. "Hard" influence tactics such as assertiveness and appeal to a higher authority might produce compliance but not commitment, and in the worst case they can lead to resistance. For example, research has shown that coalitions are often successful, but their effect may be limited to compliance rather than commitment when the coalition is assertive and threatening in its approach.[51]

This does not mean that hard tactics should not be used; but the evidence suggests that they should be adopted only when soft tactics have failed to produce the desired result, and the issue is important enough to risk resistance. The problem with hard tactics is that they can undermine trust, which can hurt future attempts to get things done through influence. For example, a manager who appeals over the head of her boss directly to the CEO to get backing for a proposal that her boss turned down might get her way; but her immediate boss might

inoculation effect
Warning an audience you are trying to influence about opposing arguments.

resistance
Refusing to perform or delaying engagement in a required behavior.

compliance
Occurs when people comply with a request, but only because they have to.

commitment
Occurs when people identify with the request of somebody trying to influence them and internalize that request, adopting it as their own.

now feel that his authority has been undermined and view that manager with suspicion going forward. Apparently this is what occurred to William Pearson at Schwab. Although Pearson was successful in drawing the attention of top management to the threat posed by the World Wide Web, the meeting with Schwab was the high point of his career. In subsequent performance appraisals Pearson's manager, whose authority had been circumvented, stated that Pearson was "not a team player."[52]

Aside from a general preference for softer influence tactics, a number of contingencies affect the choice of influence tactic. One contingency is the influencer's power base. Those with expertise tend to be more successful at influence when using persuasion, whereas those with a strong hierarchical power base are usually more successful in applying silent authority.[53]

Another important contingency concerns where the target of influence activities is located within the organization. Somebody trying to influence peers should probably focus more on persuasion, network building, exchange, and coalition formation, and less on assertiveness or appeal to a higher authority, both of which might generate resentment among peers. Assertiveness, appeal to a higher authority, and information control are particularly risky tactics when applied to a superior in a hierarchy. But it is more acceptable for superiors to influence their subordinates through information control.

Another contingency of some significance is the personal values of the target, which may be determined by sociocultural factors.[54] A general trend in North America, for example, is toward softer influence tactics because younger employees tend to have more egalitarian values than those nearing retirement. As such, silent authority and assertiveness are tolerated less than a few decades ago. Acceptance of influence tactics also varies across cultures. Canadian and American managers and subordinates alike often rely on persuasion and moderate ingratiation because these techniques minimize conflict and support a trusting relationship. In contrast, managers in Hong Kong rely less on ingratiation, possibly because this tactic disrupts the more distant roles that managers and employees expect in these cultures. Instead influence through exchange tends to be more common and accepted in Asian cultures than in the United States, perhaps due to the long tradition of reciprocity in these cultures.

A final contingency relates to gender. Men and women seem to differ in their use of influence tactics. Men seem more likely than women to rely on direct impression management tactics. Men tend to advertise their achievements and take personal credit for successes of others reporting to them, whereas women are more reluctant to force the spotlight on themselves, often preferring to share the credit with others. At the same time women are more likely to apologize (personally take blame) even for problems not caused by them. Men are more likely to assign blame and less likely to assume it.[55]

conflict

A situation that arises when one party perceives that its interests are being opposed or negatively influenced by another party.

Some research also suggests that women generally have difficulty exerting some forms of influence in organizations, and this has limited their promotional opportunities. In particular, women are viewed as less (not more) influential when they try to influence others by exerting their authority or expertise. In job interviews, for example, direct and assertive female job applicants are less likely to be hired than male applicants using the same influence tactics. Similarly, women who directly disagree in conversations are less influential than women who agree with the speaker.[56] These findings suggest that women may face problems applying hard influence tactics such as assertiveness. Instead, until stereotypes change, women need to rely on softer and more indirect influence strategies, such as ingratiation.

■ // Negotiation: The Art of Conflict Resolution

Conflict is a fact of organizational life. **Conflict** is a situation that arises when one party perceives that its interests are being opposed or negatively influenced by another party.[57] Exercising power and influence within an organization can bring a manager into conflict with other managers who perceive their own goals to be negatively impacted by the action the manager is advocating. Conflicts often arise because resources are limited in organizations, and different people, teams, or units have different views about how scarce resources should be used. Employee preferences for higher pay can conflict with the CEO's desire to reduce costs and boost profits. The wish of the marketing department to spend more on advertising and promotion can conflict with the desire of manufacturing to increase capital investments in new plants and equipment. The desire of a product development team to spend more on accelerating development can conflict with the desire of another team to keep its project on track.

Conflicts can also arise between a firm and other organizations with which it interacts. A firm can find itself in conflict with suppliers and customers over prices and delivery terms, with the government over appropriate regulations, and with labor unions over employment conditions.

Managers spend a lot of time resolving conflicts. They do this through **negotiation**, which is an interpersonal decision-making process by which two or more parties try to reach an agreement over an issue that is being disputed, such as the allocation of scarce resources.[58] For example, through negotiation a marketing department may agree to reduce its request for marketing spending this year, thereby enabling the manufacturing department to purchase new equipment, with the understanding that marketing spending will be increased in the following year. Similarly, through negotiation a firm and its suppliers may agree on pricing terms and delivery schedules.

You will recall from Chapter I that negotiation is one of the crucial roles of management.[59] Negotiating is a way of life for managers.[60] They negotiate with suppliers and customers over prices, with peers over the allocation of shared resources and about cooperative efforts, with their superiors for access to scarce resources such as capital, and with subordinates to assign employees to tasks. How do they do this?

> **negotiation**
>
> An interpersonal decision-making process by which two or more parties try to reach an agreement over an issue that is being disputed, such as the allocation of scarce resources.

// BARGAINING ZONE MODEL OF NEGOTIATIONS

One way of thinking about negotiations is called the *bargaining zone* model, shown in Figure 15.6.[61] This linear diagram illustrates a *win–lose* situation: One side's gain will be the other's loss. However, the bargaining zone model can also be applied to situations in which both sides potentially gain from the negotiations. In *win–win* situations the negotiation revolves around the allocation of gains from the deal being negotiated.

As illustrated in the bargaining zone model, the parties typically establish three main negotiating points. The *initial offer point* is the opening offer to the other party. The *target point* is the manager's realistic goal or expectation for a final agreement. The *resistance point* is the point beyond which the manager will make no further concessions.

The parties begin negotiations by describing their initial offer points for each item on the agenda. In most cases the participants know that this is only a starting point that will change

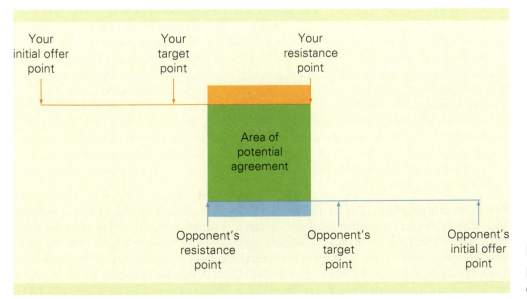

FIGURE 15.6

Bargaining Zone Model of Negotiation

as both sides offer concessions. In win–lose situations neither the target nor the resistance point is revealed to the other party. However, people try to discover the other side's resistance point because this knowledge helps them determine how much they can gain without breaking off negotiations. Put differently, they try to identify an area of potential agreement. When the parties have a win–win orientation, on the other hand, the objective is to find a creative solution that keeps everyone close to their initial offer points. They hope to find an arrangement by which each side loses relatively little value on some issues and gains significantly more on other issues.

// NEGOTIATING EFFECTIVELY

The effectiveness of negotiating depends on the situation, the relative power the parties bring to the negotiating table, and the behaviors of the negotiators. By getting the situation right, accumulating and using power, and engaging in the right behaviors, managers can increase the probability that they will come out of a negotiation with a deal that is close to their target point.

Situational Factors Four of the most important situational factors are location, physical setting, time, and audience. First, it is easier to negotiate on your own turf because you are familiar with the negotiating environment and can maintain comfortable routines.[62] Moreover, there is no need to cope with travel-related stress or depend on others for resources during the negotiation. Of course you can't walk out of negotiations easily at your own location, but this is usually a minor issue. Considering the strategic benefits of home turf, many negotiators agree to neutral territory. Telephones, videoconferences, and other forms of information technology potentially avoid territorial issues, but skilled negotiators usually prefer the media richness of face-to-face meetings.[63]

The physical distance between the parties and formality of the setting can influence their orientation toward each other and the disputed issues. So can the seating arrangements. People who sit face-to-face are more likely to develop a win–lose orientation toward the conflict situation. In contrast, some negotiation groups deliberately intersperse participants around a table to convey a win–win orientation. Others arrange the seating so that both parties face a whiteboard, reflecting the notion that both parties face the same problem or issue.

The more time people invest in negotiations, the stronger their commitment becomes to reaching an agreement. However, the more time put into negotiations, the stronger the tendency to make unwarranted concessions so that the negotiations do not fail. Deadlines may be useful to the extent that they motivate the parties to complete negotiations. However, time pressures are usually a liability in negotiations.[64] One problem is that deadlines give the parties less time to exchange information or present flexible offers. Negotiators under time pressure also process information less effectively, so they have less creative ability to discover a win–win solution to the conflict. There is also anecdotal evidence that negotiators make excessive concessions and soften their demands more than they should as a deadline approaches.

Finally, most negotiators have audiences—anyone with a stake in the negotiation outcomes, such as executives, other team members, or the public. Negotiators tend to act differently when their audience observes the negotiation or has detailed information about the process, compared to situations in which the audience sees only the end results.[65] When the audience has direct surveillance over the proceedings, negotiators tend to be more competitive, less willing to make concessions, and more likely to engage in political tactics against the other party. This "hard-line" behavior shows the audience that the negotiator is working for their interests. With their audience watching, negotiators also have more interest in saving face.

Power and Negotiation The relative distribution of power is an important factor in negotiation. When managers from Wal-Mart and Procter & Gamble sit down to negotiate the price that Wal-Mart will pay for disposable diapers, they are not working as equals. Wal-Mart has more power because it does not need to stock P&G diapers—it can instead sell products from rival companies. P&G, on the other hand, needs Wal-Mart because the company is the largest retailer in the United States, and not selling through Wal-Mart would undoubtedly hurt P&G.

■ Wal-Mart and Procter & Gamble: Power and negotiation.

P&G is more dependent on Wal-Mart than Wal-Mart is on P&G, so Wal-Mart has more power and hence has the upper hand in negotiations.

The relative power that two parties bring to the negotiating table has long been recognized as an important predictor of the outcome of a negotiation.[66] In general, the more power you have, the better you will do in negotiation. Recognizing this, parties to a negotiation often pursue tactics designed to increase their power relative to that of the other party. For example, to increase his power when negotiating with his boss for a pay raise, a manager might seek a job offer from another organization. Because the manager is less dependent on his organization for employment, he can drive a harder bargain. Increasing your options going into a negotiation, and thereby being less dependent on the outcome of the issue under negotiation, is a classic tactic for increasing negotiating power. Other tactics include trying to gain information advantage over the other party, using experts to increase power, or building a coalition of allies that support a negotiating position.

The perception of power can be just as important as actual power in negotiations, so a skilled negotiator might try to create the perception that she has more power than is actually the case. A negotiator can *bluff,* for example, by threatening action that will damage the other party unless the other party agrees to the negotiator's demands. If the other party believes the bluff, this increases the power of the bluffer to drive a hard bargain. Thus in a salary negotiation a manager might threaten to look for another job unless her employer agrees to certain terms. This may be a bluff, but if the employer believes the threat to be credible, the perceived power of the manager has increased.

Behavioral Factors Managers can adopt a number of different behaviors in negotiations to increase their probability of success. First, research has consistently reported that people have more favorable negotiation results when they prepare for the negotiation and set goals.[67] In particular, negotiators should carefully think through their initial offer, target, and resistance points. They also need to consider alternative strategies in case the negotiation fails.

Second, it is important to gather as much information as possible about what the other party wants from the negotiation—to develop an understanding of their goals and likely negotiating tactics. Managers should spend time listening closely to the other party and asking for details.[68] One way to improve the information-gathering process is to have a team of people participate in negotiations. With more people involved in the process, some people can specialize in listening to the negotiation and trying to understand the other party, while others actively participate in the bargaining process. Asian companies tend to have large negotiation teams for this purpose.[69] With more information about the opponent's interests and needs, negotiators are better able to discover low-cost concessions or proposals that will satisfy the other side.

Third, skilled negotiators communicate in a way that maintains effective relationships between the parties. Specifically, they minimize socioemotional conflict by focusing on issues rather than people. Effective negotiators also avoid irritating statements such as "I think you'll agree that this is a generous offer." Effective negotiators are often masters of persuasion. They structure the content of their message so that it is not merely understood but also accepted by others.[70]

Finally, effective negotiators understand the tactical value of making concessions. Concessions are important because they (1) enable the parties to move toward the area of potential agreement, (2) symbolize each party's motivation to bargain in good faith, and (3) tell the other party about the relative importance of the negotiating items.[71] How many concessions should you make? This varies with the other party's expectations and the level of trust between you. For instance, many Chinese negotiators are wary of people who change their position during the early stages of negotiations. Similarly, some writers warn that Russian negotiators tend to view concessions as a sign of weakness rather than a sign of trust.[72] Generally the best strategy is to be moderately tough and give just enough concessions to communicate sincerity and motivation to resolve the conflict.[73] Being too tough can undermine relations between the parties; giving too many concessions implies weakness and encourages the other party to push harder for a favorable deal.

IN CONCLUSION   WHY DOES IT MATTER?

Why should you be concerned about issues of power, influence, and negotiation in organizations? All organizations are political entities in which power and influence are important. Your ability as a manager to obtain the scarce resources required to get things done is determined by your ability to accumulate power, influence others, and negotiate for the resources you need. Without power and influence you will find it more difficult to negotiate for access to resources, to persuade your peers to work cooperatively with you for mutual gain, and to persuade your subordinates to work productively. Without power and influence you will have little impact on organizational goals, strategies, or outcomes—and you will not be effective as a manager.

At the same time, remember that power and influence are double-edged swords. Used judiciously and ethically, power and influence can help somebody with integrity to achieve great things in organizations. However, power does tend to corrupt. Power can be and has been abused by skilled managers who have used their power unethically to the detriment of others—and often themselves.

MANAGEMENT CHALLENGES

1. The exercise of what kind of power is likely to produce the most resistance in an organization? What kind of power is likely to produce the least resistance?
2. Why does power tend to corrupt? What can you do to make sure power does not corrupt you?
3. Is the accumulation and exercise of power necessary for success in management?
4. What do we mean when we say that organizations are political entities? How does organizational politics influence organizational outcomes?
5. What tactics could you adopt to increase the probability that you will be able to negotiate effectively for what you want?

MANAGEMENT PORTFOLIO

FOR THE ORGANIZATION YOU HAVE CHOSEN TO FOLLOW:

1. Where does the power of the chief executive officer come from?
2. What sources of countervailing power limit his or her power?
3. Can you find any examples of middle to lower-level managers accumulating power, exercising influence, and impacting the goals, strategy, actions, or operations of the organization? How did the managers accumulate power? How did they exercise influence?
4. Is there any evidence of political behavior and conflict within the organization? If so, give an example and explain how it was resolved.
5. Try to find an example of a negotiation between the organization and an external party (such as a supplier, a customer, or the government). What was the negotiation about? Who had the most power in the negotiation? What was the outcome? Which party was the better negotiator?

CLOSING CASE   THE RISE AND FALL OF MIKE SEARS

Mike Sears was a prodigy of Harry Stonecipher, the blunt-talking, hard-driving aerospace executive who became CEO first of McDonnell Douglas and then Boeing. Picked by Stonecipher to lead the F-18 Hornet fighter program at McDonnell Douglas in the early 1990s, Sears earned a reputation as a skilled manager who restlessly cut costs and boosted productivity, building a program that was below costs and ahead of schedule. Stonecipher admired Sears's effectiveness at assembling and managing cross-functional product development teams, establishing closer ties with suppliers, and improving controls within his organization. When McDonnell Douglas was acquired by Boeing in 1996, Sears went with Stonecipher to the acquiring company, where Stonecipher became president until his retirement in 2002. Sears was appointed as chief financial officer.

It was soon clear, however, that Sears was after the top spot. As CFO he was one of the obvious candidates in line to succeed Boeing CEO Phil Condit. Other contenders included Alan Mulally, head of Boeing's commercial aerospace group, and James Albaugh, who ran Boeing's defense systems business. According to company insiders, Sears began to take steps to amass a power base at his rivals' expense.

In 2002 Sears heard that Darleen Druyun, the top Air Force procurement officer, was looking to move into the private sector. Druyun was quite possibly the most sought-after executive-to-be in the entire aerospace industry. Because of her knowledge of the Pentagon procurement process and her contacts, Boeing and other aerospace companies tried hard to land her. James Albaugh had talked to her at least once but came up dry. Sears, however, somehow managed to persuade her to join the company. The coup gave Sears a huge advantage over Albaugh and Mulally. It also had the potential to expand his power base by making Druyun an ally. Unknown to others at the time, Sears had clinched the deal by promising Druyun a top job at Boeing while she was still in the middle of negotiating a $22 billion military contract with Boeing for a fleet of jet tankers, which Boeing was ultimately awarded.

In 2003 Sears pushed things further. He reportedly waged an all-out war with CEO Phil Condit, taking over all public relations responsibilities and controlling access to the

Corrupted by Power   Boeing CFO Mike Sears and Pentagon procurement executive Darleen Druyun both pleaded guilty and went to jail for their role in a Pentagon procurement scandal. Sears offered Druyun a job at Boeing (which she accepted) while she was still negotiating a $22 billion tanker contract with Boeing.

© AFP/Getty Images.

media and investors—roles that were normally the prerogative of the CEO. Sears also took control of Boeing's in-house leadership center at St. Louis. Banished from the sessions were Albaugh and Mulally. With almost any important executive passing through the center, control gave Sears unprecedented exposure within Boeing's far-flung organization.

Sears's stock rose further in mid-2003 when leaks to the media implied that Albaugh had withheld information from Sears about a $1.2 billion charge against earnings that Boeing was forced to take due to write-downs in its defense business. Sears was in charge of public relations at the time, and many suspected that the leak was part of a deliberate smear campaign. In an internal Boeing memo later leaked to the press, Albaugh said that "the efforts to cast the write-down as the result of me withholding information—surprising world head-quarters—is not supported by the facts . . . . If Mike (Sears) is intent on discrediting me, he does a disservice not only to me, but also to the company."

By this time it was becoming apparent to many that Sears was anxious to succeed Phil Condit, "to the extent that it got pretty disgusting" according to a Boeing board member.

The summer of 2003 turned out to be the high point in Mike Sears's career. In November 2003 the government accused Sears of "communicating directly and indirectly with Darleen Druyun about future employment when she had not disqualified herself from acting in her official government capacity on matters involving Boeing." The government went on to state that the pair had attempted to conceal this infraction from company lawyers investigating the matter. It was also alleged that Druyun broke the law by telling Boeing employees confidential information about how Airbus had priced its bid for the tanker contract. Boeing fired Mike Sears immediately, and ultimately both he and Druyun pleaded guilty to criminal wrongdoing and faced jail time.

Ironically the firing of Sears raised questions about the ethics of management at Boeing under Phil Condit, the man Sears had wanted to replace as CEO. Within a month Condit had resigned from the CEO position, a victim of the fallout from the scandal, which resulted in the loss of the military tanker contract. Condit was replaced by Harry Stonecipher, who came out of retirement to take the CEO position. However, in another disturbing power play at Boeing, Stonecipher was himself forced to step down after a leaked e-mail message revealed that he had initiated an extramarital affair with an employee at Boeing. Fearing that Boeing was becoming mired in scandal after scandal, the board of directors asked for Stonecipher's resignation. He was replaced by Jim McNeary, the CEO of 3M.[74]

CASE DISCUSSION QUESTIONS

1. From a power perspective, what do you think explains the rise of Mike Sears to the CFO position at Boeing? What were the sources of his power?

2. Once he became CFO, what did Mike Sears do to consolidate his power base at Boeing? What sources of power was he trying to accumulate? What was he trying to do with this power?

3. What do you think about the ethics of Sears's actions? Does the fall of Mike Sears prove that power tends to corrupt?

4. What does the case tell you about the nature of internal organizational politics at Boeing during this period? As incoming CEO, would you see this as a problem? If so, how would you deal with it?

5. Do you think that power is more important in an organization like Boeing than in one that has less politics? Why?

ENDNOTES

1. A. Pollack, "She's Winning Her Drug War," *The New York Times,* May 7, 2005, p. 1; D. Hamilton, "Women to Watch: Susan Desmond-Hillmann," *The Wall Street Journal,* October 31, 2005, p. R6.

2. L.A. Hill, *Becoming a Manager* (Boston: Harvard Business School Press, 1992).

3. H. Mintzberg, "Managerial Work: Analysis from Observation," *Management Science* 18 (1971), pp. B97–B110.

4. For a discussion of the definition of power, see H. Mintzberg, *Power in and around Organizations* (Englewood Cliffs, NJ: Prentice-Hall, 1983), Chapter 1; J. Pfeffer, *Managing with Power* (Boston: Harvard Business University Press, 1992), pp. 17, 30; J. Pfeffer, *New Directions in Organizational Theory* (New York: Oxford University Press, 1997), Chapter 6; J.M. Whitmeyer, "Power through Appointment," *Social Science Research* 29 (2000), pp. 535–55.

5. R.A. Dahl, "The Concept of Power," *Behavioral Science* 2 (1957), pp. 201–18; R.M. Emerson, "Power–Dependence Relations," *American Sociological Review* 27 (1962), pp. 31–41; A.M. Pettigrew, *The Politics of Organizational Decision Making* (London: Tavistock, 1973); T. Casciaro and M.J. Piskorski, "Power Imbalance, Mutual Dependence, and Constraint Absorption," *Administrative Science Quarterly* 50 (2005), pp. 167–90.

6. R. Kanter, "Power Failure in Management Circuits," *Harvard Business Review* 57 (July–August 1979), pp. 65–75.

7. J.P. Kotter, "Power, Dependence, and Effective Management," *Harvard Business Review,* July–August 1977, pp. 50–62.

8. G. Morgan, *Images of Organization* (Beverley Hills: Sage, 1985).

9. J.R.P. French and B. Raven, "The Bases of Social Power," in *Studies in Social Power,* ed. D. Cartwright (Ann Arbor: University of Michigan Press, 1959), pp. 150–67; P. Podsakoff and C. Schreisheim, "Field Studies of French and Raven's Bases of Power: Critique, Analysis, and Suggestions for Future Research," *Psychological Bulletin* 97 (1985), pp. 387–411; S. Finkelstein, "Power in Top Management Teams: Dimensions, Measurement, and Validation," *Academy of Management Journal* 35 (1992), pp. 505–38; P.P. Carson and K.D. Carson, "Social Power Bases: A Meta-Analytic Examination of Interrelationships and Outcomes," *Journal of Applied Social Psychology* 23 (1993), pp. 1150–69; Pfeffer, *Managing with Power.*

10. S. Craig, "Merrill Brokers Fired in Scandal Win $14 Million," *The Wall Street Journal,* January 6, 2006, p. C1.

11. Pfeffer, *Managing with Power.*

12. S. Pulliam and A. Latour, "Lost Connection," *The Wall Street Journal,* January 12, 2005, p. A1; S. Rosenbush, "Five Lessons of the WorldCom Debacle," *Business Week Online,* March 16, 2005.

13. P.F. Drucker, "The New Workforce," *The Economist,* November 3, 2001, pp. 8–12.

14. G. Yukl and C.M. Falbe, "Importance of Different Power Sources in Downward and Lateral Relations," *Journal of Applied Psychology* 76 (1991), pp. 416–23; B.H. Raven, "Kurt Lewin Address: Influence, Power, Religion, and the Mechanisms of Social Control," *Journal of Social Issues* 55 (Spring 1999), pp. 161–86.

15. C.R. Hinings et al., "Structural Conditions of Intraorganizational Power," *Administrative Science Quarterly* 19 (1974), pp. 22–44. Also see C.S. Saunders, "The Strategic Contingency Theory of Power: Multiple Perspectives," *The Journal of Management Studies* 27 (1990), pp. 1–21.

16. D.J. Brass, "Being in the Right Place: A Structural Analysis of Individual Influence in an Organization," *Administrative Science Quarterly* 29 (1984), pp. 518–39; D. Krackhardt, "Assessing the Political Landscape: Structure, Cognition, and Power in Organizations," *Administrative Science Quarterly* 35 (1990), pp. 342–69; J. Pfeffer and A. Konrad, "The Effect of Individual Power on Earnings," *Work and Occupations,* 1991.

17. "Corporate Culture Instilled Online," *The Economist,* November 11, 2000.

18. P.L. Dawes, D.Y. Lee, and G.R. Dowling, "Information Control and Influence in Emergent Buying Centers," *Journal of Marketing* 62, no. 3 (July 1998), 55–68; D.J. Brass et al., "Taking Stock of Networks and Organizations: A Multilevel Perspective," *Academy of Management Journal* 47, no. 6 (December 2004), pp. 795–817.

19. E.J. Zajac and J.D. Westphal, "Director Reputation, CEO–Board Power, and the Dynamics of Board Interlocks," *Administrative Science Quarterly* 41 (1996), pp. 507–30.

20. A. W. Gouldner, "The Norm of Reciprocity: A Preliminary Statement," *American Sociological Review* 25 (1960), 161–78.

21. R.A. Caro, *The Path to Power: The Early Years of Lyndon Johnson* (New York: Alfred A. Knopf, 1982).

22. Pfeffer, *Managing with Power,* p. 166.

23. J. Kotter, *The General Managers* (New York, Free Press, 1982).

24. J. Gleick, *Genius: The Life and Science of Richard Feynman* (New York: Vintage Books, 1992).

25. D.J. Hickson et al., "A Strategic Contingencies' Theory of Intraorganizational Power," *Administrative Science Quarterly* 16 (1971), 216–27; Hinings et al., "Structural Conditions of Intraorganizational Power"; Kanter, "Power Failure in Management Circuits."

26. Hickson et al., "A Strategic Contingencies' Theory of Intraorganizational Power"; J.D. Hackman, "Power and Centrality in the Allocation of Resources in Colleges and Universities," *Administrative Science Quarterly* 30 (1985), pp. 61–77.

27. Kanter, "Power Failure in Management Circuits" ; B.E. Ashforth, "The Experience of Powerlessness in Organizations," *Organizational Behavior and Human Decision Processes* 43 (1989), pp. 207–42; L. Holden, "European Managers: HRM and an Evolving Role," *European Business Review* 12 (2000).

28. J. Voight, "When Credit Is Not Due," *Adweek*, March 1, 2004, p. 24.

29. R. Madell, "Ground Floor," *Pharmaceutical Executive (Women in Pharma Supplement),* June 2000, pp. 24–31.

30. K. Atuahene-Gima and H. Li, "Marketing's Influence Tactics in New Product Development: A Study of High-Technology Firms in China," *Journal of Product Innovation Managemen*t 17 (2000), pp. 451–70; A. Somech and A. Drach-Zahavy, "Relative Power and Influence Strategy: The Effects of Agent/Target Organizational Power on Superiors' Choices of Influence Strategies," *Journal of Organizational Behavior* 23 (2002), pp. 167–79.

31. J. Kador, *Charles Schwab* (New York: Wiley, 2002).

32. D. Kipnis, S.M. Schmidt, and I. Wilkinson, "Intraorganizational Influence Tactics: Explorations in Getting One's Way," *Journal of Applied Psychology* 65 (1980), 440–52. Also see C. Schriesheim and T. Hinkin, "Influence Tactics Used by Subordinates: A Theoretical and Empirical Analysis and Refinement of the Kipnis, Schmidt, and Wilkinson Subscales," *Journal of Applied Psychology* 75 (1990), 246–57; W.A. Hochwarter et al., "A Reexamination of Schriesheim and Hinkin's (1990) Measure of Upward Influence," *Educational and Psychological Measurement* 60 (October 2000), pp. 755–71.

33. R.B. Cialdini and N.J. Goldstein, "Social Influence: Compliance and Conformity," *Annual Review of Psychology* 55 (2004), 591–621.

34. Rao and Hashimoto, "Universal and Culturally Specific Aspects of Managerial Influence." Silent authority as an influence tactic in non-Western cultures is also discussed in S.F. Pasa, "Leadership Influence in a High Power Distance and Collectivist Culture," *Leadership & Organization Development Journal* 21 (2000), pp. 414–26.

35. Rao and Hashimoto, "Universal and Culturally Specific Aspects of Managerial Influence"; Pasa, "Leadership Influence in a High Power Distance and Collectivist Culture."

36. A.T. Cobb, "Toward the Study of Organizational Coalitions: Participant Concerns and Activities in a Simulated Organizational Setting," *Human Relations* 44 (1991), pp. 1057–79; E.A. Mannix, "Organizations as Resource Dilemmas: The Effects of Power Balance on Coalition Formation in Small Groups," *Organizational Behavior and Human Decision Processes* 55 (1993), 1–22; D.J. Terry, M.A. Hogg, and K.M. White, "The Theory of Planned Behavior: Self-Identity, Social Identity, and Group Norms," *British Journal of Social Psychology* 38 (September 1999), pp. 225–44.

37. B. Carter, "How a Hit Almost Failed Its Own Audition," *The New York Times,* April 30, 2006, Section 3, pp. C1, C9.

38. D. Strutton and L.E. Pelton, "Effects of Ingratiation on Lateral Relationship Quality within Sales Team Settings," *Journal of Business Research* 43 (1998), pp. 1–12; R. Vonk, "Self-Serving Interpretations of Flattery: Why Ingratiation Works," *Journal of Personality and Social Psychology* 82 (2002), pp. 515–26.

39. C.A. Higgins, T.A. Judge, and G.R. Ferris, "Influence Tactics and Work Outcomes: A Meta-Analysis," *Journal of Organizational Behavior* 24 (2003), pp. 90–106.

40. D. Strutton, L.E. Pelton, and J.F. Tanner, "Shall We Gather in the Garden: The Effect of Ingratiatory Behaviors on Buyer Trust in Salespeople," *Industrial Marketing Management* 25 (1996), pp. 151–62; J. O'Neil, "An Investigation of the Sources of Influence of Corporate Public Relations Practitioners," *Public Relations Review* 29 (June 2003), pp. 159–69.

41. A. Rao and S.M. Schmidt, "Upward Impression Management: Goals, Influence Strategies, and Consequences," *Human Relations* 48 (1995), pp. 147–67.

42. A.P.J. Ellis et al., "The Use of Impression Management Tactics in Structured Interviews: A Function of Question Type?" *Journal of Applied Psychology* 87 (December 2002), pp. 1200–8; M.C. Bolino and W.H. Tunley, "More Than One Way to Make an Impression: Exploring Profiles of Impression Management," *Journal of Management* 29 (2003), pp. 141–60; S. Zivnuska et al., "Interactive Effects of Impression Management and Organizational Politics on Job Performance," *Journal of Organizational Behavior* 25 (2004), pp. 627–41.

43. J. Rutenberg, "At Fox News, The Colonel Who Wasn't," *The New York Times,* April 29, 2002, p. 1.

44. J. Dillard and E. Peck, "Persuasion and the Structure of Affect: Dual Systems and Discrete Emotions as Complementary Models," *Human Communication Research* 27 (2000), pp. 38–68; S. Fox and Y. Amichai-Hamburger, "The Power of Emotional Appeals in Promoting Organizational Change Programs," *Academy of Management Executive* 15 (November 2001), pp. 84–94; E.H.H.J. Das, J.B.F. de Wit, and W. Stroebe, "Fear Appeals Motivate Acceptance of Action Recommendations: Evidence for a Positive Bias in the Processing of Persuasive

Messages," *Personality and Social Psychology Bulletin* 29 (May 2003), pp. 650–64; R. Buck et al., "Emotion and Reason in Persuasion: Applying the Ari Model and the Casc Scale," *Journal of Business Research* 57, no. 6 (2004), pp. 647–56.

45. A.P. Brief, *Attitudes in and around Organizations* (Thousand Oaks, CA: Sage, 1998), pp. 69–84; D.J. O'Keefe, *Persuasion: Theory and Research* (Thousand Oaks, CA: Sage Publications, 2002).

46. Conger, *Winning 'Em Over: A New Model for Managing in the Age of Persuasion;* J.J. Jiang, G. Klein, and R.G. Vedder, "Persuasive Expert Systems: The Influence of Confidence and Discrepancy," *Computers in Human Behavior* 16 (March 2000), pp. 99–109.

47. These and other features of message content in persuasion are detailed in R. Petty and J. Cacioppo, *Attitudes and Persuasion: Classic and Contemporary Approaches* (Dubuque, IA: W. C. Brown, 1981); D.G. Linz and S. Penrod, "Increasing Attorney Persuasiveness in the Courtroom," *Law and Psychology Review* 8 (1984), pp. 1–47; M. Pfau, E.A. Szabo, and J. Anderson, "The Role and Impact of Affect in the Process of Resistance to Persuasion," *Human Communication Research* 27 (April 2001), pp. 216–52; O'Keefe, *Persuasion: Theory and Research,* Chapter 9.

48. N. Rhodes and W. Wood, "Self-Esteem and Intelligence Affect Influenceability: The Mediating Role of Message Reception," *Psychological Bulletin* 111, no. 1 (1992), pp. 156–71.

49. "Be Part of the Team If You Want to Catch the Eye," *Birmingham Post* (UK), August 31, 2000, p. 14; S. Maitlis, "Taking It from the Top: How CEOs Influence (and Fail to Influence) Their Boards," *Organization Studies* 25, no. 8 (2004), pp. 1275–1311.

50. C.M. Falbe and G. Yukl, "Consequences for Managers of Using Single Influence Tactics and Combinations of Tactics," *Academy of Management Journal* 35 (1992), pp. 638–52.

51. Falbe and Yukl, "Consequences for Managers of Using Single Influence Tactics and Combinations of Tactics"; Atuahene-Gima and Li, "Marketing's Influence Tactics in New Product Development."

52. Kador, *Charles Schwab.*

53. R.C. Ringer and R.W. Boss, "Hospital Professionals' Use of Upward Influence Tactics," *Journal of Managerial Issues* 12 (2000), pp. 92–108.

54. G. Blickle, "Do Work Values Predict the Use of Intraorganizational Influence Strategies?" *Journal of Applied Social Psychology* 30, no. 1 (January 2000), pp. 196–205; P.P. Fu et al., "The Impact of Societal Cultural Values and Individual Social Beliefs on the Perceived Effectiveness of Managerial Influence Strategies: A Meso Approach," *Journal of International Business Studies* 35, no. 4 (July 2004), pp. 284–305.

55. D. Tannen, *Talking from 9 to 5* (New York: Avon, 1994), Chapter 2; M. Crawford, *Talking Difference: On Gender and Language* (Thousand Oaks, CA: Sage, 1995), pp. 41–44.

56. S. Mann, "Politics and Power in Organizations: Why Women Lose Out," *Leadership & Organization Development Journal* 16 (1995), pp. 9–15; E.H. Buttner and M. McEnally, "The Interactive Effect of Influence Tactic, Applicant Gender, and Type of Job on Hiring Recommendations," *Sex Roles* 34 (1996), pp. 581–91; L.L. Carli, "Gender, Interpersonal Power, and Social Influence," *Journal of Social Issues* 55 (Spring 1999), pp. 81–99.

57. J.A. Wall and R.R. Callister, "Conflict and Its Management," *Journal of Management* 21 (1995), pp. 515–58; D. Tjosvold, *Working Together to Get Things Done* (Lexington, MA: Lexington, 1986), pp. 114–15.

58. L. Thompson, *The Mind and Heart of the Negotiator* (Upper Saddle River, NJ: Prentice-Hall, 2000).

59. H. Mintzberg, *The Nature of Managerial Work* (New York: Harper & Row, 1973); H. Mintzberg, "The Manager's Job: Folklore and Fact," *Harvard Business Review,* July–August 1975, pp. 49–61.

60. L. Hill, *Becoming a Manager: How New Managers Master the Challenges of Leadership* (Boston: Harvard Business School Press, 2003), pp. 41–42.

61. R. Stagner and H. Rosen, *Psychology of Union–Management Relations* (Belmont, CA: Wadsworth, 1965), pp. 95–96, 108–10; R.E. Walton and R.B. McKersie, *A Behavioral Theory of Labor Negotiations: An Analysis of a Social Interaction System* (New York: McGraw-Hill, 1965), pp. 41–46; Thompson, *The Mind and Heart of the Negotiator,* Chapter 2.

62. J.W. Salacuse and J.Z. Rubin, "Your Place or Mine? Site Location and Negotiation," *Negotiation Journal* 6 (January 1990), pp. 5–10; J. Mayfield et al., "How Location Impacts International Business Negotiations," *Review of Business* 19 (December 1998), pp. 21–24.

63. For a full discussion of the advantages and disadvantages of face-to-face and alternative negotiation situations, see M.H. Bazerman et al., "Negotiation," *Annual Review of Psychology* 51 (2000), pp. 279–314.

64. A.F. Stuhlmacher, T.L. Gillespie, and M.V. Champagne, "The Impact of Time Pressure in Negotiation: A Meta-Analysis," *International Journal of Conflict Management* 9, no. 2 (April 1998), pp. 97–116; C.K.W. De Dreu, "Time Pressure and Closing of the Mind in Negotiation," *Organizational Behavior and Human Decision Processes* 91 (July 2003), pp. 280–95. However, one recent study reported that speeding up these concessions leads to better negotiated outcomes. See D.A. Moore, "Myopic Prediction, Self-Destructive Secrecy, and the Unexpected Benefits of Revealing Final Deadlines in Negotiation," *Organizational Behavior and Human Decision Processes* 94, no. 2 (2004), pp. 125–39.

65. Lewicki et al., *Negotiation,* pp. 298–322.

66. P.H. Kim, R.L. Pinkley, and A.R. Fragale, "Power Dynamics in Negotiation," *Academy of Management Review* 30 (2005), pp. 799–822.

67. S. Doctoroff, "Reengineering Negotiations," *Sloan Management Review* 39 (March 1998), pp. 63–71; D.C. Zetik and A.F. Stuhlmacher, "Goal Setting and Negotiation Performance: A Meta-Analysis," *Group Processes & Intergroup Relations* 5 (January 2002), pp. 35–52.

68. L.L. Thompson, "Information Exchange in Negotiation," *Journal of Experimental Social Psychology* 27 (1991), pp. 161–79.

69. L. Thompson, E. Peterson, and S.E. Brodt, "Team Negotiation: An Examination of Integrative and Distributive Bargaining," *Journal of Personality and Social Psychology* 70 (1996), pp. 66–78; Y. Paik and R.L. Tung, "Negotiating with East Asians: How to Attain 'Win–Win' Outcomes," *Management International Review* 39 (1999), pp. 103–22.

70. O'Keefe, *Persuasion: Theory and Research.*

71. Lewicki et al., *Negotiation,* pp. 90–96; S. Kwon and L.R. Weingart, "Unilateral Concessions from the Other Party: Concession Behavior, Attributions, and Negotiation Judgments," *Journal of Applied Psychology* 89, no. 2 (2004), pp. 263–78.

72. J.J. Zhao, "The Chinese Approach to International Business Negotiation," *Journal of Business Communication,* July 2000, pp. 209–37; N. Crundwell, "U.S.–Russian Negotiating Strategies," *BISNIS Bulletin,* October 2003, pp. 5–6.

73. J.Z. Rubin and B.R. Brown, *The Social Psychology of Bargaining and Negotiation* (New York: Academic Press, 1976), Chapter 9.

74. Sources: S. Holmes, "Why Boeing's Culture Breeds Turmoil," *BusinessWeek,* March 21, 2005, pp. 34–36; R. Stodghill, "Combat Ready at McDonnell," *BusinessWeek,* April 29, 1996, pp. 39–41; J.C. Anselmo, "After Harry," *Aviation Week,* March 14, 2005, pp. 22–26.

16

EFFECTIVE LEADERSHIP

After Reading This Chapter You Should Be Able to:

1. Explain why good leadership is critical for success as a manager.

2. Summarize the main theoretical approaches to leadership.

3. Identify the behaviors and skills that are commonly associated with effective leadership.

4. Explain how the right approach to leadership might be influenced by important contingencies.

5. Discuss the difference between transformational and transactional leadership.

When Gordon Bethune arrived at Continental Airlines in 1994, the company was in dreadful shape. The airline was flirting with bankruptcy, ranked last in customer satisfaction, and was embroiled in severe conflict between management and employees. This was nothing new for Continental; it had gone bankrupt twice since 1983. Ten CEOs had tried running the company in as many years. Bethune's diagnosis of Continental's problems was simple: In their fervor to reduce costs, previous managers had destroyed the capacity of the airline to deliver what customers wanted—flights that departed and arrived on time (only 61 percent of Continental's flights arrived on time in early 1994). Bethune moved quickly to shut down unprofitable routes; but what really caught everyone's attention was the way he persuaded employees at Continental to join him in a campaign to improve the company's on-time performance. Bethune's analysis indicated that late and canceled flights were costing Continental $6 million a month; so he stated that if employees could help him improve Continental's performance and get the company into the top five airlines measured by on-time performance, he would split the $6 million with them, which translated into $65 a month for each employee. By the end of 1995 Bethune had paid out this sum six times, and the airline's planes arrived on time over 80 percent of the time. To drive home the message, Bethune personally went around to major Continental hubs, where he delivered the checks along with a speech to employees pitched with the fervor of an evangelical preacher, urging them to "make reliability a reality" and to "work together" for the good of the airline and everyone associated with it. By the end of the decade Continental was profitable and ranked first in the industry for customer service.[1]

Gordon Bethune was a transformational leader. He was able to do what his predecessors could not: transform Continental from a perennially troubled airline into a standout performer. He did this by articulating a clear strategic vision and then persuading employees through a combination of bonus pay and evangelism to join him on a mission to improve Continental's customer service. This tour de force landed Bethune on several lists of the most important business leaders of the decade.

You will recall from Chapter 1 that leadership is one of the central functions of management. What often distinguishes great managers from merely good ones is that great managers excel in leadership. By **leadership** we mean the process of motivating, influencing, and directing others in the organization to work productively in pursuit of organization goals.[2] Great managers are able to work through other people to achieve remarkable transformations in the performance of an organization. Exemplary leaders of the last decade include Gordon Bethune; Louis Gerstner, who transformed IBM from a money-losing computer hardware enterprise into a computer services powerhouse; Meg Whitman, whose visionary leadership helped make eBay a dominant Internet company; Larry Bossidy, who transformed AlliedSignal from a poorly performing industrial conglomerate into a textbook example of superior productivity; and Steve Jobs, whose vision and technology evangelism helped turn Pixar into the dominant animation film studio and injected new energy into the company he founded, Apple Computer, with its iPod. In this chapter we discuss what it takes to be an effective leader. We start by looking more closely at leadership as a function of management.

leadership

The process of motivating, influencing, and directing others in the organization to work productively in pursuit of organization goals.

■ // Managing and Leading

It has become fashionable to draw a sharp distinction between leaders and managers. The influential business author Warren Bennis, for example, has stated that leaders are concerned with "doing the right things," whereas managers are concerned with "doing things right."[3] He sees leaders as focusing on vision, mission, and goals, whereas managers focus on efficiency and effectiveness. He depicts managers as preservers of the status quo; leaders see themselves as promoters of change and challengers of the status quo. Bennis argues that American organizations are "overmanaged and underled." Harvard's John Kotter makes a similar point. Management, according to Kotter, is about coping with complexity. Leadership, by contrast, is about coping with change.[4] In the view of Bennis and Kotter, important as they are to the efficient functioning of organizations, managers are somehow lesser mortals than leaders.

Both Bennis and Kotter are writing for effect; but their comparisons between managers and leaders are misleading. The reason is simple: *All* managers are also leaders, and as we said in Chapter 1, they must perform the leadership function effectively to excel at the other management functions—strategizing, planning, organizing, controlling, and developing employees. This is true not just of the CEO of a corporation but also of lower-level managers, who must lead their divisions, functions, units, and teams effectively to achieve their goals. Management and leadership are not two different tasks that require different skills; they are the same thing. To be effective, whatever their position in the organization hierarchy, managers must lead.[5] Where Bennis and Kotter may be right is in asserting that too many managers have not grasped the basic truth that leading is a critical component of their job.

How important is good leadership to the performance of an organization? One stream of research looks at the impact of CEO succession on firm performance and argues that if leadership is important, a change in CEOs should explain some of the subsequent variance in enterprise profitability (with good leaders boosting performance and bad leaders depressing performance).[6] A widely quoted classic study found that CEO succession explained about 15.2 percent of a company's profit margin variance after one year and 31.7 percent of the variance after three years.[7] Another more recent study suggested that on average, the impact of CEO succession explained roughly 15 percent of the subsequent variance in company performance, after controlling for general economic conditions, industry factors, and unique company attributes.[8] This was about the same impact on performance as the industry in which an enterprise competed. These are not trivial findings; they suggest that leadership changes at the top of an organization can have a substantial impact on the subsequent performance of an enterprise.[9]

Moreover, numerous case studies suggest that these averaged figures disguise the significant impact that good or bad leaders can have on an organization in specific situations. There is little doubt that Gordon Bethune had a major impact on the performance of Continental Airlines. After having cycled through 10 CEOs in as many years, Continental was desperate for strong leadership. In contrast, bad leaders have often destroyed significant economic value at the enterprises unlucky enough to have them. Al Dunlap, for example, who was known as "Chainsaw Al" for his tough approach to cost cutting, is blamed for rapidly driving small appliance maker Sunbeam into bankruptcy due to poor leadership during his two-year tenure as CEO of that company.[10] In short, leaders matter.

■ // What Makes an Effective Leader?

Leadership may be one of the most discussed management topics. Walk into any bookstore's management section and you will see dozens of titles all claiming to explain the secrets of effective leadership. **Effective leadership** means the ability of a leader to get high performance from his or her subordinates. In the case of a CEO or general manager of a self-contained product division, effective leadership should translate into sustained high performance for the entire company or division. Literally thousands of academic studies have tried to discern the difference between effective and ineffective leadership. Despite this large body of work, there is a lack of consensus about what makes an effective leader. However, five different perspectives on leadership have emerged over the years, each of which teaches us something about the nature of effective leadership (see Figure 16.1).[11]

One perspective, the *power–influence* approach, attempts to explain leadership effectiveness in terms of the amount of power possessed by a leader, the type of power possessed, and how that power is used to influence others within the organization. Another perspective, called the *trait* or *competency perspective,* has tried to identify the traits and competencies of effective leaders. A third approach, the *behavior perspective,* asserts that certain behaviors are related to leadership effectiveness. The *contingency perspective* argues that the appropriate behaviors for a leader to adopt depend on context, and that what works in some situations will not in others. Finally, the last two decades have seen the rise of work on what is called the *transformational perspective* on leadership. The transformational perspective suggests that effective leaders "transform" organizations through their vision,

effective leadership
The ability of a leader to get high performance from his or her subordinates.

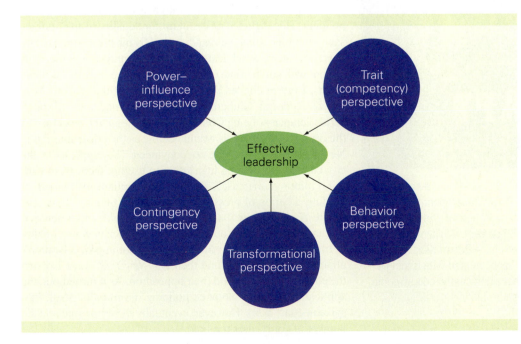

FIGURE 16.1

Perspectives on Leadership

communication, and ability to build commitment to that vision among employees. Gordon Bethune is an example of a transformational leader. He transformed Continental by articulating a different vision for the airline, relentlessly communicating that vision to all employees, rewarding employees for improving performance, and empowering them to take actions that were consistent with the vision.

These different perspectives are not mutually exclusive. For example, to be effective a transformational leader may require certain competencies, have to engage in certain behaviors, and need to accumulate and use power to achieve his or her transformational goals. Each perspective tells us something important about the nature of leadership. Together the five perspectives give us as complete a portrait as we have of what it takes to be an effective leader. In the remainder of this chapter we tour through the five perspectives to see what we can learn.

■ // The Power–Influence Perspective

■ Leadership at the NYPD.

Leaders, by definition, have legitimate power that comes from their hierarchical position, as well as power over the distribution of rewards and sanctions and over the allocation of scarce resources (see Chapter 15). However, research on the use of different forms of power suggests that effective leaders rely as much on the personal power that flows from expertise, a network of allies, and individual attributes as they do on power flowing from their formal position.[12] The power that flows from hierarchical position is a blunt instrument that does not necessarily build commitment from employees to a vision. As CEO of Continental Airlines Gordon Bethune enjoyed significant hierarchical power, which allowed him to manipulate the reward structure at Continental to improve customer service. However, his effectiveness as a leader also came from his power as an expert in the industry (Bethune had a long career in aerospace) and individual attributes such as his eloquence, energy, focus, and integrity, all of which earned him the respect of employees and helped him influence their behavior.

The Reformer   After a highly successful tenure as commissioner of the New York Police Department, during which the overall crime rate fell by 17 percent, felony crimes by 39 percent, and murders by 50 percent, William Bratton become head of the Los Angeles Police Department. In a 30-year police career, Bratton has been credited with leading a reform movement in policing that significantly reduced crime wherever he had leadership responsibility.

© AP Photo/Lee Celano

For another illustration of the nuanced position that leaders must adopt with regard to the accumulation and application of power, consider William Bratton, who gained significant credit for reducing the crime rate in New York first as leader of the New York Transit Police and then as commissioner of the New York Police Department. Bratton advocated zero-tolerance policing. This included prosecution for "quality of life" crimes such as panhandling and vandalism. His push was opposed by the city's courts, which feared the policy would swamp the court system with small crime cases. To get past the opposition of the courts, Bratton elicited the help of a powerful ally, New York Mayor Rudolph Giuliani. Giuliani explained that although zero-tolerance policing would initially increase the workload of the courts, over time this would decline as the crime rate fell in New York. The courts were not convinced. They appealed to the city council, advocating legislation to exempt them from handling minor crime cases. Bratton and Giuliani responded by holding a series of press conferences and placing their case before *The New York Times,* the city's most influential newspaper, arguing that if the courts did not help crack down on quality of life crimes, the city's crime rate would not improve. Bratton's alliance with the mayor and then *The New York Times* isolated the courts, which dropped their opposition. As it turned out, the application of zero-tolerance policing did initially result in a spike in court cases. However, eventually the crime rate and the number of court cases tumbled.[13]

The story of William Bratton illustrates how a network of allies can be a significant source of power enabling a leader to push through a policy or program against substantial opposition from an important constituency, in this case the New York City court system. What we learn from the experiences of Gordon Bethune and William Bratton is that to get things done in organizations, effective leaders rely on more than their legitimate hierarchical power. They play the power game with skill, combining their hierarchical power, their expertise, a network of allies, and personal power to achieve their goals. Effective leaders are skilled organizational politicians. They know how to use power to win over important constituencies to their cause and to remove or neutralize obstacles to their strategies.

■ // The Competency (Trait) Perspective

People have always been interested in personal characteristics, or traits, that distinguish great leaders from the rest of us. The "great person" theory of leadership assumes that leaders are "born, not made" and that leaders are gifted with traits such as tireless energy, penetrating intuition, uncanny foresight, and irresistible persuasive powers.[14] During the 1930s and 1940s hundreds of trait studies were conducted in an effort to identify the traits that marked people for greatness. Although this mass of literature yielded endless lists of traits, a lack of consistency across studies led to widespread disillusionment with the trait approach to leadership. By the 1970s research on the personality traits of leaders seemed to have reached a dead end.[15]

However, as so often happens with the history of ideas, the notion that some universal traits are associated with effective leaders reemerged. Reexamination of earlier studies suggested that certain personality traits—such as intelligence, motivation, drive, self-confidence, and desire for power—might be associated with effective leadership.[16] Subsequent research has suggested that several traits might be important predictors of effective leadership, including strategic thinking ability, achievement motivation, power motivation, charismatic traits, and emotional intelligence. Some of these traits have been renamed "competencies," implying that they can be acquired through learning. However, despite a vast supply of literature there is still no agreement about which of these traits are important or necessary.

// STRATEGIC THINKING

Strategic thinking refers to the cognitive ability to analyze a complex situation, abstract from it, and draw conclusions about the best strategy for the firm to follow. Strategic thinking requires a combination of intelligence and reasoning skills. People with a talent for big picture strategic thinking can cut straight through a lot of messy data and get to the heart of an issue. They are skilled at analyzing an industry, understanding competitive dynamics, and discerning what is important for the firm. They are the opposite of people who cannot see the forest for the trees—they see the entire forest with great clarity.

strategic thinking
The cognitive ability to analyze a complex situation, abstract from it, and draw conclusions about the best strategy for the firm to follow.

It has been argued that many great leaders have had this visionary competency. Winston Churchill, Britain's leader during World War II, understood in the early 1930s that the rise of Nazi Germany was a profound threat to peace in Europe. He saw the big strategic picture and repeatedly warned the British government about it in the years before the outbreak of war, but to no avail. Only after Germany invaded Poland in 1939 did the political majority in Britain concede that he had been correct and turn to him to lead the country. In May 1945 Churchill again demonstrated his strategic thinking abilities when we warned President Harry Truman that the Soviets were erecting an "Iron Curtain" across Europe. Churchill urged Truman not to authorize the withdrawal of American forces from parts of Eastern Germany, arguing that the U.S. presence would be replaced by Soviet control. Truman did not heed Churchill's warning, and an Iron Curtain dropped across Central Europe and remained there for the next 40 years.

Bill Gates is another example of a leader who has demonstrated strategic thinking. A few years ago this author had the opportunity to interview Gates about Microsoft's strategy.[17] Gates was still CEO of Microsoft and was very much the chief strategist. I arrived at the

■ Bill Gates: Strategic thinking.

achievement motivation
The unconscious concern for achieving excellence in accomplishments through one's individual efforts.

power motivation
The unconscious drive to acquire status and power and to have an impact on others.

interview with a long list of questions for Gates about changes taking place in the computer and communications industries and about Microsoft's strategy. As it turned out, there was no need to ask any of the questions. Gates knew I was interested in learning more about Microsoft's strategy, and he immediately launched into a high-level summary of changes taking place in the environment, how they were impacting Microsoft and might in the future, what competitors were doing, and what Microsoft's strategy would be. It was a brilliant intellectual performance. When he had finished, Gates had answered every single question on the list without a single one being asked, providing a compelling and coherent summery of Microsoft's strategy.

Leaders like Bill Gates and Winston Churchill embody the cognitive ability to see the big picture. Both individuals were naturally endowed with *high intelligence* and *superior reasoning ability,* letting them see what others could not—constructing mental maps to navigate the terrain they confronted. Although intelligence is a natural gift, some people believe that reasoning ability can to some extent be acquired. With appropriate education, aspiring leaders can be taught how to look at the big picture. Indeed, many of the models for strategic analysis that are taught in business schools, such as Porter's competitive forces model (see Chapter 2), are designed to do just that.

// ACHIEVEMENT MOTIVATION

Achievement motivation is the unconscious concern for achieving excellence in accomplishments through one's individual efforts. Achievement-motivated individuals set challenging goals for themselves, assume personal responsibility for goal accomplishment, are persistent in pursuing those goals, take calculated risks to achieve their goals, and actively use information for feedback, adjusting their efforts as necessary.[18] In other words, achievement-motivated individuals have a high degree of *intrinsic drive.* They are goal-driven. They know what they want to achieve, work hard toward that end, will take risks when necessary, and do not blame others if they fail to attain their goals.

U.S. President Lyndon Johnson was an ambitious individual who had his sights set from youth on attaining high political office. Johnson was driven and worked long and hard to attain his goals. As such, he embodied achievement motivation. The same can be said of Bill Gates. From an early age Gates wanted to be a successful entrepreneur. As teenagers he and Microsoft cofounder Paul Allen would look through issues of *Forbes* magazine, asking how people got onto the *Forbes* list of the richest people in America. Gates wanted to be one of them. Like Johnson, he was also a risk taker. When he saw an opportunity to profit from the emergence of the personal computer, he dropped out of Harvard to start his own company (Microsoft)—something most people would never do.

// POWER MOTIVATION

Power motivation is defined as the unconscious drive to acquire status and power and to have an impact on others. Psychologist David McClelland argues that effective leaders want to accumulate power so they can influence others, and that they do this because it gives them intrinsic satisfaction.[19] The power motivation is necessary for leadership effectiveness, according to McClelland, because getting things done in organizations requires individuals to accumulate power and use it to influence others.

However, McClelland stresses that effective leaders also demonstrate a high concern for the moral exercise of power. Effective leaders act with *integrity.* Employees will not follow leaders willingly unless they trust them, and trust is derived from integrity. Leadership effectiveness, therefore, requires more than power motivation: It requires an ability to use that power in a just fashion that earns the respect and commitment of followers. Interestingly, several large-scale studies have reported that integrity or honesty is the most important leadership characteristic. Employees want honest leaders whom they can trust.[20]

// CHARISMA

Robert House has proposed that charisma is also an important trait of effective leaders.[21] **Charisma** refers to the ability that some people have to charm or influence others. Charismatic individuals are often said to have "magnetic" personalities that are larger than life and that draw others toward them. Charismatic leaders have exceptionally high self-confidence, strength of conviction, and assertiveness or social dominance, and they are often superb communicators. Former U.S. President Bill Clinton is generally viewed as quite charismatic, even by those who disagree with his politics. Steve Jobs, the CEO of Apple computer, is also regarded as charismatic, as was Sam Walton, the founder of Wal-Mart. Charismatic leaders are able to command the loyalty of their followers, and this can make them particularly effective. Unfortunately some charismatic leaders have used their charisma to do harm. Jim Jones, the charismatic leader of the Peoples Temple religious cult, used his charisma first to persuade the 1,000 or so members of his church to move from San Francisco to Guyana with him, and then in 1978 to convince them to participate in a mass suicide that left 914 people dead.

Management writer Jim Collins has recently argued that although charismatic leaders can be effective, charisma can also work against effective leadership.[22] In Collins's view, leaders with charismatic personalities can use their charm to get people to do things that defy rational logic (witness Jim Jones). Leaders who lack charisma, however, have to rely on logic, fact, reason, and data to win arguments—and that can produce better decisions. Collins points to Walgreen CEO Charles R. Walgreen, who lacked charisma but built a great company nonetheless. Another example would be David Glass, who succeeded Sam Walton as CEO of Wal-Mart and helped to build Wal-Mart into the dominant enterprise it is today. Glass lacked charisma, but no one would disagree that he was an effective leader.

// EMOTIONAL INTELLIGENCE

A controversial contributor to the trait approach to leadership is a perspective called **emotional intelligence**, which refers to the ability to monitor one's own and others' feelings and emotions, to discriminate among them, and to use this information to guide one's thinking and actions.[23] The concept has been popularized by writer and consultant Daniel Goleman, who argues that emotional intelligence is a bundle of related competencies that many effective leaders exhibit.[24] According to Goleman, the key components of emotional intelligence are these:

- Self-awareness—the ability to understand one's own moods, emotions, and drives, as well as their effect on others.
- Self-regulation—the ability to control or redirect disruptive impulses or moods and to think before acting.
- Motivation—a passion for work that goes beyond money or status, and a propensity to pursue goals with energy and persistence.
- Empathy—understanding the feelings and viewpoints of subordinates, and taking those into account when making decisions.
- Social skills—friendliness with a purpose.

Goleman asserts that leaders who possess these attributes—who exhibit a high degree of emotional intelligence—tend to be more effective than those who lack them. Their self-awareness and self-regulation elicit the trust and confidence of subordinates. In Goleman's view, people respect leaders who, because they are self-aware, recognize their own limitations and, because they are self-regulating, consider decisions carefully. Goleman also argues that self-aware and self-regulating individuals tend to be more self-confident and therefore are better able to cope with ambiguity and are more open to change. Strong motivation exhibited in a passion for work can also be infectious, helping to persuade others to join in pursuit of a common goal or organizational mission. Finally, strong empathy and social skills can help leaders earn the loyalty of subordinates. Empathetic and socially adept individuals tend to be skilled at managing

charisma
The ability of some people to charm or influence others.

emotional intelligence
The ability to monitor one's own and others' feelings and emotions, to discriminate among them, and to use this information to guide one's thinking and actions.

disputes, can find common ground and purpose among diverse constituencies, and can move people in a desired direction. They can also build a network of allies.

Goleman cites some limited data to support the emotional intelligence view. In a 1996 study of a food and beverage company, David McClelland found that when senior managers had a critical mass of emotional intelligence competencies, their divisions outperformed yearly earnings goals by 20 percent. Meanwhile divisional leaders without that critical mass of competencies underperformed their goals by almost the same amount. Goleman states that his own research suggests that although intelligence and cognitive skills such as big picture thinking predict leadership effectiveness, nearly 90 percent of the difference between star performers and average performers in senior leadership positions can be attributed to emotional intelligence factors. (Interestingly, Goleman's own research has not been published, so we do not know how robust his findings and research methodology actually are.)

The emotional intelligence perspective has some appeal and has certainly generated considerable interest, but several writers have attacked it for being defined so broadly that it lacks any real discriminating power. In a stinging critique, the highly regarded management scholar Ed Locke states that the definition of emotional intelligence is "preposterously all-encompassing."[25] Critics such as Locke also point out that the evidence in favor of emotional intelligence is sketchy at best and is derived from unpublished studies and proprietary data sets that others cannot see. He also notes that those who argue that emotional intelligence is an important construct are academics turned consultants who have made a fortune out of the concept and have a stake in promoting it.

Is Locke correct? It is difficult to say. Resolution of the increasingly vitriolic debate about emotional intelligence awaits detailed research either confirming or falsifying the main proposition of the emotional intelligence perspective on competencies: that the self-regulation of emotions contributes to leadership effectiveness.

// LIMITATIONS AND IMPLICATIONS

A naive reading of the trait (or competency) perspective on leadership might lead one to believe that all of the traits just discussed are needed for effective leadership, but this is not the case. Not all the traits are equally important, and there are certainly examples of effective leaders who do not possess all of these traits. Perhaps some traits are more critical in certain situations than others are. For example, charisma may be particularly valuable when a leader needs to convince employees to commit to a widespread program of organizational change, rejecting the status quo and moving toward a new configuration of strategy and organization architecture. The importance of different traits for effective leadership, therefore, is context dependent. What works in one situation might not in another.[26] Moreover, as we saw in the case of emotional intelligence and charisma, there is still a lack of agreement over the validity and importance of some of these traits—both as coherent constructs and as predictors of leadership effectiveness.

Although the trait perspective seems to suggest that effective leaders are born, not made, again this is not strictly true. We are all gifted with a certain level of intelligence, drive, and reasoning ability; some competencies can be acquired, or at least improved, through learning. Goleman, for example, argues that although emotional intelligence is partly innate, leaders can enhance their emotional intelligence through training. They can learn to become more self-regulating and self-aware, to put themselves in the shoes of others and develop empathy. To the extent that they are successful, this may improve their effectiveness as leaders. Moreover, as stated already, leaders can improve their strategic thinking ability by using frameworks such as Porter's competitive forces model that help them see the big picture.

■ // The Behavior Perspective

The behavior perspective on leadership tries to link effectiveness of leaders with their behavior toward subordinates. The assumption is that certain leadership behaviors result in greater commitment on the part of subordinates and hence higher performance in pursuit of organization goals. Various empirical studies have distilled two clusters of leadership behaviors, or styles, from literally thousands of leadership behavior items.[27]

One cluster represents **people-oriented behavior**, which is a leadership style that includes showing mutual trust and respect for subordinates, demonstrating a genuine concern for their needs, and having a desire to look out for their welfare. Leaders with a strong people-oriented style listen to employee suggestions, do personal favors for employees, support their interests when required, and treat employees as equals. (One might argue that leaders who engage in people-oriented behaviors have a high degree of emotional intelligence.)

The other cluster represents task-oriented behaviors and includes behaviors that define and structure work roles. The style of leaders who engage in **task-oriented behavior** is to assign employees to specific tasks, clarify their work duties and procedures, ensure that they follow company rules, and push them to reach their performance capacity. Task-oriented leaders establish stretch goals and challenge employees to push beyond those high standards.

Should leaders be task-oriented or people-oriented? This is a difficult question to answer because each style has advantages and disadvantages. Research suggests that both styles are positively associated with leader effectiveness, but differences are often apparent only for leaders who score either very high or very low on a particular style. Generally measures of subordinate performance such as absenteeism, grievances, turnover, and job dissatisfaction are worse among employees who work with supervisors with very low levels of people-oriented leadership, suggesting that leaders who lack a people orientation are ineffective. However, job performance is also lower among employees who work for leaders who do not engage in task-oriented behaviors.[28]

In general, however, this research has failed to show clear patterns linking these different behaviors to leadership effectiveness. One problem may be that the two clusters are not mutually exclusive. Effective leaders may display both people-oriented and task-oriented behavior. Jack Welch, the former CEO of General Electric, routinely used both types of behaviors. He was a very task-oriented leader, setting goals and holding subordinates accountable for attaining those goals. But he could also be very people-oriented, sending handwritten notes to managers, inquiring about their personal lives, and offering to help managers in trouble. A second problem with the behavioral leadership perspective is that the two categories are broad generalizations that mask specific behaviors within each category, and the specific behaviors may be more important than the broad form. A final problem with the perspective is that the appropriate behaviors may be context dependent.[29] Different situations may require leaders to emphasize different styles—sometimes it may be best to be task-oriented, other times people-oriented. The contingency perspective on leadership tries to address this issue.

// The Contingency Perspective

At the heart of the contingency perspective is a simple proposition: The best leadership behavior to adopt depends on the context.[30] There are a number of different contingency theories of leadership, and there is little agreement among leadership researchers about their validity. Here we briefly review three important contingency perspectives to see what we can learn about the elusive topic of leadership effectiveness. These perspectives are Fiedler's contingency theory, path–goal theory, and the leadership substitutes theory.

// FIEDLER'S CONTINGENCY THEORY

In the 1960s psychologist Fred Fiedler introduced his contingency theory of leadership in an attempt to move the field of leadership research away from an obsession with leadership and behaviors. Fiedler's basic assumption was that it was difficult if not impossible for people to change their leadership style. Fiedler accepted the two basic leadership styles we have just discussed (task-oriented and people-oriented) although he came up with his own way of measuring those styles. He believed that the effectiveness of a leader should be measured by how the team, group, or organization under the leader performed. His research suggests that the

people-oriented behavior
A leadership style that includes showing mutual trust and respect for subordinates, demonstrating genuine concern for their needs, and having a desire to look out for their welfare.

task-oriented behavior
The style of leaders who assign employees to specific tasks, clarify their work duties and procedures, ensure that they follow company rules, and push them to reach their performance capacity.

■ Leadership style at General Electric.

FIGURE 16.2

Fiedler's Leadership Theory

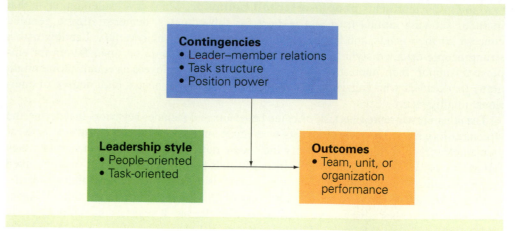

Contingencies
• Leader–member relations
• Task structure
• Position power

Leadership style
• People-oriented
• Task-oriented

Outcomes
• Team, unit, or organization performance

leader–member relations

How well followers respect, trust, and like their leaders.

task structure

The degree to which the jobs of subordinates are highly structured with clear work responsibilities, well-defined tasks, explicit goals, and specific procedures.

position power

The power that derives from formal hierarchical power over subordinates, including the legitimate power to hire, fire, reward, and punish subordinates.

effectiveness of the two basic leadership styles depends on three main situational factors or contingencies (see Figure 16.2).

The first contingency is **leader–member relations**, which refers to how well followers respect, trust, and like their leaders. When leader–member relations are good, subordinates respect, trust, and like their leaders. The second contingency is **task structure**, which refers to the degree to which the jobs of subordinates are highly structured with clear work responsibilities, well-defined tasks, explicit goals, and specific procedures. The jobs of assembly-line workers, for example, have a high degree of task structure. The job is clearly structured, and responsibilities, goals, and procedures are well understood. In contrast, creative jobs from fashion design to R&D tend to have a low degree of task structure by nature. The final contingency is **position power**, which is the power that derives from formal hierarchical power over subordinates and includes the legitimate power to hire, fire, reward, and punish subordinates.

Fiedler argued that the situational factors (contingencies) were *favorable* when leader–member relations were good, task structure was clearly defined and understood, and position power was high. Situational factors were *unfavorable* when leader–member relations were poor, task structure was ill-defined, and the position power of the leader was low. Fiedler's research showed that *task-oriented* leaders did well in two situations: when the situational factors were unfavorable or very favorable. Conversely, *people-oriented* leaders did better when the situational factors were moderately favorable (see Figure 16.3).

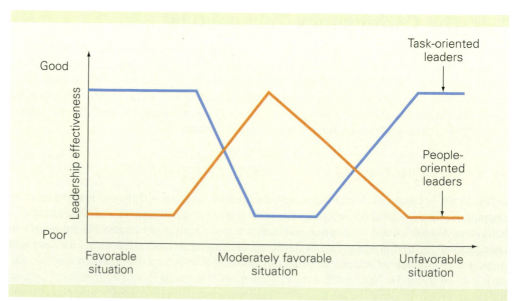

FIGURE 16.3

Predictions of Fiedler's Theory

Task-oriented leaders seem to do well in very favorable situations because everyone gets along, the task is clear, and the leader has the power needed to take charge and set the direction. According to Fiedler, task-oriented leaders also do well when situational factors are unfavorable because they can establish goals and impose structure on the tasks of subordinates, giving them direction, even if the leaders are not personally liked or trusted. In moderately favorable situations, a leader with good people skills (a people-oriented leader) can create a positive atmosphere in his or her group that improves interpersonal relationships, clarifies task structure, and helps the leader influence subordinates.

The implication of Fiedler's theory is that leaders must be matched to situations. It would not work, for example, to appoint a people-oriented leader in an unfavorable turnaround situation—a task-oriented leader would be better. People-oriented leaders, who focus on building trusting relationships, might not be the best match when hard decisions have to be made: In Fiedler's view a people-oriented leader would simply be incapable of imposing the required structure and goals. Anecdotal evidence supports this. For example, in 2001 Merrill Lynch appointed Stan O'Neal as CEO of the troubled financial institution. At the time Merrill's profits were down, it was losing market share, and outside observers believed that the company had a bloated bureaucracy and far too many stockbrokers. O'Neal is a classic task-oriented leader. Described as cold, calculating, aloof, and ruthless, O'Neal cut costs with zeal, laying off 24,000 employees, closing more than 300 field offices, and firing dozens of veteran managers, including some of his closest subordinates in 2003 after they went behind his back and tried to lobby the board to replace him. Nevertheless O'Neal engineered an impressive turnaround at Merrill Lynch with net earnings surging to a record $5.2 billion in 2005, up from $2.5 billion in 2002.[31]

■ Leadership style at Merrill Lynch.

The great virtue of Fiedler's theory is that it advocates matching the leader to the situation, which has some intuitive appeal. A weakness with this theory is that it seems simplistic. Like the behavioral theories, which it extends, classifying leadership behavior into two broad types seems an unwarranted generalization. Moreover, the division of leaders into people-oriented and task-oriented styles ignores the fact that sometimes the same leader can exhibit elements of both styles. Fiedler's theory also suggests that a leader who succeeds in changing the situation (as Stan O'Neal has done at Merrill Lynch) should perhaps be replaced by another leader more suited to the new situation. However, it seems unrealistic to "reward" an effective leader like O'Neal by removing him because he has done his job so well that an unfavorable situation has become more favorable. Finally, Fiedler assumes that leaders cannot change their style, but not everyone agrees with this. The next perspective we look at, path–goal theory, asserts that leaders can change their style to match the situation.

Unlovable but Unperturbed   Stan O'Neal is a task-oriented leader who gets low points for his people skills. Described as a cold, aloof, ruthless bean counter, O'Neal nevertheless engineered an impressive turnaround at Merrill Lynch, cutting costs and boosting profits to record levels between 2001 and 2005. O'Neal has reportedly stated that "ruthless isn't always that bad."

© Getty Images

// PATH–GOAL THEORY

Path–goal theory is the most complex leadership theory we review here. Like Fiedler's theory, path–goal theory is a contingency theory. It states that the best leadership style depends on the situation. Unlike Fiedler's theory, path–goal theory is based on the assumption that leaders can change their style to match the situation. Path–goal theory would state, for example, that having engineered an impressive turnaround at Merrill Lynch, Stan O'Neal can continue to be an effective leader by adopting different behaviors, including a more people-oriented style.

Effective Leadership   The core proposition of path–goal theory is that leaders can increase the performance of their subordinates by clarifying and clearing the "path" that subordinates have to follow to attain their goals, and by identifying and offering rewards that motivate subordinates to work toward their goals. *Clarifying the path* means leaders work with subordinates to help them identify and learn behaviors that will lead to goal attainment. In other words, they mentor and coach subordinates. *Clearing the path* means leaders try to take care of problems and remove

directive leadership

Occurs when leaders tell subordinates exactly what they are supposed to do, giving them goals, specific tasks, guidelines for performing those tasks, and the like.

supportive leadership

A leadership style in which the leader is approachable and friendly, shows concern for the welfare of subordinates, and treats them as equals.

participative leadership

A leadership style in which the leader consults with his or her subordinates, asking for their opinions before making a decision.

achievement-oriented leadership

Occurs when a leader sets high goals for subordinates, has high expectations for their performance, and displays confidence in subordinates, encouraging and helping them to take on greater responsibilities.

obstacles that make it difficult for subordinates to attain their goals. For example, they might remove unnecessary tasks, such as excessive meetings, so subordinates can focus on important work. *Identifying and offering rewards* means leaders identify what will motivate their subordinates to work toward goals attainment, and then put the appropriate rewards in place.

As the chair of an academic department, the current author once had to lead some 23 other faculty members (a difficult proposition even in the best of times)! Clarifying the path involved helping other faculty members understand what was required both for them to get a good performance review and for the business school to improve its standing in the academic community as measured by rankings. What was stressed continually was the need to publish research in the best academic journals and to get excellent teaching evaluations for their classroom performance. Time was also spent in coaching junior faculty members to help them improve both their research and teaching performance. Clearing the path involved removing obstacles impeding work to attain these goals by, for example, reducing the number of committees faculty members had to serve on. Identifying and offering rewards meant finding and using the right incentives—including pay raises, promotions, and awards—to motivate faculty members to work harder toward goal attainment.

Leadership Styles Path–goal theory describes four different leadership styles (see Figure 16.4).[32] First there is **directive leadership**, which occurs when leaders tell subordinates exactly what they are supposed to do, giving them goals, specific tasks, guidelines for performing those tasks, and the like. Directive leadership is essentially the same as the task-oriented leadership concept discussed earlier. A second leadership style is **supportive leadership**, which can be defined as a leadership style in which the leader is approachable and friendly, shows concern for the welfare of subordinates, and treats them as equals. Supportive leadership is similar to people-oriented leadership.

A third leadership style is known as **participative leadership**, in which a leader consults with his or her subordinates, asking for their opinions before making a decision. The participative leader encourages subordinates to make suggestions and to offer input into the decision-making process. The final leadership style, known as **achievement-oriented leadership**, occurs when a leader sets high goals for subordinates, has high expectations for their performance, and displays confidence in subordinates, encouraging and helping them to take on greater responsibilities.

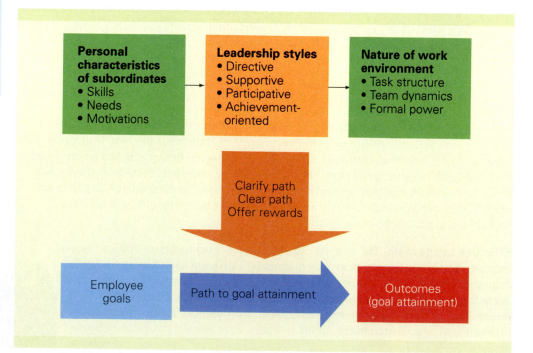

FIGURE 16.4

Path–Goal Theory

Contingencies Path–goal theory argues that a leader can change his or her leadership style, and that two important contingencies dictate the best choice of leadership style: (1) the personal characteristics of subordinates and (2) the nature of the work environment (see Figure 16.4). The personal characteristics of subordinates include factors such as the abilities, skills, needs, and motivations of employees. For example, academics are skilled and self-motivated individuals with a high sense of their own self-worth. As such, they respond poorly to directive leadership (they resent being told what to do). Conversely, they are generally open to a participative leadership style that recognizes that they have substantial expertise and experience and much advice to offer the leader. The same can be said of most professional employees, such as lawyers, doctors, and research scientists.

The nature of the work environment refers to the *task structure* (is the task well-defined and standardized or complex and varied?), the *dynamics of the work group* or team (is the team cohesive or fragmented?), and the *formal power* in the organization (is it strong or weak?). Assembly-line work, for example, is well-defined, standardized, and predictable. Such work can be dull, leading to apathy and boredom among employees. To counter this, path–goal theory suggests achievement-oriented leadership, where the leader motivates subordinates by setting challenging goals and expressing confidence in subordinates' ability to attain those goals.

Path–goal theory makes a number of key predictions. First, the theory states that if followers lack confidence, supportive leadership will increase subordinates' confidence that they can achieve goals, which raises performance. If the task of subordinates is ambiguous, directive leadership may be preferred because this helps clarify the path subordinates must follow, which again increases performance. If the task of subordinates is standardized and dull, achievement-oriented leadership can motivate subordinates by setting high goals and expressing confidence in their abilities. If the rewards offered to employees are inappropriate, participative leadership may allow the leader to clarify the needs of subordinates and change rewards to improve performance.

Contributions and Limitations A virtue of path–goal theory is that it recognizes a wider diversity of leadership styles than either behavioral theory or Fiedler's theory. The recognition that in addition to directive (task-oriented) and supportive (people-oriented) styles leaders can adopt achievement-oriented and participative leadership styles adds richness to any discussion of what effective leadership entails. Some might see another virtue in the assumption that leaders can match their style to the situation they confront. This implies that leaders are at least in part made, not born, which is an encouraging message for managers trying to improve their leadership capabilities. In addition, path–goal theory tries to predict what style is best suited to what situation, which might be useful information for managers trying to determine how they should lead.

On the other hand, path–goal theory has weaknesses. First, the implicit assumption that a leader can adopt only one style at a time seems simplistic. A leader might develop a successful individual style that combines elements of the styles discussed here. A leader can direct subordinates to perform certain tasks while still being approachable and friendly (supportive leadership), setting high goals (achievement-oriented leadership), and consulting with employees about how to improve the work environment (participative leadership). Second, despite significant research, there is still no strong empirical consensus that path–goal theory does a good job of explaining what is required for effective leadership.[33] Many of the propositions of path–goal theory are difficult to test, and they remain unexplored.

Finally, and perhaps most seriously, path–goal theory has a narrow definition of leadership effectiveness. The theory focuses on what a leader can do to increase subordinates' motivation by clarifying and clearing the path toward a goal and putting appropriate rewards in place. What is ignored are other potentially important factors in the leadership process—such as the central role of leaders in crafting a strategic vision, the need for leaders to interact with external stakeholders, the ability of the leader to energize employees through eloquent words, the importance of personality characteristics such as charisma, and the significance of leading by example. Thus as insightful as path–goal theory is, it too seems to provide only a partial definition of effective leadership.

// LEADERSHIP SUBSTITUTES

Unlike path–goal leadership, which recommends different leadership styles in various situations, the **leadership substitutes** approach identifies contingencies that may be "substitutes" for a leadership style.[34] A substitute is a situational variable (a contingency) that makes a leadership style unnecessary. The theory identifies several contingencies that substitute for task-oriented and people-oriented leadership styles. For example, it is argued that highly professional subordinates who know how to do their tasks, such as lawyers or doctors, do not need a task-oriented leader who structures their work and tells them what to do. Moreover, because such professional subordinates derive substantial intrinsic satisfaction from their work and have a high sense of self-worth, a people-oriented leadership style is also less necessary. Professionalism on the part of subordinates, in other words, substitutes for both task- and people-oriented leadership styles. Leaders of organizations with a highly professional workforce, therefore, are often considered "first among equals," and their own leadership focuses on providing strategic direction for the organization and interacting with stakeholders.

More generally, any situational variable that results in employees managing their own behavior and directing themselves toward the attainment of goals (what we might call *self-leadership*) reduces the need for proactive task-oriented and people-oriented leadership styles. For example, performance-based reward systems can keep employees directed toward organizational goals, so they might replace or reduce the need for task-oriented leadership. Similarly, cohesive self-managing work teams can be a substitute for both task- and people-oriented leadership. In a cohesive team coworkers can become substitutes for hierarchical leadership.[35] Coworkers can direct new employees, explaining to them how the team works and what the tasks entail. Coworkers can also provide the social support that might otherwise be provided by a people-oriented leader. Moreover, when bonus pay for a team is linked to team performance, peer control within the team can act as a substitute for achievement-oriented leadership, with team members stretching themselves to attain team goals and encouraging each other to work hard toward that end.[36] Such conditions are found within companies such as Toyota, 3M, and Nucor Steel, all of which group employees into self-managing teams that take on direct responsibility for a portion of the work process. In these enterprises team self-management substitutes for hierarchical leadership, enabling the firms to operate with flatter organizational structures that have fewer management layers and wider spans of control (see Chapter 8).

The idea of leadership substitutes has intuitive appeal, but the empirical evidence so far is mixed. Some studies show that a few substitutes do replace the need for task- or people-oriented leadership, but others do not. The messiness of statistically testing for leadership substitutes may account for some problems. However, other writers contend that the limited support is evidence that leadership plays a critical role regardless of the situation.[37] Probably at best we can conclude that a few contingencies such as self-managing work teams, self-leadership, and appropriate reward systems might reduce the importance of proactive leadership.

// Transformational Leadership

We opened this chapter with the story of how Gordon Bethune transformed Continental Airlines. Bethune was a transformational leader: He initiated radical change in Continental Airlines that improved the performance of that organization. Like Bethune, **transformational leaders** are agents of strategic and organizational change.[38] Transformational leaders reenergize troubled organizations, pushing them in new strategic directions and engineering wholesale changes in operational processes, organization architecture, and culture. Some of the most admired business leaders of our time—people like General Electric's Jack Welch, Gordon Bethune, Lou Gerstner at IBM, and William Bratton at the New York Police Department—are described as transformational leaders.

In recent decades leadership experts have come to recognize the importance of transformational leadership. In a world where the only constant is change, long-established organizations periodically find their competitive position under attack from new rivals who are utilizing new technology and new business models to gain market share. If established organizations confronting such challenges are to survive, they must make substantial changes in their strategy, organization, and operations, and this requires transformational leadership. Thus IBM, once the world's most profitable enterprise, found itself losing billions of dollars in the early 1990s as the center of gravity in the computer industry shifted away from its mainframe computers toward personal computers, a business dominated by scrappy new rivals such as Dell Computer, Microsoft, and Intel. It took a transformational leader, Lou Gerstner, to implement much-needed changes at IBM. Gerstner remade IBM, building a big service business where none existed and replacing IBM's bureaucratic, consensus-driven culture with a more dynamic and entrepreneurial ideology.

■ Transformational leadership at IBM.

To drive home the importance of transformational leaders, a comparison is often made between them and transactional leaders. A **transactional leader** helps an organization achieve its current objectives.[39] He or she tries to run the ship as efficiently as possible but does not try to change the organization's course. The contingency and behavioral theories described earlier adopt the transactional perspective: They focus on leader behaviors that improve employee performance and satisfaction within a given context. In contrast, transformational leadership is about changing the organization's context, altering strategies and culture to fit better with the surrounding environment.[40] Transformational leaders are change agents who energize and direct employees to a new set of corporate values and behaviors.

transactional leader
A leader who helps an organization achieve its current objectives.

// ELEMENTS OF TRANSFORMATIONAL LEADERSHIP

What does it take to be a transformational leader? Writers on the topic have identified a number of behaviors that transformational leaders seem to share (see Figure 16.5).[41] First, transformational leaders *envision* a different future for the organizations they are leading. This new vision often embraces changes in both strategy and the architecture of the organization, including the culture of the organization as captured by values and norms. Gordon Bethune envisioned a different strategic future for Continental Airlines: one where planes arrived and left on schedule and customers were satisfied.

Second, transformational leaders persistently *communicate* this new vision to employees. They use every opportunity to state what the vision is and what values employees must adopt to execute that vision. Again, Bethune used every opportunity he could to communicate his message to Continental employees. Transformational leaders frame messages around a grand purpose with emotional appeal that captivates employees and other corporate stakeholders. Such framing helps transformational leaders establish a shared mental model that subordinates can adopt as their own.[42] Transformational leaders bring their visions to life through symbols, metaphors, stories, and other vehicles that transcend plain language. Metaphors borrow images of other experiences, thereby creating richer meaning in the vision that has not yet been experienced.

Third, transformational leaders *model desired behaviors*. They recognize that to succeed, they must lead by example. They live by the values they espouse. They know that unless they do this, employees will not take them seriously, and any transformational change effort will fail. In one of the great historical stories of transformational leadership, when Lee Iacocca took over the CEO position at Chrysler, which at the time was teetering on the brink of bankruptcy, he famously announced that he would take only $1 a year in salary until the company

FIGURE 16.5

Behaviors of
Transformational
Leaders

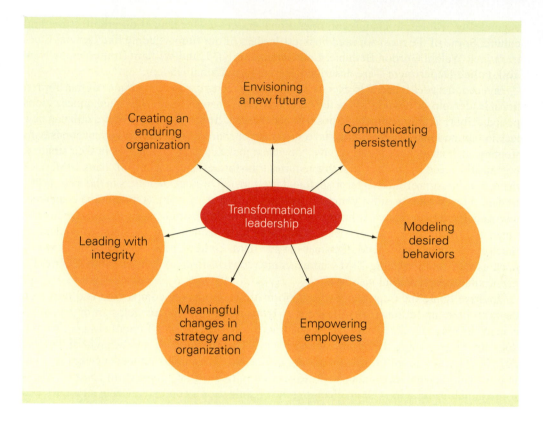

■ Transformational
leadership at Continental
Airlines.

became profitable. This symbolic act sent a very strong message to employees: We are all in this together, and we suffer and prosper together.

Fourth, transformational leaders *empower employees* to implement the grand strategic visions they have articulated. At Continental Airlines Gordon Bethune did this by asking employees to help him improve Continental's performance and by splitting the benefits with them. At General Electric Jack Welch empowered employees by introducing a methodology known as "workout," where during a three-day event employees could suggest process improvements to their bosses, who had to say yes or no to proposals on the spot. Welch went further, tying the bonus pay of managers to their success at implementing process improvements that came out of workout sessions.

Fifth, transformational leaders make *meaningful changes* in the activities and architecture of an organization. They move quickly to show that they are serious, changing organizational structure, controls, and incentive systems to promote the behaviors they see as necessary to implement their strategic vision. Transformational leaders recognize that without concrete actions, employees will soon lose faith in change efforts. They understand that to get employees' support for organizational change efforts, they need to show immediately that they mean what they say. Gordon Bethune did this by tying employee bonuses to improvements in Continental's customer service.

Sixth, transformational leaders *lead with integrity.* They recognize that people will not follow someone they do not trust, and that a reputation for fairness and candor is among the most important assets a leader can have. People respect leaders who tell them the truth (even if that truth is sometimes hard) and who manage in an ethical manner. This does not mean that transformational leaders are not tough, but they are tough in a fair way. If they have to lay off employees, they do so in an open and honest way, explaining why they have to make this difficult choice. Thus although Stan O'Neal is regarded as a tough leader who did not flinch from announcing significant job cuts when he took over the helm of Merrill Lynch, he is also regarded as having integrity.

Finally, transformational leaders *create an enduring organization* that continues to operate efficiently and effectively long after they are gone. They do not lead through a cult of personality; rather they reengineer the organization to create a new system that will persist and produce benefits for years. Although Jack Welch stepped down as CEO of General Electric in 2001, GE is still very much the organization that Welch built. Similarly, the changes William Bratton introduced in the New York Police Department persist today even though he left in the 1990s. Great transformational leaders make themselves redundant by building an organization and by developing people who can continue their work once they have moved on.

Note that we have not said transformational leaders are charismatic. They may be charismatic, but they do not have to be. Charisma is a personality trait that gives a leader power and influence over followers, whereas transformational leadership is a set of behaviors that managers use to lead a change process.[43] Charismatic leaders are born, but the aspects of transformational leadership can be learned. However, transformational leaders certainly require high intelligence and superior reasoning ability to envision a different strategic future for the organization, and intelligence at least is a trait. Many successful transformational leaders were effective but not charismatic. Although Lee Iacocca and Jack Welch were charismatic, Lou Gerstner and William Bratton were not, but they all engineered significant and persistent changes in the organizations they led.

// EVALUATING TRANSFORMATIONAL LEADERSHIP

The concept of transformational leadership has wide appeal, and it is probably the most popular perspective on leadership today. Moreover, research suggests that transformational leaders make a difference. Subordinates are more satisfied and have greater commitment to their organizations under transformational leaders. They also perform better, engage in more organizational citizenship behaviors, and tend to make decisions that are more creative.[44] However, the concept of transformational leadership faces a number of challenges.

One problem is that some writers use circular logic by defining transformational leadership in terms of the leader's success.[45] They suggest that leaders are transformational when they successfully bring about change, rather than when they engage in certain behaviors that we call transformational. Another concern is that some writers present transformational leadership as a universal rather than a contingency-oriented approach. However, recently writers have begun to explore the idea that transformational leadership may be more appropriate in some situations than in others.[46] Transformational leadership seems most appropriate when organizations are in trouble and need to improve their performance and adapt to a changing environment. For an organization based in a stable environment that is performing well, transactional leadership may be just fine. Indeed, a transformational leader who tries to change a well-oiled machine might do more harm than good.

■ // Gender Differences in Leadership

The last three decades have seen a dramatic rise in the number of women found in leadership roles within organizations. In 1972 women filled 18 percent of administrative positions in the United States according to the Bureau of Labor Statistics; by 2002 this figure had increased to 46 percent.[47] It should be pointed out, however, that women are still unrepresented at the highest levels in organizations—only 16 percent of senior management positions in American industry were held by women in 2003.[48]

The steady rise of women in the workplace raises an important question: Do women lead differently than men? Several writers think so. They suggest that women have an interactive style that includes more people-oriented and participative leadership.[49] They also believe that women are more relationship-oriented, cooperative, nurturing, and emotional in their leadership roles.

They further assert that these qualities make women particularly well suited to leadership roles when companies are adopting a stronger emphasis on teams and employee involvement. These arguments are consistent with sex role stereotypes—namely that men tend to be more task-oriented whereas women are more people-oriented.

Are these stereotypes true? Do women adopt more people-oriented and participative leadership styles? The answers are no and yes, respectively. Leadership studies in work settings have generally found that male and female leaders do not differ in their levels of task-oriented or people-oriented leadership. The main explanation is that real-world jobs require similar behavior from male and female job incumbents.[50]

However, women do adopt a participative leadership style more readily than their male counterparts. One possible reason is that, compared to boys, girls are often raised to be more egalitarian and less status-oriented, which is consistent with being participative. There is also some evidence that women have better interpersonal skills than men, which translates into their relatively greater use of the participative leadership style. A third explanation is that subordinates expect female leaders to be more participative, based on their own sex role stereotypes, so female leaders comply with follower expectations to some extent.

Several recent surveys report that women are rated higher than men on leadership qualities such as coaching, teamwork, and empowering employees.[51] Yet research also suggests that women are evaluated negatively when they try to apply the full range of leadership styles, particularly more directive and autocratic approaches. Thus, ironically, women may be well suited to contemporary leadership roles, yet they continue to face limitations on leadership through the gender stereotypes and stereotypes of leaders held by followers.[52] Overall, both male and female leaders must be sensitive to the fact that followers have expectations about how leaders should act, and leaders who deviate from those expectations may get negative evaluations from their subordinates.

IN CONCLUSION WHY DOES IT MATTER?

Why is the study of leadership important for aspiring managers? First, as we noted in the opening chapter of this book, leadership is the pivotal function of management. To be effective, managers have to lead. Subordinates expect their managers to lead; and if managers are to strategize, plan, control, organize, and develop employees, they must meet these exceptions. Moreover, advancement within organizations requires leadership skills. You do not get to run an organization or one of its subunits unless you have demonstrated that you can lead subordinates.

Second, it is important to learn what makes an effective leader. We have seen that leaders are skilled at using power to influence subordinates and other important constituencies, as well as to get things done. Although personality traits such as intelligence and charisma may define some successful leaders, many of the characteristics of effective leaders are behaviors that can be learned and improved through practice. It is possible to learn how to lead; competencies that can be learned, such as strategic thinking and emotional intelligence, are potentially important predictors of leadership success. We have also seen that it may pay managers to vary their leadership styles, matching them to the situations. Some situations call for more task-oriented leadership, others for more people-oriented leadership; if path–goal theory is correct, managers can learn the skills associated with these various leadership styles and tailor their use of them to match the circumstances they face. Finally, we have seen what it takes to be a transformational leader—to alter the strategy and organization architecture of the company or subunit that a manager leads. This requires a set of behaviors that can be learned and honed through experience. The central message of this chapter is that you can learn how to improve your effectiveness as a leader.

MANAGEMENT CHALLENGES

1. Is an understanding of power and influence critical for leadership success? If so, how?

2. In this chapter we discussed Stan O'Neal, the CEO of Merrill Lynch. What makes Stan O'Neal an effective leader?

3. Is it possible to be both a people-oriented and a task-oriented leader?

4. How would you characterize the leadership style of Gordon Bethune, the former CEO of Continental Airlines who was profiled in this chapter?

5. Are great leaders born that way, or is it possible to learn how to be a great leader?

6. In February 2005 Carly Fiorina, the CEO of Hewlett-Packard, was ousted by HP's board of directors. Through research, try to find out something about Fiorina's leadership style (several articles published at the time discussed her tenure at HP). How would you characterize it? Was she an effective leader? Why do you think she was asked to resign?

MANAGEMENT PORTFOLIO

FOR THE ORGANIZATION YOU HAVE CHOSEN TO FOLLOW:

1. What can you find out about the leadership style of the chief executive officer? How would you characterize his or her leadership style?

2. Does the leadership style he or she has adopted match the situation confronting the organization?

3. Would you characterize the CEO as an effective leader? How would you explain his or her success or lack thereof?

CLOSING CASE   A.G. LAFLEY

On the day that A.G. Lafley took the helm at consumer products giant Procter & Gamble in 2000, the stock dropped by $4. The financial markets were unimpressed with Lafley's rise to the CEO spot. Lafley, who started out at P&G in 1977 as a brand assistant for Joy dishwashing liquid, did not seem to have the stuff of which CEO legends are made. Quiet, understated, and unassuming, with a shock of white hair, wire-rimmed glasses, and the demeanor of Mr. Rodgers, he looks more like a thoughtful college professor than the stereotype of a visionary and dynamic CEO. In a profile, a *Fortune* reporter described Lafley as "a listener, not a story-teller. He's likable, not awe-inspiring. He's the type of guy who gets excited in the mop aisle of a grocery store. . . . He has rallied his troops not with big speeches and dazzling promises, but by hearing them out, one at a time. It's a little dull perhaps."[53]

Dull or not, Lafley had his work cut out for him. His predecessor, Durk Jager, had lasted just 17 months after failing to improve P&G's lackluster performance. For a decade P&G had struggled to introduce new brands, considered by many to be the lifeblood of a large consumer products company. Worse still, half of P&G's 15 top brands were losing market share, and employee morale was at an all-time low.

Lafley realized that he had to move fast: "I had to move quickly to get people focused. I didn't want everyone sitting around worrying that the stock price had dropped in half."[54] One of Lafley's first acts was to issue a manifesto of "10 things I believe in." At the top of the list was "lead change," followed by "the consumer is boss." Lafley also signaled that it was time for P&G to look outside its own organization for new product ideas—something the company had long resisted.

As Lafley saw it, P&G did not need a radical makeover; it just needed to focus on selling more of its basic brands, such as Tide and Pampers. He chose P&G's 10 best-selling brands, each of which generated more than $1 billion in sales, and he told his managers to focus on selling more. These brands would get the bulk of P&G's resources. It was a message everyone could understand. Selling more Tide was easier than inventing the next great brand. For years P&G had been struggling to invent new brands, but it had not introduced a new blockbuster since 1983 when it had a huge hit with Always (feminine protection pads). Now, Lafley told his managers, the number one task was to sell more of what they had.

Lafley went further, pushing his managers to add value to P&G's established brands by listening closely to what consumers wanted. This approach worked. For example, by watching consumers use its diapers, P&G learned that mothers were frustrated by how long it took to toilet train their children; so P&G developed a new line of its best-selling Pampers brand—Feel n Learn Advanced Trainers, which stay wet for two minutes to alert toddlers to try tinkling in the toilet. He also told managers to focus on telling customers what the brand could do for them rather than the attributes of the product; so the mission for Pampers changed from "making the driest diapers" to "helping moms with babies' development." The result: Pampers gained market share against longtime rival Kimberly-Clark.

At the same time Lafley moved to cut costs. Within months he had eliminated some 9,600 jobs, closing down several new product development projects that were consuming resources and pulling new products from the market that had not generated significant sales. He also sold off products he did not see as strategic fits, including Jif and Crisco brands. It was a classic case of triage: Focus on what is selling, pour resources into those brands, and cut the rest.

Commenting on Lafley's cost cutting, one of P&G's board members noted, "He knows how to lay down the rules when he needs to. Quiet people tend to be the toughest." Indeed, in a culture traditionally characterized by collegiality, Lafley has not been shy about pushing his managers to improve their performance. Each quarter at a meeting with top managers, Lafley reveals everyone's financial results. He notes, "It motivates people who are performance oriented. For the people that it doesn't motivate, we are probably not the right place for them."[55]

The Un-CEO   A big listener, A.G. Lafley lacks the charismatic big personality of many star CEOs. But he has been an effective leader for Procter & Gamble, helping to drive the company to improve its operating performance after a decade of stagnation.

Courtesy of Procter & Gamble

Another goal of Lafley's was to break down the barriers within P&G, getting employees from different divisions to exchange ideas. He emphasized that R&D and marketing people from different divisions should talk to each other, which they had not traditionally done. To give the idea teeth, he rewarded business units that shared their ideas with others. To drive home the importance of removing barriers between units, Lafley embarked on a highly visible symbolic redesign of the fabled 11th-floor executive suites at P&G's head office. The oak-paneled walls were torn down; the 19th-century paintings that once decorated offices were donated to a local art museum; and the CEO and other top executives were assigned to cubicles on half the floor. The other half was transformed into a center for employee learning.

Lafley also articulated the need to "reach outside for ideas." His goal is to get half of P&G's new products from external sources—up from 20 percent when he took over. P&G has started entering alliances with other companies to develop new products, including competitor Clorox, with which it codeveloped Glad Press and Seal—a product that overtook S. C. Johnson's Saran Wrap to become the top-selling food wrap in the United States.

The results of Lafley's leadership have been impressive. P&G's core brands have been gaining impetus. In 2005, 19 out of P&G's top-selling 20 brands gained market share. Costs have fallen, and sales and profits have advanced strongly. In 2000 P&G earned $5.53 billion on sales of $40 billion. In 2005 it earned $10.4 billion on sales of $57 billion. The stock price doubled over the same period.[56]

CASE DISCUSSION QUESTIONS

1. How would you characterize the leadership style of A.G. Lafley—people-oriented or task-oriented?

2. What leadership competencies does A.G. Lafley have? What competencies often associated with strong leaders does he seem to lack?

3. How did Lafley go about shifting the strategy and culture of P&G? Would you characterize Lafley as a transformational leader or a transactional leader?

4. What does the story of A.G. Lafley tell you about the attributes and style of effective leaders?

ENDNOTES

1. G. Bethune, "From Worst to First," *Fortune,* May 25, 1998, pp. 185–89; B. O'Reilly, "The Mechanic Who Fixed Continental," *Fortune,* December 20, 1999, pp. 176–83.

2. G. Yukl and R. Lepsinger, "Why Integrating the Leading and Managing Roles Is Essential for Organizational Effectiveness," *Organizational Dynamics* 34, no. 4 (2005), pp. 361–75.

3. W. Bennis, *Why Leaders Can't Lead* (San Francisco: Jossey-Bass, 1989).

4. J.P. Kotter, "What Leaders Really Do," *Harvard Business Review* 68, no. 3 (1990), pp. 103–12.

5. Yukl and Lepsinger, "Why Integrating the Leading and Managing Roles Is Essential for Organizational Effectiveness."

6. D.V. Day and R.G. Lord, "Executive Leadership and Organizational Performance: Suggestions for a New Theory and Methodology," *Journal of Management* 14 (1988), pp. 453–64.

7. S. Lieberson and J.F. O'Conner, "Leadership and Organizational Performance: A Study of Large Corporations," *American Sociological Review* 37 (1972), pp. 91–109.

8. N., Wasserman, B. Anand, and N. Nohira, *When Does Leadership Matter?* Harvard Business School Working Paper 01–063, 2001.

9. Some academics say that these results show that leadership does not matter much because the percentage of variance in profit rates is in their view relatively small. However, a 15 percent variance in profit rates is large when you consider that if a good leader follows a good leader, as is often the case, we would expect no variance at all.

10. Staff reporter, "Exit Bad Guy," *The Economist,* June 20, 1998, p. 70.

11. R.N. Kanungo, "Leadership in Organizations: Looking Ahead to the 21st Century," *Canadian Psychology* 39 (Spring 1998), pp. 71–82; G.A. Yukl, *Leadership in Organizations,* 6th ed. (Upper Saddle River, NJ: Pearson Education, 2006); G.A. Yukl, "Managerial Leadership: A Review of Theory and Research," *Journal of Management* 15 (1989), pp. 251–89.

12. Yukl, "Managerial Leadership: A Review of Theory and Research."

13. W.C. Kim and Mauborgne, "Tipping Point Leadership," *Harvard Business Review* 81, no. 4 (2003), pp. 60–71.

14. Yukl, "Managerial Leadership: A Review of Theory and Research."

15. R.M. Stogdill, *Handbook of Leadership* (New York: The Free Press, 1974), Chapter 5.

16. R.J. House and R.N. Aditya, "The Social Scientific Study of Leadership: Quo Vadis?" *Journal of Management* 23 (1997), pp. 409–73.

17. The interview was to gather information for an executive course the author was teaching at Microsoft.

18. House and Aditya, "The Social Scientific Study of Leadership: Quo Vadis?"

19. D.C. McClelland, *Power: The Inner Experience* (New York: Irvington, 1975).

20. D.R. May et al., "The Moral Component of Authentic Leadership," *Organizational Dynamics* 32 (August 2003), pp. 247–60. The large-scale studies are reported in C. Savoye, "Workers Say Honesty Is Best Company Policy," *Christian Science Monitor,* June 15, 2000; J.M. Kouzes and B.Z. Posner, *The Leadership Challenge,* 3rd ed. (San Francisco: Jossey-Bass, 2002), Chapter 2; J. Schettler, "Leadership in Corporate America," *Training & Development,* September 2002, pp. 66–73.

21. R.J. House et al., "Personality and Charisma in the U.S. Presidency: A Psychological Theory of Leadership Effectiveness," *Administrative Science Quarterly* 36 (1991), pp. 364–96.

22. E.M. Heffes, "Follow These Leaders," *Financial Executive,* April 2005, pp. 20–24; J. Collins, *From Good to Great* (New York: Harper Collins, 2001).

23. P. Salovey, and J. Mayer, "Emotional Intelligence," *Imagination, Cognition, and Personality* 9 (1990), pp. 185–211. See also J.M. George, "Emotions and Leadership: The Role of Emotional Intelligence," *Human Relations* 53 (August 2000), pp. 1027–45.

24. The term was first coined by Salovey and Mayer in 1990. See Salovey and Mayer, "Emotional Intelligence"; D. Goleman, "What Makes a Leader?" *Harvard Business Review,* November–December 1998, pp. 92–105.

25. E.A. Locke, "Why Emotional Intelligence Is an Invalid Concept," *Journal of Organizational Behavior* 26 (2005), pp. 425–31.

26. R. Jacobs, "Using Human Resource Functions to Enhance Emotional Intelligence," in *The Emotionally Intelligent Workplace,* ed. C. Cherniss and D. Goleman (San Francisco: Jossey-Bass, 2001), pp. 161–63.

27. P.G. Northouse, *Leadership: Theory and Practice,* 3rd ed. (Thousand Oaks, CA: Sage, 2004), Chapter 4; Yukl, *Leadership in Organizations,* Chapter 3.

28. A.K. Korman, "Consideration, Initiating Structure, and Organizational Criteria—a Review," *Personnel Psychology* 19 (1966), pp. 349–62; E.A. Fleishman, "Twenty Years of Consideration and Structure," in *Current Developments in the Study of Leadership,* ed. E.A. Fleishman and J.C. Hunt (Carbondale, IL: Southern Illinois University Press, 1973), pp. 1–40; T.A. Judge, R.F. Piccolo, and R. Ilies, "The Forgotten Ones? The Validity of Consideration and Initiating Structure in Leadership Research," *Journal of Applied Psychology* 89, no. 1 (2004), pp. 36–51; Yukl, *Leadership in Organizations,* pp. 62–75.

29. S. Kerr et al., "Toward a Contingency Theory of Leadership Based upon the Consideration and Initiating Structure Literature," *Organizational Behavior and Human Performance* 12 (1974), pp. 62–82; L.L. Larson, J.G. Hunt, and R.N. Osbom, "The Great Hi–Hi Leader Behavior Myth: A Lesson from Occam's Razor," *Academy of Management Journal* 19 (1976), pp. 628–41.

30. House and Aditya, "The Social Scientific Study of Leadership: Quo Vadis?"; Yukl, "Managerial Leadership: A Review of Theory and Research."

31. D. Rynecki, "Putting the Muscle Back into the Bull," *Fortune,* April 5, 2004, pp. 162–67.

32. R.J. House, "Path–Goal Theory of Leadership: Lessons, Legacy, and a Reformulated Theory," *Leadership Quarterly* 7 (1996), pp. 323–52.

33. J. Indvik, "Path–Goal Theory of Leadership: A Meta-Analysis," *Academy of Management Proceedings,* 1986, pp. 189–92; J.C. Wofford and L.Z. Liska, "Path–Goal Theories of Leadership: A Meta-Analysis," *Journal of Management* 19 (1993), pp. 857–76; House and Aditya, "The Social Scientific Study of Leadership: Quo Vadis?"

34. S. Keer and J.M. Jermier, "Substitutes for Leadership: Their Meaning and Measurement," *Organizational Behavior and Human Performance* 22 (1978), pp. 375–403.

35. D.F. Elloy and A. Randolph, "The Effect of Superleader Behavior on Autonomous Work Groups in a Government Operated Railway Service," *Public Personnel Management* 26 (Summer 1997), pp. 257–72; C.C. Manz and H. Sims Jr., *The New SuperLeadership: Leading Others to Lead Themselves* (San Francisco: Berrett-Koehler, 2001).

36. M.L. Loughry, "Coworkers Are Watching: Performance Implications of Peer Monitoring," *Academy of Management Proceedings,* 2002, pp. O1–O6.

37. P.M. Podsakoff and S.B. MacKenzie, "Kerr and Jermier's Substitutes for Leadership Model: Background, Empirical Assessment, and Suggestions for Future Research," *Leadership Quarterly* 8 (1997), pp. 117–32; S.D. Dionne et al., "Neutralizing Substitutes for Leadership Theory: Leadership Effects and Common-Source Bias," *Journal of Applied Psychology* 87, no. 3 (June 2002), pp. 454–64; J.R. Villa et al., "Problems with Detecting Moderators in Leadership Research Using Moderated Multiple Regression," *Leadership Quarterly* 14, no. 1 (February 2003), pp. 3–23; S.D. Dionne et al., "Substitutes for Leadership, or Not," *The Leadership Quarterly* 16, no. 1 (2005), pp. 169–93.

38. B.M. Bass, "From Transactional to Transformational Leadership," *Organizational Dynamics,* Winter 1990, pp. 19–32.

39. V.L. Goodwin, J.C. Wofford, and J.L. Whittington "A Theoretical and Empirical Extension to the Transformational Leadership Construct," *Journal of Organizational Behavior* 22 (November 2001), pp. 759–74.

40. A. Zaleznik, "Managers and Leaders: Are They Different?" *Harvard Business Review* 55, no. 5 (1977), pp. 67–78; W. Bennis and B. Nanus, *Leaders: The Strategies for Taking Charge* (New York: Harper & Row, 1985); R.H.G. Field, "Leadership Defined: Web Images Reveal the Differences between Leadership and Management," in *Annual Conference of the Administrative Sciences Association of Canada, Organizational Behavior Division,* ed. P. Mudrack (Winnipeg, Manitoba, May 25–28, 2002), p. 93.

41. J.M. Burns, *Leadership* (New York: Harper & Row, 1978); B.M. Bass, *Transformational Leadership: Industrial, Military, and Educational Impact* (Hillsdale, NJ: Erlbaum, 1998); B.J. Avolio and F.J. Yammarino, eds., *Transformational and Charismatic Leadership: The Road Ahead* (Greenwich, CT: JAI Press, 2002).

42. J.A. Conger, "Inspiring Others: The Language of Leadership," *Academy of Management Executive* 5 (February 1991), pp. 31–45; G.T. Fairhurst and R.A. Sarr, *The Art of Framing: Managing the Language of Leadership* (San Francisco: Jossey–Bass, 1996); A.E. Rafferty and M.A. Griffin, "Dimensions of Transformational Leadership: Conceptual and Empirical Extensions," *Leadership Quarterly* 15, no. 3 (2004), pp. 329–54.

43. J. Barbuto, J.E., "Taking the Charisma out of Transformational Leadership," *Journal of Social Behavior & Personality* 12 (September 1997), pp. 689–97; Y.A. Nur, "Charisma and Managerial Leadership: The Gift That Never Was," *Business Horizons* 41 (July 1998), pp. 19–26; M.D. Mumford and J.R. Van Doorn, "The Leadership of Pragmatism—Reconsidering Franklin in the Age of Charisma," *Leadership Quarterly* 12, no. 3 (Fall 2001), pp. 279–309.

44. J. Barling, T. Weber, and E.K. Kelloway, "Effects of Transformational Leadership Training on Attitudinal and Financial Outcomes: A Field Experiment," *Journal of Applied Psychology* 81 (1996), pp. 827–32.

45. A. Bryman, "Leadership in Organizations," in *Handbook of Organization Studies,* ed. S.R. Clegg, C. Hardy, and W.R. Nord (Thousand Oaks, CA: Sage, 1996), pp. 276–92.

46. B.S. Pawar and K.K. Eastman, "The Nature and Implications of Contextual Influences on Transformational Leadership: A Conceptual Examination," *Academy of Management Review* 22 (1997), pp. 80–109; C.P. Egri and S. Herman, "Leadership in the North American Environmental Sector: Values, Leadership Styles, and Contexts of Environmental Leaders and Their Organizations," *Academy of Management Journal* 43, no. 4 (2000), pp. 571–604.

47. J. Porterfiled and B.H. Kleiner, "A New Era: Women and Leadership," *Equal Opportunities International* 24, no. 5 (2005), pp. 49–56.

48. S.L. Bellar, M. Helms, and D.E. Arfken, "The Glacial Change: Women on Corporate Boards," *Business Perspectives* 16, no. 2 (2004), pp. 30–38.

49. J.B. Rosener, "Ways Women Lead," *Harvard Business Review* 68 (November–December 1990), pp. 119–25; S.H. Appelbaum and B.T. Shaprio, "Why Can't Men Lead Like Women?" *Leadership and Organization Development Journal* 14 (1993), pp. 28–34; N. Wood, "Venus Rules," *Incentive* 172 (February 1998), pp. 22–27.

50. G.N. Powell, "One More Time: Do Female and Male Managers Differ?" *Academy of Management Executive* 4 (1990), pp. 68–75; M.L. van Engen and T.M. Willemsen, "Sex and Leadership Styles: A Meta-Analysis of Research Published in the 1990s," *Psychological Reports* 94, no. 1 (February 2004), pp. 3–18.

51. R. Sharpe, "As Leaders, Women Rule," *BusinessWeek,* November 20, 2000, p. 74; M. Sappenfield, "Women, It Seems, Are Better Bosses," *Christian Science Monitor,* January 16, 2001; A.H. Eagly and L.L. Carli, "The Female Leadership Advantage: An Evaluation of the Evidence," *The Leadership Quarterly* 14, no. 6 (December 2003), pp. 807–34; A.H. Eagly, M.C. Johannesen-Schmidt, and M.L. van Engen, "Transformational, Transactional, and Laissez-Faire Leadership Styles: A Meta-Analysis Comparing Women and Men," *Psychological Bulletin* 129 (July 2003), pp. 569–91.

52. A.H. Eagly, S.J. Karau, and M.G. Makhijani, "Gender and the Effectiveness of Leaders: A Meta-Analysis," *Psychological Bulletin* 117 (1995), pp. 125–45; J.G. Oakley, "Gender-Based Barriers to Senior Management Positions: Understanding the Scarcity of Female CEOs," *Journal of Business Ethics* 27 (2000), pp. 821–34; N.Z. Stelter, "Gender Differences in Leadership: Current Social Issues and Future Organizational Implications," *Journal of Leadership Studies* 8 (2002), pp. 88–99; M.E. Heilman et al., "Penalties for Success: Reactions to Women Who Succeed at Male Gender-Typed Tasks," *Journal of Applied Psychology* 89, no. 3 (2004), pp. 416–27; A.H. Eagly, "Achieving Relational Authenticity in Leadership: Does Gender Matter?" *The Leadership Quarterly* 16, no. 3 (June 2005), pp. 459–74.

53. K. Brooker, "The Un-CEO," *Fortune,* September 16, 2002, pp. 88–93.

54. Brooker, "The Un-CEO."

55. Brooker, "The Un-CEO."

56. Sources: Brooker, "The Un-CEO"; P. Sellers, "Teaching an Old Dog New Tricks," *Fortune,* May 31, 2004, pp. 166–73; T. Wasserman, "Seizing the Moment of Truth," *Brandweek,* October 10, 2005, pp. M8–M13.

17

COMMUNICATION

This cartoon by Jen Sorensen nicely captures the response of many to Larry Summers's statements on the intrinsic aptitudes of women. Source: http://www. slowpokecomics. com

On February 21, 2006, Lawrence Summers, the former U.S. Treasury secretary, resigned as president of Harvard University. Summers's problems began in 2001, shortly after his appointment, when in a face-to-face meeting with noted African American scholar Cornell West, Summers apparently berated him for teaching a course on hip hop and skipping classes to help in political campaigns. West, who apparently felt Summers was criticizing his teaching and scholarship, promptly left Harvard for Princeton. Next Summers caused a stir on campus when he labeled as "anti-Semitic in their effect if not their intent" the efforts of a group of students and faculty to persuade Harvard to divest its holdings in companies that do business in Israel as a protest against the treatment of Palestinians. Some of the faculty who supported the initiative thought Summers's use of the term "anti-Semitic" was inflammatory, and feelings against him began to harden. Then in February 2005 Summers suggested that differences in "intrinsic aptitude" might explain why fewer women succeed in science and math. His comments were greeted by a firestorm of protests and accusations of gender bias. It didn't help that during Summers's presidency the proportion of Harvard tenure offers that went to women had fallen from 37 percent to 11 percent. Summers apologized for his poor communication skills and tried to make amends by allocating $50 million to efforts by Harvard to get more women into the sciences, but the damage had been done.[1]

■ Poor communication at Harvard.

communication

The process by which information is exchanged and understood between people.

The fall of Lawrence Summers from the top leadership position at Harvard illustrates the important role communication skills play in the success or failure of a manager. Many at Harvard thought Summers was doing a great job of shaking up the university's stodgy culture and pushing for needed changes, but his constant communication gaffes detracted from his efforts. In the words of writer Richard Bradley, author of the book *Harvard Rules,* Summers "seems to have a knack for putting things in a way that annoys his audience. He is constitutionally incapable of being inoffensive."[2] In fact, the brilliant but brash Summers had a long history of shooting from the hip. As president of the World Bank in the early 1990s he created an outcry for suggesting in a memo that toxic waste could be exported to third world countries (he later called the notion a "whopper" of a mistake).

In this chapter we look closely at the important role played by communication in the work of managers. **Communication** is the process by which information is exchanged and *understood* between people. We emphasize the word *understood* because transmitting the sender's intended meaning is the essence of good communication. Communication is an important part of a manager's job. Henry Mintzberg's research on managerial work (discussed in Chapter 1) suggests that managers spend 80 percent of every working day communicating with others—in face-to-face settings, on the telephone, via e-mail, in speeches, or via written memos and reports.[3]

Managers influence others through communication. They use communication to

- Transmit information about their goals, strategies, expectations, management philosophy, and values.

- Build commitment among subordinates to their programs and policies, convince allies in their network to support them, persuade their bosses that they are performing well, and influence stakeholders.

- Achieve coordination between different units within an organization, such as R&D, marketing, and production.

- Help shape the image of themselves that they present to the world (something Larry Summers did not do well).

As Lawrence Summers amply illustrated, effective communication is a major challenge for managers. To be good communicators, they must use the right media. They must decide whether a face-to-face meeting, e-mail, a video broadcast, or some other medium is appropriate for transmitting a message. They must craft their message carefully, paying close attention to the information content. They must decide what to communicate and what to keep private. They must deliver their message in a way that will have maximum effect, selecting language to convey the correct information and elicit the desired response. Moreover, managers must also use the information communicated to them by others both inside and outside the organization. They must be able to separate the information content of a message from noise, and they must be able to accurately process the information they are receiving, discern its true meaning, and employ it rationally.

We start our discussion of management communication by reviewing a simple but powerful model of the communication process. Next we discuss different media, or channels, through which information can be communicated, and we consider how to match channels to messages. This is followed by a review of communication within organizations. We move on to discuss communication barriers and breakdowns, including information overload and perceptual biases that lead listeners to misinterpret messages. We close the Chapter with a discussion of what managers can do to improve communication.

■ // The Communication Process

The communication model presented in Figure 17.1 illustrates the standard way researchers think about the communication process.[4] According to this model, communication flows through channels between the sender and receiver. The sender forms a message and encodes it into words, gestures, voice intonation, and other symbols or signs. Next the sender transmits the encoded message to the intended receiver through one or more communication channels (media).

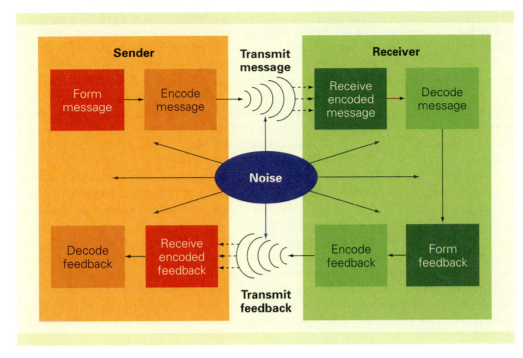

FIGURE 17.1
A Model of the
Communication Process

The receiver senses the incoming message and decodes it into something meaningful. Ideally the decoded meaning is what the sender intended (although this does not always occur).

In most situations the sender looks for evidence that the other person received and understood the transmitted message. This feedback may be a formal acknowledgment, such as "Yes, I know what you mean," or indirect evidence from the receiver's subsequent actions. Notice that feedback repeats the communication process. Intended feedback is encoded, transmitted from the receiver to the sender of the original message, received, and decoded.

This model recognizes that the communication of meaning from one person to another can be and often is altered by **noise**—the psychological, social, and structural barriers that distort and obscure the sender's intended message. If any part of the communication process is distorted or broken, the sender and receiver will not have a common understanding of the message. The results of noise can be serious. Deborah Tannen, a linguist who studies miscommunication between senders and receivers, tells the story of Judy Scott, who was applying for a job as office manager at the headquarters of an ice cream distributor, a position she was well qualified for.[5] Although her last job title was "administrative assistant," she actually ran the entire office and did it well. However, at the interview she never had the chance to explain this. The interviewer did all the talking; she left feeling frustrated and failed to get the job. Scott ran into a common structural barrier that distorted the message she was trying to transmit: The intended receiver, the interviewer, did not listen. Larry Summers might also have suffered the consequences of noise. When meeting face-to-face with Cornell West, he probably did not intend to denigrate the scholarship and teaching of one of the most famous African American academics, but Cornell West perceived the message that way. The noise that led to miscommunication may have been created in part by Summers's failure to correctly frame the message—and in part by West's unfavorable perception of Summers going into the interview and his psychological predisposition to interpret messages from the brash and blunt economist in a negative light.

noise

The psychological, social, and structural barriers that distort and obscure a sender's intended message.

▪ // Communication Channels

A critical part of the communication model is the channel or medium through which information is transmitted. There are two main types of channels: verbal and nonverbal. Verbal communication includes any oral or written means of transmitting meaning through words, including face-to-face meetings, telephone conversations, written memos, and e-mail messages. Nonverbal communication is any part of communication that does not use words. Here we review verbal and nonverbal communication channels and discuss the best channel to use.

// VERBAL COMMUNICATION

Face-to-face communication is one of the richest media channels for exchanging information. **Media richness** refers to the *data-carrying capacity of a channel*—to the volume and variety of information a sender and receiver can transmit during a specific time.[6] Face-to-face communication is a media-rich channel because oral communication is supported by important nonverbal cues such as voice intonation, facial expressions (raised eyebrows, smiles, frowns), the use of silence, posture, and the like. Furthermore, face-to-face interaction gives the sender immediate feedback from the receiver and the opportunity to adjust the emotional tone of the message and tailor content accordingly.

Telephone conversations are a step down in media richness. Although many nonverbal cues are missing from telephone conversations, such as facial expressions and posture, voice intonation can still carry an enormous amount of information. An emerging communication channel, videoconferencing over the Internet, may offer an improvement over the telephone by allowing communicators to observe some nonverbal cues, such as facial expressions. This technology, however, is still not widely used, although that may change in the future.

Electronic mail (e-mail) is now widely used to exchange information that at one time was transmitted over the telephone. E-mail has revolutionized how we communicate in organizational settings. It has become the medium of choice in most workplaces because messages are quickly formed, edited, and stored. Information can be appended and transmitted to many people easily. E-mail has become the preferred medium for coordinating work (such as confirming a coworker's production schedule or arranging a meeting) and for sending well-defined information for decision making. It often increases the volume of communication and significantly alters the flow of that information within groups and throughout the organization.[7] Most notably, it reduces some face-to-face and telephone communication but increases communication between people at different levels in an organization hierarchy. Some social and organizational status differences still exist with e-mail, but they are less apparent than in face-to-face communication. E-mail also reduces many unconscious perceptual biases because it hides our age, race, weight, and other features that are observable in face-to-face meetings and that unfortunately introduce noise into the communication process.

E-mail is not as media-rich as face-to-face meetings and telephone conversations. E-mail lacks visual and verbal cues, so there is a greater chance of misinterpreting a message. Another problem with e-mail is that it seems to reduce our politeness and respect for others, which is mostly evident through the increased frequency of **flaming**—the act of sending an emotionally charged message to others. There are two explanations for this lack of diplomacy. First, people can quickly write and post e-mail messages before their emotions subside, whereas cooler thoughts might prevail before traditional memos or letters are sent. Second, e-mail is an impersonal medium, allowing employees to write things they would never say in face-to-face conversation. Fortunately, research has found that politeness and respect increase as people get to know each other and when companies establish explicit norms and rules governing e-mail communication.[8]

Another problem with e-mail is that it is an inefficient medium for communicating in ambiguous, complex, and novel situations. The communicating parties lack mutual mental models, so they need to transmit many messages to share enough information. Two-way face-to-face communication is a much more effective medium under these circumstances, but many employees are reluctant to break out of the e-mail habit. A final problem with e-mail is that it contributes to information overload (which we discuss later in this chapter). Hundreds of messages can overwhelm e-mail users each week, many of which are either unnecessary or irrelevant to the receivers. Using e-mails, somebody can easily create and

media richness
The volume and variety of information that a sender and receiver can transmit during a specific time.

flaming
The act of sending an emotionally charged message to others.

copy a message to thousands of people through group mailbox systems, which exacerbates information overload.

Instant messaging (IM) is another form of computer-mediated information exchange that has gained popularity in some organizations. In some ways IM is more efficient than e-mail because messages are brief (usually just a sentence or two with acronyms and sound-alike letters for words), appear on the receiver's screen as soon as they are sent, and allow real-time feedback; and several people can engage simultaneously in an IM conversation. Another advantage is that employees soon develop the capability of carrying on several IM conversations at the same time. "No matter how good you are on the phone, the best you can do is carry on two conversations at once," says one New York City broker. "With IM, I can have six going at once. . . . That allows me to get my job done and serve clients better."[9] Like e-mail, however, IM lacks the media richness of face-to-face or telephone conversations.

Lower still in media richness are written letters, memos, and reports. Such media convey only the cues that are written on paper (they are now often appended to e-mail, but they lack the immediacy of direct e-mail communications). The lack of richness of this media can be an advantage in some situations. Carefully crafted written statements might clarify a message while helping the sender avoid the noise associated with perceptual biases, inappropriate nonverbal cues, and the like.

Web logs (blogs), which are in effect online diaries, have started to emerge as a novel way by which executives can communicate with many employees using the written word. Executives at Google, for example, regularly post information of value to other employees and customers on the "official" Google blog site (which can be found at http://googleblog. blogspot.com). In media richness blogs are similar to written letters, reports, and memos. The big difference is that whereas executives normally have specific targets for written letters and memos, blogs are open to all to visit, and people elect to be receivers by visiting the Web site.

// NONVERBAL COMMUNICATION

Nonverbal communication refers to messages sent through human actions and behaviors rather than words.[10] As noted previously, nonverbal communication includes facial gestures, voice intonation, posture, physical distance, and silence. Nonverbal communication occurs most in face-to-face situations, although voice intonation is detectable over the telephone. In face-to-face communication, research indicates that nonverbal cues have a greater impact on message interpretation than actual spoken words.[11] For example, how would you feel if during a meeting with your boss he kept gazing out the window? How would you feel if he looked directly at you the entire time with an interested expression on his face? The words might be the same, but the nonverbal cues would result in a very different perception on your part of how successful the meeting was. Rather like a parallel conversation, nonverbal cues signal subtle information to both parties that colors the words communicated, placing them in a richer context.[12]

Nonverbal communication differs from verbal communication in a number of ways. First, it is less rule-bound than verbal communication. We receive a lot of formal training in how to understand spoken words but little in understanding nonverbal signals. On the face of it, this may mean that nonverbal cues are generally more ambiguous and susceptible to misinterpretation. However, many facial expressions (such as smiling or raising eyebrows) are hardwired and universal, thereby providing the only reliable means of communicating across cultures.[13] In addition, many other nonverbal cues are common to a culture—so if you are from that culture, you are socialized into understanding them at an early age.

Another difference between verbal and nonverbal communication is that the former is typically conscious, whereas most nonverbal communication is automatic

nonverbal communication
Messages sent through human actions and behavior rather than words.

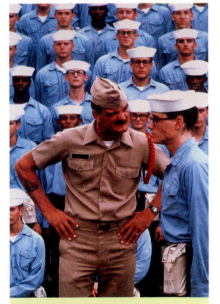

Read My Body Language, Maggot! If you think the officer in this picture is aggressively correcting the enlisted man, you are right. His body posture is enough to illustrate his strong disapproval.

© Royalty-Free/Corbis

and unconscious. We normally plan the words we say or write, but we cannot plan every blink, smile, or other gesture during a conversation. Often we involuntarily send out strong nonverbal cues, such as by blushing at an embarrassing moment; these can influence the perception that receivers might have of any message we are trying to convey.

One of the most fascinating effects of emotions on nonverbal communication is the phenomenon called **emotional contagion**, which is the automatic process of "catching" or sharing another person's emotions by mimicking that person's facial expressions and other nonverbal behavior. Consider what happens when you see a coworker accidentally bang his or her head against a filing cabinet. You probably wince and put your hand on your own head as if you had hit the cabinet. Similarly, while listening to someone describe a positive event, you tend to smile and exhibit other emotional displays of happiness. While some of our nonverbal communication is planned, emotional contagion represents unconscious behavior—we automatically mimic and synchronize our nonverbal behaviors with those of other people.[14]

Emotional contagion serves three purposes. First, mimicry provides continuous feedback, communicating that we understand and empathize with the sender. To consider the significance of this, imagine employees remaining expressionless after watching a coworker bang his or her head! The lack of parallel behavior conveys a lack of understanding or caring. Second, mimicking the nonverbal behavior of other people seems to be a way of receiving emotional meaning from those people. If a coworker is angry with a client, your tendency to frown and show anger while listening helps you share that emotion more fully. In other words, we receive meaning by expressing the sender's emotions as well as by listening to the sender's words. The third function of emotional contagion is to fulfill the drive to bond with our coworkers. Through nonverbal expressions of emotional contagion, we see others share the emotions we feel. This can strengthen team cohesiveness by providing evidence of member similarity.[15]

emotional contagion
The automatic process of "catching" or sharing another person's emotions by mimicking that person's facial expressions and other nonverbal behavior.

// SELECTING THE BEST COMMUNICATION CHANNEL

Each communication channel has advantages and disadvantages. The best channel to use depends on the situation. We have already described how the media richness of different channels varies, with face-to-face communication having the greatest media richness and written reports the least. Media richness is actually determined by three factors:

1. Rich media simultaneously use multiple communication methods. For instance, face-to-face communication scores high on media richness because it includes both verbal and nonverbal information exchange, whereas written reports rely on just verbal information.

2. Rich media such as face-to-face communication allow immediate feedback from receiver to sender, whereas feedback in lean media, such as written reports, is delayed or nonexistent.

3. Rich media let the sender customize the message to the receiver. Most face-to-face conversations are developed specifically for one or a few people (speeches being an exception to this rule). Financial reports, in contrast, have low media richness because one size fits all—everyone gets the same information.

Figure 17.2 shows that rich media are better than lean media when the communication situation is nonroutine or ambiguous. In nonroutine situations (such as an unexpected and unusual emergency) the sender and receiver have little common experience, so they need to transmit a large volume of information and receive immediate feedback. Ambiguous situations also require rich media because the parties must share large amounts of information with immediate feedback to resolve multiple and conflicting interpretations of their observations and experiences. In contrast, lean media work well in routine situations because the sender and receiver have common expectations through shared mental models.[16]

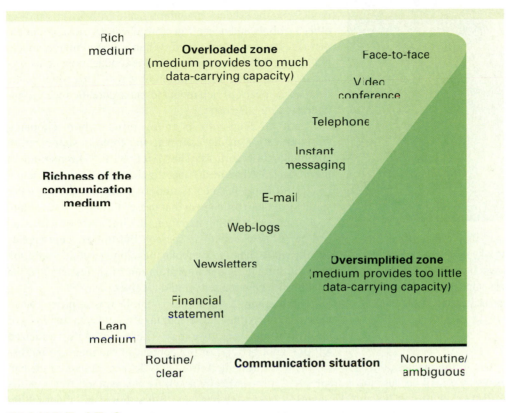

FIGURE 17.2   Matching Media to the Situation

Source: Based on R. Lengel, and R. Daft, "The Selection of Communication Media as an Executive Skill," *Academy of Management Executive*, 2(3), 1988, p. 226.

What happens when we choose the wrong level of media richness for the situation? When the situation is routine or clear, using a rich medium—such as holding a special face-to-face meeting—would seem like a waste of time. On the other hand, if a unique or ambiguous issue is handled through a written report or some other lean medium, then issues take longer to resolve and misunderstandings are more likely to occur.

For example, consider an emergency situation, such as what occurred in February 2006 when Vice President Dick Cheney, while hunting in Texas, accidentally shot one of his hunting companions, Harry Whittington (Whittington spent several days in the hospital). Cheney and his staff kept the incident secret for 24 hours. When information about the incident was released, it was through a statement by the owner of the ranch where the accident occurred to a local Texas newspaper (this could be characterized as a lean medium). Within hours the news was all over the national press. Commentators were demanding to know why Cheney was being so secretive and how the accident happened. The news coverage quickly spiraled out of control, and press reports were criticizing Cheney for his secrecy. After four days of front-page coverage, during which Cheney said nothing, President Bush apparently persuaded Cheney to go on national television, explain the incident to an interviewer, and accept responsibility, which he did. After that the controversy died down.

■ Failure to match media to message: Dick Cheney's hunting accident.

Cheney and his staff had failed to recognize that the shooting incident was a nonroutine and ambiguous incident that required face-to-face communication. A third-party news release, followed by days of silence, was too simple a media response for the situation. When Cheney finally engaged in face-to-face communication with a news interviewer he was matching the medium to the situation; this pushed the incident off the front page.[17]

A factor to consider in matching media to situations is the communicator's previous experience with the receiver. When people share mental models, less information exchange is required to communicate new meaning. People who know each other may have similar mental

Damage Control   Vice President Dick Cheney explains to Fox News interviewer Brit Hume why he kept quiet for four days while controversy swirled over his accidental shooting of a hunting partner. Cheney's reluctant decision to engage in face-to-face communication quickly defused a situation that was spiraling out of control.

© HO/Reuters/Corbis.

■ Failure to match medium to message at KPMG.

models, so the sender can communicate with fewer words or other symbols and doesn't need to check as closely that the message has been understood. When a shared mental model is lacking, the sender needs to add redundancy (such as saying the same thing in two different ways). This requires the detailed feedback of rich media to make sure the receiver has understood the message.

Another factor to bear in mind when choosing communication media concerns the famous statement by communication guru Marshall McLuhan: "The medium is the message."[18] This means that the channel of communication has social consequences as important as (or perhaps more significant than) the content that passes through that medium. McLuhan was referring mainly to the influence of television and other "new media" on society; but this concept applies equally well to how the symbolic meaning of a communication medium influences our interpretation of a message and the relationship between sender and receiver.

The medium-as-message principle was apparent when the consulting firm KPMG sent layoff notices to hundreds of its British employees via e-mail. The public swiftly criticized KPMG—not because of the content of the message but because of the medium through which it was transmitted. Ironically KPMG delivered the bad news by e-mail because most employees had specifically asked for this method. Yet even the KPMG executives who sent the layoff notices were hesitant. "I was horrified about telling staff via e-mail as I knew it would make us look callous," admitted one executive.[19] The point here is that we need to be sensitive to the symbolic meanings of communication media to ensure that they amplify rather than distort the meaning of messages.

■ // Organizational Communication

formal channels

Systems of officially sanctioned channels within an organization that are used regularly to communicate information.

informal channels

Unofficial communication channels not formally established by managers.

downward communication

Occurs when information flows from higher levels within an organization hierarchy.

So far we have discussed communication in general terms. Let us now look more closely at the nature of communication within an organization. Communication flows through two main channels in an organization: formal channels and informal channels. **Formal channels** are systems of officially sanctioned channels within an organization that are used regularly to communicate information. Formal channels tend to follow the structure of an organization, with information transmitted up and down a management hierarchy and horizontally between subunits. **Informal channels** are unofficial channels that have not been formally established by managers. Informal channels typically do not follow the structure of an organization. Informal channels include communication that flows through the personal networks of employees (that is, gossip networks).

// FORMAL COMMUNICATION CHANNELS

Within the formal communication channels of an organization, information flows in three directions: downward, upward, and horizontally. **Downward communication** occurs when information flows from higher to lower levels within an organization hierarchy. Downward communication includes information about the organization's mission, goals, values, strategies, processes, procedures, task responsibilities, and overall organizational performance, along with feedback regarding the performance of lower levels within a hierarchy. When considering downward communication, managers have to decide what to communicate, what media to use, and how to minimize noise in the system so that the receivers get the intended message. We discuss these issues in more depth later in the Chapter when we look at barriers to communication. For now note that managers need to be careful not to communicate too much information downward. To minimize the chance of overloading subordinates with information, they should focus on communicating only what is important. They also need to match media to their messages.

Upward communication occurs when information flows from lower to higher levels within an organization. Upward communication includes routine performance reports; feedback to higher-level managers about success in implementing strategies, policies, and procedures; suggestions for improving operations or strategies; alerts about unanticipated events or problems; and grievances and complaints. As with downward communication, senior executives have to decide what information they want communicated up to them regularly. They too do not want to be overloaded with information, so they normally install systems to ensure the regular upward communication of selected financial, accounting, operational, and market data. You will recall from Chapter 9 that many firms now use the balanced scorecards to help decide what information they want communicated upward.[20] In addition, managers must make sure that systems are in place so employees can make suggestions and alert senior managers to emerging problems, opportunities, and grievances or complaints. These systems can include employee suggestion boxes, regular scheduled face-to-face meetings between senior managers and lower-level employees, and other procedures for allowing employees to suggest new business ideas.

An interesting example of a formal upward communication channel can be found at Google, the fast-growing Web search company. Part of the management philosophy at Google is that employees should spend 10 percent of their work time on "far-out ideas" that might one day become a business opportunity for Google. Google founders Sergey Brin and Larry Page hold regular sessions with employees working on projects that come out of this innovation time. Employees don't get to present their ideas to Brin and Page, however, until they have first been vetted by Marissa Mayer, the company's director of consumer Web products. Anyone can post a proposal. Mayer then meets with employee groups, helping them to develop their ideas, and decides when they are ready to present before Brin and Page—something they don't get to do until the pitch has been well developed and there are hard data to back up the proposals. Then employees get just 20 minutes before Brin and Page. Ideas that have come out of this process include gmail (Google's e-mail program), Google Talk, an initiative to offer free wi-fi connections to the Internet in San Francisco, and Google Earth.

Horizontal communication occurs among employees and units that are at the same hierarchical level in an organization. Horizontal communication is essential to coordinate the activities of employees and units and to solve any problems that might arise without involving higher levels of management. For example, developing a new product often requires close coordination between R&D, marketing, and manufacturing to ensure that R&D designs products for which there is adequate demand and that can be manufactured efficiently. Such coordination requires rich communication between R&D, manufacturing, and marketing. To achieve this, firms often establish cross-functional teams, which allow face-to-face communication between personnel from different departments (see Chapter 8 for details). In other words, the teams become the communication channel. As we saw in Chapter 8 when we discussed organization structure, other communication channels for achieving coordination between different units include regular direct contact between managers from different units, liaison roles, and full matrix structures.

// INFORMAL COMMUNICATION CHANNELS

As noted, informal channels do not follow the structure of an organization, and they are often based on **personal networks** (relationships between individuals). Personal communication networks can be a valuable source of information about what is going on in an organization and a conduit for the exchange of ideas. Smart managers often proactively build a personal network precisely for this reason—it helps them discover important information. For example, in Chapter 9 we discussed how Jim Donald, CEO of Starbucks, drops into his local Starbucks store every morning on the way to work. The store employees know him well, and in effect Donald has added them to his personal network. As such they can be a useful source of information about the company that Donald

might not get from formal channels. Howard Schultz, the current chairman and former CEO of Starbucks, does the same, and it was through one of these contacts that Schultz first heard the idea that Starbucks should sell music—something that is now a big push at the company (we discussed the incident in Chapter 1).

Personal networks can also function as conduits for rumor and gossip about what is going on in an organization. The **grapevine** can spread unsanctioned information (rumor and gossip) rapidly through personal networks.[21] Grapevines *always* exist in organizations, often becoming the dominant force for transmitting information about what is going on—particularly in highly uncertain situations when information has not been released through formal channels. For example, if a firm is in financial trouble and managers have indicated that they will take "concrete steps" to cut costs but have not released any information through formal channels, the rumor mill often generates significant gossip about what managers intend. Gossip, in other words, arises to fill an information vacuum, and the flow of gossip through the grapevine will be particularly high in an ambiguous and uncertain situation.

The interesting thing about grapevines is how much communication goes through them and how accurate it often is. One study estimated that as much as 70 percent of all communication in an organization flows through the grapevine; another suggested that as much as 70–90 percent of all information passed through the grapevine is at least partly accurate.[22] Some managers might like to squash the grapevine because some of the information flowing through it can be inaccurate and because it is outside their control. However, such an approach is unrealistic. People love to gossip. A better tactic might involve listening to the grapevine for valuable feedback about what employees are thinking and correcting misperceptions by releasing information through formal channels.

// Communication Barriers and Breakdowns (Noise)

As we noted earlier in the chapter, communication is often distorted by noise. Despite the best intentions of sender and receiver to communicate, several barriers can inhibit the effective exchange of information. As author George Bernard Shaw wrote, "The greatest problem with communication is the illusion that it has been accomplished." Pervasive communication barriers that cause noise are perceptions, filtering, language, information overload, cultural differences, and gender differences. The amount of noise in a communication system increases if the communicator does not match the medium to the message. For example, Vice President Dick Cheney's decision to use lean media to communicate about his hunting accident injected noise into the communication system.

// PERCEPTIONS

Perception is the process of attending to, interpreting, and organizing information. Perceptions influence what information we notice, how we interpret that information, and how we organize it. Our perceptions are themselves shaped by our mental models of how the world works. These models are the product of our psychology and our experiences. They influence what we attend to, what we ignore, how we interpret incoming information, and how we organize it.

If we didn't have mental models to guide our perceptions, we would drown in the sea of information that is constantly bombarding us. But although mental models are generally beneficial, their presence can also cause problems. We are all prone to **selective perception**—the tendency to notice and attend to information that is consistent with our values, beliefs, and expectations while ignoring or screening out information that is inconsistent with these. We already encountered this phenomenon in Chapter 5 when we discussed decision-making biases. There we referred to the prior hypothesis bias, which asserts that decision makers attend to information that is consistent with strongly held prior beliefs while ignoring or downplaying disconfirming evidence. The prior hypothesis bias is the result of selective perception. Within the context of communication, selective perception implies that we attend to only a portion of

grapevine
The spread of unsanctioned information (rumor and gossip) through personal networks.

perception
The process of attending to, interpreting, and organizing information.

selective perception
The tendency to notice and attend to information that is consistent with our values, beliefs, and expectations while ignoring or screening out information that is inconsistent with these.

the information within a communication system—most notably information that is consistent with our prior values, beliefs, and expectations.

Another problem concerns **stereotyping**: the process of assigning traits to people based on their membership in a social category.[23] Stereotypes influence how we interpret incoming information. We stereotype people based on factors such as their age, gender, race, accent, looks, and the like. Stereotyping can lead to poor judgments. For example, there is growing evidence that white males receive better health care from doctors than black males and that this is reflected in a higher incidence of untreated heart disease among black males. This situation occurs because doctors stereotype their patients based on race, tend to discount the information they receive from black males in the clinic, make inappropriate assumptions about lifestyles that influence the treatment options given, and pay closer attention to the information they receive from white males.[24]

Another example of stereotyping is that based on looks. There is evidence that attractive people command an income premium in the labor market of 5–10 percent over the incomes of average-looking people; the incomes of unattractive people are 5–10 percent below average. Called the *beauty premium,* the higher earnings of attractive people have been attributed to their ability to elicit more favorable perceptions from others due to their looks, and seem unrelated to their actual abilities.[25] The existence of this stereotype implies that we probably pay more attention to communication from good-looking people and tend to interpret it favorably. In other words, looks are a perceptual source of noise in the communication process.

A third perceptual problem is the **attribution process**—deciding whether an observed event is caused primarily by external or internal factors. Internal factors originate within a person and concern an individual's ability or motivation. External factors originate from the environment and concern things such as availability of resources, the impact of other people, and luck. For an example of how this process works, consider an employee who does not perform well. An internal attribution arises when we believe that the poor performance is due to a lack of ability or motivation. An external attribution would occur if we believed that the employee's poor performance was due to a lack of resources.

Psychologists have discovered that we tend to attribute the behavior of other people more to internal than external factors.[26] If an employee is late for work, for example, observers are more likely to conclude that this is because he overslept than to think external factors such as unusually heavy traffic might have caused him to be late. The tendency to blame people rather than the environment for poor performance is called the **fundamental attribution error**, and it seems to be a particular problem when there is limited information about situational factors affecting people's performance.

The fundamental attribution error implies that senior managers tend to blame people, rather than external factors outside their control, for poor performance. In other words, they misinterpret the information in a communication system and make an incorrect attribution. This can and often does lead to the firing of managers when the units for which they are responsible do not perform well. For example, in August 2004 when Hewlett-Packard reported earnings below Wall Street's expectations, CEO Carly Fiorina responded by firing three senior executives on the spot. Fiorina had attributed the company's poor performance to these executives, but many observers felt that it had more to do with tough competition from rivals Dell and IBM and Hewlett-Packard's own struggles to merge the assets of Compaq Computer with HP—a merger Fiorina had championed.[27]

Another attribution error is the **self-serving bias**—the tendency to attribute favorable outcomes to internal factors and our failures to external factors. Simply put, we take credit

Don't Judge Me on My Looks   Attractive people tend to elicit more positive feedback from others.

(left) © Liquidlibrary/Dynamic Graphics/Jupiter images. (right) © Comstock/PictureQuest

stereotyping
The process of assigning traits to people based on their membership in a social category.

attribution process
Deciding whether an observed event is caused primarily by external or internal factors.

fundamental attribution error
The tendency to blame people rather than the environment for poor performance.

self-serving bias
The tendency to attribute our favorable outcomes to internal factors and our failures to external factors.

■ Fundamental attribution error at Hewlett-Packard.

for our successes and blame others or the environment for our mistakes. The existence of this bias has been well documented. In one recent example a study found that 90 percent of employees who received lower than expected performance ratings blamed them on their supervisor, the organization, the appraisal system, or other external causes. Only a handful blamed themselves for the unexpected results.[28] The self-serving bias can lead managers to misinterpret information and assume that their efforts, rather than external causes, are responsible for improvements in the performance of the organization. The converse also holds: They may attribute poor performance to external factors when their management of the organization is really at fault.

A final perceptual bias to consider is the **recency effect**, which occurs when the most recent data dominate our perception of others.[29] The recency effect often occurs in performance appraisals, for which supervisors must recall everyone's performance over the preceding year. The most recent performance information tends to dominate the evaluation because it is the easiest to recall. People who know this sometimes try to game a performance evaluation system, submitting important information to their supervisor that presents them in a favorable light just before their annual performance evaluation.

recency effect
Occurs when the most recent data dominate perceptions.

// FILTERING

A major source of noise in communication systems is **filtering**, which is the tendency to alter information in some way, or fail to pass it on at all, as it moves through a communication system. Filtering may involve deleting or delaying negative information, using less harsh language to present bad events in a more favorable light, or distorting information in other ways to achieve a personal goal.[30] Employees and managers may filter communication to create a good impression of themselves to superiors, to build support for a program or policy they favor, or to foster opposition to a program or policy with which they disagree. Filtering occurs because organizations are fundamentally political entities and because (as we saw in Chapter 15) the control and manipulation of information is a source of power and influence within organizations. Filtering tends to be most common where organizations reward employees who communicate mainly positive information and punish those who convey bad news.

filtering
The tendency to alter information in some way, or fail to pass it on at all, as it moves through a communication system.

■ Filtering at NASA.

An example of filtering occurred in 2006 when NASA scientists accused a 24-year-old political appointee at NASA, William Deutsch, of censoring reports. Deutsch was a public affairs official; he was able to shape communications issued by NASA in a way he thought favorable to his political masters. Deutsch used his position to limit media access to James Hanson, a prominent NASA scientist who was urging swift action by the U.S. government to reduce the greenhouse gas emissions that contribute to global warming (in Deutsch's view, Hanson's position was contrary to administration policy). In addition Hanson was required to submit for review any lectures, Internet statements, and requests for interviews from journalists. Unfortunately for Deutsch his filtering efforts backfired. Hanson publicly complained about the censorship; a blizzard of news reports followed; and an embarrassed NASA denied that it had ever tried to censor government scientists. Deutsch himself resigned from NASA when a journalist discovered that he had padded his résumé (another example of filtering) and did not graduate from Texas A&M University as he had claimed.[31]

// LANGUAGE BARRIERS

Language problems can be a huge source of communication noise. Recall from Figure 17.1 that the sender encodes the message and the receiver decodes it. To make this process work, both parties need to have the same "codebook" or mutual understanding of what the words or other symbols being sent mean. Even when both people speak the same language, they might interpret words and phrases differently. If someone says "Would you like to check the figures again?" he or she may be politely *telling* you to double-check the figures or may be merely *asking* if you want to do this.

Language ambiguity isn't always dysfunctional noise.[32] Corporate leaders sometimes rely on metaphors and other vague language to describe partially formed or complex ideas. Ambiguity is also used to avoid conveying or creating undesirable emotions. For example, one recent study reported that people rely on ambiguous language when communicating with people who have different values and beliefs. In these situations ambiguity minimizes the risk of conflict.

Along with ambiguity, people who generally speak the same language might not understand specific jargon within that language. **Jargon** consists of technical language and acronyms as well as recognized words with specialized meaning in specific organizations or social groups. For example, engineers at Microsoft commonly use the acronym "Win 36 API" when discussing the design of their products. The term actually means "Windows 36-bit application protocol interface"—still a somewhat jargon-filled term that refers to "hooks" in the Windows program that interface with software applications, allowing them to run on Windows.

Some jargon can improve communication efficiency when both sender and receiver understand this specialized language. However, technical experts (including university professors) sometimes use jargon without realizing that listeners don't have the codebook to translate those special words. A recent survey found that people react negatively to unnecessary jargon, which is probably contrary to many senders' intention to look "cool" by using the latest buzzwords.[33]

Another language problem that can distort information, creating noise, concerns the phenomenon known as drop-off. **Drop-off** occurs when the content of a message gets distorted as it is passed through a communication system due to the failure of people in the system to accurately decode a message and accurately encode it as they pass it on to the next person.[34] We already discussed this phenomenon in Chapter 8 when we talked about the accidental distortions that occur when information is transmitted through different layers in a management hierarchy. There we likened the process to the children's game of telephone, in which a message is passed through a communication chain of children, with each child whispering the message to the next person in the chain. The message that emerges at the end of the chain is very different from the one that started out.

In a tragic example of the consequences of drop-off, during the Vietnam War a journalist witnessed U.S. troops burning down a Vietnamese hamlet. Subsequent investigations found that headquarters staff had ordered the troops not to burn down any hamlets, but the message had been distorted as it passed through the communication chain so that troops thought that was what they were supposed to do. The original message from headquarters to the brigade was "On no occasion must hamlets be burned down." The brigade then radioed the battalion commander and said, "Do not burn down any hamlets, unless you are absolutely convinced that the Viet Cong are in them." The battalion radioed the infantry company at the scene and said, "If you think there are any Viet Cong in the hamlet, burn it down." The company commander then ordered his troops to burn the hamlet.[35]

// INFORMATION OVERLOAD

We live in an information-rich world. Many of us feel continually besieged by information, and there is good reason for this. One estimate suggests that the amount of information in the world is currently doubling every 72 days. The Library of Congress catalogs 7,000 new items every day. More than 2,000 new Web sites go online every day. At least 2,000 new books are published every day.[36] To this we can add the explosion of e-mail communication within organizations that has occurred over the last decade. Some managers receive as many as 300 e-mail messages a day.[37] If you also include voice mail, mobile phone text messages, Web site scanning, PDF file downloads, hard copy documents, and other sources of incoming information, you have a perfect recipe for **information overload**.[38] Information overload occurs when the volume of information received exceeds a person's capacity to get through it. Employees have a certain *information processing capacity*—the amount of information they can process in a fixed unit of time. At the same time jobs have a varying *information load*—the amount of information to be processed per unit of time.[39] As Figure 17.3 illustrates, information overload occurs whenever the job's information load exceeds the individual's information processing capacity.

jargon
Technical language and acronyms as well as recognized words with specialized meaning in specific organizations or social groups.

drop-off
Distortion in the content of a message as it passes through a communication system.

information overload
Occurs when the volume of information received exceeds a person's capacity to get through it.

FIGURE 17.3

Information Overload

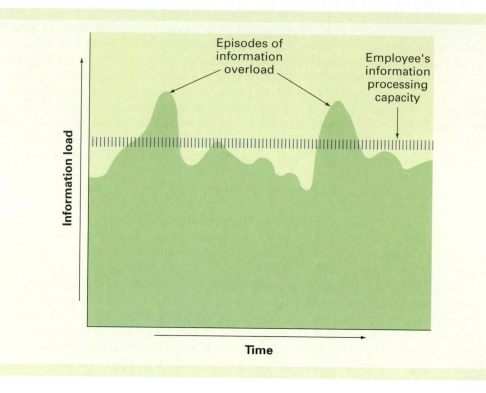

Information overload creates noise in a communication system because information gets overlooked or misinterpreted when people can't process it fast enough. It has also become a common cause of workplace stress. These problems can be minimized by increasing our information processing capacity, reducing a job's information load, or a combination of both. Information processing capacity increases when we learn to read faster, scan documents more efficiently, and remove distractions that slow information processing speed. Time management also increases information processing capacity. When information overload is temporary, information processing capacity can be increased by working longer hours.

// CULTURAL DIFFERENCES

In a world of increasing globalization and cultural diversity, organizations face new opportunities as well as communication challenges.[40] Language is the most obvious cross-cultural communication challenge. Words are easily misunderstood in verbal communication if the receiver has a limited vocabulary or the sender's accent distorts the usual sound of some words. The issue is further complicated in global organizations, where employees from non–English-speaking countries often rely on English as the common business language. The problem of ambiguous language is amplified when communication is taking place across cultures. For example, a French executive might call an event a "catastrophe" as a casual exaggeration, whereas someone in Germany usually interprets this word literally as an earth-shaking event.[41]

Mastering the same language improves one dimension of cross-cultural communication, but problems may still occur when interpreting voice intonation. Middle Easterners tend to speak loudly to show sincerity and interest in the discussion, whereas Japanese people tend to speak softly to communicate politeness or humility. These different cultural norms regarding vocal volume may cause one person to misinterpret the other.

Cultural differences in nonverbal communication can also lead to noise when people from different cultures try to communicate with each other. Nonverbal communication is more important in some cultures than in others. For example, people in Japan interpret much of a message's meaning from nonverbal cues. To avoid offending or embarrassing the receiver (particularly outsiders), Japanese people will often say what the other person wants to hear (called *tatemae*) but send subtle nonverbal cues indicating the sender's true feelings (called *honne*). A Japanese colleague might politely reject your business proposal by saying "I will think about that" while sending nonverbal signals that he or she is not interested. "In Japan, they have seven ways to say no; they never want to offend," advises Rick Davidson, global CIO at Manpower, Inc. "Sometimes they nod their head, and you think you have an agreement, but they're just saying, 'I hear you.'"[42]

Many unconscious or involuntary nonverbal cues (such as smiling) have the same meaning around the world, but deliberate gestures often have different interpretations, and this can lead to misunderstanding. For example, most of us shake our head from side to side to say "no," but a variation of head shaking means "I understand" to many people in India. Filipinos raise their eyebrows to give an affirmative answer, yet Arabs interpret this expression (along with clicking one's tongue) as a negative response. Most Westerners are taught to maintain eye contact with the speaker to show interest and respect, yet Australian Aborigines (and people in some other cultures) learn at an early age to show respect by looking down when an older or more senior person is talking to them.[43]

Even the common handshake communicates different meaning across cultures. Westerners appreciate a firm handshake as a sign of strength and warmth in a friendship or business relationship. In contrast, many Asians and Middle Easterners favor a loose grip and regard a firm clench as aggressive. Germans prefer one good handshake stroke, whereas anything less than five or six strokes may symbolize a lack of trust in Spain. If this isn't confusing enough, people from some cultures view any touching in public—including handshakes—as a sign of rudeness.

Reciprocal Bowing! In Japan it is customary to bow when you meet someone. It is a sign of respect.

© Ryan McVay/Getty Images

Communication also includes silence, but its use and meaning varies from one culture to another.[44] A recent study estimated that silence and pauses represented 30 percent of conversation time between Japanese doctors and patients, compared to only 8 percent of the time between American doctors and patients. Why is there more silence in Japanese conversations? In Japan silence symbolizes respect and indicates that the listener is thoughtfully contemplating what has just been said.[45] Empathy is also important in Japan, and this shared understanding is demonstrated without using words. In contrast, most people in Australia, India, and many other cultures view silence as a *lack* of communication and often interpret long breaks as a sign of disagreement.

Conversational overlaps also send different messages in different cultures. Japanese people usually stop talking when they are interrupted, whereas talking over another person's speech is more common in Brazil and some other countries. This difference in communication behavior is due to interpretations. Talking while someone is speaking to you is considered quite rude in Japan, whereas Brazilians are more likely to interpret this as a person's interest and involvement in the conversation.

// GENDER DIFFERENCES

After reading popular books about how men and women communicate, such as the best-selling *Men Are from Mars and Women Are from Venus,* you might come to the conclusion that they are completely different life forms.[46] In reality men and women have similar communication practices, but subtle distinctions can occasionally inject noise into communication systems and lead to misunderstanding and conflict. One distinction is that men are more likely than women to view conversations as negotiations of relative status and power. They assert their power by directly giving advice to others ("You should do the following") and using combative language. There is also evidence that men dominate the talking time in conversations with women, as well as interrupting more and adjusting their speaking styles less than women.[47]

Men also engage in more "report talk," in which the primary function of the conversation is impersonal and efficient information exchange. Women also use report talk, particularly when conversing with men; but conversations among women have a higher incidence of relationship building through "rapport talk." Rather than asserting status, women use indirect requests such as "Have you considered . . . ?" Similarly, women apologize more often and seek advice from others more quickly than men. Finally, research indicates that women are more sensitive than men to nonverbal cues in face-to-face meetings.[48]

Men and women usually understand each other, but these subtle differences are occasional irritants. For instance, female scientists have complained that adversarial interaction among male scientists makes it difficult for women to participate in meaningful dialogue.[49] Another irritant occurs when women seek empathy but receive male dominance in response. Specifically, women sometimes discuss their personal experiences and problems to develop closeness with the receiver. However, when men hear problems, they quickly suggest solutions because this asserts their control over the situation. As well as frustrating a woman's need for common understanding, the advice actually says, "You and I are different; you have the problem and I have the answer." Meanwhile men become frustrated because they can't understand why women don't appreciate their advice.

■ // Improving Communication

Now that we understand some sources of noise that lead to distortions and misinterpretations in communication it is time to look at what managers can do to improve communication and limit noise. Communication can be improved (and noise reduced) if managers match media to messages; take steps to reduce information overload; think about how best to get messages across; engage in active listening when decoding incoming messages; proactively use the grapevine to gather and disseminate information; engage in direct communication with employees; and design workspaces to facilitate communication.

// MATCH MEDIA TO MESSAGES

We have already discussed the importance of *matching media to messages*. As illustrated in Figure 17.2, lean media work well when the message to be communicated is routine and clear because the sender and receiver have common expectations through shared mental models. Ambiguous and nonroutine situations require rich media because the parties must share more information with immediate feedback to resolve multiple and conflicting interpretations of their observations and experiences. Put differently, ambiguous and nonroutine situations enhance the chances of noise. Limiting this noise requires the use of rich media.

// REDUCE INFORMATION OVERLOAD

■ Bill Gates: Strategies for managing information overload.

Matching media to messages can also help reduce information overload. Rich media are information-intensive, and heavy use of rich media can exacerbate information overload. If managers use lean media in routine nonambiguous circumstances, this can reduce the total volume of information flowing through a communication system and hence cut information overload. Managers should also be careful not to communicate too much trivial routine information. They must use their judgment to focus on communicating only what is important.

Beyond this, three strategies can help receivers manage information overload: buffering, omitting, and summarizing.[50] Consider Bill Gates at Microsoft. Gates receives approximately 300 e-mail messages daily from Microsoft addresses that are outside a core group of people; these messages are buffered—routed to an assistant who reads each and sends Gates only the 30 or so messages considered essential reading. Gates also applies the omitting strategy by using software rules to redirect e-mails from distribution lists, nonessential sources, and junk mail (spam). These messages are dumped into preassigned folders to be read later, if ever. Gates likely also relies on the summarizing strategy by reading executive summaries rather than entire reports on some issues.

// GET YOUR MESSAGE ACROSS

As noted early in the chapter, effective communication occurs when the other person receives and understands the message. To accomplish this difficult task, the sender must learn to empathize with the receiver, repeat the message, choose an appropriate time for the conversation, and be descriptive rather than evaluative.

Empathy refers to a person's ability to understand and be sensitive to the feelings, thoughts, and situation of others. Empathizing with the receiver involves putting yourself in the receiver's shoes when encoding the message. For instance, be sensitive to words that may be ambiguous or trigger the wrong emotional response.

It is also important to rephrase key points a few times. The saying "Tell them what you're going to tell them; tell them; then tell them what you've told them!" reflects this need for redundancy. Redundancy is important because it emphasizes and drives home the critical message. Many leaders have learned the importance of repeating their core message, and will do this repeatedly until it sinks in. In the last chapter, for example, we discussed how the CEO of Continental Airlines, Gordon Bethune, in his communication constantly repeated the need for the airline to "make reliability a reality." This was his core message to employees, and he communicated it relentlessly.

Choosing an appropriate time to deliver your message is important because the receiver is more likely to listen at some times than others. Your message has to compete with other messages and with noise, so it is important to find a time when the receiver is less likely to be distracted. Finally, it is important to be descriptive—to focus on the problem, not the person, when you have negative information to convey. People stop listening when information attacks their self-esteem. Suggest things the receiver can do to improve, rather than point to him or her as a problem.

// ENGAGE IN ACTIVE LISTENING

There is an old saying: "Nature gave people two ears but only one tongue, which is a gentle hint that they should listen more than they talk."[51] To follow this advice, we need to recognize that listening is a process of *actively* sensing the sender's signals, evaluating them accurately, and responding appropriately. These three components of listening—sensing, evaluating, and responding—reflect the listener's side of the communication model described at the beginning of this chapter. **Active listeners** receive the sender's signals, decode them as intended, and provide appropriate and timely feedback to the sender (see Figure 17.4). Active listeners constantly cycle through sensing, evaluating, and responding during the conversation and engage in various activities to improve these processes.[52] Most people are actually poor listeners who fail to retain or understand much of what they hear. Poor listeners frequently interrupt others, jump to conclusions about what people will say before they have said it, hurry speakers along, don't pay attention to what people are saying, and often let their perceptual biases shape the way they process information. In contrast, active listeners are better able to keep their perceptual biases in check.

Sensing Sensing is the process of receiving signals from a sender and paying attention to them. These signals include the words spoken, the nature of the sounds (speed of speech, tone of voice, and so on), and nonverbal cues. Active listeners improve sensing by postponing evaluation, avoiding interruptions, and maintaining interest. *Postponing evaluation* is important to avoid becoming a victim of first impressions and stereotyping. Active listeners try to stay as open-minded as possible by delaying evaluation of the message until the speaker has finished. *Avoiding interruptions* matters because interrupting a speaker in midstream can have two negative effects. First, it disrupts the speaker's idea, so the listener does not receive the entire message. Second, interruptions tend to second-guess what the speaker is trying to say, which contributes to the problem of evaluating the speaker's ideas too early. *Maintaining interest* is important because active listening requires conscious engagement. Too often we close our minds soon after a conversation begins because

■ Getting the message across on Continental Airlines.

active listeners
Listeners who receive a sender's signals, decode them as intended, and provide appropriate and timely feedback to the sender.

sensing
The process of receiving signals from a sender and paying attention to them.

FIGURE 17.4

Active Listening

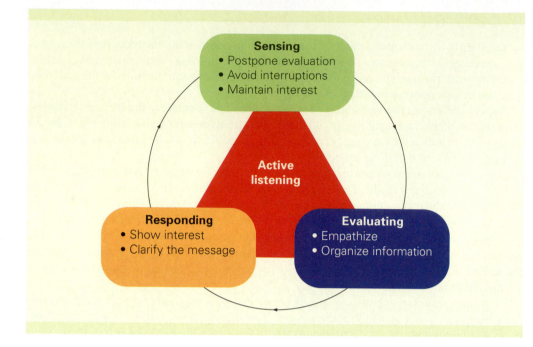

the subject is boring. Instead active listeners maintain interest by taking the view—probably an accurate one—that there is always something of value in a conversation; it's just a matter of actively looking for it.

Evaluating The evaluating component of listening includes understanding a message's meaning, evaluating the message, and remembering it. To improve their evaluation of the conversation, active listeners empathize with the speaker and organize information received during the conversation. Active listeners try to understand and remain sensitive to the speaker's feelings, thoughts, and situation. Such *empathy* is a crucial skill in active listening because it helps the listener interpret accurately the verbal and nonverbal cues in a conversation from the other person's point of view. As for organizing information, it is worth noting that human beings can, on average, process information three times faster than the average rate of speech (450 words per minute versus 125 words per minute), so they are easily distracted. Active listeners use this spare brainpower to organize the information into key points. In fact, it's a good idea to imagine that you must summarize what people have said after they are finished speaking. This can make you a better active listener.

Responding Responding, the third component of listening, gives feedback to the sender, which motivates and directs the speaker's communication. Active listeners do this by showing interest and clarifying the message. Active listeners show interest by maintaining sufficient eye contact and sending backchannel signals such as "Oh, really!" and "I see" during appropriate breaks in the conversation. To clarify the message, active listeners provide feedback by rephrasing the speaker's ideas at appropriate breaks ("So you're saying that . . . ?"). This further demonstrates interest in the conversation and helps the speaker determine whether the listener understands the message.

// PROACTIVELY USE THE GRAPEVINE

Earlier in this chapter we discussed how important personal networks are for communicating information within an organization. Information can flow very quickly through the grapevine. We noted that rather than trying to shut down the grapevine, managers should use it as a source of information about what concerns people. Skilled managers build personal networks that give them information that cannot be obtained through formal communication channels. They use these networks to tap into the grapevine and learn what is going on, and to see whether critical information is being filtered out of formal communication systems.

By quick action, such as releasing clarifying information through formal channels, managers can forestall the spread of inaccurate rumors through the grapevine. Moreover, managers can use the grapevine to test ideas. For example, they may propose an idea for consideration (often called a "trial balloon") and then listen to the grapevine for feedback about the idea. Politicians do this often—either hinting that they are thinking about a policy or releasing information through an "unnamed source" and then gauging the response before deciding whether to commit themselves formally to the policy. Similarly, there is evidence that managers and investment bankers sometimes plant rumors that two companies are engaged in merger talks to see how the market will respond.[53]

Fielding Questions   President Bush answers unscripted questions from the audience about his strategy for winning the war of terror at a town hall meeting held in early 2006. Through town hall meetings like this leaders can learn about concerns that might be filtered out through formal communication channels.

© AP Photo/Evan Vucci

// COMMUNICATE DIRECTLY WITH EMPLOYEES

Skilled managers recognize the importance of nontraditional channels that enable them to communicate directly with employees. They get out of their offices and interact with employees lower down in the organization. Nearly 40 years ago people at Hewlett-Packard coined a phrase for this communication strategy: **management by walking around**.[54] Herb Kelleher, the founder and longtime CEO of Southwest Airlines, practiced this communication strategy. He could frequently be found on Southwest flights, talking to flight attendants or the pilots and helping to hand out refreshments to customers. Similarly, Wal-Mart founder Sam Walton would often drop in on his stores unannounced, engaging employees in conversations about the business. This strategy is an effective way of counteracting filtering, and it can teach the manager things that might not be transmitted upward through formal channels.

One recent trend, popularized initially by politicians, has been for executives to directly communicate with employees via "town hall meetings." In these meetings large groups of employees hear about a merger or other special news directly from the key decision makers. An important element of a town hall meeting is that executives open the meeting to questions and respond on the spot to issues raised. Other executives attend employee roundtable forums to hear opinions from a small representation of staff about various issues. All of these direct communication strategies potentially minimize filtering because executives listen directly to employees. They also help executives acquire a deeper meaning and quicker understanding of internal organizational problems. A third benefit of direct communication is that employees might have more empathy for decisions made further up the corporate hierarchy.

// FACILITATE COMMUNICATION THROUGH WORKSPACE DESIGN

The ability and motivation to communicate is to some extent influenced by the physical space in which employees work. The location and design of hallways, offices, cubicles, and communal areas (such as cafeterias and elevators) all shape whom we speak to as well as the frequency of that communication. Pixar Animation Studios designed its campus near

Open Space, Open Communication   This office uses an open space designed to facilitate interaction and communication between employees

© AP Photo/John Cogill

■ Designing for communication at Pixar.

San Francisco, California, to let employees share knowledge through chance interactions with people on other teams. Pixar executives call this the "bathroom effect" because team members must leave their isolated pods to fetch their mail, have lunch, or visit the restroom. "It promotes that chance encounter," says Pixar creative director John Lasseter. "You run into people constantly. It worked from the minute we arrived. We just blossomed here."[55]

Another increasingly popular workspace strategy is to replace traditional offices with open space arrangements in which all employees (including managers) work in the same open area. Anecdotal evidence suggests that people communicate more often with fewer walls between them. However, research also suggests that open office design potentially increases employee stress due to the loss of privacy and personal space. According to an analysis of 13,000 employee surveys in 40 major organizations, the most important function of workspace is to provide a place to concentrate on work without distraction. The second most important function is to support informal communication with coworkers.[56] In other words, workspace design needs to balance privacy with opportunities for social interaction.

IN CONCLUSION   WHY DOES IT MATTER?

To get things done through people, managers need accurate, timely, and reliable information. In theory that information is provided to them by formal and informal communication channels within their organizations. However, as we have seen, the information that flows through these channels is often distorted by noise. As a result, managers may make decisions based on incorrect, incomplete, or biased information. In addition, to influence others, managers need to be able to communicate in an effective way; but here too messages might be distorted by the noise in a communication system, and the receivers might not get the intended message.

To avoid this, thus improving their ability to make decisions and influence others through communication, managers need to understand the communication processes in their organizations. They need to understand how information flows through communication channels and what the barriers are to the accurate transmission of information. Managers need to understand how important it is to improve the efficacy of communication within their organizations. They must know how to separate information from noise and limit the amount of noise in communication. When communicating, they need to match media to their messages. They should remember that information may be filtered by other people in a communication network. They need to know how best to encode and deliver a message so that it is understood by receivers, and they need to become active listeners to counteract perceptual biases and accurately decode the messages sent to them. Moreover, they should develop informal communication channels to supplement formal communication. They need to understand the value of the grapevine and use it proactively; and they should interact directly with employees whenever possible, using such opportunities both to communicate and to gather information that might not be flowing through formal channels. If they can do all of this, managers will be far more effective.

MANAGEMENT CHALLENGES

1. Explain how noise in a communication system might lead to misallocation of financial resources in an organization.

2. Stereotypes are pervasive in our society. Can you think of some common stereotypes? As a manager, what steps might you take to ensure that your perception of a message is not biased by unconscious stereotyping of the sender?

3. Information overload is an endemic problem in organizations. Can you think of some strategies you might adopt, as a receiver, to manage the flow of information and reduce information overload? What can you do as a sender to make sure your receivers are not overloaded?

4. Your company is the target of a hostile takeover bid from another enterprise. The bidding company is run by a CEO who has a reputation as a tough cost cutter. As a senior manager you have to explain to your employees what this takeover might mean for them. What communication media might you want to use? Why?

5. You are the communications director for a company that has just appointed a new CEO. The CEO was a senior executive at another company. The grapevine in your company is buzzing with speculation about what she might do. She is known as a charismatic change agent, and it is known that the board of directors has asked her to increase the performance of the company, which has lagged that of rivals in recent years. As communications director, what would you advise her to do? Why?

MANAGEMENT PORTFOLIO

FOR THE ORGANIZATION YOU HAVE CHOSEN TO FOLLOW:

1. How is the strategy of the organization communicated? Is this communication appropriate? Why?

2. Can you find any evidence of communication problems or breakdowns?

3. What media does the CEO use to communicate to employees and shareholders? Is the choice of media appropriate given the content of his or her messages?

4. What media are used in the company to facilitate horizontal communication? Are these media sufficient given the strategy of the company?

CLOSING CASE   THE *CHALLENGER* DISASTER

On January 28, 1986, the space shuttle *Challenger* took off from Kennedy Space Center in Florida into clear blue skies. Seventy-three seconds later *Challenger* exploded, killing all seven people on board. In the investigation that followed, attention soon focused on two factors: the O-ring seals on the rocket boosters and record cold prelaunch temperatures.

The O-ring seals on the rocket boosters were designed to keep the rocket's superhot gases from escaping out of the joints in the boosters and flaming, like a blow torch, onto the hull of the space shuttle. The investigation revealed that as early as October 1982, there had been concern that the O-rings might fail. In July 1985 a NASA analyst had warned in an internal memo that unless the O-rings were improved, "catastrophic" failure might follow. Similar concerns had been aired by engineers at Morton Thiokol, which manufactured the rocket boosters. Also in mid-1985 Thiokol's top expert on O-ring design had sent a memo to his superiors warning that the O-rings could fail and that the result would be "a catastrophe of the highest order—loss of human life." One month later yet another Thiokol engineer urged his company to tell NASA to suspend all shuttle flights until the seal problem was fixed. However, while work continued on redesign of the seals, the shuttle continued to fly.

Then there was the weather. On January 27, 1986, a cold front hit Florida, and forecasts called for temperatures at the launch site to fall to as low as 18°F. This concerned executives at Rockwell, the company that made the shuttle. They were worried that icicles that had formed on the shuttle tower might break off and damage the heat tiles on the shuttle. At 8:45 a.m. on the morning of January 28, the president of the Rockwell unit that made the space shuttle called the company's representative at the Kennedy Space Center, Robert Glaysher, and told him that Rockwell "couldn't recommend a launch because of concerns about ice on the launch site." At 9:00 a.m. Glaysher met with NASA officials and "stated more than once . . . that Rockwell's position was that it couldn't assure that it was safe to fly."

According to NASA officers at the meeting, the Rockwell executives did not make themselves clear. Arnold Aldrich, the ranking NASA official at this meeting, later stated to investigators that although Rockwell officials expressed concerns about possible ice damage to the shuttle, he didn't understand them to mean that there was a serious threat to safety. Aldrich stated that Rockwell officials "didn't ask or insist that we not launch." Richard Smith, the director of the Kennedy Space Center, who attended part of the launch meeting, supported Aldrich's interpretation of events. He stated to investigators, "I left that meeting feeling fully that everybody had signed up for launch."

Rockwell officials were not the only ones worried about the cold temperatures. The night before, engineers at Morton Thiokol in Utah, alarmed by reports of low temperatures in Florida, had called their representatives at the Kennedy Space Center and urged them to review the launch risks. The engineers were worried that in the extreme low temperatures the O-rings might fail. Fueling their worries was evidence from prior flights that at temperatures as high as

53°F the O-rings had shown evidence of erosion from hot gases. At 8:45 p.m. on January 27, several Thiokol engineers and managers had a teleconference with NASA officials. The highest-ranking Thiokol engineer on the call stated flatly that unless the temperature reached at least 53°F, the launch should be called off.

The two top NASA officials on the conference call, Mulloy and Hardy, resisted this. Hardy stated that he was "appalled" by the no-fly stance of Thiokol, insisting that there was no established link between temperature and O-ring erosion. Mulloy complained that Thiokol had not established minimum launch temperatures for the boosters, and they were now trying to change the flight criteria the night before a mission. The implication was that this was unreasonable. Mulloy then apparently said, "My God Thiokol, when do you want me to launch, next April?" After two hours of debate, the Thiokol personnel on the call took a break to consider NASA's objections. While the engineers in Utah remained opposed to the launch, the senior Thiokol manager on the call, Jerald Mason, declared, "We have to make a management decision." In front of the surprised engineers, he then polled only the management officials, getting them to join him in giving NASA a recommendation from Thiokol to launch. Thiokol then brought the NASA officials back onto the call to deliver the news that Thiokol no longer opposed the launch.

In the subsequent investigation, both Hardy and Mulloy insisted that they had exerted no pressure on Thiokol by their tough questioning of the engineers. They also stated that after Thiokol officials announced that the flight should go ahead, they had no idea that the engineers at Thiokol had remained unanimously opposed to this position.

Ultimately it was determined that the extreme cold temperatures resulted in failure of an O-ring on one of the solid rocket boosters, causing the explosion that doomed *Challenger*.[57]

CASE DISCUSSION QUESTIONS

1. Could the *Challenger* disaster have been prevented?
2. What communication problems contributed to the *Challenger* disaster? In particular, what barriers to communication distorted the flow of information between Rockwell, Thiokol, and NASA?
3. How might the communication system between Thiokol, Rockwell, and NASA have been improved?

ENDNOTES

1. A. Findler, P. Healy, and K. Zernike, "President of Harvard Resigns, Ending Stormy 5-Year Tenure," *The New York Times,* February 22, 2006, pp. A1, A19.

2. Quoted in R. Winters, "Harvard's Crimson Face," *Time,* January 31, 2005, p. 52.

3. H. Mintzberg, *The Nature of Managerial Work* (New York: Harper & Row, 1973).

4. C.E. Shannon and W. Weaver, *The Mathematical Theory of Communication* (Urbana: University of Illinois Press, 1949); K.J. Krone, F.M. Jablin, and L.

L. Putnam, "Communication Theory and Organizational Communication: Multiple Perspectives," in *Handbook of Organizational Communication: An Interdisciplinary Perspective,* ed. F.M. Jablin et al. (Newbury Park, CA: Sage, 1987), pp. 18–40.

5. D. Tannen, *That's Not What I Meant!* (New York: Ballantine, 1987).

6. R.L. Daft and R.H. Lengel, "Information Richness: A New Approach to Managerial Behavior and Organization Design," *Research in Organizational Behavior*

6 (1984), pp. 191–233; R.H. Lengel and R.L. Daft, "The Selection of Communication Media as an Executive Skill," *Academy of Management Executive* 2 (1988), pp. 225–32.

7. W. Lucas, "Effects of E-Mail on the Organization," *European Management Journal* 16, no. 1 (February 1998), pp. 18–30; D.A. Owens, M.A. Neale, and R. I. Sutton, "Technologies of Status Management Status Dynamics in E-Mail Communications," *Research on Managing Groups and Teams* 3 (2000), pp. 205–30; N. Ducheneaut and L.A. Watts, "In Search of Coherence: A Review of E-Mail Research," *Human–Computer Interaction* 20, no. 1–2 (2005), pp. 11–48.

8. G. Hertel, S. Geister, and U. Konradt, "Managing Virtual Teams: A Review of Current Empirical Research," *Human Resource Management Review* 15 (2005), pp. 69–95; H. Lee, "Behavioral Strategies for Dealing with Flaming in an Online Forum," *The Sociological Quarterly* 46, no. 2 (2005), pp. 385–403.

9. D. Robb, "Ready or Not . . . Instant Messaging Has Arrived as a Financial Planning Tool," *Journal of Financial Planning,* July 2001, pp. 12–14; J. Black, "Why Offices Are Now Open Secrets," *BusinessWeek,* September 17, 2003; A.F. Cameron and J. Webster, "Unintended Consequences of Emerging Communication Technologies: Instant Messaging in the Workplace," *Computers in Human Behavior* 21, no. 1 (2005), pp. 85–103.

10. L.Z. Tiedens and A.R. Fragale, "Power Moves: Complementarity in Dominant and Submissive Nonverbal Behavior," *Journal of Personality and Social Psychology* 84, no. 3 (2003), pp. 558–68.

11. A. Mehrabian, *Silent Messages* (Belmont, CA: Wadsworth, 1971).

12. L.Z. Tiedens and A.R. Fragale, "Power Moves: Complementarity in Dominant and Submissive Nonverbal Behavior," *Journal of Personality and Social Psychology* 84, no. 3 (2003), pp. 558–68.

13. P. Ekman and E. Rosenberg, *What the Face Reveals: Basic and Applied Studies of Spontaneous Expression Using the Facial Action Coding System* (Oxford, England: Oxford University Press, 1997); P. Winkielman and K.C. Berridge, "Unconscious Emotion," *Current Directions in Psychological Science* 13, no. 3 (2004), pp. 120–23.

14. E. Hatfield, J.T. Cacioppo, and R.L. Rapson, *Emotional Contagion* (Cambridge, England: Cambridge University Press, 1993); S.G. Barsade, "The Ripple Effect: Emotional Contagion and Its Influence on Group Behavior," *Administrative Science Quarterly* 47 (December 2002), pp. 644–75; M. Sonnby-Borgstrom, P. Jonsson, and O. Svensson, "Emotional Empathy as Related to Mimicry Reactions at Different Levels of Information Processing," *Journal of Nonverbal Behavior* 27 (Spring 2003), pp. 3–23.

15. J.R. Kelly and S.G. Barsade, "Mood and Emotions in Small Groups and Work Teams," *Organizational Behavior and Human Decision Processes* 86 (September 2001), pp. 99–130.

16. R.E. Rice, "Task Analyzability, Use of New Media, and Effectiveness: A Multi-Site Exploration of Media Richness," *Organization Science* 3 (1992), pp. 475–500.

17. G. Hitt and J.D. McKinnon, "Cheney Takes Blame for Shooting but Defends How It Was Disclosed," *The Wall Street Journal,* February 16, 2006, p. A4.

18. M. McLuhan, *Understanding Media: The Extensions of Man* (New York: M-Graw-Hill, 1964).

19. K. Griffiths, "KPMG Sacks 670 Employees by E-Mail," *The Independent* (London), November 5, 2002, p. 19; P. Nelson, "Work Practices," *Personnel Today,* November 12, 2002, p. 2.

20. R.S. Kaplan and D.P. Norton, *The Balanced Scorecard: Translating Strategy into Action* (Boston: Harvard Business School Press, 1996).

21. N.B. Kurland and L.H. Pelled, "Passing the Word: Toward a Model of Gossip and Power in the Workplace," *Academy of Management Review* 24 (2000), pp. 428–38. See also G. Michelson and V.S. Mouly, "'You Didn't Hear It from Us But . . .': Toward an Understanding of Rumor and Gossip in Organizations," *Australian Journal of Management* 27 (2002), pp. 57–67.

22. S.M. Crampton, J.W. Hodge, and J.M. Mishra, "The Information Communication Network Factors Influencing Grapevine Activity," *Public Personnel Management* 27 no. 4 (1998), pp. 569–84. D.B. Simmons, "The Nature of the Organizational Grapevine," *Supervisory Management,* November 1985, pp. 39–45.

23. C.N. Macrae and G.V. Bodenhausen, "Social Cognition: Thinking Categorically about Others," *Annual Review of Psychology* 51 (2000), pp. 93–120.

24. A. Balsa and T.G. McGuire, "Prejudice, Clinical Uncertainty, and Stereotyping as Sources of Health Disparities," *Journal of Health Economics* 22 (January 2003), pp. 89–100.

25. D. Hamermesh and J.E. Biddle, "Beauty and the Labor Market," *American Economic Review* 84 (1994), pp. 1174–94.

26. J.M. Feldman "Beyond Attribution Theory: Cognitive Processes in Performance Appraisal," *Journal of Applied Psychology* 66 (1981), pp. 127–48; H.H. Kelley, "The Process of Causal Attribution," *American Psychologist* 28 (1973), pp. 107–28.

27. "Exit Carly," *The Economist,* February 10, 2005, p. 1.

28. P.J. Taylor and J.L. Pierce, "Effects of Introducing a Performance Management System and Employees' Subsequent Attitudes and Efforts," *Public Personnel Management* 28 (Fall 1999), pp. 423–52.

29. D.D. Steiner and J.S. Rain, "Immediate and Delayed Primacy and Recency Effects in Performance Evaluation," *Journal of Applied Psychology* 74 (1989), pp. 136–42.

30. D. Goleman, R. Boyatzis, and A. McKee, *Primal Leaders* (Boston: Harvard Business School Press, 2002), pp. 92–95.

31. "Gagged Prophet," *Houston Chronicle,* February 5, 2006, p. 2.

32. L.L. Putnam, N. Phillips, and P. Chapman, "Metaphors of Communication and Organization," in *Handbook of Organization Studies,* ed. S.R. Clegg, C. Hardy, and W.R. Nord (London: Sage, 1996), pp. 373–408; G. Morgan, *Images of Organization,* 2nd ed. (Thousand Oaks, CA: Sage, 1997); M. Rubini and H. Sigall, "Taking the Edge Off of Disagreement: Linguistic Abstractness and Self-Presentation to a Heterogeneous Audience," *European Journal of Social Psychology* 32 (2002), pp. 343–51.

33. K.M. Jackson, "Buzzword Backlash Looks to Purge Jibba-Jabba from Corporate-Speak," *Boston Globe,* April 17, 2005, p. G1.

34. R.D. McPhee, "Vertical Communication Chains," *Management Communication* 1, no. 4 (1988), pp. 455–86.

35. J.G. Miller, "Living Systems: The Organization," *Behavioral Science* 17 (1972), pp. 69–80.

36. J. Davidson, "Fighting Information Overload," *Office Solutions* 23, no. 1 (2006), p. 49.

37. D. Stonehouse, "E-mail," *Sun Herald* (Sydney), June 26, 2005, p. 26.

38. T. Koski, "Reflections on Information Glut and Other Issues in Knowledge Productivity," *Futures* 33 (August 2001), pp. 483–95; D.D. Dawley and W.P. Anthony, "User Perceptions of E-Mail at Work," *Journal of Business and Technical Communication* 17, no. 2 (April 2003), pp. 170–200; "E-mail Brings Costs and Fatigue," *Western News* (University of Western Ontario–London, Ontario), July 9, 2004.

39. A.G. Schick, L.A. Gordon, and S. Haka, "Information Overload: A Temporal Approach," *Accounting, Organizations & Society* 15 (1990), pp. 199–220; A. Edmunds and A. Morris, "The Problem of Information Overload in Business Organizations: A Review of the Literature," *International Journal of Information Management* 20 (2000), pp. 17–28.

40. D.C. Thomas and K. Inkson, *Cultural Intelligence: People Skills for Global Business* (San Francisco: Berrett-Koehler, 2004), Chapter 6; D. Welch, L. Welch, and R. Piekkari, "Speaking in Tongues," *International Studies of Management & Organization* 35, no. 1 (Spring 2005), pp. 10–27.

41. D. Woodruff, "Crossing Culture Divide Early Clears Merger Paths," *The Asian Wall Street Journal,* May 28, 2001, p. 9.

42. M. Brandel, "Global CIO," *Computerworld,* November 21, 2005, pp. 39–41. Tatamae and hone are discussed in H. Yamada, *American and Japanese Business Discourse: A Comparison of Interaction Styles* (Norwood, NJ: Ablex, 1992), p. 34; R.M. March, *Reading the Japanese Mind* (Tokyo: Kodansha International, 1996), Chapter 1.

43. P. Harris and R. Moran, *Managing Cultural Differences* (Houston: Gulf, 1987); H. Blagg, "A Just Measure of Shame?" *British Journal of Criminology* 37 (Autumn 1997), pp. 481–501; R.E. Axtell, *Gestures: The Do's and Taboos of Body Language around the World,* rev. ed. (New York: Wiley, 1998).

44. S. Ohtaki, T. Ohtaki, and M.D. Fetters, "Doctor–Patient Communication: A Comparison of the USA and Japan," *Family Practice* 20 (June 2003), pp. 276–82; M. Fujio, "Silence during Intercultural Communication: A Case Study," *Corporate Communications* 9, no. 4 (2004), pp. 331–39.

45. D.C. Barnlund, *Communication Styles of Japanese and Americans: Images and Realities* (Belmont, CA: Wadsworth, 1988); Yamada, *American and Japanese Business Discourse: A Comparison of Interaction Styles,* Chapter 2; H. Yamada, *Different Games, Different Rules* (New York: Oxford University Press, 1997), pp. 76–79.

46. This stereotypic notion is prevalent throughout J. Gray, *Men Are from Mars, Women Are from Venus* (New York: Harper Collins, 1992). For a critique of this view see J.T. Wood, "A Critical Response to John Gray's Mars and Venus Portrayals of Men and Women," *Southern Communication Journal* 67 (Winter 2002), pp. 201–10.

47. D. Tannen, *You Just Don't Understand: Men and Women in Conversation* (New York: Ballantine, 1990); D. Tannen, *Talking from 9 to 5* (New York: Avon, 1994); M. Crawford, *Talking Difference: On Gender and Language* (Thousand Oaks, CA: Sage, 1995), pp. 41–44; L.L. Namy, L.C. Nygaard, and D. Sauerteig, "Gender Differences in Vocal Accommodation: The Role of Perception," *Journal of Language and Social Psychology* 21, no. 4 (December 2002), pp. 422–32.

48. A. Mulac et al., "'Uh-Huh. What's That All About?' Differing Interpretations of Conversational Backchannels and Questions as Sources of Miscommunication across Gender Boundaries," *Communication Research* 25 (December 1998), pp. 641–68; N.M. Sussman and D.H. Tyson, "Sex and Power: Gender Differences in Computer-Mediated Interactions," *Computers in Human Behavior* 16 (2000), pp. 381–94; D.R. Caruso and P. Salovey, *The Emotionally Intelligent Manager* (San Francisco: Jossey-Bass, 2004), p. 23.

49. P. Tripp-Knowles, "A Review of the Literature on Barriers Encountered by Women in Science Academia," *Resources for Feminist Research* 24 (Spring/Summer 1995), pp. 28–34.

50. D. Kirkpatrick, "Gates and Ozzie: How to Escape E-Mail Hell," *Fortune,* June 27, 2005, pp. 169–71.

51. Cited in K. Davis and J.W. Newstrom, *Human Behavior at Work: Organizational Behavior,* 7th ed. (New York: McGraw-Hill, 1985), p. 438.

52. The three components of listening discussed here are based on several recent studies in the field of marketing, including S.B. Castleberry, C.D. Shepherd, and R. Ridnour, "Effective Interpersonal Listening in the Personal Selling Environment: Conceptualization, Measurement, and Nomological Validity," *Journal of Marketing Theory and Practice* 7 (Winter 1999), pp. 30–38; L. B. Comer and T. Drollinger, "Active Empathetic Listening and Selling Success: A Conceptual Framework," *Journal of Personal Selling & Sales Management* 19 (Winter 1999), pp. 15–29; and K. de Ruyter and M.G.M. Wetzels, "The Impact of Perceived Listening Behavior in Voice-to-Voice Service Encounters," *Journal of Service Research* 2 (February 2000), pp. 276–84.

53. J.V. Bommel, "Rumors," *Journal of Finance* 58 (2003), pp. 1499–1520.

54. The original term is "management by *wandering* around," but this has been replaced with "walking" over the years. See W. Ouchi, *Theory Z* (New York: Avon Books, 1981), pp. 176–77; T. Peters and R. Waterman, *In Search of Excellence* (New York: Harper and Row, 1982), p. 122.

55. S.P. Means, "Playing at Pixar," *Salt Lake Tribune* (Utah), May 30, 2003, p. D1; G. Whipp, "Swimming against the Tide," *Daily News of Los Angeles,* May 30, 2003, p. U6.

56. G. Evans and D. Johnson, "Stress and Open-Office Noise," *Journal of Applied Psychology* 85 (2000), pp. 779–83; F. Russo, "My Kingdom for a Door," *Time Magazine,* October 23, 2000, p. B1.

57. Sources: I. Austen, **"Blemishes on NASA's Shining Image,"** *Maclean's,* March 10, 1986, p. 60; E. Magnuson, "A Serious Deficiency," *Time,* March 10, 1986, pp. 38–41; L. McGinley and E.T. Pound, "Rockwell International Aids Tell Panel They Warned NASA Launch Was Unsafe," *The Wall Street Journal,* February 28, 1986, p. 1.

18

MANAGING
INNOVATION AND CHANGE

Going Digital   Kodak is rapidly moving to digital photographing in order to stay in business as its traditional film business dies.
© Getty Images

For the best part of a century Kodak dominated the photographic business. The company's business model was simple: Sell cameras cheaply and then make money by selling and processing the film. It worked flawlessly until the 1990s when digital cameras started to appear on the scene. Suddenly consumers didn't need film, and Kodak's managers found themselves staring into an abyss. Recognizing the threat, Kodak started an aggressive program to produce digital cameras. By 2005 Kodak was the market leader, selling 22 percent of all digital cameras in the United States. However, this was little cause for celebration. The digital camera business was fiercely competitive, and profit margins were low. In the old days Kodak had sold over half the film processed in the United States and enjoyed fat margins. That business was now declining three times faster than top managers had predicted just two years earlier, contributing to a $1.4 billion loss in 2005. As its traditional business imploded, Kodak scrambled to downsize its film business, closing down factories and laying off employees. Antonio Perez, the company's CEO, noted that the company "was in the worst possible place" as it tried to shift from traditional photography to digital imaging. Nevertheless, he predicted that by 2008 things would be improving: 80 percent of revenues would then come from digital imaging, and the company would be growing at double-digit rates.[1]

The wrenching changes that Kodak is going through are the result of a technological paradigm shift in the photography market. Kodak is not the first business to confront a dramatic paradigm shift. Eventually most businesses find the market moving away from them due to the emergence of a new technology and the rise of new competitors who exploit that technology. In the 1980s and 1990s IBM faced a similar challenge as its traditional mainframe computer business shrank in the face of new competition from the companies that were driving the personal computer revolution, including Microsoft, Intel, and Dell. IBM survived by reinventing itself as a computer services company, just as Kodak is trying to survive by reinventing itself as a digital imaging company. Encyclopedia Britannica is another business that saw a paradigm shift and survived by remaking itself. For over 200 years Encyclopedia Britannica's business involved selling books. In the 1990s this market collapsed as consumers switched to first CDs and then online encyclopedias such as Microsoft's Encarta and Wikipedia, both new competitors. To survive Encyclopedia Britannica had to shut down its traditional business and move to an online format.

■ Paradigm shifts in the computer industry.

Although companies like IBM and Encyclopedia Britannica were able to survive paradigm shifts, albeit only after a difficult transition, many long-established businesses do not.[2] The advent of word processing software and personal computers decimated demand for typewriters, and in the late 1990s Smith Corona, one of the world's great typewriter companies, went bankrupt. Similarly Wang Computers, one of the technology growth companies of the 1970s, built a significant business selling word processing software for use on midrange computers. It too ultimately went bankrupt when word processing software for PCs destroyed its market. In the steel industry enterprises such as Nucor Steel have used minimill technology to take market share from established steelmaking enterprises, many of which, such as Bethlehem Steel, have now gone bankrupt.

In this final chapter we look at the nature of paradigm shifts. We discuss how the emergence of a new paradigm often revolutionizes competition, putting established incumbent companies on the defensive. We look at the inertia forces within organizations that make it difficult for incumbent companies to respond to a new paradigm, and we discuss how managers can implement major changes in their strategy and organization architecture to survive a paradigm shift. The chapter closes with a discussion of how managers can develop innovations that might initiate a paradigm shift.

■ // Paradigm Shifts

paradigm shift
Occurs when a new technology or business model comes along that dramatically alters the nature of demand and competition.

A **paradigm shift** occurs when a new technology or business model comes along that dramatically alters the nature of demand and competition. Faced with paradigm shifts, incumbent enterprises have to adopt new strategies to survive. Paradigm shifts appear to be more likely in an industry when one or more of the following conditions are in place.[3] First, the established

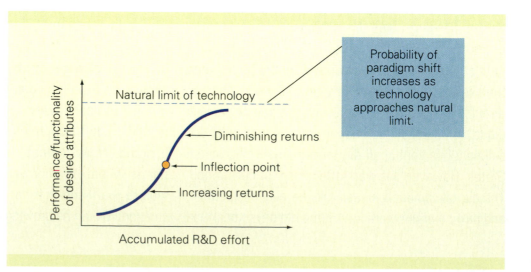

FIGURE 18.1

Technology S-Curves

technology in the industry is mature and approaching or at its natural limit. Second, a new disruptive technology has entered the marketplace and is taking root in market niches that are poorly served by incumbent companies that use the established technology. Third, a company develops a new business model that is radically different from that used by competitors, enabling it to capture more demand and put its rivals on the defensive.

// NATURAL LIMITS TO TECHNOLOGY

Richard Foster has formalized the relationship between the performance of a technology and time in what he calls the *technology S-curve* (see Figure 18.1).[4] This curve shows the relationship over time between *cumulative* investments in R&D and the performance (or functionality) of a given technology. Early in its evolution, R&D investments in a new technology tend to yield rapid improvements in performance as basic engineering problems are solved. After a while diminishing returns to cumulative R&D begin to set in, the rate of improvement in performance slows, and the technology starts to approach its natural limit where further advances are not possible. For example, one can argue that there was more improvement in the first 50 years of the commercial aerospace business following the pioneering flight by the Wright Brothers than there has been in the second 50 years. The first 50 years took us from Kitty Hawk to the jet age—from slow propeller-driven planes made of wood, wire, and cloth to the Boeing 707, the world's first successful commercial jetliner. Today's commercial jetliners, such as the Boeing 787, although far more efficient than the 707, are recognizable as direct descendants of the 707. In commercial aerospace we are now in the region of diminishing returns and may be approaching the natural limit to improvements in the technology of jetliners.

What does this have to do with paradigm shifts? According to Foster, when a technology approaches its natural limit, research attention turns to possible alternative technologies. Eventually one of those alternatives might be commercialized and replace the established technology. That is, the probability that a paradigm shift will occur increases. Thus sometime in the next decade or two another paradigm shift might shake the foundations of the computer industry as a new computing technology replaces silicon-based computing. If history is a guide, when this happens many of the incumbents in today's computer industry will go into decline and new enterprises will rise to dominance.

Foster pushes this point further, noting that initially the contenders for the replacement technology are not as effective as the established technology in producing the attributes and features

■ Natural limits to technological progress in aerospace.

consumers demand in a product. For example, in the early years of the 20th century, automobiles were just starting to be produced. They were valued for their ability to move people from place to place, but so were the horse and cart (the established technology). When automobiles originally appeared, the horse and cart were still quite a bit better than the automobile at doing this (see Figure 18.2). The first cars were slow, noisy, and prone to breakdowns. Moreover, they needed a network of paved roads and gas stations to be useful, and that network didn't exist. Thus for most applications the horse and cart were still the preferred mode of transportation—and cheaper.

However, in the early 20th century automobile technology was at the very start of its S-curve and was about to experience dramatic improvements in performance as major engineering problems were solved (and those paved roads and gas stations were built). In contrast, after 3,000 years of continuous improvement and refinement, the horse and cart were definitely at the end of their technology S-curve. The result was that the rapidly improving automobile soon replaced the horse and cart as the preferred mode of transportation. At time T_1 in Figure 18.2 the horse and cart were still superior to the automobile. By time T_2 the automobile had surpassed the horse and cart.

Highly Evolved Technology   After some 3,000 years of development the horse and cart are high on their technology S-curve, and few improvements are likely. The maturity of this technology made it vulnerable to a paradigm shift, which occurred when Henry Ford started to mass-produce automobiles.

FIGURE 18.2

Established and Successor Technologies

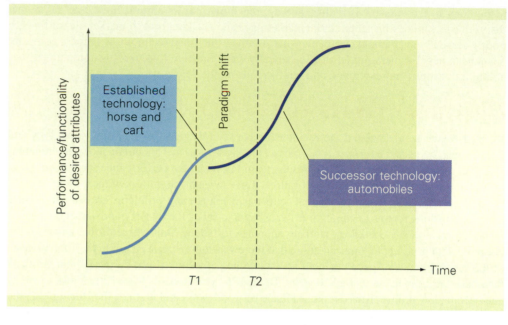

Foster notes that because the successor technology is initially less efficient than the established technology, established companies and their customers often make the mistake of dismissing it, only to be caught off guard by its rapid performance improvement. A final point here is that often there is not one potential successor technology but a swarm of potential successor technologies, only one of which might ultimately rise to the fore (see Figure 18.3). When this is the case, incumbent enterprises are at a disadvantage. Even if they recognize that a paradigm shift is imminent, they may not have the resources to invest in all the potential replacement technologies. If they invest in the wrong one—something that is easy to do given the uncertainty that surrounds the entire process—they may be locked out of subsequent development.

// DISRUPTIVE TECHNOLOGY

disruptive technology

A new technology that gets its start away from the mainstream of a market and then, as its functionality improves, invades the main market.

Clayton Christensen has built on Foster's insights and his own research to develop an influential theory of disruptive technology.[5] Christensen uses the term **disruptive technology** to refer to a new technology that gets its start away from the mainstream of a market and then, as its functionality improves, invades the main market. Such technologies are disruptive because they revolutionize industry structure and competition, often causing the decline of established organizations. They cause a technological paradigm shift.

Christensen's greatest insight is that established companies are often aware of the new technology but do not invest in it because they listen to their customers, and their customers do not want it. Of course this occurs because the new technology is early in its development and thus only at the beginning of its technology S-curve. Once the performance of the new technology improves, customers want it; but by this time, it is new entrants, as opposed to established companies, that have accumulated the knowledge required to bring the new technology into the mass market.

Christensen supports his view with several detailed historical case studies. One concerns the story of how disruptive technology revolutionized the market for excavation equipment. Excavators are used to dig foundations for buildings and trenches to lay pipes for sewers and the like. Before the 1940s the dominant technology used to manipulate the bucket on a mechanical excavator was based on a system of cables and pulleys. These mechanical systems, known as "steam shovels," could lift large buckets of earth; but the excavators themselves were large, cumbersome, and expensive. Thus they were rarely used to dig small trenches for house foundations, irrigation ditches for farmers, and the like. In most cases small trenches were dug by hand.

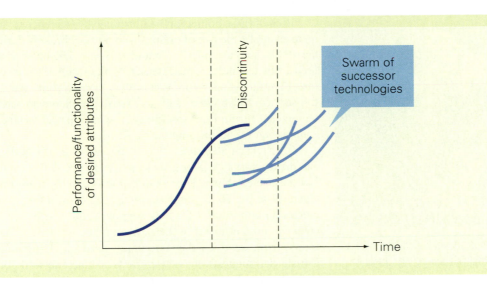

FIGURE 18.3

Swarm of Successor
Technologies

In the 1940s a new technology appeared: hydraulics. In theory hydraulic systems had advantages over the established cable and pulley systems. Most important, their energy efficiency was higher: For a given bucket size, a smaller engine would be required using a hydraulic system. However, the initial hydraulic systems also had drawbacks. The seals on hydraulic cylinders leaked under high pressure, effectively limiting the size of bucket that could be lifted using hydraulics. Notwithstanding this drawback, when hydraulics first appeared, many of the incumbent firms in the mechanical excavation industry took the technology seriously enough to ask their primary customers whether they would be interested in products based on hydraulics. Because the primary customers of incumbents needed excavators with large buckets to dig the foundations for large buildings and trenches, their reply was negative. For this customer set, the hydraulic systems of the 1940s were not reliable or powerful enough. Consequently, after consulting with their customers, these established companies in the industry made the strategic decision not to invest in hydraulics. Instead they continued to produce excavation equipment based on the dominant cable and pulley technology.

It was left to a number of new entrants, including J.I. Case, John Deere, J.C. Bamford, and Caterpillar, to pioneer hydraulic excavation equipment. Because of the limits on bucket size imposed by the seal problem, these companies initially focused on a poorly served niche in the market that could use small buckets: residential contractors and farmers. Over time these new entrants solved the engineering problems associated with weak hydraulic seals; and as they did this they manufactured excavators with larger buckets. Ultimately they invaded the market niches served by the old-line companies: general contractors that dug the foundations for large buildings, sewers, and so on. At this point Case, Deere, Caterpillar, and their kin rose to dominance in the industry, whereas the majority of established companies from the prior era lost market share. Of the 30 or so manufacturers of cable-actuated equipment in the United States in the late 1930s, only four survived to the 1950s.

In addition to listening too closely to their customers, as the manufacturers of cable-activated excavators did, Christensen identifies a number of other factors that make it difficult for established companies to adopt a new disruptive technology. He notes that many established companies have declined to invest in new disruptive technologies because initially these technologies served such small market niches that they seemed unlikely to affect company revenues and profits. As the new technologies started to improve in functionality and invade the main market, companies' investment was often hindered by the fact that exploiting the new technology required a new business model different from the established model, which was thus difficult to implement.

■ Disruptive technology in the excavation industry.

Victim of Disruption   The steam shovel was the dominant excavation technology until hydraulics came along. Despite the advantages of hydraulic systems, most steam shovel companies did not invest in this new technology, and most ultimately went out of business.

© Corbis

Both of these points can be illustrated by reference to one more example: the rise of online discount stockbrokers during the 1990s such as Ameritrade and E*Trade. The enterprises used a new technology, the Internet, to allow individual investors to trade stocks for a very low commission fee; at full-service stockbrokers, such as Merrill Lynch, orders had to be placed through a stockbroker who earned a larger commission for performing the transaction.

Christensen also notes that a new network of suppliers and distributors typically grows up around the new entrants. Not only do established companies initially ignore disruptive technology, but so do their suppliers and distributors. This creates an opportunity for new suppliers and distributors to enter the market to serve the new entrants. As the new entrants grow, so does the associated network. Ultimately, Christensen suggests, the new entrants and their network may replace not only established enterprises, but also the entire network of suppliers and distributors associated with established companies. Taken to its logical extreme, this view suggests that disruptive technologies may kill entire networks of enterprises.

// NEW BUSINESS MODEL

business model

The way in which an enterprise intends to make money.

The term **business model** refers to the way in which an enterprise intends to make money. For example, the business model of Hewlett-Packard's printer division has been to sell printers at cost and then make money by selling replacement ink cartridges at a price far in excess of their cost of production. This is known as the *razor and razor blades* business model because it was pioneered by Gillette, which would sell razors at cost and then sell replacement blades for a substantial premium. Another example of a business model is the search-based paid advertising model popularized by Google. Google offers free Web-based search products, but it makes money from the advertising associated with each search—particularly the "sponsored links" that pop up whenever anyone enters a search term into Google. Advertisers pay Google a small fee every time someone clicks on one of the sponsored links and is directed to the sponsor's Web site. Advertisers bid against each other to appear high on the list, with the advertiser featured on the top of the list paying the most.

■ New business models: Google, Dell, and Southwest Airlines.

The development of a new business model can radically alter the competitive playing field, disrupting competition by capturing demand from established enterprises. In other words, the development of a new business model can cause a paradigm shift. Google's search-based advertising model, for example, is creating problems for traditional media (from television to print magazines) as they see advertising dollars diverted toward Google and its competitors (Yahoo and Microsoft's MSN). Similarly, Southwest Airlines created a new business model in the airline industry that has seriously disrupted competition. Southwest decided to bypass hubs and fly "point to point" between cities, often from smaller airports not used by established airlines. Customers value the convenience and speed associated with this business model. The company also stripped costs dramatically by not offering meals during flights or assigned seating, departure lounges at airports, or baggage transfers to other airlines. So Southwest and its imitators such as Jet Blue and Europe's Ryan Air have taken progressively more market share from established airlines, many of which are now in financial trouble. Another example is Dell Computer, which pioneered the business model of direct selling in the personal computer industry. Dell's rivals, which sell through retail channels, have been struggling to find their equilibrium since Dell took advantage of the superior value proposition and low costs associated with its business model to grab market leadership.

What Google, Southwest Airlines, and Dell have done (and are continuing to do) is reshape competition in their respective markets by developing novel business models that offer more value to consumers, enabling them to take demand from established enterprises. The development of new business models is often predicated on the emergence of a new technology. Thus Google's business model could not have existed until the Web had emerged and until the technology for searching Web pages had been perfected. Similarly, the emergence of Web browsing made Dell's direct selling model particularly powerful and disruptive. Technological innovation, in other words, offers fertile ground for the development of new business models. But new business models can sometimes emerge in the absence of new technology: No new technology underlay the business model developed by Southwest Airlines.

// PUNCTUATED EQUILIBRIUM

Paradigm shifts are episodic events in the history of an industry. Studies have revealed that most industries are characterized by long periods of stability in which the development of technology proceeds along a well-established trajectory (a given S-curve) and established business models are adopted by all; but these periods of stability are interspersed with periods of rapid change. Normally such change is due to the emergence of a new technology, a new business model, or some combination of these that triggers a paradigm shift. This view of the evolution of an industry, referred to as **punctuated equilibrium**, holds that long periods of equilibrium, when an industry's structure is stable, are punctuated by periods of rapid change when industry structure is revolutionized by innovation.[6]

Figure 18.4 shows what punctuated equilibrium might look like for one key dimension of industry: competitive structure. From time t_0 to t_1 the competitive structure of the industry is stable and highly concentrated, with a handful of companies sharing the market. At time t, a major innovation is pioneered by either an existing company or a new entrant. The new technology lowers barriers to entry into the industry; new companies enter the market using the new technology; and the industry structure becomes more fragmented and competitive. After a while incumbent companies that cannot adapt go out of business, as do the new entrants that cannot gain enough market share to reap economies of scale. By time t_2 the industry becomes consolidated again, but now *different* firms dominate the market. Thus there is a period of turbulence between t_1 and t_2, after which the industry settles down into a new equilibrium with different industry leaders.

During a period of rapid change when industry structure is being revolutionized by a technological innovation, value typically migrates to business models championed by new entrants and based on new strategies.[7] In the photography industry value has migrated away from a

punctuated equilibrium

A view of industry evolution asserting that long periods of equilibrium are punctuated by periods of rapid change when industry structure is revolutionized by innovation.

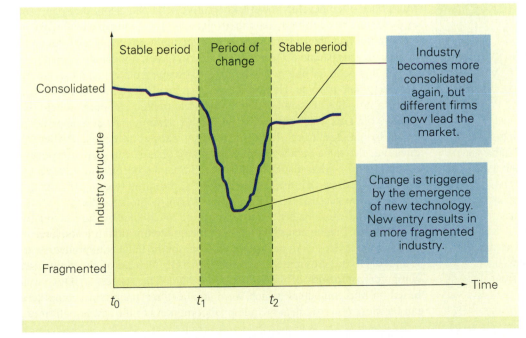

FIGURE 18.4

Punctuated Equilibrium

business model based on the sale of film and film processing services and toward digital imaging. Kodak was the champion of the old business model; Hewlett-Packard and Sony have championed the new model (and now makers of wireless phones, such as Samsung, are getting into the market with camera phones). In the stock brokerage industry value migrated away from the full-service broker model championed by the likes of Merrill Lynch to the online trading model championed by E*Trade. In the book-selling industry value has migrated away from small neighborhood bookshops toward large bookstore chains like Barnes & Noble and online bookstores such as amazon.com, both of which reap enormous economies of scale. As value migrates during these periods of change, many incumbent enterprises go into decline or at least go through periods of wrenching change such as the one Kodak is experiencing. In the next section we discuss why this is the case.

■ // Organizational Inertia

organizational inertia

Internal and external forces that make it difficult to change the strategy or organization architecture of an enterprise.

We have noted that when confronted with paradigm shifts, many incumbent businesses decline. This decline is normally due to the inability of an enterprise to change its strategy and organization architecture as rapidly as the environment is changing due to organization inertia.[8] By **organizational inertia** we mean internal and external forces that make it difficult to change the strategy or organization architecture of an enterprise. These inertia forces include cognitive schemata, internal political constraints, organizational culture, strategic commitments and capabilities, and external institutional constraints.[9]

// COGNITIVE SCHEMATA

cognitive schema

A manager's mental model of the world his or her enterprise inhabits.

■ Cognitive schemata and inertia at Digital Equipment.

In the course of their work managers form **cognitive schemata**, which are mental models of the world their enterprise inhabits. These mental models include beliefs about what works and does not work in their business and about what is important and unimportant. These models are based on experience. When a management team has worked together for some time, they often come to share the same worldview—the same cognitive schema—and this can influence their decision making.[10] Although this can lead to quick decisions, management teams with a shared cognitive schema tend to ignore events, data, and suggestions that fall outside their schema: They have cognitive blind spots.[11] Consequently they may not understand the threat posed by new technologies and new enterprises.[12]

Cognitive schemata are usually adopted because they have worked in the past. Danny Miller has postulated that senior managers in successful enterprises often develop powerful cognitive schemata about the right way to do business, and this makes them particularly vulnerable to cognitive blind spots when new competitors or new technologies emerge. Miller calls this the "Icarus paradox."[13] Icarus, a figure in Greek mythology, used a pair of wings—made for him by his father—to escape from an island where he was being held prisoner. He flew so well that he climbed higher and higher, ever closer to the sun, until the heat of the sun melted the wax that held the feathers onto his wings and he plunged to his death in the sea. The paradox is that his greatest asset—his ability to fly—caused his demise. Miller argues that the same paradox applies to many once-successful enterprises. According to Miller, managers at such companies become so dazzled by their early success that they believe more of the same type of effort is the way to future success: They develop powerful cognitive schemata about what works. Unfortunately these ideas can be invalidated by the rise of new technologies, but the managers may not recognize this until it is too late.

One of Miller's examples is Ken Olson, the brilliant entrepreneur who founded Digital Equipment Corporation (DEC), one of the dominant computer companies of the 1970s and 1980s. The success of DEC was based on minicomputers, which were smaller than mainframe computers but far more powerful than the personal computers of the day. For all of his

The Fall of Icarus   A figure from Greek mythology, Icarus flew too close to the sun, which melted the wax holding feathers onto his wings, and he fell to his death. When confronted with new technology and new competitors, high-flying corporations can suffer the same fate if they adhere too closely to the cognitive schemata (and business models) that made them great. Their greatest assets can become their greatest weaknesses.

© The Art Archive/Corbis

brilliance, Olson and his management team at DEC failed to see the threat posed by the rise of the personal computer, primarily because it fell outside their cognitive schema. DEC made powerful machines that were sold to businesses and accessed through terminals. Olson believed that such machines were the way of the future. In 1977 Olson was asked what he thought of personal computers, which were just starting to emerge. He replied, "There is no reason anyone would want a computer in their home." Olson didn't get it! His company missed the personal computer revolution. Meanwhile, people who did get it, such as Steve Jobs at Apple, Bill Gates at Microsoft, and Michael Dell at Dell Computer, were busy laying the foundations for a revolution in the industry.

// INTERNAL POLITICAL CONSTRAINTS

Organizations can be thought of as political systems within which there is an existing distribution of power and influence.[14] As we saw in Chapter 15, the power and influence enjoyed by different managers is a function of several things, including their position in the hierarchy, their control over valuable resources and information, and their perceived expertise. For example, a well-regarded marketing vice president whose sales database gives her access to important information about customer preferences might enjoy significant power in an organization otherwise dominated by engineers. Personal attributes are also a source of power, including a manager's energy, eloquence, empathy with others, and physical endurance. Senator Ed Muskie, one of the most powerful members of the Senate during his day, was reputed to be able to get things done, and thus accumulate power, in part because of his enormous physical stamina. When a bill was being debated in committee, he never left the room, *not* even to go to the bathroom—proving the old adage that a large bladder can be an asset in a bureaucracy.[15]

However power is accumulated, managers who possess it are unlikely to give it up willingly, and this is the problem. Any change, almost by definition, tends to alter the established distribution of power and influence within an organization. Those whose power is threatened by change will naturally tend to oppose it, often arguing that the change is inappropriate. Because they have power, this opposition may be considerable. To the extent that they are successful, this constitutes a source of organizational inertia that might slow or stop change.

For example, in the 1990s the large Dutch multinational enterprise Philips NV increased the roles and responsibilities of its global product divisions and decreased those of its foreign subsidiary companies. The idea was to consolidate power in the hands of divisional heads, letting them reap economies of scale and lower costs by closing down factories in various countries and consolidating production in a few efficient plants. This implied that managers running the foreign subsidiary companies, who had wielded considerable power within Philips, would see their power and influence decline. As might be expected, the managers of foreign subsidiary companies did not like this change and resisted it, which slowed the pace of change and put Philips at a competitive disadvantage relative to rivals like Sony and Matsushita, both of which had powerful global product divisions.

// ORGANIZATIONAL CULTURE

Another source of organizational inertia is the existing culture of the enterprise as expressed in norms and value systems (see Chapter 10). Closely related to cognitive schemata, value systems reflect deeply held beliefs; as such they can be hard to change. If the formal and informal socialization mechanisms within an organization have emphasized a consistent set of values for a prolonged period, and if hiring, promotion, and incentive systems have all reinforced these values, suddenly announcing that those values are no longer appropriate and need to be changed can produce resistance and dissonance among employees. At Philips, for example, the culture had long placed a high value on granting autonomy to the managers running foreign subsidiaries. The changes of the 1990s implied a reduction in this autonomy, which contradicted the established values of the company and was thus resisted.

■ Organizational inertia at Philips NV.

// COMMITMENTS AND CAPABILITIES

■ Strategic commitments in the auto industry.

A major determinant of the ability of an incumbent firm to respond to new competition is the nature of that firm's prior strategic commitments.[16] **Strategic commitments** are a firm's investments in tangible and intangible assets to support a particular way of doing business (a particular business model). Tangible assets are buildings, plants, and equipment. Intangible assets include capabilities (skills and knowledge) that are accumulated over time. Once a firm has made a strategic commitment, it will have difficulty responding to new competition if doing so requires a break with this commitment. When established firms have deep commitments to a particular way of doing business and have developed supporting capabilities, they may be slow to imitate an innovating firm's strategy or adopt radical new technology. In part this is because they are unwilling to walk away from their existing commitments; and their capabilities may not be well suited to the new competitive environment, so they stick with what they know best even if that is no longer working.

The history of the U.S. automobile industry offers an example. From 1945 to 1975 the industry was dominated by the stable oligopoly of General Motors, Ford, and Chrysler, all of which geared their operations to making large cars, which American customers demanded at the time. When the market shifted from large cars to small, fuel-efficient ones during the late 1970s, U.S. companies lacked the assets and capabilities required to produce these cars. Their prior commitments had built the wrong assets and capabilities for this new environment. As a result, foreign producers, particularly the Japanese, stepped into the market breach by providing compact, fuel-efficient, high-quality, low-cost cars. The failure of U.S. auto manufacturers to react quickly to the entry of Japanese auto companies gave the latter time to build a strong market position and brand loyalty, which subsequently has proved difficult to attack. Ironically the same thing seems to be occurring now, with high fuel prices switching demand away from the large SUVs made by Ford and General Motors and toward small fuel-efficient cars, such as the Toyota Prius, built by foreign manufacturers.

Another example is IBM. In the 1980s IBM had major investments in the mainframe computer business. When the market shifted toward personal computers, IBM was stuck with significant assets specialized to the declining mainframe business: Its manufacturing facilities, research organization, and sales force were geared to the production of mainframes. Because these assets and capabilities were not well suited to the emerging personal computer business, IBM's difficulties in the early 1990s were in a sense inevitable. Its prior strategic commitments locked it into a business that was shrinking. Shedding these assets was bound to cause hardship for all organization stakeholders.

Source of Inertia   IBM's investments in the mainframe computer business, once a source of strength, became a source of inertia once the PC revolution gained speed.

(left) © Bob Rowan; Progressive Image/Corbis. (right) © Kimberly White/Reuters/Corbis.

// EXTERNAL INSTITUTIONAL CONSTRAINTS

External constraints imposed by powerful institutions, such as government agencies or labor unions, can also act as a source of inertia.[17] Unions, for example, might resist job cuts or attempts to introduce flexible work rules, thereby slowing a firm's ability to meet new competition. The ability of established airlines such as United to respond to low-cost competitors such as Jet Blue and Southwest, for example, has been hindered by strong labor unions that have resisted attempts to change aspects of their employment contracts and to restructure pensions, which has kept the cost structure of United Airlines high.[18] Similarly, government regulations can limit the ability of an organization to change its strategy and organization to meet new competition. In some countries, for example, local content rules specify that a certain percentage of a product sold in a country must be produced there. This can make it difficult for a business to counter low-cost competition by moving parts of its production system to countries where costs are lower.

// Organizational Change

As we have just seen, organizations are characterized by considerable inertia forces that impede organizational adaptation to new competitive realities. According to many scholars, the failure of organizations to adapt rapidly to new market realities is a major cause of corporate decline.[19] This raises the question of what managers can do to implement organizational change quickly and successfully. Research on organizational change suggests that there are four steps in a successful organizational change process: leadership committed to change, unfreezing the organization, moving the organization toward a new strategic and organizational configuration, and refreezing the organization in its new configuration (see Figure 18.5).[20]

// LEADERSHIP COMMITTED TO CHANGE

Organizations cannot change unless their leaders recognize the need for change and are committed to pushing it through. This is not as easy as it sounds. As we have seen, the shared

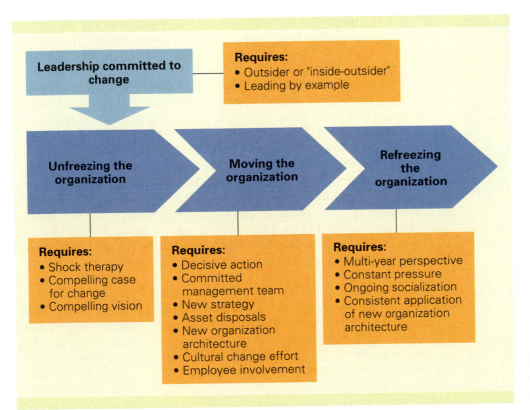

FIGURE 18.5

The Process of Organizational Change

cognitive schemata of a leadership group might be a source of inertia, causing failure to recognize the need for change. In many cases change is reactive instead of proactive because leaders are unable to recognize quickly enough that change is necessary and are pushed to accept reality by declining financial performance.

■ Change agents at IBM, 3M, and Xerox.

When managers decide to institute radical change, they often turn to an outsider who does not share their ideas and cultural values. When IBM was in deep trouble during the early 1990s (IBM lost $14 billion between 1990 and 1993) the board of directors appointed an outsider, Lou Gerstner, to the CEO position. Similarly, when the board of 3M decided that it was time to shake up the company's culture after a decade of mediocre performance, they hired Jim McNerney from General Electric, the first outsider ever to hold the CEO position at 3M. Alternatively, appointing an "outside–insider" to the leadership role—someone who is a manager in the firm but does not share the dominant cognitive schema and cultural values—can work. Jack Welch, who transformed GE, fits this description, as does Anne Mulcahy, who was the surprise pick of the Xerox board to lead that troubled company in 2001. A successful longtime Xerox executive, Mulcahy had never been considered CEO material. Not only was she a woman in a male-dominated organization, but she was also a salesperson in an engineering culture. Four years later, after guiding Xerox through an impressive turnaround, this "outside–insider" was being heralded as one of the best CEOs in America.[21]

A leader who is committed to organizational change not only recognizes the need for change and can communicate this eloquently to employees, motivating them to support the change effort, but must also "walk the talk." Jack Welch worked as hard as he was asking his employees to, and he embodied the values he was asking managers at GE to adopt. Anne Mulcahy logged 100,000 miles visiting employee locations during her first year as CEO, spreading the gospel of change. When Lee Iacocca became CEO of the troubled Chrysler Corporation in the 1970s, he accepted pay of only $1 a year until Chrysler made money. These leaders showed through personal commitment that they were serious about change. They led by example.

// UNFREEZING THE ORGANIZATION

Unfreezing an organization involves confronting all employees with the need for change and getting them to believe that change is necessary. Because organizations are by nature static, attempts at incremental or gradual change will usually be successfully resisted by those within the organization who stand to lose from the change effort. Thus many experts recommend bold, dramatic action to signal to employees that change is coming. What is needed, they say, is something akin to shock therapy. Sometimes, as at IBM and Xerox, poor financial performance provides the necessary shock. In other cases leaders have to create a sense of crisis by warning that unless the organization changes its ways, decline is inevitable. Jack Welch commented that one of the biggest problems he faced early on at General Electric was convincing a company that was performing reasonably well that it was facing a crisis of competitiveness. Managers have adopted some interesting tactics to push reluctant organizations to change. One CEO reportedly deliberately engineered the largest accounting loss in the company's history to startle employees out of their comfort zone. Another manager commissioned the company's first customer satisfaction survey, knowing that the results would be awful, and used those findings to push for change.[22]

To convince employees of the need for change, leaders may have to draw on all their communication abilities. They need a compelling message that tells employees why change is necessary, along with a credible strategic vision for the firm; and they must deliver that message and vision in an eloquent manner so that it resonates among employees. Sometimes bold symbolic action may also help awaken employees to the need for change. Frustrated by a lack of progress after four years of trying to change the culture at General Electric, Jack Welch fired 12 of the top 14 managers in a single day. Welch came to this decision after realizing that the inner circle of senior managers at GE was among those most resistant to

Turnaround Queen   When Anne Mulcahy took over as CEO of Xerox, the company was a shambles. It was losing market share to rivals because it had been slow to move from analog to digital copiers and from black and white to color. The company was bleeding red ink and only a few quarters from bankruptcy. Four years later the company was turning a profit and gaining market share.

Courtesy Xerox Corporation

change. This action sent an unmistakable signal to other GE managers that Welch was serious about changing the organization.[23]

// MOVING THE ORGANIZATION

Moving an organization entails changing management, strategy, organization architecture, and employee behavior. Movement requires action. At Xerox the action was decisive, as it needs to be in these situations because slow action is often successfully resisted. Anne Mulcahy quickly assembled her own management team, handpicking people from within and outside Xerox to work with her on the change effort. These people shared loyalty to Mulcahy and to what she was trying to achieve (as opposed to the old Xerox). Indeed, building a top management team that is committed to the change effort is recognized as an important first step in the movement process.[24] This helps consolidate power and authority in the key change agent, the leader.

While still recruiting senior managers, Mulcahy moved to change strategy, directing R&D resources toward accelerating Xerox's development of digital copiers while simultaneously shutting down several of Xerox's factories and selling others to third-party manufacturers. She even closed down the desktop copier division, a business she had created. Asset disposals like this are also characteristic of many organizational change efforts as the enterprise reconfigures itself to pursue a different strategy. Layoffs are a tough but necessary aspect of many such disposals. To remove the uncertainty and adverse motivational consequences associated with not knowing where layoffs will strike next, it is suggested that managers move through any downsizing phase as rapidly as possible and then signal to the remaining employees when it is completed.

Along with changes in strategy, resource allocation, and asset disposals, significant reengineering of the organization architecture is a standard part of many change efforts. Often the idea is to clarify who is responsible for what within an organization and to push down responsibility and accountability, stripping away unnecessary layers of management. At General Electric Jack Welch reduced the number of management layers between himself and the lowest-level employees from as many as 11 to as few as 4. At the same time he pushed responsibility for strategic and operational decision making further down in the organization. He also initiated sweeping changes in GE's control and incentive systems, boosting incentive pay and linking it to output targets like division profitability. The message behind these organizational changes was clear: "GE is now a performance-driven culture." Changes in organization architecture also disturb the distribution of power and influence within a firm, breaking the hold of those who are trying to protect the status quo.

At the heart of many organizational change efforts is an attempt to shift the culture of the enterprise. To some extent this can be done by rewarding people who manage according to the new values, letting go those who do not, and hiring people who support the new values rather than the failed culture. In addition, leaders often introduce systematic employee development programs aimed at socializing employees into the new culture. A classic example occurred in the 1980s when British Airways launched a cultural change effort. At the time customers often referred to the initials of the airline, BA, as standing for "bloody awful." After deciding that British Airways was in the customer service business rather than the transportation business (a strategic shift), the CEO put the entire 37,000-strong workforce through a two-day cultural change program called "Putting People First." Almost all the 1,400 managers went through a five-day version titled "Managing People First." To drive home the customer service message, BA also changed its control and incentive systems. In the new scheme managers were rewarded not only for how

■ Organizational change at Xerox.

■ Organizational change at British Airways.

From Bloody Awful to Bloody Awesome in Five Years   After large losses, British Airways went through an organizational change effort that transformed the culture of the airline and helped make it into one of the best and most profitable in the world.

© Linsey Parnaby/epa/Corbis

Transformational Tool   Jack Welch used management development classes held at GE's Crontonville Management Education Center as a forum for socializing managers into the cultural values that he believed were important for success at GE.

Courtesy of GE

■ Organizational change at GE.

well they performed, but also for how they behaved—and in particular whether that behavior was consistent with the new customer-centric focus of the airline. Five years later British Airways had gone from registering massive losses to having the highest profit rate in the entire airline industry and was winning awards for customer service.[25]

A critical component of many change efforts is involving employees in the change process, thereby giving them a sense of ownership. At General Electric Jack Welch created a process known as "workout" to involve employees in his attempt to turn GE into a performance-driven culture. Employees would meet for two to three days and come up with ideas for improving productivity in their work units. At the end they would make presentations to their managers, who had to approve or reject the suggestions on the spot. To put pressure on the managers, subordinates would be in the room, observing. If accepted, ideas had to be implemented. The process placed real power in the hands of employees and was responsible for some of GE's dramatic gains in productivity during the 1990s. To help cement employee empowerment Welch introduced 360-degree performance evaluations for all managers, enabling Welch, in his words, to identify "those who smiled up and kicked down."[26]

// REFREEZING THE ORGANIZATION

Refreezing an organization involves trying to solidify the new strategy and architecture of an organization so that the desired employee behavior becomes second nature. This is not easy. In the 1980s the Scandinavian airline SAS went through a major organizational change effort similar to that adopted by British Airways. Initially it seemed to work; but after a few years the CEO noticed that the old culture seemed to be trying to reassert itself, so he launched a second organizationwide training effort to try to solidify the new culture. Trying to alter an organization's culture is difficult because culture includes deeply held and persistent shared values. Effecting a change may require years of effort.

Refreezing an enterprise in a new strategic and organizational configuration requires constant attention and pressure. Leaders within the organization must stay on message and embody the desired behavior persistently. Control and incentive systems have to foster the desired behavior and reward managers and employees who perform well while acting in a manner that is consistent with the values and norms of the new culture. Ongoing attention is required for hiring and employee development policies. Some companies, for example, use extensive in-house management education programs to socialize managers into a new culture, explaining to them why it is important. At GE Jack Welch used the company's Crontonville Management Education Center as a socialization mechanism. He taught in every class, constantly emphasizing the entrepreneurial, performance-oriented values that he wanted to see managers adopt at GE.

A striking feature of Jack Welch's two-decade tenure at GE is that he never stopped pushing his change agenda. He kept thinking of new programs and initiatives to push the culture of the organization along the desired trajectory. That seems to be what is required to refreeze an organization in a new configuration.

■ // Failed Change Efforts and the Secrets of Success

Many managers have tried to push through radical change efforts in their organizations. Many have failed. By his own count John Kotter of Harvard Business School has studied over 100 organizational change efforts, both as an academic researcher and as a consultant who participated in the change effort. According to Kotter, there are eight errors that leaders often make when implementing a change effort.[27] First, Kotter estimates that over 50 percent of companies that fail to implement change do so because from the outset, they do not *establish a great enough sense of urgency.* In other words, they do not create a sense of crisis that startles employees out of their comfort zone. Second, Kotter says many leaders do not create *a powerful enough guiding coalition* to push through the change. They do not understand the importance of power and the fact that many incumbent managers can be a source of inertia. As we saw, Anne Mulcahy at Xerox dealt with this problem by handpicking her own top management team, and Jack Welch fired 12 of his 14 top managers, replacing them with managers who shared his values and sense of urgency.

Third, many change efforts fail because the leader *lacks a compelling vision* that tells employees what the organization is trying to achieve by its change effort. Fourth, and related to this, the leader may have a vision, but *the vision may be poorly communicated.* According to Kotter, many managers do not understand the need to communicate the vision consistently, often over a period of years, and to make sure it is heard by employees at all levels in the organization.

Fifth, Kotter comments that many change efforts fail because leaders *fail to remove obstacles to the change effort.* The obstacles may include managers who are unable or unwilling to buy into the new culture or an organization architecture that continues to foster old habits. Change efforts that fail to remove obstacles are cosmetic because the leaders have failed to change either the balance of power within the organization (shifting it away from managers who have a vested interest in maintaining the status quo) or an organization structure that reinforces the status quo.

Sixth, transformation efforts can fail due to a loss of momentum. Kotter sees the biggest error here as *not planning for and creating short-term wins.* People need to see evidence that the change effort is working—or they will fail to believe that change is possible and revert to the old ways of doing things. They need feedback to convince them that the change effort is making progress.

Seventh, Kotter believes that a big mistake is *declaring victory too soon.* As we have already stated, successful change efforts can take years, and persistence is required. If leaders declare victory too soon, the pressure for improved performance is released, and employees might slide back to the old way of doing things. Finally, Kotter notes that *change fails when it is not anchored in the organization's culture.* Without cultural change (change in the values that guide behavior in the organization) managers and employees revert to the old culture, and the change effort will not take.

Although not in Kotter's list, there is another important reason for failed change efforts: *failure to empower employees and lower-level managers to implement the change.*[28] As we have seen, a critical element of driving change efforts is to give employees a sense of ownership—to give them the power to push through changes. Often employees far down in the organization can be the greatest allies of senior managers. This was what Jack Welch understood when he created the workout process at General Electric. Change is not something you drive just from the top. It can also be driven from the bottom.

So what is required to make a change effort work? In summary, change demands leaders who are committed to the change effort, who can create a sense of urgency, who can form a powerful guiding coalition to push through the change, who can craft a compelling vision for the organization to strive toward, and who can successfully and persistently communicate that vision to all within the organization. Also required are quick and decisive changes in management and organization architecture to remove obstacles to change (to neutralize inertia forces). Managers should also arrange short-term wins to keep the momentum going. They should develop and implement processes that empower employees, enlisting them in the change effort as Jack Welch did at GE with the workout process. Finally, they must not only push the culture of the organization in a new direction but also institutionalize that culture by creating supporting reward and incentive systems, hiring the right people, and socializing employees into the culture through training and development programs. Moreover, they must do this consistently and persistently for years to stabilize the change.

■ // Driving Innovation

In this chapter we have discussed what managers must do to overcome inertia forces and lead a change in the strategy and organization of their enterprise so it can survive a technological paradigm shift in their industry. In this final section we discuss what a business might do to generate technological innovations—to be proactive and drive change in its industry. These might be **quantum innovations** that incorporate new technology and disrupt competition, shifting the dominant paradigm; or they might be **incremental innovations** that represent improvements in product functionality within an established technology (that is, an established S-curve). For example, eBay's adoption of Internet technology to run an auction business can be considered a *quantum innovation:* It involved a radically different technology (compared to a human auctioneer running an auction), and it effectively transformed the auction industry. In contrast, the latest personal computers represent cumulative incremental improvements of a technology that was introduced in the 1970s (the first personal computers, in contrast, were quantum innovations because they represented a distinct break with the past).

In many ways innovation is the most important source of competitive advantage for a business organization. This is because innovation can create new products that better satisfy customer needs, improve the quality of existing products, or reduce the costs of making products customers want. The ability to develop innovative new products, processes, or business models gives a business a major competitive advantage, allowing it to differentiate its products and charge a premium price or lower its cost structure below that of its rivals. Competitors, however, attempt to imitate successful innovations and often succeed. Therefore, maintaining a competitive advantage requires a continuing commitment to innovation.

Successful new product launches are major drivers of business success. Robert Cooper looked at more than 200 new product introductions and found that of those classified as successful, some 50 percent achieve a return on investment in excess of 33 percent; half have a payback period of two years or less; and half achieve a market share in excess of 35 percent.[29] Many companies have established a record of accomplishment for successful innovation: Sony, whose successes include the Walkman, the compact disk, and the PlayStation; Nokia, which has been a leader in the development of wireless phones; Pfizer, a drug company that during the 1990s and early 2000s produced eight blockbuster new drugs; and 3M, which has applied its core competency in adhesives to develop a wide range of new products.

> **quantum innovations**
>
> Innovations that incorporate new technology and disrupt competition, shifting the dominant paradigm.

> **incremental innovations**
>
> Innovations that represent improvements in product functionality within an established technology.

// NEW PRODUCT FAILURES

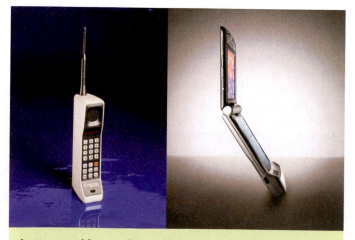

Incremental Innovation   While the first cell phones were a true quantum innovation, improvements since then have been incremental additions to existing technology.

Although promoting innovation can be a source of competitive advantage, the failure rate of innovative new products is high. Research suggests that only 10–20 percent of major R&D projects give rise to commercially viable products.[30] Well-publicized product failures include Apple Computer's Newton, a personal digital assistant; Sony's Betamax format in the video player and recorder market; and Sega's Dreamcast video game console. Although many reasons have been advanced to explain why so many new products fail to generate an economic return, five explanations for failure appear on most lists.[31]

First, many new products fail because the demand for innovations is inherently uncertain. It is impossible to know before market introduction whether a new product has tapped an unmet customer need or if there is sufficient market demand to justify making the product. Good market research can reduce but not eradicate uncertainty about likely future demand for a new technology, so some failures are to be expected.

Second, new products often fail because the technology is poorly commercialized. This occurs when there is definite customer demand for a new product, but the product is not well adapted to customer needs because of factors such as poor design and poor quality. For instance, the failure of Apple Computer to establish a market for the Newton, a handheld personal digital assistant that Apple introduced in the summer of 1993, can be traced to poor commercialization of a potentially attractive technology. Apple predicted a $1 billion market for the Newton, but sales failed to materialize when it became clear that the Newton's handwriting software (an attribute Apple chose to emphasize in its marketing) could not adequately recognize messages written on the Newton's message pad. Subsequently Palm entered this market with the Palm Pilot, a very successful product that racked up over $1 billion in sales.

Third, new products may fail because of poor strategy, including inappropriate pricing, weak promotion, or a poor distribution strategy. Apart from poor product quality, another reason for the failure of the Apple Newton was poor positioning strategy. The Newton was introduced at such a high initial price (close to $1,000) that there would probably have been few buyers even if the technology had been well commercialized.

Another reason why many new product introductions fail is that companies often market a technology for which there is not enough demand. A company can be blinded by the wizardry of a new technology and fail to examine whether there is sufficient customer demand for the product. Finally, companies fail when they are slow to get their products to market. The more time that elapses between initial development and final marketing—the slower the "cycle time"—the more likely it is that someone else will beat the company to market and gain a first-mover advantage.[32] In the car industry General Motors has suffered from being a slow innovator. Its product development cycle has been about five years, compared with two to three years at Honda, Toyota, and Mazda and three to four years at Ford. Because they are based on five-year-old technology and design concepts, GM cars are already out of date when they reach the market.

■ New product failure at Apple Computer.

// GENERATING SUCCESSFUL INNOVATIONS

Managers can take a number of steps to build innovation skills in their organizations and avoid failure. Six of the most important steps seem to be

- Building skills in basic and applied scientific research.
- Developing a good process for project selection and project management.
- Using cross-functional integration.
- Creating product development teams.
- Implementing partly parallel development processes.
- Placing a radically new technology in an autonomous organization unit.[33]

Building Skills in Basic and Applied Research Building skills in basic and applied research requires the employment of research scientists and engineers and the establishment of a work environment that fosters creativity. A number of top companies try to achieve this by setting up university-style research facilities, where scientists and engineers are given time to work on their own research projects in addition to projects that are linked directly to ongoing company research. At Hewlett-Packard, for example, company labs are open to engineers around the clock. Hewlett-Packard even encourages its corporate researchers to devote 10 percent of company time to exploring their own ideas and does not penalize them if they fail. 3M allows researchers to spend 15 percent of the workweek researching any topic that intrigues them, as long as there is the potential of a payoff for the company. The most famous outcome of this policy is the ubiquitous Post-its. The idea for them evolved from a researcher's desire to find a way to keep the bookmark from falling out of his hymnal. Post-its are now a major 3M business, with annual revenues of around $300 million.

Project Selection and Management Project management is the overall management of the innovation process, from generation of the original concept through development and into final

FIGURE 18.6

A Development Funnel

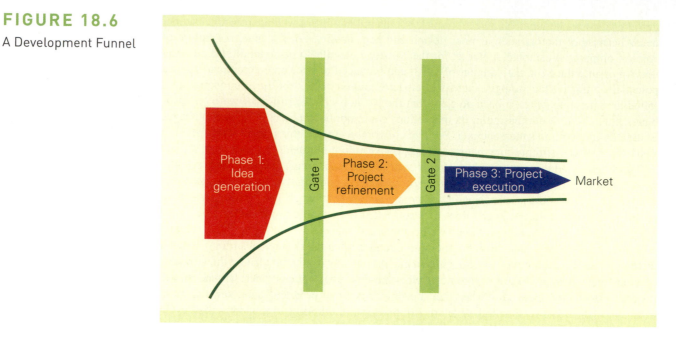

production and shipping. Project management requires three important skills: the ability to generate as many good ideas as possible, the ability to select among competing projects at an early stage of development so that the most promising receive funding and potential costly failures are killed off, and the ability to minimize time to market. The concept of the development funnel, divided into three phases, summarizes what is required to build these skills (see Figure 18.6).[34]

The objective in phase 1 is to widen the mouth of the funnel and encourage as much idea generation as possible. To this end, a company should solicit input from all its functions as well as from customers, competitors, and suppliers. At gate 1 the funnel narrows. Here ideas are reviewed by a cross-functional team of managers who did not participate in the original concept development. Concepts that are ready to proceed then move to phase 2, where the details of the project proposals are worked out. Note that gate 1 is not a go/no-go evaluation point. At this screen ideas may be sent back for further concept development and then resubmitted for evaluation.

During phase 2, which typically lasts only one or two months, the data and information from phase 1 are put into a form that will enable senior management to compare proposed projects. Normally this requires the development of a careful project plan, complete with details of the proposed target market, attainable market share, likely revenues, development costs, production costs, key milestones, and the like. The next selection point, gate 2, is a go/no-go evaluation point. Senior managers review the projects under consideration and select those that seem likely winners and make the most sense from a strategic perspective given the long-term goals of the company. The overriding objective is to select projects whose successful completion will help to maintain or build a competitive advantage for the company. A related objective is to ensure that the company does not spread its scarce capital and human resources too thinly over too many projects, instead concentrating resources where the chances of success and potential returns are most attractive. Any project selected to go forward at this stage will be funded and staffed with the expectation that it will be carried through to market introduction. In phase 3 the project development proposal is executed by a cross-functional product development team.

Cross-Functional Integration Tight cross-functional integration between R&D, production, and marketing can help a company to ensure that

- Product development projects are driven by customer needs.
- New products are designed for ease of manufacture.
- Development costs are kept in check.
- Time to market is minimized.

Close integration between R&D and marketing ensures that product development projects are driven by the needs of customers. A company's customers can be one of its primary sources of new product ideas. The identification of customer needs—particularly unmet needs—can set the context within which successful product innovation takes place. As the point of contact with customers, the marketing function can provide valuable information. Moreover, integrating R&D and marketing is crucial if a new product is to be properly commercialized. Otherwise a company runs the risk of developing products for which there is little or no demand.

The case of Techsonic Industries illustrates the benefits of integrating R&D and marketing. This company manufactures depth finders—electronic devices that fishers use to measure the depth of water beneath a boat and to track their prey. Techsonic had weathered nine consecutive new product failures when the company decided to interview sportspeople across the country to identify what they needed. They discovered an unmet need for a depth finder with a gauge that could be read in bright sunlight, so that is what Techsonic developed. In the year after the $250 depth finder hit the market, Techsonic's sales tripled to $80 million, and its market share surged to 40 percent.[35]

Integration between R&D and production can help managers ensure that products are designed with manufacturing requirements in mind. Design for manufacturing lowers manufacturing costs and leaves less room for mistakes—and thus can lower costs and increase product quality. Integrating R&D and production can help cut development costs and speed products to market. If a new product is not designed with manufacturing capabilities in mind, it may prove too difficult to build. In that case the product will have to be redesigned, and both overall development costs and time to market may increase significantly. For example, making design changes during product planning could increase overall development costs by 50 percent and add 25 percent to the time it takes to bring a product to market.[36] Moreover, many quantum product innovations require new manufacturing processes, which makes it even more important to achieve close integration between R&D and production: Minimizing time to market and development costs may require the simultaneous development of new products and new processes.[37]

Product Development Teams One of the best ways to achieve cross-functional integration is to establish product development teams composed of representatives from R&D, marketing, and production. The objective of a team should be to take a product development project from the initial concept development to market introduction. A number of attributes seem to be important for a product development team to function effectively and meet all its development milestones.[38]

First, **a heavyweight project manager**—one who has high status within the organization and the power and authority required to get the financial and human resources the team needs—should lead the team and be dedicated primarily (if not entirely) to the project. The leader should believe in the project (that is, be a champion) and be skilled at integrating the perspectives of different functions and helping personnel from different departments work together for a common goal. The leader should also be able to act as an advocate of the team to senior management.

Second, the team should have at least one member from each key function. The team members should possess a number of attributes, including the ability to contribute functional expertise, high standing within their functions, willingness to share responsibility for team results, and the ability to put functional advocacy aside. It is generally preferable if core team members are 100 percent dedicated to the project for its duration. This keeps their focus on the project, not on the ongoing work of their function.

Third, the team members should be physically colocated to create a sense of camaraderie and facilitate communication. Fourth, the team should have a clear plan and clear goals, particularly for critical development milestones and development budgets. The team should have incentives to attain those goals, such as pay bonuses when major development milestones are hit. Finally, each team needs to develop processes for communication and conflict resolution. For example, one product development team at Quantum Corporation, a California-based

heavyweight project manager

A manager who has high status within an organization and the power and authority required to get the financial and human resources that his or her team needs to succeed.

FIGURE 18.7A
A Sequential Process

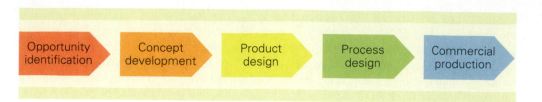

manufacturer of disk drives for personal computers, instituted a rule that all major decisions would be made and conflicts resolved at meetings that were held every Monday afternoon. This simple rule helped the team meet its development goals.[39]

Partly Parallel Development Processes   One way to compress the time it takes to develop a product and bring it to market is to use a partly parallel development process. Traditionally product development processes have been organized sequentially, as illustrated in Figure 18.7a. A problem with this kind of process is that product development proceeds without manufacturing issues in mind. Because the basic product design is completed prior to the design of a manufacturing process and full-scale commercial production, there is no early evaluation of manufacturability. Consequently the company may find that it cannot efficiently manufacture the product and have to send it back for redesign. Cycle time lengthens as a product bounces back and forth between stages.

To solve this problem, organizations can use a process similar to that illustrated in Figure 18.7b. In a partly parallel development process, development stages overlap so that, for example, work starts on the development of the production process before the product design is complete. By reducing the need for expensive and time-consuming product redesign, such a process can significantly reduce the time it takes to develop a new product and bring it to market.

Creating an Autonomous Unit   When a firm develops a quantum innovation—one that might usher in a technological paradigm shift in its industry—there is a danger that managers within the firm may fear the consequences of unleashing this innovation on the established business of the enterprise.[40] They may worry that the innovation will cannibalize sales of the firm's established business. Thus even though Kodak was a leader in developing digital imaging, for years Kodak reportedly hesitated to aggressively push digital cameras because managers knew the new technology would disrupt the industry and cut film sales.

In addition, a quantum innovation often requires a radically different business model. It may require a different manufacturing system, a different distribution system, and different pricing strategies from those used by the established business. For example, the business model associated with digital cameras is radically different from the business model associated with Kodak's traditional film business. Research suggests that it is almost impossible for two distinct business models to coexist within the same organization. Almost inevitably the established business model will suffocate the business model associated with the disruptive technology.[41]

■ Creating an autonomous unit at Hewlett-Packard.

The solution to these problems is to separate the new technology and place it in its own autonomous division. For example, during the early 1980s Hewlett-Packard built a successful laserjet printer business. Then HP invented inkjet technology. Some people in the company believed inkjet printers would cannibalize sales of laserjets and consequently argued that HP should not produce inkjets. Fortunately for HP, senior managers at the time saw inkjet technology for what it was: a potentially powerful disruptive technology. They allocated significant R&D funds toward its commercialization. Furthermore, when the technology was ready for market introduction, they established an autonomous inkjet division at a different geographic location with its own manufacturing, marketing, and distribution activities. HP managers accepted that the inkjet division would take sales away from the laserjet division and decided that it was better to have an HP division cannibalize the sales of another HP division than have those sales taken by another company.

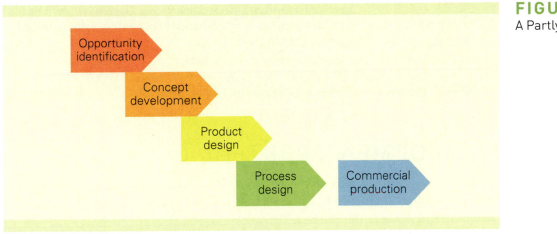

FIGURE 18.7B
A Partly Parallel Process

IN CONCLUSION \ WHY DOES IT MATTER?

In this chapter we have seen that industries are periodically revolutionized by new competitors that champion new technology. If established businesses are to survive the paradigm shifts initiated by new technology, they must change their strategy and organization architecture. This requires managers to adopt a systematic approach to organizational change that neutralizes inertia forces that defend the status quo and forges ahead with meaningful business transformation. We have also discussed what steps managers must take to make their own organizations successful at generating both quantum and incremental innovations.

Why does this material matter for students of management? We live in a world in which change is constant. Competition is a process that is driven by the development of new products, processes, and business models some of which destroy old business models, while creating entirely new product market opportunities. To succeed as a manager you must understand how this process works and be ready to play a part in leading it. You must be able to stay ahead of the competition by pushing your organization to develop better innovations, recognizing paradigm shifts when they occur. You must be ready to push for change in the strategy and organization architecture of your company so that it can adapt, survive, and prosper when facing a new competitive reality. For change to be successful, you must be able to identify inertia forces in your organization and know how to counteract them, helping the organization overcome the inevitable resistance to change. These skills mark truly great managers.

MANAGEMENT CHALLENGES

1. Where do you think Kodak's traditional film business and digital imaging business are located on their respective S-curves? What are the competitive implications of your answer?
2. Paradigm shifts don't occur only in high-technology industries. Can you think of a paradigm shift that occurred in a business not normally thought of as being high-tech? When did this paradigm shift occur, and what were its consequences?

3. During the late 1990s the discount broker Charles Schwab was faced with a paradigm shift. Research the cause of this paradigm shift and document how Schwab responded. What lessons can be drawn from the Schwab example?

4. General Motors is currently facing considerable challenges in its core U.S. market. What are the natures of these challenges? What must GM do to respond to these challenges? What inertia forces might make it difficult for GM to respond?

MANAGEMENT PORTFOLIO

FOR THE ORGANIZATION YOU HAVE CHOSEN TO FOLLOW:

1. Select a technology the organization uses. Where is that technology positioned on its S-curve?

2. Is the organization facing a paradigm shift, or has it faced one in the near past? If so, describe the nature of that shift and how the organization is responding (or did respond) to the paradigm shift.

3. Did the organization pioneer, or help pioneer, a paradigm shift in the past? If so, describe what occurred.

4. What inertia forces does the organization confront? If a future paradigm shift disrupts the organization's business model, how easy do you think it will be for the organization to adapt? What steps will it have to take to change the organization?

CLOSING CASE   TRANSFORMING REUTERS

London-based Reuters is a venerable company. Established in 1850 and devoted to delivering information around the world by the fastest means available—which in 1850 meant a fleet of 45 carrier pigeons—by the late 1990s the company had developed into one of the largest providers of information in the world. Although Reuters is known best to the public for its independent, unbiased news reporting, 90 percent of Reuters' revenues are generated by providing information to traders in financial markets. In the 1990s the company used a proprietary computer system and a dedicated telecommunications network to deliver real-time quotes and financial information to Reuters terminals—devices that any self-respecting financial trader could not function without. When Reuters entered the financial data business in the early 1970s, it had 2,400 employees, most of them journalists. By the late 1990s its employee base had swelled to 19,000, most of whom were on the financial and technical side. During this period of heady growth Reuters amassed some 1,000 products, often through acquisitions, such as foreign-language data services, many of which used diverse and sometimes incompatible computer delivery systems.

The late 1990s were the high point for Reuters. Two shocks to Reuters' business put the company in a tailspin. First came the Internet, which allowed newer companies, such as Thompson Financial Services and Bloomberg, to provide real-time financial information to any computer with an Internet connection. Suddenly Reuters was losing customers to a cheaper and increasingly ubiquitous alternative. The Internet was commoditizing the asset on which Reuters had built its business: information. Then in 2001 the stock market bubble of the 1990s finally broke; thousands of people in financial services lost their jobs; and Reuters lost 18 percent of its contracts for terminals in a single year. Suddenly a company that had always been profitable was losing money.

In 2001 Reuters appointed Tom Glocer as CEO. The first nonjournalist CEO in the company's history, Glocer, an American in a British-dominated firm, was described as "not part of the old boys' network." Glocer had long advocated that Reuters move to an Internet-based delivery system. In 2000 he was put in charge of rolling out such a system across Reuters but met significant resistance. The old proprietary system had worked well, and until 2001 it had been extremely profitable. Many managers were therefore reluctant to move toward a Web-based system that commoditized information and had lower profit margins. They were worried about product cannibalization. Glocer's message was that if the company didn't roll out a Web-based system, Reuters' customers would defect in droves. In 2001 his prediction seemed to be coming true.

Once in charge, Glocer again pushed an Internet-based system, but he quickly recognized that Reuters' problems ran deeper. In 2002 the company registered its first annual loss in history, £480 million, and Glocer described the business as "fighting for survival." Realizing that dramatic action was needed, in February 2003 Glocer launched a three-year strategic and organizational transformation program called Fast Forward. It was designed to return Reuters to profitability by streamlining its product offering, prioritizing what the company focused on, and changing its culture. The first part of the program was an announcement that 3,000 employees (nearly 20 percent of the workforce) would be laid off.

To change its culture Reuters added an element to its Fast Forward program known as "Living Fast," which defined key values such as passionate and urgent working, accountability, and commitment to customer service and team. A two-day conference of 140 managers, selected for their positions of influence and business understanding rather than their seniority, launched the program. At the end of the two days the managers collectively pledged to buy half a million shares in the company, which at the time were trading at an all-time low.

After the conference the managers were fired up; but going back to their regular jobs, they found it difficult to convey that sense of urgency, confidence, and passion to their employees. This led to the development of a follow-up conference: a one-day event that included all company employees. Following a video message from Glocer and a brief summary of the goals of the program, employees spent the rest of the day in 1,300 cross-functional groups addressing challenges outlined by Glocer and proposing concrete solutions. Each group chose one of "Tom's challenges" to address. Many employee groups came up with ideas that could be rapidly implemented—and were. More generally, the employees asked for greater clarity in product offerings, less bureaucracy, and more accountability. With this mandate managers launched a program to rationalize the product line and streamline the company's management structure. In 2003 the company had 1,300 products. By 2005 Reuters was focusing on 50 key strategic products, all delivered over the Web. The early results of these changes were encouraging. By the end of 2004 the company recorded a £380 million profit, and the stock price had more than doubled.[42]

CASE DISCUSSION QUESTIONS

1. What technological paradigm shift did Reuters face in the 1990s? How did that paradigm shift change the competitive playing field?

2. Why was Reuters slow to adopt Internet-based technology?

3. Why do you think Tom Glocer was picked as CEO? What assets did he bring to the leadership job?

4. What do you think of Glocer's attempts to change the strategy and organizational culture at Reuters? Was he on the right track? Would you do things differently?

ENDNOTES

1. D. Henry, "A Tense Moment at Kodak," *BusinessWeek,* October 17, 2005, p. 84; W.M. Bulkeley, "Kodak Scales Back Short-Term View but Sees Revival," *The Wall Street Journal,* September 29, 2005, p. B4.

2. J.M. Utterback, *Mastering the Dynamics of Innovation* (Boston: Harvard Business School Press, 1994); A.J. Slywotzky, *Value Migration: How to Think Several Moves Ahead of the Competition* (Boston: Harvard Business School Press, 1996).

3. C.M. Christensen, *The Innovator's Dilemma* (Boston: Harvard Business School Press, 1997); R.N. Foster, *Innovation: The Attacker's Advantage* (New York: Summit Books, 1986).

4. Foster, *Innovation.*

5. See Christensen, *The Innovator's Dilemma;* and C.M. Christensen and M. Overdorf, "Meeting the Challenge of Disruptive Change," *Harvard Business Review,* March–April 2000, pp. 66–77.

6. The term *punctuated equilibrium* is borrowed from evolutionary biology. For a detailed explanation of the concept, see M.L. Tushman, W.H. Newman, and E. Romanelli, "Convergence and Upheaval: Managing the Unsteady Pace of Organizational Evolution," *California Management Review* 29, no. 1 (1985), pp. 29–44; C.J.G. Gersick, "Revolutionary Change Theories: A Multilevel Exploration of the Punctuated Equilibrium Paradigm," *Academy of Management Review* 16 (1991), pp. 10–36; R. Adner and D.A. Levinthal, "The Emergence of Emerging Technologies," *California Management Review* 45 (Fall 2002), pp. 50–65.

7. Slywotzky, *Value Migration: How to Think Several Moves Ahead of the Competition.*

8. M. Hannah and J. Freeman, *Organizational Ecology* (Cambridge, MA: Harvard University Press, 1989); M.T. Hannah and J. Freeman, "Structural Inertia and Organizational Change," *American Sociological Review* 49 (1984), pp. 149–64.

9. C.J. Fombrum, *Leading Corporate Change* (New York: McGraw-Hill, 1992).

10. C.K. Prahalad and R.A. Bettis, "The Dominant Logic: A New Linkage between Diversity and Performance," *Strategic Management Journal* 7 (1986), pp. 495–501.

11. E.J. Zajac and M.H. Bazerman, "Blind Spots in Industry and Competitor Analysis," *Academy of Management Review* 16 (1991), pp. 37–57.

12. M. Tripsas and G. Gavetti, "Capabilities, Cognition, and Inertia: Evidence from Digital Imaging," *Strategic Management Journal* 21 (2000), pp. 1147–61.

13. D. Miller, *The Icarus Paradox* (New York HarperBusiness, 1990).

14. G. Morgan, *Images of Organization* (Beverly Hills: Sage, 1986); J. Pfeffer, *Managing with Power: Politics and Influence within Organizations* (Boston: Harvard Business School Press, 1992).

15. H. Smith, *The Power Game: How Washington Works* (New York: Ballantine, 1988).

16. P. Ghemawat, *Commitment: The Dynamic of Strategy* (New York: Free Press, 1991).

17. P.J. DeMaggio and W.W. Powell, "The Iron Cage Revisited: Institutional Isomorphism and Collective Rationality in Organizational Fields," *American Sociological Review* 48 (1983), pp. 147–60.

18. J. Ott, "United No More," *Aviation Week and Space Technology,* May 16, 2005, p. 28.

19. Hannah and Freeman, *Organizational Ecology;* Hannah and Freeman, "Structural Inertia and Organizational Change."

20. M. Beer, *Organization Change and Development: A Systems View* (Santa Monica, CA: Goodyear Publishing, 1980); Fombrum, *Leading Corporate Change;* K. Lewin, *Field Theory in Social Sciences: Selected Theoretical Papers* (New York: Harper Brothers, 1951); M.L. Tushman and C.A. O'Reilly, *Winning through Innovation: A Practical Guide to Leading Organizational Change and Renewal* (Boston: Harvard Business School Press, 1997); M.L. Tushman and C.A. O'Reilly, "Ambidextrous Organizations: Managing Evolutionary and Revolutionary Change," *California Management Review* 38, no. 4 (1996), pp. 8–31; M. Washington and M.J. Ventresca, "How Organizations Change," *Organization Science* 15 (2004), pp. 82–97.

21. B. Morris, "The Accidental CEO," *Fortune,* June 23, 2003, p. 58.

22. J.P. Kotter, "Leading Change: Why Transformational Efforts Fail," *Harvard Business Review* 73 (March–April 1995), pp. 55–63.

23. *GE's Two-Decade Transformation: Jack Welch's Leadership* (Harvard Business School Case 9-399-150).

24. Fombrum, *Leading Corporate Change.*

25. Tushman and O'Reilly, "Ambidextrous Organizations: Managing Evolutionary and Revolutionary Change."

26. Quoted in *GE's Two-Decade Transformation: Jack Welch's Leadership.*

27. J.P. Kotter, "Leading Change: Why Transformational Efforts Fail," *Harvard Business Review* 73 (March–April 1995), pp. 55–63.

28. G. Labianca and B. Gray, "A Grounded Model of Organizational Schema Change during Empowerment," *Organization Science* 11 (2000), pp. 235–57; P.J. Gade and E.L. Perry, "Changing the Newsroom Culture: A Four-Year Case Study of Organizational Development at the *St. Louis Post-Dispatch*," *Journalism and Mass Communication Quarterly* 80 (2003), pp. 327–47.

29. R.G. Cooper, *Product Leadership* (Reading, MA: Perseus Books, 1999).

30. Cooper, *Product Leadership;* A.L. Page, *PDMA's New Product Development Practices Survey: Performance and Best Practices* (PDMA 15th Annual International Conference, Boston, MA, October 16, 1991); E. Mansfield, "How Economists See R&D," *Harvard Business Review,* November–December 1981, pp. 98–106.

31. S.L. Brown and K.M. Eisenhardt, "Product Development: Past Research, Present Findings, and Future Directions," *Academy of Management Review* 20 (1995), pp. 343–78; M.B. Lieberman and D.B. Montgomery, "First Mover Advantages," *Strategic Management Journal* 9 (Special Issue, Summer 1988), pp. 41–58; D.J. Teece, "Profiting from Technological Innovation: Implications for Integration, Collaboration, Licensing, and Public Policy," *Research Policy* 15 (1987), pp. 285–305; G.J. Tellis and P.N. Golder, "First to Market, First to Fail?" *Sloan Management Review* Winter 1996, pp. 65–75; G.A.Stevens and J. Burley, "Piloting the Rocket of Radical Innovation," *Research Technology Management* 46 (2003), pp. 16–26.

32. G. Stalk and T.M. Hout, *Competing against Time* (New York: Free Press, 1990).

33. K.B. Clark and S.C. Wheelwright, *Managing New Product and Process Development* (New York: Free Press, 1993); M.A. Schilling and C.W.L. Hill, "Managing the New Product Development Process," *Academy of Management Executive* 12, no. 3 (August 1998), pp. 67–81.

34. Clark and Wheelwright, *Managing New Product and Process Development.*

35. P. Sellers, "Getting Customers to Love You," *Fortune,* March 13, 1989, pp. 38–42.

36. O. Port, "Moving Past the Assembly Line," *BusinessWeek,* Special Issue: Reinventing America, 1992, pp. 177–80.

37. G.P. Pisano and S.C. Wheelwright, "The New Logic of High-Tech R&D," *Harvard Business Review,* September–October 1995, pp. 93–105.

38. K.B. Clark and T. Fujimoto, "The Power of Product Integrity," *Harvard Business Review,* November–December 1990, pp. 107–18; Clark and Wheelwright, *Managing New Product and Process Development;* Brown and Eisenhardt, "Product Development"; Stalk and Hout, *Competing against Time.*

39. C. Christensen, *Quantum Corporation—Business and Product Teams* (Harvard Business School Case #9-692-023).

40. Christensen, *The Innovator's Dilemma;* C.W.L. Hill and F.T. Rothearmel, "The Performance of Incumbent Firms in the Face of Radical Technological Change," *Academy of Management Review* 28 (2003), pp. 257–77.

41. Christensen, *The Innovator's Dilemma.*

42. A.M. Bell, "Inspiring Organizational Change at Reuters," *Strategic Communication Management,* August–September 2005, pp. 18–23; K. Brooker, "London Calling," *Fortune,* April 2, 2001, pp. 130–34; J. Matloff, "Can Reuters Recover?" *Columbia Journalism Review* 42 (July–August 2003), pp. 49–53.

\\ GLOSSARY \\\

A

achievement motivation The unconscious concern for achieving excellence in accomplishments through one's individual efforts.

achievement-oriented leadership Occurs when a leader sets high goals for subordinates, has high expectations for their performance, and displays confidence in subordinates, encouraging and helping them to take on greater responsibilities.

action plans Plans that specify with precision how strategies will be put into effect.

active listeners Listeners who receive a sender's signals, decode them as intended, and provide appropriate and timely feedback to the sender.

adaptive culture An organizational culture in which employees focus on the changing needs of customers and other stakeholders and support initiatives to keep pace with these changes.

adverse (or disparate) impact The effect of a policy or practice that appears neutral but has a significant and unintentional negative influence on one or more protected groups.

affirmative action Policies and practices to assist members of protected groups that are underrepresented in the organization.

anticompetitive behavior Behavior aimed at harming actual or potential competitors, most often by using monopoly power.

aptitude test A selection method that measures a person's potential ability, such as general intelligence and finger dexterity.

artifacts The observable symbols and signs of an organization's culture.

assembly-line production Systems used to mass-produce large volumes of a standardized product.

assertiveness Applying hierarchical power to influence others.

asset utilization The extent to which assets are "working," generating income for the organization.

attitudes Clusters of beliefs, assessed feelings, and behavioral intentions toward a person, object, or event.

attribution process Deciding whether an observed event is caused primarily by external or internal factors.

autonomous subunit A unit that has all the resources and decision-making power required to run its operation daily.

availability error Arises from our predisposition to estimate the probability of an outcome based on how easy the outcome is to imagine.

B

backchannel An informal channel through which managers can collect important information.

balanced scorecard (BSC) A reward system that pays bonuses for improved results on a composite of financial, customer, internal process, and employee factors.

balanced score card (BSC) A control approach that suggests managers use several different financial and operational metrics to track performance and control an organization.

bargaining power of buyers Ability of buyers to bargain down prices charged by firms in the industry or to raise the costs of firms in the industry by demanding better product quality and service.

bargaining power of suppliers Ability of suppliers to bargain up prices charged by firms in the industry or to raise the costs of firms in the industry by supplying lower-quality products and service.

barriers to entry Factors that make it costly for potential competitors to enter an industry and compete with firms already in the industry.

barriers to exit Factors that stop firms from reducing capacity even when demand is weak and excess capacity exists.

barriers to imitation Factors that make it difficult for a firm to imitate the competitive position of a rival.

bicultural audit The practice of diagnosing cultural relations between companies and determining the extent to which cultural clashes will likely occur.

Big Five personality dimensions The five abstract dimensions representing most personality traits: conscientiousness, agreeableness, neuroticism, openness to experience, and extroversion.

bounded rationality Limits in human ability to formulate complex problems, to gather and process the information necessary for solving those problems, and thus to solve those problems in a rational way.

brand loyalty The preference of consumers for the products of established companies.

broad market strategy Serving the entire market.

buffer stocks Inventories held for some unexpected contingency.

build to order Taking an order first, then building the product.

build to stock Stocking a distribution channel in the anticipation that a customer will purchase those products.

bureaucratic control Control through a formal system of written rules and procedures.

business ethics Accepted principles of right or wrong governing the conduct of businesspeople.

business model The way in which an enterprise intends to make money.

business-level strategy Strategy concerned with deciding how a firm should compete in the industries in which it has elected to participate.

C

centrality The degree and nature of interdependence between the power holder and others.

centralization The concentration of decision-making authority at a high level in a management hierarchy.

ceremonies Planned activities conducted specifically for the benefit of an audience.

charisma The ability of some people to charm or influence others.

coalition A group of people that comes together to cooperate in attaining a certain goal.

cognitive biases Decision-making errors that we are all prone to making and that have been repeatedly verified in laboratory settings or controlled experiments with human decision makers.

cognitive dissonance An uncomfortable tension experienced when behavior is inconsistent with our attitudes.

cognitive schema A manager's mental model of the world his or her enterprise inhabits.

commitment   Occurs when people identify with the request of somebody trying to influence them and internalize that request, adopting it as their own.

commodity product   A product that is difficult to differentiate from those produced by rivals.

communication   The process by which information is exchanged and understood between people.

competencies   A manager's skills, values, and motivational preferences.

competitive advantage   Advantage obtained when a firm outperforms its rivals.

competitive structure   The number and size distribution of incumbent firms in an industry.

competitive tactics   Actions that managers take to try to outmaneuver rivals in the market.

complementors   Firms providing goods or services that are complementary to the product produced by enterprises in the industry.

compliance   Occurs when people comply with a request, but only because they have to.

conceptual skills   The ability to see the big picture.

conflict   A process in which one party perceives that its interests are being opposed or negatively affected by another party.

consolidated industry   An industry dominated by a few large companies.

contingency plans   Plans formulated to address specific possible future events that might have a significant impact on the organization.

contingent work   Any work arrangement in which the individual does not have an explicit or implicit contract for long-term employment, or one in which the minimum hours of work can vary in a nonsystematic way.

continuance commitment   An employee's calculative attachment to an organization, whereby an employee is motivated to stay only because leaving would be costly.

continuous flow production   Production systems that continuously produce a standardized output that flows out of the system.

control   The process through which managers regulate the activities of individuals and units.

controlling   The process of monitoring performance against goals, intervening when goals are not met, and taking corrective action.

controls   Metrics used to measure the performance of subunits and to judge how well managers are running those subunits.

corporate-level strategy   Strategy concerned with deciding which industries a firm should compete in and how the firm should enter or exit industries.

countervailing power   Power that subordinates have over their superiors.

crisis management plan   Plan formulated specifically to deal with possible future crises.

cultural control   Regulating behavior by socializing employees so that they internalize the values and assumptions of an organization and act in a manner that is consistent with them.

D

decentralization   Vesting decision-making authority in lower-level managers or other employees.

decision heuristics   Simple rules of thumb.

deep-level diversity   Differences in the psychological characteristics of employees, including personalities, beliefs, values, and attitudes.

delayering   Reducing the number of layers in a hierarchy.

demographic forces   Outcomes of changes in the characteristics of a population, such as age, gender, ethnic origin, race, sexual orientation, and social class.

design for manufacturing   Trying to increase productivity by designing products that are easy to manufacture.

developing employees   The task of hiring, training, mentoring, and rewarding employees in an organization, including other managers.

devil's advocacy   The generation of both a plan and a critical analysis of the plan by a devil's advocate.

dialectic inquiry   The generation of a plan (a thesis) and a counterplan (an antithesis) that reflect plausible but conflicting courses of action.

differentiation strategy   Increasing the value of a product offering in the eyes of consumers.

directive leadership   Occurs when leaders tells subordinates exactly what they are supposed to do, giving them goals, specific tasks, guidelines for performing those tasks, and the like.

discontinuous change   Change that fundamentally transforms the nature of competition in the task environment.

discretion   The freedom to exercise judgment—to make decisions without referring to a specific rule or receiving permission from someone else.

disruptive technology   A new technology that gets its start away from the mainstream of a market and then, as its functionality improves, invades the main market.

distinctive competency   A unique strength that rivals lack.

diversification   Entry into new business areas.

downward communication   Occurs when information flows from higher to lower levels within an organization hierarchy.

drives   Instinctive tendencies to seek particular goals or maintain internal stability.

drop-off   Distortion in the content of a message as it passes through a communication system.

E

80–20 rule   A heuristic stating that 80 percent of the consequences of a phenomenon stem from 20 percent of the causes.

economies of scale   Cost advantages derived from a large volume of sales or production.

economies of scope   Cost reductions associated with sharing resources across businesses.

effective leadership   The ability of a leader to get high performance from his or her subordinates.

emotional contagion   The automatic process of "catching" or sharing another person's emotions by mimicking that person's facial expressions and other nonverbal behavior.

emotional intelligence   The ability to monitor one's own and others' feelings and emotions, to discriminate among them, and to use this information to guide one's thinking and actions.

emotions   Physiological, behavioral, and psychological episodes experienced toward an object, person, or event that create a state of readiness.

employee assistance programs (EAPs)   Counseling services that help employees overcome personal or organizational stressors and adopt more effective coping mechanisms.

employee engagement   Employees' emotional and cognitive (rational) motivation, their perceived ability to perform the job, their clear understanding of the organization's vision and their specific role in that vision, and their belief that they have been given the resources to get the job done.

employee orientation   The organization's systematic process of helping new employees make sense of and adapt to the work context.

employee stock ownership plans (ESOPs)   Reward systems that encourage employees to buy company stock.

employer brand   The package of functional, economic, and psychological benefits provided by employment and identified with the company as an employer.

employment discrimination   Any situation in which some people have a lower probability of being hired, promoted, financially rewarded, or receiving valuable training and development opportunities due to non–job-related demographic characteristics.

empowerment   A psychological concept represented by four dimensions: self-determination, meaning, competence, and impact of the individual's role in the organization.

enacted values   Values that actually guide behavior.

environmental degradation   Taking actions that directly or indirectly result in pollution or other forms of environmental harm.

equity theory   A theory that explains how people develop perceptions of fairness in the distribution and exchange of resources.

escalating commitment   Arises when decision makers, having already committed significant resources to a project, commit even more resources if they receive feedback that the project is failing.

espoused values   What people say is important to them.

ethical dilemmas   Situations in which there is no agreement over exact accepted principles of right and wrong.

ethical values   Values that society expects people to follow because they distinguish right from wrong in that society.

ethnocentric staffing   A staffing policy in which all key management positions are staffed by home country nationals.

exchange   The promise of benefits or resources in exchange for another party's compliance with your request.

exit–voice–loyalty–neglect (EVLN) model   A model that outlines the consequences of job dissatisfaction.

expatriates   Home country executives sent to a foreign post.

expectancy theory   A motivation theory based on the idea that work effort is directed toward behaviors that people believe will lead to desired outcomes.

exporting   Producing a good at home, and then shipping it to another country.

external environment   Everything outside a firm that might affect the ability of the enterprise to attain its goals.

extrinsic reward   Anything received from another person that the recipient values and is contingent on his or her behavior or results.

F

filtering   The tendency to alter information in some way, or fail to pass it on at all, as it moves through a communication system.

five-forces model   Model of competitive forces that determine the intensity of competition in an industry.

fixed costs   The costs that must be borne before the firm makes a single sale.

flaming   The act of sending an emotionally charged message to others.

flat hierarchies   Organizations with few layers of management.

flexible production technologies   A set of methodologies that allows enterprises to produce a wider range of end products from a given production system without incurring a cost penalty.

focus strategy   Serving a limited number of segments.

foreign direct investment   Investments by a company based in one nation in business activities in another nation.

formal channels   Systems of officially sanctioned channels within an organization that are used regularly to communicate information.

four-drive theory   A motivation theory based on the innate drives to acquire, bond, learn, and defend that incorporates both emotions and rationality.

fragmented industry   An industry with many small or medium-sized companies.

framing bias   Bias arising from how a problem or decision is framed.

franchising   Licensing the right to offer a service in a particular format.

frontline managers   Managers who manage employees who are themselves not managers.

functional managers   Managers responsible for leading a particular function or a subunit within a function.

functional structure   A structure that follows the obvious division of labor within the firm, with different functions focusing on different tasks.

fundamental attribution error   The tendency to blame people rather than the environment for poor performance.

G

gainsharing plan   A reward system in which team members earn bonuses for reducing costs and increasing labor efficiency in their work process.

general adaptation syndrome   A model of the stress experience, consisting of three stages: alarm reaction, resistance, and exhaustion.

general environment   Political and legal forces, macroeconomic forces, demographic forces, sociocultural forces, technological forces, and international forces.

general managers   Managers responsible for the overall performance of an organization or one of its major self-contained subunits or divisions.

geocentric staffing   A staffing policy that seeks the best people for key jobs throughout the organization, regardless of nationality.

geographic structure   A structure in which a firm is divided into different units on the basis of geography.

global standardization strategy   Treating the world market as a single entity, selling the same basic product around the globe.

globalization   The process whereby national economies and business systems are becoming deeply interlinked with each other.

globalization of markets   The merging of historically distinct and separate national markets into one huge global marketplace.

globalization of production   Sourcing goods and services from locations around the globe to take advantage of national differences in the cost and quality of factors of production.

goal   A desired future state that an organization attempts to realize.

goal setting   The process of motivating employees and clarifying their role perceptions by establishing performance objectives.

grapevine   The spread of unsanctioned information (rumor and gossip) through personal networks.

groupthink   Arises when a group of decision makers embarks on a course of action without questioning underlying assumptions.

H

heavyweight product manager   A manager who has high status within an organization and the power and authority required to get the financial and human resources that his or her team needs to succeed.

horizontal communication   Occurs among employees and units that are at the same hierarchical level in an organization.

horizontal differentiation   The formal division of the organization into subunits.

human capital   The knowledge, skills, and capabilities embedded in individuals.

human resource (HR) planning   The process of ensuring that the organization has the right kinds of people in the right places at the right time.

human skills   Skills that managers need, including the abilities to communicate, persuade, manage conflict, motivate, coach, negotiate, and lead.

I

illusion of control   The tendency to overestimate one's ability to control events.

impression management   The process of actively shaping one's public image.

incentive   A factor, monetary or nonmonetary, that motivates individuals to pursue a particular course of action; also, a device used to encourage and reward appropriate employee behavior.

incremental change   Changes that do not alter the basic nature of competition in the task environment.

incremental innovations   Innovations that represent improvements in product functionality within an established technology.

industry-specific regulators   Government agencies with responsibility for formulating, interpreting, and implementing rules specific to a particular industry.

influence costs   The loss of efficiency caused by deliberate information distortion for personal gain within an organization.

influence tactics   Steps that people can take to exert influence over others in an organization.

informal channels   Unofficial communication channels not formally established by managers.

information manipulation   Situations in which managers use their control over corporate data to distort or hide information to enhance their own financial situations or the competitive position of the firm.

information overload   Occurs when the volume of information received exceeds a person's capacity to get through it.

ingratiation   Attempts to increase the extent to which someone likes you.

inoculation effect   Warning an audience you are trying to influence about opposing arguments.

intangible resources   Nonphysical assets that are the creation of managers and other employees, such as brand names, the reputation of the company, processes within the firm for performing work and making decisions, and the intellectual property of the company, including that protected through patents, copyrights, and trademarks.

integrating mechanisms   Mechanisms for coordinating subunits.

internal environment   Everything inside a firm that affects managers' ability to pursue actions or strategies.

internal governance skills   The ability of senior managers to elicit high levels of performance from the constituent businesses of a diversified enterprise.

international trade   The sale of a good or service across borders.

intrinsic reward   A positive emotional experience resulting directly and naturally from the individual's behavior or results.

inventory holding costs   The capital cost of money tied up in inventory and the cost of the warehouse space required to store inventory.

inventory turnover   The speed with which inventory is replaced.

J

jargon   Technical language and acronyms as well as recognized words with specialized meaning in specific organizations or social groups.

job analysis   The systematic investigation and documentation of duties performed, tools and equipment involved, conditions surrounding work, and competencies required by job incumbents to perform the work.

job characteristics model   A job design model that relates the motivational properties of jobs to specific personal and organizational consequences of those properties.

job enrichment   A job design practice in which employees are given more responsibility for scheduling, coordinating, and planning their own work.

job satisfaction   A person's evaluation of his or her job and work context.

job shop   Production systems used when items are ordered individually.

joint venture   An agreement between a firm and a partner to establish a new enterprise in which they each take an equity stake.

just in time   Inventory that enters a production process just in time to be used.

justice theories   Theories that focus on attaining a just distribution of economic goods and services.

K

knowledge network   A network for transmitting information within an organization based on informal contacts between managers within an enterprise and on distributed information systems.

L

leader–member relations   How well followers respect, trust, and like their leaders.

leadership substitutes   Contingencies that may act as substitutes for a leadership style.

leadership   The process of motivating, influencing, and directing others in the organization to work productively in pursuit of organization goals.

leading   The process of motivating, influencing, and directing others in the organization to work productively in pursuit of organization goals.

learning effects   Cost savings that come from learning by doing.

legacy constraints   Prior investments in a particular way of doing business that are difficult to change and limit a firm's ability to imitate a successful rival.

legitimate power   Power deriving from an implicit agreement that people higher in a hierarchy can request certain behaviors of their subordinates.

licensing   Licensing a foreign firm to produce its product in a country or region in return for royalty fees on any sales that the licensee makes.

local customization strategy   Varying some aspect of product offerings or marketing messages to take country or regional differences into account.

location economies   The economies that arise from performing a business activity in the optimal locations for that activity.

low-cost strategy   Focusing managerial energy and attention on doing everything possible to lower the costs of the organization.

M

macroeconomic forces   Forces that affect the general health and well-being of a national or the regional economy, which in turn affect the profitability of firms within that economy.

management   The art of getting things done through people.

managerial roles   Specific behaviors associated with the task of management.

market controls   Regulating the behavior of individuals and units within an enterprise by setting up an internal market for some valuable resource such as capital.

market economy   An economy in which businesses are privately owned and prices are set by the interaction of supply and demand.

MARS model   A model that outlines the four factors that influence an employee's voluntary behavior and resulting performance— motivation, ability, role perceptions, and situational factors.

Maslow's needs hierarchy theory   A motivation theory of needs arranged in a hierarchy, whereby people are motivated to fulfill a higher need as a lower one becomes gratified.

mass customization   The ability to customize the final output of a product to individual customer requirements without suffering a cost penalty.

matrix structure   An organization with two overlapping hierarchies.

media richness   The volume and variety of information that a sender and receiver can transmit during a specific time.

mission   The purpose of an organization.

motivation   The forces within a person that affect his or her direction, intensity, and persistence of voluntary behavior.

multidivisional structure   A structure in which a firm is divided into different divisions, each of which is responsible for a distinct business area.

multinational enterprise (MNE)   A business that has productive activities in two or more countries.

N

needs   Mostly conscious deficiencies that energize or trigger behaviors to satisfy those needs.

negotiation   An interpersonal decision-making process by which two or more parties try to reach an agreement over an issue that is being disputed, such as the allocation of scarce resources.

network building   Actively seeking and establishing relationships with people who may prove useful in the future.

noise   The psychological, social, and structural barriers that distort and obscure a sender's intended message.

nonverbal communication   Messages sent through human actions and behavior rather than words.

norms   The informal rules and shared expectations that groups establish to regulate the behavior of their members; the social rules and guidelines that prescribe appropriate behavior in particular situations.

O

operating plans   Plans that specify goals, actions, and responsibility for individual functions.

operating strategy   Strategy concerned with the actions that should be taken at the level of individual functions, such as production, logistic, R&D, and sales, to support business-level strategy.

operations   The different activities involved in creating an organization's products and services.

operations managers   People who manage operations.

opportunistic exploitation   Unilaterally rewriting the terms of a contract with suppliers, distributors, or complement providers in a way that is more favorable to a firm, often using its power to force the revision through.

organization architecture   The totality of a firm's organization, including formal organization structure, control systems, incentive systems, organizational culture, and people.

organization structure   The location of decision-making responsibilities in the firm, the formal division of the organization into subunits, and the establishment of integrating mechanisms to coordinate the activities of subunits.

organizational commitment   An employee's emotional attachment to, identification with, and involvement in a particular organization.

organizational culture   The values and assumptions shared within an organization.

organizational inertia   Internal and external forces that make it difficult to change the strategy or organization architecture of an enterprise.

organizational socialization   The process by which individuals learn the values, expected behaviors, and social knowledge necessary to assume their roles in an organization.

organizing The process of deciding who within the organization will perform what tasks, where decisions will be made, who reports to whom, and how different parts of the organization will coordinate their activities to pursue a common goal.

output controls Setting goals for units or individuals to achieve and monitoring performance against those goals.

outside view Identifying a reference class of analogous past strategic initiatives, determining whether those initiatives succeeded or failed, and evaluating a project at hand against those prior initiatives.

P

paradigm shift Occurs when a new technology or business model comes along that dramatically alters the nature of demand and competition.

participative leadership A leadership style in which the leader consults with his or her subordinates, asking for their opinions before making a decision.

patterned behavior description interview A structured employment interview method that asks applicants to recall specific incidents in the past and describe how they handled the situations.

peer control Occurs when employees pressure others within their team or work group to perform up to or in excess of the expectations of the organization.

people The employees of an organization, the strategy used to recruit, compensate, motivate, and retain those individuals, and the type of people they are in terms of their skills, values, and orientation.

people-oriented behavior A leadership style that includes showing mutual trust and respect for subordinates, demonstrating genuine concern for their needs, and having a desire to look out for their welfare.

perception The process of attending to, interpreting, and organizing information.

performance ambiguity A situation that occurs when the link between cause and effect is ambiguous.

performance appraisal A systematic process of evaluating an employee's performance.

personal control Making sure through personal inspection and direct supervision that individuals and units behave in a way that is consistent with the goals of an organization.

personal networks Relationships between individuals.

personality The relatively stable pattern of behaviors and consistent internal states that explains a person's behavioral tendencies.

personalized power orientation Seeking power for personal gain.

persuasion The use of reason through factual evidence and logical arguments.

piece rate systems Systems that reward employees based on the number of units produced.

planning A process whereby managers select goals, choose actions (strategies) to attain those goals, allocate responsibility for implementing actions to specific individuals or units, measure the success of actions by comparing actual results against the goals, and revise plans accordingly.

planning horizon How far out a plan is meant to apply.

political and legal forces Industry changes resulting from changes in laws and regulations.

polycentric staffing A staffing policy in which key management positions in a subsidiary are staffed by host country nationals.

position power The power that derives from formal hierarchical power over subordinates, including the legitimate power to hire, fire, reward, and punish subordinates.

power The potential of a person, team, or organization to require others to do certain things.

power motivation The unconscious drive to acquire status and power and to have an impact on others.

primary activities Activities having to do with the design, creation, and delivery of the product; its marketing; and its support and after-sales service.

prior hypothesis bias Decision makers who have strong prior beliefs about the relationship between two variables tend to make decisions on the basis of these beliefs, even when presented with evidence that their beliefs are wrong.

process losses Resources (including time and energy) expended toward team development and maintenance rather than tasks.

production system How the flow of work is configured.

productivity The output produced by a given input.

productivity of capital Sales divided by the total capital (money) invested in a business.

productivity of labor Unit output divided by some measure of labor inputs.

profit-sharing plan A reward system that pays bonuses to employees based on the previous year's level of corporate profits.

psychological harassment Repeated and hostile or unwanted conduct, verbal comments, actions, or gestures that affect an employee's dignity or psychological or physical integrity and that result in a harmful work environment for the employee.

punctuated equilibrium A view of industry evolution asserting that long periods of equilibrium are punctuated by periods of rapid change when industry structure is revolutionized by innovation.

Q

quantum innovations Innovations that incorporate new technology and disrupt competition, shifting the dominant paradigm.

quota A limit on the number of items of a good that can be imported from a foreign nation.

R

realistic job preview (RJP) Giving job applicants a balance of positive and negative information about the job and work context.

reasoning by analogy The use of simple analogies to make sense out of complex problems.

recency effect Occurs when the most recent data dominate perceptions.

recruitment A set of activities that improves the number and quality of people who apply for employment and the probability that qualified and compatible applicants will accept employment offers.

regional trade agreements Agreements to remove barriers to trade between nations within a geographic region.

related diversification Diversification into a business related to the existing business activities of an enterprise by distinct similarities in one or more activities in the value chain.

reliability How consistently a selection method measures a person's characteristics.

representativeness Generalizing from a small sample or even a single vivid anecdote.

resilience The capability of individuals to cope successfully in the face of significant change, adversity, or risk.

resistance Refusing to perform or delaying engagement in a required behavior.

resource-based view A view that resources of an enterprise can be a source of sustainable competitive advantage.

resources Assets that managers have to work with in their quest to improve the performance of an enterprise.

rights theories The view that human beings have fundamental rights and privileges.

rituals The programmed routines of daily organizational life that dramatize the organization's culture.

role A set of behaviors that people are expected to perform because they hold certain positions in a team and organization.

S

satisfice Aiming for a satisfactory level of a particular performance variable rather than its theoretical maximum.

scenario planning Plans that are based on "what if" scenarios about the future.

selection The process of deciding which job applicants will make the most suitable employees.

selective perception The tendency to notice and attend to information that is consistent with our values, beliefs, and expectations while ignoring or screening out information that is inconsistent with these.

self-actualization The need for self-fulfillment in reaching one's potential.

self-control Occurs when employees regulate their own behavior so that it is congruent with organizational goals.

self-dealing Situations in which managers find a way to feather their own nests with corporate funds.

self-directed teams Teams organized around work processes that complete an entire piece of work requiring several interdependent tasks and have substantial autonomy over the execution of those tasks.

self-serving bias The tendency to attribute our favorable outcomes to internal factors and our failures to external factors.

sensing The process of receiving signals from a sender and paying attention to them.

sexual harassment A type of harassment that includes unwelcome conduct of a sexual nature that detrimentally affects the work environment or leads to adverse job-related consequences for its victims.

shared values Values held in common by several people.

silent authority Occurs when someone complies with a request because of role expectations and the requester's legitimate hierarchical power.

single-use plans Plans that address unique events that do not reoccur.

small batch Production systems used when customers order in small batches but when each order is different.

social culture The system of values and norms that are held in common by people living in a society.

social loafing Occurs when people exert less effort (and usually perform at a lower level) when working in groups than when working alone.

social responsibility A sense of obligation on the part of managers to build certain social criteria into their decision making.

socialist economy An economy in which businesses are owned by the state and prices are set by state planners.

socialized power orientation Accumulating power to achieve social or organizational objectives.

sociocultural forces The way in which changing social mores and values affect an industry.

span of control The number of direct reports a manager has.

stakeholder An individual, institution, or community that has a stake in the operations of an organization and in how it does business.

standard A performance requirement that the organization is meant to attain on an ongoing basis.

standing plans Plans used to handle events that reoccur frequently.

stereotyping The process of assigning traits to people based on their membership in a social category.

stock options A reward system that gives employees the right to purchase company stock at a future date at a predetermined price.

strategic commitments A firm's investments in tangible and intangible assets to support a particular way of doing business (a particular business model).

strategic plan A plan that outlines the major goals of an organization and the organizationwide strategies for attaining those goals.

strategic thinking The cognitive ability to analyze a complex situation, abstract from it, and draw conclusions about the best strategy for the firm to follow.

strategizing The process of thinking through on a continual basis what strategies an organization should pursue to attain its goals.

strategy An action that managers take to attain the goals of an organization.

strategy implementation Putting action plans into effect.

stress An adaptive response to a situation that is perceived as challenging or threatening to a person's well-being.

stressors Any environmental conditions that place a physical or emotional demand on a person.

subgoal An objective that, if achieved, helps an organization attain or exceed its major goals.

substandard working conditions Tolerating unsafe working conditions or paying employees below-market rates to reduce costs of production.

substitutability The availability of alternative resources.

substitute products The goods or services of different businesses or industries that can satisfy similar customer needs.

superordinate goals Common objectives held by conflicting parties that are more important than the departmental or individual goals on which the conflict is based.

supply chain   The chain of suppliers that provides raw materials, partly finished products, or finished products to an organization.

support activities   Activities that provide inputs that allow the primary activities to occur.

supportive leadership   A leadership style in which the leader is approachable and friendly, shows concern for the welfare of subordinates, and treats them as equals.

surface-level diversity   Observable demographic or physiological differences in people, such as their race, ethnicity, gender, age, and physical disabilities.

sustainable competitive advantage   A distinctive competency that rivals cannot easily match or imitate.

switching costs   The time, energy, and money required to switch from the products offered by one enterprise to those offered by another.

SWOT   Strengths, weaknesses, opportunities, and threats.

T

tactical plans   The actions managers adopt over the short to medium term to deal with a specific opportunity or threat that has emerged.

tall hierarchies   Organizations with many layers of management.

tangible resources   Physical assets, such as land, buildings, equipment, inventory, and money.

tariff   A tax on imports.

task environment   Actual and potential competitors, suppliers, and buyers (customers or distributors); firms that provide substitute products to those sold in the industry; and firms that provide complements.

task interdependence   The extent to which team members must share common inputs to their individual tasks, need to interact in executing their work, or receive outcomes (such as rewards) that are partly determined by the performance of others.

task-oriented behavior   The style of leaders who assign employees to specific tasks, clarify their work duties and procedures, ensure that they follow company rules, and push them to reach their performance capacity.

task structure   The degree to which the jobs of subordinates are highly structured with clear work responsibilities, well-defined tasks, explicit goals, and specific procedures.

team building   Any formal activity intended to improve the development and functioning of a work team.

team cohesiveness   The degree of attraction people feel toward a team and their motivation to remain members.

team effectiveness   The team's effect on the organization, individual team members, and the team's existence.

teams   Groups of people who interact and influence each other, are mutually accountable for achieving common goals associated with organizational objectives, and perceive themselves as a social entity within an organization.

technical skills   Skills that include mastery of specific equipment or following technical procedures.

360-degree feedback   Performance feedback received from a full circle of people around an employee.

transactional leader   A leader who helps an organization achieve its current objectives.

transformational leader   A leader who is an agent of strategic and organizational change.

trust   A psychological state comprising the intention to accept vulnerability based on positive expectations of the intent or behavior of another person.

U

uncertainty   An inability to predict with accuracy the nature, magnitude, timing, and direction of change in the environment.

unit plans   Plans for departments within functions, work teams, or individuals.

unrelated diversification   Diversification into a business not related to the existing business activities of an enterprise by distinct similarities in one or more activities in the value chain.

upward communication   Occurs when information flows from lower to higher levels within an organization hierarchy.

utilitarian approaches   The view that the moral worth of actions or practices is determined by their consequences.

V

validity   How well a selection method predicts an applicant's suitability as an employee.

values   Stable, evaluative beliefs that guide our preferences for outcomes or courses of action in a variety of situations; the philosophical priorities to which managers are committed.

value innovation   Using innovation to offer more value at a lower cost than competitors.

vertical differentiation   The location of decision-making responsibilities within a structure.

vertical integration   Moving upstream into businesses that supply inputs to a firm's core business or downstream into businesses that use the outputs of the firm's core business.

virtual teams   Teams whose members operate across space, time, and organizational boundaries and are linked through information technologies to achieve organizational tasks.

visibility   The extent to which a power holder is known, or visible, to others.

vision   A desired future state.

W

wholly owned subsidiary   A foreign subsidiary that is fully owned by a firm.

work sample test   A selection method that requires job candidates to demonstrate their behavior and performance in a real-time situation.

workforce diversity   Differences in the demographic, cultural, and personal characteristics of employees.

work–life balance   A state of minimal conflict between work and nonwork demands.

Page numbers followed by n indicate notes.

SUBJECT INDEX